RODALE'S ILLUSTRATED
ENCYCLOPEDIA OF
organic
GARDENING

RODALE'S ILLUSTRATED ENCYCLOPEDIA OF

organic
GARDENING

THE HENRY DOUBLEDAY RESEARCH ASSOCIATION

Editor-in-chief Pauline Pears

DK Publishing

LONDON, NEW YORK, MUNICH,
MELBOURNE, and DELHI

Project editor Louise Abbott
Senior art editor Stephen Josland
Art editor Alison Lotinga
Photography Peter Anderson
Illustrations Marian Hill
Managing editor Anna Kruger
Managing art editor Lee Griffiths
DTP design Louise Waller
Media resources Romaine Werblow
Picture research Samantha Nunn
Production controller Ruth Charlton

RODALE INC.
Executive editor Margot Schupf
Art director Patricia Field
Copy manager Nancy N. Bailey
Project manager Deborah L. Martin
Editor Nancy J. Ondra
Copy editor Sarah S. Dunn
Photo editor Jackie Ney
Researcher Sarah Wolfgang Heffner
U.K. liaison editor Joanna Chisholm
U.K. liaison art editor Alison Lotinga
Media resources Richard Dabb
Picture research Samantha Nunn

First American Edition, 2002
00 01 02 03 04 05 10 9 8 7 6 5 4 3 2 1

Published in the United States by
DK Publishing Inc.,
375 Hudson Street,
New York, New York 10014

A Cataloging-in-Publication record for this book is available from
the Library of Congress
ISBN 0-7894-8908-2 HARDBACK
ISBN 0-7566-0932-1 PAPERBACK

Color reproduction by Colourscan, Singapore
Printed and bound in Spain by AGT

This book is printed on chlorine-free paper from sustainably
managed forests, manufactured by an
environmental award-winning mill

See our complete product line at
www.dk.com

RODALE

Organic Gardening Starts Here!

Here at Rodale, we've been gardening organically for more than 60 years—ever since my grandfather J. I. Rodale learned about composting and decided that healthy living starts with healthy soil. In 1940 J. I. started the Rodale Organic Farm to test his theories and today the nonprofit Rodale Institute Experimental Farm is still at the forefront of organic gardening and farming research. In 1942 J. I. founded *Organic Gardening* magazine to share his discoveries with gardeners everywhere. His son, my father, Robert Rodale, headed *Organic Gardening* until 1990, and today a third generation of Rodales is growing up with the magazine. Over the years we've shown millions of readers how to grow bountiful crops and beautiful flowers using nature's own techniques.

In this book you'll find the latest organic methods and the best gardening advice. We know—because all our authors and editors are passionate about gardening! We feel strongly that our gardens should be safe for our children, pets, and the birds and butterflies that add beauty and delight to our lives and landscapes. Our gardens should provide us with fresh, flavorful vegetables, delightful herbs, and gorgeous flowers. And they should be a pleasure to work in as well as to view.

Sharing the secrets of safe, successful gardening is why we publish books. So come visit us at www.organicgardening.com, where you can tour the world of organic gardening all day, every day. And use this book to create your best garden ever.

Happy gardening!

Maria Rodale

Maria Rodale
Rodale Organic Gardening Books

THE EDITOR-IN-CHIEF

Pauline Pears M.Sc.
An expert in organic vegetable growing and composting, with 25 years' experience working in the organic movement. Ran H.D.R.A.'s Information and Education department for many years; now a Senior Horticultural Advisor with H.D.R.A. Author, trainer, and broadcaster.

THE CONTRIBUTORS

Kathleen Askew Sustainable landscape gardener and garden designer. Awards include a Gold Medal garden at the Chelsea Flower Show.

Anna Corbett Organic gardening specialist with a particular interest in growing herbs and vegetables. Writer, author, and teacher.

Sally Cunningham H.D.R.A. deputy head gardener, a biker with a lifelong passion for plants and anything classed as natural history. Also paints, keeps hens, and uses a community garden.

Patsy Dyer H.D.R.A. Advisor and garden designer. Has worked in Botanical Gardens in America and the U.K.

Alan Gear Chief Executive, H.D.R.A. A well-known figure on the organic scene. Regularly writes, broadcasts, and lectures on organic gardening, farming, and food.

Jackie Gear Executive Director, H.D.R.A. Organic gardening and food writer, respected for her creative energy and forthright views on all things organic.

Dr. Isabelle Van Groeningen Garden consultant; co-designer of H.D.R.A.'s Paradise garden and the award-winning "Go Organic" garden at Hampton Court 2000.

Andrew Miller B.A. Dip.L.A. M.L.I. Chartered landscape architect; co-designer of H.D.R.A.'s Paradise garden and the award-winning "Go Organic" garden at Hampton Court 2000.

Adam Pasco Editor, B.B.C. *Gardeners' World* magazine. Passionate gardener, enthusiastic composter, and qualified horticulturist, with a growing interest in organic gardening.

Bernard Salt Writer with 60 years' practical experience in organic gardening.

Colin Shaw MA Freelance writer, photographer, and lecturer. Enjoys applying technical solutions to gardening problems. Pioneered Square Foot gardening in the U.K.

Bob Sherman BA MIoH Organic gardener for 25 years. Head of Horticulture at H.D.R.A.; Vice Chairman of the R.H.S. Fruit Group.

Owen Smith Founder of "Future Foods." A botanist with a special interest in unusual edible plants and sustainable food production.

Janet Walker Plant lover and experienced vegetable grower, fascinated by the life cycle of plant pests and diseases. Past member of H.D.R.A.'s Advisory team.

John Walker Writer, author, and Permaculture designer committed to developing sustainable gardening techniques. Grows his own food in a small urban garden.

Dr. Martin Warnes Runs Pestwatch, advising and training growers and retailers on garden pest control and promoting sustainable pest management.

For full contributor credits see p. 416

Contents

Organic gardening: an introduction   9
What's in it for you and what you can do, from the
smallest contribution to a whole way of life

Organic by design   20
Are organic gardens designed differently? Plans and
practicalities

THE BASICS

Soil and soil care   33
Understanding and improving your soil; composting,
manures, and leaf mold

Water and watering   63
Effective watering; recycling rain and household
water; ways to cut water use

Weeds and weed control   73
Weed prevention for less work; clearing neglected sites

Plant health   84
Natural controls; encouraging pest predators; traps
and barriers; last resorts

Raising plants   104
How to propagate plants from seed and cuttings;
saving and storing seed

LOOKING GOOD

The garden framework   126
From paving to pond liners, advice on choosing
landscaping materials

Woody plants and climbers   142
Choosing and caring for the lasting elements in your
planting schemes

Garden flowers   158
Right plant, right place; flower power; the new
naturalistic planting styles

Lawns and lawn care   174
Can an organic lawn be perfect? Seed, grass, and
meadow choices

Gardening for wildlife   186
Simple ways to provide food and shelter for wildlife
in the garden; ponds and pond life

Container gardening   203
Fruit, vegetables, and flowers in pots; choice of
containers; plant care

Gardening under cover   216
How to make the best use of greenhouses and hoop
houses; using cloches and other crop covers

GROW YOUR OWN

Growing fruit   237
Tree and bush fruit, strawberry beds, vines, and nut
trees for fresh fruits in season

Growing herbs   282
Best choices for the kitchen; harvesting and storing

Growing vegetables   293
From traditional kitchen gardening to the "no-dig"
technique and edible landscaping

REFERENCE SECTION

A–Z of vegetable and salad crops   337
Detailed sowing, spacing, care, and harvesting advice,
from artichokes to zucchini

A–Z of plant problems   367
Diagnostic advice and organic solutions for pests,
diseases, and disorders

U.S.D.A. Plant Hardiness Zone Map   396

**H.D.R.A. Organic Guidelines
for Gardeners**   397

Resources   402
Useful addresses, Web sites, further reading

Index   404

Acknowledgments   416

Organic gardening: an introduction

ORGANIC METHODS ALLOW YOU TO CREATE ANY GARDEN YOU
WANT; THE METHODS ARE PRACTICAL AND EFFECTIVE

PUT SIMPLY, ORGANIC GARDENING is an environmentally friendly, people-friendly style of gardening. Organic gardening methods can be used by everyone to create and maintain almost any shape, size, and style of garden, in any location, from a city center to a rural paradise.

Organic gardening gives you the chance to create the garden you want, safe in the knowledge that you are also doing your part to protect the wider environment in which we all must live.

From food to flowers

The organic movement really started in the middle of the 20th century, when forward-thinking, visionary individuals such as Lawrence D. Hills and Lady Eve Balfour began to question the direction that farming and food production—and in their wake, gardening—were taking. Their concern was, in particular, healthy food production, and it is in the area of food production that organic growing is most advanced. But organic methods are not just for the fruit and vegetable patch. They can be applied to all areas of the garden, from lawns to flowerbeds and windowsills. Interest is now growing in managing public parks, sports fields, playgrounds, and even parking lots organically.

The future is organic

The last decade has seen a phenomenal rise in interest in all things organic. The organic movement—for a long time an energetic, committed, active but relatively small group of enthusiasts—has really come of age. Organic food is widely available in both major supermarket chains and specialty stores throughout America, governments are supporting organic farming and research, and more and more people are turning to organic methods of gardening. Every time there is another food scare or the dangers of another pesticide come to light, more people turn to eating and growing organically.

The bigger picture (facing page)
Organic methods are used today to create and maintain every sort and style of garden, however large or small. They are no longer confined to the kitchen garden or vegetable patch.

Pots and troughs (left)
Any growing space can benefit from organic principles, even one as small as plants in pots.

The development of the organic movement

Work in progress
Today's organic movement looks to the past and to modern science to find sustainable techniques. Above: trialling slug repellents. Below: J. I. Rodale studied soil health.

Although artificial fertilizers were invented 150 years ago, they did not gain widespread acceptance until the mid-1940s, in the years following World War II. For a long time, farmers were suspicious of "artificial manure," believing that only proper "muck" put "heart" into the soil. Modern pesticides, many of which were developed as nerve poisons during the war years, have a similarly short history. Prior to 1950, the number of chemicals that were used by farmers against pests was surprisingly limited. Nevertheless, it would be wrong to think of farming at the turn of the century as being the same as the organic growing that is practiced today. The fundamentals may not have changed much, but the modern, improved techniques, equipment, and plant varieties used by today's organic farmers would have astonished their Victorian ancestors.

Organic pioneers

The post-war years were marked by a huge drive by the government to increase agricultural production. Most farmers jumped aboard the chemical bandwagon, spurred on by subsidies and other incentives. As a result, crop yields, aided by improvements in plant breeding, rose sharply. On the face of it the new policy was an unqualified success, yet, even in the beginning, a small number of voices were raised in protest.

Their essential concern was that, by abandoning the use of animal manure in favor of artificial nutrients, the very health of the soil was being jeopardized. An impoverished soil, it was argued, produces unhealthy plants that undermine rather than enhance the health of people and livestock.

Lady Eve Balfour, one of the chief exponents of this theory, founded the Soil Association in 1945 in order to highlight the vital relationship between the health of soil, plants, animals, and man. This marked the start of the "Organic Movement" in Britain.

Going so blatantly against the advice of government and of virtually every academic and research establishment in the land, it took a brave soul to stand out against the doctrine of the time. In general, it was the farmers who noticed the deterioration of their soil or who suffered pesticide mishaps, so it was they who rallied to the organic cause in those early years.

In gardens of the time, too, the desire to be "modern" persuaded many people to switch to ready-bagged fertilizers and "miracle" products like D.D.T. But here, also, a tiny minority stood their ground—among them Lawrence D. Hills, who was one of the founding members of Britain's Soil Association. In 1958 he set up an organization for organic gardeners and called it the Henry Doubleday Research Association, or "H.D.R.A.— the organic organization," as it is better known today. He named it after a Victorian, Essex-based Quaker and experimental horticulturist, whose work and philosophy he greatly admired.

The movement grows

Throughout the years, interest in organic principles was growing in the U.S., too. In 1942, J. I. Rodale founded *Organic Farming and Gardening*, one of the first publications to promote the organic method. A small segment of U.S. farmers adopted organic practices, and more gardeners became aware of their options. During the 1960s, a more widespread backlash against the use of pesticides began, fueled by Rachel Carson's revelations in her hard-hitting book *Silent Spring*, which highlighted the harmful environmental consequences of these chemicals. This gained pace with the public's increasing environmental awareness during the 1970s and 1980s. Organic food began to go on sale at about this time, though only in small specialty stores. During the final decade of the 20th century, a series of food scares, including B.S.E. (Bovine spongiform encephalopathy, or Mad Cow Disease) and the issue of genetic modification (G.M.; see also p. 294), produced an explosion in demand. Now, in the new millennium, the outlook for organic production could not be brighter. Some even predict that, at current rates of growth, organic farming will have all but replaced conventional agriculture within the next 25 years.

So today, who says what is organic?

If food is to be marketed as "organic," the consumer needs to have confidence that it really has been grown organically. To maintain consumer confidence it is now, in many countries, illegal to sell produce as organic unless it carries a recognized organic symbol, which confirms that it has been grown to an approved set of organic standards. These standards—the practical application of the basic organic principles—cover every aspect of growing, storing, and processing food, including soil management, animal welfare, and pest and weed control.

There are, at the time this was written, no legal standards governing public horticulture—parks, gardens, golf courses, parking lots, and so on—but these may come in the future. Organic gardeners know that it is perfectly possible to manage the entire garden—including roses, lawns, shrubs, and flower borders—without using chemical fertilizers and sprays. So why should the same not apply to public gardens and parks, school grounds, and the

like? In some countries, such as Germany, Denmark, and Switzerland, such initiatives are already underway. In the U.K., H.D.R.A. is working with the horticultural industry to draft a set of organic standards for public horticulture and landscaping.

Gardeners in all countries can choose to work to H.D.R.A.'s Organic Guidelines for Gardeners (see p. 397), which are adapted from the standards for commercial growing. The information provided in this book is based on those guidelines. Gardening, on whatever scale, obviously includes many aspects, such as lawns and patios, that do not concern farmers. H.D.R.A. guidelines cover some of these nonfood areas; others are under consideration.

Related systems

The fundamental principles of organic growing are also at the heart of the growing systems used by two other movements—biodynamics and permaculture. Biodynamic methods, used by farmers and gardeners alike, are based on the teachings of Rudolf Steiner, an Austrian radical philosopher working in the 1920s. Permaculture is an interdisciplinary ecological design philosophy developed by Australian Bill Mollison in the late 20th century. Both biodynamics and permaculture provide, for some people, a philosophy for life.

Organic gardening products

One area of gardening where it would be helpful to have legally recognized standards is that of garden products—fertilizers, potting soils, and pesticides, for instance. Currently an item can be labeled as organic as long as it is "of living origin" (the dictionary definition of the word.) This means that manure from intensive henhouses, for example, can be sold as "organic manure" although it is not acceptable for use in an organic garden.

Increasingly, however, gardening products are carrying an organic symbol or a statement that they are suitable for use in an organic garden. If not, buy from an organic organization, or check with the supplier before buying. The H.D.R.A. guidelines and the relevant chapters in this book will help you to ask the right questions.

There is an increasing range of organic—and so-called organic—gardening products available. See p. 19 for more information.

RELATED SYSTEMS

Biodynamic agriculture
Biodynamic thinking recognizes a spiritual dimension to life, enlarging the basis of science to include the cosmic and what is beyond the sense-perceptible. It has a holistic worldview that, for example, sees the influence of planetary rhythms on the growth of plants and animals as of equal importance to a purely chemical analysis.

It is the regeneration of the forces that work through the soil to the plants, aided by "enlivened" compost or manure, that is the central aim of biodynamics and that makes it conspicuously different from other organic systems. When crops are harvested from the land, it is not only their substance that is removed but also the forces and vitality that make them worth eating. To give back this vitality, biodynamic gardeners use special therapeutic preparations for the soil, plants, compost, and manure. Biodynamic produce carries the Demeter symbol.

Permaculture
Permaculture is an ecological design system that helps find solutions to the many problems facing us—both locally and globally.

Permaculture tackles how to grow food, build houses, and create communities while minimizing the environmental impact. It encourages us to be resourceful and self-reliant. By thinking carefully about the way we use our resources, it is possible to get much more out of life by using less. We can be more productive for less effort, reaping benefits for our environment and ourselves, for now and for generations to come. This is the essence of permaculture—the design of an ecologically sound, sustainable way of living—in households, gardens, communities, and businesses.

What can organics offer you?

The organic way has so much to offer you, your family, and your wider environment.

Healthy eating

Organically grown produce can never be guaranteed as pesticide-free—our world is too polluted to claim that—but it is grown without relying on the arsenal of pesticides that may be used in conventional growing. Deaths from pesticide poisoning in the western world are few, but we have really no idea about the cumulative, chronic effects of the cocktail of low levels of pesticides that we all consume in and on conventionally grown food. Babies and young children, with their low body weight, are particularly at risk. Pesticides are even found in breast milk.

By growing your own organic fruit, herbs, and vegetables, you can be sure the food you and your family eat is as healthy—and as fresh—as it can be. You can enjoy a much wider range of varieties than you find in the stores, too. Plus, research shows that organically grown food tends to be nutritionally superior with respect to vital ingredients such as vitamin C.

And it is not just food that can contain pesticide residues. Cut flowers, often imported from countries where pesticide use is less strictly controlled, may have been sprayed with substances that have been banned in other countries—so growing your own makes sense.

Healthy gardening

By gardening organically, you can avoid using any pesticides at all. You, your children, and visiting wildlife can enjoy the garden environment in safety.

Healthy wildlife

Wildlife has inevitably suffered—both in numbers and species range—as the environment has become progressively degraded. It is alarming to find that once-common species of birds such as bluebirds are now less abundant than they were 50 years ago. Countless lesser-known species maintain only a precarious existence.

Not surprisingly, wildlife flourishes on organic farms and in organic gardens, and one would hope that, as more farmers and gardeners abandon chemicals, the steady decline of wildlife will be reversed. Scientific studies have shown that organic farms support a greater number and diversity of wild creatures than most conventionally managed farmland. In spite of the relatively small area of land devoted to gardens in comparison with farmland, it is still significant. Even a modestly sized organic garden can attract a diverse and plentiful wildlife community. In fact, one of the great pleasures of gardening organically is enjoying the birds, butterflies, and other smaller creatures that inhabit your garden with you. With diversity comes balance, so pests are less of a problem where wildlife flourishes.

Reaping the rewards
Organic gardening creates a healthy environment and food for your family. Growing your own fresh, healthy crops will allow you to rediscover the seasonal pleasures of harvesting and also grow lesser-known, even traditionally local varieties of fruits and vegetables. In addition, border plants and good-looking cutting flowers for the house can be managed using only organic methods.

Healthy environment

Environmental pollution is an increasingly common factor in modern life. Waste disposal sites and incinerators, designed to dispose of the ever-increasing mountains of trash, do not make pleasant neighbors. Organic gardening encourages reuse and recycling of items often thrown away or burned, helping to reduce the waste mountain.

It is hard to overestimate the damage to the environment that has been caused by intensive agricultural practices during the last half-century. Precious landscape features, such as fencelines, wildflower-rich meadows, and wetlands, have been destroyed on a massive scale. Overuse of fertilizers has polluted lakes and rivers, in many cases choking them almost to death through the proliferation of algae blooms and waterweeds. Pesticides are everywhere in the environment: on land, in the sea, and even at the North and South Poles, where they accumulate in the body fat of creatures such as seals, penguins, and polar bears.

Organic farming and gardening, which do not rely on artificial additives, cause little pollution. They preserve and enhance landscape features that are habitats for wildlife, which is vital for pest control. It is little wonder that scientific research consistently rates organic growing as the most sustainable method there is.

Healthy "pocket"

The hidden costs of conventional agriculture are huge. In the U.K. alone, the annual costs of cleaning up drinking water to reduce the pesticide content to an "acceptable" level are in the region of $170 million a year. Removing nitrates costs another $22 million. These costs are even higher in the U.S., of course, and they are paid for by you, the consumer, directly from your pocket.

Organic gardening methods can cut your costs. Making compost and leaf mold, for example, can eliminate the need to purchase soil amendments and fertilizers, and you can save considerable amounts of money on organic produce by growing your own.

Healthy future

The idea that we do not inherit the earth from our ancestors but borrow it from our children is a compelling one. Organic methods help us to fulfill this philosophy.

Worldwide, pressures are to intensify food production, increasing reliance on chemical additives and the rapidly declining range of crops and cultivars bred to respond to those additives. Genetic modification (G.M.) is the latest and most worrying embodiment of this trend, which is the antithesis of organic growing. These developments deny local knowledge, traditional expertise, sustainability, diversity, and equal distribution of power and control. Industrial agriculturalists may protest that theirs is the only way to feed the world, but many would take issue with this. The organic movement offers a healthy, sustainable alternative view of the future.

Best of both worlds
Growing plants to attract wildlife may bring an appreciation of the gentle beauty of wild and native plants, but organic gardening is not all nostalgia. It uses the best of traditional methods (especially those that, like the "no-dig" potatoes below left, save on labor) but also searches for ways to use and recycle today's materials.

What is organic gardening?

Organic gardening is not just a matter of replacing chemicals such as synthetic fertilizers and pesticides with more natural products, as it is often simplistically described. There is a great deal more to it than that, in both theory and practice.

Basic principles

The organic approach recognizes the marvelous complexity of our living world: the detailed and intricate ways in which all living organisms are interconnected. It aims to work within this delicate framework in harmony with nature.

Feeding the soil

Conventional fertilizers are generally soluble (their ingredients are directly available to plants). The organic method, on the other hand, relies on creatures that live in the soil to make food available to plants.

Unbelievable as it may sound, a single teaspoonful of fertile soil can contain more bacteria and fungi than the number of people living on the planet. These microorganisms, which are invisible to the naked eye, break down compost, manure, and other organic materials that are added to the soil to provide a steady supply of nutrients for plants to absorb. Their activities also help to improve soil structure. Soil fed in this way tends to produce healthier plants that are better able to withstand attack from pests and diseases, or have a much better chance of recovery.

Natural pest control

All creatures, whatever their size, risk attack by pests and diseases. They are part of a great food chain. In the words of Jonathan Swift, "... a flea has smaller fleas that on him prey, and these have smaller fleas to bite 'em, and so proceed *ad infinitum.*"

So, lady beetles prey on aphids, robins eat cutworms, and toads devour slugs. It is nature's way. As an organic gardener, you can capitalize on the situation by creating the right conditions to attract these unpaid pest controllers—the gardener's friends. There are other strategies in the organic cupboard too—barriers and traps, pest- and disease-resistant plant varieties, companion planting, and crop rotation. These are just some of the techniques that, alone or in combination, provide realistic alternatives to the use of pesticides.

Managing weeds

Weeds can be a valuable resource as a compost ingredient or food for wildlife, but they can also smother plants, compete for food and water, and spoil the appearance of a path or border. There are currently no organic weedkilling sprays, but there are plenty of effective alternatives, both for clearing weedy ground and for keeping weeds under control. You just need to choose the one that suits the circumstances. Options include hoeing, mulching, cultivation, hand-weeding, and the use of heat in the form of a flame weeder.

Incentives and benefits
Organic methods can be applied to the whole garden, not just food crops; it is nurturing the soil that is essential. Recycling helps to prevent unnecessary waste, and other, natural cycles can be used to advantage: If you grow plants that attract wildlife, the wildlife will in turn help control pests.

Conservation and the environment

By taking a holistic approach to the use of finite resources and by minimizing impact on the environment, organic growing makes a positive contribution toward creating a sustainable future for all life on earth. This means recycling and reusing instead of dumping, burning, or buying new; providing habitats where wildlife can flourish; and avoiding the use of non-reusable resources. It also involves choosing locally available materials rather than those transported over long distances.

Welfare considerations

Animal welfare is an important element of organic farming. There is no place in the organic philosophy for factory farming, such as intensive hog farms or battery and broiler henhouses. As a logical extension, organic gardeners do not use by-products—such as manures—from intensive agriculture. There is concern for people, too—the standards governing the trade in organic food are increasingly coming together with those concerned with "fair trade," to provide better livelihoods for those employed in farming, particularly in developing countries.

"Animal-free" gardening

The use of animal manures is an integral part of most organic farming systems, but it is quite possible to garden without using any products of animal origin. Garden compost, green manures, leaf mold, and plant-based fertilizers are all "animal-free" organic gardening ingredients.

ORGANIC GARDENING "DOS"

Do:
• Manage the whole garden organically— edible crops, ornamentals, lawns, and paths.
• Make the garden wildlife-friendly, encouraging wildlife to control pests.
• Learn to distinguish pests from predators.
• Play to your garden's strengths, capitalizing on its particular characteristics.
• Make soil care a priority.
• Make garden compost and leaf mold to feed the soil.
• Reuse and recycle to cut down the use of finite resources and reduce disposal problems such as landfill.
• Use organically grown seeds where possible.
• Consider the environmental implications when choosing materials for hard landscaping, fencing, soil improving, and so forth.
• Collect rainwater, and reduce the need for watering by improving soil and growing appropriate plants.
• Make local sources your first choice.
• Use traditional methods where appropriate.
• Make use of the latest scientific findings where acceptable organically.
• Stop using synthetic fertilizers.
• Give up burning trash.
• Control weeds without herbicides.
• Avoid the use of pesticides and preservative-treated wood.
• Say "no" to genetically modified cultivars.
• Recognize the value of genetic diversity and the preservation of threatened cultivars.

Materials and methods
Using both traditional methods and equipment and the latest and best "high-tech" materials fits in with the organic belief, provided that sustainability is always kept in view. Why use imported wood, for example, when a local industry may be able to supply materials such as wooden stakes and fencing.

Preserving heirloom vegetables

Diversity is a keystone of organic growing, and freedom of choice is something that all gardeners appreciate, particularly when it comes to plant choice. Seed-saving organizations help to maintain both within the plant kingdom.

Our gardening heritage

Every fall, "heirloom" gardeners harvest the seeds that will keep little bits of history alive for one more year. The seeds they gather are those of heirloom plants—varieties of plants grown in the 18th, 19th, and early 20th centuries.

If they were not preserved in backyard plots by such dedicated gardeners, many of these old-time plants would not exist today. They are not suited to large-scale production because they cannot be harvested mechanically or transported long distances to markets. But they are often ideal for home gardeners, whose needs and preferences remain unchanged through the generations.

Many heirloom crops taste better or are more tender than their hybrid replacements, and many spread their harvest over a longer period. If grown for years in one location, they can adapt to the climate and soil conditions of that area and may outproduce modern cultivars. Others may be less productive than today's hybrids but offer greater disease and insect resistance.

A taste of history

Heirloom plants are a tangible connection with the past. Like fine old furniture and antique china, the garden plants of earlier generations draw us close to those who have grown them before us. Some heirloom varieties have fascinating histories. 'Anasazi' corn, found in a Utah cave, is thought to be more than 800 years old. And 'Monstoller Wild Goose' bean was said to have been collected from the craw of a goose shot in 1864 in Somerset County, Pennsylvania. Varieties such as these are eagerly sought by seed collectors, who maintain them for their historic value just as archivists maintain old papers and books.

Genetic diversity

A more vital reason for growing old cultivars is that heirloom plants represent a vast and diverse pool of genetic characteristics—one that will be lost forever if these plants are allowed to become extinct. Even cultivars that seem inferior to us today may carry a gene that will prove invaluable in the future.

The federal government maintains a National Seed Storage Laboratory in Fort Collins, Colorado, but the task of preserving seed is so vast that the government cannot do the job on its own. Heirloom gardeners recognize the importance of maintaining genetic diversity, and many feel a real sense of urgency and importance about their preservation work.

To get started as an heirloom gardener, try ordering seed from specialty houses that carry old cultivars. You can also contact nonprofit organizations that work with individuals to preserve heirloom plants. One of the best known is the Seed Savers Exchange (see *Resources*, p. 402, for details). Another good way to find heirloom plants is to check readers' letters in gardening magazines, or seed exchange forums on the World Wide Web—many participants offer homegrown seed in exchange for postage.

Growing for seed
When grown for seed, crops such as this giant leek may need to be isolated in an insectproof cage when in flower to keep the cultivar true. This prevents cross-pollination with other leek cultivars.

HEIRLOOM HIGHLIGHTS

The plants pictured and described here are just a few examples of heirloom vegetable varieties that you can find through seed-saving organizations and specialty seed companies.

'Alderman' pea
Introduced in 1891, this shelling pea (far left) produces vines 5–7 ft. (1.5–2.2 m) tall and needs sturdy support. The vines are very productive and the peas have excellent flavor and keeping quality.

'Babington' leek
Not a true leek but a species on its own, found growing in the wild in the U.K., where it may be a relic of early cultivation in monasteries. The flowerheads form bulbils, giving them a rather extraterrestrial appearance (left). These, and bulbils formed at the bottom of the plant, are used for propagation. It is used like garlic—the green shoots are cut for eating, while bulbs, which can be strongly flavored, can be dug up and stored.

'Cherokee Trail of Tears' climbing French bean
The Cherokee nation was forced out of its homeland in the 1830s on a march that became known as the Trail of Tears. They took their most precious possessions with them, including, naturally, their seeds. One of those was this climbing bean (far left). The small, black, shiny seeds, produced in purple pods, are usually dried for winter use.

'Brandywine' tomato
Perhaps the most famous heirloom in the garden, this Amish cultivar (left) originated in Pennsylvania's Brandywine River valley. The rose-pink fruits are large, flavorful, and borne on vigorous, indeterminate plants.

Going organic

As this book will show, "going organic" is not simply a question of changing your brand of spray or fertilizer (though you may well do this). It involves a change of approach, treating the garden as a complete entity where natural systems are promoted and allowed to thrive. You will start developing long-term strategies for maintaining soil fertility and managing pests and diseases.

Getting started

The best way to go organic is to take the plunge—to start using organic methods and give up chemical ones in every area of the garden at once. This book is full of practical advice to help in the conversion process, whether you are starting with a blank plot, clearing a weedy patch, or converting an existing garden.

In this book, the chapter *Soil and Soil Care* helps you to get to know your soil, and learn how to get the best from it. *Weeds and Weed Control* gives advice on clearing a weedy plot and keeping weeds under control. Prevention is the most effective strategy when dealing with pests and diseases. *Plant Health* and *Gardening for Wildlife* are both full of hints and tips. Organic methods do not stop at the edge of the flowerbed—they are used for lawns, too (see *Lawns and Lawn Care*). It is also important to "think organic" in relation to hard landscaping (see *The Garden Framework*) and in the greenhouse (*Gardening under Cover*).

H.D.R.A.'s Organic Guidelines for Gardeners (p. 397) list techniques and materials suitable for use in an organic garden. These are divided up into three categories: Best Practice, Acceptable, and Qualified Acceptance. When starting out, you may find that you are mainly using techniques in the second and third categories, advancing to Best Practice as you and your garden adjust to organic methods.

How long does it take?

Commercial growers converting to organic methods are required to go through a "conversion period," commonly 2 years. During this period, the land is managed organically but produce cannot yet be sold as organic. Depending on past management, you may find that your garden also goes through a conversion period while it is adapting to the change—or everything may flourish from the start!

Outside help

If you are new to organic gardening or simply need some advice or new ideas, there are organizations that can help. The Rodale Institute, based in Maxatawny, Pennsylvania, sponsors many outreach programs, both at its 333-acre experimental farm and around the country. If you visit the farm, you can take guided or self-guided tours of both the farm and the gardens. It's a wonderful opportunity to see a diverse range of organic practices and ask questions. The magazine *O.G.* (formerly known as *Organic Gardening*), published by Rodale, Inc., is also an excellent source of information on the latest issues and advice relating to organic gardening. (For more information, see *Resources*, p. 402.)

Revamp problem areas

There may be areas of your garden that you are not able, for whatever reason, to effectively manage organically. A common example is weed control on paths, drives, and patios. With some thought, it should be possible to redesign these areas to make organic management a more practical option.

Dispose of unwanted pesticides

If the garden shed is full of pesticides and herbicides not suitable for an organic garden, dispose of these safely; check with your municipality for advice.

Change the way you shop

Organic gardening products are available in some garden centers. Specialty mail-order catalogs usually supply a greater range. In an ideal world, anything you use in an organic garden would itself have been grown or produced organically. Unfortunately, this is not yet possible; although supplies are growing, at times you will have to use conventionally grown seed, for example, or manure from animals not raised organically. Suggestions for alternative options are given where appropriate. To conform to the organic principles of sustainability, always try to reuse and recycle waste materials from your own garden and locality in preference to bringing them in.

THE ORGANIC GARDEN SHOP

	Item	Organic choice	Notes	Other options
Plants and seeds	Seeds and sets	Organically grown vegetable and herb seed, onion sets, and garlic bulbs; also some flower seeds	Look for a recognized organic symbol. Recent development; range still limited but expanding quickly.	If organic seed is not available in the cultivar you want, use untreated seed (see p. 314) or save your own. Do not use genetically modified cultivars.
	Transplants	Organically grown vegetable "plug" plants; also some wildflowers	Look for a recognized organic symbol.	Raise your own.
	Bulbs	Organically grown bulbs	Limited range from few sources. Look for a recognized organic symbol. Never buy bulbs taken from the wild.	
	Potato tubers	Organically grown seed potatoes; select pest- and disease-resistant cultivars where appropriate	Reasonable range available. Look for a recognized organic symbol.	If organic seed potatoes are not available in the cultivar you want, use conventional ones, or grow micropropagated plants, then save your own tubers.
	Flowers, shrubs, fruit trees, and bushes	A limited range and supply of organically grown plants is available from specialist nurseries	Look for a recognized organic symbol.	Raise your own from seed and cuttings.
	Herb plants	A good range is available	Look for a recognized organic symbol.	
Pots and growing media	Pots and trays	Biodegradable compressed paper and cardboard	Reuse plastic pots.	Make your own paper pots for plant raising; recycle household items.
	Growing bags	Available containing organic growing media		Grow in soil or large pots.
	Growing media	Organic seed, multipurpose, and potting soils are available		Make your own using organic ingredients.
	Moisture retainer	Seaweed-based products		
Soil fertility	Soil improvers	Composted animal manure and plant waste; wide range from low- to high-fertility materials	Buy products that have some form of organic approval if available. Do not buy products that originate from intensive farming systems.	Make your own from recycled garden waste, composted manure, autumn leaves, etc.
	Green manure seeds	Not yet commonly available as organically grown		Purchase conventionally grown, or save your own.
	Fertilizers	A wide range of plant-, animal-, and mineral-based products; some from organic sources	Buy products that have some form of organic approval if available. Do not use chicken manure from intensive farming systems.	Use other means of improving soil fertility.
	Liquid fertilizers	A range of plant-, animal-, and mineral-based products; some from organic sources	For container plants, baskets, etc., buy products that have some form of organic approval if available.	Make your own from comfrey or nettle leaves.
Compost-making	Compost bins	Wood or recycled plastic	Check for wood preservatives that may have been used.	Make your own, or use a simple covered pile.
	Compost activators	Bacterial and herbal		Use grass clippings or comfrey leaves.
	Worm compost bins	Wood, recycled plastic, compressed paper		Make your own or convert a plastic trash can.
Weed control	Loose mulch	Biodegradable mulch, occasionally of organic origin	Buy products that have some form of organic approval if available.	Use shredded garden prunings or bark.
	Mulch membranes	Biodegradable and synthetic mulches		Use recycled cardboard and newspaper.
	Flame weeders	Gas-powered		
Pest control	Pesticides	All those permitted for use in an organic garden are available	See p. 103 for acceptable products.	
	Barriers and traps	Row cover, slug traps, grease bands, etc.		Improvise some with household materials.
	Biological controls	Good range but mostly mail order		
	Wildlife habitats	Boxes for birds, lacewings, and other predators		Make your own.

Organic by design

CREATE AND MAINTAIN AN ORGANIC GARDEN WHATEVER ITS
SHAPE, SIZE, AND DESIGN

GETTING THE GARDEN YOU WANT

• Visit other gardens to look at their design, structure, and materials used, and see what you like and do not like in a garden.

• Decide on the style of garden you would like.

• List all the elements that are required in the garden.

• Take photos and collect pictures from garden magazines to build up a file of ideas.

• Mark out shapes of borders, patios, and paths with a garden hose, sand, or strings, and live with them for a while before you start digging.

• Make sure that seating areas are large enough to accommodate your table and chairs comfortably.

WHETHER YOU ARE REVAMPING an existing garden or starting a new one from scratch, it pays to think organic from the very start. An organic garden relies as much on careful planning as the actual gardening to be successful. Within reason, whatever the design you have planned for your garden, you can make it organic—whether you have several rural acres or a tiny urban plot.

Find a comfortable seat, sit back, relax, and take your time to develop your plans. Discuss your ideas with others who will use the garden. Always consider maintenance, and be realistic when deciding how much time you will want to spend working in the garden. Now is the time to build in low-maintenance features. Plan in solutions and avoid potential problems.

With the help of a miniature to-scale plan of the existing garden, a sharp pencil, and an eraser, you can gradually work out a suitable master plan for the garden, incorporating all the elements you require. Make lots of copies of the basic plan or use a tracing paper overlay so that you can try out all sorts of options.

When faced with a major overhaul of your garden, work out the complete plan before you begin any work. Then prioritize the tasks. If time, courage, or financial restraints mean that you cannot take on the whole garden in one season, plan phases over several years, completing one area at a time. This is better for morale than having a half-finished garden that drags on for years, giving little pleasure but much frustration.

Site assessment

When putting in a new garden, it pays to take your time to familiarize yourself with the site.

• **Take a close look** at the soil and the existing vegetation for vital clues about soil condition and fertility—whether there are particularly wet or compacted areas, for example. (See *Soil and Soil Care*, pp. 33–37, for further information on soil assessment.)

• **Observe the position** of the sun throughout the day, remembering that the winter sun may not make it over the top of trees or buildings. Identify hot spots and, equally important, likely frost pockets: low areas where frost gets trapped and the winter sun cannot reach to thaw it. Note the prevailing wind direction to see where windbreaks may be helpful. Some areas may be cold and exposed, while other parts can be sheltered pockets, with quite a different microclimate. Mark all these features, and the direction of North, on your plan.

• **Consider the relationship** between your garden and its surroundings. Are there unsightly buildings or objects that need screening, or to have attention drawn away from them? Are there views of trees or buildings that could add to the pleasure in your garden? You can create a focal point by borrowing from the surrounding landscape and give an illusion that your garden is larger than it is in reality.

• **Assess existing vegetation** for wildlife potential.

• **Watch out** for cables, pipes, and drains, and make a note of where they are. If you are likely to need access to them at any time, avoid laying hard surfaces or planting big trees and shrubs over them.

When taking on an existing garden, it can be very hard to imagine it looking any different from what is there already. It is always worth living with a garden that is new to you for a year before making major changes. You may find that boring shrubs burst into unexpected glory, bare patches erupt with an explosion of spring bulbs, and oddly positioned trees actually provide just the right amount of shade. Do not be afraid to contemplate removing existing elements to introduce new, better ones. If you do not like a plant, or it is not performing well enough because of old age or disease, take it out.

Before creating permanent paths, watch where you and your family walk. It is against human nature to go the long way on a path if there is an easier shortcut. To allow for these "desire lines," you may need to change the location of your paths or make the shortcuts inaccessible.

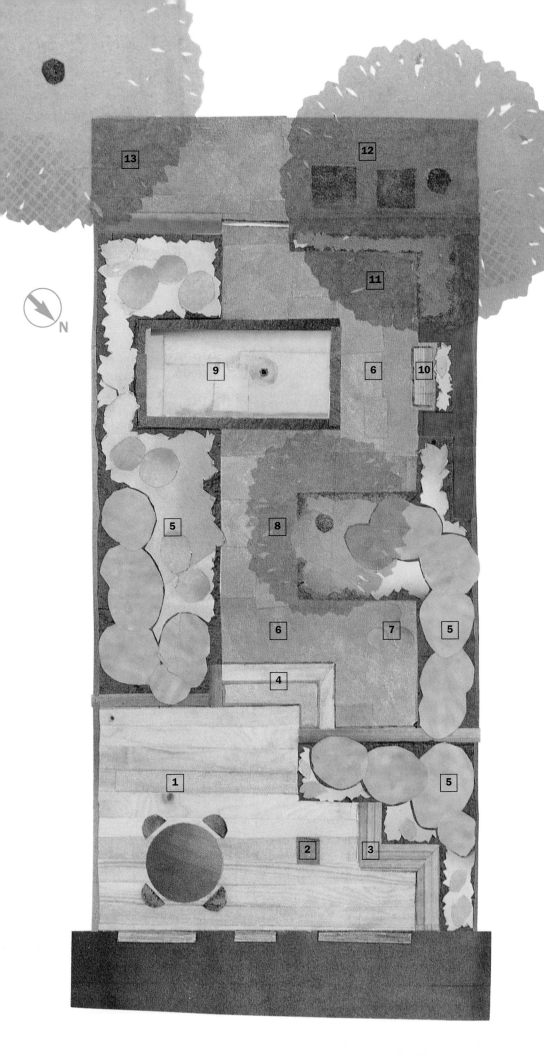

CHIC CITY GARDEN

An elegant but low-maintenance design for a busy working couple who want somewhere to relax and entertain friends.

1 Decking and patio furniture of Western red cedar; all wood from renewable sources
2 Sculpture—look for interesting pieces using local, natural, or recycled materials rather than mass-produced "artwork"
3 Wooden seating for party guests
4 Wide wooden steps, with low retaining wall of rot-resistant wood on either side
5 Low-maintenance planting of native species shrubs to attract and give shelter to wildlife
6 Paths of broken slate (by-product of slate quarrying) laid over weed-suppressing landscape fabric
7 Frostproof terra-cotta pots (renewable material)
8 Ornamental spring-flowering tree to support wildlife, especially birds—allies in controlling garden pests
9 Solar-powered fountain in shallow formal pool—the garden's focal point; water encourages birds into the garden to bathe and drink and forms a habitat for other creatures
10 Secluded wooden bench, enclosed by formal pruned hedges
11 Planting of hostas and ferns, which tolerate dry shade under tree
12 Recycling area for compost bin and leaf mold cage, screened by pruned hedge; the hedge provides a nesting place for birds
13 Storage area for additional garden furniture and for woody branches until a shredder is rented

Planning considerations

A garden should be considered an extension of the house, providing you with open-air rooms that can be used for both work and play. While much attention is given to the functional, decorative layout of a house, that of the garden quite often tends to be ignored. The same level of thought can be put into the layout and furnishing of a garden. Compile a wish list, including all the elements you must have—the basics such as clotheslines and compost pile, as well as those you would like to have. Remember to include organic essentials (see p. 26). Once you start planning, you will see how much fits into the space.

Living spaces

As well as looking good, a garden should remain practical. Make a separate list of the functional elements and give these priority. Fresh herbs are best positioned near the kitchen door (as long as the site is a sunny one), as is a generous seating area if you like to eat your meals outdoors. On the other hand, a relaxing area with comfortable chairs and a small table where you can enjoy a quiet lunch or have an evening drink should be away from the house so that you can savor the view across the garden. Or put the chairs in a secluded garden "room," surrounded by scented flowers. Somewhere quiet and private gives you the chance to have a peaceful afternoon nap, while at the opposite end of the garden an open space allows children to kick a ball around safely.

If you have small children, position the play area within view of the patio or kitchen window so that you can keep an eye on them. When they are older and prefer privacy, you may also prefer to have them out of sight.

Suburban orchard

Designs can often be based on existing features. This garden has been planned for a couple whose children have left home. They want to grow a few vegetables and give the garden an "orchardy" feel by emphasizing some beautiful old apple trees.

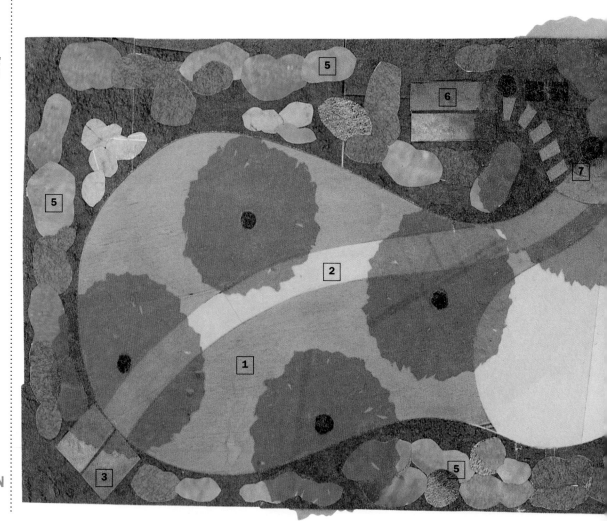

N

Productive areas

Nothing tastes better than home-grown vegetables and fruit. If you have room, you may want a separate vegetable garden. If not, vegetables—and fruit and herbs—can be incorporated into flower borders. Where space is an issue and growing food a high priority, give some thought as to how you can create a vegetable area that, even in the depths of winter, will still look good. The easiest way to achieve this is by creating a formal layout with edged beds. This way the bed boundaries will stay defined, giving the garden a tidy look all year.

Espalier-grown fruit trees or arches can provide height. Although yielding less than free-standing trees, trained fruit takes up less space and can make a decorative screen. To add a decorative, colorful note, edge the beds with herbs or annual flowers, which will be beneficial as they attract predatory insects. (See *Growing Fruit*, p. 237, and *Growing Vegetables*, p. 293.)

Compost and other organic recycling

Somewhere to recycle green garden waste—weeds, old plants, autumn leaves, kitchen scraps, and on—is essential in any organic garden. In most cases, this means a compost pile or piles. Resist the temptation to place your compost pile in an out-of-the-way, inaccessible spot at the back of the yard. Compost bins can come in a range of designs and sizes to suit all properties, so it is not always essential to hide them. It may be more practical to have several scattered around a larger yard, rather than one permanent site. An area to temporarily stack material for composting and shredding can be invaluable. A worm compost bin used to recycle kitchen scraps is best located in a sheltered spot near the kitchen door. Leaf mold piles can usually be accommodated somewhere among trees and shrubs, as they require little attention. In a small garden, stuff autumn leaves into black plastic bags to store out of sight while decomposing.

KEY TO THE SUBURBAN ORCHARD

1 Wildflower area beneath apple trees will attract pollinating insects; take care when mowing meadow areas not to damage tree trunks or bark
2 Mown path leads to gazebo; having short and and long grass creates habitats for a wide range of creatures, from thrushes (short grass) to amphibians (long grass)
3 Sedum roof on wooden gazebo provides an additional wildlife habitat
4 Vegetables grow within flower borders; ornamentals "camouflage" the vegetables, making them less vulnerable to some pests
5 Native species shrubs support wildlife
6 Shed with sedum roof and water barrel to collect and store rainwater
7 Circular wooden seat under tree
8 Flowers grow among vegetables for cutting and to attract beneficial insects
9 Arches over rolled gravel path (heavily rolled surface helps to control weeds) support climbing vegetables as well as ornamental climbers
10 Lawn, managed organically
11 Red cedar decking with pergola
12 Pond (in former sandbox) uses rainwater from roof and has overflow pipe to garden
13 Bench on paved terrace; mortared joints eliminate weeds in paving
14 Low hedge separates terrace from rest of garden
15 Urn/vase creates focal point

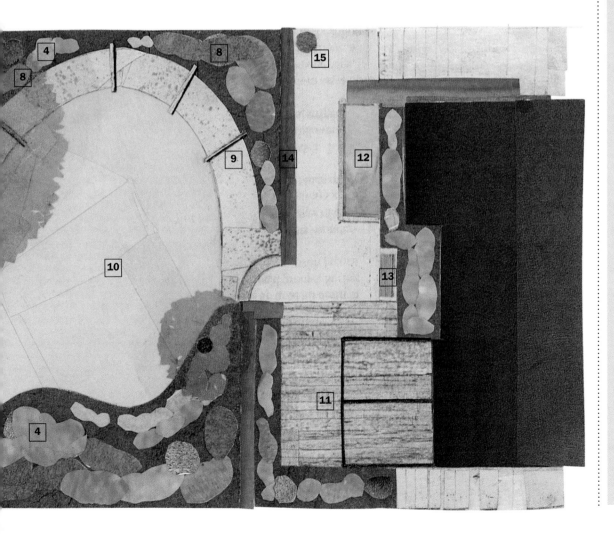

Greenhouses and coldframes

If you are eager to grow food or exotic plants, or to do more out-of-season gardening, a greenhouse is a wonderful addition to a garden. It does, however, require regular attention. (See *Gardening under Cover*, p. 216, for advice on greenhouses.) A hoop house is more economical to buy but less visually appealing. A coldframe can be useful for growing some early crops or as a hardening-off area. Place it away from frost pockets, in a sunny location. If none of these is possible, a small heated propagator positioned on a north-facing windowsill is useful for rooting cuttings and raising seedlings.

Plant selection

In a natural environment, plants are never artificially fertilized, mulched, or watered. They obtain all the necessary nutrition and moisture from their surroundings. Rainfall provides the moisture, and nutrients are supplied by soil organisms, which decompose vegetation and animal remains. The plants that survive and thrive are adapted to that particular environment. If the conditions change, the vegetation pattern will adapt itself accordingly. By choosing the right plants for the growing environments in your garden, and by selecting plants that fit the available space, you will find gardening becomes easier and relatively trouble-free. It will cut down on watering, fertilizing, staking, and pest and disease control, as well as pruning.

Wildlife

Native wildlife is your friend in the garden. Apart from keeping you company, the local fauna perform a vital function in the garden. Provide suitable board and lodging and in return these creatures—from

Traditional backyard garden

Most designs have to cater to an assortment of needs. This is a practical family garden for growing a small range of edibles as well as growing ornamentals, hanging out the laundry, and giving the children their own "private" space.

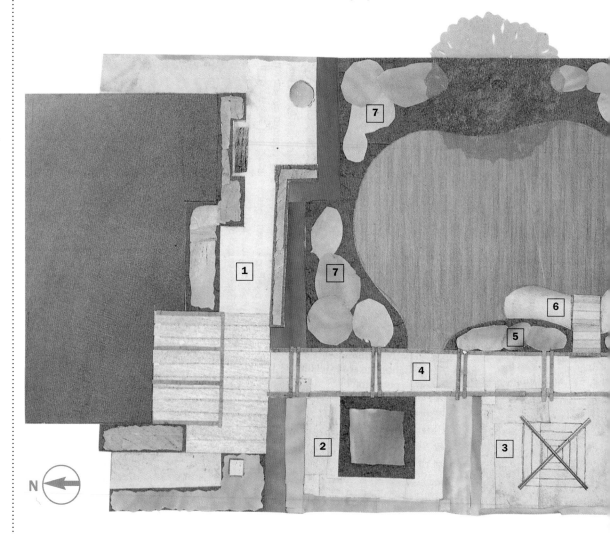

microbes to birds—will help you keep the garden thriving, free from pests and diseases.

Thickets, shrub borders, mixed hedges, dead wood, ponds, and scrubby growth all help to provide shelter and habitats for these useful creatures. Planting fruiting trees and shrubs such as hollies, hawthorns, viburnums, crab apples, and shrub roses will not only provide a colorful touch for the garden in autumn and winter but will also provide a vital food source for these animals. Annual and perennial flowers attract nectar-feeding insects into the garden. Some hybridized forms, particularly those with double flowers, are sterile and are of no value to nectar-feeding insects; they also do not set seed, depriving birds and mammals of food.

Water is always welcomed by wildlife. A pond (see *Gardening for Wildlife*, pp. 198–201), situated in a quiet corner of the garden, can become home to many beneficial creatures. Install it near shrubs, trees, and some long grass to extend the habitat variety. If an informal pond is not an option, consider some other form of water feature, such as a small fountain, container water garden, or even a simple bird bath.

KEY TO THE TRADITIONAL BACKYARD GARDEN

1 Low-maintenance sitting area, part cedar, part paved; mortared joints keep out weeds; wooden pergola over deck covered with climbers provides welcome shade, as the area is south-facing. In family gardens, ensure that children, whether sitting with you or in their own play areas, have some sort of protection from hot sun

2 Herb garden provides culinary essentials and also attracts beneficial insects

3 Clothesline is screened by trellis and space-saving espalier and fan-trained fruit trees

4 Path of natural broken slate (by-product of slate industry) laid over landscape fabric to control weeds

5 Bog garden makes best use of a badly drained "problem" area

6 Small pond provides habitat for pest-controlling creatures such as frogs, and drinking and bathing water for birds

7 Vegetables and flowers for cutting combined in ornamental borders

8 Trained fruit trees around fruit-bearing shrubs

9 Raised beds for easy-to-reach vegetables give improved drainage and avoid compaction caused by treading on soil

10 Greenhouse, for propagation and a few specialist plants, has barrel to collect rainwater for use on vegetables

11 Shed for storing tools and toys; water barrel

12 Recycling area for making soil improvers—compost and leaf mold—and stacking manure

13 Planting of native, shade-tolerant species, mainly shrubs, to support wildlife

14 Secluded play area for older children

DESIGN ELEMENTS TO CONSIDER

Barbecue
Brush pile
Clothesline
Coldframes
Composting areas ★★
Food sources for wildlife ★★
Fruit
Greenhouse
Hedging and screening
Herbs
Irrigation
Leaf mold piles ★★
Lighting
Manure storage area ★
Parking
Paths
Play areas
Pond or water feature ★
Power sources
Rainwater collection ★★
Seating areas
Shrubs and flowers
Storage for logs or coal
Trees
Vegetables
Wildlife habitats ★★
Worm compost bin ★

★★ organic essentials
★ high on organic priority list

Design elements

Even when you are not aiming for a formal garden, it pays to create a good structural layout—the bones of the garden. This will ensure that it looks attractive in winter as well as summer. Some of Britain's most famous gardens, such as Sissinghurst and Hidcote, are highly structured, consisting of a sequence of garden rooms, all laid out in simple but nonetheless strict geometric patterns. It is the opulent mass of flowers breaking out of their boundaries that softens the harsh lines during the summer months. Once winter returns, the crisp straight lines of paths and hedges provide a totally different but equally attractive picture.

Paths and seating areas

Hard surface areas—paths, terraces, and patios—are an expensive but long-lasting investment. The choice of material you use should be influenced by the style of the house, the cost, local availability, and the environmental impact of the production of that material (see *The Garden Framework*, p. 126, for more information). Options include real or reconstituted stone paving slabs, engineering bricks, wooden planks, gravel, and slate chippings.

Screens and windbreaks

A screen may be created in a garden to provide privacy, shelter, a visual barrier, noise absorption, or to keep animals in (or out). A decorative screen creates spaces or garden rooms, which are part of the intrigue in a garden. Rather than taking in the whole garden in one glance, it is often much nicer to leave some of the garden to your imagination and just provide an enticing glimpse of what's around the corner.

Screening for privacy requires a solid, preferably quick, answer. A brick or stone wall is instant and long-lasting, but expensive. It provides an attractive background to planting and is ideal for climbers and trained plants. It can also create shelter, providing a special microclimate in the garden, but it is not the best choice as a windbreak. Wooden fencing is a quick and affordable solution but is often treated with preservatives and has a restricted lifespan. A hedge is in many ways an attractive option. Although it will take some years to establish, a hedge is inexpensive, long-lasting if well maintained, and a barrier to noise and pollution, and if well chosen adds wildlife interest to the garden. It is also the most effective windbreak.

If a screen is to act as a windbreak, it should be around 50% permeable to be effective. A solid wall or fence deflects the wind upward, causing turbulence on the other side. A hedge, living fence (see p. 140), or slatted fence will slow down the air as it passes through.

Screens do not need to be opaque; it can be more interesting to create a net-curtain effect, stopping the eye at that point, yet allowing a glimpse of the garden beyond.

Design principles

• **Focus** Focal points, which draw the eye, are an important design feature. Use a specimen tree, statue, or sculptural plant.
• **Scale** Plants and features should be in scale with the garden. Avoid too many large trees and shrubs in small gardens; select small- to medium-size ones. In larger gardens, use more prominent groups.
• **Unity** Elements in the garden, including hard landscaping and the house itself, should relate harmoniously to one another.
• **Rhythm** It is pleasing to have a repetition of elements. Repeat plants in a border, or a pattern in paving along the length of a walkway.
• **Contrast** Contrast in color, texture, and pattern can be achieved both in planting and hard landscaping.

> ### ENVIRONMENTALLY SOUND CONSTRUCTION MATERIALS
> Choose materials that make the least impact on the environment.
> • Recycled or waste materials: Reuse old bricks, paving slabs, and stone, available from reclamation yards. Some quarrying processes produce by-products such as small slate pieces, ideal for surfacing paths. Plastics, such as polystyrene, are recycled into imitation wood products, which will not decompose.
> • Wood: Try to use native wood, preferably naturally resistant hardwoods rather than those treated with preservatives (see *The Garden Framework*, p. 126, for more details).

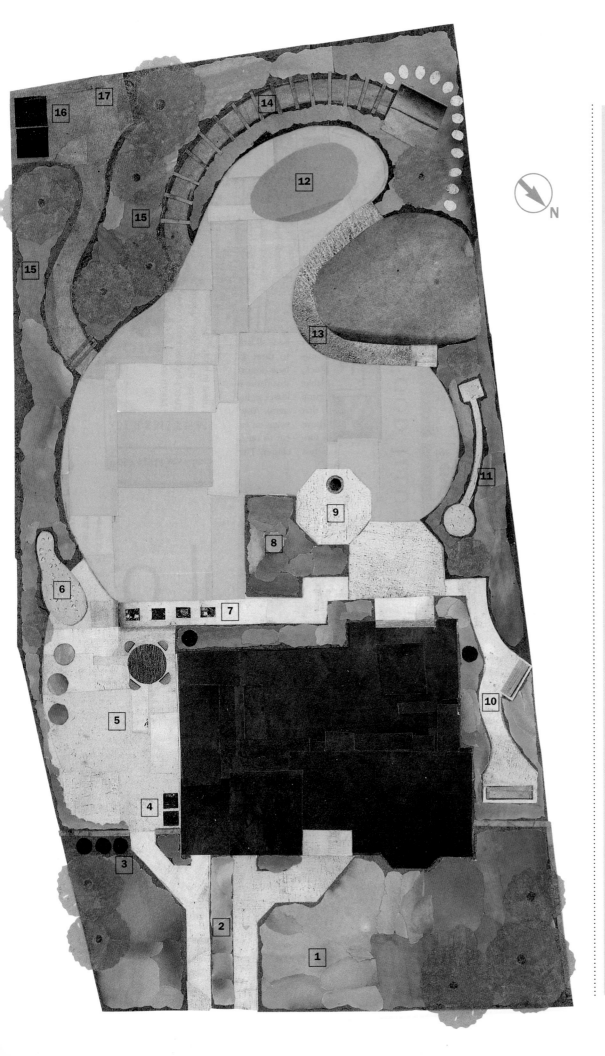

FAMILY GARDEN

A family with two children wants a garden that will be fun as well as a place to foster their interest in wildlife.

1 Low-maintenance, dense planting in front garden gives good weed control

2 Driveway of gravel, crushed stone, or crushed brick is laid on compacted base over weed-suppressing landscape fabric; mat-forming plants in center

3 Recycling bins for storing paper, glass, and cans

4 Worm bins for providing high-nutrient compost

5 Sitting area. Herbs in planting pockets between reclaimed stone or brick; tubs for lettuce and edible flowers chosen and planted by children

6 Small pond to support wildlife, covered with secure metal grid while children are small

7 Mosaic slabs, made by family, set into path

8 Bird table to encourage birds to visit and nest in garden

9 Barbecue and bench on patio of reclaimed stone or brick

10 Secret garden with benches; planted with ferns that will enjoy the shade

11 Shallow stream, for toy boat races, connects reservoir and pebble fountain

12 Wildflower meadow with longer grass, set within lawn, to attract beneficial insects and other creatures

13 Lavender "moat" separates children's play area from lawn; play area has floor of play-grade wood chips with split-rail edging

14 Living-willow tunnel, with floor of deep, weed-suppressing wood chips to children's den

15 Planting of small native trees and shrubs to support wildlife

16 Compost/leaf mold bins

17 Logs to give shelter to beetles, frogs, and toads (good pest-controllers) and to grow shiitake mushrooms

KEY TO THE EDIBLE PARADISE

1 Diverse food plants, including hazelnuts, mulberries, wild strawberries, Japanese wineberries, blackberries, and sunflowers
2 Meadow containing edible leaves such as sorrel, dandelion, and salad burnet; close-mown edges control their spread and give access
3 Raised beds for lettuce and edible flowers
4 Paved area using reclaimed wood
5 Solar greenhouse provides natural warmth for tender crops and solar-heated hot tub

6 Composting toilet
7 Worm compost bins, outside log and vegetable storage
8 Barrels store water from all roofs
9 Paths of reclaimed brick and crushed brick aggregates; planting pockets for herbs
10 Lavender, thyme, bee balm, and oregano to attract beneficial insects
11 Hedge of *Rosa eglanteria* and *R. rugosa*, providing fruits for humans and birds
12 Chicken house; adjoining orchard doubles as chicken run
13 Soft fruit; peach trained against sunny wall
14 Shady area; leaf mold and

compost bins, logs to grow mushrooms, ivy for nesting birds
15 Vegetable beds allowing for 4-year rotation (see p. 303)
16 Greenhouse and coldframes; tool shed; area surfaced with bark mulch
17 Pool, with gentle slope for wildlife access; leads into bog garden
18 Comfrey for making liquid fertilizer
19 Patio of log rounds, grooved for nonslip surface, set into bed of fine crushed brick aggregate
20 Lawn

Edible paradise

This plan shows a highly productive plot for food-loving gardener-cooks who want to grow unusual crops as well as more conventional fruit and vegetables.

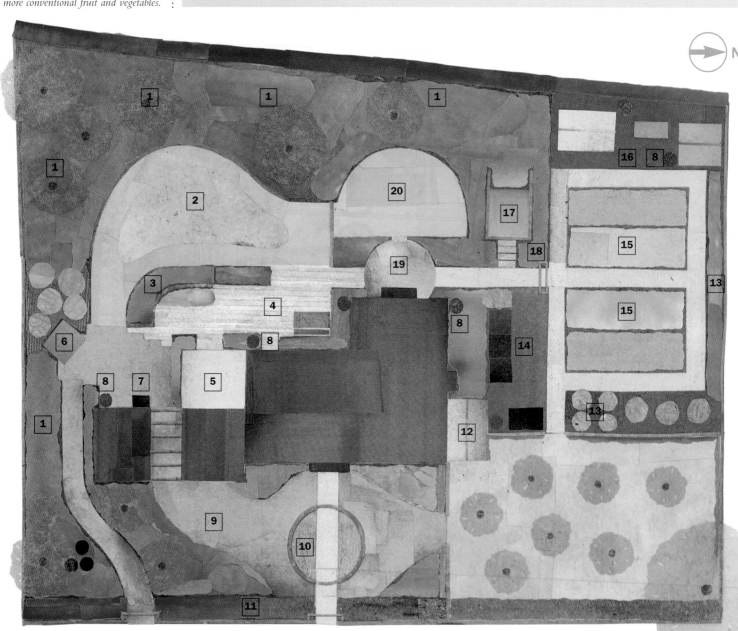

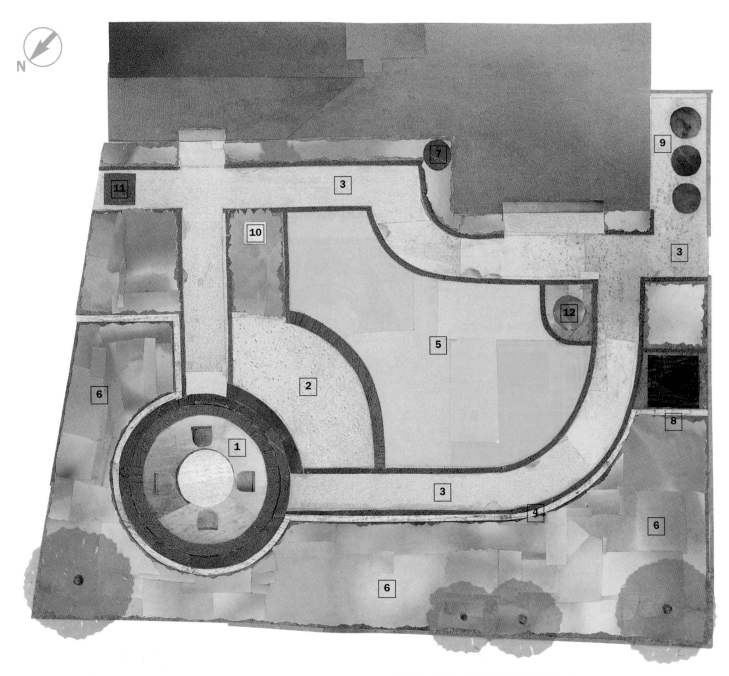

N

KEY TO THE CITY GARDEN

1 Patio, with table and chairs for outdoor eating, uses only natural materials—reclaimed bricks encircle paving of broken tiles
2 Pond attracts wildlife such as pest-controlling birds, insects, and amphibians; gentle slope on flowerbed side gives creatures easy access
3 Retaining wall, needed after leveling slope, constructed from heavy, vertical, reclaimed wooden beams
4 Paths of crushed slate (by-product of slate industry) edged with brick contain pockets for groundcover plants to accent the slate's dark tones
5 Small flowery lawn contains spring bulbs, daisies, and clover, which help increase wildlife diversity; requires little mowing or maintenance
6 Low-maintenance, all-year-interest planting of shrubs will also provide food and shelter for birds and other creatures
7 Water barrel collects rainwater from house roof for use on plants in pots and for the pond
8 Compost bin
9 Household recycling bins for paper, glass, and cans
10 Bird table attracts pest-controlling birds
11 Worm compost bin for recycling kitchen waste
12 Terra-cotta pot (focal point) can be used for herbs or lettuce plants

City garden
A garden on a small sloping site is designed to provide relaxation and refreshment in an urban surrounding.

The
basics

KEY ORGANIC TECHNIQUES FOR A GREENER GARDEN

Soil and soil care

THE SOIL IS A LIVING ENVIRONMENT, WITH AS MUCH
INFLUENCE ON PLANTS AS THE ENVIRONMENT ABOVE GROUND

TO AN ORGANIC GARDENER, the soil is the
most important aspect of the garden. Building and
maintaining fertile, healthy soil is the first priority.
Much can be done to improve poor soil, but before
work begins it is important to find out more about
your soil type, its texture, and its structure. Soil
texture or type depends on the physical location and
the geology of the area. Soil structure is determined
by previous cultivation—how the soil has been
managed, if at all, in the past. Both texture and
structure have an effect on soil chemistry—whether
it is more acid or alkaline. This in turn will
determine which plants are likely to grow well and
the amount of life in the soil.

What is soil?

Soil is often just taken for granted—treated like dirt.
Although it may look lifeless, soil is a complete
underground living environment, teeming with life.
It supports plants and provides them with the food
and water they need. The soil environment is just as
important to plants as the environment above ground.

Understanding the particular characteristics of
the soil in your garden will help you to get the best
from it and to look after it effectively. The type of
soil and its past history of cultivation will influence
what you can grow, how and when (or if) you
should cultivate it, how easy it will be to work, its
nutrient- and water-holding capacity, how freely it
drains, and how quickly it warms up in the spring.

Getting to know a soil

As you garden, you will gradually get to know your
soil as you cultivate, sow, plant, weed, and notice
which plants thrive and which are less successful. If
you are just getting to know a new garden or plot,
however, take a close look at the soil from the start.
Pick up a handful and feel it to get an idea of the
texture (see p. 34); dig a hole and look at the "soil
profile" to find out more about the structure, or
send a sample for analysis (see p. 37) to measure the
pH and identify nutrient imbalances.

Soil structure

The fertility of soil is not simply a question of
the quantity of plant foods that it contains—it is
the sum of all the features that are necessary for
plant growth. The structure of the soil—the way
it is put together—is just as important. A heavy
clay soil, for example, can be rich in plant foods
but still grow poor plants because it is too heavy and
waterlogged for adequate root growth. Simply
improving its structure—allowing more air into the
soil by adding bulky organic matter—can make a
dramatic difference. Light, sandy soils may be low in
nutrients, but the simple addition of a low-fertility
soil improver such as leaf mold, which increases the
soil's ability to hold on to food and water, can again
make a dramatic improvement.

Unlike soil type, soil structure is something that
the gardener can alter. This chapter describes how
to understand and improve soil structure and, just
as importantly, how to avoid destroying it.

**Get to know your soil
(facing page)**
*The simplest activities—walking and
digging in your garden, or examining
the soil when it's both wet and dry—
will tell you a lot about your soil. The
more you garden and grow plants the
more you will learn, almost without
being aware of it.*

SOIL STRUCTURE INDICATORS

Good structure	Poor structure
· Plant roots penetrate deeply.	· Plants have shallow roots.
· Sweet, earthy smell.	· Unpleasant smell.
· Water does not sit long in the bottom of a hole after rain.	· Water sits in holes or on the surface (below), or drains through immediately.
· The soil is relatively easy to dig.	· Soil sticky or in hard lumps, or very dry.
· No hard "pan"—compacted layer—in the topsoil.	· Few worms.
· Lots of worm channels.	· Compacted layer in topsoil.
· Top layers of soil crumbly and friable when both wet and dry.	· Surface layer slumps when wet and dries out to a crust.

What's in a soil?

Approximately half the volume of soil is made up of mineral particles from weathered rocks, organic matter, and living organisms; the other half is water and air. Together these ingredients form an effective medium to support plant growth. Plant foods are supplied by mineral particles and the breakdown of organic matter. The chemical composition of the soil also determines its pH—its acidity or alkalinity. This will affect what plants you can grow and possibly the availability of certain nutrients.

Soil type

Over millions of years rocks are weathered down into small particles, which form the basic ingredient of almost all soils. The size and chemical composition of the particles depend on the rock they came from and determine the type of soil you have. There are three types of weathered rock particles that make up soil: sand, silt, and clay.

The proportion of the different particles found in a soil determine its type—what name it is given—and how it behaves and should be managed. Most soils contain a mixture of all three particle types. If they are in roughly equal proportions, the soil is called a loam. If one type begins to predominate, then it will be called a sandy, silt, or clay loam—and the soil will begin to take on the characteristics of that particular particle type. It is not always easy to determine exactly what type of soil you have, particularly in a garden where different soils may have been brought in. However, handling a sample of moist soil, rolling it between your fingers into a "sausage," can give you some indication of the predominating particle types (see *Appearance and feel* in the table below). Take a handful of soil and add water to it. Work the soil in your hand until it is evenly moist and take out any stones or lumps.

• **Clay soils** Soils where clay particles predominate tend to be dense, sticky, and heavy to work. The tiny clay particles settle together, with little room for air.

• **Sandy soils** At the other extreme, soils with a high sand content tend to be dry. The relatively large spaces between sandy soil particles are too big to hold water, so it drains through quickly, taking plant nutrients with it.

• **Silt soils** Fall somewhere between clay and sand.

• **Peat soils** These form where wet, acid conditions prevented full decomposition of organic matter. They are rich in organic matter and may be very

Soil type

All soils, except peaty ones, are rock-based. Their differing particle sizes, although they may seem minimal to us, are critical to their different textures. If a particle of clay were enlarged until it was as big as a grain of sand, the grain of sand, similarly enlarged, would be a boulder as tall as a person.

WHAT TYPE IS YOUR SOIL?

Soil type	Appearance and feel	Advantages	Disadvantages
Peaty soils and soils very rich in organic matter	Black or very dark, feels spongy; will not maintain any shape, cannot be rolled into a ball	Easy to work, makes a good seedbed	Can be very dry in summer and wet in winter; suitable only for acid-loving plants
Clay soils	Sticky, heavy feel; holds together well in a ball; can be rolled into a "sausage" shape: the higher the clay content, the thinner the sausage	Can be rich in plant nutrients and water	Roots may find it difficult to penetrate the soil to reach nutrients and water
Sandy soils	Feels gritty, makes a rasping sound when rubbed between the fingers; a light sand will not stick together or form a ball, a sandy loam is slightly more cohesive	Sandy soils warm up quickly and are easy to cultivate	Usually low in nutrients; water drains away rapidly, often washing out nutrients with it
Silty soils	Soapy, very silky feel; makes a squeaky sound when rubbed, leaving fingers dirty	Reasonably moisture-retentive and nutrient-rich	Compacts easily, so can be heavy to work
Saline (salt-affected) soils	Found mostly in arid regions; high pH	None	High salt content harms many plants; gypsum can help

SOME VISIBLE GROUND-DWELLERS

Earthworms
Slugs
Centipedes
Millipedes
Sowbugs (far left)
Leatherjackets
Ground beetles and their larvae (near left)

Most soil-dwelling organisms are invisible to the naked eye. Tiny soil life forms include nematodes and a fungus that traps and consumes them.

acid and infertile, but can be fertile and productive.
• **Saline soils** These tend to be alkaline and infertile. They form in arid climates.

Air and water

Air and water are vital for soil-living creatures and for effective root and plant growth. Air and water are found in the spaces, or pores, between soil particles. Larger pores between sand or soil particles contain air, but they are usually too large to hold on to water. Medium-size pores hold water that roots can take up. A soil that contains a good mixture of both pore sizes can be described as well-drained and moisture-retentive. In a waterlogged soil, water replaces air in larger pores, making it difficult for plants and creatures to survive.

Soil life

Soil teems with many different kinds of life—from microscopic bacteria and fungi to more noticeable creatures such as earthworms, beetles, slugs, and insect larvae. Many of these creatures are responsible for recycling organic matter, breaking it down so that the nutrients it contains are once again available to plants. Their activities also build soil structure.

Some soil-living organisms can be plant pests and others may cause disease—but most do no harm or are beneficial. As in the environment above ground, the more diverse and active the community, the less likely it is that one particular organism will get out of hand. Problems are less

likely to arise in a soil with good structure that is rich in organic matter, which encourages a diverse and active microflora and -fauna.

Worms are the most obvious and well-known creatures found in soil. They are sometimes on the surface of the soil—they are unearthed when soil is cultivated. They help process organic matter by dragging it down into the soil before eating it. Their tunnels serve to aerate the soil and help it to drain; their casts provide a source of nutrients, and they help to form soil crumbs (see right).

Useful microorganisms

There are many microscopic organisms living in the soil. Despite their size, or lack of it, they perform functions vital to soil health. They include bacteria that can take up nitrogen from the air (nitrogen-fixing), and beneficial mycorrhizal fungi.

Nitrogen-fixing bacteria exist in a symbiotic relationship with the plant, living in nodules on the roots. Mycorrhizal fungi live by attaching themselves to the roots of plants. They work in harmony with the plant by helping it to absorb more water and nutrients; in return the plant provides food for the fungi. The surface area of the fungi is much greater than the area of the roots, so the fungi effectively extend the feeding area of the plant. Mycorrhizal fungi are fragile and are very sensitive to fungicides. They prefer soil that is not disturbed and thrive in "no-dig" gardens and those with a high organic soil content.

SOIL CRUMBS

The various types of mineral particles in a soil form, along with organic matter, what are called soil "crumbs," which are a few millimeters in diameter. The network of pores between the crumbs holds air and water, and this is where roots grow and soil creatures live. Where soil structure is good, these crumbs do not break down easily—and can survive battering by rain and cultivation. Where structure is poor, the crumbs easily collapse. A common example of this collapse is a hard crust, or "cap," which forms at the surface when poor soil dries out.

WHAT PLANT NUTRIENTS DO

Different nutrients are needed for different aspects of plant growth. Among the major nutrients, or "macronutrients," nitrogen fuels the growth of leaves and shoots, while magnesium is important in the production of chlorophyll, the pigment that makes leaves green (magnesium deficiency shown far right). Phosphorus is important in the growth of roots; potassium is vital to flowering and fruiting and "hardens" growth, increasing resistance to pests, diseases, and frost.

CHEMICAL SYMBOLS

Plant nutrients are commonly referred to by their chemical symbols—usually one or two letters—especially in the world of synthetic fertilizers, where the "NPK" ratio is a prominent aspect of labeling. However, organic gardeners may also find it useful to learn this convenient "shorthand."

Macronutrients
Nitrogen (N)
Phosphorus (P)
Potassium (K)
Magnesium (Mg)
Calcium (Ca)
Sulfur (S)

Micronutrients, or trace elements
Iron (Fe)
Manganese (Mn)
Copper (Cu)
Zinc (Zn)
Boron (B)
Molybdenum (Mb)

Symbols may also appear together to indicate chemical compounds—usually simply a common or more manageable form in which the nutrient can be applied. For example, rock phosphate may be written as P_2O_5, potash as K_2O, and limestone or calcium carbonate as $CaCO_3$.

Organic matter

Organic matter is the term used to describe the dead and decomposing remains of living things, such as plant debris, animal remains, and manures. It is a crucial part of the soil, providing food for soil-living creatures; for plants in particular, it is a major source of nitrogen. Without it, soil would be just sterile rock dust.

Organic matter is continually being broken down by soil creatures and by natural oxidation. In nature it is replenished in the natural cycles of life and death. Humus is the final product in the breakdown of organic matter. It acts as a valuable reservoir of water and plant nutrients, and it helps to form stable soil crumbs.

In short, organic matter:
• Feeds soil-living creatures
• Encourages a diverse flora and fauna in the soil
• Improves the physical structure of the soil
• Supplies plant foods
• Absorbs water
• Holds on to plant foods
• Buffers soil against pH changes

Plant nutrients

Plant foods are supplied by the breakdown of mineral particles and organic matter. Soil contains a wide range of nutrients that are required, in larger (macronutrients) or smaller (micronutrients or trace elements) amounts, for healthy plant growth. Most nutrients required for plant growth come from the basic mineral particles that make up the soil skeleton. They are also found in organic matter. Nitrogen is found only in living (or decaying) tissue, so bulky organic matter is a major source.

The complete range of plant foods can be found in most soils. Depending on what you are growing, you may need to augment the levels of nitrogen, phosphorus, potassium, and possibly magnesium—the nutrients that plants use in greatest amounts. Other minerals can occasionally be lacking, causing plant mineral deficiencies, which result in a variety of symptoms (see p. 89).

However, deficiency symptoms in plants are not always due to a shortage of a particular nutrient in the soil. An excess of one nutrient—caused by adding too much fertilizer, for example—can alter the chemistry of the soil to make other nutrients unavailable to plants. Poor structure, water shortage, and an unsuitable pH can also prevent plants from obtaining the nutrients that they need. Some nutrients, including nitrogen, are easily washed out of the soil.

There is generally no need to be concerned about the precise levels of plant foods in your soil. Using organic methods of soil management, you should be able to provide plants with a good, balanced diet. In a new garden, however, or where plants are failing for no obvious reason, a soil analysis may be useful to highlight any particular deficiency or imbalance that may exist. Ideally, use a soil analysis service designed for organic growers; this will indicate the potential of the soil, not simply the nutrients currently available.

Soil chemistry

An important characteristic of soil is its level of alkalinity or acidity, known as the pH. The pH scale runs from 1, extremely acidic, to 14, extremely alkaline. The range found in most soils is 4–8, with the majority of plants growing in the range 5.5–7.5. Ornamentals tend to tolerate quite a wide pH range, although some, such as many rhododendrons and heathers, will grow only in more acid soils, while others can tolerate a high pH. Vegetables prefer a pH in the range 6.5–7, fruit 6–6.5 (see those chapters for more details). The calcium level in the soil controls pH. Calcium can be washed out of the soil, especially if well-drained, making the soil more acid.

What effects does pH have?

The pH of a soil governs the availability of nutrients to plants. In very acid soils, plant foods may be washed out, or dissolve in the soil water at toxic levels. At the other end of the scale, plant foods may be locked up in the soil, unavailable to plants. Plants that can grow in more extreme pHs have adapted to deal with these problems.

Soil pH also has an effect on the diversity and activity of the soil life. Certain diseases, such as potato scab, are more troublesome in alkaline soils, while clubroot is much less so. Leatherjackets and wireworms are more common in acid conditions, but earthworms dislike acid soils.

Why test the pH?

An initial pH test when you take over a new garden (see below) can help you to choose the appropriate plants for the site. Always test the pH before adding lime to the soil, for example in the vegetable plot. Excessive liming can lock up certain nutrients, making them unavailable to plants.

LEARNING MORE ABOUT YOUR SOIL

Soil profiles

A good way to learn more about the structure of your soil is to dig a hole and have a look at what is known as the "soil profile." This will involve a fair amount of digging but can tell you a lot, and it may save disappointment in the future.

Dig a hole at least 3 ft. x 3 ft. (1 m x 1 m) and 3 ft. (1 m) or so deep. Clean up one vertical face of the hole and see what you can see.

The soil is likely to show two, or sometimes three, distinct layers:
• The upper layer, called topsoil, will be the darkest in color, with the top few inches being darker still if the soil has been well cared for. This is where most organic matter and soil life is concentrated. The topsoil layer can be from 2 to 24 in. (5–60 cm) deep. Its depth and composition depend on the geographical location and past soil management. You might even find wide variations in different parts of your garden.
• Topsoil ends where there is a distinct color change to the subsoil. Deep roots will penetrate the subsoil layer to find water; it will contain little else in the way of organic matter. The state of the subsoil will affect how the soil drains.
• In particularly shallow soil you may also see a third layer, the bedrock.

Taking a soil sample

If you are going to send soil for analysis to test for nutrient levels or measure the pH, it is important to take a representative sample; otherwise, the results will be meaningless. Only a small quantity of soil is required for analysis, but it must be representative of the thousands of pounds of soil in your garden.

If you are sending a sample for analysis, contact the testing service first to find out the quantity of soil required.

Do:
• Take soil to a depth of 6 in. (15 cm).
• Take separate samples from distinct areas or plots that have been treated differently.
• Take soil from at least 10 places in each plot, distributed randomly over the area. Put the soil into a clean plastic bucket and mix it thoroughly, using a trowel or other implement. Take the final sample for analysis from this.

Don't:
• Sample soil that has been recently limed or manured, or from near compost piles, bonfires, or hedges.
• Just take one trowelful of soil.
• Touch samples with your hands.

Measuring pH

There are several ways to measure pH.

Meters
Buy a simple pH meter, consisting of a probe inserted into the soil that displays a readout almost immediately. It may not be very accurate, but it will give you a rough and ready reading, with the advantage that you can take spot-readings at various points in the garden.

Kits
The easiest and cheapest pH testing kits use a liquid color change to indicate pH. These are a little more involved than the simple probe or meter, but can give reasonably accurate results. Take samples from various parts of the garden.

Analysis
For the most accurate reading, send a sample to a soil analysis laboratory, preferably one that provides a service for organic growers. It is important that the sample, or samples, are representative of the garden (see left).

Indicator plants

Look at the plants already growing in your garden and in the surrounding area. These "indicator plants" may be able to tell you a lot about soil chemistry. Be aware, though, that plants that thrive in extreme soil types are also usually just as happy in more average soil, so take a good look around at both wild and cultivated areas to see if you can get a broad picture. One other note of caution: If you have moved into a newly built home where a garden area has been created from scratch, remember that it is common practice for developers to import topsoil (often to cover a multitude of sins), and this may not match the soil in the locality.

• **Heavy clay/wet soil** Coltsfoot, cattails, horsetail (mare's tail)

• **Peaty/acidic soil** Azaleas, rhododendrons, blueberry, mountain laurel; blue hydrangeas retain their color only in acid soils

• **Sandy, dry soil** Purslane, butterflyweed

• **Alkaline soil** Pennycrest, pepperweed, scabious, beech, clematis

Managing soil organically

How you treat your soil depends on the soil type, how it has been managed in the past, and what is growing—or will be growing—in it. If drought-loving plants are chosen for a poor, well-drained soil, for example, it will need little attention. A wildflower meadow, which needs a low-nutrient soil to flourish, will soon be taken over by other species if you start to feed it. On the other hand, a compacted clay soil in the garden of a newly built house will need considerable effort to improve it. Shrubs growing in loamy soil will need no more than the occasional organic mulch, while a vegetable plot should have a planned program to maintain its performance.

The organic approach

The organic approach to soil care is a combination of good horticultural practice and the use, as needed, of bulky organic materials such as compost, animal manure, and green manure, supplemented with organic fertilizers (natural products of animal, plant, or mineral origin). Organic additives are often

Working from paths
Narrow beds are an ideal solution for heavy soils; raising the beds enables plenty of organic matter to be added, and working from paths avoids compacting the ground by walking on it.

PRINCIPLES OF ORGANIC SOIL CARE

• **Feed the soil** Bulky organic soil improvers feed the soil-living creatures that build soil structure and fertility.
• **Walk with care** A compacted soil is airless, difficult for roots to penetrate, and a poor environment for soil-living creatures.
• **Dig only when necessary** Digging has its uses, but it can destroy soil structure.
• **Keep it covered** A covering of plants, or a mulch, protects the soil structure.
• **Take care with plant nutrients** More problems are caused by overfertilizing than underfertilizing. The performance of your plants should be your guide.
• **Check the pH before you add lime** Too much lime can make nutrients unavailable.

---

recycled waste products. As well as benefiting the soil, their use helps to avoid the pollution that their disposal—in landfill sites or from burning—would cause. Organic gardeners, following nature's example, recycle plant and animal wastes, feeding the soil, rather than feeding plants directly. Soil-living creatures break down bulky organic materials in the soil. In the process, structure is improved and foods are made available to plants. A biologically active soil is a healthy place to grow.

Bulky soil improvers

Bulky organic materials (see p. 40), being of living origin, contain a wide range of essential plant foods and trace elements, as compared with the "quick-fix" fast-food diet of synthetic fertilizers with their readily soluble, limited selection of plant foods—which do nothing for the soil life or soil structure. They may be dug into the soil or spread over it as a mulch (see opposite). Plants fed on an organic diet are less attractive to some pests and diseases; organic composts can help to control soilborne pests and diseases.

Avoiding soil compaction

Compaction occurs when soils are walked on regularly or cultivated in wet conditions. It is a particular problem on heavy soils. Avoid it by creating paths or growing in beds that are narrow enough to be worked on from surrounding paths. Regular use of a mechanical cultivator can also cause a compacted layer or "pan" below the soil surface.

Digging and cultivating

Dig only when necessary, keeping it to a minimum. Digging is essential to break up hard and compacted ground, but regular digging increases the rate that organic matter—that essential component of a good soil—breaks down. Digging can encourage weeds, too; every time you turn the soil over, a new batch of weed seeds is brought to the surface to germinate.

Dig only when soil conditions are right, especially if your soil is heavy. It should not be so wet that it sticks to your shovel, nor so dry that you have to break up huge clods.

It is quite possible to garden without regular digging. The chapter *Growing Vegetables* gives information on the no-dig system (see p. 326).

Covering the soil with mulches

Regular mulching with an organic soil improver will do wonders for the structure of the vital surface layers of the soil—so emerging seedlings and water will penetrate it more easily. It will also help to keep the soil moist. Mulches insulate the soil from rapid changes in temperature and moisture. For this reason it is important not to mulch a dry soil until it has been soaked through by the rain. Wait until the soil has warmed up before mulching young plants. (Mulching a cold soil will keep it cool, slowing growth, making young plants more susceptible to

DIGGING TO BREAK UP COMPACTION

- Divide the area to be dug in half, lengthways.
- Remove a trench of soil, one spade deep—or as deep as the topsoil, if this is less than one spade deep.
- Loosen the soil in the bottom of the trench with a fork. Stab the tines in vertically and move the fork gently back and forth.
- Dig the next trench, using the soil to fill in the first trench.
- Continue to the end of the plot, then turn around and come back in the other direction.
- Fill in the final trench with the soil taken from your first trench.

---

pest damage.) As an added bonus, mulches suppress weeds (see pp. 76–77) and attract beetles, centipedes, and other pest-eating creatures, which enjoy the dark, moist conditions created. Keep mulches away from the base of most plants, particularly those with woody stems, to avoid encouraging stem rot.

Living mulches or green manures

Green manures (see pp. 56–57) are grown to cover bare soil—over winter, for example, or between widely spaced plants. They are specific plants grown to protect and build soil structure and to prevent nutrients from washing out of the soil. Leguminous green manures can be a useful source of nitrogen, which bacteria living in nodules on their roots take up from the air. These "nitrogen-fixers" can be valuable when growing vegetables, particularly if you do not want to use animal manures.

Altering soil chemistry

Organic fertilizers can be used, where necessary, to supply additional nutrients to the soil. Other mineral-based compounds can be used to change the pH of the soil; most commonly to raise it (increase alkalinity) by adding lime (see p. 61).

Distributing weight
When ground is wet, working from a board will distribute your weight and protect the soil structure, especially on clayey and silty soils.

Bulky organic soil improvers

Bulky materials of living origin maintain and improve soil structure—helping light soils to hold onto food and water, and heavy soils to drain more effectively. They may also supply plant foods, released as they are broken down by soil-living creatures. The table opposite lists a range of bulky organic soil improvers. Each has a "fertility rating" as a guide to its nutrient value, especially nitrogen content. These can be only a broad indication, as the exact nutrient content of this type of material can vary quite widely, depending on the basic ingredients and how it has been stored. Remember that there is often no need to use a nutrient-rich material. Low-fertility soil improvers can be extremely effective in maintaining soil fertility, despite their low nutrient value.

Many materials, such as kitchen and garden waste and animal manure, are usually composted before use to stabilize the plant nutrients they contain and to make them easier to apply.

Sources of organic soil improvers

Recycling, one of the basic tenets of organic growing, reduces the need to bring in outside additives and cuts down on the volume of "waste" to be disposed of. It is rarely possible to be totally self-sufficient in a garden situation, but all bulky organic materials from the house and garden should be recycled for use in the garden. These can be augmented with supplies brought in from other appropriate sources in the area.

Commercial soil improvers, such as composted manures and plant wastes, can be purchased if you are unable to make enough of your own. Where possible, choose a product that has some form of accreditation from an organic certifying organization. When in doubt, check with the supplier for the source of the ingredients. The word "organic" is not sufficient on its own; it may simply mean that the ingredients are "of living origin," not that they are appropriate for an organic garden.

Applying organic matter to the soil

All soil improvers can be applied as a mulch. Most can also be dug into the soil. Keep them in the top 6–8 in. (15–20 cm) or so, where the main feeding

---

MAXIMUM YEARLY APPLICATION RATES

- **High-fertility soil improvers**—up to one full builder's wheelbarrow (11 gal.) per 50 sq. ft. (50 liters/5 sq. m). This makes an evenly spread layer approximately ¼ in. (5 mm) deep.
- **Medium-fertility soil improvers**—up to two full builder's wheelbarrows (22 gal.) per 50 sq. ft. (100 liters/5 sq. m), making an evenly spread layer approximately ½ in. (1 cm) deep.
- **Low-fertility soil improvers** can be applied in greater quantities, and more frequently if needed. As mulches, use a 6-in. (15-cm) layer of lightweight materials such as bark and straw; up to 4 in. (10 cm) for heavier materials and those such as leaf mold that pack down densely.

Bulky organic soil improvers
Below, from left to right: manure and other waste from a chicken pen; cow manure with straw bedding (see also p. 58); seaweed; spent mushroom compost; hop waste; leaf mold; garden compost; shreddings from a municipal green waste composting site.

SOME ORGANIC SOIL IMPROVERS

Material	Fertility rating*	Mulch	Dig in	Notes
Bark, fine grade	Low	•	•	See *Mulches for Weed Control*, pp. 76–77
Compost, garden	Medium	•	•	See pp. 42–49
Compost, municipal	Low	•	•	Compost from large-scale composting facilities, recycling green waste; a good source of potassium; little nitrogen
Compost, worm (mostly from vegetable waste)	High	•	•	See pp. 52–55
Hay	Medium	•		Apply as a mulch only
Leaf mold	Low	•	•	Composted autumn leaves
Manure, animal	Medium to high	•	•	Should be well-rotted before use; obtain from non-intensive or organic farms
Spent mushroom compost	Medium	•	•	Tends to be alkaline; obtain from organic growers to avoid pesticide contamination
Commercial products— composted manures, plant wastes, and food wastes	Variable	•	•	Bagged materials available for purchase
Prunings, shredded green	Low to medium	•		Compost before use (see pp. 42–49)
Prunings, shredded woody	Low	•		Apply as a mulch around trees, shrubs, and perennial plants only; compost before use (see pp. 42–49)
Straw	Low	•		Obtain from an organic farm if possible
Wood chips and coarse bark	Low	•		Apply as a mulch around trees, shrubs, and perennial plants only

*This relates to the nutrient content of the material, particularly nitrogen.

roots of plants are at work and where good structure is most critical. Apply medium- and high-fertility materials in the spring and summer only; their nutrients will be wasted if applied over winter when plant growth is minimal. As for application rates, the maxim "if some is good, more must be better" does not apply when adding nutrient-rich materials to the soil. Too much nitrogen, for example, encourages leafy growth rather than fruits and flowers. Any excess may just be wasted, washed out of the soil and into our water supplies. Let the performance of your plants be your guide.

Making garden compost

The finished product
Garden compost is a rich, dark, soillike material. It has a pleasant, earthy smell when mature.

A place for a pile
A compost bin can be tucked into a corner of the ornamental garden or take center stage in the vegetable plot.

A compost pile is both a recycling facility for kitchen and garden waste and a small processing plant, producing a first-class, medium-fertility soil improver—garden compost. No garden should be without one—or two, or three....

Making compost is often seen as a complex art, but in fact it is not that difficult. Anyone can learn to do it. The actual process of converting waste into compost is carried out by naturally occurring creatures, from worms to microbes, that appear as if by magic. All you have to do is to supply a suitable mixture of ingredients and let them get on with it.

Where to make compost

You can make compost in a simple, covered pile in the corner of your yard, but a compost bin (see pp. 46–47) looks neater and can be easier to maintain. Your compost pile or bin should be situated on bare earth or grass, not on a hard surface such as a patio. It can be in sun or shade; what is important is that it is accessible, with plenty of room around it for adding, removing, and turning material.

The size of the pile or bin will depend on how much material you generate. Larger piles are better, but choose a size that suits you. If you have a large garden, you may need more than one bin. If you do not generate much garden waste but want to compost kitchen scraps, consider a high-fiber pile (see p. 44) or a worm bin (see p. 52).

What goes on a compost pile?

The main ingredients in a garden pile are likely to be weeds, grass, and other green waste, plus fruit and vegetable scraps from the kitchen. Other items, such as strawy manure, can be brought in to augment supplies. Anything once alive will compost, but some items are best avoided for health or practical reasons.

"Greens" and "browns"

The key to making good compost is to use a mixture of types of ingredients. Young, moist materials, such as grass clippings, rot quickly to a smelly sludge; these are known as "greens." They need to be mixed with tougher, dry items like old

What to compost (right)
*A huge variety of organic waste can be recycled onto the compost pile. Large quantities of items marked * are best dealt with in heaps of their own. Other miscellaneous compostable items include wood ash and eggshells. However, do **not** add:*
- *Meat and fish scraps*
- *Glass and cans*
- *Dog feces*
- *Used cat litter*
- *Disposable diapers*
- *Coal ashes*
- *Plastics*
- *Synthetic fibers*

INGREDIENTS FOR THE COMPOST PILE

"Greens"—quick to rot	Intermediate	"Browns"—slow to rot
Comfrey leaves	Fruit and vegetable scraps	Old straw
Grass clippings	Rhubarb leaves	Tough vegetable stems
Poultry manure (without bedding)	Coffee grounds	Herbaceous stems
Young weeds and plants	Tea bags	Old bedding plants
Nettles	Vegetable plant remains	Autumn leaves*
	Strawy animal manures	Woody prunings*
	Cut flowers	Tough and evergreen hedge clippings*
	Soft hedge clippings	Cardboard tubes, egg cartons, paper bags, and similar paper items, crumpled up
	Herbivore pet bedding	Newspaper
	Perennial weeds*	

bedding plants—"browns," which are slow to rot on their own. Browns add the necessary fiber to give the compost a good structure.

Many compostable items themselves contain a good balance of green and brown. When you have been making compost for a while, you will get a feel for the right mixture. If the contents of your compost pile tend to be wet and smelly, mix in more browns; if they are dry, bring in the greens.

The only other ingredients needed are air and water. Mix materials that tend to pack down and exclude air, such as grass clippings, with more open items to ensure a supply of air. Water dry items, or mix them with the moister greens.

High-fiber composting
A research project by the Centre for Alternative Technology in Wales has identified that one of the main problems in composting, especially for those

with smaller gardens, is a lack of brown materials to balance the greens, which tend to be predominately kitchen waste. To address this problem, they have developed the "high-fiber" composting technique, which uses scrap paper and packaging—kitchen paper, paper bags, cardboard cartons, and tubes, for example—to provide the balance of ingredients required. These are crumpled up before being added to the pile. Roughly equal volumes of kitchen waste and paper products are added as they become available. The composting process is slow but requires no further attention.

Compost activators
Greens, which are quick to rot, will activate a pile (get it started). There are various types of commercial activators on the market said to speed up the composting process, but a mixed pile should compost perfectly adequately without.

To be composted
From left to right: general household waste; old straw; weeds; spent bedding plants; soft hedge clippings; dead cut flowers; bedding from rabbit and hamster cages; grass clippings, with the addition of some crumpled sheets of newspaper.

Chopping and shredding
Mashing and chopping up tough material will help it compost. A sharp spade can be used to chop most items, including tough vegetable stems. A mechanical shredder will make short work of woody hedge prunings, for example, which can then be composted or used as a mulch.

Composting weeds and diseased material

To avoid the risk of spreading troublesome weeds, compost them before they seed. Put perennial roots in a black plastic bag, mixed with some grass clippings, and leave to rot for a year. When dead, add to the compost pile.

The biological activity in a compost pile is so great that it can break down many plant diseases. Any heat produced will help the process. Even so, it is probably wise not to add plants infected with very persistent diseases such as clubroot and white rot. Likewise, keep foliage infected with potato (late) blight out of your compost bin. It poses a risk to commercial potato crops and should be destroyed.

Hedge clippings and woody prunings

Add soft young clippings—from a regularly pruned hedge, for example—to the compost pile. Tougher prunings in any quantity, including evergreen hedge clippings, are best composted separately, preferably after shredding. Pile them up or put them in a compost bin, and water well. Mix with a green material, or water with a nitrogen-rich liquid fertilizer, such as nettle or comfrey liquid (see p. 207), to speed up the process. Use after 6 months or more as a mulch on established shrubs and trees.

Recycling woody waste

Tough and chunky material will compost much more quickly if chopped up into smaller pieces. A sharp spade will chop all but the most woody items. For these, use a shredder. Rent a shredder for occasional use or buy the most powerful one you can afford. Try out a range—some are much quieter and easier to use than others.

Wear adequate safety protection when using a shredder. Don goggles, hearing protection, and

A SIMPLE BIN

This compost bin is simple and cheap to make. It is also an excellent way to recycle cardboard boxes.

Hammer four posts into the ground in a square, and unroll chicken wire around the posts on the inner and the outer sides, stapling or nailing it in place (**1**). Be sure when you trim it to size to fold over any sharp edges. Slide cardboard between the two layers (**2**) for insulation. You can leave the front open for easy access (**3**), or make a hinged fourth side, like a gate, that will keep the heap neat. Cover the heap with old carpet, a tarp, or a similar material (**4**).

sturdy gloves, and never use your hands to clear out clogged or jammed material.

If you have space, woody items can be stacked in an out-of-the-way corner and left to decay over a period of years. They will make a valuable wildlife habitat (see also p. 190). Some may be suitable for use around the garden—as plant supports, for example. Your local waste disposal site may recycle woody items if you cannot. Avoid burning, which causes pollution and nuisance, unless you have diseased woody plants to dispose of.

Compost bins

Compost bins can be purchased or homemade, preferably from recycled or reused materials. As long as it fulfills the basic criteria listed, the design choice is yours. Choose one that suits your needs and garden. Place it in an accessible spot, directly onto bare ground. It can have a permanent location or, depending on the model, it can be moved to different parts of the garden between batches.

Once you have started making compost, you may find that two or more containers are needed,

Compost bins
Fom left to right:
• Four posts, some wire netting, and a slatted wooden front make a simple, economic bin.
• A sectional or slatted wooden box (see also facing page, above) makes filling and removing the compost simple.
• A traditional wooden "New Zealand" box. Two of these side by side is ideal. One bay is filled while the other is maturing. Removable slats allow easy access to the compost.
• Recycled plastic containers are compact and usually have no base; simply lift them off the ground to get the compost.

A BEEHIVE BOX

One of the easiest wooden bins to construct, the beehive type has the advantage of looking neat in a garden setting. It can be painted and stained; some people make wooden lids to complete the effect. The wooden layers are all built the same way, with the battens that hold them together slightly elevated (**1**) so each will fit securely on top of the one below. The bin can be built up at the same rate as you add the compost (**2,3**), up to a height of 3 ft. (1 m) or so. As the contents decompose the compost will sink, and layers can be removed to start a new heap. Turning the compost is easy with this type of bin, provided that the piece of ground next to it is left clear. Simply take off the layers and restack them next to the heap, turning the compost into the "new" bin as you go (**4**).

although it is possible to get by with just one. Once maturing, compost can be covered with carpet or a plastic sheet, freeing up the bin that it was in.

Making compost

• Collect a mixed batch of greens and browns suitable for composting, as much as you can find.

• Add it to the compost bin, spreading it out to the edges. Tamp down gently and water if dry.

• Continue to add to the bin as material becomes available. If you add kitchen waste on its own, mix it

WHAT MAKES A GOOD COMPOST BIN?

• Solid sides.
• Open base.
• Wide top opening for easy filling.
• Rainproof lid or cover that does not blow away.
• Minimum volume of 66 gal. (300 liters), or 30 in. x 30 in. x 39 in. (75 cm x 75 cm x 1 m).
• Removable side, or lift-off container, to access compost.

The composting process
If you fill a bin gradually, the bottom layers will be the first to decompose (right), generating heat that will rise through the pile and be lost from an open bin or uncovered pile. The heat is valuable to the composting process, so cover the pile to keep it in. A cover will also conserve moisture, while keeping out the rain. You can add extra insulation by making a compost "blanket"—a padded plastic pad (far right).

in with what is already in the bin.

• You may never fill the bin completely, as everything decreases in volume as it decays.

• After 6–12 months, or sooner if the bin is almost full, stop adding any more.

• Leave it to finish composting, and start a new bin that can be used in the meantime.

• Alternatively, check progress. Remove any compost that has formed in the lower layers. Replace the uncomposted material in the bin, adjusting the mixture if it is too wet or dry. Continue to add to this heap.

Hot tips for quicker compost

• **Fill the compost bin all at once** with a good mixture of materials. The heap should get quite hot, speeding the process and killing weed seeds.

• **Turn the heap.** Remove everything from the bin, mix it all up, and replace it in the container. Turning a "hot" heap that has cooled will reactivate it; this can usually be repeated once or twice. Turning a slow heap now and again gives you an opportunity to see how it is working and to adjust the mixture if necessary.

• **Chop up** tough and bulky items with a spade or shredder.

How long does it take?

Compost is ready to use when it looks like dark soil (as shown on p. 42) and none of the original ingredients are recognizable—apart from the odd twig, eggshell, or corn cob. It can be ready to use in as little as 12 weeks in summer, if you follow the "hot tips" above, but it can also take up to a year or more. Both quick and slow compost can be equally valuable.

Using compost

Garden compost can be classified as a medium-fertility soil improver. Apply it where required at a rate of up to two full builder's wheelbarrows (22 gal.) per 50 sq. ft. (100 liters/5 sq. m). This is a layer of approximately ½ in. (1 cm) thick spread out evenly over the ground. Apply compost in spring or summer as a mulch, or dig it into the top 8 in. (20 cm) of the soil.

TRENCH COMPOSTING

Another way to recycle kitchen and vegetable waste is to bury it in a trench or pit, and grow peas, beans, squash or pumpkins on top of it. It is an effective way of providing a source of nutrients and moisture where it is required.

In the autumn, dig a trench or pit, one spade deep. For peas and beans, dig it one spade wide, and as long as the row. Make a pit approximately 3 ft. x 3 ft. (1 m x 1 m) for each cucurbit plant. Gradually fill with vegetable scraps and kitchen waste, covering each addition with soil. When full, cover with the rest of the soil and leave it for a couple of months.

Sow or plant into the trench at the appropriate time for the crop, after the soil has settled.

LEAF MOLD AGING

1 Freshly collected leaves in autumn.
2 The following autumn—rough, year-old leaf mold makes an excellent mulch.
3 Two-year-old leaf mold is much finer and can be used as a soil improver or an ingredient in growing media (see pp. 116–117).

Leaf mold containers
The simplest cages are made from four wooden stakes driven into the ground, wrapped with chicken wire or rabbit fencing. A cage full of leaves decreases in volume dramatically as they decay to form leaf mold.

Making leaf mold

When leaves fall from trees in the autumn, they decay on the ground to form a rich, dark material called leaf mold, which is an excellent soil conditioner. Making leaf mold in your garden is easy to do. All you need is a supply of autumn leaves and a simple container to keep them from blowing away. Throwing leaves out with the trash or burning them is a waste of a very valuable resource.

Which leaves to use?

Any leaves fallen from deciduous trees and shrubs can be collected in autumn to make leaf mold. Do not use evergreens, such as laurel and holly. Leaves of some species take longer than others to decay, but all rot eventually. To supplement supplies, collect leaves from quiet streets or, with permission, from parks and cemeteries. Leaves from busy roadsides can be polluted with oil and vehicle emissions. Local authorities may be prepared to deliver a supply. Never collect leaves or leaf mold from woodland. An easy way to collect leaves from a lawn is to run the mower over them. The grass and chopped-leaf mixture collected by the mower will rot easily.

Alternatively, mow without the leaf bag on the mower. The chopped leaves will soon be absorbed into the lawn.

Making the leaf mold

Collect fallen leaves in the autumn, preferably after rain so they are wet. If the leaves are dry, soak them well with water. Stuff the leaves into a container or stack them in a corner. Leave them to decay.

Simple leaf mold containers can be made with netting and posts, or bought. There is no need for a lid or solid sides, nor is size critical—just big enough to hold your supply of leaves. Smaller quantities can be stuffed into plastic bags. Make a few air holes with a garden fork when the bags are full, and tie the top loosely. An even simpler method is to just pile the leaves in a sheltered corner and wait.

A leaf mold pile may heat up slightly, but the process is generally slow and cold. It can take anything from 9 months to 2 or more years to make a useable batch, depending on the tree species and the particular use. The information on the facing page suggests ways to use your leaf mold.

USING LEAVES AND LEAF MOLD

Leaf mold can generally be used as a low-fertility soil improver (see pp. 40–41) and a moisture-retaining mulch after 1 year. It should be darker and more crumbly than newly fallen leaves but does not have to be fully rotted. For a finer product for use in seed and potting mixes or as a topdressing for lawns, leave it to decay for another year, or even 2 if the leaves are very slow to rot.

Apply leaf mold in a layer up to 4 in. (10 cm) thick, leaving it as a surface mulch or lightly forking it in if required. It can be applied to any plants at any time of year.

• Leaf mold is particularly valuable as a winter cover for bare soil, especially where small seeds, such as carrots, are to be sown. Newly fallen leaves can also be used for winter cover, raking them off in the spring before sowing.

• Leaf mold also makes a good moisture-retentive mulch, applied once the soil has warmed up in the spring.

• Protect the crowns of tender plants such as penstemons with a blanket of leaf mold or newly fallen leaves, held down with conifer prunings. It will keep off frost in the winter and help to retain moisture in the summer.

• To make a more nutrient-rich material for use in a potting mix, add comfrey leaves to 1-year-old leaf mold (see also p. 207) and allow them to decay together for a few months.

• Two-year-old leaf mold can be mixed with loam and sand to make a topdressing mix for a lawn (see p. 179).

Worm composting

Certain types of earthworm, found naturally in piles of leaves and in manure and compost piles, specialize in decomposing plant wastes. Colonies of these worms can be housed in a container and fed kitchen and garden waste, which they will convert into a rich manure known as worm compost—a high-fertility soil improver.

A worm compost system can be kept working year-round. It is a good alternative to a traditional compost pile when the main material available for composting is kitchen scraps and vegetable waste. It cannot cope with large volumes of material at once.

Worms and worm bins

Common or garden earthworms seen in soil are not suitable for use in worm composting bins. Brandling worms (*Eisenia foetida*) are the type most commonly used. They are very efficient recyclers of organic waste and will reproduce quickly in the confines of the bin. It is a good idea to start a worm bin with at least 1,000 worms—about 18 oz. (500 g) in weight. They can be extracted from a maturing compost pile, a manure stack, or another worm bin, or they can be purchased by mail order. The dark, moist

conditions that worms need to live in can be provided by keeping them in a plastic bin or a wooden box. Worm bins can be purchased, or you can make your own—or adapt existing containers such as wooden crates or boxes (see facing page), or a plastic trash can (see below). Because worms like to feed near the surface, the most effective bins have a relatively large surface area. Good drainage is vital, as kitchen waste can produce a lot of moisture, and the worms will drown if conditions are too wet. If there is no reason to move your worm bin, there is no need for it to have a base; it can simply be set directly on to the soil. There is no need for the container to be "wormproof;" the worms will stay put if the conditions are right for them.

Where to keep a worm bin

Worms work best at temperatures between 50 and 77°F (12–25°C). They will survive considerably lower temperatures, but the rate at which they produce compost will slow down. Keep a worm bin where temperatures do not fluctuate widely—out of direct sunlight in summer. Move the bin into a shed

Worms for a worm bin
Brandling worms, also called red wigglers or manure worms, have a characteristic red-and-yellow banding. Their eggs are borne in tiny, lemon-shaped cocoons.

Trash can worm bin
Cross-section through a plastic trash can converted into a worm composting bin (see far right).

MAKING A WORM BIN FROM A TRASH CAN

1 Drill two rings of holes all around the can, one 4–6 in. (10–15 cm) from the bottom, the other 3–4 in. (7.5–10 cm) below the rim.
2 To create a drainage reservoir so that the worms do not drown in accumulated liquid, fill the base of the bin with a layer of gravel approximately 6 in. (15 cm) deep. This also stabilizes the bin with its weight.
3 Cut a circle of plywood to fit over the gravel and drill holes in it—or use a perforated disc of heavy-duty polyethylene.
4 Add a 6–12 in. (15–30 cm) layer of damp bedding material. This can be strips of newspaper, shredded cardboard, old compost, or leaf mold; it must not be raw, uncomposted material.
5 Add the worms.
6 Add a thin layer of suitable food (see facing page); spread loosely over half of the surface.
7 Cover the food with a layer of damp newspaper. Replace the lid of the trash can.

or warm greenhouse in winter, or insulate it well before the cold weather starts. A worm bin with an integral drainage system can be kept indoors, in a shed or porch for example, and moved out in the summer. Other bins may need to be set on bare soil to absorb any excess liquid produced.

Feeding the worms

A worm compost bin is typically used to process kitchen and vegetable scraps, which are usually available "little and often." This suits the worms, which cannot process large quantities at once. Remember that they are, in effect, livestock, with limited appetites! Excess food will "turn" before they can process it—resulting in an unpleasant smell. The worms will not process rotting food, and may well die. A worm bin can also be used to process garden waste if it is added in small quantities. A sprinkling of ground limestone (see p. 61) every month will help to keep conditions in the bin sweet.

How much your worm bin can process in a week depends on the temperature and the number of worms. Add no more than 5–7 pints (3–4 liters) of suitable food at a time. Start slowly, and build up the feeding gradually. It is important to judge what is happening before adding any more. Chop up

---

WHAT CAN I PUT IN MY WORM BIN?

Yes
- Vegetable peelings
- Vegetable crop waste
- Eggshells
- Fruit peelings
- Cooked leftovers
- Shredded paper
- Paper bags
- Coffee grounds
- Tea leaves
- Onion skins
- Egg cartons
- Kitchen paper

No
- Large amounts of citrus peel
- Dairy products
- Meat and fish
- Cat/dog feces
- Purchased flowers
- Plastic, glass, cans, and other items not of living origin

---

larger items to speed up the process. A worm bin will survive many weeks without food being added. Do not be tempted to add lots of extra food before you go away on vacation.

Common problems

A worm compost system that is working well does not smell. If a worm bin begins to smell unpleasant and the food you add is not being processed, this is a

WOODEN WORM BIN

This homemade worm bin is useful where quantities of waste are very small and space is limited. It consists of two wooden boxes from which the bases have been removed, one within the other, with a thick layer of straw packed between the two as insulation—this helps avoid extreme fluctuations of temperature, and in cold weather will ensure that the worms keep on doing their work. The box needs a sturdy lid. Thick plastic around the inner sides of the inner box keeps moisture in and helps to keep the worms warm. Add small amounts of food to the existing compost in a different spot each time, and cover it with damp newspaper to keep it moist.

Additional visitors
Small white, threadlike enchytraid worms may appear in large numbers in a worm bin. They are quite harmless, but can be a sign that the contents of the bin are rather acid. They are not young compost worms.

Extracting the worms
When the finished worm compost is spread out on the ground, the worms will automatically move to gather in the cooler, damper conditions under the sheet of wet newspaper. This worm-rich compost can then be gathered up and returned to the bin.

sure sign that something is wrong. The two main causes are overfeeding and excess moisture, which may be the result of poor drainage or overfeeding. If there are still some live worms in the compost, stop feeding for a while. Mix in moisture-absorbing materials, such as newspaper, egg cartons, paper towels, and cardboard tubes. Add a sprinkling of limestone and clear any drainage holes.

If on investigation you cannot see any active worms at all, you will have to assume that they are dead. Clear out the bin and start again.

Tiny black fruit flies may appear in a worm bin, especially in summer. They are not a health hazard, but can be annoying. Burying waste as you add it may cut down their numbers. Alternatively, they can be caught in a homemade trap. Never use pesticides on a worm compost bin.

Removing the compost

After a few months of regular feeding, the worms will have begun to produce a rich, dark compost in the bottom of the bin. To remove a small amount, scrape back the top layer of uneaten material and worms and take what you need.

If you want to remove larger quantities of compost, first scoop off the top layer of semi-decomposed food and worms and set this aside, and then replace this material when you have emptied out the compost.

Extracting the worms

You may find that the compost is full of worms. These should be extracted if you are to use the compost in growing media, or you may just want them back in your worm bin. On a dry, sunny day, spread the compost out on a hard surface, in a layer no more than 2 in. (5 cm) deep. Place a layer of wet newspaper, several sheets thick, over one-third to one-half of the compost. Go away and do something else for several hours. The worms will hide under the newspaper and can be shoveled up in the damp compost below. By repeating the process, you can collect nearly all of the worms.

Using worm compost

Worm compost made from vegetable waste is a high-fertility soil improver (see also p. 41), with a fine, crumbly texture. It tends to be richer than garden compost, and the plant foods it contains are more readily available. It is rich in humus and has good water-holding capacity. These qualities, and the fact that it tends to be available in relatively small quantities, mean that it is usually used more like a concentrated fertilizer than a bulky organic compost (see facing page for some suggestions).

Worm liquid

Vegetable waste has a very high moisture content. Water will tend to accumulate in plastic worm bins,

Collecting liquid
This commercial worm bin has a tap at the base to drain off liquid rich in nutrients. Put the bin on bricks so that you can get a bowl under it.

Mountains of food
Heavy feeders such as young melon and squash plants enjoy the richness of worm compost in their compost mix.

and the worms may drown unless adequate drainage is provided. If there is a reservoir at the bottom of the bin, the liquid can be drained off through a standard water barrel tap. This liquid contains some plant foods, which can be recycled by watering it onto the compost pile. It may also be used to feed container-grown plants (diluted at least 10:1 with water), but the results are likely to be variable.

WAYS TO USE WORM COMPOST

• Apply as a topdressing to greedy feeders such as squash and other fruiting vegetable crops during the growing season.
• Apply as a topdressing for patio pots or house plants—if necessary, remove the top 1 in. (2 cm) of the potting mix (see also *Container Gardening*, p. 203), and replace with worm compost. Water as usual.
• Add to a commercial potting mix to enrich it and improve its water-holding capacity—for hanging baskets, for example.
• Use as an ingredient in homemade potting soils and other growing media (see right, and also pp. 114–117).

POTTING MIX WITH WORM COMPOST

This is a rich potting mix, suitable for tomatoes, eggplants, and hanging baskets, for example. Mix together:

• One or two 2-gal. (9-liter) buckets of worm compost.
• One bucket of sharp sand or horticultural sand.
• Three buckets of well-rotted leaf mold or other peat alternative.
• 2½ oz. (75 g) ground limestone (see p. 61).

Green manures

Green manures are plants grown to improve the soil, rather than for food or ornament. Their beneficial characteristics include nitrogen-fixing, dense foliage for weed suppression, and extensive or penetrative roots, ideal for opening up heavy soils and improving light soils.

Why grow green manures?

• **To add plant foods** Clovers and related green manures absorb nitrogen from the air and fix it in nodules on their roots. It becomes available to plants when the green manure is dug in. Some extract minerals from deep in the soil, bringing them up for subsequent shallow-rooted plants.

• **To protect soil** Green manures protect soil from compaction by heavy rain, particularly important on heavy clay. Green manures also mop up plant foods from the soil, so they are not washed out by rain.

• **To improve structure** Winter rye, with its very extensive fine root system, improves heavy soil by opening up the structure; on lighter soils, the roots bind with soil particles, helping them to hold water.

• **To smother weeds** Green manures germinate quickly and grow rapidly, smothering weed seedlings. (See *Weeds and Weed Control*, p. 73.)

• **To control pests** Frogs, beetles, and other natural predators appreciate the cool, damp cover provided by a green manure. Some insects can be confused by the presence of a green manure crop planted between food crops. (See *Plant Health*, p. 84.)

• **To "rest" your soil** To give your soil a rest, sow a longer-term green manure and leave it to grow for a whole season. This will help soil recover from constant cultivation and improve fertility and structure with little effort.

Choosing a green manure

The specific green manure you choose will depend on what you want to achieve, how long the ground needs to be covered, what was there before, what you will be planting next, the time of year, and the type of soil you have. At first, the list of possibilities seems long and confusing, but if you apply some simple rules you can choose the best plant for your situation. These are the questions you need to ask when choosing which green manure to use:

• **How does the green manure fit into my crop rotation?** (See *Growing Vegetables*, p. 293.)

• **When do I want to sow?** Choose hardy varieties to overwinter.

• **How long do I want the green manure to grow?** Some mature more quickly than others.

• **What I am going to plant next?** Winter rye can inhibit seed germination for several weeks after it has been incorporated, so it is best not grown before sowing small seeds.

• **What variety suits the garden soil best?**

• **Is nitrogen-fixing required?**

Armed with this information, you can choose a suitable green manure from the table opposite. Whichever one you use, the principle is the same— the seeds are sown, the plant grows, and at a certain

Green manures
Below, from left to right: buckwheat, which if allowed to flower is a magnet for beneficial insects; alfalfa; clover; winter rye.

Digging in a green manure
Green manure plants need to decompose rapidly once incorporated into the soil. Younger plants will rot more quickly, so dig them in before growth begins to toughen up—before flower buds appear, ideally. If you leave the plants to flower (which mustard, far left, can do after just a few weeks), you run the additional risk of seed forming and ripening.

point it is incorporated back into the soil. Dig the plants into the top 6–8 in. (10–15 cm) of soil, chopping them up with a sharp spade as you do so.

When to dig in

Digging in is best done some weeks before you want to use the ground. Early spring is usually a good time when green manures have been used over winter. Allow anything from a week to a month or more for the foliage to decompose and the soil to settle before using the ground again. The younger the plants and the warmer the soil, the quicker the turnaround can be.

No-dig green manures

If you are using the "no-dig" technique (see p. 326), you can still grow green manures. Instead of digging in the plants, simply cut them down and leave the foliage on the surface to decompose; you can plant through this layer, treating it exactly as a mulch, or move it to one side to sow seeds. Alternatively, cut, remove, and compost the crop.

Perennial green manures and grazing rye may regrow after cutting down. It may be possible to hoe off regrowth. Alternatively, kill it off with a light-excluding mulch or a crop of potatoes grown under straw (see p. 327).

CHOOSING GREEN MANURES

Green manure	Sowing time	Growing period	Soil type	Nitrogen-fixer?
Alfalfa (ha) *Medicago sativa*	Late spring–midsummer	1 year +	Avoid acid or wet soils	Yes†
Buckwheat (hha) *Fagopyrum esculentum*	Late spring–late summer	1–3 months	Thrives on poor soils	No
Beans, field (ha) *Vicia faba*	Autumn–early winter	Over winter	Prefers heavy soil	Yes
Clover, crimson (ha) *Trifolium incarnatum*	Early spring–late summer	2–3 months; may overwinter	Prefers lighter soil	Yes
Clover, red (hp) *Trifolium pratense*	Spring–late summer	3–18 months	Good loam	Yes
Fenugreek (hha) *Trigonella foenum-graecum*	Early spring–late summer	2–3 months	Well-drained	Yes†
Lupine (ha) *Lupinus angustifolius*	Early spring–midsummer	2–4 months	Light, acid soils	Yes
Mustard (hha) *Sinapis alba*	Early spring–late summer	1–2 months	Most	No
Phacelia (ha/hha) *Phacelia tanacetifolia*	Early spring–late summer	1–3 months; may overwinter	Most	No
Rye, winter* (ha) *Secale cereale*	Late summer–early winter	Over winter	Most	No
Trefoil (hb) *Medicago lupulina*	Spring–late summer	3 months +	Will stand light dry soils, pref. not acid	Yes
Vetch, common (ha) *Vicia sativa*	Spring/late summer–early autumn	2–3 months; may overwinter	Avoid acid and dry soils	Yes

(ha) hardy annual; **(hha)** half-hardy annual; **(hp)** hardy perennial; **(hb)** hardy biennial
*Will inhibit germination of small seeds for a few weeks after digging in   †Nitrogen-fixer only in soils that contain suitable bacteria

FARMYARD MANURE WITH BEDDING

Straw is a traditional animal bedding material, which rots down to make a useful soil improver when mixed with animal manure. However, some livestock, especially horses, are bedded on wood shavings, which, although fine for the animals, are not as ideal for the gardener. Wood shavings are very slow to break down and can actually rob the soil of nitrogen rather than contributing to fertility if they are not very well composted before use. To avoid such a risk, mix shavings-based manures with grass mowings, poultry manure, or other high-nitrogen material and leave to rot for a year or two. If in doubt, use it only on perennial plants where the soil will not be cultivated—for example, in a shrub border.

Animal manures

Animal manures—from chickens and other poultry, cattle, horses, and goats—are a traditional source of soil fertility in an organic garden. They are most valuable when composted with some form of bedding material. The resulting medium- to high-fertility soil improver provides bulk (to build soil structure) and nutrients, which are made available to plants as the manure decomposes in the soil.

Urine is the main source of the plant nutrients, particularly nitrogen and potassium, in manure. It is soaked up by bedding (see facing page). These nutrients are easily washed out of fresh manure if not stored under cover. With birds, the urine is in fact the dab of white on the droppings, so the manure itself can be very rich.

Obtaining manure

Most organic farmers recycle their manure on the farm. Any other manure is likely to be polluted with residues of veterinary products used to treat the animals. If manure from an organic farm is not available, try to get it from "free range" and less-intensive livestock. Never use manure from intensive "factory" farms. It is easy to find local stables eager to give away their manure, but remember that horses are wormed regularly, and the mixtures used contain pesticides, which remain for 2 or more weeks in the manure. Check with the stable when its horses were last treated for worms.

Storing manure

Animal manure should be composted or well-rotted before use. This is to stabilize the nutrients, which might otherwise be washed out by the rain, and avoid any risk of damage to plants. Manure can be added to a compost pile, or if mixed with bedding it can be heaped up as a separate manure pile. If poultry manure has no bedding material with it, add it to the compost pile or mix it with straw.

MAKING A MANURE HEAP

• Heap the manure in a position where it can remain undisturbed for several months.
• If the bedding is dry, soak it well.
• Pack down the material.
• Cover with a waterproof sheet.
• Leave for 3 months if from an organic source, otherwise 6 months, to allow for any unwanted pollutants to break down. If based on wood shavings, at least a year will be needed (see facing page).

Chicken little
Manure from free-range chickens will be rich in nitrogen, so use it sparingly in the garden.

USING MANURE

Well-rotted manure can be dug into the soil or spread over it (right) as a mulch, especially if it contains plenty of straw. Don't let it touch living plant stems.

A sack or mesh bag of manure can be soaked in water (far right, suspended in a rainwater barrel) to make manure "tea," which can be used as a liquid fertilizer. Because the makeup of the liquid can be so variable, it is difficult to give precise instructions for its use. Apply it occasionally in place of water to plants that need a boost.

Buying composted manure
Commercial brands of composted manure are also available. Where possible, choose a product that has a symbol, logo, or some other form of accreditation from an organic certifying organization. When in doubt, check with the supplier for the source of the raw ingredients. The word "organic" is not sufficient recommendation on its own; this may simply mean that the ingredients are "of living origin," not that they are appropriate for use in an organic garden (see also p. 11).

Other manure-based products
Guano, bat, or bird excrement that has been dried and aged is a highly concentrated source of nutrients and should be regarded as a fertilizer rather than a manure (see facing page for more information). Again, check labeling carefully to ensure that the product is suitable for an organically managed garden. Farmyard manure is also used as the basis of some commercial liquid fertilizers, usually with the addition of trace elements.

Using animal manures
Well-rotted manure improves soil structure and water-holding capacity and supplies nitrogen, potassium, and other plant foods. Its nutrient content will vary with the proportion of manure and urine to straw or other bedding, and if it has been stored under cover (nitrogen and potassium are easily washed out in the rain). However, it should be a medium- to high-fertility soil improver. Apply at a rate of one or two wheelbarrow loads (11–22 gal.) per 50 sq. ft. (50–100 liters/5 sq. m).

The main use for manure is in the vegetable garden, on hungry crops such as potatoes, zucchini, eggplants, pumpkins, squashes, tomatoes, and brassicas. It also makes a good topdressing for roses that are pruned hard every year, and for herbaceous plants, applied every 2 or 3 years. Manure can be used more widely on poor soils, but should not be applied where root crops such as carrots are to grow, or on plants that prefer a poor, dry soil. Well-rotted manure can also be used in potting mixes (see pp. 114–117).

When handling manure and other animal-based products, keep cuts covered, wash your hands under running water before handling food, and keep anti-tetanus protection up to date.

Alternatives to manure
For those who wish to avoid animal products, remember that it is not essential to use manure in an organic garden. Soil fertility can be equally well maintained using other soil improvers, fertilizers, and green manures described in this chapter.

Adding fertilizers and altering soil pH

Organic fertilizers are products of plant, animal, or mineral origin. The nutrients they contain are generally released slowly over a period of time as the fertilizer is broken down by microorganisms. This slow-release feeding is generally much better for plants than the quick fix of chemical fertilizers, avoiding the fast, sappy growth that can cause plants to be more susceptible to insect attack and late-spring frosts. Some organic fertilizers, such as soybean meal, alfalfa meal, seaweed meal, and the compound mixtures, supply a range of plant foods. Others, such as rock phosphate, are more specific. As these products are all of natural origin, they will also tend to contain a range of minor and trace elements as well.

It is sensible to follow basic hygiene rules when applying any fertilizer, especially the animal-based products. Wear gloves and wash your hands after application. Always follow the instructions, and do not be tempted to add extra "just for luck."

Where specific mineral deficiency symptoms occur on plants (see p. 89), the cause may not be a simple shortage of that mineral. The *A–Z of Plant Problems*, p. 367, has more details. The solution should be to deal with the cause rather than symptoms, but for short-term relief more soluble mineral sources can be used. The major ones are Epsom salts (magnesium), borax (boron), and seaweed with iron (iron). Wood ash is a good natural source of potash, but as it is very soluble it is generally best recycled through the compost pile.

Altering the pH of the soil

If you need to raise the pH of your soil (make it more alkaline), use ground limestone (calcium carbonate) or dolomitic limestone (calcium magnesium carbonate). These slow-acting limestones are gentler on the soil than slaked or hydrated lime. They are usually applied in autumn to allow them to act on the soil before the next growing season, but it can take a year for the full effect to develop. The rate used will depend on the pH change required. As a general rule, add 7 oz./sq. yd. (200 g/sq. m) annually until you reach the desired pH. Dolomitic limestone is the preferred choice where magnesium levels tend to be low.

Making a soil more acidic is much more difficult. Composted pine needles can have some effect, and sulfur dust (a natural-mined product) can slowly make a soil slightly more acid, but where the soil is basically alkaline you are better advised simply to grow plants that suit the soil.

ORGANIC FERTILIZERS

Fertilizer	Major nutrients	Function	Use
Bonemeal	P_2O_5 20%	Promotes strong root growth	As a base dressing before planting shrubs, fruit, and other perennials
Alfalfa meal	N 5%; P_2O_5 1%; K_2O 2%	General fertilizer for leaf and root growth	Apply in spring and early summer
Hoof and horn	N 12%	Slow-release supply of nitrogen, where strong growth is required	Apply in spring and early summer as required
Soybean meal	N 7%; P_2O_5 0.5%; K_2O 2.3%	High nitrogen source	Annual vegetable beds; base dressing on poor soils
Seaweed meal	N 2%; K_2O 2.7%	Helps build up humus levels in soil	Annual beds; fruit trees and bushes; lawns and turf
Phosphate, rock	P_2O_5 27%	Corrects a phosphate deficiency	Good non-animal alternative to bonemeal
Potash, organic garden (plant source)	K_2O 20%	Supplies potash, released over one season	Fruit and vegetables
Ground limestone	Calcium carbonate	Raises pH; supplies calcium	Use where an increase in pH is required
Dolomitic limestone	Calcium magnesium carbonate	Raises pH; supplies calcium and magnesium	Use where an increase in pH is required
Gypsum	Calcium sulphate: S 13%; Ca 16%	Supplies calcium without altering pH	A gypsum:dolomitic limestone mix (80:20) can be used to help lighten heavy clay soils

See p. 36 for key to chemical symbols. Mixed organic fertilizers for specific uses, such as on vegetables or lawns, are also available.

Water and watering

WITH SENSIBLE WATERING STRATEGIES AND GOOD CHOICE OF PLANTS, ORGANIC GARDENERS CAN CUT BACK ON WATER USE

EVERY LIVING THING needs water—without it, life cannot exist. Plants need water so that the vital processes of photosynthesis, respiration, and absorption of nutrients can occur. In other words, they need water to grow, flower, and fruit.

Being an organic gardener means being aware of the resources used in the garden and the wider implications of their use—and this includes water. Water conservation, storage, and recycling are essential organic gardening strategies. Organic methods of soil care and management, careful plant choice, and correct timing and appropriate delivery of water help to minimize use of this valuable resource and avoid problems of drought—and of overwatering.

A shortage of water affects plants in a number of ways, depending on the type of plant and the extent of the shortage. Even before plants show obvious signs of drought stress such as wilting, their growth and performance may be reduced. As with most resources, not only too little but also too much water presents plants with problems (see p. 64).

Problems caused by water shortage

• Leafy vegetable crops such as spinach and cabbage will be much less productive. Plant vigor in general will be lower, resulting in smaller, slower-growing plants. Flowers may drop and fruits may be reduced in both size and quality.

• Some plants will "bolt" (flower prematurely) if they fail to receive enough water. Annuals will flower for only a very short period before dying.

• Trees and shrubs will shed their leaves in a severe drought; shoots and even branches may die and snap off. Herbaceous perennials will wilt, lose their leaves, and eventually die back to ground level.

• A shortage of water can result in nutrient deficiencies or imbalances because the plants are unable to absorb what they need through their roots. In very dry climates, the buildup of various salt deposits in the soil due to high evaporation exacerbates this tendency.

• Plants become more susceptible to disease and pest attack when water is scarce. Powdery mildew, for example, is much more common on roses,

WATER CONSERVATION

On a global scale, fresh water is a scarce resource. Although our planet has vast reserves of water, approximately 94% of it, located in the oceans, is unsuitable for irrigation purposes. The remaining 6% is fresh water, but is mostly held either as ice and snow in glaciers and polar ice caps (nearly 2%) or deep underground within rock strata (4%). Very little is easily accessible for human use. Rivers, for example, contain 0.00008% of the earth's water. Areas of high rainfall are also localized and global warming may alter the existing patterns of precipitation. Our current levels of use for domestic, industrial, and agricultural purposes both deplete water reserves and contaminate them and cannot be sustained in the long term. The cost of cleaning up water to drinking standards is high—so it is wasteful to squander it on our gardens.

The construction of large dams for irrigation and hydroelectric purposes have radically altered or destroyed whole ecosystems. As our demand for fresh water increases globally, we must develop much more prudent and equitable strategies for its use. Responsible use—reducing consumption and recycling— by organic gardeners is part of this process.

Domestic water use accounts for some 65% of the total water used by humanity, so it is clear that any savings made at home and in the garden are worth pursuing.

The arid approach
Desert gardens demand good water conservation and thoughtful planting— strategies useful to all organic growers.

grapevines, soft fruit, and many other plants when the soil is dry. Potato scab is also worse in dry soil. Blossom end rot is a disorder of tomatoes and peppers caused by water shortage (see also p. 88). Stressed plants are also favorites of pests such as aphids and whitefly.

Excess water

An overly wet soil or growing medium will also affect plant growth. A wet soil warms up much more slowly in the spring; growth is slow, and young plants are more likely to succumb to pest and disease attack. When the pore spaces are filled with water, oxygen is driven out of the soil, creating anaerobic conditions. This can lead to the death of roots through oxygen deficiency.

There are several symptoms associated with excess water. Root diseases may become more common; sickly, yellow, drooping foliage is often indicative of overwatered or poorly drained plants whose roots have rotted. Very moist conditions also allow slugs and snails to feed and breed at increased rates. Some plants, including camellias and geraniums, develop edema, where watery blisters develop on the leaves. These blisters may become corky or burst.

Problems caused by excess watering

• Washes nutrients away.
• Wastes water—a valuable resource.
• Damages soil structure if applied by sprinkler, causing crusting (see p. 109) and puddling.
• Encourages leafy growth at the expense of flowers.
• Encourages shallow rooting, making plants more susceptible to water shortages.
• Provides ideal conditions for slugs and snails.
• Promotes root diseases.
• Becomes expensive if water is metered.
• Reduces flavor of fruit crops.

Soils with too much water

Poorly drained soils can be improved by installing a drainage system, which usually takes the form of perforated pipes buried below the soil surface. This is a major undertaking and it is worth trying to improve the soil structure first (see pp. 38–41). The easiest option is to accept the soil as it is and convert the area into a bog garden, which will provide a great deal of beauty and interest.

HOW TO WATER LESS

There is a whole range of techniques that can be used in the garden to reduce the need for watering—saving a great deal of time and water.
• Choose plants that suit the soil and climate. Where water is scarce, attractive ornamental plantings can be made using succulents and drought-resistant perennials, grasses, and shrubs.
• Increase the soil's water-holding capacity or, in the case of heavy clay, increase the availability of the water to your plants by incorporating bulky organic soil improvers (see p. 41). Applied as a mulch, they will improve the structure of the soil at the surface, allowing rain to be absorbed more effectively and reducing runoff and puddle formation.
• Dig, where appropriate, to break up compacted ground to encourage extensive plant rooting.
• Do not dig soil in dry weather, as this increases the rate at which it dries out.
• Mulch the soil surface (see *Mulches for Weed Control*, pp. 76–77) with low-fertility soil improvers (see p. 41) such as leaf mold, shredded bark, or other bulky material to help cut moisture loss and reduce weed growth. Make sure that the soil is moist before applying a mulch. You want the mulch to keep moisture in rather than out. If the ground is dry, water thoroughly before laying down the mulch. In dry climates, a mulch of rocks and gravel will often trap and condense moisture and direct it to the soil surface.
• Remove weeds. Weeds will compete with plants for scarce water supplies.
• Where a tree or shrub has been planted into grass, keep a 3-ft. (1-m) area around it grass-free (preferably mulched) for at least 2 years.
• Shelter plants from drying winds by building or growing windbreaks to protect them. Hot, dry winds can increase water loss dramatically.
• When making new lawns, sow drought-tolerant grass types (see p. 183). Allow grass to grow longer—up to 3 in. (7.5 cm)—in dry weather. Grass that is not mown too frequently develops deeper roots and is more drought-resistant.
• Shade young seedlings in hot weather.
• Use drip and soaker hose irrigation systems rather than overhead sprinklers.

CHOOSING DROUGHT-RESISTANT PLANTS

Plants that cope well with water shortage often have gray foliage (for example, eucalyptus). They may also be covered in hairs, or felted, like santolina and lavender. Leaves may be reduced to thin needles; think of pines in coastal areas, where winds are strong and drying. Alternatively, leaves and stems may be fleshy and succulent, storing reserves of water; sedums and sempervivums are good examples, as are cacti, which also protect their water reserves with tough skins, spines, and prickles.

Drought-resistant plant choices for the garden include:

Trees and shrubs

Junipers; lavenders; *Microbiota* (Siberian carpet cypress); pines; *Potentilla* (cinquefoil); *Prunus besseyi* (western sand cherry); *P. maritima* (beach plum); *Rhus* (sumac); *Sarcococca* (sweet box); lilacs; *Taxus* (yews)

Perennials

Achillea (yarrow); agapanthus; alliums; crambe; *Cynara* (artichokes and cardoons); *Dianthus* (pinks); *Eryngium*, including sea holly (pictured); *Euphorbia* (spurges); gypsophila; *Iberis* (candytufts); *Kniphofia* (red hot pokers); lychnis; *Oenothera* (evening primroses); osteospermums; penstemons; perovskia; sedums; *Sempervivum* (houseleeks); *Stachys* (lamb's ears); verbascums; yuccas

Using water well

A plant's requirement for water varies depending on its stage in the life cycle. Seedlings, which have a small root system, are very susceptible to water shortage and may not recover if they dry out. Newly planted trees and shrubs, especially bareroot transplants, will need additional watering in dry conditions for a year or two; once established, most will survive without supplemental water.

Some plants have a critical period when water is essential if they are to perform to your requirements. Peas and beans, for example, need a good water supply to encourage flowering and seed set, but not until the flowers start to form. A camellia may drop all its flower buds in the spring if it has been deprived of water in the previous early autumn.

The type of plant can govern its water needs. Drought-resistant plants, adapted to surviving extremely dry conditions, positively thrive where water is scarce and may fail if the soil is too wet.

The location of the plant also influences its watering requirements. Plants in containers, for example, rely on you, the gardener, for their supply.

> **MAKING BEST USE OF WATER**
> • Give priority to seedlings, transplants, and newly planted specimens.
> • Water in the early morning.
> • Apply water directly to soil, not plants.
> • Soak ground well; do not just wet the surface.
> • Water at critical growth stages.
> • Do not water plants that do not need it.
> • Use a soaker hose rather than a sprinkler.
> • Use a timer to control supply.
> • Do not water lawns.

Plants in "rain shadow" locations—such as next to a house, wall, or fence, where the soil receives less rain—are more likely to need supplemental watering.

When to water

The most effective time to water is in the early morning or in the evening, when the air and soil are cool and less water will be lost by evaporation.

PLANTS IN CONTAINERS

Plants in pots, tubs, seed trays, baskets, and other containers need careful watering. They should never dry out completely, but neither should the growing medium be waterlogged. Supply water as it is needed rather than sticking to a routine. In hot, dry weather when plants are growing vigorously, a hanging basket or a tomato plant in a large pot may need to be watered twice a day. A slow-growing houseplant may need watering no more than once over the winter.

If a pot has dried out, water applied from above may simply run through without wetting the soil. Where possible, set the tray or pot in a container of water, leaving it until the surface of the growing medium is moist. Remove and allow to drain well. A very dry pot may need total immersion in a bucket of water.

WATERING CROPS IN DRY WEATHER

All vegetable crops need regular watering in the early stages, as seedlings and young plants. The least thirsty vegetable crops to grow, once established, are beets, broccoli, Brussels sprouts, hot peppers, carrots, leeks, onions, parsnips, radishes, rutabagas, and turnips. Critical times for watering other crops—only, of course, if the weather is dry—are:

While flowering
Peas and all types of beans;
  continue as pods start to form
Potatoes
Sweet corn

While fruiting
Peas and beans
Sweet corn, as cobs swell
Tomatoes
Zucchini

All the time
Leafy vegetables, such as lettuce and spinach; summer cabbage

Avoid watering slug-susceptible plants in the evening, though; watering leaves a film of moisture on plants and soil, creating ideal conditions for slugs and snails.

> Water shortage is not the only cause of wilting— root rots, wilt diseases, and root-eating pests such as vine weevil are also possible

How much water?

It is not easy to specify how much water you should apply and how often, as this depends on the plants you are growing, the temperature, and many other factors. The golden rule is to give plants an occasional thorough soaking rather than watering little and often. During dry weather, 2 gal. per sq. yd. (11 liters per sq. m) on row crops should be sufficient to moisten the root zone successfully.

Once you have watered a plant or a bed, check the soil to make sure that the water has penetrated down to the roots. A wet soil surface may hide dry soil beneath. Water again if necessary.

Watering vegetables

Vegetables respond to watering in different ways, depending on the crop and its growth stage. Water encourages vegetative (leaf and shoot) growth, which is useful for leafy crops but can delay production of peas, beans, and tomatoes, and may reduce flavor. More leafy growth does not necessarily mean higher yields of root crops. Where time and water are short, water only those plants that will benefit at the key stages that will give maximum response (see above).

Methods of applying water

You can deliver water to plants in many ways, ranging from the most basic to very high-tech. It depends on your budget, the time you have available, and how much water you have. Water is best directed to the plant's roots, avoiding soaking the leaves, flowers, and stems, where it may encourage disease. Sprinklers are one of the least efficient ways of watering and should be avoided where possible because much of the water is blown away or evaporates before it reaches the plants. In dry climates, where watering is an essential and often daily task, it makes good sense to avoid surface evaporation by directing the water below ground level to the plant roots using soaker hose irrigation (see below).

Hand systems

Water can simply be applied with a watering can or hose. This has the advantages of allowing you to give individual plants water when they need it, in the correct quantity. The disadvantage is that this can take up a lot of time, and plants can die if you are away. Hoses fitted with a trigger-operated mechanism reduce the water wasted as you move between plants. Water delicate seedlings with a fine rose to avoid damaging them. If they are in a seed tray or pot, stand it in a tray of water until the medium is moist, rather than watering from above.

You can increase the efficiency of hand-watering by directing the water below ground to where the roots are. This reduces evaporation and keeps the surface dry, which helps to prevent weed growth. One way to do this is to bury an unglazed pot next to a plant, then pour water into the pot. This seeps out gradually. Other possibilities include a large funnel or an inverted plastic soda bottle, with the base cut off and the cap loosened so that water can seep out. For trees and shrubs, a piece of perforated drainage pipe laid with one end at root level and the other at the surface works well.

Irrigation systems

Elaborate, gravity-fed irrigation channels are found in many parts of the world. The same principles can be adapted to garden-scale operations if you have a suitable water source and sloping site.

Soaker hose irrigation is more practical for most sites where there are rows of plants with the same water requirements. Water passes along porous or "leaky" pipes, soaking into the surrounding soil through small holes. If the pipes are buried below the surface or under a loose mulch or weedproof landscape fabric (see *Mulches for Weed Control*, pp. 76–77), evaporation is virtually nonexistent, ensuring that the plants get to use all the water. The water supply is turned on only for as long as is necessary to water the plants, then switched off—or an automatic timer can be used.

For more widely spaced plants, drip irrigation, where individual drippers are fitted at specified locations along a pipe, is more appropriate. This sort of system can also be used for a series of hanging baskets or planters.

A basic system that can be used in a greenhouse or for houseplants uses a series of wicks connected to a central reservoir. Water is drawn along the wicks by capillary action to the soil in the pots, thus maintaining moisture levels. All you need to do is fill the reservoir regularly.

Methods of watering
Always direct water at plant roots, either with a hose or spray (below left), or by filling reservoirs sunk into the soil, such as porous clay pots, open lengths of pipe, or upside-down plastic bottles with the lids loosened. The clay pots between the lettuces (below right), have been given lids to reduce evaporation, a traditional method known as "pitcher irrigation." A porous soaker hose, laid between plants (bottom) or just below the soil, is one of the most valuable modern contributions to water conservation.

What water to use?

Water used to irrigate a garden can be obtained from a number of sources. There is little need to use drinking-quality water on garden plants and crops.

Municipal water

Municipal water is clean, usually available whenever you want it, and supplied at high pressure. The provision of this service, however, may come at an unnecessary cost—both financial and environmental. The chlorine in municipal water may harm your soil's microbe population and damage sensitive plants. Municipal water may also have a high pH, making it unsuitable for use on lime-hating plants.

Rainwater

Rainwater is generally of good quality, free from contaminants, and has a relatively low pH, making it suitable for use on all types of plants. Surprisingly large volumes can easily be collected from roofs using the gutters, then stored in water barrels, tanks, and ponds. To figure out how much water you are likely to be able to collect, you need to know your roof area and average rainfall in your region. By multiplying these you can calculate the likely volume of water your roof will yield. Bear in mind that there will be some inefficiencies—so a figure of about 75% of the total is realistic.

Store as much water as you can. The supply from a single water barrel will not last long in dry weather. A container with a tight-fitting, light-excluding cover is preferable to reduce evaporation; help to discourage mosquitoes, leaves, and other detritus from accumulating; prevent algae from growing; and keep children out. If your tank or barrel is situated above the garden, you may be able to allow gravity to do the work of watering, using a hose attached to the tap. If not, a small pump may be needed, or simply use a watering can.

Rivers, springs, and wells

If you are lucky enough to have one in your garden, water from clean natural sources such as wells, lakes, springs, and rivers is perfectly suitable for use in the garden. Check with your local water authority that you have permission to extract water, and whether

WATER STORAGE RECEPTACLES

Storage container	Pros	Cons
Water barrel, plastic	Relatively cheap, many sizes; reused/recycled barrels available	Damaged by UV (sunlight)
Water barrel, wood	Attractive	Heavy, often leaks if not kept full
Tank, steel	Durable	Unattractive, will rust
Tank, concrete	Durable, suitable for underground use	Expensive to construct
Tank, reinforced concrete	Durable, fairly cheap, design and shape can be customized	Need to be fairly skilled to construct

restrictions or charges are in operation. Excessive use of natural supplies could cause them to run out, threatening the local ecology, so be reasonable in your usage. You may also need to pump or filter the water before using it in irrigation pipes. Be aware of the possibility of contamination by agrochemicals in intensively farmed areas.

Gray water

Gray water is the term used for domestic waste water, excluding sewage. As the volumes produced are quite large, gray water can be valuable for garden use as long as it is handled correctly and it is not too contaminated with soaps, detergents, fats, and grease. Waste water from dishwashers is unsuitable; the detergents they use can harm plants. Water from the bath or shower (avoid bubble bath and oils) and that used for washing vegetables are most suitable. Be aware, though, that many plumbing and health codes do not allow gray water reuse because of assumed health risks. For the legal status of gray water in your community, consult your local building codes or health officials.

Gray water, unless it has been used only to wash vegetables, should not be used on plants for eating. Nor is it suitable for use on acid-loving plants. Rotate gray water applications around the garden to avoid potential buildup of harmful substances. Bath or shower water is likely to contain bacteria, some of which could be potentially harmful to health, so it should not be stored—use it immediately. It can be run through a straw filter or a reed bed before use if greater purity is required.

A reed bed is a large, more long-term project that will take some time to establish (see facing page). To make a simple straw filter, fill a well-perforated bucket with straw, and allow your gray water to flow through it before directing it onto permanent plantings. Empty the bucket onto the compost heap at regular intervals and replace the straw.

Reed beds for purification

One of the best ways of cleaning up gray water is through a reed bed system, where the water flows through a gravel-filled trough or tank containing reeds and other water plants. The vast numbers of bacteria living on the roots of the reeds break down the waste materials in the water into a form that is safe for plants to use. Their numbers are especially high because the reeds are able to transport oxygen down to their roots via their hollow stems. The gray water leaves the reed bed in a safe state for irrigating the whole garden, including vegetables.

Reed beds do not work as efficiently at low temperatures, so if you live in a cold climate it may be necessary to divert your gray water back into the main drainage system during the winter. Plumbing in a separate pipe with a valve that can be opened and shut will allow you to direct the water to the reed bed or down into the sewer at will. A "surge tank" large enough to hold all the water leaving the house at one time allows the water to flow at a controlled rate into the reed bed via another valve.

Types of reed beds

There are two basic types of reed beds: horizontal and vertical. In horizontal reed beds, the waste water enters at one end of a waterproof trough and flows through it in a horizontal direction, whereas in vertical beds it pours into the center of the trough

and flows downward to the bottom before leaving. Vertical systems are now more popular, as they take up less space and are believed to be more efficient.

In the vertical reed bed, the base of the trough contains about 20 in. (50 cm) of coarse gravel, with an 8-in. (20-cm) layer of pea gravel on top. The reeds are planted into this, spacing them about 20 in. (50 cm) apart. The most commonly used species is common reed (*Phragmites australis*), but others that are locally common in your region could also be used. A rough guide for the size of the trough is 1.5–3 sq. yd. (1.5–3 sq. m) for each person in the household. Beds need to be rested at frequent intervals, so it is a good idea to have several small ones that can be used alternately. The processed water can be collected or allowed to trickle away into the ground.

Using flowforms

A recently developed method of further improving the quality of the water that leaves a reed bed is the "flowform." This consists of a series of stepped bowls into which the water flows. The design of the cascade makes the water flow in a figure-eight pattern as it progresses downward. This oxygenates it and is believed by some to further enhance its qualities on other, more subtle levels. A flowform is certainly a beautiful addition to the garden and to the purification process.

Water diverter
A homemade device allows water from the downspout to be diverted into a collecting pipe, or in times of surplus simply to drain away normally.

FLOWFORMS

The rhythmic oscillation of water passing through a flowform is fascinating to watch and soothing to hear, as well as an effective means of oxygenating water. Though all flowforms consist basically of a pattern of interlocking pools, various designs are available. Moisture-loving plants such as ferns will thrive in the cool, moist atmosphere created by the cascading water. The rims of the shallow pools will become favorite perching spots for garden birds.

Weeds and weed control

"IS THIS A WEED?" IS A COMMON QUESTION ASKED BY NOVICE GARDENERS. THE ANSWER IS, "IT DEPENDS."

WHETHER A PLANT IS A WEED simply depends on the identity of the particular plant, where it is growing, and the effect it is likely to have on the plants around it. Simply put, a weed is an invasive plant, growing where you do not want it. A weed can be an annual, a biennial, an herbaceous or shrubby perennial, or even a tree. This chapter introduces you to the way that weeds work—how and why they are so efficient—and the range of organic methods that you can employ to clear weeds and keep them under control.

The aim in an organic garden is not to eradicate every weed but to keep them at an acceptable level appropriate to the situation. Plants that can be weeds can also make a positive contribution to a garden—in which case they are no longer weeds!

What makes a weed?

Plants that become weeds are aggressive colonizers, the invaders of the plant world. Some are wild plants, others are plants that were deliberately introduced into gardens. Japanese knotweed (*Polygonum cuspidatum*), for example, was introduced into British gardens in 1825, as "a plant of sterling merit." It is now Britain's most troublesome weed, and a serious problem in many parts of the U.S., too.

We can still unwittingly plant potential weeds today. Russian vine (*Fallopia baldschuanica*), for example, is a useful, fast-growing creeper that can cover an ugly fence or garden shed in a few months but in a few years it can overwhelm a full-size tree. Yellow archangel (*Lamium galeobdolon*) and periwinkle (*Vinca minor*) give quick groundcover but can soon take over the whole border.

PRINCIPLES OF ORGANIC WEED CONTROL

• Know your weeds. Knowing how a weed survives and reproduces helps to choose the most effective method of dealing with it.
• Design out problem areas; design in effective weed prevention.
• Take time to clear perennial weeds effectively before any permanent planting—even if this could take a year or more.
• Choose methods to suit the time and energy that you have available.
• When clearing ground, be realistic. Do not clear more than you are able to keep weed-free.
• Never leave soil bare: Plant it, cover it, or sow a green manure.
• Mulches can both prevent and eradicate weeds—for little effort.

Take up the hoe (facing page)
A hoe can be a particularly effective tool for controlling weeds at varying stages of growth.

WEEDS IN THE GARDEN

Pros	Cons
Weeds can be: • Attractive—such as field pansy and scarlet pimpernel • Edible—such as chickweed, lamb's quarters, purslane • Food and shelter for birds—for example teasel, thistles, ivy • Food for beneficial insects (such as yarrow) and host to creatures that will eat pests • Attractive to butterflies (dandelion) • Useful additions to the compost pile; deep-rooted weeds such as dandelions can bring up potassium and phosphorus for other plants	Weeds can: • Spoil the appearance of beds and borders • Overwhelm other plants, smothering them with vigorous growth • Compete for soil moisture and nutrients • Reduce yields of fruit and vegetables • Make harvesting more difficult • Act as host plants for pests and diseases

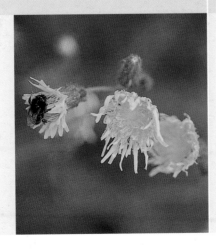

How weeds work

Knowing how weeds reproduce, spread, and survive adverse conditions can help you to develop an effective weed management and control strategy.

Weeds use a variety of techniques to achieve their aim: survival and invasion.

• **Annuals and biennials** Annual weeds grow, set seed, and die in the space of a year. Some may produce several generations in one year. Seed is their mechanism for spread and survival. Some weeds can even set seed after they have been hoed off when in flower. Annual weeds are most common in regularly disturbed ground such as vegetable plots and annual borders.

Biennials flower in their second year and spread as seed. They are more common in perennial and shrub beds and plantings, where ground is not disturbed every year.

• **Perennials** Perennial weeds make use of a range of mechanisms for their long-term survival and spread. This can include both seed and vegetative means, such as runners, rhizomes, and long, deep taproots.

HOW WEEDS SPREAD

1 Seeds
Often produced in huge quantities, seeds are spread by wind, water, animals, and mechanical propulsion.

2 Runners (stolons)
Runners are creeping stems that grow along the ground. Buds along them produce plantlets that root quickly. Sometimes the stems arch over and produce roots at the tip, even before touching the soil.

3 Roots and rhizomes
Tough, fleshy taproots can regrow after cutting or dying back. Even chopped-up pieces of taproot may also regrow, as can small chopped or broken-up sections of the rootlike, underground creeping stems known as rhizomes.

4 Bulbs and bulbils
Bulbs, bulbils, or tubers that break off easily when the plant is dug up or pulled out will easily produce a new plant. Cultivation simply spreads them.

Weed prevention

Prevention is always better than cure where weeds are concerned, and making simple adjustments to the way you garden—or adopting new techniques—can greatly reduce the chances of weeds getting a toehold among your plants.

Closer planting, for example, not only makes displays look good more quickly but also cuts down on space where weeds can grow. Removing intermediate plants at a later date will prevent overcrowding. In the same way, close, evenly spaced vegetables (see p. 316) will soon cover the ground and smother out weeds.

Simply cutting down on digging can reduce weed problems. Turning over the soil encourages the germination of thousands of weed seeds from the soil's "weed bank" by exposing them to the light. There is no need to dig soil on a regular basis, even when growing vegetables (see also p. 326).

Rethink your watering techniques. A hose or sprinkler wets a large area of soil, encouraging weed germination. Instead, use a drip or soaker-hose irrigation system, or water into sunken pots.

Crop rotation

Vegetable crops tend to be associated with weeds that have a similar life cycle. Crops also differ in their ability to compete with weeds and in how easy it is to weed between plants. Potatoes and squashes, for example, compete well and are also easy to weed; other crops, such as onions, are poor competitors and are less easy to weed. Using a crop rotation (see p. 301) that alternates different crops can help you to keep weeds under control in a vegetable plot.

Stale seedbed

A stale seedbed is one that is prepared 2 to 3 weeks in advance of sowing to allow a flush of weeds to germinate. Hoe or flame these off (see p. 78), then sow or plant as usual. This technique is useful when broadcast sowing—as with grass for a lawn—where weed control would be difficult or when direct-sowing slow-germinating crops such as carrots or parsnips. A variation on this technique is to mulch ground with black plastic before sowing. Research has shown that covering soil with a black plastic mulch for 4 to 8 weeks, then removing it before sowing or planting vegetables, can reduce annual weeds and increase yields significantly.

A quick start

Using transplants rather than sowing direct gives plants a head start over any weeds, and also allows time for a stale seedbed to be used. Also, if you are concerned about distinguishing between seeds you have sown and weed seedlings, using transplants helps to avoid confusion.

> The most effective time to weed carrots is 4 weeks after half the crop has come up

Preventing path weeds

Weeds in a path, patio, or other hard surface may grow up from below, or blow in as seeds. Effective ground preparation and weedproof fabrics laid beneath the surface can stop weeds from growing up. To prevent seedling weeds from getting a hold in paving, point the joints between bricks or slabs (see p. 132). Regular brushing with a stiff brush can also be effective. Use a high-pressure hose to remove algae from a path or patio. Frequent walking over gravel is a good way of keeping weeds down. If large areas of hard surface are unused and weedy, consider converting them to some other use.

Cover the ground

One of the most formidable weapons that the organic gardener can deploy to prevent weeds is mulching to exclude light from the soil, effectively stifling their growth.

Weeds rapidly colonize bare ground. Seeds already in the soil will germinate, and others will move in from outside. Keeping the soil covered with a mulch or growing plants will keep the weeds at bay. Mulches can be used in almost any location, including paths. Simply choose the appropriate material(s) for the job—with an appearance that suits the location and an appropriate life span.

NATURAL WEED KILLERS

Some plants inhibit the growth of others by producing toxic substances, either when growing or decaying. This effect, known as allelopathy, is often selective, working against some species and not others. It is particularly effective in preventing the germination of annual broad-leaved weeds. Buckwheat, an excellent smother crop, is thought to produce allelopathic chemicals. Winter rye is another weed-smothering green manure. When it is dug into the soil, or cut and left as a mulch, it releases chemicals as it decomposes that inhibit the germination of small seeds for a few weeks. It is, however, quite safe to plant young plants into or through the decomposing foliage, taking advantage of its weed-suppressing capacity.

APPLYING A LOOSE MULCH

1 Wait until the soil has warmed up and is well soaked.

2 Clear the ground of weeds.

3 Add any soil improvers or fertilizers required.

4 Level the ground.

5 Apply the mulch within a few days of clearing weeds.

Tips
• Apply a thick layer of mulch that will settle to the required depth; to be effective, at least 4 in. (10 cm) deep.
• Do not mulch right up to plants; leave a few inches bare around the stems or trunk.
• A retaining edge may be needed to keep mulch from migrating to surrounding areas.
• Add mulch as needed to maintain required depth.

Effective mulches
Below, from left to right: a living mulch of thyme grown as groundcover; clover, a green manure, covering the ground beneath sweet corn plants; coarse shredded bark; lawn clippings spread over layers of newspaper; rotted straw; ornamental bark; cardboard around crops; synthetic landscape fabric in the fruit garden.

Mulches for weed control

Weed-controlling mulches come in two forms—loose mulches, such as shredded wood or bark, and mulch membranes, sheets of material such as cardboard or synthetic landscape fabric. These can be biodegradable or synthetic. As with all areas of organic gardening, the first choice should be a recycled biodegradable material such as cardboard or wood chips, but for longer-term, low-maintenance control synthetic materials may be the most effective option.

Living mulches

Living mulches may be ornamental—permanent plantings of groundcover shrubs and perennials—or functional—the so-called green manures, or smother crops, which are used to cover ground temporarily and improve the soil.

Effective groundcover plants are tough, rapidly spreading ornamentals that will compete successfully with weeds for food, water, and light (see also *Woody Plants and Climbers*, p. 147). Groundcover plants are particularly useful for weed control in areas where access is difficult.

Green manures (see pp. 56–57), such as buckwheat, winter rye, and clover, make good weed-preventing smother crops (living mulches). Grow them where ground is to be left bare for a few months or more—over the winter months, for example, or when you have prepared a plot but are not yet ready to plant it. They can also be sown between widely spaced shrubs. Vigorous, fast-growing annual flowers such as sweet alyssum and candytuft can be used in the same way.

Trefoil, a low-growing green manure that tolerates some shade, can be sown between rows of sweet corn. Sow trefoil, broadcast, when the corn is around 6 in. (15 cm) high. When the corn is cut down at the end of the season, the trefoil can be left to protect the ground over winter.

Loose mulches

On weed-free ground, a loose mulch, 4 in. (10 cm) deep, will provide effective weed control. Any weeds that may appear are easily removed. You can reduce the depth of mulch needed, and hence the cost, by spreading it over a mulch membrane (see facing page for details). A durable mulch membrane, such as landscape fabric, will also stop gravel or similar materials from working into the soil.

Mulch membranes

Mulch membranes can be used to clear weeds from open ground and beds, as long as there are no woody weeds present. They are also used to prevent weeds from growing on ground that has been cleared. Holes can be cut to allow planting through the barrier as appropriate. Membranes are usually covered with a loose mulch to hold them in place, extend their lifespan, and improve their appearance. A mulch membrane must be permeable to allow air and water into the soil, unless it is intended to be kept in place for only a few months.

MULCHES FOR WEED CONTROL

Loose mulches

Composted bark products (P; B)
Attractive, dark-colored mulch.

Wood chips (P; B)
Forest waste, or chipped scrap wood, composted before sale.
Available in stained colors. Lower cost than bark.
Apply a high-nitrogen fertilizer before mulching young plants.

Coarse-grade municipal compost (P; B)
Recycled green waste. Quicker to degrade than bark or wood
chips.

Shredded prunings (P; B)
Home-produced or from a tree service. Compost for a few months
before use, or use fresh on paths.

Straw and hay (A; B)
Informal appearance. Should last for a season. Use a layer 6 in.
(15 cm) thick. Hay will feed plants as it decays, but may produce
its own crop of seedling weeds.

Gravel and slate waste (P)
Good around plants that like dry, hot conditions.

Leaf mold (A; B)
A homemade, short-term mulch. Best used over a membrane.

Buckwheat hulls (A; B)
Very light and fluffy. Top with a heavier mulch in windy locations.

Cocoa shells (A)
Waste product of the chocolate industry. Apply in a layer at least
2 in. (5 cm) deep. Water lightly after application to moisten
surface. Higher in nitrogen than wood-based mulches.

Membranes

Newspaper (A; B)
No-cost option for a single season. Lay opened-out newspapers,
at least 8 sheets thick, around and between existing plants. Top
with grass clippings or leaf mold to keep in place.

Cardboard (A; B)
No-cost option for a single season. Lay on soil, overlapping well
to prevent weeds growing through. Keep in place with straw or
hay. Vigorous plants such as pumpkins can be planted through
the cardboard.

Paper mulch (A; B)
Sturdy paper in a roll, for use on annual vegetable beds.

Landscape fabric (P)
Long-term weed control; cover with loose mulch to protect from
light.

Woven plastic (P)
Medium-term weed control. Cover with loose mulch to extend life.

Black plastic sheeting (400–600 gauge)
Suitable only as a ground-clearing mulch (see also p. 79). Do not
cover ground for more than a few months without removing the
plastic to allow air and water into the soil. Hold in place by
burying edges in the ground or weighting with heavy items such
as wooden planks or car tires.

PLANTING THROUGH A MULCH MEMBRANE

1 Clear the ground, or cut down existing vegetation.

2 Add any soil improvers required, bearing in mind the lifespan of the mulch.

3 Level the ground if necessary.

4 Spread the membrane over the soil. Cover the outer edges (10–12 in.; 25–30 cm) with soil, secure with wire staples, or hold down with heavy planks, bricks, or stones.

5 Set the plants out in their proposed positions.

6 With a sharp knife, cut crosses in the membrane where each plant is to go.

7 Plant your plants, and water them in.

8 Top with 2 in. (5 cm) of loose mulch.

Perennial weeds may grow up around the planting cut. Cut them off with a knife or scissors.

A single-season mulches for annual or perennial beds   **P** mulches for perennial beds only   **B** biodegradable, the preferred choice

Weed control and removal

Preventive measures can never be rigorous enough to eliminate the need for some weeding. Hoeing and hand-weeding can be a relaxing and satisfying occupation. The key is to do the weeding when the weeds are small. Only when you put it off does it become a chore. Hand-clearing neglected ground (see facing page) can be a long job, but here again knowing your weeds will help. Some tested strategies that can beat some of the most persistent perennial weeds, using the general techniques that are outlined here, are given on pp. 80–81.

Hand-weeding

Hand-weeding is the only really "selective" organic method of weed control, allowing you to remove the real weeds and retain self-sown ornamentals and other "weeds" that you would like to keep. Use a hand fork or weeding hoe to loosen weeds when necessary; even annual weeds can regrow if the top breaks off as you are trying to pull the whole plant out. Hand-weeding is easiest after a good rainstorm and on uncompacted soil, such as in beds, that are never walked on and those that are well-mulched.

Paths and patios can also be hand-weeded. There is a range of tools available to help extract weeds from cracks between paving slabs.

Hoeing

Once you have learned the art, hoeing can be a quick and effective method of keeping ground and gravel paths weed-free. Hoeing works best against seedling weeds (annual and perennial), but it can also be quite effective in removing the tops of perennial weeds, though regular hoeing over a period of years will be needed to kill them completely.

Hoes come in many shapes and sizes—for large or restricted areas, for use standing up or kneeling. If you can, try a hoe before buying to see that it suits you and the handle is the correct length.

Thermal weeding

Modern thermal weeders kill weeds with a short blast of heat lasting no more than a few seconds. The plants do not burn, they simply wilt and die. The heat may be applied as a flame, hot air, or even as steam. The main use for thermal weeders in the organic garden is on hard surfaces—paths, drives, and patios. Seedling weeds are easily killed with a single pass. More established annuals and biennials may need from three to six treatments. Perennial weeds will be gradually weakened and may eventually die. Thermal treatment should also kill weed seeds on the ground.

TIPS FOR EFFECTIVE HOEING

• Choose a hoe that you find easy to use.
• Keep the hoe sharp.
• Cut plants off just where the stem joins the root.
• Hoe regularly when weeds are small.
• Hoe on a dry day.
• Pick up the weeds if rain is likely.
• Leave sufficient space between crop rows to allow for easy hoeing.

Clearing weed-infested ground

Weeds rapidly colonize bare ground, either newly created by building developments or where a garden or empty lot has fallen into disuse. At first there will probably be a mixture of annual and perennial weeds, but, if the land continues to be neglected, perennials will soon dominate. However daunting the task may look, overgrown land can be cleared without herbicides, using one or a combination of the methods below.

Cutting down

Simply cutting down weeds can be a quick, short-term solution to a weed problem, preventing seeding and spreading. Repeated cutting can, eventually, clear even persistent perennial weeds over a period of years. The most effective time to weaken the roots of perennials and avoid seeding is when flower buds are just beginning to show. Scything is the most peaceful method and can be quick and effective—but of course needs skill. The alternative is an electric- or gas-powered string trimmer.

Digging or forking

Turning the ground over, removing weeds and roots, is a relatively quick but physically challenging way to clear ground of many perennials. Breaking up the ground first with a spade or a digging hoe will ease the work, as will covering the ground with a mulch membrane for a few weeks or more before starting. This method is good for weeds with taproots such as dandelions and docks, and can be effective against quackgrass if you are diligent.

Never strip off the top layer of soil along with the weed roots. You will be removing the most fertile soil from the area.

Mechanical cultivation

A mechanical cultivator (rotary tiller) can be useful when clearing a large area of ground, but it does have its drawbacks. Using a tiller can be hard work if the ground is thick with perennial weeds and grasses. If perennial weeds are present, they will be chopped up into many pieces; each portion of root or rhizome may regrow, potentially increasing the problem manyfold. Till in late spring or early summer when the soil is dry and weeds are growing

well. Leave the ground until it is "greening up" with weed regrowth, then till again. Repeat as necessary. If you can till only once, it may be possible to hoe off the regrowth. Otherwise, choose another method. It is much more difficult and time-consuming to dig out hundreds of chopped-up pieces of root than it is whole plants. Lightweight mechanical cultivators can be used for weed control between row crops.

Clearing ground without digging

A light-excluding mulch membrane will stop weeds growing and will, in time, kill them. If you want to convert an area of lawn into a vegetable garden or flowerbed, mulch it in the spring and it will be clear by the autumn, if not before.

Persistent perennials may take a couple of years or more to die. Vigorous annual plants, such as squashes and sunflowers, can be planted through the mulch, though perennial weeds may grow up through the holes cut for the plants. Mulching is most effective during the season when weeds are actively growing.

Grassing down

Where there is a severe perennial weed problem such as bishop's weed or horsetail, plant grass—either by sowing seed or laying turf. Regular mowing for 2 or 3 years should solve the problem. A rather extreme measure, perhaps, but worth it in the long run.

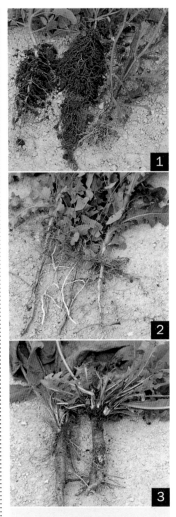

KNOW YOUR ROOTS

1 Some weeds, particularly annuals such as groundsel, bittercress, and chickweed, have shallow, fibrous roots that are easily removed.

2 Weeds with spreading, creeping roots such as creeping thistle, bindweed, and quackgrass need to have the soil around their roots well loosened so that every piece of root can be removed.

3 The long taproots of weeds such as dandelion and dock must be removed in their entirety to prevent regrowth.

Forking
For weeds such as Canada thistle, loosen the soil all around the root area in order to pull out the entire root run.

PERENNIAL WEED PROFILES

◁ Field bindweed
Convolvulus arvensis (see also Hedge bindweed, facing page)
Survival and spread
An extensive network of roots and rhizomes, which can give rise to new plants. Roots can reach a depth of 30 ft. (10 m). Rarely seeds; more in dry years.
Control
· Hoe frequently over a period of years.
· Fork out early infestations, removing every piece. Probably not worth trying where well established.
· Cover with membrane for 2+ years.

◁ Ground ivy
Glechoma hederacea
Survival and spread
An attractive plant that flowers in early spring. Spreads rapidly in shady areas, particularly where the soil is moist and fertile.
Control
· Smother with mulch membrane.
· Dig or pull out, being careful to get as much of the plant as possible.

Blackberry/bramble ▷
Rubus fruticosus
Survival and spread
A prickly, fast-growing woody weed. Spreads by stolons and seed.
Control
· Dig out young plants as soon as seen.
· Cut back established plants regularly. Dig out where practical.

Creeping buttercup ▷
Ranunculus repens
Survival and spread
Common on moist soils and lawns. Spreads by runners; new plants form and root at intervals in late spring and early summer. Also seeds.
Control
· Hoe when small.
· Established plants are hard to pull out by hand. Dig out or cover with a mulch membrane for a year or two.

◁ Quackgrass
Elymus (Agropyron) repens
Survival and spread
Has shallow, creeping, tough, white rhizomes, often thought of as roots. Rhizome tips are very sharp—can grow through potatoes. Rarely seeds.
Control
· Hoeing regularly in late summer reduces production of new rhizomes.
· Fork over soil, removing all rhizomes.
· Cover with mulch membrane for 2–3 years.

◁ Dandelion
Taraxacum officinale
Survival and spread
Plants can regenerate from any part of the substantial taproot. Seeds freely, early spring to autumn.
Control
· Cut down before seeding.
· Dig out.
· Cover with mulch membrane for 2–3 years.

Dock ▷
Rumex spp.
Survival and spread
Plants can regenerate from top 6 in. (15 cm) of the taproot. Seeds prolifically.
Control
· Hoe off seedlings.
· Cut down plants before seeding.
· Dig out established plants.
· Cover with mulch membrane for 2–3 years.

Bishop's weed ▷
Aegopodium podagraria
Survival and spread
White, underground creeping stems just under the surface. New leaves produced at every node. Few seeds.
Control
· Persistent regular hoeing.
· In small areas dig out plants, including every bit of root.
· Plant grass and mow for a few years.
· Cover with mulch membrane for at least 2–3 years.

◁ Horsetail
Equisetum arvense
Survival and spread
Extensive, creeping, black underground stems that can penetrate 6 ft. (2 m) or more down into the soil.
Control
· May be smothered out by vigorous plant growth.
· Persistent hoeing.
· Cover with mulch membrane for several years.

◁ Poison ivy
Rhus toxicodendron
Survival and spread
Grows as a low shrub or as a vine. Spreads by seed and by underground roots that can spread widely.
Control
· Pull, cut, or hoe seedlings (wear gloves to avoid irritating oil).
· Smother for 2 years with mulch membrane.
· Do not burn.

Stinging nettle ▷
Urtica dioica
Survival and spread
A valuable plant for wildlife and for making a liquid plant food. The stems, purplish at first, creep along the soil surface. They become erect and green in spring. Seeds abundantly.
Control
· Fork out, or undercut with spade.
· Cover with mulch membrane for 2–3 years.

Broadleaf plantain ▷
Plantago major
Survival and spread
Leaf rosettes have deep taproots. Also seeds.
Control
· Dig out.
· Do not allow to produce seed.
· Cover with mulch membrane.

◁ Common yellow wood sorrel
Oxalis stricta
Survival and spread
· Low, bushy plants grow from taproots. Prolific seed production.
Control
· Pull, hoe, mow, or cut plants before they set seed.
· Smother with a mulch membrane for a full growing season.

◁ Perennial sow-thistle
Sonchus arvensis
Survival and spread
Creeping roots grow new shoots—even from small fragments. Main roots grow deep—down to 2 ft. (60 cm)—and extensively. Also seeds.
Control
· Do not allow to produce seed.
· Regular, persistent hoeing for several years.
· Cover with mulch membrane.
· Smother out (see Canada thistle).

Canada thistle ▷
Cirsium arvense
Survival and spread
Aerial shoots develop from white, creeping, brittle, horizontal roots. Stout, fleshy taproot. Few seeds.
Control
· Hoe off young plants.
· Cover with mulch membrane.
· With a dense stand, allow plants to grow large. Before they flower, cut down. Repeat. Cultivate ground and sow a vigorous, medium-term green manure crop such as vetch or crimson clover.

Hedge bindweed ▷
Calystegia (Convolvulus) sepium
Survival and spread
Spreads by white, brittle, creeping underground stems. Rarely seeds.
Control
· Hoe frequently over a period of years.
· Fork out early infestations, removing every piece. Probably not worth trying where well established.
· Cover with mulch membrane for several years.

CHOOSING WEED-CONTROL MULCHES AND TECHNIQUES TO SUIT THE SITUATION

Used for	Cardboard	Paper mulch	Newspaper	Tree mats	Landscape fabrics	Black plastic sheeting	Ornamental bark or wood chips	Leaf mold	Cocoa shells	Municipal compost (coarse grade)
Clearing rough ground	●				●	●				
Annual vegetables	●	●	●					●		
Annual flowers								●	●	
Shrubs	●	●	●	●	●		●	●	●	●
Herbaceous perennials					●		●	●	●	●
New plantings	●	●	●	●	●		●	●	●	●
Fruit trees and bushes	●	●	●				●		●	●
Trees	●	●	●	●	●		●	●	●	●
Paving					●					
Gravel paths					●					
Ground not in use	●				●		●	●		

See pp. 76–77 for advice on using mulches effectively; pp. 78–79 for other techniques

Gravel	Pine needles	Straw	Cutting down	Groundcover plants (ornamental)	Green manure crops	Hand-weeding	Hoeing	Digging/ forking	Rotary tilling	Stale seedbed	Thermal weeding
			●		●	●		●	●		
		●	●		●	●	●			●	
	●					●	●			●	
●	●			●		●	●	●			
●	●					●	●	●			
●	●	●		●		●	●	●			
		●				●		●			
●	●		●	●	●	●	●	●			
						●	●				●
				●		●	●				●
		●				●		●			

Plant health

USE ORGANIC METHODS OF SOIL AND GARDEN MANAGEMENT
TO PROTECT YOUR PLANTS THE NATURAL WAY

IT IS ONLY RECENT GENERATIONS that have come to rely on artificial chemical additives for pest and disease control, and in doing so many gardeners have forgotten that it is possible to produce good food and maintain beautiful gardens without pesticides. In this chapter, the nature of plant pests and diseases will be described, along with the extensive range of methods, both ancient and modern, that organic gardeners can use to maintain a healthy garden and keep pest and disease problems at acceptable levels.

A natural balance

Organic gardening emphasises soil health and the link between a healthy soil, healthy plants, and our own health. A healthy soil leads to healthy plant growth in a stable and sustainable environment. Natural environments, or ecosystems, usually contain a diversity of plant and animal species, including plant pests and the causal agents of plant disease; all the organisms live in balance with each other (equilibrium). In organic gardens we try to emulate this balance of species and the ecological stability that results. Although gardens are never natural ecosystems, sensitive planting and design can create gardens that attract wildlife (including beneficial animals) and encourage diversity: productive gardens where plants and animals live in stable equilibrium.

Working with the system

Organic gardeners seek to work with nature to limit damage from pests and plant disease rather than to control nature artificially. The dream of the organic gardener is sustainable gardening. It is a different dream from the utopia of a pest- and disease-free garden promoted by the garden industry. It is a more realistic approach to gardening, accepting that plants occasionally show spots and blemishes just as our bodies from time to time show imperfections. This is

Striking sight (facing page)
Wildlife brings a beauty of its own into the garden, and gardeners should think twice before automatically seeking to banish creatures like this striking black swallowtail caterpillar. Diversity is crucial to achieving a natural balance between pests and predators.

Contemporary bird scarer (right)
There is nothing new about protecting crops from birds, but organic gardeners are always ready to explore the potential usefulness of new materials—especially when they provide an opportunity to recycle, as with these discarded CDs.

not to say that organic vegetables are inevitably maggot-infested or that organic flowers are moth-eaten—far from it—but that, rather than the intolerance promoted by the gardening industry, tolerance is required. Instead of quick fixes with their environmental side-effects, organic gardeners aim for prevention and sustainable management of pests and disease.

Strategies old and new

There is a wide range of organic techniques and strategies to keep plants healthy. Going organic is not, as newcomers often assume, simply a question of replacing artificial or chemical additives with natural alternatives. There is a lot more to it than just changing your brand of pesticide. Traditional methods of good husbandry—such as appropriate soil care, crop rotation, encouraging natural predators, picking off pests and diseased growth by hand, good hygiene, and timing of sowing and planting—are combined with more modern techniques, including biological controls, resistant cultivars, pheromone traps, and lightweight crop covers. A few so-called "organic" pesticide sprays are available to be used as a last, not a first, resort.

The ideal is to use good gardening techniques to promote and maintain plant health, combining this when necessary with more direct methods of prevention and control. This strategy generally results in a flourishing garden. There will inevitably be times when there is nothing that can be done to save a plant—in extreme weather conditions, for example, or if it is in an inappropriate location. The organic solution is then to give in gracefully!

CAUSES OF PLANT PROBLEMS

To combat problems and, where possible, bring plants back to health it is important to understand the cause of the complaint and whether it is an environmental or growing problem (see p. 88), nutrient deficiency (p. 89), disease (p. 90), or pest attack (p. 92).

1 The plant's environment includes the soil conditions; these peas are showing heat and drought stress.

2 The element magnesium is a plant nutrient required for the production of the green substance chlorophyll; here, deficiency causes a characteristic yellowing of the leaves between the veins.

3 Potato blight, a fungal disease, starts with brown patches on the leaves but soon completely destroys the top-growth, before the spores are washed down to infect the tubers.

4 Pests are animals that eat our plants. Japanese beetles often arrive in large numbers, skeletonizing leaves and damaging buds, flowers, and fruits. Plants that survive the feeding injury may be severely weakened.

What can go wrong?

Most plants in a well-kept garden or any natural ecosystem are healthy most of the time. Like animals, they have well-ordered defense mechanisms against invaders and only occasionally submit to ill health. When plant health problems arise, they can be caused by:

• environmental factors, such as water shortage
• mineral deficiencies, such as magnesium deficiency
• disease, such as potato blight
• pests, which are animals that eat green plants

Resisting attack

Healthy plants have a great tolerance for pests and diseases and, like healthy young people, can readily shake off minor infections. If environmental conditions are not as good as they might be and as a result the plant is stressed, or if it is very young or old, the same infections could be life-threatening. As a general principle, the bigger the plant, the more disease or pest damage it can tolerate. A large oak tree, for example, supports many thousands of insects and mites on its leaves—not to mention fungi feeding on the leaves, stems, and roots—without showing any ill effects. At the other extreme, a small lettuce seedling is totally vulnerable to the damping-off fungus *Pythium* and the very weak biting mouths of sowbugs. But as the seedling grows, the epidermis thickens and sowbugs cannot bite through to the soft tissue inside; the thickened epidermis also offers protection from fungal invasion.

Getting the diagnosis right

Accurate identification of plant health problems followed by knowledge of when intervention is necessary are the keys to successful organic pest and disease control. Identification requires close inspection; the most obvious symptoms may not be the real problem. Sooty mold on camellias, for example, is caused by the presence of soft scale (a sap-sucking insect). These pests secrete a sticky waste substance called honeydew on which sooty molds thrive. Control can be achieved only by taking action against the scale insects, not the more obvious sooty molds.

Refer to reference books or contact your local Cooperative Extension Service office (garden centers may also be able to help) before deciding on a

course of action, and remember that most maladies that plants suffer are not life-threatening. Discovering the most appropriate action (when to act and when not to act) and formulating control strategies comes with experience. Gaining this experience is part of the fun and intellectual challenge of organic gardening.

Knowledge of plant taxonomy—how plants are grouped into families—is helpful (see also *Crop Rotation*, pp. 301–313). Plants within the same family tend to suffer from similar maladies. These family groups are not always obvious: Stocks (*Matthiola*), for example, are in the same family as cabbages and other brassica crops, and cabbage white butterflies are just as happy on stocks as they are on cabbage and sprout plants.

Inspect damaged or diseased plants closely. A magnifying glass or eye piece (of no more than 10x) is useful. Be sure to take a look at night as well because many animals that eat plants are nocturnal and will be hiding out of view during the day. Monitoring traps are useful for early warning of the presence of certain pests; the yellow sticky cards widely available from garden retailers, for example, will reveal the presence of whitefly in the greenhouse long before the average gardener notices any significant problem with plant health. Early knowledge of a problem means that measures to nip it in the bud can be implemented before the plants suffer. Prevention, rather than cure, is the key to resisting attack.

GETTING THE DIAGNOSIS RIGHT

Even if the symptoms seem obvious, it is possible to make the wrong diagnosis.
1 Wilting can be caused not just by drought but by fungal diseases called "wilts," or by pest damage to the liquid transport system further down the plant.
2 This leaf looks diseased, but the malformations are caused by the feeding of tiny blister mites.
3 Sooty mold is a secondary problem; the fungal growth is feeding on waste from soft scale insects, the cause of the problem.

A closer look
A photographer's magnifying eye glass or "loupe" can be a useful tool in identifying plant problems.

Growing problems

Tightly bound
A severely potbound plant may never thrive when planted out. New roots are unable to grow out from the tightly coiled rootball.

The environment plants experience includes the conditions in the soil as well as the weather, or climate above ground. So mineral deficiencies or excesses can be classified as environmental problems, just as an inappropriate level of moisture or exposure to too much wind are environmental problems. Environmental problems can have both direct effects and indirect effects because they leave plants more vulnerable to attack from pathogens or pests.

Water

Shortage of water causes plants to wilt, which even for short periods weakens plants, leaving them more vulnerable to attack from pests or invasion by pathogens. Prolonged water shortages can result in stunted growth and tissue death in all or parts of the leaves. Other factors can cause plants to wilt: pest damage to the roots that prevents them from taking up water, for example, or some fungal infections called "wilts." Water shortages can have delayed effects on plants; flower drop in camellias in spring is caused by dry conditions the previous autumn.

Plants can also wilt as a result of too much water in the soil, caused either by poor drainage or over-watering. Waterlogged soil prevents the roots from breathing. The initial response is wilting, as the roots cease to function. This is followed by tissue death, allowing fungal and bacterial pathogens and rots to enter. Always ensure the soil is dry before watering, especially with indoor and container plants. (See *Water and Watering*, pp. 63–71, for more information.)

Frost

Even frost-hardy plants occasionally have parts that are subject to frost damage, notably spring buds, young shoots, and blossom on fruit. As water in the plant cells freezes, it expands, causing the cells to burst; the cells die off leaving black/brown areas of dead tissue, usually on the growing tips. Avoid frost damage by choosing later flowering or frost-hardy cultivars of some plants, delaying sowing dates, or using protective row covers or cloches.

Mechanical damage

Mechanical damage can be caused by hail, heavy rain and wind, and over- or underexposure to sun. Scorch, caused by excessive sun, is aggravated by the presence of a thin film of water on the surface of the leaf that acts like a tiny magnifying glass. The leaf surface turns brown and dries up. In tomatoes, scorch on the ripening fruits causes a condition known as green shoulders, where the tops of the fruit fail to

A REGULAR WATER SUPPLY

Blossom end rot (right) is a disorder of tomatoes and peppers resulting from calcium deficiency, but usually caused by lack of water. The calcium may be present in the soil but unavailable to the plant due to dry conditions around the roots; this is common in pots where water supply fluctuates.

Runner beans, grown well, are prolific (far right); poor production may be caused by insufficient water at the flowering stage, which is critical to pod set.

redden, remaining a yellow/green color. Scorch can be minimized by watering early in the morning or in the evening, or by shading. Mechanical damage can also be caused to plants by trampling or misuse of equipment, especially nylon string trimmers.

Other disorders

Splitting in vegetables, bolting (flowering too early), blindness (failing to produce flower heads and fruit), and edema (swelling) can occur in plants that, usually for environmental reasons, have suffered disturbed growth patterns. The difficulty with these conditions is isolating the cause and avoiding it.

Mineral deficiencies

Mineral deficiencies can cause plants to fail and show symptoms of "disease" (technically disorders), but in a well-ordered organic garden, with continual emphasis on the health of the soil, these are seldom a problem. When managed organically, most garden soils will provide all the nutrients plants require.

Occasionally, especially in alkaline soil, trace elements, although present, may not be soluble due to the high pH and are therefore unavailable to the plant. On these occasions additional sources might need to be added (see p. 61). Mineral deficiencies can also be caused by an excessive application of particular elements; overdo potassium-rich fertilizers, for example, and you may alter the soil chemistry, "locking up" magnesium so that plants develop symptoms of magnesium deficiency.

Mineral deficiencies are often difficult to confirm from symptoms alone and can easily be confused with diseases, especially viruses. If a problem persists, it may be necessary to have the soil or the plant analyzed professionally (see *Soil and Soil Care*, pp. 34–37).

MINERAL DEFICIENCIES

Mottling, marking, and even crisping of leaves can all be the result not of disease but of mineral deficiencies. Fruits may also spoil and wither.

1 Iron deficiency is one of the most common plant disorders and almost always presents as a yellowing of leaves, especially between the veins. It is especially common in alkaline soils, when it is known as lime-induced chlorosis.

2 Manganese deficiency (on potato leaves), common in poorly drained soils.

3 Phosphorus deficiency (on tomato leaves)—often seen in acid soils.

4 Potassium deficiency (on French beans), often seen in light or sandy soils.

5 Bitter pit in apples, caused by calcium deficiency—common in light, sandy soils.

6 Boron deficiency on sweet corn; overliming can disrupt the uptake by plants of this trace element.

Plant diseases

Plant diseases result from the invasion of plant tissue by microscopic organisms. These can be fungi, bacteria, or viruses. Living on the plant tissue as parasites, they cause cell damage, death, and sometimes distortions of growth rather like tumors or cancers. Organisms that cause disease are known as pathogens, and the study of plant disease is the study of plant pathology. It is important to note that some organisms that are closely related to plant pathogens have beneficial relationships with our plants. Examples include the mycorrhizal fungi that act as extensions to the root hair system, and the *Rhizobium* bacteria that form the nitrogen-fixing nodules on the roots of legumes (see also p. 35).

Fungal diseases

Fungi are plants without chlorophyll; they are incapable of producing their own energy by photosynthesis. Most are saprophytic (feeding on dead and decaying tissue), but some have developed the ability to overcome plant defenses and feed on living plant tissue.

Common destructive fungal diseases include potato blight, clubroot in brassicas, damping off in seedlings, mildews, and rusts. Some of these, like the organism that causes clubroot, have protected dormant spores that can remain viable in the soil for 40 years or more. The organism that causes potato blight is carried over from year to year on infected seed tubers, but is spread from plant to plant in the form of spores, as is the case with most fungi. The fungus that causes apple scab overwinters on infected plant remains such as leaves on the orchard floor.

The majority of fungi that cause disease usually go unnoticed, apart from their symptoms. Honey fungus, with its distinctive honey-colored toadstools, is one obvious exception.

Most fungal diseases are more prevalent in warm, damp conditions, which allow the fungal spores to move freely in moist air and on a film of water on the surface of leaves. Fungal spores, which either pass through the soil or are carried in the wind, arrive on the plant's surface. From here they invade the plant cells. Fungal diseases are very diverse, but are grouped according to the type of disease (or symptoms) that they cause. Within these groups pathogens can be specific to their particular hosts. For example, the organism that causes powdery mildew on apples (*Podosphaera leucotricha*) is different from the organisms that cause the seemingly identical powdery mildews on plums (*P. tridactyola*) or roses (*Sphaerotheca pannosa*). On the other hand, the grey mold fungus *Botrytis cinerea* can affect a wide range of plants and plant parts.

Control of fungal pathogens is limited to trying to avoid or prevent the conditions in which they thrive. Good garden hygiene, ensuring adequate ventilation around plants, avoidance of over-watering, the use of resistant cultivars, and the judicious use of permitted fungicides (see p. 103) all help avoid or limit damage.

Bacterial infections

Bacteria are single-celled organisms; they reproduce rapidly simply by dividing into two. Plant-pathogenic bacteria cause numerous soft rots, wilts, cankers,

Plant diseases
Symptoms, from left to right, of: canker on apple branch; rust on fuchsia leaf; fungal leaf spot; pear scab; apple powdery mildew; blossom wilt; rose black spot; gray mold on a pelargonium blossom; brown rot; honey fungus— fruiting bodies on tree bark.

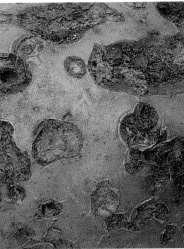

TYPES OF DISEASE

Fungal diseases (left)
The spores of fungal diseases are spread in air or, as with peach leaf curl, in water, especially rainwater.

Bacterial infections (center)
Potato scab is more common on dry alkaline soils, low in humus.

Viruses (right)
These (here, cucumber mosaic virus on wisteria) cannot be cured; instead, control the pests that transmit them.

blights, and galls on plants. Unlike fungi, bacteria usually enter plant tissue only through wounds, caused by pruning or pests, for example. Treatment is limited to removing the affected material and prevention is usually reduced to simple cleanliness.

Examples of bacterial infections include common scab on potatoes; fireblight on apples, pears, and other members of the Rosaceae family; and many of the cankers on fruit trees.

Viruses

Viruses are simply genetic material encased within a protein coating. They invade the cells of higher organisms, including plants, and "hijack" the cells' genetic codes for replicating themselves, diverting the cells' energy into the production of masses of viral material that spreads to adjacent cells, often severely restricting the host's growth or causing malformations and malfunctions of parts of the plant. Viruses cannot exist independently and usually rely on insects or other animals to act as "vectors" to carry them from infected to uninfected plants. Bugs such as aphids, whiteflies, and leafhoppers, with their sap-sucking habits, are particularly important as plant virus vectors. Viral infections can also be passed on by vegetative reproduction from infected plants. Certification plans exist in many countries that ensure that only virus-free plant stock is sold, most particularly of very susceptible fruits such as raspberries. "Certified Seed Potatoes" are free of viral material; they are produced in cooler climates (Maine is a major producer in the United States), where the aphid vectors of potato viruses are somewhat less likely to survive in sufficient numbers to spread the viral material between plants.

Viruses are too small to be seen with a conventional microscope, so they usually are named after the plant in which they were first discovered and the symptoms they cause. Control of plant viruses is restricted to planting virus-free material, the use of resistant varieties, and controlling the insect vectors of the virus.

Plant pests

Pests are those animals—large, small, and microscopic—that cause unacceptable damage to plants in the garden or reduce our enjoyment of the space that is the garden. Most creatures in the garden, however, are not pests. Many are beneficial, acting either as pollinators or helping to recycle nutrients for plants. Others feed on pest species and act as nature's own pest controllers, and there are those that have no effect on the activities of the gardener but are part of the rich biodiversity of the garden ecosystem. The beauty of many of these animals and their interesting behavior enhances the enjoyment of any garden, and as such they should be encouraged by organic gardeners.

Some animals do not fit comfortably into either the pest or beneficial group, as their habits change with the seasons, with their life cycle, or as the vulnerability of certain plants to pest attack changes. Earwigs are notorious for destroying dahlia blooms, but in other circumstances and at other times of year they are significant predators of pests such as aphids and moth and vine weevil eggs. Even the most notorious garden pests such as slugs and snails have their part to play in breaking down rotting vegetation. It is only when plants are young and tender, or when particularly vulnerable plants such as hostas and delphiniums are left unguarded, that these animals cause so much damage.

Also, many animals feed on plants without causing significant damage and therefore in an organic garden do not deserve pest status. A good example would be the froghopper or spittle bug, often found on roses in the late spring and summer. These sapsuckers are usually present only in ones and twos on each plant (one bug per mass of spittle), whereas aphids can often appear in colonies of several thousands. Other animals are pests only when the plant is young and tender, moving on to feed on other material as it ages.

Most pests achieve pest status by feeding directly on plants, but some creatures might be considered pests because they incidentally damage plants or because they foul the soil with their droppings. The domestic cat is one such example; it also demonstrates that pest status is often something in the eye of the beholder. Some gardeners tolerate cats, but others despise them.

Pests are frequently classified according to where they feed on the plant and their feeding habits. Although this is convenient for the smaller pests, it is in some ways an artificial distinction. Many leaf feeders also feed on stems; some sapsucking aphids also feed on roots and flowers.

Sapsuckers

Animals such as aphids, whitefly, and red spider mite, for example, have needle-like mouthparts and are known as sapsuckers. They pierce the outer epidermis of the plant and suck up the sap. Loss of sap results in reduced vigor and growth distortions. Sapsuckers can transmit plant viruses, and their waste (honeydew) soils plants, providing a sugar-rich food

TYPES OF PESTS

From left to right:
Sapsuckers (aphids); root feeders (here, wireworms in a potato tuber); leaf feeders (capsid bug damage and a sawfly larva—some leaf feeders also eat stems); flower feeders (Japanese beetles); fruit feeders (wasps on an apple); gall formers (here, a gall on an oak branch caused by a gall wasp).

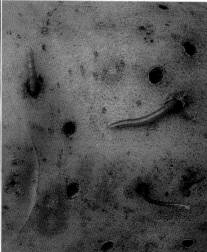

source on which fungal molds will thrive. Bacterial infections can also enter the plant via the wounds made by their tiny mouthparts.

Root feeders

Many insect larvae, including the caterpillars of some moths (cutworms); beetle grubs such as wireworms, vine weevil, chafer beetles, cabbage root fly, and carrot flies; and many species of microscopic pest nematodes graze on plant roots. Some move between plants and others invade the root, feeding on the taproot and stem. Damage restricts nutrient and water uptake, restricting and weakening growth and causing wilting.

Leaf feeders

Many butterfly, moth, and sawfly caterpillars; adult beetles and their grubs; and of course slugs and snails graze on leaves. Other moth and fly larvae mine the leaves, leaving characteristic patterns with the transparent epidermis intact on either side of the leaf. Birds and mammals also occasionally graze on foliage. Leaf damage reduces the area where photosynthesis occurs, restricting growth and fruit set and spoiling the appearance of ornamental plants.

Stem feeders

Some moth caterpillars mine heartwood and mammals will strip bark, causing dieback in trees. Many leaf-feeding pests also consume stems. Since the stems support the leaves, damage resulting from stem-feeding is similar to that resulting from leaf-feeding.

Flower feeders

Earwigs, thrips, blossom weevils, and Japanese beetles all feed directly on flowerheads and buds, which damages ornamental displays and reduces fruit set. Some animal pests, including rabbits, squirrels, deer, and birds, feed on the buds of fruit trees and bushes in late winter and early spring, when food is scarce and the creatures are at their hungriest. This damage significantly reduces yields.

Fruit feeders

Caterpillars of some moths and sawflies, as well as some beetle grubs and fly larvae, feed directly on developing fruit. Birds and wasps also feed on ripe and ripening fruit. Direct damage is usually limited, but the disfiguring of fruit renders it unpalatable, and indirect damage caused by the opening up of fruiting bodies to bacterial and fungal rotting agents is often serious.

Gall formers

Many fly and wasp larvae, as well as some mites, cause galls to develop on plants. Galls are enlarged masses of a plant's own cells, grown into weird shapes in response to feeding pests. Usually plants can function perfectly well in the presence of these galls because the pest feeds within on the gall tissue. Occasionally, however, gall-forming pests cause significant plant injury. Big bud mite, also known as filbert or hazelnut bud mite or hazel bud gall, produces gall-like swellings on the tip or lateral buds, dramatically reducing yields. Galls on plants can also be caused by fungal, bacterial, or viral infections.

Earwig (female with eggs)
Earwig populations should be tolerated in gardens, as they do a great deal of good. Although they are often found in holes in fruits, they are almost invariably only taking advantage of damage caused by other creatures.

Reducing problems by good gardening

A number of techniques can be used by organic gardeners to ensure that pests and diseases stay below an acceptable threshold. Most are not new and could be described simply as "good husbandry," an aspect often overlooked by conventional (chemical) gardening in the drive to achieve other aims. Good husbandry techniques are essentially preventive. Many are common sense and have other advantages as well as reducing losses to pests and diseases.

Start with the soil

Soil can have a dramatic effect on plant health. Get to know your garden soil (see pp. 34–37) and try to choose plants that will suit it. Where necessary, improve soil structure and fertility to encourage strong, balanced growth. Composted organic materials can help to reduce pest and disease levels in the soil and to grow plants less prone to attack.

Garden cleanliness

The carry-over of pests and diseases between seasons can be prevented with good housekeeping practices. Compost garden waste and ensure that anything that might be infected with fungal or bacterial pathogens or insect pests is well mixed into the middle of the pile, where heat generated by the breakdown of the organic material will kill them. Any plant material infested with persistent pathogens, such as clubroot-infected brassica roots, and material resistant to composting, such as the woody prunings from canker-infected trees, should be burned.

Plants carrying a viral infection should be removed and composted as soon as symptoms are identified. Viruses are incapable of existence without a living host and will die with their hosts on compost piles. Remove self-set (volunteer) potato and tomato plants, which often spring up on compost piles; such plants could be infected with blight. Lift and remove any pest-infested plant rather than leaving it for the pests to complete their development. Ensure also that pest colonies in overwintering plants, particularly brassicas, are removed where possible, and any plant remains from these crops are composted immediately or buried in a trench to prevent them acting as a reservoir for overwintering pests and fungal spores.

Winter digging can expose many of the overwintering stages of pests for predation by birds and surface predators like ground beetles. When tidying up the garden, spare a thought for the beetles and centipedes that play a vital role in pest control. They need safe, undisturbed locations to thrive.

Plant choice

Choose plants that are suited to the climatic conditions and soil types in your garden. These will grow well and will be less susceptible to pests and diseases. When buying plants ensure that they are healthy—not carrying infections or potbound—only use certified seed from a reputable source, and be wary of gifts of plants. The primary means of dispersal for many pests and pathogens is on plants transported between gardens.

Resistance

Certain cultivars, or varieties of plants, show resistance to some pests and diseases. Resistance does not imply immunity and on its own is seldom

Seed potatoes
Virus-free certification plans exist for seed potatoes and some fruits; always look for these and for disease-resistant varieties.

Compost pile hygiene
The heat generated by the process of decay will kill many pathogens, but material infected with certain very persistent diseases, such as clubroot, should be discarded.

sufficient to protect crops completely. Nonetheless, resistant varieties can be an important part of an integrated control strategy, especially against virus diseases. They can be invaluable where the threat from particular pests and diseases is high.

Companion planting

Companion planting is a term used to describe the growing of different species of plants together to the benefit of one or both. The technique is often, perhaps misguidedly, thought of as a mainstay of organic pest and disease control. While there is certainly evidence to show that some plants can help to keep others healthy, it would be unwise to rely solely on companion planting to keep pests and diseases at bay. Much is written on the subject, with accompanying definitive lists of "good" and "bad" companions, but there is little hard evidence to show that these companionships work or advice on what proportion of each plant is required to be effective.

Monoculture creates a pest and disease paradise, so it is worth growing a diversity of plants where possible—in all parts of the garden, not just the vegetable patch. Mixed planting can be effective and attractive, and, if particular combinations work in

your garden, stick with them. What works in one situation may not be effective in another.

There is some evidence to show that the strong scent of French marigolds (*Tagetes patula*) may keep whitefly out of a greenhouse, but only when the marigolds are in flower. On a field scale, it has been shown that carrots grown with onions are less damaged by carrot fly as long as there are four times as many onions as carrots, but that the effect lasts only while the onions are actively growing and stops once they start to produce bulbs. This may not be as effective on a garden scale.

Research is beginning to show that mixed planting can cut down on pest damage simply by reducing the chance of a pest landing on a suitable host. Cabbages interplanted with an unrelated crop such as French beans or undersown with clover show much lower infestations of cabbage aphid and cabbage root fly. When a cabbage root fly lands on a plant, it "tastes" it with its feet. If it lands on several suitable plants in a row, it stops to lay eggs. If the next plant is not suitable, it may fly off elsewhere.

Interplanting a disease-susceptible cultivar with a resistant one is a technique that also looks promising, at least on a field scale. Research trials

COMPANION PLANTING

Pests that find their host plant by responding to its characteristic odor are often confused by strong-smelling companion plants. Traditional gardening tips like interplanting carrots with onions (top) and growing French marigolds in the greenhouse (below) may have a basis in science.

Mixed planting
Planting flowers around vegetables encourages pollinating and predatory insects, as well as enhancing the beauty of some vegetable crops.

have shown that lettuces can be protected from downy mildew by planting alternate resistant and susceptible plants.

Plants that attract beneficial predators and parasites (see below, and also pp. 98–99) are of course "good companions" in the vegetable patch and around fruit trees and bushes to encourage natural pest control.

Timing

With vegetable crops and some annual flowering plants, careful timing of sowing or planting can avoid pest attack. In areas where potato blight is prevalent, for example, planting and cropping early potatoes usually misses the period when the threat from blight peaks. Sowing peas early or late ensures that flowering and pod development are completed before or start after the threat from pea moth is present, avoiding damage to the peas. In general,

early sowing, provided that conditions are warm enough, allows plants to be well established before the threats from pests and diseases arrive, giving them more chance of resisting pest attack. Raising plants indoors or on heated benches allows an early start when the conditions outside are not favorable. Sturdy transplants are more able to resist attack than seedlings slowly emerging from cold, wet soil.

Crop rotation

Keeping to a strict rotation for vegetable crops not only allows better use of nutrients but also prevents the buildup of pests and pathogens in the soil (see also p. 301). With perennial crops, such as roses, strawberries, apples, and pears, do not replant with the same species in the same place. New plants may fail to thrive due to high levels of host-specific pests or pathogens in the soil. The old established plants may have built up tolerance to these.

PLANTS TO ATTRACT PREDATORS

Many adult insects visit flowers for nectar or pollen even though their juvenile stages or larvae are predators. Insects are attracted to flowers by their color (including colors that we cannot see) and sometimes by their scent. Big, bold, open flowers and the tiny florets of umbelliferous flowers, such as Queen Anne's lace, are particularly effective.

Typical examples of flowers that will attract beneficial insects are:
1 Gaillardias
2 Sweet alyssum, *Lobularia maritima*
3 Carrot (an umbellifer), flowering in its second year
4 Poached egg flower, *Limnanthes douglasii*

See also *Gardening for Wildlife*, pp. 186–201.

Predators and parasites for natural control

A major component of working with nature for organic pest management is allowing the natural balance of predators and parasites of pests to thrive and keep pest populations in check. The use of pesticides upsets this balance. Often pesticides are more harmful to predator populations than they are to the target pest species. In the past, pesticides have actually given new species pest status as the pesticide wiped out the predator populations. The fruit tree red spider mite is a perfect example, emerging as a pest of fruit trees only after the introduction of tar-oil winter sprays in the 1930s.

Natural predators

Many animals in the garden feed on pests. Some are more obvious than others and get much of the attention, such as praying mantids. Some we like for aesthetic or sentimental reasons and readily notice their importance in the pest control stakes, such as lady beetles. But many insignificant creatures work unnoticed, keeping pest populations below threshold levels. The chart on pp. 98–99 shows animals that are effective pest control agents in the garden. It is important to recognize these so they can be encouraged and left alone to perform their business.

To build up the numbers of natural predators and parasites in your garden, aim to avoid the use of pesticides (even those mentioned at the end of this chapter). Pesticides not only have a direct effect on predators and parasites (killing them) but also the indirect effect of removing their food supply. Mixing flowering plants with vegetables and fruit encourages many general predators, such as parasitic wasps, hoverflies, and lacewings, the adults of which feed on the nectar from flowers (see also facing page).

Habitats and shelters

Maintain a pond for predators that have an aquatic phase in their life cycle. Provide artificial nesting sites, such as piles of wood for solitary wasps and overwintering boxes for lacewings (see *Gardening for Wildlife*, p. 192). A good mulch and minimal cultivation create ideal conditions for ground beetles (the number-one slug predator), and dense, matted grass at the base of hedges provides overwintering sites for these and lady beetles.

Lady beetle on the march
Adult lady beetles will prey on aphids, but the growing larvae (see pp. 98–99) inflict the most damage on aphid populations.

Robin feeding young
Like most songbirds, robins capture countless insects to feed their hungry young.

ANIMALS THAT FEED ON GARDEN PESTS

◁ Nematodes

Parasitic, microscopic roundworms; available as biological control agents for the control of slugs and vine weevil. These parasites are host-specific and are completely harmless to nontarget organisms. Here *Heterorhabditis megidis* is multiplying within the parasitized body cavity of a vine weevil.

◁ Centipedes

General ground-based predators, distinguished from millipedes, which are vegetarian, by having only one pair of legs per segment. They also move much faster than millipedes. Centipedes feed on slugs, slug eggs, and soil-dwelling insects.

Predatory bugs ▷

Many bugs from several families (notably capsids and anthocorids) are predators of other plant-feeding bugs; they are especially important in orchards. Here, an anthrocorid bug nymph attacks a small aphid.

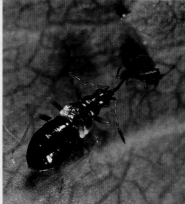

Lacewings ▷

The larvae are ferocious predators of aphids and similar insects, consuming upwards of 300 during development; encourage overwintering of populations by erecting lacewing boxes (see p. 192). They can also be purchased as biological control agents, in the form of eggs. A green lacewing larva feeds here on a Western flower thrip.

◁ Hoverflies

Larvae of many common species are predatory mainly on aphids. Their color varies but is usually bright, and they resemble flattened fishing maggots. Adults can be encouraged by planting open-flowered plants. Here, a number of bright green larvae are feeding on aphids on a rose shoot.

◁ Predatory midges

A number of species of tiny midges have wandering, predatory larvae that feed exclusively on aphids. Some can be purchased as biological control agents. *Aphidoletes* midge larvae prey on an aphid colony.

Tachinid flies ▷

Adult females of these flies, which resemble very bristly houseflies, lay eggs on or near other insect hosts, especially butterfly and moth larvae. The larvae, or maggots, develop as parasites within the host. Adults are encouraged by open-flowered plants.

Wasps ▷

The adult females of solitary species like this mason wasp collect insect pests to provide food for grubs; encourage them by keeping a pile of rotting logs as a nesting site. Social wasps are also useful predators in spring/early summer, when adult females collect insect pests to feed the grubs; however, they become pests of ripening fruit in late summer and autumn.

◁ Parasitic wasps
Adult females lay eggs in other insects and the larvae develop as parasites, killing the host. Most insect species have specific wasps parasitizing their larvae. A number of them can be purchased as biological control agents. This *Apantales glomeratus* is an important predator of cabbage white butterfly larvae.

◁ Beetles
Many species of ground beetle are predatory both as adults and larvae, feeding on juvenile and egg stages of slugs, snails, and ground-based insects. These rove beetles are similar to ground beetles; many species are good fliers, feeding on a range of plant-feeding pests. Encourage beetles by minimizing soil disturbance and with use of mulches.

Lady beetles ▷
Both the adults and larvae are predatory on aphids and other bugs. Lady beetles can be purchased as biological control agents. These lady beetle larvae are feeding on a colony of black bean aphids.

Mites ▷
Many predatory mites feed mainly on plant-feeding mites. A number can be purchased as biological control agents. *Phytoseiulus persimilis* is a biological control agent against red spider mite; here it is feeding on red spider mite eggs.

◁ Harvestmen
These are roving, spindly legged, ground-based predators related to spiders. Unlike spiders, these have only one body part.

◁ Spiders
All spiders are predatory on insects and other arthropods, although catching systems vary and not all spiders use webs as traps. Spiders can be differentiated from harvestmen by their two clearly defined body parts.

Frogs, toads, and newts ▷
The adults of all these creatures feed on many pest species; the young are aquatic, so a pond is required (see pp. 198–201). Green frogs such as this one may be found wherever there is shallow, fresh water.

Lizards ▷
Many species feed exclusively on insects and other invertebrate pests, including slugs and snails. This adult glass lizard (a legless lizard) is a predator of slugs.

Yellow sticky traps
These traps are used to monitor the presence of pests—they cannot effectively control infestations.

MIGHTY MITES

The red spider mite (RSM) is a major pest of most greenhouse plants. The predatory mite *Phytoseiulus persimilis*, if introduced early enough, will completely control populations of RSM. *Phytoseiulus* are introduced, usually in an inert carrier such as vermiculite, by sprinkling into the crop. (Make sure the container is left on its side for an hour or so before this, otherwise all the mites congregate in the top layers of the vermiculite.) For *Phytoseiulus* to work, the temperature needs to be 68°F (20°C) for at least part of the day, and the humidity should be kept high (at around 60%). High humidity suits the predator, but not the prey, switching the balance further in the predator's favor. As with most biological control agents, the aim is not pest eradication but control: Hopefully some RSM will remain in the crop to maintain a population of *Phytoseiulus* ready to kick in if the pest population starts to expand again.

Biological controls

Many predators and parasites of pests can be purchased, usually by mail order, for introduction into the greenhouse or garden. These are known as biological control agents. Some, such as lacewings and lady beetles, boost the natural populations; more often they are exotic species that are introduced to control a specific pest, like the parasitic wasp *Encarsia formosa*, a parasite of the greenhouse whitefly. Many biological control introductions work best indoors (in greenhouses, conservatories, and hoop houses), where movement is restricted and climatic conditions can be controlled to suit the predators' biology, but some predatory insects and mites can be used outside, provided that conditions are favorable and the nighttime temperature stays above the minumum required. The range of biological control agents available to the amateur is increasing all the time.

Using the controls

Details of how to use biological control agents vary, depending on the organism, but these are live cultures and the instructions must be followed to the letter (see left for one example). Since biological control agents usually arrive by mail order and sometimes more than one release is required, check the shipping dates and likely date of arrival. Plan ahead so that you are there to receive the live material and are in a position to use it immediately.

Take careful note of the conditions, especially temperature and humidity, that are needed, and avoid using all pesticides before as well as during application. Finally, ensure early introduction by closely monitoring plants for pests. Predator populations usually grow at a much slower rate than pest populations. In order to prevent the pest population from getting away from the predators, early introduction is essential. Yellow sticky traps will pick up the first pioneers of an infestation of greenhouse whitefly, for example, indicating that it is time to introduce the biological control parasitic wasp *Encarsia formosa*.

SOME BIOLOGICAL CONTROL AGENTS

Whitefly control

Pest	Agent	Special requirements
Greenhouse whitefly	*Encarsia formosa* (parasitic wasp)	Optimum temperature 64–77°F (18–25°C)
Red spider mite	*Phytoseiulus persimilis* (predatory mite)	Optimum temperature 64–77°F (18–25°C). Humidity 60%
Mealybug	*Cryptolaemus montrouzieri* (predatory beetle)	Optimum temperature 68–77°F (20–25°C). Humidity 70%
Aphids	*Aphidoletes aphidimyza* (predatory midge larva)	Optimum temperature 70°F (21°C). Humidity 80%
Vine weevil	*Heterorhabditis megidis* (parasitic nematode)	Minimum soil temperature 57°F (14°C). Moist soil essential
Soft scale	*Metaphycus helvolus* (parasitic wasp)	Temperature 68–86°F (20–30°C). Good light levels needed
Slugs	*Phasmarhabditis hermaphrodita* (parasitic nematode)	Minimum soil temperature 40°F (5°C). Moist soil essential
Thrips	*Amblyseus cucumeris* (predatory mite)	Optimum temperature 77°F (25°C)
Leatherjackets	*Steinernema feltiae* (parasitic nematode)	Minimum soil temperature 50°F (10°C). Moist soil essential
Chafer grubs	*Heterorhabditis megidis* (parasitic nematode)	Minimum soil temperature 54°F (12°C). Moist soil essential. Apply from mid- to late summer

Traps, barriers, and deterrents

Barriers such as walls or fences around gardens to keep rabbits out have been used since medieval times; fruit cages, too, are a traditional way of protecting soft fruit crops from birds. By contrast, barriers against insect pests are a relatively recent advance. They usually consist of a net with openings so small that insects cannot get in—usually less than ¹⁄₁₆ in. (1.5 mm). This lets maximum light, water, and air through, while keeping insect pests out. Insect mesh is not to be confused with row cover, an unwoven fabric. Row cover protects young plants from climatic damage and also some pests (see p. 233), but its continued use prevents ventilation and provides ideal conditions for slugs and fungal pathogens to proliferate.

Know the pest's habits

Sometimes, as with carrot fly, a simple fence 18–20 in. (45–50 cm) high will act as a barrier. The host-seeking female carrot flies keep low to the ground, as they are weak fliers and subject to being blown off-course by wind. The fence prevents the low-flying carrot flies from getting into the carrot patch and also acts like a chimney, taking the carrot odor upward and away from the host-seeking females.

Stronger fliers, like cabbage white butterflies, need complete crop cover to keep them out. This also protects crops from insect pests like cabbage root flies, which lay their eggs adjacent to cabbage stems after a response is triggered by alighting on appropriate leaves (see p. 95). Collars (see p. 304) or upside-down yogurt cups with the base removed prevent access to the base of cabbage family plants by egg-laying female cabbage root flies. Insect barrier glue is a sticky, nonset glue that prevents walking insects from passing. It is especially effective at controlling winter moths in orchards. The female winter moth has no wings; it climbs the tree in autumn or winter. On trees less than 4 years old, the glue or fruit tree grease should be applied on a paper band, not directly to the trunk itself. If the tree is staked, remember to put a sticky band around the stake as well.

Keeping slugs and snails away

A small isolated bed protected with strips of copper sheeting can be an effective way to keep slugs and snails away from vulnerable plants such as tender salad crops. Some scientific studies indicate that copper is effective because slugs and snails actually get an electric shock when they touch it. Their slimy coating may interact chemically with the copper, creating an electric current.

A number of materials are marketed as slug barriers. Most consist of a scratchy substance, such as a mined material known as diatomaceous earth, that is dry and unpleasant for slugs to pass over. However, these barriers tend to be less effective in wet weather and seldom stay in place for long; also, slugs can move under them through the soil.

Trapping and hand-picking

In small gardens, the value of hand-picking pests should not be underestimated. Removing or squashing a few invaders at the start of an infestation

Suds for slugs
Set with its rim at the soil surface, a beer-filled trap lures slugs to a sudsy demise. Traps such as this work best when filled with fresh beer; check them daily to empty and refill when you're battling a heavy infestation.

Ringing the changes
Birds soon become accustomed to scaring devices, so use a variety of devices and replace or move them around from time to time. Effective bird deterrents use sound, such as humming tape, or movement and light, like the reflective mirror ball (1). This windmill (2), made from a detergent bottle, uses sound and movement. The hovering "bird of prey" (3), made from feathers and a potato, is a very old idea.

can prevent colonies from becoming established, and continued action can control numbers of persistent pests such as slugs. Removing badly affected plants, pruning out damaged sections, or sometimes removing the sensitive part of an uninfested plant (as when pinching out the tender shoot tips of broad beans, which attract aphids) can prevent pests from spreading or becoming established.

Traps for garden pests can be used in conjunction with hand-picking. This is especially effective for slugs. As most slug activity is after dark, nighttime forays into the garden with a flashlight are usually the best time for slug collection. Traps baited with beer or chocolate, or simply items that provide daytime refuge (such as plastic plant trays or old bits of wood or carpet) for slugs, allow slugs to be picked during the day. A simple slug trap can be made from a plastic carton filled with beer. Keep the rim just above soil level to prevent beetles from falling in. Slugs will happily climb over the lip.

Introducing ducks or chickens into a garden can also control slugs. Ducks and bantams are particularly useful in this respect, as they tend not to cause significant damage to plants. On vegetable plots, chickens can be introduced for a short period between crops as part of a rotation.

The primary use of insect traps is to monitor populations, but in sufficient numbers in small areas they can help prevent pests from becoming established.

Pheromone traps are available for many moth pests, usually consisting of a protected sticky board and a sachet of the female sex pheromone. Male moths find the females by homing in on this pheromone's scent and are easily fooled into entering a trap and alighting on the sticky board. The removal of males has little effect on the population's viability since surviving males will readily cover for their deceased colleagues, but in small gardens a few such traps can often either take out enough males to have an effect, or disrupt the mate-seeking process sufficiently to reduce the viability of the next generation.

Feeding pests

When young vegetable and bedding plants are transplanted into a newly prepared bed, they become an attractive source of food for hungry slugs. Distract them with young lettuce plants, or old lettuce leaves tucked under bricks and tiles, put out several days in advance. Replace the leaves, taking the slugs away with the old ones, every few days. Some gardeners report success using French marigolds as similar "trap" crops among other bedding plants.

A pile of cut comfrey leaves can help to clear a bed of slugs before it is planted. The leaves, and the the slugs feeding on them, are left in place for a few days and removed at night. Surrounding new plants with a protective ring of cut comfrey leaves can distract slugs until the plants become established.

BARRIERS

• Individual cloches made from old plastic bottles (right) offer protection from slugs to young vulnerable plants.
• Older cabbage family plants can be protected from birds with "cages" made from twigs (far right). Netting or floating row cover, supported by canes to keep it off the plants, can protect rows.

Pesticides in the organic garden

As a final resort, organic gardeners may use a small range of insecticides and fungicides. Although often less harmful or persistent than many synthetic pesticides, these "organic" pesticides are still poisons, and like synthetic pesticides can adversely affect beneficial organisms. Their use is constantly under review by the bodies that set organic standards.

Safety considerations

It is often thought that any pesticide of natural origin—and this usually means plant extracts—is acceptable in an organic garden. Although some such products might be effective and relatively harmless environmentally, their use cannot be recommended unless they have been tested for efficacy and safety and officially approved for use. As the cost of testing and approval are very high, this is unlikely to happen. Some homemade products, such as nettle tea or boiled rhubarb leaves, may be relatively innocuous, but other homemade plant concoctions can be extremely poisonous.

There are a number of commercial, plant-based sprays (commonly referred to as botanicals) available to gardeners today. Many of these are broad-spectrum insecticides, which means they kill many types of insects, and they are marketed as natural equivalents to synthetic pesticides. But these powerful compounds kill beneficial insects as well as pests, seriously disrupting the natural balance of pests and predators that organic gardeners are striving to achieve. Some botanicals, such as rotenone, are also moderately toxic to people and most animals, and very toxic to birds and fish. Others, such as neem or pyrethrins, may be acceptable when the alternative is serious crop damage by a particular pest.

Spray only as a last choice. And while you are spraying, think about the possible options for preventing the problem from arising in future!

IF YOU MUST SPRAY, SPRAY SAFELY
- Don't use a spray as a preventive measure.
- Read the label and follow instructions precisely.
- Use a good-quality sprayer.
- Spray only where necessary. Spray contact insecticides directly on the pests, or spray the whole plant if it is to be eaten by the pests.
- Mix only as much spray as you need; never store premixed spray.
- Spray only in still weather to avoid drift.
- Never spray when bees are working—the evening is often safest.
- Wear protection when spraying—rubber gloves, mask, and goggles.
- Always wash your hands after spraying.

Sulfur dust on grapes
A traditional remedy, sulfur dust can be applied on grapes to control powdery mildew.

PERMITTED PESTICIDES

Spray	Source/derivation	Use against	Notes
Neem	From the seeds of *Azadirachta indica*	A wide range of pests, including aphids, leafminers, beetles, thrips, and whitefly	Might be harmful to some beneficial insects
Pyrethrum	Extracted from flowerheads of *Chrysanthemum cinerariaefolium*	Aphids	Can harm beneficial insects but does not persist for long
Insecticidal soap	Fatty acids extracted from plant material	Aphids; whitefly; red spider mite; soft scale; rose slug	Makes the pests slip off rather than harming them. Can damage some sensitive plants
Vegetable oils	Agricultural crops	Aphids; whitefly; thrips; scale; red spider mite	Do not use on fuchsias, begonias, or seedlings as it can damage leaves
Bordeaux mixture	Compound containing copper and sulfur	Apple scab; peach leaf curl; potato blight	Harmful to fish, livestock, and worms (due to the buildup of copper in the soil)
Sulfur	Naturally occurring mineral	Powdery mildew; rose black spot	Can harm predatory mites; do not use on young apples and gooseberries
Bacillus thuringiensis	Bacterial spores that produce an insect-toxic protein	Pest caterpillars	Protein causes paralysis of mouthparts and gut in host; degrades in sunlight; usually needs repeat applications

Raising plants

SOWING SEEDS AND TAKING CUTTINGS COMES AS NATURALLY
TO THE ORGANIC GARDENER AS COMPOSTING AND MULCHING

**Tools and techniques
(facing page)**
*Taking cuttings needs a little skill but
is not difficult to master. A clean, sharp
knife that feels comfortable to use is
your greatest ally. An ordinary
pocketknife can be perfectly adequate.*

RAISING PLANTS can be a fascinating occupation
with many benefits, especially for the organic
gardener. Propagation, as it is known, can be carried
out on many different scales and in all sorts of
situations. Most of the equipment required is
relatively cheap and easy to obtain. You can even
take the enterprise one step further and produce the
seed itself in your own garden.

There are two main methods of propagation.
Vegetative propagation—taking cuttings, for
example—produces plants that are genetically
identical to the parent; in effect, clones. Sowing seed
produces more varied results, especially if you save
your own seed from the garden, but the diversity in
the plants produced is all part of the fun.

The secret to successful propagation is to
understand the basics. Give your seeds and cuttings
the best conditions you can and they will repay you
by growing well. Correct temperature, light levels,
moisture, and ventilation are all crucial. A greenhouse
and heated bench (see p. 220) will open up all sorts
of possibilities, but excellent results can be yours
using sunrooms and windowsills—and many seeds
and cuttings can be grown outdoors.

Seeds of success
*Those bitten by the propagation bug
soon find every corner of the garden
and greenhouse filled with
"experiments" at various stages of
growth. Taking good care of them all
can be a full-time job.*

WHY PROPAGATE YOUR OWN PLANTS?

• **It's fascinating** Propagating plants can
enhance your understanding and enjoyment of
gardening. There is something endlessly
fascinating about sowing seeds, taking cuttings,
and dividing plants. You could even discover or
develop your own new plant varieties.

• **Avoid pests and pesticides** Purchased
plants may harbor pests, such as vine weevil, in
the growing medium or on the plant. Many
commercially produced plants are regularly
sprayed with chemicals that you do not want in
your garden or home, and the growing medium
may also contain pesticides. By raising your
own stock, you can be certain that you are not
introducing unwanted pollutants into your
organic garden.

• **Save yourself money** Cut costs by investing
a little time and effort in producing your own
seeds and plants. You can produce just the right
quantity for your own needs, or grow a few
extra if you have the space. The seed saved from
one tomato will give dozens of plants; one
squash will provide more than enough seed for
the average gardener. Many cuttings can be
produced from a single plant. A surplus of
plants need never go to waste. Grow plants for
your friends, for schools, for community
gardens, or to raise funds for local good causes.

• **Extend the range** Organically grown seeds
and plants are available, but the range is still
limited. By raising your own, you can extend
this range. Many rare and unusual varieties
of fruits, vegetables, and ornamentals are
impossible to obtain through seed companies
and nurseries. Under these circumstances,
you will need to rely on your own or other
people's skills in propagation to get hold of
the plants you want.

• **Think locally** Reduce transportation
costs by growing what you need where you
need it, instead of relying on expensive and
environmentally damaging deliveries from
far away.

Vegetative propagation

Propagation means growing a whole plant from a part of a plant. It can be used for all plants except annuals and biennials, which are always grown from seed. Don't forget, though, that many of the bedding plants we grow as annuals and discard every year are in fact tender perennials that can be propagated by cuttings over winter, provided that you can give them warmth and shelter.

Stems, roots, and even single leaves can be used, depending on the species. The advantage of raising plants in this way is that the offspring will be identical to the parent, without the genetic variation that can result when you save seed from a plant. And it is the only way to propagate plants that do not produce viable seed—for example, the lawn chamomile 'Treneague', bred not to flower.

Division

Division—cutting or pulling clump-forming plants into sections, each with roots and shoots—is the quickest and easiest way to propagate herbaceous perennials (see p. 173) and gives large, flowering plants in a short time. It also reinvigorates them. Most can be divided in spring or autumn. Division also works well for plants that form clumps of fleshy storage organs—bulbs, corms, or tubers—below ground, such as Jerusalem artichokes and daffodils. These can be harvested at the end of the season, separated, stored, and planted out the next spring.

Divisions of fist-size dimensions, or fully formed bulbs, can be planted out as they are, with no need for extra warmth or protection. Smaller parts of plants, including the little bulblets resembling garlic cloves that form around clumps of bulbs, benefit from being potted up for a year or two.

Stem cuttings

Both tips and sections of stem can be put in pots of compost or into the soil to develop their own roots. While all cuttings root faster with bottom heat

TAKING SOFTWOOD STEM TIP CUTTINGS

Choose strong, nonflowering shoots 3–4 in. (8–10 cm) long, severing them just above a leaf joint (**1**).

Trim the cutting to just below a leaf joint (**2**), and remove the leaves from the bottom half of each cutting (**3**).

Insert into a pot containing a 1:1 mix of coarse sand and peat moss, so that the first leaf is just above the level of the rooting medium (**4**). Keep this moist but not sodden.

Cover with a plastic bag to maintain high humidity. Use two pieces of bent wire to construct a frame to support the bag so that cuttings do not touch it and rot. Keep it out of direct sunlight.

Once rooted, harden off gradually (see pp. 113 and 232) before potting up, to acclimate cuttings to the reduced humidity and more intense light levels.

provided by a heat mat or heated bench, most do not need it. Shelter under glass or on a windowsill is necessary only for cuttings taken from soft growth that would quickly dry up and fail if exposed outside. While these cuttings need a humid atmosphere, it is important that they do not become waterlogged or the soft tissue will rot, so the compost you use must be well-drained, opened up with grit or sand (see *Growing Media*, p. 114).

Hormone rooting powders are not regarded as a suitable organic additive. Most plant species root effectively without any special treatment.

Types of stem cuttings

While there is no harm in experimenting if the opportunity presents itself, in general take the right type of cuttings at the appropriate time, and take more than you need, for the best chance of success.

• **Softwood cuttings** are nonwoody shoots taken primarily from hardy perennials and tender bedding plants in spring and early summer while they are producing strong, soft, fleshy growth. Stem tips are the easiest to take and root (see facing page). Some of the most successful for beginners are coleus, geraniums, and catmints. Because the shoots are actively growing, you need to provide adequate levels of moisture, light, and warmth to encourage rooting, so the cuttings must be potted up and kept under cover.

• **Semi-ripe cuttings** are taken just as the current season's growth starts to harden at the base. They are useful for all types of woody plants, including small

---

ROOTING CUTTINGS IN PLASTIC BAGS

This is an alternative to rooting softwood cuttings in pots or open ground that works particularly well for carnations and fuchsias. Cut an opaque plastic bag to make a long strip about 10 in. (25 cm) wide, and fold in half lengthwise to form a crease. Spread a gritty potting mix along the crease. Lay the cuttings on this so that the top third sticks out at the top, then roll up the plastic like a jelly roll and secure it with a rubber band. Water carefully, since there are no drainage holes, and stand in a warm place out of direct sunlight. When the cuttings root, remove the rubber band, unroll the plastic, and pot them up.

---

shrubs such as lavenders and dwarf boxwood, so are ideal for making quantities of edging plants. Conifers and many climbers also root well from semi-ripe cuttings. They are usually taken from deciduous species in early to late summer; cuttings from evergreens often root better if taken in early autumn. In some cases, getting the timing right is critical for success. Treat as for softwood cuttings.

Recent research has shown that longer cuttings than traditionally used can be very successful, giving bigger plants in a shorter time. Semi-ripe shoots of 1 ft. (30 cm) or more of most shrubs can be rooted. In the case of climbers, shoots of up to 3 ft. (1 m) can be used. Both ends are inserted into the pot and will often root. The arched stem will then produce multiple shoots, giving much denser growth than a normal cutting.

• **Hardwood cuttings** (see right) are taken from trees and shrubs while dormant. When taken from ready-rooting, hardy plants—for example, black currant, gooseberry, willow, and dogwood—they need very little attention. Prepare a "nursery bed" (see p. 314) for them outdoors in a cool, shaded area. These cuttings are most usually taken in late winter.

Layering

Many woody plants and climbers have a tendency to develop roots on stems where they touch the ground (some climbers, such as ivy, even develop aerial roots). You can take advantage of this habit—or stimulate it in some other woody plants—to make new plants, cutting the rooted stem from the parent and either potting it up or planting it out, if well-developed enough. Layering is especially useful to increase clematis, rhododendron, camellia, and magnolia, none of which roots easily from cuttings.

Layer shrubs in spring and climbers in early summer. Rooting usually takes at least a year, sometimes several. Dig a hole next to the parent plant and bend a stem into it, leaving about 6 in. (15 cm) of the growing tip above ground. Peg the shoot down with a piece of bent wire, replace the soil, and put a rock on top to hold the shoot down and conserve moisture. Wounding the buried stem can speed up rooting. Cut a slice out or twist it so the bark is damaged. When the stem beyond the stone begins to show more vigorous growth, it has rooted and can be severed from the parent plant.

TAKING HARDWOOD CUTTINGS

Cut vigorous shoots, formed during the summer, into 9-in. (23-cm) lengths. Remove leaves if necessary (**1**). Trim the lower end of each to just below a bud with a sharp knife. Cut off any soft growth at the top to just above a bud (**2**).

In a sheltered location, make a narrow slit or slits in the soil with a spade and fill the bottom with coarse sand. Place cuttings in this nursery bed, so that at least 3 in. (7.5 cm) remains above ground (**3**). Refill with soil. Leave for 1 year, watering and weeding during the growing season as necessary. The rooted cuttings should be ready for transplanting by the following autumn.

TOUGH SEED COATS

Many members of the pea family, such as sweet pea, broom (*Cytisus*, top), and wisteria have tough seed coats, which give their seeds long-term viability while waiting for the right germination conditions. Aid germination by scarifying the seed—nicking the seed coat with a knife or rubbing gently between a folded sheet of sandpaper (above).

Starting from seed

A seed is the product of a fertilized flower. It contains an embryo plant enclosed in a protective seed coat. The seed also contains food reserves that nourish the germinating embryo until it is able to feed itself.

Large-scale organic seed production is a relatively recent development. A limited but increasing range, mainly of vegetable seed, is now available through standard seed catalogs. There are also companies supplying only organically grown seed. If you cannot find an organic supply of the seed you are looking for, the next best thing is to buy seed without any chemical seed treatment, or consider growing your own seed.

What seeds need

For successful germination, seeds require moisture, air, and an appropriate temperature. Most prefer to germinate in darkness, although some, especially fine seeds, need exposure to light. Success also depends on the vigor of the seed. Fresh seed or seed that has been stored in good conditions (see p. 123) will germinate more rapidly and produce more vigorous seedlings than old or poorly stored seed.

Seed can be sown directly into the soil or into a specialty growing medium, such as a seed or multipurpose potting mix, in a pot or tray. This will supply the necessary mixture of moisture and air that the seed needs. An appropriate temperature in the soil or growing medium is essential for germination. Seeds have particular requirements, which govern where and when particular species should be sown.

Depending on the species of plant, both low and high temperatures can inhibit germination. The most temperature-sensitive stage in the process is when the seed is first absorbing water. The growth of some tender crops, such as sweet corn and French beans, can be permanently impaired by temperatures that are too low at this stage. The germination of onions, lettuces, and celery, on the other hand, can be inhibited when the temperature is too high.

Special treatments

Over the years, vegetables and many ornamentals have been bred for fast, regular germination.

Wildflowers, shrubs, and trees often germinate much more erratically and may refuse to germinate unless given special treatment:
• A tough seed coat may require "scarification"—wounding so that water and air can enter (see *Tough Seed Coats*, left).
• Many trees, shrubs, and wildflowers, such as hawthorn, holly, and cowslip, which are native to colder climates, need a period of low temperature before they will germinate. After sowing, stand the seed trays or pots outdoors over winter.

Alternatively, mix larger seed with moist sand and store in a refrigerator for a few months. This is known as stratification.

When seedlings fail to emerge, there can of course be causes other than poor germination, such as pest and disease attack or poor growing conditions (see pp. 112–113).

GERMINATION TEMPERATURES

Seed	Temperature range
Cabbage	41–90°F (5–32°C)
Leeks and onions	45–70°F (7–21°C)
Celery	50–66°F (10–19°C)
Sweet corn	Over 50°F (10°C)
French bean	Over 54°F (12°C)
Lettuce (butterhead)	Below 77°F (25°C)
Tomato	Over 59°F (15°C)
Poppy	59–70°F (15–21°C)
French marigold (*Tagetes*)	64–77°F (18–25°C)
Begonia	64–77°F (18–25°C)
Impatiens	68–77°F (20–25°C)
Morning glory	64–75°F (18–24°C)
Nasturtium	59–70°F (15–21°C)
Broad bean	41° (5°C)

Sowing seeds outdoors

The simplest and most direct way of raising many plants is to sow seed outdoors. The key to success is to ensure that you sow when the soil conditions—temperature and moisture content—are just right. This skill will develop with experience.

Preparing the soil

A few weeks before the anticipated sowing date, prepare the soil to suit the plants that are to be sown. Where practical, apply a leaf mold mulch to sowing areas the previous autumn. This will improve the structure at the soil surface, where germinating seedlings need it. Even freshly fallen autumn leaves will be of benefit; these can be raked off before sowing.

Do not work the soil if it is too wet—this will destroy the soil structure and give poor germination and growth rates. If mud sticks to your boots, you should abandon the work until the soil is drier.

The soil condition known as "crusting," also weather-related, will prevent the emergence of seeds, but you can take measures to help germination when you sow (see *Coping with Crusting*, right).

Making a seedbed

Rake the surface to create a fine "tilth." Compacting a seedbed is sometimes recommended, but it is better to allow the soil to settle for a few weeks rather than risk damaging the soil structure. This has the added advantage of creating what is known as a "stale seedbed." Disturbing the soil stimulates weed seeds near the surface to germinate. As they germinate quickly and grow vigorously they can easily swamp young seedlings. To prevent this, leave a prepared seedbed empty for a few weeks, hoe off the weeds that germinate, and sow immediately. This will give your seedlings a head start on the next batch of weeds to appear.

Soil temperatures

Avoid the temptation to sow seeds too early in the spring. If soil temperatures are below 45°F (7°C), the majority of seeds will germinate very slowly or not at all, and seedling growth will be slow. The longer seeds remain in cold, wet soil, the more likely they are to rot or be attacked by pests. Seeds sown in warm soil will frequently overtake those sown many weeks earlier in cooler soil. A soil thermometer is an invaluable tool, giving you a good idea of how quickly your soil is warming up. Speed this process by covering the soil with a cloche or sheet of black or clear plastic for a month before you want to sow.

How to sow

Most seeds do not need to be buried deeply; ⅛ in. (3 mm) is quite sufficient. Larger seeds can go in at a depth of twice their diameter. Peas can take a depth of 1–1½ in. (2.5–4 cm) and beans 1½–2 in. (4–5 cm). Seed can be sown in rows, in individual positions or "stations," or broadcast over a larger area.

• **Sowing in rows** Seed is sown in a shallow trench, created with the corner of a hoe or a stick. It may be sprinkled along the row, for later thinning, or placed at the final spacing required. Water the bottom of the trench before sowing; rake back the soil to cover the seeds.

• **Station sowing** Seed is sown in individual "stations" at the final spacing required. Two or three seeds can be sown at each station if necessary, then thinned to one seedling. Station-sow along a row, or

Soil thermometer
Different soils warm up at different rates; a soil thermometer provides accurate information as to when the soil is warm enough for sowing.

COPING WITH CRUSTING

Crusting is a condition prevalent in soils with poor structure. Rain causes soil particles to coalesce; a hard crust then forms on top of the soil during dry weather. If your soil is prone to crusting, cover seeds with a mixture of soil and leaf mold, or even a seed or potting medium, instead of soil. Water the seedbed before sowing, then do not water again until the seedlings have come up. Mulch the soil with a low-fertility soil improver, particularly over winter, to improve the surface structure. Reduce the frequency of digging—or give it up entirely (see *The "No-Dig" Approach*, p. 326).

GEL SOWING

Start seeds off indoors on some moist paper towel in a plastic box (**1**). Put the lid on, and keep the box at about 70°F (21°C) until roots begin to appear.

When the roots are about ¼ in. (5 mm) long (**2**), carefully wash them off the towel and into a fine-gauge plastic strainer.

Make up some fungicide-free wallpaper paste at half the normal strength, and when it has thickened, add the seeds to it (**3**), stirring gently. Try not to touch the delicate seeds.

Pour the paste and seed mix into a plastic bag and seal the top with a knot. Make a shallow trench in the soil using a draw hoe and moisten it. Cut the corner off the plastic bag and squeeze the seeds and paste out into the trench (**4**). You could also use a cake-icing bag if you have one. Cover the seeds and firm gently with the back of a rake. Keep the row moist in dry weather.

dig individual small holes. Station sowing can cut down on the amount of seed you use, especially for widely spaced plants.

• **Broadcast sowing** Seed is scattered over the soil and gently raked in. Useful for sowing grass, green manures, and other small to medium-size seed that has to be evenly distributed over an area. As it is difficult to cover every seed, some protection against birds may be needed. Row cover is particularly effective as it also speeds germination by warming the soil. Water after sowing if rain is not forecast.

Gel sowing

Gel sowing (see above) is a useful way of speeding germination indoors and sowing the germinating seeds outside without damaging their delicate roots.

Seedling emergence is often 2–3 weeks earlier than with dry-sown seeds. Gel sowing has been shown to give higher yields of slow-germinating crops such as early carrots, parsnips, and onions. Outdoor tomatoes can be sown direct in climates where the season is usually considered to be too short.

Thinning

Once seedlings have emerged, they will usually need thinning. Competition for light, water, and nutrients is intense, and if you do not remove the surplus you will end up with a mass of stunted plants. First remove weak, spindly, and slow-germinating seedlings, simply pinching them out of the ground, then continue if necessary until no seedling touches another. You may need to thin once or even twice again as the seedlings grow and encroach on each other once more. Most seed packets give an ideal "final spacing" for the plant being grown. In the vegetable garden, this can be varied according to the way you are growing your crops (for example, in narrow beds as opposed to traditional rows) and the size you wish to harvest roots, bulbs, or leafy heads.

Pest problems

Even though a seed germinates, a seedling may not emerge. Slugs, bean seed fly, mice, and millipedes may destroy it before it sees the light of day. Covers, traps, and barriers (see p. 101) keep some pests at bay.

Sowing under cover

Raising seedlings in pots and trays in a greenhouse, hoop house, or on a windowsill allows plants to be started earlier than might be possible outdoors and helps to keep them safe from pests. This method is particularly appropriate for the more tender plants but can be useful for hardy plants, too. Seedlings can be growing in trays while the ground where they will be planted is still occupied by other plants.

Where to sow

A greenhouse or coldframe is an excellent place in which to raise plants, providing good all-around light. "Bottom heat" is the most economic way of providing warmth—either with a thermostatically controlled heated propagator or on a heated bench (see also p. 220). Flat, roll-out heating mats can be used as a flexible heat source, or soil-warming cables can be buried in sand in a deep bench or box. Temperatures in the range of 65–70°F (18–21°C) will be sufficient for most plants.

Seedlings can be raised in the house, though it can be difficult to provide enough light to prevent them from becoming spindly. A propagator is useful if extra warmth is needed for germination, though the top of a refrigerator or radiator can be used instead. Check the temperature there over a few days before you sow to be sure it stays within acceptable limits. As soon as the seedlings emerge, transfer them to a sunny windowsill. They need to be turned every day so that the plants do not become lopsided as they grow toward the light. An open-topped foil-lined box, with the side facing the window cut away, will reflect light onto seedlings from all angles and produces more regular growth.

What to sow in

You can sow in a wide range of containers, either purchased or recycled from household items. The basic requirement is that whatever you use allows adequate drainage, is robust enough for the job, and is free from disease organisms and chemicals that are poisonous to plants.

• **Pots** Clay pots are porous, allowing air to reach the roots and moisture to evaporate through the clay,

Perfect for propagating
A sturdy workbench situated in dappled shade with an easily swept floor makes an ideal spot for sowing and potting on.

COVERING SEEDS

Covering pots and seed trays with plastic will help maintain moisture levels during the critical germination phase. Once germination starts, remove the covering so that the seedlings are able to emerge properly.

Shading

Young plants on windowsills can be given temporary protection from scorching sunlight simply by taping a sheet of paper onto the glass. Open windows in hot weather to make sure that plants do not stifle in hot, still air.

reducing problems caused by overwatering. They are, however, more expensive than plastic, and cleaning them is much more difficult. Plastic pots need less watering, which is advantageous when using soilless growing medium, which dries out faster than a loam-based one. Biodegradable pots, made of paper or similar materials, are transplanted along with the plant to minimize root disturbance.

• **Seed trays** Trays 2–3 in. (5–7 cm) deep and of variable size. Wooden trays are rare these days. Plastic ones are cheaper and easier to clean.

• **Cell packs** Multicelled seed trays—also known as module trays—are available in plastic and polystyrene. The plastic ones are easier to remove plants from and thus use again. Seedlings grow in individual "mini pots," so their root system is not disturbed on transplanting. "Root trainers," deeper than cell packs, encourage a healthy root system, and are ideal for sweet peas, beans, and sweet corn, for example.

• **Homemade pots and seed trays** Aluminium foil take-out containers, ice cream and margarine tubs, polystyrene coffee cups, and yogurt cups can all be used. Clean them thoroughly and make drainage holes in the bottom. Egg cartons can be used as module trays. Toilet paper rolls and homemade paper tubes are useful for plants that resent root disturbance. Just plant them straight into the ground when the plants are ready.

Sowing the seeds

Use a commercial seed mix or a multipurpose organic medium (see *Growing Media*, p. 114). The finer the seeds, the finer the growing medium needs to be. After filling pots or trays, lightly firm the medium before sowing so it is less likely to become compacted when watered. For seed trays, a wooden block is ideal for firming evenly and gently. Fine seeds can be sown on the surface of the medium and covered by gently sifting a little more over the top. Large seeds can be pushed in individually with a finger, or dropped into holes made with a pencil or small stick.

Keeping seedlings healthy

Manage the growing environment carefully to keep seedlings and young plants healthy. Good growth is the best defense against pest or disease attack. Make sure that you start with healthy, viable seeds; a good-quality sowing medium; and clean, disease-free pots. Washing used pots in soapy water will normally remove most potential hazards. Scrub off all old soil before rinsing and allowing them to dry.

• **Temperature** Keep seedlings at the correct temperature. This varies according to species and is influenced by the light levels reaching the seedlings. As a general rule, the higher the temperature, the more intense the light required. Rapid fluctuations can stunt, and even kill, plants. Do not sow warmth-loving species early unless you have the facilities to keep the seedlings adequately warm and light once they have germinated.

• **Light** Too little light leads to spindly, weak plants. Be careful about exposing delicate seedlings to direct sunlight, however. They burn very easily, especially if they have been growing in diffuse light for a while.

• **Watering** Make sure the growing medium stays moist, but do not overwater. Waterlogged conditions deprive the seedling roots of oxygen, while disease organisms thrive. Use clean, uncontaminated water. For seedlings, tap water is best. An occasional spraying with seaweed extract helps to encourage sturdy growth. An effective way to water seedlings without wetting the foliage is to stand pots or trays in water. Remove them when the surface of the growing medium is just moist, and allow to drain.

• **Stroking** Gently brushing or stroking seedlings raised indoors helps to produce stocky, firmly rooted plants (see right).

Problems

A rot problem known as damping off is common in seedlings and can spread rapidly through whole batches. It is caused by fungi that thrive in cool, wet, still conditions. Otherwise healthy seedlings will collapse at ground level, as the stem and roots become blackened and thin. To avoid damping off:

• Practice good hygiene (see also pp. 228–229).

• Don't overwater.

• Ensure that ventilation is good without exposing seedlings to cold drafts.

• Don't let seedlings become overcrowded.

Ants and sowbugs, not normally plant pests, can play havoc with seedlings. You can keep them off greenhouse benches with grease smeared around the legs or by standing the legs in saucers of water, provided that no part of the bench touches the walls to give them an alternative way up.

Space

Give seedlings space to grow. Densely sown seedlings compete for limited light, water, and space, and diseases thrive in these conditions. Plants that suffer damage at this stage may never catch up. Spacing properly at planting time is one of the best ways to avoid the problems caused by overcrowding. Alternatively, you must ruthlessly thin the seedlings, or prick them out, as early as possible. Select the healthiest, most vigorous ones and remove the rest.

Seedlings in trays need transplanting (also known as pricking out) when the first pair of true leaves, rather than the initial seed leaves, appears (see below). Growing in cell packs avoids the need for this.

Hardening off

Young plants must be acclimated gradually to cooler and less humid growing conditions. This is known as "hardening off" (see also p. 232). The best place to do this is in a coldframe. You can also cover plants with a cloche or row cover and remove it gradually over a number of days.

Stroking seedlings
Seedlings raised under cover tend to be taller and weaker than those growing outside. Gently stroking or brushing seedlings makes them grow shorter and sturdier without harming them in any way. The plants do not need to be stroked individually. A piece of cardboard brushed gently back and forth 10–20 times over a tray of seedlings is all that is required on a daily basis. Plants seem to respond best when stroked early in the day.

TRANSPLANTING

A chopstick or swizzle stick makes an excellent tool for transplanting seedlings. Before transplanting, water the planting medium well. Pry the seedlings gently out and very carefully hold them by one of the seed leaves as you lower them into a hole poked into the new container. Make sure the seed leaves are well above the surface; if not, they are likely to rot.

COMPOST IN POTS

Aged, screened garden compost is an excellent addition to potting mixes but, contrary to what you might think, pure compost isn't recommended as a growing medium. Pure compost is far too rich for most ornamentals but, combined with topsoil, sand, and other ingredients, it is ideal. Compost supplies nutrients for the container plants and improves the drainage, aeration, and nutrient-holding qualities of the mix. It even includes organisms that help suppress fungal diseases.

Growing media

To produce healthy seedlings and grow plants in pots and containers, use a specific growing medium—a seed, potting, or multipurpose mix. Garden soil on its own gives poor results; the complex balance of microorganisms, air spaces, and nutrient levels is easily lost in the restricted, artificial conditions of a container. You can buy organic growing media, or make your own mixture.

The ideal growing medium

- Is both moisture retentive and well aerated
- Contains an appropriate quantity of nutrients
- Allows a vigorous root system to develop
- Is uniform in consistency and predictable in behavior
- Is free from pathogens

Soil-based and soilless mixes

Growing media, whether commercial or homemade, usually contain a carbon-rich bulk material with some other ingredient, such as sand, to improve drainage. The majority of commercial mixes now available are soilless; they do not contain any loam (which in this context means a sterilized, or pasteurized, fine-textured topsoil). This makes them lighter to handle, if not necessarily easier to manage. They are, for example, very difficult to rewet once they have dried out.

Some plants, like chrysanthemums and fuchsias, prefer a soil- or loam-based mix. These are also useful for patio and container growing, where their added weight, higher nutrient content, and moisture-retaining abilities are helpful.

Commercial mixes are usually clearly labeled with their intended uses; however, the development of multipurpose media, which can be used for both sowing and growing in, has tended to blur these distinctions. Here are general guidelines:

- **Seed mixes** Soilless; consist of equal parts of fine-textured bulking material (such as peat) and vermiculite, which ensures effective drainage and aeration for germinating seeds. They contain little in the way of additional fertilizers; high nutrient levels are not necessary and can inhibit germination.
- **Rooting media** Very similar to the above. Often horticultural grit or perlite is used instead of sand to open up the mix still more, reducing the risk of cuttings rotting off instead of rooting.
- **Potting mixes** Used to pot up cuttings once rooted, or plants once they have grown beyond the seedling stage. Similar in texture and ingredients to seed mixes, but with the addition of fertilizers to sustain plant growth for an extended period of time.
- **Multipurpose media** Similar to potting mixes but with more moderate levels of fertilizer, so that they can be used for seeds and cuttings. As a result, older plants will need more fertilizing than those in potting mixes.

Making your own growing media

It is also possible to make your own seed and potting mixes using readily available ingredients. This is, after all, the way most gardeners did things a few generations ago. From an organic standpoint it makes good sense, too—by minimizing the use of purchased ingredients and products it reduces the need to transport heavy materials around the country; it allows garden materials and wastes to be reused and recycled; and it gives you a more intimate understanding of your garden soil, and what plants need from a growing medium. The aim is to get the right balance of bulk material, nutrients, aeration, and drainage to suit the plants you are growing. For ingredients and "recipes," see pp. 116–117.

PASTEURIZING SOIL

Method 1 (Conventional oven)
Place moist, not wet, soil in a shallow tray to a depth of about 4 in. (10 cm). Cover with foil. Put in a preheated oven at 180°F (80°C) for 30 minutes. Remove promptly, uncover, and let cool. This process does tend to impart a rather earthy aroma to the kitchen.

Method 2 (Microwave oven)
Put moist soil in a loosely covered bowl. It must not contain any stones, as these can explode. Set to maximum and allow 2½ minutes for 2 lb. (900 g) of soil, 7 minutes for 10 lb. (4.5 kg). Spread the soil out on a tray to cool.

Steam sterilizers are available from horticultural suppliers for processing larger quantities.

THE PEAT ISSUE

Over the last 50 years, soilless products have almost entirely replaced loam-based growing media. They are light, easy to handle, and more versatile than their predecessors. The chief reason for their success has been the use of peat: the decayed remains of sphagnum moss or other bog plants. Peat extraction, however, is responsible for the destruction of rare habitats—the unique and fragile ecosystem of a bog—so its use is not encouraged in an organic garden.

Peat-based growing media are permitted for use in commercial organic horticulture, but gardeners generally do not need them. In response to the concerns of organic gardeners, wildlife organizations, and environmental groups, "peat-free" products have been developed. These are based on a variety of bulk materials, including various composted waste products, such as bark, crop residues, and municipal compost. Using these recycled products rather than disposing of them reduces environmental pollution.

It is important to recognize that growing media based on different bulk products will each have their own characteristics. They should not be assumed to perform in an identical way to each other, particularly with regard to watering. Experiment on a small scale with any new medium before undertaking any large-scale growing.

INGREDIENTS SUITABLE FOR USE IN GROWING MEDIA

Composted bark
· pH 5–6.5
· Low-nutrient bulking agent
· May suppress root diseases
· Good buffering against high nutrient levels
· Unsuitable for capillary matting systems
· Too well-drained on its own, best mixed with other finer material
· Unsuitable for small cell packs

Coir
· pH 5.8–6.5
· Adds bulk
· High potassium content
· Good aeration and water-holding capacity
· Encourages root growth
· Surface dries out quickly, while underneath remains moist—easy to overwater

Sawdust
· Low pH
· Good bulking agent when used in combination with loam for potting mixes
· Very well-drained
· Locks up nutrients
· Needs thorough composting before use

Peat
· Low-nutrient bulking agent
· Low pH
· Hard to rewet when dry
· Choose other materials whenever possible

Leaf mold (2 years old)
· Low-nutrient bulking agent
· Good moisture retention and consistency
· Contains disease-combating microorganisms
· Makes a good seed sowing medium on its own
· May grow weed seedlings
· Excellent addition to potting mixes, helps to maintain an open structure

Sand
· Washed sand, free of salt and other contaminants, is best
· Use coarse sand for loam-based growing media (particle sizes 0.2–2mm)
· Use fine sand for soilless mixes

Perlite and vermiculite
· Lightweight materials to improve drainage

Garden compost
· Adds bulk and nutrients
· Best used in potting media
· May help suppress diseases
· May contain weed seeds
· Batches may vary in quality and consistency

Municipal compost
· Variable pH of 6–9
· Adds bulk and some nutrients (high in potassium)
· Suppresses disease
· Good buffering capacity
· Unsuitable for acid-loving plants
· Requires addition of inert material to balance nutrient status

Mushroom compost
· High pH
· Unsuitable for acid-loving plants
· Adds bulk and nutrients

Animal manures
· Unsuitable for acid-loving plants
· High nutrient content
· Best composted with straw or other bulking agents
· Useful for heavy feeders such as tomatoes

Comfrey leaf mold (see p. 207)
· Nutrient-rich bulking agent, high in potassium

Worm compost
· Ideal for plants requiring a rich mix
· Good topdressing for pot plants
· Holds large amounts of water, making it useful for inclusion in hanging baskets

Loam
· Good quality topsoil

Limestone
· Used to raise pH

Organic fertilizers (see p. 61)
· Provide plant nutrients for potting mixes

MAKING TOPSOIL FROM SOD

Never waste sod that you have removed to increase planting areas or convert to hard surfaces. Made into a turf stack, it will rot down into a crumbly, even-textured loam, ideal for use in growing mixes. Stack the pieces upside down. Cover with light-excluding black plastic or old carpet for 6–12 months. The resulting loam should be crumbly and ready for screening. Pasteurize the loam (see p. 114) for use in seed-sowing mixes to destroy harmful pathogens and weed seeds. Do not sterilize it; this kills beneficial microflora and affects the way nutrients behave.

MIXING YOUR MEDIA

If garden soil will form part of your mix, first screen it to remove stones (**1**). It is important to mix ingredients well. Make sure that the ingredients (other than any fertilizers) are damp, but not overly wet. Fertilizers are best mixed with some sand in a bucket, which will help spread them evenly through the mix. Spread the ingredients out in layers on a flat table or bench, or heap them on a hard surface (**2**), then sprinkle the sand and fertilizers evenly over the top of them. Mix the ingredients thoroughly using your hands. For larger quantities, use a spade (**3**) or a cement mixer. Do not store growing media for long; make up small quantities at regular intervals.

PLANT RAISING AND POTTING MIXES

Use	Ingredients	Ratio (by vol.)	Comments
Seed-sowing mixtures	Leaf mold alone		Often sufficient on its own if sieved.
	Leaf mold : loam	1 : 1	Gives good results with most seeds. Has enough nutrients until seedlings are transplanted. Too coarse for small seeds. Needs careful watering.
	Comfrey leaf mold : sand	4 : 1	Will provide sufficient nutrients until transplanting stage.
Potting mixtures	Coir alone		Transplant seedlings promptly to avoid nutrient deficiencies.
	Loam : leaf mold : garden compost	1 : 1 : 1	A good basic mix, well-drained and fertile.
	Peat : sand : loam : garden compost	2 : 1 : 3 : 0.5	Nutrient-rich.
	Leaf mold : worm compost	3 : 1	Nutrient-rich.
	Loam : aged manure : leaf mold	3 : 1 : 1	Very rich mix for heavy feeders such as pot-grown tomatoes and peppers.
	Comfrey leaf mold alone		Good for flowering and fruiting container-grown plants.
	Comfrey leaf mold : sand	4 : 1	To every 8 gal. (35 liters) add 5 oz. (144 g) general organic fertilizer and 1 oz. (28 g) seaweed meal.
	Leaf mold : loam	1 : 1	Good for permanent plantings in pots. Loam does not require pasteurization. Use comfrey leaf mold for a richer mix.
	Loam : coir	1 : 1	To every 8 gal. (35 liters) add 8 oz. (225 g) seaweed meal; 4 oz. (110 g) bonemeal; 3 oz. (85 g) hoof and horn; 2 oz. (55 g) ground limestone. Nutrient-rich.
Rooting mixtures	Peat : sand or perlite	1 : 1	
	Sieved leaf mold : coarse sand	1 : 1	Use well-rotted leaf mold.

Saving seed from the garden

Seed-saving is something all gardeners can do. You might simply save a few seeds from a favorite flower or vegetable for the next season, or you might take on the more specialized task of maintaining a specific variety from a seed library or collection. The techniques you use will depend on the type of plant and on how important it is that it is kept pure, or true to type.

When are seeds set?

A flower must be pollinated to set seed. Pollen is transferred from the male part of the flower, the anther, to the female part, the stigma. The pollen grain then grows down the style to the ovary, where it fertilizes the eggs. These then develop into embryos, which will be enclosed in the seed, ready to grow into new plants.

• **Self-pollinators** Self-pollinators are plants that produce flowers that are normally fertilized by their own pollen. This can happen even before the flowers open, so there is little or no danger of one variety crossing with another.

GOOD REASONS FOR SEED SAVING

• Seed saving adds another dimension to gardening. It's a fascinating process that extends your knowledge of how plants work.
• It is not possible to buy organically grown seed of every plant. Saving your own in an organic garden helps to ensure a supply of what you want.
• Many old and less commercial cultivars are dropped from seed catalogs and may disappear altogether. Some of these may have excellent characteristics, particularly suited to the gardener, or may simply be your favorite flower or vegetable. By saving seed of threatened cultivars and sharing them with others, you will be helping to conserve our genetic heritage.
• Leaving a few plants to flower and set seed will give you many more seeds than you could ever get in a seed packet, for virtually no cost. It will be fresh, too. Home-saved seed often has a high germination rate and produces vigorous seedlings.

• **Cross-pollinators** Cross-pollinators need pollen from another flower, or sometimes even another plant, to produce healthy, viable seed. Pollen is transferred by insects and/or the wind. Keeping seed of cross-pollinators pure is more difficult because they may be pollinated by other cultivars of the same plant, close relations of the same species, or by pollen from wild relatives.

Another point to consider is whether the plants are annual, biennial, or perennial. Annual plants will flower and set seed in a few months, whereas biennials, such as carrots and parsnips, may require up to 18 months to do so. Many perennials may not produce seeds until several years after sowing.

Saving seed from F1 hybrids is rarely done. F1s are produced by crossing two specific parent plants; seed produced from the resulting F1 hybrid will not be true to the original, though the results might be interesting!

Selection for health and purity

It is important to keep seed free from disease (which may be transmitted in the seed) and, depending on your requirements, true to type.

• Save seed from plants that have the typical characteristics of the variety.
• Choose plants that are healthy, vigorous, and yield well. Do not just choose the first plant to go to seed; you will be selecting for this characteristic, which is not usually what you want. If it is the roots of a biennial plant that are the important part, as in the case of carrots, dig them up in the autumn to choose the best. You will then need to replant them, to flower and set seed the following summer.

Cull any plants that are diseased, weak, or do not appear true to type. This is known as "rogueing out."
• With self-pollinating plants, a bean with the wrong-colored pods or a tall pea among a dwarf variety, for example, should be removed before seed is harvested. Off-type cross-pollinating plants need to be removed before they flower so their pollen cannot fertilize other flowers.
• Do not grow different cultivars of the same plant

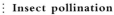

Insect pollination
Encourage beneficial insects into the garden to help plants set seed. As they move from flower to flower, pollen travels with them.

HOW THEY ARE POLLINATED

Self-pollinated
French bean
Lettuce
Pansy
Pea
Sweet pea
Tomato
Zinnia

Wind-pollinated
Beet
Hazelnut
Love-lies-bleeding (*Amaranthus*)
Spinach
Sweet corn

Insect-pollinated
Basil
Broad bean
Cabbage
Celery
Columbine
Foxglove
French marigold
Leek
Nasturtium
Pepper
Poppy
Primrose
Radish
Runner bean
Summer squash
Sunflower
Winter squash and pumpkins

next to each other if you are saving seed. It is remarkably easy to confuse different varieties, especially if plants have died down prior to harvest.
• Save seed from several plants, if possible, to maintain the genetic diversity. Although all plants of a variety may look alike, over the generations small mutations will occur, giving variations in height, maturity, color, and yield. To retain this variation, you should save seed from several plants. If you are aiming to maintain a variety for the long term, then larger numbers of plants are needed.

Keeping it true

If different varieties cross, then the results can be unpredictable. Generally speaking, on a garden scale, keeping true to type is more important in vegetables—where you want to be sure that you are going to get a good crop—than it is with ornamentals, where diversity can be a bonus.

If you are saving seed of a cross-pollinating plant, make sure that none of its close relatives, including weeds, is in flower in your garden at the same time. Of course pollen can be brought in from surrounding gardens and fields, too. The distance that pollen can travel varies from species to species. Hedges, fences, and other barriers will cut down the risk of crossing. Where it is vital to maintain absolute purity—when growing seed for a seed exchange, for example—you may need to go to the lengths of growing cross-pollinating plants such as brassicas, carrots, and onions in isolation cages (see p. 16).

Generally, keep varieties of the same species of self-pollinating plants 6 ft. (2 m) apart to be fairly sure that seed saved from them will stay true to type.

HAND-POLLINATING SQUASH FOR SEED

Squash flowers are pollinated by insects. Cross-breeding is common as the pollinators move from plant to plant. For plants to breed true, you must ensure that a female flower is pollinated by a male flower of the same variety.

In the evening, choose selected flowers of both sexes before they are fully open (**1**). The females are recognizable by a swelling on the stem below the petals: This will develop into the fruit. Cover the plant with row cover overnight (or tie up or tape the flowers, as in picture **4**). The next morning, to hand-pollinate the female flower with the male, pick the male flower, tear off the petals (**2**) and insert it into the female flower (**3**), making sure pollen is rubbed from the anthers onto the stigma. Immediately tie the petals of the female up with raffia or twine (**4**), or seal with tape, to ensure that no insects can enter with foreign pollen. Leave until the flower drops off.

CLEANING TOMATO SEED

Crush the tomatoes and add a little water, then leave the mixture in a warm place to ferment. Gradually the pulp will form a moldy cap or crust, while the seeds sink to the bottom (far left).

Drain the seeds (left) and rinse them with copious amounts of cold water, and then drain and dry them as quickly as possible.

Seed harvest and storage

Seeds come in a great variety of shapes and sizes and are produced within an equally diverse range of pods and fruits. For seed-saving purposes they can be divided into two basic categories: those that can be stored in a dried state, and those that will die if they are allowed to dry out. The latter types, sometimes described as "recalcitrant," include trees with large oily seeds, such as oaks, and many tropical plants. In this instance storage is limited to keeping the seeds in a cool, moist environment such as a sand-filled pot in the refrigerator and sowing them within a few months.

Luckily, most of the seeds produced by garden plants can be stored dry. There are two main sub-divisions according to how the seeds are produced: those borne within soft fruits, such as tomatoes and squashes, and those that are dry-seeded at maturity. Dry-seeded types should be allowed to mature on the plants until the pods or seedheads have dried out. Dry pods should have a crisp feel when squeezed and should not contain any sap, moisture, or green pigment when scratched with a fingernail. In climates where the seed harvest is affected by rain, harvest plants when they are as close to maturity as possible and hang them upside down in a dry, well-ventilated place to allow the seed to ripen further. Harvest soft fruits when ripe. Members of the pumpkin family require additional ripening after harvest to produce the best-quality seeds because their seeds continue to mature after the fruit is ripe.

Seed cleaning

• **Soft-fruited plants** (for example, squashes, tomatoes, melons, and cucumbers). Scoop out the seeds from the fruit, place in a bowl, and wash off the adhering pulp. Alternatively, the seed can be mixed with water and fermented for several days (see above), allowing the action of bacteria and fungi to help clean the seed and eliminate some seedborne diseases. Drain off the pulp and any floating seeds, leaving the viable seeds at the bottom.

To prevent the seeds from becoming moldy or germinating, they need to be dried quickly. Spread out washed seed on a plastic, glass, or metal sheet to dry. Place the sheet in a well-ventilated spot, out of intense sunlight. Stir the seeds every few hours to speed the drying process. Another option is to place the seeds close to a fan set to run at a cool temperature; hot air could damage the seeds. For larger seeds, construct drying trays from fine wire mesh. These will provide excellent conditions for rapid moisture loss.

• **Dry-seeded plants** (for example, beans, brassicas, cosmos, lettuce, love-in-a-mist, peas, and poppies). Seedheads and pods are harvested from the plants and threshed to clean off the dry debris when fully dry. Various threshing techniques can be used to release them.

• Put the seedheads in a sack, then walk on it or beat it with a stick.

• Crush small pods between planks or boards.

• Open large pods individually and extract the seeds.

Dry-seeded plants
Members of the carrot family produce seeds in flattish heads called umbels. Choose the biggest umbels—these contain the best quality seed. Harvest them when the seeds are ripe and leave them to dry; they can then be winnowed.

Winnowing, the separation of seeds and chaff, can be achieved by placing the seeds in a bowl and blowing carefully—the debris is usually lighter than the seeds and is ejected from the container. A more reliable result can be obtained by using a hair dryer on a cool setting. When you are winnowing seeds, it is a good idea to wear a face mask. Some fine chaff can irritate the lungs, throat, and nasal passages.

One of the best methods involves the use of two screens or sieves, of different gauges. The first, which is just big enough to allow the seeds to pass through, retains any chaff larger than the seeds themselves. The second, with a gauge smaller than the seeds, lets the remaining chaff drop through, leaving the seeds clean.

Pest and disease control

Having obtained your freshly winnowed seeds, look through them carefully and remove any that are diseased, moldy, or eaten by maggots. There is no

point in storing seed that is already weakened by disease or pest attack.

Seeds, like any other parts of plants, can harbor unwanted organisms. These may be capable of killing the seeds or ruining the subsequent crop. The fermentation method, used for tomatoes, has already been mentioned. Provided that seeds are very well-dried, they can also be placed in the freezer for a couple of days. This will kill some, though not all, types of weevils and their eggs.

Hot water treatment

By soaking seeds in water heated to 122°F (50°C) for 25 minutes, you can eliminate a number of seedborne diseases. Among these diseases are black leg, black rot, and black leaf spot in cabbage; target spot and bacterial canker in tomato; and downy mildew in spinach. Do this after extracting or threshing the seeds. You need to keep the temperature just right—use a thermometer and a double boiler and make sure the temperature is constant before adding the seeds. Stir them into the water and continue to stir for the duration of the treatment. Remove, drain, and dry the seeds as usual.

Seed storage

Whether home-saved or purchased, store your seeds in the correct conditions to maintain their ability to germinate and grow for as long as possible. The drier and cooler the seeds are kept, the better. Seeds stored in breathable envelopes or packets in a cool, dry room will fare much better than in a warm, damp one. Never keep seeds in a greenhouse.

There is no point in storing seed already weakened by pest or disease attack

The moisture content of seeds is usually the critical factor in determining how long they remain viable. Seeds stored in humid climates can have a depressingly short life. The answer is to dry the seeds further, to 8% moisture levels, in airtight containers. Glass jars with rubber seals are probably the best. These can be kept in a refrigerator or freezer, which will increase the life span of the seed even further, often up to ten times that of seed kept at room temperature and humidity. The process of seed drying is quite simple and involves the use of color-indicating silica gel as the desiccant (drying agent). As the granules absorb moisture, they change from blue to pink; when saturated they can be dried and used again. A very low oven (200°F/95°C) or a microwave will remove the moisture and reverse the color change. Repeat this whenever you need to dry the silica gel.

Drying seeds with silica gel

Put dry seeds into breathable packets or envelopes, label, and weigh them. Place them in an airtight jar with an equal weight of dry silica gel. Seal the lid tightly. After a week the seeds will have reached the correct moisture content and can be stored in another airtight container and placed in the freezer or refrigerator for long-term storage. Before opening the jars and removing seeds, let them reach room temperature, which reduces the amount of moisture condensing on the inside of the jars and on the seeds they contain. It is also a good idea to let very dry seeds reach ambient humidity levels before sowing—just keep them in a room for a few days.

Getting started

The list on the right shows some of the easiest seeds to save—judged on their overall score for ease of pollination, maintenance of purity, and ease of harvest and cleaning—together with more challenging projects. You can learn more about seed-saving, and even start seed-swapping, by joining your local gardening club or society—and by becoming a member of organizations such as the Seed Savers Exchange, which are dedicated to preserving and giving gardeners access to old and unusual varieties.

ROUGH GUIDE TO EASE OF SEED SAVING

Easy
Basil
Broad bean
Calendula
Columbine
Coriander
French bean
Nasturtium
Phacelia
Pea
Poppy
Rocket
Tomato

Moderate
Amaranth
Cabbage
Carrot
Cucumber
French marigold
Leek
Lettuce
Onion
Parsley
Peppers
Radish
Runner bean
Squash
Sunflower

Challenging
Beet
Parsnip
Spinach
Sweet corn
Turnip

SEED LIFE SPANS

1–3 years	Up to 5 years	5+ years
Begonia	Basil	Artichoke
Carrot	Beet	Borage
Delphinium	Broad bean	Calendula
French bean	Cabbage	Chicory
Leek	Cauliflower	Cosmos
Lily	Celery	Cucumber
Onion	Lettuce	Endive
Parsley	Nasturtium	Lupin
Parsnip	Pansy	Mallow
Pea	Pepper	Morning glory
Rocket	Radish	Pumpkin
Rosemary	Sunflower	Squash
Runner bean	Tomato	Watermelon
Sweet corn	Turnip	

Looking
good

NATURAL BEAUTY IN THE ORGANIC ORNAMENTAL GARDEN

The garden framework

THE ORGANIC APPROACH CAN BE APPLIED TO ALL ASPECTS OF HARD LANDSCAPING IN THE GARDEN

Using wood (facing page)
Choose sustainable sources and avoid potentially toxic preservatives when selecting wood.

Long-lasting materials (below)
Building with reclaimed materials like these edging tiles preserves their use and beauty for another generation.

AS INCREASINGLY LARGE TRACTS of land are suffocated below asphalt or concrete, or diminished by industrial agriculture, the living landscape of our gardens becomes ever more important. The potential of our gardens as thriving ecosystems is affected by the design and composition of the garden framework.

Purchasing power

Gardens are usually multiuse environments, and they need a "framework" to meet these needs. This includes all aspects of garden construction or hard landscaping—patios, paths, driveways, fences, walls, garden buildings, and special features. To apply the philosophy of organic gardening to hard landscaping, we need to take a detailed and critical look at materials, including the extraction of the raw materials, processing, transport, their use in the garden, how they affect garden ecology, and, finally, recycling. Organic gardeners should be searching for sustainable ways of providing and maintaining the garden framework from the planning stage onward, while also being mindful of how those decisions will support the green living world. We need to consider not only the design of the garden and the selection of the materials but also maintenance requirements.

There is a greater choice of building materials for the garden today than ever before. Gardening television programs and magazines inspire us to make full use of these materials for everything from basic paths and fences to expressing a creative talent.

Forming the guidelines

Assessing the environmental costs of garden building materials and practices is a comparatively new area, and the situation is constantly changing as companies set about improving their environmental policies. As yet there are no organic standards for hard landscaping, which is a relatively new concept. In the U.K., H.D.R.A. is working to create organic standards for public horticulture and landscaping, in conjunction with the amenity horticulture industry. At the time of this writing, there are no similar nationwide movements in the U.S., but they may come in time.

In the meantime, the basic principles of organic gardening—sustainability and low environmental impact—can be applied. Some materials, such as locally purchased and well-managed lumber, will always score highly in terms of being sustainable and environmentally friendly. Other materials should be avoided, due to toxicity perhaps or the fact that extraction of the raw materials may damage natural habitats or if their manufacture causes pollution. Sometimes compromises have to be made; some materials, such as glass, fall between these two extremes. This chapter raises the issues and should help you to make sustainable, organic choices whether you are building a new garden or adding structures to an existing one.

THE PROBLEMS WITH PLASTICS

There are many different types of plastic. Some of them are implicated in serious environmental pollution, and some governments are restricting their use. It is hard for the layman to distinguish between the most and least harmful types. New and recycled P.V.C. have been particularly highlighted by environmental organizations. P.V.C. contains dioxin, a persistent organic pollutant (P.O.P.), which accumulates in the food chain and can be released during manufacture and disposal. P.V.C. can also contain phthalates, plasticizers that make materials flexible. Phthalates have been linked to cancer, kidney damage, and problems with the reproductive system. Furthermore, most types of plastic will not rot. At the end of their lives, they will end up in a landfill site or in an incinerator where they can produce toxic fumes and residues. Until manufacturers, or other bodies, guarantee a safe disposal or recycling service for these plastic items, they will remain an environmental problem.

Counting the environmental costs

Building materials and products carry environmental costs that you may not have considered. The information below and the table on the facing page will help you start to make more environmentally sound choices. Unfortunately, products rarely fulfill all the criteria that we would wish, so there will have to be compromise somewhere along the line. A balance must be struck. For example, although natural stone is a nonrenewable resource, it is extremely durable and should last for many generations.

Making your choices

The information needed to make informed decisions may not always be available or easily accessible, but it is always worth asking. Where do the raw materials come from? Does the manufacturer have an environmental policy? What steps do they take to repair environmental damage?

How you can help

If your questions cannot be answered satisfactorily, let producers know that you will be making an alternative choice. Over the last decade it is public demand that has fueled the enormous increase in the availability of organic food and "fair-trade" products (which guarantee a fair price to producers). Ecological awareness has led to huge developments in products to replace peat, in composting green waste, and in avoiding garden furniture and related products made from tropical hardwoods. Public interest and pressure can improve things.

THE COSTS

- **Extracting the raw material** Quarrying and other extraction processes can damage habitats, water tables, and wildlife. The process may cause pollution. The company may not take responsibility for repairing damaged landscape. Processes may be hazardous to human health, and products may not be fairly traded.
- **Transportation** Long-distance transportation consumes energy and causes pollution.
- **Processing** Industrial processes may use fossil fuels and could cause pollution of air, land, or water.
- **Sustainability** Materials may be from finite, rather than renewable, sources and may be used inefficiently. The techniques used to install them may be energy intensive.
- **Disposal** If the product cannot be composted or reused in another form, an environmental and financial cost will be attached to its disposal.
- **Durability and maintenance** The material may not serve its purpose well, and it may require frequent maintenance.
- **Toxicity** Treated wood and masonry may leach harmful substances into the environment, and they can be hazardous to the person using them. Seek out nontoxic alternatives.

THE SOLUTIONS

- **Plan carefully** Design the garden framework to meet your needs but also create habitats to support wildlife.
- **Consider maintenance** Hard landscaping can be designed to minimize maintenance, such as string trimming, and reduce weed problems. This will cut down on the use of fossil fuels, engine noise, pollution, and work time.
- **Conserve soil** Use excavated soil on site. Do not mix good soil with nonorganic waste.
- **Avoid damage** Be aware of products and practices that harm people or the environment.
- **Use sustainable or renewable resources** Look for wood from well-managed forests and home-grown bamboo.
- **Use nonrenewable resources sparingly and efficiently** For example, use metal only where its properties of strength and lightness are essential.
- **Reuse and recycle** Can existing materials in the garden be put to new uses? Are reclaimed building products available locally? Can purchased materials be recycled or composted at the end of their life?
- **Use local resources** Locally available materials reduce pollution caused by transportation.
- **Use labor rather than industrial or mechanical processing** Labor and craftsmanship are a renewable source of energy.

BUILDING MATERIALS AND THE ENVIRONMENT

Material	Sustainability	Applications	Durability	Cautions	Recycling
Wood	Sustainable if from well-managed forests	Practically all garden landscape work	Variable according to species	Ensure from sustainable forests; avoid toxic preservatives	Can be reclaimed or, ultimately, allowed to rot to "compost"
Preformed concrete slabs or blocks	Quarried materials, reserves limited; cement manufacture currently polluting	Paving	Very durable	Avoid large areas of unbroken, sterile paving	Use recycled slabs if available; some new slabs are made of recycled materials
Fired clay bricks or blocks	Quarried materials, energy-intensive manufacture	Walls or paving	Very durable		Can be reclaimed and recycled
Natural stone and stone chippings	Quarried material, reserves limited	Walls or paving	Very durable, variable according to type	Use most local supply	Can be reclaimed and recycled
Reconstituted stone	Secondary raw materials, using reclaimed aggregates	Walls or paving	Very durable	May contain resins or cement	Can be reclaimed and recycled
Cement mortars, concrete	Quarried materials; polluting, energy-intensive manufacture	Walls or paving	Very durable	Avoid inhaling cement powder, avoid skin contact	Can be recycled
Sand and gravel	Quarried materials	Paving, mortars, or concrete	Very durable		Can be recycled
Plastics	Can be made from natural materials; most are derived from petroleum	Paving, soil reinforcing, or walls	Durable, but variable according to type; some may become brittle	Avoid plastics such as P.V.C., which can be expensive to recycle safely; never burn plastics	Plastics can be recycled, but facilities for safe recycling are scarce
Plastics, recycled	Recycled plastic and polystyrene waste	Fencing, paving, compost bins, bed edging, and in other situations in place of wood	Very durable	Will never biodegrade; do not burn; check recycled content	Can be recycled again to produce more of the same, but it rarely is
Lime	Quarried material, reserves limited	Used in cement manufacture and in lime mortars	Very durable if used correctly	Avoid skin contact, as very caustic	Old lime mortars can be reclaimed for foundation material
Wrought iron work	Quarried material; energy-intensive manufacture	Railings and decorative screens and gates	Fairly durable	Check that any metal paints used are eco-friendly	Can be reclaimed or recycled
Steel and other metals	Quarried material; energy-intensive manufacture	Sometimes used in garden barriers, also fittings, nails, etc.	Fairly durable	Use only where particular properties of steel are essential	Can be reclaimed or recycled; plastic-coated metals are difficult to recycle
Wood treatments	Some products highly toxic	Used to preserve nondurable woods	—	Use only nontoxic products	Some wood preservatives cause burning wood to emit toxic fumes
Glass	Quarried materials and lime, potash, and metallic oxides	Greenhouse, glass bricks, or mosaics	Fairly durable		All glass can be recycled
Landscape fabrics	Can be made of plastics or natural biodegradable materials	Weed-suppressing membrane; also used to separate soil from paving material	Plastics durable, biodegradability varies according to material		Not widely recycled (biodegradable plastics rot harmlessly)
Pond liners, bentonite lining membrane	Quarried material, plus polypropylene geotextile	Water retention in ponds, reed beds, or wetlands	Very durable; self-sealing		Geotextile can be separated from bentonite
Pond liners, synthetic	Butyl preferable to P.V.C. as does not contain carcinogenic plasticizers and does not pose same risk of chlorine pollution	Ponds or bog gardens	Will last up to 20 years, and can be repaired	Avoid P.V.C. liners	Not recyclable, but can be made into granular fillers (although this requires a lot of energy)
Bamboo	Sustainable, but incurs transport costs; can be home-grown	Plant supports, screening, pergolas, or gutters	Variable according to size and variety		Can be composted
Natural-fiber ropes (hemp, flax)	Sustainable	Plant supports, and between wooden posts for boundaries	Variable according to size of rope		Can be composted

Choosing wood for the garden

Wood is potentially the most environmentally friendly of all building materials and can provide attractive and durable decking, fences, screens, and supports. In an organic garden it is important to use lumber that comes from sustainably managed forests, whatever the type of wood and the country it comes from. Look for wood with the Forest Stewardship Council (F.S.C.) label, which guarantees that it comes from a well-managed sustainable forest. Coppice wood (see p. 138) is also a sustainable resource, cut from mixed temperate woodlands. A managed coppice forest also provides an incredibly diverse habitat for plants and animals.

Well-weathered wood
Naturally resistant woods such as oak and cedar can last for years without any preservative treatment.

Natural resistance

To avoid the use of wood preservatives (see also below), try to use wood that is naturally resistant to decay. The heartwood of more naturally rot-resistant species, such as oak, can be used untreated. Other woods that last well without treatment are larch (*Larix decidua*), which will last about 10 years in contact with the soil or up to 20 years if not in contact with soil; Western red cedar (*Thuja plicata*), which will give service for about 20 years; and black locust (*Robinia pseudoacacia*), traditionally used for stakes and posts. Untreated pine lasts for about 5 years. See the table on the facing page.

Well-seasoned wood that has been allowed to dry out evenly is more expensive than green wood (freshly cut undried wood), but, in its favor, it tends to last longer and can be less prone to distortion as it weathers.

Once you begin to think about it, your own garden may well be able to provide a useful harvest of material for making plant supports and screens (see also pp. 138–141).

Wood preservatives

Lumber, posts for outdoor use, and many ready-made wooden products, such as fence panels and compost bins, are usually treated with some sort of preservative before sale. Organic gardeners should, if possible, avoid treated lumber and products unless a relatively environmentally friendly product has been used. Be aware that pretreated lumber may not have any form of label to indicate that it has been treated.

Items in contact with the soil, such as posts and compost bins, are at most risk from decay, so they are often made of lumber that has been pressure-treated with toxic chemicals such as copper arsenate and chromium arsenate (C.C.A.), which is a very effective, long-term wood preservative. Manufacturers claim that if properly applied, the chemicals in the preservative, which are themselves highly toxic, are held very tightly within the fibers of the wood, but there are doubts concerning leaching and the release of vapors. Such chemicals have no place in the organic garden. If the use of C.C.A. pressure-treated lumber is unavoidable, always wear gloves when handling it, and wear a face mask if you are sawing. This type of lumber should never be burned because it releases highly toxic fumes.

Alternatives to conventional preservatives

Boron rods provide an alternative wood preservative that is considered safe for people and the environment. They are made of boron compounds that have been subjected to high temperatures to form water-soluble, glasslike rods. These rods are placed in holes drilled in the wood, strategically placed where decay is most likely and then plugged to secure them. When the wood becomes wet, boric acid is released, which prevents fungal decay. Boron pastes have a similar effect. Both the rods and the paste are becoming more widely available and provide an excellent option for wood preservation.

Wood that is not in direct contact with the ground and so is less prone to rot is usually treated with less-toxic preservatives. Until the use of more environmentally friendly methods of preservation are used as standard throughout the lumber industry, you may want to ask a sawmill or fencing supplier to

supply untreated wood. You can treat this yourself using eco-friendly products based on natural plant oils, resins, and less-toxic materials. Creosote is sometimes sold as "organic" as it is derived from material of living origin (coal tar), but it is not regarded as suitable for use in an organic garden due to its hazardous nature.

Think about how you will use the wood before making a final decision about the use of preservative-treated wood (untreated being the preferred, organic option). If it is absolutely necessary, then consider how long it needs to last. Tree stakes generally need to last only a couple of years, after which time the tree should support itself—so using a C.C.A.-treated stake that will survive for 25 years is totally unnecessary. Non-structural timbers, such as bed edging and wood for a compost bin, could simply be left untreated. It will rot eventually, but you can then simply replace it.

Railroad ties are not generally appropriate in an organic garden because of the tar that permeates them, which may leach out in some conditions. Some ties are made of hardwood that has not been treated.

"SYNTHETIC WOOD"

Waste polystyrene and plastic can be recycled and made into a material that looks remarkably like wood. Products include fencing, furniture, and sheets, planks, and posts with which to make your own structures. It may not have quite the same flexible strength as real wood (check with your supplier to ensure that the material you buy is suitable for the proposed use), but has the advantage of needing no treatment to prevent decay. While it would be preferable not to use any form of plastic at all in an organic garden, this material is at least finding a use for a common waste product. But beware—some products contain only a small amount of recycled material. Check before you buy.

DURABILITY OF NATURAL WOODS IN A GARDEN SETTING

Species	Durability	Uses
Black locust (*Robinia pseudoacacia*)	Very durable	Very strong and hard; excellent for fence posts
Cherry (*Prunus avium*)	Moderately durable; will last about 10 years	Not widely available, but can be used in light garden structures if local stock is found
Douglas fir (*Pseudotsuga menziesii*)	Moderately durable; will last 10 years	Can be used for fencing, compost bins
Larch (*Larix decidua*)	Moderately durable—10 years in contact with the soil, up to 20 years above ground	Used extensively for fencing and pergolas; larch logs can be used for paving
Oak (*Quercus robur*)	Durable—20 years in contact with the soil, up to 40 years above ground	Ideal for fence posts, compost bins, fencing, decking, boardwalks, and garden buildings; can be used for paving (old beams or log rounds)
Pine (*Pinus* spp.)	Most types are not durable, lasting about 5 years; maritime pine moderately durable (10 years)	Can be used in all types of garden construction from fences to compost boxes and path edges, but plan to replace on a 5-year cycle or use an eco-friendly preservative to extend life
Western red cedar (*Thuja plicata*)	Durable	Frequently used for fences, trellises, and light, non-load-bearing structures; not as strong as oak
White cedar (*Chamaecyparis thyoides*)	Durable	Fencing, furniture, trellises

NOTE: Durability comparisons are made using heartwood—virtually all sapwoods are considered perishable.

Hard surfaces

Hard surfaces, such as patios, pathways, drives, and pads for utility areas, account for a large proportion of the building materials used in gardens. They often require a substantial depth of foundation material, which involves excavating topsoil.

Planning

Keep areas of continuous, unbroken paving to a minimum. They may provide a suitable setting for plants in containers, but they cannot support the same biodiversity as a border with soil.

However, paving such as broken random natural stone, with herbs or rock-garden plants in the gaps, can provide a valuable habitat for garden wildlife. The stones absorb heat in summer and give a welcome sunbathing place for lizards and other small animals, while the nearby plants provide safe cover. If laid only on a minimal foundation of sharp sand, the stones will also provide cover for invertebrates such as beetles.

Minimizing weeds in paving

If you want a very neat garden, there are ways to reduce weeds. First, provide an impenetrable foundation layer: landscape fabric under gravel, or a substantial foundation construction underneath. If the paving includes joints—filled-in gaps of about ½ in. (1 cm) between each unit—they should be pointed with mortar, rather than filled with sand, which gives weeds an ideal rooting medium. Cement and concrete products are not the most environmentally sustainable materials (see *Cement or Lime?*, facing page) and you may wish to consider more sustainable options. Lime mortars can be used in place of cement in many areas, including paving foundations and pointing.

ROCK FEATURES

Garden rock features raise considerable anxiety and opposition from environmentalists. This is because some of the rock that makes the most convincing and attractive garden features is taken from valuable habitats.

Natural stone is a limited resource that is best reserved for building purposes. You could consider using reconstituted stone made from stone dust, or reclaimed stone. A rock garden using stone chips or crushed brick fragments is another effective way to display rock-garden plants.

Paving stones
Mortars for laying and pointing paving materials can be made using lime in place of cement.

Excavations

Establishing an area of paving will often necessitate the excavation of topsoil. Consider, at the planning stage, how the soil is to be removed and what is to be done with it. Can it be used elsewhere in the garden—for example, for a raised bed or berm—or somewhere nearby? If machines are used, ensure they are the lightest and smallest possible. Do not forget that energy and materials are used to create the machine, although the environmental cost of this will be spread over its working life. The fuel it consumes and the noise and pollution it creates while working are all part of the equation.

Using stone

Natural stone, such as granite, sandstone, limestone, and slate, is a very limited resource but provides very durable building materials. Reconstituted stone products are made using stone dust from quarrying operations, bonded with cement or synthetic resins. Synthetic stone is made from minerals such as sand and ash bonded with synthetic resins. More energy is required to produce a reconstituted or synthetic product than to use stone in its natural state, and the production of the resins used can cause pollution.

Local stone may be a good choice for paving. It forms the character of the varied regions in which we take pride. All stone extraction involves quarrying, and it is potentially environmentally

USING LIME IN STONEWORK

Always use lime mortars consistently throughout a construction project; do not use cement for part of the project or for repair work, as it has different properties of porousness, expansion, and contraction.

General foundation mix for laying paving slabs and other hard surfaces
3½ parts coarse sand
1 part slaked lime
25% pozzolan

Wall foundations depend on the height and construction of the wall. The following mixes can be used for paving or walls:

Bedding mortar for granite
3 parts sand
1 part slaked lime
20% pozzolan

Bedding mortar for sandstone
3½ parts sand
1 part slaked lime
10% pozzolan

Coping course mortar
3 parts sand
1 part slaked lime
20–30% pozzolan

CEMENT OR LIME?

The use of cement has been heavily criticized by environmentalists, for both the energy and emissions involved in its manufacture and its inappropriate use. At the time of writing, cement manufacture accounts for at least 7% of the world's emissions of carbon dioxide (CO_2), and this figure is steadily rising.

Lime can be used in place of cement in mortars and foundations in garden building work. While both cement and builder's lime are produced by burning limestone in a kiln to produce calcium oxide (quicklime), the cement process requires higher temperatures and more energy. Another important difference is that when water is added to calcium oxide, it turns into calcium hydroxide, known as "slaked lime" or "lime putty," which can then reabsorb CO_2 from the atmosphere to become calcium carbonate once again. This cycle can be repeated indefinitely, whereas the lime component in cement cannot behave in the same way.

Lime mortars can be bought, made using lime putty mixed with sand, or made by mixing quicklime with wet sand. The latter is the more traditional method and is known as "sand-slaked" or "hot-mix" mortar. A "pozzolan"—a substance that aids the carbonation process—is added to lime mortar to increase its strength and frost resistance.

Like cement, builder's lime is caustic when wet, and thick protective gloves are required. It does not, as cement does, pose the additional risk to the user of inhaling silicon dioxide.

Collecting materials
Small quantities of reclaimed materials can be snapped up when seen and stored until matching or complementary items are found. Here, a stack of tiles in a corner makes a mini-wildlife habitat in the meantime; many creatures will appreciate the warmth that the tiles retain after the sun has left this spot.

dense bricks, such as reclaimed engineering bricks, generally last longer as paving than facing brick, although some types of fired clay facing bricks can be extremely hard-wearing. Ask a reputable dealer if you are uncertain. Pleasing designs can be achieved by combining a number of different materials such as quarry tiles, bricks, and bottle ends. If the area is to appear in harmony with its surroundings, some aspect of it, such as a color or matching brick, should relate to the nearby buildings. If a combination of materials is being used, a repeated pattern of materials will make the area look well-planned. This can also be achieved by surrounding random materials with a uniform edging material. Selecting materials of similar depth and preparing foundations carefully will make a uniform finished level easier to achieve.

Different materials may require different laying techniques. An area that consists only of reclaimed granite pieces would require a bedding layer of sharp sand, rather than mortar. Well-compacted stone can be used for the base layer. For normal garden use in an average soil, the base layer for stones, bricks, or slabs will need to be 3–4 in. (7–10 cm) deep. This should be increased to 6 in. (15 cm) for clay soils. A bedding layer of at least ½ in. (1.5 cm) of mortar can then be used to fix and point the surface materials. Cement mortar is normally used for bedding and pointing paving materials, and concrete is often used as the base material. Lime mortar is generally recognized as an environmentally friendly alternative (see p. 133).

Gravel and stone chips

Gravel and crushed rock—stone chips—are obtained by quarrying. Some gravels are collected by dredging, which destroys marine environments. However, secondary aggregates, such as crushed rubble from demolition works, offer an alternative to newly quarried materials and make an attractive, durable surface in a variety of colors and textures.

For general garden use, a 1–2-in. (2.5–5-cm) layer of gravel or stone over a weedproof landscape fabric will suffice. For areas of heavy pedestrian or vehicular use, lay a foundation of compacted rubble, 4 in. (10 cm) deep for paths, and double that for driveways. Regular traffic can help to prevent seedling weeds from establishing.

destructive, depending on how the company manages and restores the site. This cost is offset to some extent because natural stone should last for many generations. If it is used in its natural form, the requirement for energy-intensive processing is minimal and local craft skills are kept alive.

Reclaimed materials

Reclaimed building materials, such as brick, stone, concrete slabs, wood, and quarry tiles can all be used to create new paving. Ensure that secondhand bricks for outdoor use are weather-resistant. Heavier, more

To keep the gravel in place, use an edging of wooden planks or reclaimed bricks or tiles. Driveways need a heavier edging material; thicker lumber, for example, or mortared bricks laid on a suitable foundation.

Hoggin

Hoggin is a mixture of clay, sand, and gravel that can be rolled to give a durable surface to patios, paths, and drives. The clay content acts as a binder. The surface is hardest in dry conditions and requires excellent drainage facilities if waterlogging and surface erosion are to be avoided. When hoggin is well laid and compacted, it suppresses weed growth.

Certain types of subsoil with a high percentage of gravel or grit can be reused as a hard-wearing surface material. A proportion of new aggregate may be necessary to give a stable surface, but this will be a much smaller quantity than if the whole area was paved.

Wood as a paving material

Wood is potentially the most environmentally friendly of all building materials, and it makes attractive and durable garden surfaces. However, it can be treacherous when wet, and surfaces should be grooved to create a nonslip surface.

Wood paving may take the form of decking, log rounds, heavy-duty lumbers (reclaimed or new beams), pavers, or bark and wood-chip mulches. (For general advice on choosing wood and wood preservatives, see pp. 130–131).

Wooden decking may be constructed from new or reclaimed wood, preferably a durable hardwood like oak, which not does require a preservative. Where the deck has a structural purpose, always consult a structural engineer to check both the design and suitability of the wood.

Precut heavy lumber paving can be used for patios, paths, and drives. It combines well with other materials such as decorative aggregates or reclaimed slate to create attractive patterns. Log rounds (see below) make good stepping-stones or an informal paving material, held in place with a retaining edge. A base layer may be needed on damp, clay soils. Use the spaces between as planting pockets, or fill with gravel or with fine sand, soft enough to be walked on barefoot.

For the ultimate soft surface, choose bark or wood mulch, in a thick layer over a weedproof barrier, which is both economical and easy to lay.

GRASS PAVERS

To strengthen grass for pedestrian and vehicle use, a recycled plastic grass paver system can be laid as a mat, and then spread with topsoil and seeded with grass. The result looks like, and is maintained as, ordinary grass, but it will not be eroded by frequent pedestrian or vehicular traffic. Grass pavers benefit the environment because they provide a grass ecosystem. Even if a foundation is required for areas of heavy use, they use less masonry than a conventional drive or pathway. Many suppliers use 100% recycled plastic.

Concrete grass pavers provide an excellent compromise between grass and heavy-duty paving. They are designed to be placed directly onto existing subsoil, so there is no need for base or bedding materials in most gardens. Grasses quickly become established in the soil pockets. The area is maintained like an ordinary lawn.

WOOD FOR GARDEN PATHS AND SURFACES

Decking

Wood decking can be constructed in a great variety of different patterns. It may be set above or level with adjacent surfaces. A ¼-in. (5-mm) gap should be allowed between each decking board for drainage.

Decking may also be available as preformed squares (see below), but check for preservative use when purchasing these.

Mulches

Bark and wood-chip mulches come in many grades, styles, and colors, which you can select to suit the location. A "play grade" bark mulch can provide a soft landing area underneath play equipment. The recommended depth for a domestic play area with no high equipment is 12 in. (30 cm). For paths, use a 4-in. (10-cm) layer. A retaining edge of planking, for example, may be needed. Replenish mulches annually.

Wood rounds and pavers

Log rounds are short lengths of round branches or tree trunks, which may or may not have had their bark removed. They can be used as stepping-stones in a mulch or grass path, or butted together as an informal surfacing material. Use shallow rounds, 4–6 in. (10–15 cm) deep, for pedestrian areas. Chunkier rounds, up to 8 in. (20 cm) deep, are more suitable for heavy use.

Garden wall
Low walls need only simple building skills and can increase the planting opportunities in your garden. This small retaining wall creates a raised bed with good drainage for sun-loving plants. Leave gaps in the mortar, or poke holes in it with a pencil when it is wet, to about 6 in. (15 cm) deep; you may encourage the nesting of masonry bees, a beneficial insect.

Walls, fences, and screens

Boundary and screening walls perform the same function as fences, but a wall is normally more solid and bulky, requiring substantial foundations. If well built, walls afford greater strength and durability. Walls absorb more heat than fences; this is slowly released during the night, providing a slightly warmer microclimate to adjacent plants. Solid walls standing alone do not make good windbreaks; they can create more turbulence than permeable barriers, which filter the wind.

Garden walls

Walls in gardens account for the use of many tons of quarried materials, a finite resource, so use recycled materials wherever possible. Stone walls should ideally be built only where their strength and durability are actually needed. Substantial walls can also be built from reclaimed heavy-duty wood, and they do not require large quantities of quarried foundation materials.

Walls can be a wildlife habitat in the garden. The dense evergreen growth and protection of an ivy-covered wall will shelter nesting or roosting birds and many insects. Dry stone walls are an ideal habitat for small mammals and reptiles.

Alternatives to brick and stone

In areas where wood and natural stone were scarce or too expensive, walls were traditionally made of adobe—local mud mixed with straw. A well-built adobe wall can last for years. They are usually less weatherproof than stone, and to last need dampproof foundations and a coping—like a tiny roof overhanging the sides, traditionally of thatch or slate. A coating of lime mortar will protect the sides. Mud can also be made into unfired bricks for "lump-wall" construction, but unless you have a suitable clay soil, lime or cement must be added to make the bricks durable.

Compacted earth or "pisé" walls consist of clay-containing earth built up in layers between removable forms. "Wattle and daub," a stick lattice covered in mud and straw, or a mixture of mud, straw, and cow manure, is another variation on the theme. If you have space, straw bales make cheap building units but need a good coat of lime mortar.

An effective and environmentally friendly acoustic barrier consists of a framework of woven, freshly cut willow, filled with soil, into which the willow stems root. Variations include a soil-filled framework of dried willow, in which groundcover plants are established. Dense, compressed reed walls designed to reduce noise are also available.

A hedge (see pp. 148–149) is without doubt the most environmentally beneficial garden barrier. But hedges take time to mature, require trimming, and occupy space. Fences provide a practical alternative where space is limited and a secure definition of boundaries is an immediate priority.

Fences

Wood is the most commonly used fencing material and is potentially the most environmentally friendly. Unfortunately, most fencing is made from nondurable softwoods, and strong chemicals may have been used to preserve it (see also p. 130). In fact, as fence panels are rarely in contact with the ground, which is where wood is most at risk from decay, a simple water-repellent stain should protect them. Fence posts are most at risk from decay at ground level, where wood, air, and soil meet. Posts made of cedar or black locust are recommended for their

natural durability. Concrete post bases extend the life of wooden posts and make them easier to replace.

Conventional wooden fencing includes the familiar post-and-rail, solid board, and picket. However, fencing panels can also be made from compressed woody prunings and other natural materials, such as reed and willow. Such panels can be homemade or bought. They are particularly suitable for lightweight screening within the garden, as are trellises and screens made from bamboo.

Bamboo canes may have traveled half a world to the U.S. Growing your own for plant supports, light structures, and screens is an environmentally friendly alternative. The canes must be dried slowly for 3 to 6 months. Tie them together with rope. They can also be drilled, but do not nail as they will split.

Other materials

Fences, barriers, and posts made from "synthetic wood" (see p. 131) can be useful; they have a long life span and never rot. There is, however, the question of how they are to be ultimately disposed of. Other fencing products made of plastic or a combination of plastic and wire can be difficult to separate and recycle, and at present only add to the problems caused by landfill and incineration.

Metals, also nonrenewable and using energy-intensive production processes, are best reserved for special applications; for example, around balconies and roof gardens where their strength and lightness is essential. Decorative iron work may also be required to preserve the architectural style of a building, and it can often be found in salvage yards.

Preferred fencing choices
• *Homemade or locally made panels from garden prunings*
• *Untreated woods from sustainable forests*
• *Panels made of natural vegetative materials such as willow, reed, or bamboo*
• *Sustainable woods treated only with eco-friendly products*
• *Recycled or scrap wood*

Avoid
• *C.C.A. pressure-treated wood*
• *Creosote-treated wood*
• *Tropical woods and any wood from poorly managed forests*
• *Plastics and recycled P.V.C.*

BAMBOOS FOR CANES

Many hardy species can be grown for canes in the U.S. Canes 6–10 ft. (2–3 m) long take around 3 years to grow. Cut them above a joint, where they are solid, to stop rain from getting into the base of the cane, leading to rot. Look for:
Phyllostachys aureosulcata var.
  aureocaulis (far left), P. nigra
  (center), and P. vivax
Pseudosasa japonica (near left)
Semiarundinaria fastuosa
Yushania anceps
Be aware that some bamboos have fast-spreading rhizomes that can become invasive.

Coppice products

THE SUSTAINABLE BARBECUE

Rather than buying charcoal made from unsustainable, poorly managed woodlands, look for charcoal from managed woods. Many avid grillers enjoy using natural charcoal because it has no added chemicals and imparts only natural flavors and odors to their food.

Coppiced poles
Below: using a bill hook to harvest hazel poles from a regularly coppiced stool. Center: cut poles stacked for drying. Far right: one of the simplest screens to construct is trimmed poles lashed together with twine. This one will support runner beans.

Renewable and sustainable, natural and versatile coppice branches and poles can provide the organic gardener with a number of indispensable building materials.

Coppice wood is the term given to poles and branches produced by a "stool"—a tree stump or root plate that is cut at ground level every few years. The stool continues to live, and grows new wood after each harvest. A pollarded tree is managed in a similar way, except that the branches are cut at a greater height.

Most deciduous trees are suitable for coppicing, and they can be harvested on a cycle, ranging from annually for willow to every 20 years for larger ash or locust poles.

Coppice products are produced commercially in various parts of the U.K. These growing systems are not common in the U.S. at this time, but there is some interest and experimentation. Of course, gardeners with moderate to large properties can produce coppice products right at home.

An ancient craft

Coppicing and pollarding usually extend the natural life of a tree. An ash tree typically lives for about 200 years, whereas if it is coppiced regularly it might be expected to continue to grow from the same plate for 1,000 years or more.

The most commonly coppiced trees in Europe include hazel, ash, sweet chestnut, oak, alder, sycamore, willow, hornbeam, maple, and lime. When carefully managed, an area of coppice can support a great diversity of flora and fauna and is one of the richest habitats of a temperate climate.

Using stems from the garden

Branches from garden pruning can be used in the same way as coppice wood. Garden trees and shrubs can provide small-diameter wood with a huge range of durability, flexibility, strength, and color. It is well worth experimenting with the species in your own garden.

Ornamental dogwoods (*Cornus alba* cultivars), willows (*Salix* spp.), and ash trees (*Fraxinus* spp.) provide some of the richest bark colors for decorative panels in woven screens. For a paler, cleaner look, branches can be stripped of their bark. Other useful material includes the pruned lower limbs of larger trees, such as cedar and cypress. These and other conifer species often have naturally curved lower branches and branchlets, which lend themselves to bentwood trellis work if they have to

be removed. Conifers do not in general lend themselves to coppicing. Many will die if cut back to bare wood. However, both yew and the shrubby juniper (*Juniperus communis*) regrow well from hard pruning, provided that it is not done very often. If you need to cut an overgrown specimen of either down to size, it will generate useful material.

Many species that are normally brittle can be used if they are cut in spring when the rising sap makes the branches more flexible for bending and weaving, especially if very young shoots are used. Otherwise, the normal time to cut coppice wood is during winter, when the trees are dormant.

Hedge clippings from species such as privet (*Ligustrum*) are flexible enough to be used for small trellises and edgings. Older, thicker hedge wood from renovation work is useful for making frameworks for larger panels.

All types of prunings, especially those with twigs too small for other applications, can be made into compressed brushwood panels.

Making plant supports

Supports for climbing plants can be made from coppiced wood, or even shrub and hedge prunings that are of a suitable length. They will last for a year or two if in contact with soil, longer if not. Twiggy materials are best for plants such as sweet peas that cling on with tendrils; straight stems work well for twining climbers.

When using willow, strip the bark from the lower part of the rod (or whole stem if you like) to keep it from rooting. This is easily done when newly cut.

Create tepees with flexible stems. For greater stability for heavier climbers such as roses, weave fine willow twigs in spiral fashion around the tepee frame to create a continuous woven band around the base. You can also use lengths of strong-stemmed climbers such as wisteria and honeysuckle for weaving.

To make an arch-shaped bentwood trellis, use a large bench or area of firm ground and lay out the framework pieces: two uprights and main crosspieces. Wire together the tops of the two uprights to form an arch. Either nail or tie the crosspieces between the uprights to strengthen the arch. Then use finer stems to crisscross the framework in the pattern of your choice.

A use for Leylandii wood

A little-known fact about the notoriously fast-growing Leyland cypress (x *Cupressocyparis leylandii*) is that it can provide durable wood for outdoor use. Its wood is not often available in the U.S., so you may look upon an inherited overgrown screen of Leyland cypress with renewed interest and begin to think of it as a more valuable resource than fodder for the chipper or shredder. If you can, dry the poles in a shed or garage for a year or more before you use them; they will last longer than if used when they are freshly cut.

Depending on the size of the trees, their trunks may be used to make fence posts, pergolas, and arches; side branches with a natural curve are useful for the tops of arches and pergolas, while others can be woven into trellises. Sadly, the trees will not regrow from the cut stump.

MAKING A HAZEL OR WILLOW SCREEN

Drive main uprights into the ground. For a screen up to 4 ft. (1.2 m) high, their diameter should be around 1½–2 in. (4–5 cm). Set them about 2 ft. (60 cm) apart, with 12 in. (30 cm) of their length below ground.

Position vertical spacers between the main uprights. These are usually of a smaller diameter than the main uprights (about 1 in./2.5 cm) and are pushed into the soil just until stable enough to weave around.

Cut green wood for the weavers, about ½ in. (1.5 cm) in diameter. Weave these rods in and out of the posts. Make sure that each new weaving rod you add in overlaps the last weaver securely and is neatly tucked into the weave. The ends of the weavers should overlap the end uprights by about 2 in. (5 cm) for stability. Use a single weave as shown, or if fine willow or hazel is available, three rods or more can be used for each row.

For taller screens, posts 3–4 in. (7.5–10 cm) in diameter are required every 4–6 ft. (1.2–2 m), with uprights and spacers set in between, as above.

Living willow screens and structures

Freshly cut green willow rods can be made into an elegant lattice fence, which subsequently takes root and grows to produce a green, living screen. Vigorous species of willow such as *Salix daphnoides*, *Salix purpurea*, and *Salix alba* hybrids are most commonly used, although any species with flexible branches of sufficient length and strength will suffice. The flexibility of willow stems allows them to be made into all kinds of structures, including arbors, tunnels, domes, and sculptures. Screens made from living willow are very strong, and they make effective windbreaks where other materials fail. The rods are cut and used fresh during winter to ensure that they will root. As the willows become established, vigorous new growth is made each season. This must be pruned back in the winter to maintain the structure. When siting a willow screen, sometimes known as a "fedge" because it is a cross between a fence and a hedge, remember that the summer growth can be widespread—up to 3 ft. (1 m) on either side.

Living willow structure

Live willow can be used to create an amazing range of screens, tunnels, domes, and other structures. If neglected, the willows will grow into full-size trees. Sadly, you won't be around to take care of your structure forever, so in clay soils prone to shrinkage, a willow structure should not be planted closer to a building than the final mature height of the willow species being used.

Making a simple willow wall

You need a selection of willow stems, sorted into bundles of similar length, and a length of weed-suppressing membrane approximately 3 ft. (1 m) wide to run the length of the screen, plus a metal rod, hammer, pruners, and twine.

• First, roll out the membrane and secure it either by digging in the edges or with large wire staples.

• Using the metal rod, make planting holes in a straight line down the center of the membrane, 6–8 in. (15–20 cm) apart and 1 ft. (30 cm) deep. Select fairly thick, straight stems and push these into the holes to form the uprights.

• Use thinner stems to establish diagonals. Make an angled planting hole at 45° beside each upright. Push stems in and weave them diagonally across four uprights. Mirror this on the other side with planting holes angled in the opposite direction on the other side of each upright.

• Using long, thin stems, create a band of firm weaving across the top. Finally, tie down the loose ends in decorative arcs across the top.

SPECIES SUITABLE FOR COPPICE CRAFTS

Species	Bendability	Durability	Applications/Notes
Hazel (*Corylus avellana*)	Good	Good 3–8 years	All types of bent and straight wood trellis work, woven panels
Ash (*Fraxinus excelsior*)	Good when young	Moderate 2–3 years	All types, traditionally used for fences; can be riven (split) into fine wands or spars for binding
Grape (*Vitis* spp.)	Very good	2–3 years	Excellent for weaving
Common oak (*Quercus robur*)	Only young branches	Good 3–8 years	Round wood used for frameworks and posts—saplings flexible
Sycamore (*Acer pseudoplatanus*)	Moderate	Poor 1–3 years	Can become weak when dry; can be used for small panels
Willow (*Salix* spp.)	Excellent	Moderate 3–5 years	Suitable for tight weaving and also living screens or "fedges," where it will survive much longer
Elm (*Ulmus* spp.)	Good	Low–moderate 1–4 years	Easy to work when young and green; young rods used as bonds (ties)
Poplars (*Populus* spp.)	Good	Moderate 1–3 years	Traditionally used for making brooms
Birch (*Betula* spp.)	Good when young, becomes brittle when dry	Poor	Besom brooms; small fence panels
Privet (*Ligustrum* spp.)	Good	Moderate–good 3–5 years	Bentwood trellis
Juniper (*Juniperus* spp.)	Good	Good	All types of trellis and light structures
Bamboos (see p. 137)	Flexible when fresh	4–8 years, depending on diameter	Cannot be nailed—predrill or tie together with rope
Dogwoods (*Cornus* spp.)	Good, very flexible	Moderate 3–5 years	Retains color when dry
Apple (*Malus* spp.)	Good	Poor 1–3 years	Suitable for small trellis
Peach, cherry, plum (*Prunus* spp.)	Poor–fair	Poor 1–3 years	Suitable for plant supports
Sumac (*Rhus* spp.)	Very good	Moderate–good 3–5 years	Highly flexible for more complex weaving—handle with gloves since some species have highly irritant sap
Lime (*Tilia* spp.)	Fair	Poor	Woven panels in larger works
Holly (*Ilex* spp.)	Fair	Poor	Suitable for weaving
Eucalyptus	Good	Moderate	Suitable for all types of bentwood or woven panel
Bay laurel (*Laurus nobilis*)	Good	Moderate	Good for weaving
Cotoneaster	Good, esp. fine shoots	Moderate	Good for weaving
Broom (*Cytisus* spp.)	Good	Fair	Good for weaving and making besom brooms
Honeysuckle (*Lonicera* spp.)	Good	2–3 years	Useful for weaving around a framework of other wood
Wisteria	Good	2–3 years	Useful for weaving
Clematis	Good	2–3 years	Fine stems useful for decorative weaving around framework of other wood; larger older stems more suitable for trellis frameworks

GARDEN USES FOR POLES AND PRUNINGS

- **Twiggy supports** for peas and tall-growing perennials.
- **Poles, screens, and tepees** for climbing beans.
- **Decorative tripod supports** for ornamental climbers.
- **Woven baskets and screens**—look for local classes in weaving to learn how to make simple projects.
- **Edging for beds**—nail stout poles between pegs, as shown left, or weave more flexible stems between more closely spaced pegs to create "mini-fences."
- **Making besom brooms**—bind bunches of brush from birch or broom tightly with twine, then drive a sharpened pole into the top of the bunch.

Woody plants and climbers

LIKE THE SET ON A STAGE, TREES, SHRUBS, AND CLIMBERS
PROVIDE THE BACKDROP FOR THE FLOWERS' PERFORMANCE

TREES AND SHRUBS supply the permanent setting for a garden. Trees provide structure and height, create shade, and add depth and character to a garden scene. Hedges are planted to enclose the garden or to create subdivisions and rooms within it. Shrubs offer structure and seasonal interest and create a permanent background for flowers. They demand relatively little attention, cover large areas of soil efficiently, suppress weed growth, and with some careful selection can provide year-round variety and interest.

Woody plants provide excellent cover for birds, mammals, and insects, and are an important source of food and nesting material. In exchange for board and lodging, these creatures will play a vital part in maintaining a garden organically. Woody plants are the slowest to develop, but in return live longest. During the first few years little progress is noticeable, but then you suddenly become aware that the tiny sapling planted years ago has matured into a wonderful tree.

The importance of trees

The old saying, "Weed as if you die tomorrow, plant trees as if you will live forever," should be put into practice more often. Many people are reluctant to plant trees, thinking they will never see them reach maturity. If the word maturity conjures up visions of old, gnarled oaks, then you are right. If, on the other hand, you would be satisfied with a trunk sufficiently large to comfortably wrap your arms around and a canopy that will provide afternoon shade, then you should be out there digging a hole for it now. Planting a tree is always special, making it the perfect way of commemorating a landmark occasion such as a birth or a wedding.

Plant a tree to celebrate a special person or event

Trees play a vital role in our environment. They clean up the air we breathe, absorb dust and noise, provide food and shelter for wildlife, and play an important role as a climatic thermostat. During summer they create welcome shade that is several degrees cooler than that cast by a building. During cold winter weather their network of branches creates air pockets, trapping air and creating a sheltered microclimate.

Choosing the right tree

The main criteria to consider when planting a tree are its suitability for the soil conditions and climate, and its ultimate size. There is a wide range of small

TREES FOR SMALL GARDENS

Acer griseum, A. campestre, and
  A. palmatum and cultivars
Amelanchier (many)
Cornus kousa var. *chinensis*
Crataegus (many)
Laburnum anagyroides
Liquidambar styraciflua
Malus 'Golden Hornet' (and
  others)
Oxydendrum arboreum
Prunus (many)
Sorbus (many)
Stewartia (many)
Styrax japonicus

Color and shape
The red stems of Cornus alba *(facing page) add brilliant color to the winter garden. The narrow growth habit of* Liquidambar styraciflua *(right) makes it ideal for small gardens, providing height without taking up too much space. In autumn its foliage turns stunning deep shades.*

FOR ATTRACTIVE BARK

Acer capillipes, *A. griseum*,
  A. pensylvanicum
Arbutus unedo
Betula (most)
Cornus alba cultivars,
  C. stolonifera 'Flaviramea'
Eucalyptus gunnii
Euonymus alatus
Hydrangea aspera cultivars
Lagerstroemia indica
Pinus bungeana
Prunus serrula
Rosa glauca
Rubus cockburnianus
  R. thibetanus 'Silver Fern' (right)
Salix alba 'Britzensis'
Stewartia (most)

FOR AUTUMN COLOR

Acer (many; right, the field
  maple, *Acer campestre*)
Amelanchier lamarckii
Aronia melanocarpa
Berberis thunbergii
Cercidiphyllum japonicum
Cercis canadensis
Cornus alba, *C. controversa*,
  C. 'Eddie's White Wonder',
  C. kousa var. *chinensis*
Cotinus coggygria
Crataegus monogyna
Ginkgo biloba
Hamamelis mollis
Hydrangea quercifolia
Laburnum anagyroides
Liquidambar styraciflua
Malus 'Golden Hornet',
  M. tschonoskii
Nyssa sylvatica
Oxydendrum arboreum
Parrotia persica
Prunus sargentii
Quercus coccinea,
  Q. palustris, *Q. rubra*
Rhus typhina
Sorbus alnifolia, *S.* 'Joseph Rock'
Viburnum opulus, *V. plicatum*
  'Mariesii'

trees suitable for small gardens, such as those in the genera *Sorbus* and *Cornus*, many maples, crab apples, and *Amelanchier lamarckii*. In a small garden in particular it is also important that the tree rewards you with maximum interest all year. Attractive bark, leaf color, autumn color, and fruits—ornamental and edible—are all options. The proposed location of the tree will also have a bearing on your choice.

Make sure the tree is suited to your garden. You may have wonderful childhood memories of the weeping willows at the lake's edge in the park, but these trees really need the moisture to be found by a lakeside and the amount of space provided by a park with a lake, rather than the average backyard with a pond.

Siting trees

Horror stories often blame trees for damage to houses—foundations ruined by tree roots, drains completely blocked, and so on. Tree roots themselves, however, rarely cause damage to buildings. Most problems occur only in clay soils where the clay either shrinks following severe dry weather, or heaves (expands), usually after a tree has been removed. A healthy tree takes up large quantities of water from the soil and during exceptionally dry spells clay soils can dry out and shrink. When a tree is removed, it is no longer drawing water out of the soil; this can cause clay soils to heave.

Tree roots sometimes do find their way into broken drains, where over time they expand, causing the drains to crack. On heavy soils in particular, birch, cherry, apple, pear, and plum should be planted at no less than 12 ft. (4 m) from the house. Ash, false acacia, chestnut, linden, plane, sycamore, and willow should be planted no less than 22 ft. (7 m) away, while oak and poplar are safest kept at a minimum distance of 40 ft. (12 m) from the house or substantial outbuildings.

Use common sense when planting trees. Look at the sun's position during the day, and imagine where the shadows will be. Make sure your favorite breakfast corner will not be cast in deep shade. Remember tree roots will spread beyond the crown, affecting moisture and nutrient levels in the soil in the surrounding area.

Pleaching, pollarding, and coppicing

With regular pruning and training, it is possible to grow potentially large trees in confined spaces. Beech, linden, sycamore, and hornbeam can be used for a hedge or stilted hedge, which is like a hedge grown on tall trunks, creating a clearing underneath. They can also be pleached, in which case the branches are trained horizontally along a framework and sideshoots are pruned back to the main branches. All these styles provide height and screening without taking up much room, but will be successful only if pruned annually to give them the trim, crisp outline required.

In established gardens, people often struggle with large trees that cast too much shade and overpower the whole scene. Many tall trees, such as lindens and willows, can be pollarded, meaning that they are cut back to the main stem at about head height. This needs to be done every 7 to 10 years. Traditionally, trees were pollarded to provide wood for domestic use while keeping the young shoots out of reach of grazing animals. Coppicing, a similar practice,

FOR ORNAMENTAL FRUIT

Amelanchier lamarckii
Arbutus x *andrachnoides* ★,
  A. unedo ★
Aucuba japonica △
Berberis (esp. deciduous ones)
Callicarpa dichotama
Chaenomeles
Cornus (many species)
Cotoneaster ★ (some)
Daphne mezereum
Ilex aquifolium cultivars ★
Mahonia aquifolium ★
Malus 'Adams', *M.* 'Golden
  Hornet', *M.* 'Sentinel'
Photinia davidiana ★
Prunus laurocerasus ★
Pyracantha
Rosa glauca, *R. moyesii*,
  R. rugosa
Sambucus nigra
Skimmia japonica ★ △
Symphoricarpos (left, white berries)
Sorbus aucuparia
Vaccinium
Viburnum betulifolium, *V. opulus*
  (left, red berries)
Vitis

★ evergreen △ female form

FOR SHADE

Aesculus parviflora
Alnus glutinosa, *A. incana*
Amelanchier lamarckii
Aralia elata
Berberis
Camellia japonica ★
Cornus (many)
Corylus maxima 'Purpurea'
Euonymus europaeus, *E. fortunei* ★
Hedera ★
Hydrangea quercifolia
Ilex ★
Juniperus x *pfitzeriana* ★
Mahonia aquifolium ★
Pieris japonica
Prunus laurocerasus ★, *P. lusitanica* ★
Rhododendron ★
Robinia pseudoacacia 'Frisia'
Sarcococca ★
Skimmia ★
Stephanandra incisa
Viburnum davidii ★

★ evergreen

involves cutting the wood down to a stool at ground level. Coppiced hazel is popular as it provides pliable stakes that are useful in the garden.

Eucalyptus trees are often grown as coppiced or pollarded shrubs in warm-climate shrub or mixed borders. Their bluish white foliage is very attractive as a backdrop to other plants and is particularly popular with flower arrangers.

Choosing the right shrub

Interesting foliage shapes and colors, attractive stems, flowers and fruits, and bird life are some of the features brought into the garden by shrubs. They can act as backdrop, groundcover, or feature plant depending on how and where they are used. They may be evergreen, have special colored foliage, be variegated, or have good autumn color. Some shrubs are as tiny as rock roses, suited to the front of a border or rock garden, while some rhododendrons can attain the size of a house.

We have a huge selection of shrubs to choose from, suiting most conditions and tastes. A little homework will help you to find the right plants for your garden. These few hours spent will save you many hours tending shrubs in the years to come. The acid-loving, stately rhododendrons, in all colors and sizes, flower between late winter and early summer; hydrangeas announce the coming of

MATCHING TREES AND SHRUBS TO SOIL TYPES

Clay soil	Dry soil	Alkaline soil
Acer platanoides △	Acer negundo, A. tataricum subsp. ginnala	Acer campestre, A. platanoides
Aesculus △	Betula (below)	Aesculus glabra
Betula pendula	Calluna vulgaris	Arbutus unedo *
Chaenomeles △	Catalpa speciosa	Catalpa speciosa
Cornus △	Enkianthus campanulatus	Cornus mas
Corylus avellana	Erica	Cotoneaster * (some)
Cotinus coggygria	Fothergilla monticola	Euonymus
Cotoneaster * (some) △	Gaultheria *	Forsythia
Euonymus alatus	Genista	Fuchsia magellanica
Hedera helix *	Gleditsia	Hypericum *
Hypericum calycinum * △	Ilex aquifolium *	Lonicera * (some)
Ilex aquifolium cultivars * △ (below)	Juniperus *	Morus nigra
Laburnum x watereri 'Vossii' △	Pieris	Paeonia delavayi, P. lutea
Mahonia * (below far right)	Pinus *	Philadelphus
Philadelphus (some) △	Rhododendron *	Prunus (Japanese cherries)
Prunus	Robinia	Pseudosasa japonica
Ribes sanguineum △	Rosa pimpinellifolia	Quercus macrocarpa
Roses	Santolina *	Sophora japonica
Salix (many)	Syringa	Sorbus aria, S. intermedia
Viburnum lantana △ , V. opulus △	Vaccinium *	Syringa
Weigela		Tilia
	* evergreen	Vinca *
* evergreen		Weigela
△ particularly suited for alkaline soils		
		* evergreen

autumn with their dainty lacecaps or spherical snowballs; viburnums with gorgeous scents flower at virtually every time of year; and ground-covering euonymus is tough and reliable. *Viburnum tinus* can be planted as an evergreen hedge or back-of-the-border shrub, while *V. plicatum* 'Mariesii', with its elegantly layered habit and lacecap-like white flowers, is a feature in its own right, deserving a prominent position.

Dogwoods such as *Cornus alba* 'Sibirica' and *C. stolonifera* 'Flaviramea' offer little in the way of flower, but start performing in autumn when their leaves turn pink and red, followed by stems that glow deep red and shine lime green, respectively. This effect can be enjoyed until late winter, when they should be cut back again. They can be planted on their own, but the effect becomes much more intense when planted in groups of five or more, where space allows.

Establishing a shrub border

Once established, shrubs, especially those that are evergreen, are effective weed suppressants, but until they have reached that stage there are several ways of dealing with the bare soil. Shrubs can be planted more densely than needed, thinning them out as they mature. If carefully dug up during the dormant season, the thinned-out shrubs can be transplanted to a new area. Alternatively, the space surrounding the shrubs can be filled with ground-covering herbaceous perennials, such as pulmonaria and the ornamental deadnettles (*Lamium*), which will gradually disappear as competition from the growing shrubs increases. Another option is to plant through a permeable weedproof barrier, which is then covered in a gravel or bark mulch to hide it. (See *Mulches for Weed Control*, pp. 76–77. See also pp. 154–157 for planting, maintaining, and pruning shrubs.)

Groundcover shrubs

Plants for groundcover have become very popular since the mid-20th century because they can reduce labor requirements considerably. A successful scheme should require little or no maintenance once it is well established, making it the most labor-saving type of planting available. Starting with a weed-free area, even young plants require little care during

the establishment years. The best plants to use as groundcover are evergreen or densely twigged ones with a low, spreading habit, such as *Stephanandra incisa* 'Crispa' and cotoneasters. This prevents light from penetrating through to the earth, discouraging weed growth.

Several conifers such as *Juniperus communis* cultivars, *J. horizontalis* cultivars, and *Tsuga canadensis* 'Cole's Prostrate' are effective, but are sometimes criticized for not offering any seasonal changes. Hypericums, on the other hand, produce flowers over a period of several months, but some can be short-lived, particularly in colder areas. Certain groundcover roses, such as 'Max Graf', grow into a colorful, animal- and intruder-repellent cover, though as they lose their leaves in winter they are not the most effective weed-suppressing plants, and their thorns can make weeding unpleasant!

GROUNDCOVER SHRUBS

Calluna vulgaris ★
Cotoneaster horizontalis ★ (left),
  C. microphyllus ★
Erica ★
Euonymus fortunei and cultivars ★ ⚘
Gaultheria ★ ⚘
Hedera ★ ⚘
Hypericum calycinum ★ ⚘
Leucothoe walteri and cultivars ★ ⚘
Mahonia aquifolium ★ ⚘,
  M. repens ★ ⚘
Microbiota decussata ★ ⚘
Pachysandra terminalis ★ ⚘
Rubus calycinoides ★
Sarcococca hookeriana var. *humilis* ★ ⚘
Skimmia japonica ★ ⚘
Stephanandra incisa 'Crispa'
Vinca ★ ⚘

★ evergreen
⚘ shade-tolerant

TIPS FOR PLANTING GROUNDCOVER

• Young plants give the quickest effect.
• Space plants at a little less than their maximum spread.
• Prepare soil well to encourage quick growth.
• Mulch for initial weed control and to aid establishment.
• Avoid invasive plants where this could be a problem.
• Match vigor if mixing plants.
• Control weeds by hand or hoe until plants have covered the ground.

Hedges and windbreaks

When low-level screening or a windbreak is required in a garden, a hedge is ideal. It will create an attractive background while also offering food and shelter to wildlife. In a very exposed location, if space is available, it is worth planting a proper shelter belt, consisting of several rows of mixed trees and shrubs that will catch the wind and disperse it to protect the garden from severe winds. A mixture of deciduous and evergreen trees and shrubs is best, planting the lowest ones on the windward side. This way the force of the wind is broken as it filters through and is pushed upward.

Which plants to use

Both trees and shrubs can be used for hedging. Your choice of plant or plants will depend not only on appearance and how you want to maintain the hedge—neatly clipped, for example, or billowing with blossom—but also whether the plants are suited to your soil and climate, and whether the hedge is in a very windswept site. Among the best choices for cold-exposed sites are beech, privet, and *Cornus mas*. Plants chosen for coastal sites must in addition tolerate salt-laden winds. And if the hedge is intended to keep out browsing animals such as deer, you must obviously choose species that do not appeal to the marauders but are not toxic as (for example) yew is.

Formal hedges

Evergreens are the classic choice for clipped hedges, giving a solid backdrop of color and structure year-round. Yew (*Taxus baccata*) and boxwood (*Buxus* spp.) are traditional garden hedges with a smooth finish; boxwood is ideal for lower hedges as it grows more slowly than yew. An interesting alternative to boxwood is *Ilex crenata*, an evergreen holly with small, rounded leaves that also lends itself to crisp clipping. Privet (*Ligustrum* spp.) is commonly planted. It is tough but only partially evergreen, and can look somewhat dull in winter. Beech (*Fagus sylvatica*) and hornbeam (*Carpinus betulus*) are deciduous but will retain their dried leaves, rustling in the wind as they glow coppery orange in winter sunlight (see below right). A fast effect is often obtained with Leylandii cypress (x *Cupressocyparis leylandii*) but, being a tall forest tree, it will grow rapidly to a huge height unless you are very strict with the pruning from an early age. Let it grow to within 12 in. (30 cm) of the desired height, and then start pruning the top. The hedge will need pruning at least twice a year to control it.

Semiformal hedges

Not all hedges need to be crisply trimmed, and flowering and fruiting hedges are among the richest food sources for wildlife (see also pp. 193–197). For a more relaxed effect, try *Viburnum tinus*, which can be loosely clipped into cloudlike shapes. In warmer climates, *Oleander* makes an attractive hedge, as do nandinas. Several flowering shrubs lend themselves to being grown as a hedge, either crisply or loosely cut. For a late winter show, the soft yellow flowers of *Cornus mas*, followed in late summer by shiny, red, edible berries, are unusual. The spring-flowering forsythias can also make a good hedge. Berberis, with its prickles, will discourage intruders; it makes a good flowering boundary.

Another way of creating an informal screen is to plant a willow "fedge," or living willow screen. Fresh willow branches are inserted into the ground during the winter months and are woven into a screen. By spring they will root and start growing. The new shoots can then be woven into the existing structure. (See also *The Garden Framework*, p. 140.)

HEDGE-PLANTING TIPS

• Bareroot plants are the cheapest. Buy mixed bundles of native species, or grow your own plants from hardwood cuttings (see p. 107).
• Plant evergreens in autumn and deciduous species from autumn to early spring.
• Don't just dig individual holes, prepare a strip 2–3 ft. (60–90 cm) wide.
• Don't forget tree guards to protect from grazing animals.
• Provide shelter initially in windy areas.
• Mulch for weed control and water retention. Water in dry weather during the first year.

CLIPPING HEDGES

With the exception of fast-growing hedges such as privet and *Lonicera nitida* that need to be pruned twice or even three times a year to keep them tidy, most established hedges, like the beech hedge, right, can be pruned once. If you prune twice, give the first cut after the last frost, as sensitive shoots of boxwood, for example, can be damaged. Otherwise it is best to prune in late summer after the main growth season is over. This way you can enjoy a crisp, neat hedge until the following spring. Prune hard, getting as close to the last cut as possible, or your hedge will soon get too fat or too tall. Only the looser-growing flowering hedges such as forthysia should be pruned with a light hand, following the natural contours formed by the shrubs.

HEDGING PLANTS

Aucuba ★ ⚑
Berberis gagnepainii △,
  B. thunbergii △, *B. thunbergii* f.
  atropurpurea △
Buxus (boxwood) ★ ⚑ △
Carpinus betulus (hornbeam)
Chamaecyparis cultivars ★
Cornus mas ⚑ △
Crataegus monogyna (hawthorn) ★
x *Cupressocyparis* cultivars ★
Elaeagnus x *ebbingei* ★ ●
Euonymus fortunei cultivars ★ △ ●
Fagus sylvatica (beech, left)
Forsythia △
Hippophae rhamnoides ★ △ ●
Ilex cultivars (holly) ★ ⚑
Kolkwitzia amabilis
Laurus nobilis (bay) ★
Ligustrum (privet) ★ ⚑ ●
Lonicera nitida and cultivars ★ ⚑
Nandina domestica ★
Nerium oleander ★ △
Potentilla fruticosa cultivars ★
Prunus laurocerasus cultivars ★ ⚑,
  P. lusitanica ★ ⚑
Rhododendron (some) ★ ⚑ △
Rosa rugosa and cultivars
Taxus baccata (yew) ★ ⚑ △
Thuja ★
Viburnum ★

★ evergreen   ⚑ shade-tolerant
△ rabbit and/or deer proof
● tolerates salty conditions

Climbing plants

Climbers are a versatile way of increasing height and variety in planting, while taking up little space. Traditionally, climbers are guided along walls, fences, and trelliswork, or up pergolas and freestanding supports. They can also, however, be grown through other plants. You might, for example, let a climbing rose such as 'Sombreuil' clamber through a tree or shrub.

Climbers in host plants

When climbers are planted in association with trees or shrubs, it is best to choose ones that will not strangle their host and that will flower at a time when the host plant is not in flower, fruit, or autumn color. This way one will not detract from the other, and a long-lived partnership can be established.

To avoid a shrub being smothered and strangled, opt for climbers that are not too vigorous and can be cut back regularly. Suitable plants include the summer-flowering clematis hybrids, such as the *C. viticella* and *C. texensis* cultivars, which can be cut back to 12 in. (30 cm) in winter, or the truly herbaceous climbers such as the golden hop (*Humulus lupulus* 'Aureus'). Alternatively, annual climbers can be used, like the stunning blue morning glory or evocatively scented sweet peas. More tender perennials like *Eccremocarpus scaber* can also be grown as annuals. Care must be taken when planting annuals at the base of woody plants to give them sufficient water since there will no doubt be strong root competition.

Plant the climber as far away from the root of the tree or shrub as is practical—and remember that it will tend to grow toward the light.

Vigorous climbers such as wisterias can be grown on a freestanding support as long as they are pruned rigorously. If you shy away from rigorous pruning, grow them at the very least on a sturdy, chunky pergola or on a house wall—somewhere you can enjoy their scent. The most powerfully fragrant climbers for arches and arbors include wisteria, honeysuckles, many roses, and *Jasminum officinale*.

Climbing techniques

Climbing plants have different adhesion techniques. The easiest to deal with—perfect for surfaces where you cannot attach climbing supports—are the self-clinging ones such as ivy and *Parthenocissus*, which have tiny roots or suction pads that adhere to the surface. Care must be taken that they do not cause damage to old brick, mortar, or stucco. If you live in an old house, it is safer to screw vine eyes into the mortar, attach galvanized guiding wires, and grow climbers that need support. Some, such as wisteria, are twiners that wind up ropes, poles, or branches. Others, like sweet peas, cling on with the help of little tendrils, while the leafstalks of clematis twine themselves around twigs, string, or wire.

Cascade of scent
Site a wisteria, one of the most elegant of climbers, where you can enjoy its delicious scent when laden with flowers in early summer.

Thorny plants, such as roses, claw their way up by hooking themselves onto their support. This is effective when they are scrambling up vegetation masses, as would happen in the wild, but they need to be tied in if you want to guide them along walls or posts.

Wall shrubs are usually grouped with climbers, but they tend to be shrubs that are slightly frost sensitive and need the shelter of a wall. Others have a lax growing habit and benefit from some kind of support (*Pyracantha coccinea*, for example). They are usually pruned and tied back to the wall, so they can benefit fully from the sheltered, sunny position in which they grow.

Training climbers

It pays to spend some time during spring and early summer, when climbers are growing rapidly, to guide them along their support. For many plants, particularly roses, terminal buds are the ones producing flower buds, while the sideshoots produce only foliage. When branches are trained in a near horizontal position, all those sideshoots will start growing vertically, and, like the terminal bud, will produce flowers. So, by tying the branches down to an existing framework and training them across rather than upward, you will ensure a much better crop of flowers, which can be enjoyed at eye level.

Tying in
Ties made of natural fibers rot with time and are unlikely to cause constriction. But check ties regularly on a plant whose stems are expanding rapidly and loosen them if necessary.

Never use plastic or metal ties, as these will cut into the wood as the branches grow and fatten, cutting off the sap stream and creating a weak point. Natural fibers will rot eventually and will snap and release the branch as it expands. By then the plant has usually been reattached at a higher point and will stay in place. It is still advisable to check climbers regularly, loosening tight ties and tying in new shoots. The younger the growth, the more pliable it is.

If you are allowing your climber to scramble up into a difficult-to-reach spot, make sure you choose one that does not need regular pruning to do well.

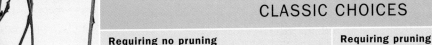

CLASSIC CHOICES

Requiring no pruning

Clematis montana is one of the more vigorous spring-flowering clematis. Its dark green foliage complements well the blush-pink flowers that appear in late spring. Although it dislikes being pruned, its vigorous habit occasionally necessitates severe cutting back. This should take place after flowering.

Hydrangea petiolaris will happily work itself up a north-facing wall, making it ideal to hide unsightly garage walls or sheds. Although it will take a few years to establish, its flaky, rust-brown stems will soon charm you as it produces its fresh green foliage in spring, soon to be followed by the delicately scented, white lacecap flowers.

Parthenocissus quinquefolia is a deciduous, self-clinging climber that has attractive foliage and stunning autumn color. Its vigor makes it ideal to cover a wall or let it clamber through a tall pine, where its autumn foliage can contrast beautifully.

Requiring pruning

Clematis viticella is a summer-flowering clematis with many cultivars and hybrids that lend themselves well to annual cutting back to 12 in. (30 cm). This promotes vigorous new growth that can then be carefully trained to produce flowers at eye level.

Climbing roses should be pruned annually, removing the old flowering stems, and thinning out some of the older stems to encourage new growth at the base. The flower stems should be cut back to the main stem, leaving approximately two eyes, before they are tied in again in as horizontal a position as possible.

Wisteria sinensis needs to be pruned in two stages. In summer, when the main growing season is over, the new shoots are pruned back by about half. In winter these shoots are then further shortened to two buds. This may seem elaborate but will give much joy when the heavily scented trusses of delicate, lilac flowers appear the following spring.

RESISTANT ROSES

Old and English roses
'Charles de Mills'
Gertrude Jekyll ★
Redouté ★
Winchester Cathedral ★

Rugosa roses ★
'Blanc Double de Coubert'
'F. J. Grootendorst'
'Roseraie de l'Haÿ'

Hybrid musks ★
'Buff Beauty'
'Penelope'

Modern shrub and groundcover roses
Bonica ★
'Country Dancer'
'Marie Pavie'

Wild roses and their hybrids
R. filipes 'Kiftsgate'
R. pimpinellifolia hybrids
R. sericea f. pteracantha

Hybrid teas and floribundas ★
'Just Joey'
'Knock Out'

Miniature roses
'Snow Carpet'
'Sun Sprinkles'

Climbers (cl) and ramblers
'Climbing Cécile Brünner'
'Félicité Perpétue'
'Maigold' ★ (cl)
'Paul's Himalayan Musk'
R. banksiae 'Lutea'

★ repeat-flowering

Roses

Loved by many gardeners, roses are often considered one of the most noble of garden flowers. They can be difficult to grow and account for a high proportion of pesticides used in nonorganic gardens. With careful selection and good growing conditions, however, roses can be grown successfully organically. Few are truly disease resistant, but some species and cultivars are known to be less susceptible than others (see left). Providing good growing conditions will help to keep them healthy.

Choosing which roses to grow

Certain roses are less suited to organic gardening than others. Bush roses, such as the hybrid tea and floribunda (cluster-flowered) types, dislike competition at root level and so often are grown as a monocrop in a rose bed. They require ample spacing, dislike underplanting, and, due to the fact that they are grown en masse, tend to be more susceptible to pest and disease outbreaks.

Species and shrub roses are better suited to the organic garden. They are less sensitive to competition from other plants and are often less susceptible to diseases and pests. Most are of greater value to wildlife and are much less labor demanding, as they require less pruning and deadheading. Look out for roses with rose hips. These are popular with pollinating insects, provide an excellent food source for birds and mammals, and create a colorful seasonal display. The more informal habit of species and shrub roses means that they look more at home in a mixed border. Species roses, such as *R. glauca* or *R. moyesii*, can be mixed into a shrub or perennial border. Most rugosa roses make a good, thorny hedge with glossy hips.

How and where to plant roses

Roses will perform at their best in an open, sunny site. Good air circulation and a moisture-retentive, well-drained soil will help to prevent disease build-up. Avoid planting in sites susceptible to waterlogging, in very acid or alkaline conditions, or on sand or heavy clay soils.

Where possible, grow roses in a mixed border. Low-growing plants can be grown around the outer edge of a bed of bush roses—which dislike competition—to add diversity and encourage natural predators. If replanting roses in the same place is unavoidable, exchange the soil with that from another part of the garden, to a minimum depth of 18 in. (45 cm).

Prepare a deep planting hole, and incorporate well-rotted manure or garden compost with a sprinkling of bone meal for a kick-start. Plant during the dormant season. If container-grown, it is also possible to plant when in leaf. Trim the roots of bareroot plants, removing damaged ends, and soak them in water while preparing the hole (see also p. 155). All bush roses should be pruned hard when planting, cutting stems back down to the second or third bud, depending on where you find an outward-pointing one.

Aftercare

Mulch the soil each spring. Depending on its richness, use a medium- to high-fertility soil improver (see p. 40). Where necessary, water roses growing against a wall or up a tree where the soil will tend to be rather dry in spring and early summer. Deadhead bush roses, such as floribundas or hybrid teas, regularly to encourage continuous flowering. Cut the flowering stem back to a complete, outward-pointing leaf. Do not deadhead roses that will later bear attractive fruit. Watch out for aphid attack, particularly early in the season. Other pests to look out for include frog hoppers and Japanese beetles, as well as the diseases black spot, powdery and downy mildew, and rose rust (see *Plant Health*, pp. 84–103, and the *A–Z of Plant Problems*, pp. 367–395). Remove fallen leaves, and renew the mulch in early spring before the buds start to grow.

Pruning roses

Prune roses when they are dormant. As part of general hygiene, remove dead or diseased wood. Cut this out and make sure you destroy all twigs and debris after pruning. Always cut above an outward-pointing bud (see p. 156). Even if no actual bud is visible at a leaf scar, one will be formed if cut at that point. Roses can be kept young and vigorous by cutting out the oldest stems entirely on a 3- to 4-year cycle. Each year, remove one or two of the oldest stems at the base of the plant. This is the only pruning required by species roses. All shrub roses should be left unpruned for the first few years. Repeat-flowering shrub roses should be pruned

to one-half to two-thirds of their height. The less they are pruned, the more natural the shape of the shrub; the harder they are pruned, the better the flowers will be. If at all, once-flowering roses should be lightly pruned, reducing them by one-third. Bush roses, including floribundas, hybrid teas, polyanthas, and miniatures, tend to be kept as compact roses, taking them down to one-half or even one-quarter of their original height.

Fruit for the birds
Roses that flower only once in summer, such as Rosa glauca, R. moyesii, *and* R. rubiginosa, *will produce colorful, bird-attracting rose hips in the autumn.*

Resistant roses
Breeders are still searching for the fully disease-resistant rose, but these roses (below, from left to right) all show some resistance: 'Charles de Mills', 'Blanc Double de Coubert', 'Buff Beauty', Bonica, R. filipes 'Kiftsgate', 'Frühlingsmorgen', Gertrude Jekyll, *and* 'Just Joey'.

Caring for woody plants

All plants benefit from being planted in a well-prepared site. The better the soil, the quicker they will establish themselves. Remove all weeds, particularly perennial ones (see *Weeds and Weed Control*, pp. 78–81). Starting with a clean slate eliminates unnecessary competition for water and nutrients.

If you are planting a new border, prepare the whole area—digging and adding soil improvers as necessary, depending on the state of the soil and the type of plants. Acid-loving (ericaceous) plants such as azaleas are happy with leaf mold or, at most, garden compost. Rapidly growing shrubs and repeat-flowering plants such as lavatera rely on a lot of energy to perform their task. They prefer a high-nutrient soil improver such as well-rotted manure.

Native species, such as birch and hawthorn, should not need any additional feeding.

When planting a mixture of species with different requirements, prepare the whole area with a low-fertility material such as leaf mold, then add compost or well-rotted manure to individual planting holes, as appropriate.

When planting a single specimen tree or shrub, particularly on poor soils, prepare a generous hole 3–5 ft. (1–1.5 m) in diameter, and 12 in. (30 cm) deep, or as deep as the rootball. If planting in a lawn, chop up the sod and put it in the bottom of the hole. In heavy soils, gently loosen the base and sides of the hole to allow roots to penetrate.

Selecting and obtaining stock

As there are not yet recognized organic growing standards for ornamentals in the U.S., the supply of organically grown trees and shrubs is very limited. The options are to make do with conventionally grown plants or raise your own organically.

Woody plants are either container- or field-grown. The latter are usually larger and stronger than container-grown plants, giving you more plant for your money. Unless they have been rootballed—lifted with a ball of earth around the roots, which is subsequently wrapped in a burlap-type cloth—the roots must not dry out, and need to be covered in soil quickly, either by heeling the plant in temporarily or planting it right away.

It can be tempting to plant a large tree, hoping it will mature quickly. In fact, a young tree will establish more quickly, require less aftercare, and will soon catch up with or even overtake a larger specimen. However, if there is a need to screen an eyesore, it may justify the extra cost of starting big.

When to plant

Although container-grown stock can be planted at any time of year, the ideal planting season for all woody plants, bareroot or not, is between autumn and spring. Trees planted in early autumn will benefit from the still-warm soil, making new roots before winter sets in. Spring-planted stock may not get the chance to establish their roots before the start of the drier season, making them more

Bareroot plants
Never let bareroot stock sit around drying out. Unwrap the bundles, separate out the young trees (here including field maple, hazel, blackthorn, and hawthorn), and plant them as soon as possible.

susceptible to drying out. In mild climates, it is possible to plant throughout winter as long as the ground is not frozen or waterlogged.

Planting woody plants

Soak the rootball well before planting. As you position the plant in the hole, stand back to check that it is upright and showing its best side. Spread out its roots, if bareroot, or gently tease the roots from the edge of the rootball if container-grown. If staking is required (see below), put in the stake now to avoid damaging the roots. Backfill the hole with the soil you removed when digging. Firm the soil, then water well.

Traditional wisdom advised cutting back up to one-half of the topgrowth on newly planted trees and shrubs, supposedly to balance the top with the reduced root system. New evidence, however, shows that this practice may not help—and may even harm—the plants. Hard pruning promotes new shoot growth, and those vigorous shoots put a high demand for water on the limited root system. Limit post-planting pruning to remove broken, dead, or diseased branches, or to making needed corrections to the plant's shape.

To promote rapid establishment, keep young plants moist and free from weeds or grass. Mulch an area of at least 3 ft. (1 m) around each plant with a loose mulch or a mulch mat (see below and also pp. 76–77). For really low maintenance, plant through a landscape fabric, covered in mulch or gravel.

Stakes and shelters

Trees shorter than 5 ft. (1.5 m) do not need a stake unless planted on a very windy site. Larger trees and shrubs usually need to be staked (see right) or even anchored when planted. This is to stop the wind from rocking the plants in the soil, which impedes good root establishment, and to prevent them from being blown over. A large semimature tree with a good, solid rootball can be anchored by constructing a square or triangular wooden frame over the rootball, attached to posts pounded into the soil. This underground structure firmly anchors the rootball.

A tree planted as a large specimen may need to be staked for 3–5 years, until it is securely anchored by its own roots, but in most cases the stake can be removed after a year or two. Use a stake to suit the situation; there is no point in using a preservative-treated stake that will last for 25 years or more when the tree is only to be staked for a couple of years. Attach the tree to the stake with a rubber or natural tree tie. To prevent it from rubbing, attach the tie at the top of the stake and use a spacer, or tie the tie in a figure 8.

Check tree ties at least once a year, and loosen or remove them as necessary. If they are allowed to tighten around the stem, they will reduce the sap flow, impeding growth.

Where necessary, young plants can be given extra protection with tree or shrub guards. These are tubes manufactured from plastic, wire mesh, or wood strips. These guards protect plants from rabbit, deer, and nylon string trimmer damage.

Aftercare

Water new plantings during dry periods. When planting larger trees, it is advisable to coil a special perforated plastic irrigation and aeration pipe around the rootball, leaving one end exposed at ground level, blocked off with a cap. When watering, the

Single and double stakes
Use a short stake, supporting the trunk or stem at around one-quarter of its height, rather than supporting the entire stem to the crown. A low-level stake allows the upper part of the tree to move in the wind, which encourages it to make strong, new anchoring roots and strengthens the whole trunk. Double stakes are useful where a large or containerized rootball prevents staking against the stem.

PLANTING IN GRASS

If planting a tree or shrub in a lawn, clear the sod from an area at least 3 ft. (1 m) all around it to limit competition from the grass plants. Keep the area weed-free with a loose mulch or by planting through landscape fabric or a mulch (tree) mat (see also pp. 76–77).

Where to cut
Prune at an angle (top) just above an outward-pointing bud. Shrubs with opposite buds (above) should be pruned level, as close to the buds as possible.

water can be poured straight into the pipe so that it reaches the roots directly as it seeps out through the holes, avoiding waste.

Mulching with an organic soil improver (see pp. 40–41) during establishment years will help to retain moisture and suppress weeds, which will promote rapid growth. If a tree or shrub has been planted into grass, keep an area of 1 sq. yd. (1 sq. m) around it mulched and weed-free. Vigorous grass growth can outmatch a newly planted tree.

Rhododendrons should be deadheaded after flowering when young or if under stress so the plant can concentrate all its efforts on producing new growth. Once established, this is no longer necessary.

Pruning trees, shrubs, and roses

As part of general hygiene measures, check plants regularly for any dead or diseased wood. Cutting this out will help to control disease outbreaks.

Formative pruning is usually applied to young plants, correcting the shape where necessary. It may also be applicable where a mature plant has outgrown its space, or when a neighboring plant has been removed, leaving the remaining plants lopsided.

A rejuvenating, or renewing, trim will encourage a shrub or tree to produce strong new shoots.

Think before you prune, making sure that the cut will enhance the shape of the bush. Generally, this means cutting just above an outward-pointing bud. If the cut is made above an inward-pointing bud, the new shoot will grow through the center of the bush, spoiling its natural shape, as well as making it dense

and airless, increasing the risk of disease. Furthermore, inward-growing shoots tend to receive little direct light, making them weak and straggly.

When to prune

If you are unsure when is the best time to prune a shrub, be guided by its flowering time. Spring-flowering shrubs, such as forsythia, produce flower buds along the stems during the preceding autumn. These buds open to flower in the spring. When flowering is over, the shrub will come into growth; this is the time to prune it. Shrubs flowering in late spring and summer, such as mock orange (*Philadelphus*), will come into growth in early spring, producing new shoots, which in turn will have flower buds by early summer. These can be pruned at any stage between leaf-fall in autumn through to late winter. If you are concerned about the hardiness of the plant, it is better to prune at the end of winter, as the network of branches will trap air, creating a protective microclimate in cold weather.

How to prune

Generally speaking, it is safe to prune hard those trees and shrubs that put on more than 12 in. (30 cm) of growth in a season. The harder these plants are pruned, the more vigorously they regenerate. Plants that grow slowly, putting on less than 12 in. (30 cm) per year, do not take kindly to severe pruning, so avoid it unless absolutely necessary. Any cuts you do make should be gentle, formative trimming.

PRUNING SHRUBS

Shrubs that perform well with annual hard pruning

Buddleia davidii, B. alternifolia
Caryopteris
Cornus alba and *C. stolonifera*
   cultivars
Cotinus coggygria cultivars (right)
Deutzias
Eucalyptus
Forsythia
Fuchsias (hardy)
Hydrangeas (some)
Hypericums
Philadelphus
Roses (some)
Rubus
Salix (some)

Shrubs that need only light pruning

Aucuba japonica and cultivars
Berberis
Buxus sempervirens
Cotoneasters
Daphnes (right)
Magnolias
Potentilla fruticosa cultivars
Prunus
Rhododendrons
Taxus baccata
Viburnums

These shrubs could be pruned hard to rejuvenate, but would take several years to recover completely.

Regenerative pruning of old shrubs

In established gardens, it is sometimes necessary to prune old, mature shrubs that have outgrown their allocated space. If you want your plants to perform well, pay them back for the efforts they will have to make to recover their vigor. After pruning, feed the plants and keep the soil moist, particularly during dry periods, by applying a generous mulch of medium- to high-fertility organic matter, such as garden compost or well-rotted manure, depending on the species.

Some shrubs take well to hard treatment, while others have to be tackled gently. Plants that have been pruned regularly cope better with a hard prune than those that have never been touched. If in doubt, the pruning can be undertaken over a 2- to 3-year period, selecting each year one-half or one-third of the oldest wood. Not all old shrubs will cope with such treatment, and you must be prepared for some losses.

Pests and diseases

In organic gardening, pest and disease management is all about prevention rather than cure. By choosing the right plant and planting it in the optimum position to ensure strong, balanced growth, the likelihood of it suffering a disease attack is small. Prepare the soil well and provide good aftercare, observing sensible hygiene rules, such as removing and destroying dead and diseased material and promoting good air circulation (see also *Plant Health*, pp. 94–96).

A little tolerance is also to be advised. Plants are part of the natural world and are inevitably going to be less than perfect; a few leaf spots here or a nibbled leaf there is not going to be life-threatening.

Propagation

Although a slow process, there is something enormously satisfying about growing a tree from seed. A species of any woody plant (that is, without a cultivar name) can be grown from seed, but will take years to reach any size. Plants grown by means of vegetative propagation reach flowering stage much sooner but still take several years to become sizable. Remember that if you want to reproduce special characteristics in a named cultivar, such as flower or foliage color, vigor, and habit, it is important to propagate the plant by vegetative means.

• **Seeds** Many woody plants do not shed their seeds until late summer or autumn, a rather inhospitable season for small seedlings to germinate and survive. Nature has therefore incorporated a protective mechanism, hardening off the seeds so they need to undergo prolonged exposure to cold weather before they can germinate. You may need to imitate this and chill, or stratify, the seeds (see p. 108). If unsure of the conditions required, sow the seeds as soon after harvest as possible, keeping them outdoors in a cool, shady place. If they have not germinated after the first winter, do not despair; some need two cold spells before coming to life. Keep the soil moist at all times. For these slow germinators, use a general-purpose potting medium. Cover the seeds with a layer of compost as thick as the seed itself.

• **Cuttings** Most woody plants are propagated from either semiripe or hardwood cuttings (see pp. 106–107). Collect semiripe cutting material in late summer, particularly from evergreen shrubs such as *Prunus laurocerasus* 'Otto Luyken' and conifers. With conifers it is often possible to take heeled cuttings, pulling off new sideshoots from the main stem with a little heel of hardened wood. Otherwise take stem-tip cuttings. Shrubs such as dogwoods and willows root easily from hardwood cuttings taken at the end of winter.

• **Layering** If only one or two plants are needed, many woody plants can be layered (see p. 107).

SOME PESTS AND DISEASES OF WOODY PLANTS AND CLIMBERS

Aphids (left)
Bacterial canker
Caterpillars (various)
Clematis wilt
Fireblight
Honey fungus
Japanese beetles
Peach leaf curl
Phytophthora root rot
Powdery mildews
Rose black spot
Scale insects
Silver leaf
Vine weevil

For more information, see the *A–Z of Plant Problems*, pp. 367–395.

Garden flowers

WHILE A PERMANENT BACKGROUND IS CREATED BY TREES
AND SHRUBS, HERBACEOUS PLANTS ADD SEASONAL VARIETY

Show time (facing page)
*Nothing beats flowering plants for
creating impact in the garden. The
scene-stealing flamboyance of oriental
poppies may be fleeting, but these
perennials will flower year after year.*

Nature's way (below)
*A naturalistic planting where the soil
is covered by a mix of groundcover
plants interspersed with pockets of
seasonal color. Clumps or drifts of
plants are scattered through as accents.*

THE TERM "HERBACEOUS" APPLIES, botanically, to
plants that do not form a persistent woody stem.
"Herbaceous" is, however, sometimes used as
shorthand for "herbaceous perennial," to mean plants
such as hostas, delphiniums, and the like that die
down in the winter and return every spring.
These plants are commonly referred to simply as
"perennials." This chapter covers the whole
spectrum of herbaceous plants—annuals, biennials,
bulbs, and half-hardy perennials grown as annuals, as
well as herbaceous perennials, including grasses.

Hardy annuals and bedding plants create long-
lasting color, while perennials come and go like
performers on a stage, each contributing its part
to create a spectacular show.

There is a huge range of plants to choose from
in this group, from tiny to gigantic, that flower
from winter through to autumn. Plants may be
grown for their foliage, for their flowers, or for
both. The color spectrum is unrivaled, covering all
shades imaginable. It is possible to find suitable plants
for all garden environments, from dry to wet, sunny
to shaded.

Herbaceous perennials

Although a few early perennials such as *Doronicum
orientale* kick off the spring season, the main
performance starts in early summer and lasts into
autumn, with delights like *Aster pringlei* 'Monte
Cassino' carrying on until the start of winter. Many
border perennials, such as helianthus, originate from
prairie environments and stand up to hot, dry
summer conditions. Others come from woodland
habitats, preferring cool shade. Many of these finish
flowering before summer, as by then trees leave little
moisture for comparatively shallow-rooted perennials.
Cranesbills (hardy geraniums), decorative deadnettles
(*Lamium*), and tiarellas are reliable, shade-loving
plants. Other perennials originate from wetland
areas, growing along streams and lakes, and require

moist soil. Many have large leaves from which high levels of moisture evaporate. Gunneras, ornamental rhubarb (*Rheum*), and rodgersias are very bold in character, adding drama to a garden scene.

Annuals and biennials

Plants, both hardy and half-hardy, that germinate, flower, set seed, and die within 1 year, such as marigolds, are known as annuals. Biennials, such as foxgloves, take 2 years to complete this process. Both can be more labor-intensive than bulbs, perennials, and woody plants because you have to sow them each year—though if content, some may self-seed and return year after year.

Tender perennials

Perennials that do not normally survive a cold winter are usually classified, with annuals, as bedding plants, as they too need to be replanted annually.

Plants such as zonal geraniums can be overwintered in a frost-free greenhouse, cutting them back and repotting them at the start of spring.

Bulbs

Most bulbs flower in late winter and spring, but there are those that flower in summer and autumn. Shade-loving woodland bulbs like cyclamen and snowdrops (*Galanthus*) come to life much earlier when winter-bare branches allow water and light to penetrate to the woodland floor. They then come into leaf, flower, and set seed before spring really sets in. Others, such as tulips, originate from areas where summer creates near desertlike conditions. They, too, come to life between autumn and late spring. Avoid large, highly hybridized tulips and daffodils, as they can have difficulty building up enough energy to keep on producing those huge flowers. Instead opt for the species, or closely related selections.

HOW THEY GROW

Annuals
Completing the cycle of seed to seed in one year, annuals (**1**, the annual poppy 'Danish Flag') can create an intense patch of color over many months.

Biennials
These plants need 1 year to build up a large, strong, basal plant which will flower, set seed, and die the following year. A few short-lived perennials are often treated as biennials to avoid disease (for instance hollyhocks, **2**, which are prone to rust).

Perennials
Faithfully returning year after year, perennials (such as columbines, **3**) provide reliable color, with attractive foliage and seedheads if the right ones are chosen.

Bulbs
Late winter and early spring flowering bulbs (such as tulips, **4**) are ideal to interplant among perennials and spring bedding and under deciduous trees and shrubs. Planting among other low plants will help disguise the leaves as they die down.

GRASSES

Strictly speaking, grasses are either herbaceous perennials or annuals but deserve to be in a category of their own. Their care and planting method are very similar to that of perennials. Some, such as the infamous gardener's garters (*Phalaris arundinacea* var. *picta*), are invasive and should be used with caution, but many, such as most species and cultivars of *Stipa*, *Miscanthus*, and *Calamagrostis*, are well-behaved and deserve a warm welcome. *Stipa arundinacea* and *S. tenuissima* may self-seed, but unwanted seedlings can be hoed off.

Grasses can play an important role in our gardens. The flowering spikes of the taller ones, such as *Molinia caerulea* subsp. *arundinacea* 'Transparent' and *Stipa gigantea* (left), provide great height while remaining translucent, creating a net-curtain effect. Grasses' slender, elegant foliage and feathery flowers add softness to a planting scheme. Grasses bring movement into the garden, creating ripples when planted in larger masses and rustling in the breeze. Many dry gracefully to warm tones of yellow and rust, adding a statuesque note to winter scenery, particularly on frosty mornings when *Miscanthus* cultivars such as *M. sinensis* 'Malepartus' can be seen standing at attention.

With their simple elegance and boldness, grasses look stunning en masse. In smaller gardens, use them individually as feature plants, either repeating through a planting or alone. Most grasses have sufficient personality to stand completely on their own. A single specimen of *Molinia* 'Windspiel' creates a sparkling fountain of very fine flower spikes, effortlessly reaching 6 ft. (2 m). They arch gracefully when weighed down with dewdrops, only to spring upright again when dry, and in autumn turn a coppery orange that fires up in late afternoon sunlight.

Planting styles

Perennials can be planted in beds or borders by themselves, or mixed with bedding plants, shrubs, or roses. They can be placed in bold groups, lingering drifts, or small clumps, all depending on the plant, its character, and the effect you are trying to achieve. You can opt for a special color scheme, using one, two, three, or more colors, suiting your taste and the garden situation.

Traditional borders

Britain is renowned for its sumptuous perennial borders. They display carefully coordinated color schemes where plants blend with each other in seasonal succession. Popular at the start of the 20th century, perennial borders were usually part of larger gardens maintained by small armies of gardeners, and had to be stunning for only 6 or 8 weeks of the year. Today, many garden owners expect the same of their gardens but have a great deal less space. The mixed border provides an answer, offering a home for shrubs, roses, and all kinds of herbaceous flowers, so that height, structure, and interest can be provided year-round. There are perennial and annual climbers, which look particularly effective scrambling over and through shrubs and trees (see *Climbing Plants,* p. 150). Annuals and bedding plants can be used to extend the season, filling gaps where early bulbs and perennials have finished.

Traditional perennial and even mixed borders can be hard work to maintain to the immaculate standards needed for them to look stunning. The secret is careful planning (see pp. 164–169) and regular attention to keep everything looking its best (see pp. 170-173).

The naturalistic approach

To cut down on the labor and other requirements of a traditional perennial border, a new naturalistic, environmentally sound approach to perennial

Consider the environment
To a large extent, site and soil dictate planting style. Moisture-loving plants, such as the mimulus, irises, and ferns below, must have damp conditions if they are to thrive and look "at home." Facing page: Brown and dry, many plants, especially grasses, can give the winter garden a haunting beauty.

planting was initiated in Germany during the 20th century. Having been further developed in the Netherlands and other European countries, it is broadly referred to as the "new European" style.

This style is usually applied to large-scale planting, and is particularly suited to public spaces, but there is no reason why the basic principles cannot be used in small gardens.

Creating the look

The principles of naturalistic planting, based on common sense, are easy to understand. Plants are chosen to suit the habitat. Unlike our traditional borders where plants are grouped simply for their aesthetic value, the aim is to create plant communities that will require management rather than maintenance. These communities are allowed to evolve and develop. Plant species can migrate, increase, or decrease as circumstances change, just as they would in a natural setting.

> # Seek out the right plants for the provided habitat and plant them the way nature intended

Out of a permanent groundcover rise perennials, bulbs, and grasses, planted in drifts, clumps, or as accents. Plants, categorized by habitat, are used accordingly, regardless of geographic origins. Depending on whether they originate from woodland, woodland margin, meadow, rock, water margin, or water, they will be used in the corresponding environment in the garden.

Furthermore, by observing a plant's natural growth habit, it is possible to mimic its normal growing patterns. Certain plants, such as mulleins, scatter themselves about by shedding their seeds away from the plant. Others, such as asters and goldenrods, have spreading rootstocks and are best planted in drifts or clumps. By imitating these reproduction processes a much more natural effect will be obtained than when perennials are planted in the traditional clumped manner. Finally, to discourage weeds, the ground is covered (as would be the case in nature) with a permanent mulch such

as gravel or crushed stone, or with groundcovering vegetation. For a naturalistic effect, it is preferable to work with generous drifts of one or more intermingling species, repeating key plants.

Reducing the workload

This naturalistic style of planting does not depend on regular maintenance. Initial ground preparation should ensure freedom from perennial weeds. If plants have been chosen correctly to suit the site, there is no need to add soil improvers or fertilizers. Groundcover means weeding is reduced to a minimum once plants are established. The plants receive no fertilizers, nutrient-rich mulches, or additional watering, so they tend to be compact and sturdy, cutting out the need for staking. Apart from some selective deadheading, the plants are cut down only once a year, in the late winter. Many plants have attractive seedheads that provide homes during winter for predatory insects. Frosts enhance their architectural outlines, while their caps of snow give a cozy look to the winter garden.

It is important to monitor the progress of more vigorous plants or those that self-seed in great quantity. Remove as necessary to prevent them from taking over completely.

ATTRACTIVE AUTUMN AND WINTER SILHOUETTES

Allium cristophii,
  A. sphaerocephalon
Asters
Calamagrostis x *acutiflora* 'Karl
  Foerster' ★, *C. brachytricha* ★
Eremurus robustus (foxtail lily)
Foeniculum vulgare 'Purpureum'
  (purple-leaved fennel)
Heleniums
Iris sibirica cultivars
Miscanthus sinensis cultivars ★
Molinia caerulea cultivars ★
Oenothera cultivars
Phlomis russeliana
Rudbeckia fulgida var. *sullivantii*
  'Goldsturm'
Sedum 'Herbstfreude',
  S. spectabile cultivars,
  S. telephium 'Matrona'
Solidago (goldenrod)
Stipa arundinacea ★,
  S. calamagrostis ★, *S. gigantea* ★,
  S. tenuissima ★
Yarrows

★ grass

Planning a flowerbed or border

Whichever style of planting you opt for, it is important to adapt the planting to suit the space. Long or deep beds and borders framed by wide spaces and seen from a great distance need to be planted boldly with large clumps so that the plants retain their identity, even from far away. Failing to do this will make the scheme look chaotic, with little flecks of color blurring into one another. Small planting areas in confined spaces are viewed intimately and should be planted accordingly. Use a wide range of plants in small numbers to create optimum variety.

Siting a border

The most versatile sites are free of shade from trees or tall buildings to ensure the maximum amount of sunlight during the day, in both summer and winter. Hedges provide a dark green backdrop for the flowers, while walls or fences offer support for

climbers. They will also create a warmer, sheltered microclimate where more delicate plants that normally would be classified as half-hardy (for instance, *Melianthus major* or some of the more exotic euphorbias) should be able to survive the winter with little or no extra protection. A sheltered area also helps to reduce the need for staking taller perennials like delphiniums.

Accent plants

To avoid the whole bed looking fussy or busy, repeat one or two instantly recognizable "accent plants" at regular intervals. Particularly suited are those with striking large or vertical leaf shapes, or a bold, long-lasting flower. Sedums, grasses, and daylilies (*Hemerocallis*) are good examples. These plants will create a rhythm, and their repetition will enable you to draw all parts together into a coherent unity. A well-chosen accent plant—for example, a

FLOWERS FOR CUTTING

Perennials
Acanthus mollis and *A. spinosus*, *Anaphalis triplinervis*°, anthemis, astilbes, asters, *Bergenia cordifolia*, *Centaurea dealbata*°, columbines, coreopsis, *Dianthus* (pinks), dictamnus, *Doronicum orientale*, echinops°, eryngiums°, *Gypsophila paniculata*°, foxgloves, heleniums, *Helianthus* (sunflowers), heuchera, hostas, *Lathyrus latifolius*, *Liatris spicata*, *Limonium platyphyllum*°, linaria, honesty (*Lunaria annua*)°, lychnis, monardas, peonies, poppies: *Papaver nudicaule* seedheads°, phlox, physostegia, rudbeckia, salvias, scabious, *Trollius europaeus*, zantedeschia

Bulbs and tubers
Agapanthus, alliums°, alstroemerias, crocosmias, dahlias, *Dierama pulcherrimum*, *Galtonia candicans*, lilies, narcissus, *Schizostylis coccinea*

Grasses
Cortaderia°, molinias°, stipas°

° suitable for drying

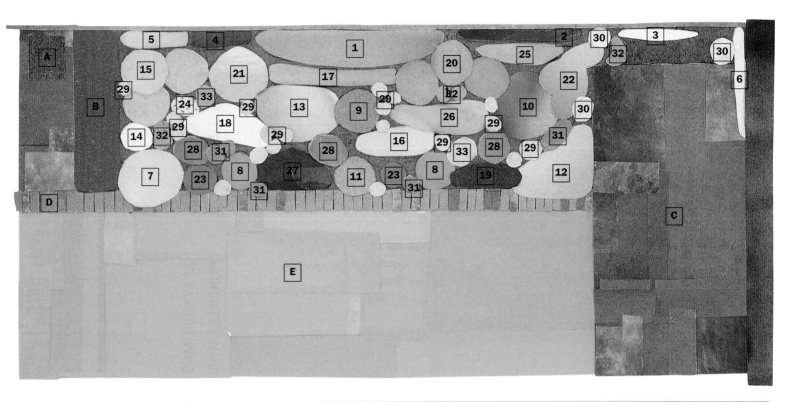

grass or hosta—can also stand alone, creating a focal point for a planting scheme in a small bed, or in a well-chosen container.

Flowers for picking

Even in the smallest garden, it is possible to grow flowers that can be harvested (see facing page). Some, such as lilies, are useful as scent providers in the house. Nasturtiums, calendulas, daylilies (*Hemerocallis*), and violets are edible and make wonderful decorations in salads (see also p. 331 for more edible flowers). Many cut flowers available for purchase are produced using pesticides. There is a wide choice of plants that you can grow organically to grow your own flowers for cutting, to be used fresh or dried.

Planting annuals and bedding plants

Some gardeners like to dedicate beds especially to bedding but, from an ecological point of view, they are best mixed in with other plants, even in the vegetable garden. Besides adding a colorful note, their flowers attract predatory insects such as hoverflies and lacewings, which control pests. Short-lived plants like forget-me-nots, cornflowers (*Centaurea cyanus*), and California poppies (*Eschscholzia*) are perfect gap-fillers around newly planted perennials, trees, and shrubs.

A TRADITIONAL MIXED BORDER

This plan shows a traditional border, facing southwest and backed by a wood fence. Climbers cover the fence, while a few woody plants provide a permanent outline. The perennials are planted in drifts. The bulbs should be planted in the background, as they flower when the perennials are still low, so their dying foliage will be hidden by the emerging perennials as spring progresses.

KEY TO PLANTS USED

Climbers/wall shrubs
1 *Ceanothus* x *delileanus* 'Gloire de Versailles'
2 *Chaenomeles speciosa* 'Nivalis'
3 *Clematis armandii* 'Apple Blossom'
4 *Clematis* 'Perle d'Azur'
5 *Rosa* 'Maigold'
6 *Schizophragma integrifolium*

Shrubs
7 *Artemisia* 'Powis Castle'
8 *Caryopteris* x *clandonensis* 'Heavenly Blue' x 2
9 *Perovskia atriplicifolia* 'Blue Spire'
10 *Rosmarinus officinalis*
11 *Salvia officinalis* 'Purpurascens'

Perennials
12 *Alchemilla mollis* x 4
13 *Agapanthus campanulatus* x 3
14 *Aster pringlei* 'Monte Cassino'
15 *Campanula lactiflora* 'Prichard's Variety' x 3
16 *Coreopsis verticillata* x 5
17 *Doronicum orientale* x 3
18 *Echinacea purpurea* 'White Swan' x 4
19 *Geranium* x *magnificum* x 2
20 *Helenium* 'Butterpat' x 3
21 *Helianthus* 'Lemon Queen'

22 *Hemerocallis citrina* x 5
23 *Nepeta racemosa* 'Walker's Low' x 2
24 *Papaver orientale* 'Black and White'
25 *Pulmonaria saccharata* 'Mrs Moon' x 3
26 *Rudbeckia fulgida* 'Goldsturm' x 7
27 *Salvia* x *sylvestris* 'May Night' x 4
28 *Sedum* 'Autumn Joy' x 3

Bulbs
29 *Allium cristophii* x 20
30 *Cyclamen hederifolium* x 6
31 *Muscari azureum* x 50
32 *Narcissus* 'Tête-à-Tête' x 50
33 *Scilla siberica* x 100

Design elements
A Compost pile
B Beech hedge
C Terrace
D Brick mowing edge
E Lawn

Preparing a planting plan

Prepare a scaled drawing of the planting area. Using the same scale as for the plan, cut out circles of paper to represent the expected spread of each plant so you will know how many plants fit into the area. Position the key plants and any shrubs or roses first, then place the larger perennials, which are often the late summer ones, gradually working down to the smaller ones near the front.

Avoiding gaps

Place shade-loving, spring-flowering woodland perennials and bulbs such as scented violets (*Viola odorata*) and lungwort (*Pulmonaria*) near the base of deciduous shrubs at the rear of the border. Many early spring flowerers, such as *Doronicum orientale* and bulbs, die back long before summer starts. Although their small size and early flowering period may tempt you to put them near the front, they will leave you with a gap for the rest of the year. If you place them further back in the border, taller plants can grow up in front of them, not only hiding the empty gaps but also masking the dying foliage. Likewise with an oriental poppy. Once it has finished flowering in early summer, it dies back

totally. Put a spreading, midsummer-flowering plant such as baby's breath next to it, allowing it to fill in the space left by the poppy. Remember that your aim is to have an even spread of color and interest throughout the year. Use foliage plants to supplement and complement the flowers.

Doing your homework

When faced with the choice of many cultivars, there are several criteria to assist in making your choice. Hardiness and suitability to soil type are the starting point. Color also plays an important role. Considering period and length of flowering enables you to provide color during the months when little happens. Flowering height depends on whether you need a plant to attain a particular size to fit in with its neighbors. If height is not important, consider a smaller plant that is less likely to require staking.

Disease resistance is another important factor in any garden, let alone an organic one. Certain plants are more susceptible to diseases like mildew or rust. Breeders have been working hard to produce cultivars that are more resistant. If in doubt, opt for an old, well-established cultivar that has proved its worthiness. Wildlife value is also important in organic

PLAN FOR A DRY, SUNNY SITE

This plan is inspired by the naturalistic movement and would suit a dry, sunny front yard. It requires little care but looks interesting the whole year round. Low, woody plants such as lavenders, hyssop, and lavender cotton (*Santolina*) provide a permanent structure. Key plants, such as the fennel, grass, and eryngiums, add seasonally changing interest. The whole area could be covered in a permeable landscape fabric before planting and mulched afterward with gravel.

KEY TO PLANTS USED

1 *Aurinia saxatilis* x 3
2 *Crocosmia* x *crocosmiiflora* 'Solfatare' x 39
3 *Eryngium alpinum* x 11
4 *Eryngium variifolium* x 14
5 *Euphorbia characias* subsp. *wulfenii* x 4
6 *Foeniculum vulgare* 'Purpureum' x 2
7 *Hyssopus officinalis* x 7
8 *Lavandula angustifolia* 'Hidcote' x 12
9 *Lavandula* x *intermedia* Dutch Group x 14
10 *Molinia caerulea* subsp. *arundinacea* 'Windspiel' x 4
11 *Santolina chamaecyparissus* x 33
12 *Sisyrinchium striatum* x 17
13 *Thymus serpyllum* x 18

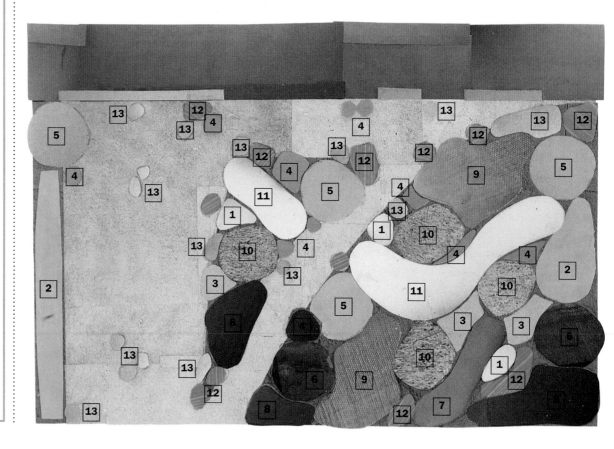

EVERGREEN PERENNIALS AND GRASSES

Acanthus mollis, A. spinosus
Achillea 'Coronation Gold',
  A. 'Moonshine', *A.* 'Taygetea'
Agaves
Ajuga reptans
Anthemis punctata subsp.
  cupaniana
Anthemis tinctoria
Armeria maritima
Artemisias (many)
Asarum europaeum
Bergenias
Campanula latiloba,
  C. persicifolia
Carex pendula
Cerastium tomentosum
Dianthus (pinks)
Dierama pulcherrimum
Doronicum orientale
Epimediums (many)
Eryngiums (some)
Euphorbia amygdaloides var.
  robbiae, E. characias, E. x *martinii*
Geranium x *cantabrigiense*
  G. macrorrhizum
Helictotrichon sempervirens
Hellebores
Heuchera
x *Heucherella*
Iris foetidissima
Kniphofia (red hot pokers—
  larger cultivars)
Lamium galeobdolon,
  L. maculatum
Limonium platyphyllum
Liriope muscari
Luzula sylvatica
Sisyrinchium striatum
Stachys byzantina
Stipa arundincea, S. gigantea
Tellima grandiflora
Verbascum olympicum,
  V. phoeniceum
Veronica gentianoides 'Variegata'
Viola riviniana Purpurea Group
  (syn. *V. labradorica*)

gardens; choose plants providing edible seeds or berries, nesting material, or shelter (see pp. 186–197).

Improving an existing border

Many borders are a collection of interesting plants accumulated over years. Memories from gardens visited and presents from friends and family have been popped into convenient spaces, with little regard for their neighbors. The best intentions of moving them into a more deserving position at a later date are soon forgotten. The result can be an uncoordinated collection without color or texture associations, and an erratic spread of flowering through the seasons. It is worthwhile to consider reworking such collections completely.

During the season, make a list of the plants, noting flowering height, color, and period of interest. Assess it to see which seasons are underrepresented, and look for plants that will cover those periods. Many borders look stunning from early to midsummer, after which they gradually fade into autumn. There are many wonderful perennials, particularly from the daisy family (Compositae, or Asteraceae), that are excellent color providers during late summer and autumn. Heleniums, helianthus, rudbeckias, and echinaceas are just a few.

To avoid staring at a neatly cut stem field for the whole of late autumn, winter, and early spring, plant early spring perennials and bulbs (see also *Avoiding Gaps*, facing page) and some perennials that are evergreen (see right) or whose flowers are followed by attractive seedheads. Birds love the seeds, and insects occupy the hibernation hotels provided by the empty stems and seedpods. The slightest frost will transform the garden into a magic winter landscape (see also *Attractive Autumn and Winter Silhouettes*, p. 163).

Having drawn up your planting plan, you can get to work. During autumn, winter, or early spring, deal with existing plants. When the ground is not too wet and there is no frost, remove plants that are to be moved or need dividing. Heel them in elsewhere, or cover with a damp sheet or tarp if they are to be replanted shortly. Be ruthless, discarding any that do not perform well or that you simply dislike. Take this opportunity to dig out any perennial weeds, too. Divide the crowns of plants you are keeping (see p. 173) before replanting; this will rejuvenate them and give you several more specimens.

Color schemes

The perception and use of color are very personal. What one person perceives as dark blue, another sees as dark green. A person may love pinks, while another hates them, preferring oranges. You are the person who spends the most time with your garden, so choose the color combinations that please you. Although it is an exciting challenge to plant a border according to a very specific color combination, simply following the colors dictated by the seasons can be equally rewarding.

Color theories and their applications

As white light shines through a prism, it breaks up into the colors of the rainbow—red, orange, yellow, green, blue, indigo, and violet. With the exception of indigo, the same color arrangement is obtained when mixing various combinations of the primary colors of yellow, red, and blue. Yellow and red make orange, red and blue produce purple and violet tones, while blue and yellow create green. These colors, when brought together, form the "color wheel." All the color theories below draw on this concept.

Opposing or contrasting colors

Using the colors that lie opposite each other on the color wheel, the following combinations can be found: red and green, blue and orange, or yellow and purple. In gardening terms, these are usually restricted to yellow and purple, and blue and orange. The effect of using these combinations can be bold and lively if intense shades are used, while the opposite is achieved if pastel tones are selected.

Using the right proportions of these mixtures is vital. Although a wonderful flower color, blue reflects little light and needs to be used in association with a higher proportion of the lighter orange tones to provide a good contrast. Likewise, dark purple is a rich color but will show to best effect only when surrounded with twice as much refreshing yellow.

HOW COLORS CHANGE WITH THE SEASONS

Spring starts off with masses of fresh color. By early summer everything still looks fresh and crisp, with pure whites, clear pinks, true blues, and reds dominating the scene. As summer progresses and the heat shimmers on the horizon, it is time for warm yellows, velvety reds, and rusty oranges. By the time autumn arrives, the faded colors of asters and chrysanthemums announce that the year is coming to its close.

Throughout the year, the importance of green as a color should not be underestimated. Evergreens give the garden much needed structure in winter, and throughout the growing season the changing backdrop of greens forms a perfect foil for colorful flowers. Tapestries of color both subtle and striking can be created using the many varying shades of foliage alone.

Adjoining colors

A more subtle arrangement can be achieved by using adjoining colors from the wheel. Yellows, oranges, and reds are known as the hot colors, while pinks, purples, blues, and mauves are known as the cool ones.

Many gardeners tend to shy away from hot colors, preferring the soft pastel tones in the cool range. Warm colors have the ability to brighten up a dull day, bringing sunshine into the garden when the weather fails to cooperate. When using these hot reds and yellows, it is important to include the shades that lie between these two main colors—the range from pale to deep yellow, orange to dark red—mirroring this color spectrum in flower and foliage where possible throughout the garden. Failing to do this can create harsh contrasts, as the linking colors are missing. The result would be like decorating a room in just black and white. The gray tones are the ones that would bring harmony into the space, removing the harshness.

Monochrome planting

Monochrome planting schemes are thrilling when good, but a bland anticlimax when not carefully orchestrated. The secret to successfully using one flower color only is to introduce as many different shades as possible in both foliage and flower to create the variety and contrast needed. When planting a white garden, for example, make full use of silver, gray, and blue foliage as well as pale, midtone, and dark greens. Besides pure white, include cream and green-tinged flowers, and those that are white with an undertone of blue, pink, mauve, or yellow. These color variations, mixed with interesting foliage shapes, create variety and add a degree of apparent spontaneity that makes the garden more exciting and interesting.

All but one

Although it is possible to have different color schemes for each season, in reality it is hard to orchestrate such a display, particularly at the change-over stage between seasons. Depending on weather conditions, some plants may come into flower earlier or later than usual, upsetting the carefully planned succession. In small gardens it can be particularly difficult for a plant lover to adhere strictly to a specific color scheme. You may love cool colors, using only blues, pinks, and purples, but at the same time have a soft spot for oriental poppies, with their huge, fire-engine red flowers. Try omitting one color from the spectrum, creating a display with the remainder. The awkward colors to blend are oranges and pinks—the notorious clashers. Remove shades of pink and reddish pink and you are left with blues, purples, yellows, oranges, and reds. Eliminating oranges and orange-reds will leave blues, purples, yellows, and pinks.

Complementary blues
The metallic blue of eryngiums can add a harmonious touch to a border of cool, blending colors or a vibrant contrasting note when placed among oranges and reds.

Planting and caring for garden flowers

When planting a new perennial flowerbed or border, it is vital to start with a clean base, free from perennial weeds. If the area was previously lawn, chop up the sod and dig it into the soil. If time allows, grow a green manure (see pp. 56–57) in the season prior to planting to improve the soil.

For a traditional perennial border, add a medium- to high-fertility organic soil improver such as compost or well-rotted manure at the digging stage—or spread it over the surface before planting. On poor soils you may also add a general fertilizer such as alfalfa meal to help plant establishment and promote growth. Grasses and bulbs cope better with less fertile soil, requiring a low- to medium-fertility soil improver, if anything at all. Where a naturalistic perennial garden is planned with plants selected to suit the existing soil conditions, no soil improvers should be required.

For annuals, provide a moisture-retentive soil rather than nitrogen-rich feeding, which will encourage leafy growth instead of flowers.

Beautiful bulbs

Bulbs such as Allium giganteum *(here among the oatlike* Stipa gigantea*) can provide many years of color, requiring little attention.*

Buying plants

Most herbaceous plants are transplanted into their final growing spot; hardy (and some half-hardy) annuals can also be sown direct.

Whether home-grown or purchased, plant out vigorous, healthy plants to give them the best start. You may be able to find organically grown plants and bulbs, but these are not yet widely available.

Few nurseries sell bareroot perennials these days, although this is preferable from both an environmental and economic standpoint. When buying container-grown plants, those in smaller pots are usually the better buy. A full pot of herbaceous perennials can often be divided before planting, giving you more for your money.

Some tender perennials, such as F1 hybrid geraniums and impatiens, can be grown from seed, but most are vegetatively propagated (see pp. 106–107). If you have a bright, frost-free spot, purchase small plantlets in early spring, and grow them indoors until they can be planted out. When buying annuals such as lobelia, choose young plants that are not pot- or tray-bound. Once the roots have been restricted in this way, the plants tend to flower before they are fully grown.

Starting from seed

Starting from seed is a cost-effective way of obtaining large quantities of plants, particularly annual bedding plants, and you can be sure that they are raised organically. Most hardy annuals and many half-hardy annuals, particularly the large-seeded ones such as French marigolds (*Tagetes*) and nasturtiums, are easy and inexpensive to grow from seed. Raising your own plants also gives you the chance to try some of the more unusual annuals, such as the blue lace flower (*Trachymene coerulea*) or the green-flowered tobacco plant (*Nicotiana langsdorffii*).

Perennials grown from seed will take a year or two to reach flowering size. Raising perennials from seed is mostly restricted to true species; seed sown from those with a cultivar name is unlikely to produce a plant identical to the parent. Some perennials, such as columbines, will self-seed freely. The flower color may bear no relation to the parent plant, but that is not necessarily a bad thing.

Most seed packets recommend a suitable sowing period for annuals, but it is worth experimenting with later sowings to fill gaps left by early-flowering perennials or bulbs. A display for late spring or early summer can be achieved from autumn sowings of hardy annuals such as love-in-a-mist (*Nigella*), which can be sown direct, or raised in cell packs and planted out after the ground has been cleared.

Many hardy annuals, such as calendula (pot marigold), *Phacelia tanacetifolia*, and the poached egg plant (*Limnanthes douglasii*), will self-seed. Self-sown plants tend to be much sturdier and to flower earlier than those you sow yourself. Unwanted seedlings can simply be hoed off or transplanted to a more appropriate site.

Harden off young transplants well before planting out. If necessary, protect against slugs and late frosts.

Planting perennials and grasses

Bareroot plants are available only at certain times of year, but container-grown plants can be planted at any time. Soak the plants well in a bucket of water before planting, so that the medium is thoroughly moist. Dig a hole large enough to take the rootball comfortably, loosening the soil at the base to help the roots penetrate to lower levels of soil moisture. Firm plants in after planting, and water, even if the soil is moist. This will eliminate air pockets, ensuring the roots make good contact with the soil.

Planting bulbs

Bulbs prefer a well-drained, humus-rich soil. If you fear the location may be too wet or the soil too heavy, incorporate plenty of sharp sand into the soil or put some gravel or coarse sand in the bottom of the planting hole. As a rule of thumb, plant bulbs at a depth twice that of the size of the bulb.

Avoid planting bulbs at the front of a bed or border. The dying foliage will be unsightly and it is vital that you allow the leaves to die back naturally for around 6 weeks after flowering, rather than cutting them off or tying them up in knots.

Bulbs are normally planted when dormant. Only the very small bulbs, such as snowdrops and winter aconites, are best transplanted while in leaf, just after flowering, as they can easily dry out. If you have to plant them as dry bulbs, soak them for 24 hours in lukewarm water prior to planting. For spring

displays, bulbs must be put into the ground in autumn; plant summer- and autumn-flowering bulbs in spring.

Watering plants

Where possible, select plants to suit the soil type to reduce the need for additional watering. Prepare the ground well before planting, breaking up any compaction to encourage extensive rooting. If appropriate, improve the soil's water-holding capacity with bulky organic soil improvers (see pp. 40-41) before planting, and keep the ground well mulched once planted (see p. 172). If watering is needed, soak the soil thoroughly rather than giving it a light sprinkling. To reduce evaporation losses, water in the early morning. Alternatively, water in the evening, though this increases the risk of slug damage.

HARDY ANNUALS THAT SEED READILY

Many hardy annuals readily self-seed and perpetuate themselves year after year. They include poppies, calendulas, California poppies, nasturtiums, snapdragons, and nigella, whose feathery leaves (above) decorate a late summer show of *Salvia patens* 'Cambridge Blue' and ageratums. These young self-seedlings, produced by summer-flowering plants, will survive winter and flower early the following year. You may need to thin them and, if you like, transplant some to other parts of the garden.

Reasons for mulching

After planting, apply a mulch. A deep layer helps to both conserve moisture in the soil and control weeds. Choose a mulching material that is in keeping with the style of planting.

RABBITPROOF PERENNIALS

Aconitum (monkshoods)
Astilbes
Campanula lactiflorae,
    C. latifolia
Cortaderia (pampas grass) ★
Crinum
Crocosmias
Foxgloves (*Digitalis*)
Epimediums
Euphorbias (★)
Hardy geraniums (★)
Helianthus (sunflowers)
Hostas
Hypericum (★)
Irises
Red hot pokers (*Kniphofia*)
Leucojum
Melissa
Nepeta (Cat mint)
Peonies
Poppies (★)
Veratrum
Vinca (periwinkle) ★

★ evergreen
(★) some species evergreen

Staking perennials

The flowers of taller perennials, such as delphiniums, may need support of some sort to prevent wind damage or simply to keep them from flopping onto their neighbors. Excess food and water will also encourage taller and less sturdy growth that requires staking. The need for support can be reduced by selecting shorter, stockier varieties or cultivars or, in the case of peonies, those with lighter, single flowers.

Traditionally, perennials are staked with bushy twigs, put in place as the plants begin to sprout. They provide a sturdy and unobtrusive support that can be removed at the end of the season and composted. Place twigs around the base of the plant and fold over the center at two-thirds of the final height, creating a dense network of fine branches that supports the flowering stems as they grow up through the twigs. Brush trimmed during late winter and spring pruning provide an ample supply of staking material for most gardens. Another option is to circle the plant with bamboo canes and then create a network of garden twine between them.

There are all sorts of commercial supports available. Quick and easy ones include the galvanized metal or plastic circles with a grid, or L-shaped plastic-coated wires that hook into each other. Suitable candidates for this type of staking are clump-forming perennials such as heleniums, phloxes, and chrysanthemums. Large clumps that threaten to fall in one direction can quickly be propped up with hefty supports made from a metal stake, bent to form a semicircular hoop.

Some very tall plants, such as delphiniums, may require individual staking. Each stalk may need its own stake, supporting the bloom for most of its height.

Always use natural fibers for tying up plants. They are less likely to strangle a plant and can safely be composted afterward in a bin or on a pile. To avoid eye injuries, top canes with purchased or homemade cane toppers.

Mulching and feeding

There should be no need to feed annuals and biennials. A suitable short-term mulch, such as leaf mold or fine bark, will help to keep the soil moist. Cocoa shells are also suitable for annual plantings but may be too rich for fertile soil.

A much wider range of mulches can be used on perennial plantings to retain moisture, control weeds, and feed the soil (see also pp. 76-77). Choose one that is appropriate to the planting. Gravel, for example, would suit a dry, prairie-style bed, whereas bark or leaf mold is more appropriate in a woodland setting. Always apply a mulch to moist, weed-free soil.

Fertile soils should be mulched with bark, leaf mold, or green-waste compost, whereas poorer ones may need a medium- or high-fertility material like garden compost, mushroom compost, or well-rotted manure until fertility builds up. Alternatively, apply a topdressing of a general organic fertilizer.

Avoid using the same mulch every year if it is likely to alter the soil pH. Mushroom compost, for example, tends to be alkaline, whereas pine needles tend to acidify the soil.

Deadheading and cutting back

Regular removal of flowers as they die will help to keep annuals and biennials looking good, and may extend the flowering period. Avoid doing this with plants such as honesty and love-in-a-mist (*Nigella*) if you want to retain their attractive seedheads.

Removing flowers from some perennials, such as phlox, will encourage sideshoots to flower, and delphiniums, lupins, and many yarrows may develop a second flush of flowers if cut back. Otherwise, resist the temptation to remove flowerheads as they fade. Be patient, and wait a few weeks to see if the plant produces seedheads that will provide a decorative element during winter months, food for birds and small mammals, and hiding places for insects. Dead stalks and leaves also protect plants against severe cold weather. Some, such as sedums, remain attractive right through winter. Others start rotting at the base and will succumb to wet and windy weather. Clean up occasionally, removing unsightly material. What is left at the end of winter can be raked off.

Dividing perennials

While annuals and biennials must be grown from seed, perennials can also be propagated by vegetative means—division and cuttings. Splitting perennials reinvigorates the plant as well as producing more identical plants, so it should be done regularly once plants are mature whether you need to increase your stock or not. Divide herbaceous perennials when plants begin to die back in the center, look congested, or show a reduction in vigor. This can be after 2 to 3 years in the case of vigorous plants, while those that are slow to establish may stay undisturbed for 15 years or more.

During autumn, winter, or early spring, when the ground is not too wet to work and there is no risk of frost, lift plants and divide. Grasses prefer to be divided in the spring. With the exception of woody-based perennials such as *Achillea* 'Moonshine', other perennials can easily be divided. Dig up a clump and insert two forks, back to back, into the middle. By rocking the two handles toward and away from each other, the roots are gradually teased apart. Repeat this until you have the number of plants you require. Really tough or fleshy rootstocks, such as hostas, may have to be chopped up with a spade or knife.

Once bulbs become overcrowded they do not flower as freely. Lift bulbs as they are dying back or when they are dormant. The clump can usually be teased apart by hand, and individual healthy bulbs can then be replanted.

Other ways of making more plants

Soft, stem-tip cuttings (see p. 106) can be taken from early spring through early summer from many perennials, including penstemons and veronicas.

With some perennials, including delphiniums and dahlias, you can take basal stem cuttings; in spring, pull new shoots carefully from the base or crown of the plant when they have four or five leaves, trim the base neatly, and root them in small pots of well-drained rooting medium.

Spring cleanup
Dead or dried growth left on plants over winter can provide wildlife with food, shelter, and nesting materials. In spring, clear away old stems and foliage and divide and plant new plants as necessary, then remove any weeds before mulching.

Lawns and lawn care

FROM PERFECT TURF TO MEADOW MIXTURES, ALL TYPES OF LAWN CAN BE MANAGED ORGANICALLY

Clean sweep (facing page)

Autumn leaves need to be raked or swept from the lawn to keep it healthy, but should never be burned; pile or bag them instead to make leaf mold (see p. 50). You can fashion a besom, or lawn broom, yourself by tying a bundle of twigs to a wooden shaft. An alternative if leaf fall is not too heavy is to mow the leaves and leave them, shredded, in place as a light mulch. They will soon disappear as worms and other creatures help take them into the soil.

DESPITE NEW TRENDS in decks and patios, for many gardeners the lawn remains an essential part of the home landscape for both its aesthetic and practical value.

Lawns provide different things for different people, forming an important part of a garden's design, a foil for more colorful planting, access through the garden, or simply an area for play and relaxation. A lawn creates a sense of space, to be used or viewed as an open area that lets in light and provides views to the garden beyond. Managed organically, this green carpet can also contribute richly to the biological diversity of the garden.

For the organic gardener, the lawn is as much an ecosystem as the pond or hedge. Nature abhors a monoculture, and "weeds" will soon try to move in to a new lawn. You may want a formal, relatively weed-free lawn, or you may prefer a more relaxed green expanse made up of a diversity of plant species. Both types of lawn can be created organically, though the former will require a lot more care and attention than the latter.

Organic lawns are exciting habitats in their own right, full of variety and of great value to insects, birds, and other wildlife. By accepting that a wide variety of different plants can exist together in a lawn in addition to grass, organic gardeners can create rich habitats that support a range of insects and other creatures. Adjusting mowing and cultural regimes can create meadows or wild areas, allowing flowers to self-seed, insects to feed and breed, and birds to forage for food and collect nesting materials.

PRINCIPLES OF ORGANIC LAWN CARE

- Choose grass seed to create the type of lawn you require and to suit the location.
- Maintain good soil structure to promote grass growth.
- Increase frequency of mowing as growth increases, but never mow too short.
- Leave clippings on the lawn during summer to feed the grass.
- Rake out moss before it accumulates and smothers grass.

Grass roots level

An organic lawn containing a variety of grasses and flowers can become a useful habitat for insects and a feeding ground for birds.

MOWING TIPS

Lawn mowers are one of the most dangerous tools used regularly in the garden, so do follow safety advice provided by the manufacturer. Wear protective clothing and shoes when mowing, clear the lawn of any stones or debris, and keep children and pets away from the area. Always check cords and plugs on electric models before mowing, and use a ground-fault interrupter (G.F.I.) outlet. Turn the power supply off at the electrical box immediately if the cord is damaged during mowing.

• Noise pollution is a growing problem in urban areas; choose a hand-powered mower or a quieter power model. Mow with consideration for neighbors.

• Have blades sharpened regularly, and replace them if badly damaged by stones.

• Check that frogs or small animals are not hiding around the edges of lawns or in longer areas of grass before cutting.

• Check the mower's blade height before mowing.

• Start by mowing the edges of the lawn, including any island beds or features.

• For formal lawns, determine the longest run, and mow in a single straight line from one end of the lawn to the other. Mow back in the opposite direction, slightly overlapping the previously cut strip, and using its line as your guide.

• Do not strain the mower by tackling very long, wet, or rough grass. Cut long grass in several stages, starting with the mower blades set high and lowering in stages until the grass is the desired height.

• To avoid damaging trees or other features in the lawn, replace an area of grass around them with a mulch.

• Get power mowers serviced before putting them away for the winter.

Cutting the grass

The frequency and height of cut of an organic lawn should be adjusted to suit the use to which the lawn will be put. By varying them you can create a formal appearance, or a more natural look. With such a vast range of mowers available it is important to choose one that suits you and your lawn. The table below describes the three main types, which use cylinder blades, rotary blades, or nylon string. For a small, level lawn, a hand-powered mower is ideal, but for larger areas of grass, powered mulching mowers bring several benefits.

Cutting the lawn

Grass can grow year-round provided conditions are warm and moist enough, but you will need to mow regularly only between spring and autumn. Frequency of mowing depends on the speed of grass growth. During spring, a weekly trim may be sufficient, but for neater lawns and play areas this can be increased to twice a week from late spring on. Grass growth decreases again in autumn, requiring less frequent mowing. In winter grass may still grow slowly, but conditions are usually too wet to mow, so it is best to avoid mowing except during prolonged warm, dry periods. The length of cut depends very much on the quality of grass in your lawn and how the lawn is being used. Long grass withstands drought better than shorter grass and also provides stronger competition for weeds. Most lawn areas can be cut to about 2½ in. (6 cm).

Family lawns used for play can be cut shorter, to perhaps 2 in. (5 cm) in spring and autumn, but slightly shorter in summer. For a fine lawn finish, grass can be cut very short, down to as low as 1½ in. (4 cm) in summer on level, quality lawns. Take care not to scalp the surface if the area is slightly bumpy, and always leave grass longer if weather is dry to help it withstand drought.

What to do with grass clippings

Grass clippings are a good source of nitrogen, which is released as they decompose. Where possible, leave them on the lawn to feed the grass; otherwise recycle them in other ways. During the main mowing season, from late spring to summer, mow regularly so that short clippings can be left on the lawn to decompose naturally. Consider investing in a mulching mower, which cuts and then recycles finely chopped grass back down to the soil surface.

In early spring and autumn and when the grass is long, clippings are best collected in the bag on your mower. Left on the lawn, they can smother growth, cause discoloring, or encourage disease. They are a useful material for recycling elsewhere in the garden and should never be burned or discarded.

• Use them as a compost activator.

• Add to the compost pile (see p. 44).

• Mix with autumn leaves in a leaf mold pile.

• Use as a mulch around trees, shrubs, fruit bushes, and vegetables.

CHOOSING A MOWER

Hand-powered	Rotary	Mulching mowers	Trimmer mowers
Use a cylindrical blade cutting against a solid base plate. Cylinder hand-powered mowers are cheap, efficient, and economical to use on small formal lawns, providing extra exercise, too. They are a good choice for organic gardeners who do not wish to use electricity or gas. Hand mowers cannot cope with long grass, so mow frequently. Keep blades sharp and well adjusted.	Rotary mowers have a single blade rotating at great speed. Cheaper models do not collect clippings; it is usually worth buying one that does. Power supply: gas, electric, and battery models available.	This development of the rotary mower is an excellent choice for organic gardeners with large lawns. Grass cuttings are chopped finely, then blown down into the lawn. Deposited close to the soil surface, they quickly decompose or are taken down by worms to feed the soil. Mulching mowers have been shown to improve grass growth, recycling nutrients back into the lawn and decreasing the need for additional feeding.	Trimmer mowers use a nylon or heavy plastic trimming line set on a spinning head. Essentially a string trimmer on two wheels, these gas-powered mowers are well suited to long grass, tall weeds, rocky areas, and sloping sites. They are not ideal for high-quality lawns.

Clear contrast
These grass paths may not be immaculately maintained, but they look well-groomed in this context, forming neat strips of green carpet between "beds" of rough grasses and wildflowers.

Mowing patterns

Elaborate patterns can be created on large areas of grass by cutting to different heights to add interest and enhance design. Leaving some areas uncut can create wildlife habitats. Summer mowing is a regular task and for some a time-consuming chore, so simply mowing paths or formal areas keeps these looking good while leaving some areas undisturbed for wildlife. Trimmer mowers are excellent for creating mown paths through areas of tall grass and meadow plantings. A trim once every few weeks will keep the paths neat and easy to walk on. You can vary the routes easily; just trim a new path each year as the mood strikes you.

Edging the lawn

Neatly cut edges really set off a lawn, and regular trimming keeps them in good condition. Start by cutting a clean edge, using a spade or half-moon edge cutter. Long-handled shears allow you to clip edges without bending. Power tools, including adapted nylon string trimmers with wheeled heads that allow both horizontal and vertical edges to be cut, make light work of edging large lawns. They are fast and efficient, but larger models can be heavy for extended use. Most are electrically powered, but some use rechargeable batteries that free you from the cord but add weight to the unit. Follow safety advice carefully, and wear goggles as debris can be

thrown up into your face. Where a section of lawn edge has become damaged it can be easily repaired.

Repairing damaged edges

Use a spade to cut out damaged sections of lawn, removing a patch with a clean, straight edge along the inside. Lift and rotate this 180°, replacing the outer edge with the cleanly cut inner edge. Fill the damaged area, now within the lawn, with seed medium mixed with grass seed (see pp. 182–183), and cover with clear plastic until the seed germinates.

Trimmed to shape
Use shears to shape and maintain this play furniture made from grass-covered mounds.

Improving the lawn

A lawn is made up of millions of plants and, as elsewhere in the organic garden, good soil structure and adequate fertility are essential for vigorous growth. Strongly growing grass prevents weeds from getting established, shrugs off pests and diseases, and withstands drought. Lawns are one of the few areas of the garden permanently covered with growth, preventing bulky organic soil improvers from being dug in. However, they can be applied as a topdressing, to build and maintain soil structure and health. Supplementary feeding may also be necessary.

Feeding the lawn

Feeding is not an annual necessity. If grass growth and color are good then do not feed; you will only encourage more grass growth, which means more mowing! If growth is poor then apply a general organic fertilizer (see p. 61) or a complete organic lawn feed over the whole lawn in early spring. Garden compost, spread thinly, can also be used if you have enough to spare. An application of seaweed meal or extract in spring and summer improves grass growth and color. If growth continues to be slow, feed again in summer, and consider topdressing in autumn to improve soil structure.

Liming lawns

Acid soil conditions encourage a buildup of thatch (see below) and cause poor grass growth. Acid soil also favors moss and certain other weeds, like sheep's sorrel. If the pH is below 5.5–6.0, lime the area to bring it up to around 7. Ground limestone or dolomitic lime (see p. 61), evenly sprinkled over the lawn and gently raked in, is the appropriate organic treatment. Repeat annually until the required pH level is reached.

Dethatching

Thatch is the name given to the layer of fibrous material and organic debris that can accumulate on the soil surface in the depths of a lawn. It can prevent water from reaching the soil, encourage diseases, and stop grass from thickening up. Where necessary, remove thatch by vigorous raking, using considerable downward pressure. This process is

LAWN CARE TOOLS

Lawn rake (right)
Useful for scarifying—raking out accumulated debris and moss, which can build up over time. A lawn rake is also useful for collecting fallen autumn leaves.

Besom or yard broom
Used to scatter worm casts, spread a topdressing, and brush off morning dew before mowing.

Garden vacuums and wheeled leaf collectors
These make life easier when collecting autumn leaves from large areas. A lawn mower can also be used for this task, chopping the leaves as they are collected before adding to the compost pile.

known as dethatching. Powered dethatchers are also available to buy or rent. Dethatching is best done in early autumn, when it will encourage the grass to thicken up. If large bare patches appear after dethatching, sow with grass seed.

Aerating

This process creates holes in the soil to allow air and water to penetrate. It can be very beneficial on compacted areas of lawn. It can also be very hard work, so attempt it only where compaction is a real problem. The best time to aerate a lawn is early autumn, when the soil is moist. If you use a hollow-tined aerator, which takes out a core of soil about 4 in. (10 cm) deep, then once every 3 years should be enough. The alternative is to simply spike the grass, using a fork on small areas, or a powered machine on larger lawns. However, spiking does compress the surrounding soil, so a hollow-tined aerator is preferable, particularly on heavy soils.

Topdressing

The sprinkling of various soil-improving materials onto the lawn surface is a process known as topdressing. These materials are applied in layers thin enough for the grass to grow up through. For a greater effect, particularly on compacted areas of the lawn, use a hollow-tined aerator before applying the topdressing, which can then be brushed down into the channels. Good soil structure encourages worm activity, which in turn improves drainage. Worms also help take surface debris down into the soil.

Applying a topdressing

Autumn and spring are both good times to apply a topdressing. Start by mowing the grass to a length of about 1 in. (2.5 cm). Do not cut lower or the dressing may smother the grass. If the lawn contains thatch, moss, or large weeds, then scarify before mowing. If you are going to aerate the soil with a hollow-tined aerator, do it at this point.

Sprinkle the topdressing mix evenly over the whole area to a depth of up to ½ in. (1 cm). Hollows can be filled slightly more, and by adding a topdressing regularly through the year these can be firmed and filled to gradually level the lawn surface.

Brush or rake the topdressing through the grass onto the soil surface below using a stiff broom. Heavy rain will help do this if you time the treatments to coincide with wet weather.

MATERIALS FOR TOPDRESSING

A topdressing mix is made by mixing together a bulky organic material with loam and/or sharp sand or fine gravel. Fine leaf mold and municipal compost are ideal bulky organic materials for autumn use. Richer materials like garden compost, if you have it to spare, can be used in the spring. The following general recipes can be adapted to suit your particular soil type. All quantities are parts by volume.

For heavy soils where the soil sits wet, or moss is a problem
3 parts sharp sand
1 part loam
1 part bulky organic material

For light, well-drained sandy soil
2 parts loam
3 parts bulky organic material

AT-A-GLANCE GUIDE TO SEASONAL LAWN CARE

Spring	Summer	Autumn	Winter
• Rake vigorously to remove moss and thatch.	• Continue to mow regularly, lowering the height of cut if growth is strong. Take care not to scalp lawns, leaving bare patches where moss and weeds can establish.	• Collect fallen leaves from lawns.	• Continue collecting fallen leaves, which can smother grass.
• Aerate poorly drained lawns; brush sand into the holes to create drainage channels.		• Aerate compacted areas.	• If soil is acid, apply ground limestone to reduce acidity.
• At the start of the season set the mower blades high to leave grass longer. Adjust frequency of mowing according to grass growth.	• Leave grass slightly longer during hot, dry periods and when drought is forecast.	• Dethatch if necessary to rake out moss and accumulated thatch.	• Avoid walking on frosted lawns.
• Cut new lawn edges, and repair damaged ones.	• Trim edges after mowing.	• Reduce frequency of mowing, and raise height of cut.	• Mow during very mild spells if grass is looking untidy.
• Repair bare patches.	• Continue raking out moss.	• Apply a topdressing mix to improve soil structure.	• Get mowers cleaned and serviced before storing away for winter in a dry place.
• Feed lawns with an organic fertilizer or compost.	• Dig out weeds by hand, filling holes with potting soil.	• Fill in hollows in lawns by spreading potting soil or a topdressing.	
	• If growth is poor, feed with an organic fertilizer to improve vigor and color, and to increase resistance to weed infestations.	• Plant crocus and dwarf bulbs under sod for spring displays.	

THE VALUE OF CLOVER

Far from treating clover as a problem, organic gardeners should consider actively encouraging it. During periods of drought, the greenest part of a lawn is often an area covered with clover, which stays green when surrounding grasses have turned brown.

Rather than wait for wild clovers to find a way into your lawn, you can oversow the existing turf with white Dutch clover. Scarify the lawn first to remove debris and expose the soil surface. Then sow clover sparingly over the required area at a rate of about ¼–½ oz. per sq. yd. (7.5–15 g per sq. m). This produces an even carpet of small-leafed clover that should grow in the company of grasses to create an attractive lawn.

Clover flowers are a rich source of nectar for bees, and the ability of clover to take nitrogen from the air and convert it into useful nitrogen fertilizer for itself in its roots means the clover will grow well even in poor soils without the need for additional feeding.

Lawn problems

A single-species lawn is a virtual monoculture— a very unnatural state of affairs. Left to its own devices, a lawn soon becomes a more varied community of plants, including coarser grasses and wildflowers, and much more attractive to a wider range of wildlife. Some gardeners spend a great deal of time preventing anything other than grass from growing in their lawns. Others take a more balanced approach, and are happy to tolerate "weeds" such as clover and daisies.

Some weeds can be positively beneficial. The roots of clover (see also left) fix nitrogen from the air in the soil, providing the plant with a ready source of this essential nutrient and cutting down on the need to add fertilizer. Grasses growing in close association with clover can take up small amounts of nitrogen released into the soil. Small-leaf clover resists drought well, remaining green in dry conditions. And how do you make a daisy chain without daisies?

Weed control

By following the advice on lawn care in this chapter, your lawn should reward you by growing strongly and resisting weed infestations. If weeds do become a problem there are various methods you can use.
• Remove individual weeds like daisies, plantains, and dandelions by hand, using an old kitchen knife or special tool, such as an asparagus fork.
• Fill in holes left after removing weeds with soil or a potting soil, and sow grass seed into this.
• Avoid mowing too low; short grass offers less competition for weeds, and cutting too short can weaken grass, which will make it easier for weeds to invade.
• Scarify to remove debris and improve conditions for grass growth.
• Improve drainage with a hollow-tined aerator to prevent waterlogged conditions, which harm grass and encourage moisture-loving weeds and moss.

Common lawn weeds

Different soils and situations encourage their own types of weeds. Identifying problem weeds can tell you something about these and help point you in the right direction to control them. Ground ivy, for

instance, quickly spreads in moist, shaded areas. Chickweed is a good indication of somewhat alkaline soil. Dandelions are more numerous on compacted soil and on lawns mown very short. Clover grows well on poor soils. Feeding the lawn will tend to deter it (but see also *The Value of Clover*, left). Sheep's sorrel can become a problem where acid soil conditions prevail. Liming soil to bring soil pH back to neutral can help. Plantain and thistles grow where grass is thin or patchy.

Lawn pests include ants, leatherjackets, and moles (see the *A-Z of Plant Problems*, pp. 367–395, for advice).

How to control moss

Moss can develop for a variety of reasons. It relishes moist areas where drainage is poor, and it will also thrive in drier soils where soil fertility is poor and acidity high. Moss colonizes in shaded areas and spreads over soil where grass is mown too short. Rake out moss regularly with a lawn rake, each spring and autumn if the problem is bad. Bare patches should be reseeded. Feed a poor lawn to strengthen grass growth, and set mower blades to about 2 in. (5 cm) to avoid mowing too short. Improving drainage and making an acid soil more alkaline by applying ground limestone or dolomitic lime (see p. 178) will also discourage moss.

Remember that moss is valued by birds for nest building, so consider leaving a mossy patch for them to obtain nesting materials, or leave piles of raked-out moss in an open location for them to collect.

Renovating a neglected lawn

If you need to renovate a lawn, a series of simple steps (see facing page) should bring it back into fine form. Although this can be done at almost any time during the growing season, it is best done in spring when grass is in active growth. Do not expect instant results, but in time you will bring the lawn area back under control. This approach should certainly be easier and cheaper than digging up the old lawn and sowing or laying a new one. One exception is where the old lawn is very uneven, with bumps and hollows over the whole area. In these circumstances a fresh start would be best.

LAWN RENOVATION

1 Cut long grass down. For this you will probably need a powerful rotary mower, setting the blades at their highest cutting height. Mow the area, collecting all the clippings. Lower the blade a little and mow the area again. Continue this routine until the long grass has been brought down to about 2 in. (5 cm) in height.

2 Rake over the lawn to remove debris and congested growth. As this leaves a very untidy surface, mow the area again.

3 Dig out large weeds by hand. Check the soil pH with a kit. If below pH 5.5–6.0, add lime to the area to bring the pH back to around 7.

4 Fill any holes with potting soil, then sprinkle a pinch of grass seed over the top. This will grow over and spread to fill the hole.

5 Apply a suitable lawn fertilizer evenly to the whole area.

6 If areas appear waterlogged, use a hollow-tined aerator to make holes up to 6–8 in. (15–20 cm) deep over the area and brush sharp sand down into the holes to create drainage channels.

7 Repair any bare patches by raking over the surface with a lawn rake, removing stones, dead grass, weeds, and debris, and loosening the soil surface. Add potting soil to level the surface if necessary. Sow a suitable grass seed mixture, and keep watered until germinated.

8 Over the coming weeks mow more often, at least once a week, and twice if possible.

9 Follow the annual care regime outlined on pp. 178–179 to maintain the lawn in top condition, encouraging strong grass growth and discouraging weeds. Gradually fill hollows and remove bumps, and topdress the whole lawn area each autumn.

LAWN PROBLEMS

Many lawn problems can be solved using cultural methods.

1 Worms benefit grass growth, but their casts can cause problems if trodden on and compacted. Disperse worm casts by brushing with a broom when dry.

2 Standing water after heavy rain can be a sign of surface compaction or poor drainage. Try to alleviate it by hollow-tined aeration.

3 Prevent thick layers of moss from building up by raking it out or by scarifying. Identify and remedy the cause to prevent it from recurring.

4 Rosette-growing weeds like plantains cleverly avoid being damaged by mowing by hugging the ground. Hand-digging them out individually is the best solution. An old kitchen knife makes an ideal weeding tool.

Making a new lawn

Good preparation lays the foundation for a healthy lawn. Check out soil structure and fertility (see *Soil and Soil Care*, pp. 33–37) and make any necessary improvements a month or two in advance of laying the sod. Soil improvement is much easier to do at this stage than when the lawn is established.

The site should be firm, level, and free from bumps, hollows, and perennial weeds. If it has been dug over, compress the soil by walking up and down the area on your heels. Rake the area to remove stones and lumps, leveling the surface by eye. A topdressing of general organic fertilizer can be raked in at the same time.

Sod or seed?

Seed is cheaper than sod, involves less work, and gives a greater choice of grass mixes, but:
• Weeds may overwhelm grass seedlings.
• It may be a year before the lawn can take hard use.
• Seed is more dependent on good weather.
Sod gives an immediate effect and the lawn can be used after a few weeks; there is also no need to

protect sodded areas from birds or cats, as there is with seeded ground. However:
• Sod must be laid within 48 hours of arrival.
• The choice of grass mixes is limited.
• Quality sod may be hard to find and expensive.

A new lawn from sod

The quickest way to create a lawn is by laying sod. You may not be able to find organically grown sod, but it is always worth checking with suppliers, as the range of organically grown products is increasing all the time. It pays to invest in good-quality, seed-raised sod unless you are growing a natural meadow and do not mind coarser grasses and wildflowers. These days it comes delivered in narrow rolls rather than in squares. Lay it as soon as possible, certainly within a day; it will quickly deteriorate if left rolled up.

How to lay sod

Sod can be laid almost all year round but is best laid during the moister spring and autumn months, when warm temperatures encourage growth and

Designing in practicalities
Areas of lawn used for access can soon show signs of wear (near right), so stepping-stones or a path may need to be installed. Edges of lawns can be protected from damage by sinking an edging strip along them. These usually come as flexible rolls of plastic or metal, and must be pushed well down so that they will not damage the mower. Where border plants spill over onto the lawn (far right), consider laying an edging of bricks or paving slabs flush with the lawn surface. This will act as a path for wet weather as well as allowing the mower to be run over the edge of the grass and onto the paving when cutting the grass.

rainfall reduces the need to water. Start by rolling out one roll along a straight-edged board. Tamp down the sod with the back of a rake to settle it onto the soil. Once a single row is in place, put the board on the laid sod to distribute your weight evenly. Working from it, unroll more sod alongside. Butt adjoining strips tightly, as sod can shrink slightly and leave gaps. Continue, staggering any joints so that you do not get a seam running across the lawn.

When creating a curve, do not stretch and bend lengths of turf, as this can result in a very uneven surface. Cut curves once turf is laid with a sharp, long-bladed knife. Use a length of hose to mark out a smooth curve; for a straight edge use a board as a guide, cutting with a knife or half-moon edger. Keep the final level of the sod slightly above any paths, paving, or patio alongside it so that you will be able to run the mower right over the edge. Finally, draw a little soil up along edges to stop them drying out until the grass has rooted down and established. Once it has, the edge can be recut.

Aftercare

Sod takes a few weeks to root down into the soil. Until then it will need regular watering using a lawn sprinkler to prevent it drying out or shrinking, if daily showers do not do this for you. If shrinking does occur, fill gaps between adjoining strips with a seed medium and sow with grass seed.

Once it has settled, your new lawn will start to grow and require mowing. Wait until the sod has rooted down before walking over it with a mower. You can gauge this by tugging at an area to see if roots hold it down. Set mower blades high for the first few cuts, just topping the grass to keep it neat. Lower the height once it has established.

A new lawn from seed

Sowing grass seed is the cheapest way to produce a lawn. You can choose a seed mix that suits growing conditions and the use to which the lawn will be put. You can also sow wildflowers and clover at the same time to create a richer environment that will be more attractive to wildlife. Sow in the damper months of spring or autumn, although lawns can be sown in summer in wetter areas. When preparing the site, make sure the finished surface is firm and level.

Complete soil preparations well before you intend to sow, to allow time to create a "stale seedbed." Leave the area bare for a few weeks, and weed seeds close to the soil surface will germinate. If the weather is dry during this period, water the soil to encourage weed germination. Hoe the weeds off just before sowing the new lawn, leaving a fine tilth on the surface. This removes many weed seedlings that would otherwise have competed with the grass.

How to sow

To sow seed evenly it helps to divide up the area into square-yard (square-meter) plots with string or long canes. Measure out sufficient seed for a single plot, then divide it in half. Sprinkle the first half evenly over the soil in one direction, then sow the second batch perpendicular to this. Mixing the seed with sand can help you to sow more evenly, as you can see where you have sown. Gently rake the seed into the soil surface to cover it slightly and hide it from birds. On small areas, consider spreading netting over the area to keep off birds until the seed has germinated. Always sow at the recommended rate given on the package. Sowing too thickly results in weak, congested grass growth; sowing too thinly leaves gaps where weeds can take over.

Aftercare

If the weather is dry, irrigate with a lawn sprinkler to keep the soil surface just moist. During warm weather grass seed should germinate within 14–21 days. Bird protection netting can then be removed, but continue irrigating gently if conditions turn dry. Try to avoid walking over newly emerged grass until it is about 1 in. (2.5 cm) tall. Check over the area regularly and pick out any emerging weeds by hand. Once the new grass has grown to about 2½–3 in. (6–7.5 cm) it can be given a light trim. If you have a mower with a rear roller, run this up and down to gently firm the new grasses and settle the soil surface. About 3 days later, the grass will have grown up straight again and can be mown. Mow lightly, setting the blades high to trim off the very tips of the grasses. Over the coming weeks, increase cutting frequency and lower the blades for a shorter cut. Regular mowing encourages grasses to develop new growth from the base, eventually producing a thicker and more robust lawn.

GRASS SEED MIXTURES

Beautiful lawns are made up of many different grasses, each offering different growth characteristics that together make a dense green lawn. Choosing the right mix of grasses is important in the organic garden. If you are sowing a new lawn from scratch, then you can select a blend of different grass types that will suit the conditions of the area, the use the lawn will be put to, and the finish required. Hard-wearing mixes can be chosen for lawns used for sports and play, while different mixes would be better for a shaded site or for growing into a manicured lawn. Grasses grown in meadows or left longer to flower and seed will attract a variety of insects and butterflies.

Rye grass
Hard-wearing perennial grass that provides a good utility lawn, withstands a certain amount of drought, and looks superb.

Red fescue
Both slender and creeping varieties of red fescue grow strongly to provide thick growth that is hard-wearing and reasonably tolerant of drought.

Meadow grasses
Smooth-stalked varieties are used in blends for fine lawns.

Other grasses
Chewings fescue and Kentucky bluegrass are just some of the other grasses used in lawn seed mixtures. By choosing blends that combine grasses with a variety of characteristics you will produce a lawn that looks good and performs well in your chosen situation.

Country casual

The tranquility of a traditional flowering meadow can be recreated in all but the smallest gardens.

CUTTING CONSIDERATIONS

Always aim to cut meadows on a sunny day after a period of dry weather. The process of cutting and raking away the debris is designed to release as much seed back onto the soil surface as possible. In addition to ensuring that the seedheads of the majority of flowering plants are ripe and splitting, a period of dry weather will make the whole process easier.

Small areas can be cut by hand using shears. On larger sites the growth can be scythed. There is a knack to using a traditional scythe, with its long, curved blade, that can soon be learned. Today the gardener is more likely to use a nylon string trimmer. Gas-powered models are available to rent, and are very useful for cutting growth on banks and uneven sites, although the noise is a drawback.

Meadows and wildflowers

For the organic gardener eager to encourage wildlife into the garden, an area of rough grass and flowers is a rich habitat enjoyed by butterflies, bees, spiders, other insects, invertebrates, and small mammals. Compare a meadow to a clean-cut lawn and you will see how one is teeming with life while the other is bereft of visible activity.

You can simply leave an area of grass uncut and see what grows. Grasses and flowers (plants otherwise regarded as weeds in this situation) will develop, flower, and set seed. The grass must be cut at some point or shrubby plants will start to move in. Cutting at the correct time ensures that seeds are released and scattered to grow another year. To encourage spring-flowering species, cut beginning in midsummer; to encourage summer-flowering species, delay mowing until early autumn.

Leave the mown grass on the surface for 2 or 3 days to release any ripe seeds, then rake away all the debris, which can be composted. Removing the cut grass helps to keep the fertility down, allowing wildflowers to flourish.

The floral content of these rough, weedy lawns can be enriched by clearing small areas and sowing or planting specific wildflowers. From field scabious to primrose, yarrow to clover, a wide range of flowers is available to suit different soils and situations and to flower at different seasons.

Sowing a wildflower meadow

Numerous seed mixes are available that contain different selections of wildflowers and grasses, suited to different soil types and situations. Ideally, choose species that are native to your locality. Do not collect seed from the wild. You could perhaps collect seed from a friend's meadow planting. Sowing this fresh seed often results in far better levels of germination than purchased packets of seed.

Wildflowers grow best in poorer soils, not in cultivated and enriched garden soil. The poorer the soil the better, as this will help prevent invasion by vigorous weeds such as thistles and docks, and also reduce the vigor of the grass, which can be very competitive. If a new wildflower lawn is being sown, start by digging over the area, turning over the richer topsoil and burying it beneath poorer subsoil. If your topsoil is deep, remove it and replace it with poorer soil.

Firm the soil down and rake it level as you would when preparing a new lawn, but without adding any compost or fertilizer. Leave the area for a few weeks after preparation, then hoe off any germinating weeds to produce a stale seedbed (see also p. 183) to sow into. Wildflower seeds and grasses can be broadcast over the area and raked into the surface, or plugs of wildflowers can be planted out between areas of sown grass. New meadows are best established in spring, sowing seed at the specified rate and keeping areas watered until seeds have germinated and seedlings are established.

Alternatives to a traditional meadow

If your soil is very fertile, a wildflower meadow is unlikely to do well. For a similar visual effect, consider instead sowing a mixture of annual meadow flowers such as cornflowers, field poppies, and corn marigolds combined with oat or barley seed (see also p. 194). This gives a magnificent spring and summer annual display, but the ground will be bare over winter. As long as the plants are allowed to seed and the ground is gently dug over each year in early spring, one sowing should last for many years.

Another way to give flowering interest to an existing lawn is by adding small bulbs (see right).

Raising wildflowers as plug plants

Flower seed can be expensive to buy, especially if you have a large meadow to develop. While a basic seed mix may provide a good general meadow, it is worth choosing a few other, more choice wildflowers to raise separately in "plug" or cell trays. These should be grown until they have reached a larger size before planting out, as you would summer annuals. Planting out in clumps or wide drifts will add character to the meadow, although the greater the diversity of plant species included in the meadow, the wider its appeal and value to wildlife. It helps to raise and keep a few plants in reserve to fill gaps where the germination of seed sown directly was poor.

Never dig up plants from the wild, however successful they appear to be in their natural habitat.

BULBS IN GRASS

Autumn is the ideal time to plant bulbs under your lawn to create spring flower displays. These will enrich the lawn environment with blooms that are attractive to many insects. Crocus, snowdrops, snake's head fritillaries (above), and dwarf narcissus grow up well through grass to produce a colorful seasonal display. Some can be planted using a bulb planter, taking out a core of soil and sod, dropping in the bulb, then replacing and firming down the plug. Smaller bulbs can be spread out over an area after peeling back the sod just 1 in. (2.5 cm) or so deep. Loosen the soil slightly, space out the bulbs, then fold back and water down the sod.

After flowering in spring, allow 6 weeks before cutting down the leaves of bulbs. This foliage is needed to produce food for the bulb to ensure a repeat flowering performance the following year.

Aim to give the lawn a trim in late autumn, or even during winter if conditions allow, so that bulbs grow up through a neat, low green carpet.

Meadow mowings
Leave mowings on the surface to dry out, then shake them well to release their seed as you collect them.

Gardening for wildlife

ORGANIC GARDENS ARE AT AN ADVANTAGE WHEN IT COMES TO
ATTRACTING AND VALUING WILDLIFE

**Inviting in the guests
(facing page)**
*You can attract a variety of beautiful
visitors such as birds and butterflies
into your garden by creating the right
habitats and conditions for them.*

A GARDEN TEEMING WITH WILDLIFE is a pleasing, relaxing place to be—good for your well-being and for the feelings it brings of continuity and interaction with the wider world. Butterflies and birds are as much of a delight as flowers and fruits, but lesser creatures can be equally stunning and are a vital part of the natural food chain.

Safe havens

With the continuing increase in urban sprawl and the intensification of modern farming, which places great reliance on the use of pesticides, the private garden has become vitally important as a safe habitat for wildlife. It is estimated that the collective area of domestic gardens in the U.K., for instance, covers twice the area of existing nature preserves. More and more wild creatures are finding in gardens not just a refuge but their only chance of long-term survival.

Organic gardens have a head start when it comes to attracting wildlife because pesticide use is minimal. Natural predators and parasites, which keep pests and diseases under control, in turn provide food for larger creatures. The use of bulky organic manures encourages a thriving microflora and -fauna in the soil—and these in turn are the first vital link in the food chain. There is no need to be concerned that more wildlife will result in more pests: Studies have shown that organic farms support a greater abundance and diversity of wildlife species than conventionally managed farms, and there is, if anything, a decrease rather than an increase in the number of pests.

Creating the right conditions

With a little extra planning you can easily increase the range of creatures visiting and living in your own garden. If you are really eager to promote the right conditions for wildlife, you can create a mini-nature preserve, with every plant carefully selected for its wildlife value. You can also incorporate plenty of wildlife-friendly ideas into an existing garden without having to make it look untidy or wild. A wildlife-friendly garden can look just as good as, or even better than, any other garden plot.

The basic requirements of all the creatures that visit your garden are the same: food, somewhere to live and breed in safety, and water for drinking and bathing. This chapter describes how you can provide these necessities of life in your garden to support a diverse range of creatures.

Don't expect too much too soon; you can only create the most suitable conditions for visits by wild birds, beasts, and insects—not drag them into your garden by force. Despite your best efforts, you may find totally different species are drawn to your garden than those you originally intended to attract.

CREATURES GREAT AND SMALL

Birds and small mammals are obvious delights for the wildlife gardener, but smaller creatures can be just as beautiful and fascinating to observe. These are just some of the invertebrates that might visit a summer garden.
Dragonflies (top) **and damselflies** will fly some distance from water. Watch some of the males defend their territory against any other insect—even butterflies.
Shield bugs (center) feed on grasses, wild legumes, and shrubs. They are often devoted parents.
Velvet mites, tiny red creatures, are garden friends. They swarm on hot, dry sidewalks and eat pests such as red spider mites.
Violet ground beetles (see p. 35) are one of the most spectacular ground beetles, with iridescent purple edges on their black wing cases.
Crab spiders (bottom) have as many distinctly different colors as birds. Females are often paler but both sexes can change color according to their background.

PLANTS FOR WILDLIFE

Hedge plants for shelter and food for wildlife
Beech (*Fagus sylvatica*)
Cranberrybush viburnum
  (*Viburnum trilobum*))
Crab apple (*Malus* spp.)
Elderberry (*Sambucus nigra*)
Hawthorn (*Crataegus crus-galli*)
Hazel (*Corylus avellana*)
Highbush blueberry
  (*Vaccinium corymbosum*)
Holly (*Ilex opaca*)
Hornbeam (*Carpinus betulus*)

Shrubs providing shelter and food for birds
Cotoneaster
Ilex verticillata
Ligustrum
Prunus 'Otto Luykens'
Pyracantha
Rubus phoenicolasius

Climbers for shelter and food for birds
Blackberry (*Rubus* spp. and
  related hybrids)
Dog rose (*Rosa canina*) and
  other related species roses
Grapes (*Vitis*)
Honeysuckle (*Lonicera
  periclymenum*)
Ivy (*Hedera helix*)
Virginia creeper
  (*Parthenocissus quinquefolia*)

Making wildlife feel at home

Every creature needs somewhere safe to rest, sleep, and breed, so it makes sense to provide some shelter for the wildlife in your garden. This may be in the form of a custom-built home, such as a birdhouse (see pp. 191–192), but creatures will also live very happily in compost piles, under mulches, and in log piles, as well as being quite content to make their home in or under a hedge.

Before you rush to dig a pond or put up a bat house, first take a look around your garden and identify the areas that are already attractive to wildlife. Then earmark any other areas that, with a little change in management, could be improved on.

Hedges and edges
A hedge is an excellent place for creatures to take shelter from predators or the weather, court, mate, feed, and build a nest. In windy winter conditions a hedge is warmer and stays dry at the base. A

hedge base full of leaf litter is also a rich food source for insect eaters—not only birds but also voles and shrews.

To avoid disturbing any nesting birds, hedge cutting should be delayed until mid- to late summer. Fruiting hedges can be left uncut until the birds have eaten the berries. The base of the hedge should remain undisturbed; there is no need to rake out fallen leaves.

If your garden is small, try creating a "fedge" along your boundary by growing ivy, honeysuckle, and clematis through a chain-link fence, or cover your walls and fences with climbing plants. Train the plants so that the base of the support is well covered, and do not trim growth back too closely. Dense evergreen climbers make the most effective wildlife refuges. Many small birds, such as wrens, will hide in thick ivy on cold winter nights. Larger birds also appreciate tall, ivy-clad trees, and if some of the branches are decaying, woodpeckers will welcome both the source of food and possible nest sites. Leave dead branches in place if they are not in immediate danger of falling so that they, too, can provide food for insects and shelter for birds.

Wildlife corridors
Creating wildlife corridors through your garden will enable smaller creatures to come and go while remaining hidden from their predators. Thick shrubs and hedge bases provide excellent protection, but groundcover plants linked to areas of longer grass and perennial beds will also provide good cover for creatures on the move. If you erect a fence, try to raise it off the ground a little so that small animals can squeeze underneath.

Lawns
To create the best variety of habitat, alternate areas of mown grass with patches of longer grass. Birds such as robins and starlings need open areas of short grass to feed on, while amphibians require longer grass. Try to leave uncut grass wherever you can without making things look too untidy—along the base of an informal hedge, for example, or under trees. A neat, short-mown path through slightly taller grass that grows next to uncut areas of vegetation

Wildlife refuge
Though we do not understand all the intricacies of the natural world, keeping your garden free of harmful chemicals and providing the right habitats ensures that as many creatures as possible, such as this female stag beetle, can continue to share your garden.

NEAT vs. NATURAL

One of the harder aspects of wildlife gardening is to strike a balance between super-tidy and messy designs. A happy medium is one of beneficial neglect with a careless abandon in the planting— think of a trailing wild rose bush sprawling its stems across long grass, a group of sunflowers left to self-seed, or a drift of cowslips romping unchecked through a lawn.

But the nostalgic country or cottage style of gardening is not the only option with wildlife appeal; there's no need for your garden to look neglected or old-fashioned. More modern styles of "meadow" planting, with drifts of herbaceous perennials threading through grasses (see also pp. 162–163), are not only visually spectacular but benefit wildlife as well. Flowers and seedheads provide food for butterflies, goldfinches, and other seed-eating birds, and leaving the seedheads over winter will give birds a long-lasting "store cupboard," as well as being easy on busy gardeners.

Nooks and crannies

If you want to encourage creatures into your garden, make a leaf mold pile or leave a log pile in a sheltered spot (above) for them to nest in. Frogs, beetles, and hoverflies may all make use of a cool, dark, probably damp site. By contrast, shrews, wood mice, toads, spiders, and even pupating butterflies and moths will be attracted to the crevices and gaps in sunny stone walls (above right) and stony banks.

can add structure to an area that might otherwise look unkempt and neglected. Do not cut or mow all areas of long grass on the same day. If you have to cut a large area of rough grass, start at one end and work inward from one side to allow creatures an escape route. Never cut grass in a circle—mice and frogs become trapped like rabbits in a hayfield.

Sheds and compost piles

Garden sheds can provide useful hiding places for different species. Butterflies may creep inside to hibernate, so leave the shed door open on sunny autumn afternoons and shut it late in the evening. Remember that garden birds will sometimes nest in the most unlikely places; they might appreciate your shed as much as you do!

If you regularly make a compost or leaf mold pile, you may well have an opossum or other animals sleeping in it for at least part of the year. If you don't want to encourage these creatures, make sure wire bins don't have any gaps, or use solid-sided bins.

Grass snakes occasionally lay their eggs and hibernate in compost piles. If you are privileged enough to have snakes visiting your garden and want them to stay, make a large compost pile in a sunny position. Snakes, like swallows, often return to the same nest site year after year, but they need the heat of decaying vegetation to hatch their eggs, so you

will need to rebuild the pile every year. The safest times to disturb the pile are during early October, or from mid-April to mid-May when the snakes have emerged.

Under cover

Small creatures love to lurk under mulches. A wood-chip or bark mulch will shelter beetles, centipedes, and the like, while thicker mulches of hay and straw may be frequented by frogs, toads, shrews, spiders, and newts. In winter try to leave some mulch undisturbed for creatures to hibernate in.

Make mounds or banks in a sunny part of the garden by piling up rubble and packing it loosely with topsoil, leaving small gaps between stones. Not only is this a good site for attractive plants that need good drainage, such as thymes, sea campion (*Silene maritima*), and rock roses (*Helianthemum*), but it is also the best habitat for hibernating amphibians or, in summer, basking lizards. Weasels also love to hide between stones, though they may also like short lengths of drainpipe in dry, undisturbed garden areas.

Many small mammals prefer a more substantial log pile, with the base logs stacked at least 4 in. (10 cm) apart. Position the logs in a sheltered spot, under trees or thick shrubs where they will not be disturbed. Some will gather dry leaves to make their nests, so make sure there are some leaves close by.

Buying and building shelters

You can buy a variety of custom-built boxes for a whole range of creatures to shelter and raise a family in. The design can be simple or intricate, as long as it fulfills the needs of whatever it is you aim to attract. The residents are unlikely to be fussy.

Toad and frog houses

Toad houses can be particularly important in urban areas where shelter is scarce. Finding a suitable shelter for winter is hard in neat gardens, so keep toads happy by placing a house (below) under a hedge or thick shrub where it will be undisturbed. Frog houses can also be of benefit in a garden: Place these in a north-facing, shady spot out of the wind.

Birdhouses

Even if there are already many suitable nest sites, a birdhouse may encourage a normally shy species of bird to stay on your plot. Birdhouses can be made of untreated wood or "woodcrete" (a commercial concrete/sawdust composition). The latter version is useful if your garden has predatory squirrels or even woodpeckers with a taste for young birds. All birdhouses should be positioned with an easy means

of access for you to be able to clean the house out periodically. Site your birdhouse on a warm, sheltered wall, tree trunk, or shed, well away from predators, rain, and direct sunlight. Cats can climb up and reach into houses from all sorts of unlikely angles, as can gray squirrels, so position it carefully. If there are a lot of cats nearby, it may be worth having several different designs of nesting houses in your garden. Predators often learn that a particular house design may contain food—chicks or eggs.

> ## A birdhouse may encourage a normally shy species of bird to stay in your yard

Ideally, birdhouses should be cleaned out every autumn. Remove any nest material and rinse the house with hot soapy water to keep it fresh for the next visitors. Bird fleas do not attack humans, but it is probably a good idea to wear gloves. Allow the house to dry thoroughly before closing it up again.

WHAT HOUSE FOR WHICH BIRD?

The size of the entrance hole determines which species can, and cannot, use a birdhouse.
• Houses with entrances just over 1 in. (2.5 cm) in diameter are suitable for chickadees.
• Entrances that are 1¼ in. (3 cm) in diameter are suited to downy woodpeckers, titmice, nuthatches, and house wrens.
• Houses with entrances that are 1½ in. (4 cm) will attract bluebirds, tree swallows, violet-green swallows, prothonotary warblers, and hairy woodpeckers.

Prefab house
A ready-made, terra-cotta toad house provides a cool, moist shelter that welcomes pest-eating toads to your garden. Tuck one in amid your flowers or vegetables to make toads feel at home.

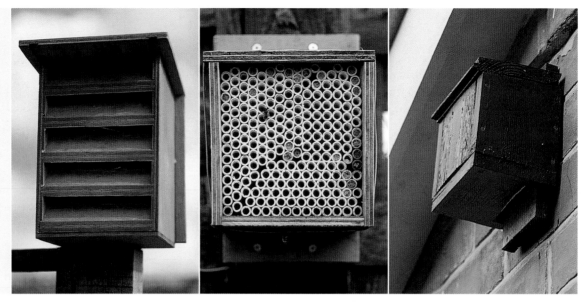

FIVE-STAR ROOMS
These sophisticated, ready-made boxes are designed to house (from left to right) lacewings, mason bees, and bats. Though some birds may use a bee box as a "feeder," don't panic—they will be unable to reach the deeper layers of eggs in their self-contained cells. Place bat houses 10 ft. (3 m) or more off the ground on trees, posts, or the sides of buildings. If you live close to an old-fashioned yellow sodium street light, you may be able to watch the bats feeding on any insects attracted to the light.

Insect hotels
Insects also appreciate having somewhere to live in winter. Lady beetles, earwigs, and other insects hibernate naturally in tufts of rough grass, dead leaves, and hollow plant stems, so delay cutting down flower stems and clearing your borders until spring.

You can buy neat wooden boxes for lacewings to hibernate in, or make a simple insect "hotel" from a plastic bottle and some corrugated cardboard (below).

Making your own lacewing hotel
• *Saw the bottom off an empty 2-liter soda bottle (it does not need to be washed out).*
• *Cut a piece of corrugated cardboard about 32–36 in. (80–100 cm) long, roll it up, and slide it inside the bottle.*
• *Push some thin wire through both sides of the bottle base to keep the cardboard from falling out.*
• *Tie a string around the bottle neck, leaving the top on, and hang the "hotel" near your garden in late summer to early fall.*

Plastic food containers can also be pressed into service for housing lady beetles and other predators. Make a series of small holes in the lid of a margarine tub with a knitting needle and stuff the inside with straw, then place the tub on its side under a bush or large perennial plant to keep it dry over winter.

Bees, especially orchard mason bees (*Osmia*), which are useful early-season pollinators, can be given extra help with supplementary shelter. They will happily colonize holes drilled in blocks of wood or paper drinking straws stacked in a waterproof box, or you can buy special bee boxes. Mason bees emerge early, so the boxes need to be erected in early spring before the apple buds burst. An open, sunny, preferably southwest-facing site is essential.

Bat roosts
Bats are quite common in built-up areas, even in large cities. They need temporary and permanent roosts. Some can eat up to 2,000 small insects, such as midges, per hour, so they are good to have around!

A bat house should be made of untreated lumber and have rough wood inside so the bats can happily hang upside down. It should be situated as high as possible—at least 10 ft. (3 m) above ground level, away from bright lights and prevailing winds. There should also be plenty of air space in front of it. Planting night-flowering annuals nearby will encourage moths and other insects to feed, which will in turn attract bats. Try night-scented stock (*Matthiola bicornis*) or tobacco plants (*Nicotiana*). As with birdhouses, the bats may take a while to settle in.

Food for all

Wild birds in gardens are often very reliant on food put out for them because supplementary feeding encourages a larger population than the habitat can naturally support. Once you have started to feed birds you must continue, as they will always come to the bird table for food rather than searching for their own during the short winter days.

Feed the birds with black sunflower seeds, fat balls, and mixed seeds (rather than peanuts, which can contain harmful aflatoxins). Keep bird feeders as clean as possible—food poisoning is not confined to humans! If possible, move the feeder's position every few months to avoid a buildup of harmful bacteria.

It is better, wherever possible, to grow plants that will supply birds with their own food source rather than develop their overdependence on humans. Berried shrubs attract a number of species, as do seedheads and grasses; leave some herbaceous plants to go to seed. Sunflowers, rudbeckias, and echinaceas make excellent garden plants as well as good food for many garden birds—hang up an old seedhead for cardinals. Once birds find a good food supply they return regularly, which is greatly to the gardener's

advantage. It has been estimated that a single bird may eat more than 10,000 caterpillars, flies, snails, and other pests during a single breeding season. Note, however, that many cultivated fruits are as attractive to birds as they are to humans.

Birds are not the only creatures that come to a garden to feed. An organic garden is likely to provide rich pickings for both vegetarian and carnivorous wildlife visitors of all shapes and sizes. With a little extra thought you can provide them with even better fare. Natural foods that can easily be included on your menu for wildlife include nectar, pollen, aphids, caterpillars, slugs, berries, and seeds.

Flower food

Flowers are not only pleasing to our eyes but also attractive to many insects, which flock to feed on the energy-rich pollen and nectar they supply. In turn, these insects will feed birds, bats, and other predators. Flowers grown to feed wildlife do not have to be native wildflowers—cultivated blooms can be even more nectar-rich and will extend the season. Many of the best-suited flowers for insects

SHRUBS WITH FRUITS OR SEEDS FOR BIRDS

Cherries (*Prunus*): robins, bluebirds, woodpeckers, catbirds, thrushes, cardinals, blackbirds, orioles, waxwings.

Dogwood (*Cornus*): catbirds, mockingbirds, robins, thrushes, woodpeckers, song sparrows, bluebirds, cardinals, waxwings.

Elderberries (*Sambucus*): bluebirds, grosbeaks, sparrows, thrashers, catbirds, vireos, finches, woodpeckers, flickers, waxwings.

Juniper (*Juniperus*): bluebirds, catbirds, purple finches, mockingbirds, thrushes, waxwings.

Viburnums (*Viburnum*): robins, catbirds, thrushes, thrashers, cardinals, bluebirds, waxwings.

WILDFLOWERS FOR WILDLIFE

A meadow (see also pp. 184–185) is one of the richest habitats of all for wildlife, containing not only flowers but also the grass species that are essential to the life cycle of many butterflies (see facing page, below right).

The rich insect population will in turn attract small mammal predators such as voles and shrews, which can forage in safety among the long growth. Never isolate a patch of meadow in the midst of a mown lawn or completely surrounded by paths or hard surfaces. Allow the meadow to lead and blend into denser growth so that creatures have a secure route in and out.

Annual meadows

A meadow does require time to develop and a careful mowing regime. For a quick and easy-to-grow colorful display that will positively crackle, buzz, and hum with wildlife in the garden, try sowing a patch with a mixture of annual meadow flowers. For a really authentic effect, mix in some oat, barley, or wheat seed.

Sow the seed in autumn or spring into weed-free ground. Once the plants have set seed in late summer or autumn, remove the remains to the compost pile. Turn the ground over in late winter and see what comes up the following spring. Some species may need to be resown if they have not seeded well, or if the seeds have been eaten by birds.

If you want to tailor your own mix, look out for white campion, corn cockle, cornflower, corn marigold, wild pansy, scarlet pimpernel, and the red poppy, *Papaver rhoeas*.

Unlike many meadow species, these annual flowers thrive in ground that is disturbed every year, so you can move your wildlife attraction around if necessary—this being particularly ideal if you are gradually reclaiming a large garden.

are smaller, old-fashioned cottage garden varieties; avoid overbred, blowsy double blooms. Different flowers suit different feeding methods, so grow a range of flowers to suit all tastes. Bumblebees, for example, have much shorter tongues than Red Admiral butterflies, but longer ones than hive bees. Grow deep-throated flowers such as sage, marjoram, foxgloves, and nasturtiums for bumblebees; nemesia, lemon balm, mahonia, and viburnums for hive bees; and sedum and buddleia for butterflies to feed on. Simple, flat-opening flowers such as fennel are best for hoverflies, parasitic wasps, and other small insects.

Most insects prefer different food plants at various stages of their life cycle, or even at different times of day. The peak nectar flow of flowers varies from species to species throughout the daylight hours, and you may find it interesting to plot a butterfly's progression from one food source to the next as the nectar ebbs and flows.

Plants as nurseries

Butterflies also need somewhere to lay their eggs. Caterpillars feed on foliage rather than nectar and pollen, and they can be quite specific about which plants they will eat; some species are quite limited in their range of food sources. It is best to identify which butterflies are visiting your garden before you plant specific caterpillar food plants. A great many

butterfly and moth species feed on grass, so leaving an area where the grass can grow tall is important. Some caterpillars hibernate and many pupate on grass stems over winter, so wait until late spring before cutting back long grass.

Grubs and caterpillars are in turn food for birds, predatory beetles, parasitic wasps, voles, and amphibians. Many creatures regarded as garden pests are actually a valuable food source for other creatures. A pair of meadowlarks, for example, may feed their nestlings up to 10,000 grasshoppers, plus many other kinds of bugs. Aphids and codling moth pupae are favorite winter food for several bird species. So give nature a chance before you take action against a pest attack; you may find that the job has been done for you. Clusters of aphids left on strong, established plants that can tolerate them, for example, will make a "nursery" for parasitic wasps and predators to feed and breed on.

Frogs and toads will live year-round in a garden if they can find a food supply, and their taste for small invertebrates—especially slugs—makes them the gardener's friends. Mealworms and angler's maggots make good extra amphibian fodder—buy them from specialty pet stores or fishing shops. Toads in particular can be taught to take food from your finger and will quickly learn to reappear at the same place at their regular feeding time.

NATIVE SPECIES

Most—though not all—creatures in this country are adapted to feeding on native plant species. If you would like to grow native species, try to find out what would naturally grow in your area before you plant—these plants will stand the best chance of attracting most creatures and of thriving, not just surviving, in your individual site and soil.

Fortunately, some nurseries are becoming attuned to the desire for native plants, and these can be excellent sources of seeds and plants. Many states also have native plant societies; ask at a local botanical garden or search the World Wide Web to find a society near you.

FOOD PLANTS FOR CATERPILLARS

Many butterfly and moth caterpillars are specific to just a few species of plant. Here are just a few:

Alfalfa (*Medicago sativa*): Marine blue, orange-bordered blue, and especially the brightly colored orange sulphur (also know as the "alfalfa butterfly")

Aster (*Aster*): Aster checkerspot and other checkerspots; field crescentspot and other crescentspots

Dill (*Anethum graveolens*): Eastern black swallowtail

Dutchman's pipes (*Aristolochia*): Pipevine swallowtails

Maypop (*Passiflora incarnata*): Gulf fritillary

Milkweed (*Asclepias*): Monarch (left)

Pawpaw (*Asimina triloba*): Zebra swallowtail

Scarlet runner bean (*Phaseolus coccineus*): Gray hairstreak

Violets (*Viola*): Most species of orange and black fritillaries

FLOWERS FOR HONEYBEES

Arabis
Broad and field beans (*Vicia faba*)
Borage (*Borago officinalis*)
Blackberry, raspberry, and hybrid berries
Carrots
Candytuft (*Iberis*)
Dog rose (*Rosa canina*, right)
Heather (*Erica*)
Mignonette (*Reseda odorata*)
Parsnips (*Pastinaca sativa*)
Russian sage (*Perovskia atriplicifolia*)
Rosemary (*Rosmarinus officinalis*)
Rosebay willowherb (*Epilobium angustifolium*)
Verbascums
Vervain (*Verbena officinalis*)
Virginia creeper (*Parthenocissus quinquefolia*)
Wallflowers (*Erysimum*)
Woad (*Isatis tinctoria*)

FLOWERS FOR BUMBLEBEES

Anise hyssop (*Agastache anisata*)
Bee balm (*Monarda*)
Bird's foot trefoil (*Lotus corniculatus*)
Clover, red and white (*Trifolium*)
Globe artichoke (*Cynara scolymus*)
Goldenrod (*Solidago*)
Horehound (*Marrubium vulgare*)
Honeysuckle (*Lonicera*, especially *L. periclymenum*, right)
Knapweed (*Centaurea scabiosa* and *C. nigra*)
Lobelia cardinalis
Lungwort (*Pulmonaria saccharata*)
Perennial cornflower (*Centaurea montana*)
Phacelia (*Phacelia tanacetifolia*)
Red valerian (*Centranthus ruber*)
Shasta daisy (*Leucanthemum* x *superbum*)
Viper's bugloss (*Echium vulgare*)
Yarrow (*Achillea vulgaris*)

FLOWERS FOR HOVERFLIES AND OTHER BENEFICIAL INSECTS

Brambles (*Rubus* spp.)
Buckwheat (*Fagopyrum esculentum*)
California poppy (*Eschscholzia californica*)
Convolvulus, annual (*Convolvulus tricolor*)
Corn marigold (*Chrysanthemum segetum*)
Cornflower (*Centaurea cyanus*)
Coriander (*Coriandrum sativum*, left)
Cow parsley (*Anthriscus sylvestris*)
Dog rose (*Rosa canina*)
Fennel (*Foeniculum vulgare*)
Figwort (*Scrophularia*)
Hawthorn (*Crataegus monogyna*)
Ivy (*Hedera helix*)
Phacelia (*Phacelia tanacetifolia*)
Sweet alyssum (*Lobularia maritima*)
Yarrow (*Achillea millefolium*)

FLOWERS FOR ADULT BUTTERFLIES

Aster, left (especially *Aster* x *frikartii* 'Mönch')
Aubrieta
Buddleia (especially *B.* x *weyeriana* and *B.* x *weyeriana* 'Sungold')
Candytuft (*Iberis umbellata*)
Field scabious (*Knautia arvensis*)
Hemp agrimony (*Eupatorium cannabinum*)
Honesty (*Lunaria annua*)
Hyssop (*Hyssopus officinalis*)
Ivy (*Hedera helix*)
Lavender ('Munstead' is one of the best)
Marjoram (*Origanum*; wild forms are best)
Mint (*Mentha* spp., especially apple mint)
Showy stonecrop (*Sedum spectabile*)
Small scabious (*Scabiosa columbaria*)
Sweet rocket (*Hesperis matronalis*)
Sweet William (*Dianthus barbatus*)

Ponds for wildlife

A pond, even a tiny one, can be the heart of your wildlife oasis. Your pond will be used by a wide range of creatures for many and various purposes. Some will drink from it or hunt for food over it. Others will use it for cover to feed and breed in. Some will spend their whole lives in the pond, and others will use it for only part of their life cycle.

A pond is not the only worthwhile water supply in a garden. Even the smallest water container will act as an "outside aquarium" and be excellent for birds and amphibians. Birds need water for daily bathing as well as drinking. They will come to fresh, clean water in any shallow container; even an upside-down trash can lid can be pressed into service. Sink the container into the ground, or build a ramp of bricks up to one edge to make it accessible for thirsty animals as well.

If you have young children and an open pool is inappropriate, consider a bubble-fountain or a wall-mounted basin, or cover your pond with a safety grating of rigid mesh until they are older.

Ponds for wildlife

A pond is best sited in a sunny position, away from overhanging trees, with an area of rough grass or plants along at least one edge to act as a refuge and feeding ground for amphibians. A pond in shade will support some life, but there will be a greater diversity of species in full sun. If your pond is visible from the house, create an area of short grass on the side of the pond nearest the window so you can watch what is going on.

Creating a wildlife pond

The size of a pond depends obviously on the site available—but it should be at the very least a yard (meter) square. At least one side should gently slope to allow small creatures safe access. Most wildlife will inhabit areas of shallow water around the edges. There should also be a deeper area, at least 24 in. (60 cm) in the center, which will remain frost-free during winter and cool in summer. There are various materials available to line a pond—you can choose from concrete, bentonite clay, ready-made plastic molds, or a butyl sheet liner (see *The Garden Framework*, p. 129). A butyl liner is the most flexible, and probably the easiest to deal with when creating an irregularly shaped pond. Natural clay, available in a mat form, will last the longest. You need to allow plenty of overlap to anchor the liner securely around the edges—your supplier will be able to help with the size required if given the intended dimensions of the pond. The pond can be filled with rain- or tap water. If using tap water, wait at least 48 hours

NEW FRIENDS

Creatures that may visit or live in garden ponds:

Frogs (right)
Newts
Bats
Whirligig beetles
Pond skaters (center)
Water measurers
Water boatmen
Water snails
Diving beetles
Damselflies and dragonflies—
    some of them are inquisitive
    and will investigate people!
Swallows (far right)

for the chlorine to dissipate before introducing floating or oxygenating plants. Wildlife will move in rapidly of its own accord, and within a year your pond should have a full complement of creatures.

New ponds often suddenly turn an alarming vivid green, caused by a sudden surge in the number of small algae. The water clears eventually, but to hurry things along put some barley straw or lavender clippings in a fine-mesh plastic net bag and weight it so it just floats. Beneficial microorganisms rapidly colonize the straw or lavender and destroy the algae.

Planting the pond

A good assortment of plants will provide food and shelter for an extensive range of creatures. Plant a mixture of floating, oxygenating, and shallow-water species. Algae growth is encouraged by sunlight, so, to keep the water clear, aim to keep one-half to

DIGGING AND LINING A POND

Early spring is the best time to create a new pond. This gives plants and wildlife time to settle in before the following winter.

• Dig the hole slightly larger than you want the pond to be to allow for any protective underlay. At least one side should slope gently (15–30°), and there should be an area 24 in. (60 cm) deep, depending on the severity of your winters, which will remain frost-free. A shelf at the edge for plants in pots is useful.

• Remove all sharp stones, roots, and anything else that might puncture the lining. Firm the sides and edges and make sure that the edges are all level. For additional protection gently smooth a 4-in. (10-cm) layer of builder's sand all around the inside of the hole. Lay a protective underlay, such as old carpet, cardboard, or a custom-made pond underlay.

• With assistance (a butyl liner is heavy), lay the liner over the hole, with a 12-in. (30-cm) overlap around the edges. Let it dip halfway into the hole, and weigh down the edges with heavy stones. Put some soil in the middle if you are going to plant directly in the soil.

• Fill the pond. The weight of water will mold the liner to the shape of the pond. Bury the edges of the liner under grass or stones to protect it from the light.

PLANTS FOR PONDS

Oxygenating/submerged	Floating plants	For shallow water
Anacharis (*Egeria densa*) Water milfoil (*Myriophyllum*) Water starworts (*Callitriche*) Wild celery (*Vallisnera americana*)	Waterlilies (*Nymphea*) for a small pond need to be carefully selected because the native species are too vigorous. Try the smaller cultivars, such as 'Chromatella' and 'Hermine', or *N. pygmaea* and *N. tetragona*	Aquatic canna (*Canna*) Arrowhead (*Sagittaria sagittifolia*) Brooklime (*Veronica beccabunga*) Flowering rush (*Butomus umbellatus*) Irises (*Iris*) Sweet flag (*Acorus calamus*) Taro (*Colocasia*) Water plantain (*Alisma*)

two-thirds of the surface covered with plant growth. Use species as native to your area as possible. Avoid planting some of the more invasive alien species—often on sale in garden centers—especially if there is any chance that they may be inadvertently released into the wild. Particular pond thugs to resist include Hydrilla (*Hydrilla verticillata*), water hyacinth (*Eichornia crassipes*), water lettuce (*Pistia stratiotes*), and Eurasian water milfoil (*Myriophyllum spicatum*). When planting in baskets, use a special, low-nutrient aquatic medium or garden subsoil.

Pond maintenance

Once a pond is established, it may not need much maintenance from the wildlife's point of view. Some insects prefer overgrown, muddy ponds, and frogs certainly don't mind weedy water. You may prefer a slightly more "managed" pond, but try not to disturb it unless really necessary.

During the summer, remove excess blanket weed; twist it around a stick or rake it out. Free-floating plants such as duckweed can be lifted out with a sieve. Leave any debris or plant matter on the pond side overnight to allow creatures to escape back into the pond, then add it to your compost pile.

Vigorous and invasive pond plants can be cut back or removed gradually; reduce the volume of submerged plant foliage, such as pond weed, by one-third. Late summer is the best time, before creatures hibernate. Avoid disturbing a pond early in the year or in very cold weather. Other pond plants can be divided every 2 or 3 years if necessary.

Cover the pond with netting for a few weeks in autumn if it collects large quantities of falling leaves, or remove the leaves by hand. Also remove dead and decaying foliage, or this will add nutrients to the water, encouraging algae growth. Always leave some debris at the bottom of the pond, however.

POND ALLIES

1 Tadpoles
Migrating frogs will tend to colonize a suitable pond within a year or two. If none appears, the pond is either unsuitable or cut off from their migration. If the latter, introduce some frog spawn taken from a healthy garden pond within, if possible, 0.5 mile (1 km) of yours. Do not take it from the wild.

2 Floating leaves
Floating leaf cover helps to prevent a pond from clogging up with algae growth. Aim for a 50–60% cover of the surface of the pond.

3 Plants with submerged and semisubmerged stems and leaves
These plants (here, for instance, golden club, *Orontium aquaticum*) provide food and shelter for water-dwelling creatures and make egg-laying sites for newts.

4 Ramshorn snails
These snails are scavengers, helping to keep pond water clean by feeding on algae and plant debris.

The rest of the garden

Amphibians spend more time on land than in the water, so if you want these creatures to visit be sure to provide some safe cover for them. Undisturbed areas, such as long grass, thick mulches, and piles of stones or logs, provide safe havens and hibernating sites for frogs, toads, and newts. At least part of the pond edge should consist of plants to provide good cover. You may also like some mown grass to allow a good view of the pond. To avoid harming emerging frogs, mow this grass regularly, starting in midspring before young creatures start to leave the pond. Always check for froglets after heavy rain.

Algae blooms

One of the most common pond problems is an algae "bloom"—the water turning the color of pea soup, or silting up with clumps of blanket weed. This is usually a symptom of warm, nutrient-rich water. The "pea soup" is generally a short-lived phenomenon, appearing in spring as the weather warms up, then vanishing once the oxygenating plants begin their spring growth. Blanket weed can be more persistent; it can be physically removed by winding it around a stick or raking it out. Barley straw or lavender clippings can also be used (see p. 199), and the following measures will help to avoid it:

• Have submerged oxygenating plants occupying around 25–33% of the volume of water.

• Let floating plant foliage cover at least one-half and no more than two-thirds of the surface to shade the water.

• If it is necessary to add to the water level, use rainwater rather than mineral-rich tap water.

• Use aquatic medium rather than the usual garden growing media when planting aquatics in pots, or a very low-nutrient, homemade potting mix.

• Clear the pond annually, if necessary.

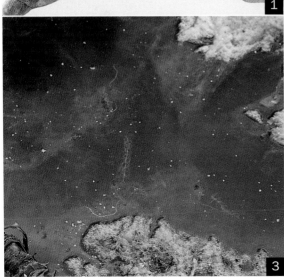

THE UNWANTED LIST

1 Great pond snail
While this snail (*Lymnaea stagnalis*) will eat algae and organic debris, it can also damage plants. If there are too many in your pond, float fresh lettuce leaves on the surface in the early evening. Remove, with attached feeding snails, in the morning.

2 Invasive plants
Avoid planting invasive and alien plant species (such as this parrot's feather). Sadly, you may find that some pond and garden centers sell inappropriate species, so check before you buy.

3 Algae
Blanket weed (shown) and other algae thrive in light conditions in nutrient-rich water. An algae "bloom" can turn a pond to green soup overnight.

4 Fish
Don't introduce fish to a wildlife pond—they will upset the natural ecosystem. Some, such as this stickleback, may arrive as eggs on birds' feet. They should survive only in numbers that the pond can sustain.

Container gardening

CONTAINER-GROWN PLANTS CAN GIVE THE GARDEN A
WELCOME INJECTION OF COLOR, FRAGRANCE, AND FOCUS

GROWING PLANTS IN CONTAINERS allows you to create a garden within a garden, or even where there is no soil at all. If you simply want to maximize your growing space, then the plainest plastic tubs will do. But with a wider choice of pots, window boxes, urns, troughs, and other improvised containers, moods and styles can be created—perhaps a lush tropical theme, an exotic Eastern look, or even the glory of an old-fashioned cottage garden. By using containers you can let your imagination run wild, following fashion or your latest enthusiasm, safe in the knowledge that you can change it all next year with little effort.

Deciding what to grow

Use containers to grow almost any type of plant—ornamental or edible, annual or perennial, dwarf or climbing. A shrub or climber in a large pot (see p. 208) can act as an attractive focal point, while a colorful assortment of pots and planters will revitalize a backyard or liven up a dull corner where nothing much will grow. You could also grow a pot full of mixed lettuce on your patio (see p. 210), or provide a tumbling riot of fragrance and color throughout the summer from a hanging basket or a wall-mounted pot (see p. 215). You can even create your own miniature wildlife garden in a window box. The potting mix can also be tailored to grow plants that would not thrive in your garden's soil. The main rule of container gardening is to select the most appropriate plants for the conditions where the container will be.

Containers and the organic approach

One of the prime tenets of organic gardening is to create a healthy, fertile soil that provides plants with all they need—so growing plants in the restricted environment of a container cannot be considered truly organic. Container-grown tomatoes could not, for example, truly be considered an organic crop. But containers do have a valuable role in our gardens—especially in towns and cities—and they can certainly approximate organic growing, with the appropriate choice of potting mix and without the use of synthetic fertilizers and pesticides.

**Creative use of space
(facing page)**
Evergreens with strong shapes are good value in small spaces, and sticking to one choice of material for the pots prevents a cluttered look. A sheltered corner or patio may allow you to grow more tender plants such as the oleander and citrus here; they will appreciate the extra heat stored and reflected by the stone patio.

Urban oases
Devoted container gardeners are liable to let their enthusiasm spread to cover the tops of walls, posts, windowsills, and even garden benches with a growing collection of plants. Introducing such variety into urban environments, especially with flowering plants, softens the hard landscape and turns the smallest paved courtyard, balcony, or even rooftop into a welcome refuge for wildlife.

Container considerations

Plants will grow in anything, from terra-cotta pots to an old bucket. A container can be new, reused, or recycled, as long as it has drainage holes and is sturdy enough to be filled with potting soil. Where freezing is likely, containers should also be frostproof.

Choose the container to suit the site or design style you have in mind. A half-barrel or stone urn will give a very different feel than floral buckets or a brightly painted wooden box. You don't have to spend a lot to be stylish. Simple containers such as the tubs below can be used for a formal effect if planted identically and arranged with care.

Drainage

All containers must have drainage holes in the base. To allow good drainage, fill the bottom of the container with coarse material before adding the growing mixture. To add weight, use large (1¼-in./ 3-cm) gravel. Broken-up styrofoam packaging is a lightweight alternative and also a good way of recycling material. Aim for a layer 1½ in. (4 cm) deep for most containers. If the pot is made of stone or terra-cotta and freezing is likely, a drainage layer one-fifth of the total depth of the pot will give it some protection. Standing the pot on bricks or ready-made "feet" also improves drainage, if necessary.

Container sizes

The size you choose depends on what plants you intend to grow. For ease of management—both feeding and watering—the larger the container the better; do not, however, put a small, slow-growing plant straight into a too-large pot. A large pot containing several plants is easier to care for than

MATERIALS AND FINISHES

Wood and wicker
Rough-sawn wood gives a rustic look and may deter slugs. Oak and cedar do not need a preservative. Planed wood can be neatly painted for window boxes, for example. Wickerwork baskets can be lined with plastic.

Stone and terra-cotta
Sales and salvage yards are good sources for old stone troughs, sinks, and clay pots. "Age" new terra-cotta by painting with yogurt and keeping the pot in a damp, shady spot. Paint manufactured pots with tile or blackboard paint. Glazed pots need less watering (see p. 66) and look good with bamboos and Japanese maples for an Eastern theme.

Plastic
Good-quality plastic pots can be long-lasting and are light enough to move around easily. They can be reused and painted.

Metal
Use galvanized buckets for a modern look—or recycle large tin cans for a cheerful display.

many individual pots. Any container should be at least 6–8 in. (15–20 cm) deep; most plants like a deeper pot. Remember that containers that taper in toward the top can make planting difficult. If the container needs to be moved from time to time, for example under cover in winter, remember that you may have to lift it. For large pots, improvise a cart: a strong board fitted with four wheels.

Growing media

Use an organic, multipurpose, or potting soil—homemade or purchased—to fill pots and other containers. Do not skimp on quality; your plants will be growing in a restricted environment and need the best. The growing medium should suit the plants you are growing. Plants that thrive in dry situations will need a quick-draining, poorer mix than a pot full of leafy vegetables. A tub of annuals can get by with a general multipurpose mix, while a fruit tree, which will be in the container for many years, will need a richer mix, preferably one based on loam or soil. These have the advantage of being heavier, and the additional weight can keep pots of tall plants from blowing over. A soilless mix, which is lighter, is useful for hanging baskets, on balconies, and where containers need to be moved around. Recipes for a range of homemade potting mixes can be found on pp. 116–117.

Feeding and watering

Feed plants in tubs, pots, and other containers with the same range of composted organic materials and organic fertilizers that are used in the ground (see *Soil and Soil Care*, pp. 33–61). Apply these as a topdressing in the container. In addition, liquid fertilizers (see p. 206), which supply nutrients in a more readily available form, can be watered on or applied as a foliar spray. How much and how often container plants need to be fed will depend on the richness of the growing medium used, the volume of the container, and the plants being grown. Some guidelines are given throughout this chapter.

How often a container plant needs watering also depends upon the plant type, its size in relation to the container, the type of container (terra-cotta dries out more quickly than plastic), the site (a windy site increases the demand for water), the weather, and the season. Never let containers dry out—plants are

much more prone to problems if they are underwatered, and dry soil is difficult to rewet. A regular water supply is particularly important for fruits and vegetables. Most container plants need daily watering during summer, even after rain, and very little in winter. Always water the soil, not the foliage. (See also *Water and Watering*, p. 66.)

Pests and diseases

As with all organic gardening, keeping plants healthy is the best defense against pests and diseases. Potbound plants in overcrowded pots with an erratic supply of water will be more prone to pests such as red spider mite and aphids. Pots and tubs are often in hot, dry locations, where plants may suffer from pests that would not be found in the open ground.

By using clean soil, you can avoid many soil-borne pests and diseases, but root-eating creatures may still move into a pot, where their effects can be devastating. Vine weevil grubs can easily kill plants in containers and baskets; use a biological control agent (see p. 100). Grow flowers to attract predators to keep other pests in check (see p. 96), and deal with any problem as it arises; check plants regularly and pick off pests and diseased shoots or leaves as you notice them. Remove sickly and badly infested plants.

Winter protection

Move tender plants indoors over winter if necessary, or cover plants with fabric. Wrap up pots so that neither the pot nor the plant roots freeze.

Pest control
Slugs and snails may be less of a problem in containers than in the open ground; however, if they make the climb, there will be nothing to distract them from the prized plant within. Try deterring them with a barrier around the pot: a strip of grease, nondrying glue, or copper, as shown here.

HOMEMADE MOCK STONE PLANTER

1 Select two strong cardboard boxes, one smaller than the other by 2 in. (5 cm) on all sides.
2 Mix 3 parts sand with 1 part each coarse coir and cement. Mix in water to form a stiff mortar.
3 Cover the bottom of the larger box with 2 in. (5 cm) of the mortar, tamp it down to remove air bubbles, and insert 5 corks to form drainage holes.
4 Center the smaller box within the larger one.
5 Fill the space between the boxes with mortar to a depth of about 6 in. (15 cm). Tamp the mortar down with care.
6 Leave for a week to harden.
7 Remove the boxes and the corks. Brush with a wire brush.
8 Brush with yogurt or liquid manure. Green algae will grow.

Organic liquid fertilizers

Liquid fertilizers provide plants with nutrients in a readily available form. Although this goes against the organic principle of feeding the soil, not the plant, there are times when a liquid fertilizer is necessary in an organic garden. Suitable fertilizers are made from manure, plant and animal wastes, and rock minerals. These are basically the same materials that are used for feeding the soil but in a different form, and they are subject to the same cautions regarding their source.

Suitable organic liquid fertilizers can be bought from most good garden centers or from specialty suppliers, or they can be homemade. The latter are almost as easy to make since their principal ingredients, comfrey and nettles, are easy to grow.

GROWING COMFREY IN THE GARDEN

Comfrey is a fast-growing hardy perennial, growing up to 3 ft. (1 m) tall. The cultivar 'Bocking 14' was selected by Lawrence D. Hills, the founder of H.D.R.A. and one of the pioneers of organic gardening. 'Bocking 14' is high-yielding and has a particularly high potash content. It does not set seed, nor does it have a creeping root—features of other species of comfrey that enable them to spread rapidly and become invasive.

Plant 'Bocking 14' in spring and summer as root cuttings or pot-grown cuttings. Once established, the leaves can be cut three or four times a year. The last cut should be in early autumn at the latest. Feed the plants every year or two with a high-fertility soil improver or high-nitrogen fertilizer. Grass clippings applied in spring, with shredded prunings added in the autumn, can be an effective feeding schedule.

When to use liquid fertilizer

Container plants, where the volume of soil is limited, are the main candidates for liquid feeding. Young plants being raised in cell packs may also need feeding if planting out is delayed. Liquid fertilizers should be used in the garden only as a short-term solution: where soil is poor, or when soil conditions or root damage prevent a plant from absorbing enough nutrients. Then the fertilizer is best applied as a foliar spray to the leaves. Never use organic liquid fertilizers as an alternative to good soil care.

Feeding plants in pots

How much and how often you need to apply a liquid fertilizer will depend of the type of plant, its size in relation to the volume of the container, how vigorously it is growing, how big you want it to grow, and the quality of the growing medium. Observation, with experience, is the key. A young tomato plant newly transplanted into its own pot, for example, should not be fed, whereas a tomato plant covered in fruit may need feeding three times a week. A slow-growing shrub will not require feeding, while a tub full of annuals may benefit from a weekly dose.

Remember that you can overdo it. It is counter-productive to encourage excess leafy growth in a tomato plant or a pot of annual flowers, for example; you will only delay the production of fruit or flowers. And slow growth does not necessarily mean a shortage of food. Cold weather, root damage, or overwatering can also slow growth, especially in young plants. In these cases, liquid feeding could simply make things worse.

Purchased liquid fertilizers

When buying a liquid fertilizer, check the ingredients to ensure that nonorganic ingredients have not been added. Choose one with an organic symbol of approval if available. Purchased liquid fertilizers may contain a mixture of ingredients to give a balanced product—either for general use, or with a high potash content for feeding tomatoes and other fruiting plants. Ingredients used to produce commercial organic liquid feeds are:

• **Liquid manures** Usually cow, poultry, or sheep

manure (not from intensive systems).

• **Fish emulsion** A by-product of the fishing industry, not from fish caught specifically for this purpose.

• **Rock phosphate** Pulverized so that it stays in suspension.

• **Plant extracts** For example, comfrey leaf extracts and seaweed (see also below).

Seaweed extract

Seaweed extract is a plant growth stimulant similar to liquid fertilizer; it contains little in the way of major plant foods. What it does contain is a wide range of trace elements, plus ingredients such as plant hormones and specific carbohydrates that can stimulate plant growth.

Seaweed extract can be used in various ways, at various stages of plant growth to produce a range of effects. It seems to work best if applied to the soil or roots early on in the life of the plant, and as a foliar spray later on. To use seaweed extract, soak seeds in seaweed extract for a few hours prior to sowing to increase the rate of seedling emergence, or apply extract to the soil around young plants to increase their root growth (two applications at 4-week intervals); or apply to the soil or foliage of young plants to "green up" leaves, which increases the chlorophyll content. Seaweed extract can also be applied to the soil to reduce the possibility of some root diseases, and as a foliar spray to discourage sap-feeding insects and possibly increase resistance to frost.

Homemade liquid fertilizers

Liquid fertilizers from comfrey or nettle leaves are easy to make but can have a strong smell.

Comfrey leaves are rich in plant foods. The leaves decay rapidly, releasing the nutrients they contain. They can also be used as a mulch or compost activator. Comfrey leaves tend to be slightly alkaline, so don't use this fertilizer on acid-loving plants. Comfrey liquid is high in potash and has reasonable levels of nitrogen and phosphate; it is good for fruiting plants, although its nitrogen levels may not be sufficient for a fully grown hanging basket.

Nettles make an all-purpose fertilizer that is a little low on phosphate but also supplies magnesium, sulfur, and iron. Young nettles cut in spring contain the highest levels of major nutrients.

RECIPES FOR LIQUID FERTILIZERS

Comfrey
• Steep 6 lb. 12 oz. (3 kg) comfrey leaves in 12 gal. (45 liters) of water.
• Cover with a lid.
• Use undiluted after 4 weeks.

Nettle
• Steep 2 lb. 4 oz. (1 kg) leaves in 2¼ gal. (10 liters) of water.
• Cover with a lid.
• Use after 2 weeks, diluting 1 part nettle liquid in 10 parts water.

Comfrey concentrate

Comfrey leaves can also be made into a concentrate. Pack cut leaves into a plastic container with a hole in the bottom (a water barrel, bucket, or drainpipe with an end cap are all good options) and cover with a lid. Place a collection vessel under the hole, and after 2 to 3 weeks a dark liquid will drip out. To use, dilute the concentrate in 10–20 parts water. For example, tomatoes in pots can be fed with concentrate diluted 1:15 with water three times a week once the fruits start to form. The concentrate can be stored for a few months in a cool, dry place.

Concentrate collector
Stuff a pipe with comfrey leaves and collect the concentrate as it drips out. For smaller quantities, use a plastic bottle inverted over a container.

COMFREY LEAF MOLD

Comfrey leaf mold can be used alone as a potting medium, or as an ingredient of a potting mix. Fill a plastic bucket or trash can with alternate 4-in. (10-cm) layers of damp, 2- to 3-year-old leaf mold (see p. 50) and chopped comfrey leaves. As the comfrey leaves decompose, the goodness they contain is soaked up by the leaf mold. When the comfrey leaves have disintegrated (usually after 2 to 5 months), the leaf mold is ready to use.

Ornamentals in containers

In addition to the usual annual bedding plants, shrubs, perennials, grasses, and even small trees can be grown in pots and planters, provided that you choose them carefully. Take a good look at the site where you will place your containers; plants will grow well as long as they are in the right place. Gloomy shade is not the right place for sun-loving geraniums, and ferns will turn brown and sad if they are scorched and dry. Most rock-garden plants, succulents such as sempervivums, and drought-tolerant shrubs such as lavender and rosemary will thrive in the hot, dry conditions of a sunny patio. Shade-loving shrubs that grow well in pots include mophead hydrangeas, *Mahonia* 'Charity', skimmias, and *Viburnum davidii*. Dwarf trees and shrubs are ideal, but others can do well even if they would naturally grow quite large. As the pot restricts the roots, the topgrowth will also be limited. There are many small conifers to choose from in greens, grays, and golds that are attractive year-round. Many are sold as rock-garden plants, but larger specimens also look good: Try *Chamaecyparis pisifera* 'Boulevard' or *Abies balsamea* 'Nana'.

The best perennials for containers are those with a long season of interest—bold foliage plants such as ferns and hostas, for example, or long-flowers such as the hardy geraniums. In a shady corner, elegant dicentras and astilbes are striking.

Container size

Large plants like climbers and small trees need plenty of space for their roots to develop; they will not thrive if you skimp on the pot size. The bigger the container, the more plants you can plant. A planter measuring 3 ft. x 12 in. x 12 in. (1 m x 30 cm x 30 cm), for example, will support three small shrubs (for example, small species of euonymus or spirea) and a couple of ivies. Underplant with bulbs for winter and spring interest; in summer, bedding plants can be tucked around the edges. By contrast, rock-garden plants, sedums, and sempervivums will all thrive with a smaller, shallower root run.

Growing media

Choose the medium to suit the needs of the plant. Many shrubs will do well in a nutrient-rich, soil-based medium. Add up to 20% extra grit for plants that need good drainage. Add sulfur to reduce the pH to below 6 for acid-loving plants. A soil-based or soilless multipurpose medium will suit most annuals, grasses, and bulbs. Use a mulch such as coarse bark or stone chips for a decorative finish that also helps to retain moisture.

Feeding and watering

In spring, repot shrubs or other perennials that you want to grow to a larger size. Use a pot 2–3 in. (5–7.5 cm) wider than the previous one, and fill the gap with fresh medium. Otherwise, topdress the

Clematis 'Arctic Queen'
Containers are not only for low-level patio groupings. Climbers such as this clematis can add a dramatic flourish of color and height to a corner or grouping.

existing pot annually in spring, adding a 1-in. (2.5-cm) layer of a nutrient-rich organic material such as garden compost. If you have used a decorative mulch, just push it to one side, add the organic material, then redistribute the mulch. If plants need extra nutrients during the growing season, a scattering of a general organic fertilizer will help, or feed regularly with a liquid fertilizer. Never let the plants dry out.

Climbers in pots

Climbers in containers can be tied to an existing wall, fence, or trellis, or they can be given their own independent supports in the pot. Use twiggy garden prunings replaced annually, for example, or a more permanent wire, cane, or trellis framework. A compact cultivar of clematis that can be cut down to the ground each winter will grow happily in a 14-in. (35-cm) diameter pot; try *Clematis florida* 'Flore Pleno' or 'Sieboldii', or *C.* 'Comtesse de Bouchaud'. Plant in a well-drained, soil-based potting medium with the crown 3 in. (7.5 cm) below the surface. Provide tall twigs for support. Pinch off new shoots to two leaves until flower buds appear to get a bushy plant covered in flowers. Other good choices for pots are scented climbers such as jasmine and honeysuckle, or annual climbers such as sweet peas and nasturtiums.

Grasses in pots

Some perennial grasses like hot, dry conditions and grow well in containers. Grow blue-gray *Festuca glauca* and *Koeleria glauca*, or bronze *Carex comans* in pots of their own, or as a contrast to flowering plants. The mosquito grass *Bouteloua gracilis*, with distinctive purple-brown flowers, makes a more unusual container specimen. Grasses are less demanding of nutrients than many other container plants.

Hardy annuals and biennials

Many hardy annuals will give only a short display; grown in pots, they can easily be replaced. They are among the best plants for attracting bees and beneficial insects into the garden. Try alyssum, *Convolvulus tricolor*, dwarf rudbeckias, calendulas, or even some of the modern dwarf sunflower cultivars. Biennials such as wallflowers, daisies, and forget-me-nots give valuable early flowers the following spring.

A pot full of bulbs

A selection of bulbs planted in a pot in early autumn can provide a succession of flowers from midwinter through late spring. Choose bulbs that flower at different times and that are planted at different depths. Plant at least two or three of each cultivar. A small, colorful summer-flowering shrub in the middle of the pot will continue the show.

Stunning displays
Exploit the flexibility and adaptability containers can provide. Grow a tree or shrub in a large container (above, far left) as a central feature in a garden without soil; plant a combination of annuals and bulbs (center) for an instantly eye-catching temporary display; or tailor your compost mix to include a greater range of plants, such as sempervivums (right), in containers.

Vegetables and herbs in containers

Almost any vegetable can be grown in a container. Zucchini, tomatoes, potatoes, and eggplants do well in large individual containers in an appropriate location. Lettuces, spring onions, chard, bush beans, beets, carrots, radishes, and oriental brassicas can be grown in a mixed pot (see facing page for some planting suggestions) or in greater quantities on their own. Avoid vegetables with deep roots such as parsnips; with a long, slow growing season such as cauliflower and Brussels sprouts; or with high demands for food and water, such as pumpkins.

Both useful and beautiful

Remember that vegetables can look good too, and an "edibles" container can look as striking as one filled with ornamentals. You might also like to add some herbs and edible flowers. Container growing is particularly useful where herbs do not like your soil conditions. If you garden in heavy clay, for example, a well-drained potting mix can allow you to grow herbs such as rosemary, sage, and thyme. In cool climates, pots of basil can be started in the greenhouse and moved outside to a warm, sunny spot when the weather improves.

Grow annual flowering plants such as calendula (also edible) or *Convolvulus tricolor* to attract predators to improve pest control, too.

Container size and soil mix

Vegetables have different growing requirements. A seedling lettuce crop (see p. 332) can be grown in medium that has already been used once, while heavy feeders need a stronger mix (see *Growing Media*, pp. 114–117). Generally, the larger the container the better because vegetables need a good supply of food and a consistent supply of water to thrive. Growing several plants in one large container may give better results than using individual pots, and the plants will be much easier to care for.

As containers come in all shapes and sizes, it is easier to describe them in terms of volume rather than dimensions (see below left for some examples). Measure the approximate volume of a container by filling it with medium from a premeasured bucket. In general, use a container that is at least 8 in. (20 cm) deep. Lettuce seedlings can go in shallower pots or trays as long as you keep them watered. Heavy feeders like tomatoes and zucchini need a container at least 10–12 in. (25–30 cm) deep. Carrots grow well in containers and are easily protected from carrot fly by draping row cover over the pot. Grow early, short-, or round-rooted varieties, such as 'Little Finger', 'Thumbelina', and 'Planet', in a container at least 6 in. (15 cm) deep. Pull the bigger carrots first, leaving the others to grow.

GROWING MEDIA REQUIREMENTS OF SOME VEGETABLES

Eggplant 2½ gal. (10 liters) per plant.
Bush beans 4 pints (2.5 liters) per plant.
Beet, kohlrabi Minimum depth of potting mix 8 in. (20 cm); plants 3–4 in. (7.5–10 cm) apart.
Leaf beet and chard 7 pints (4 liters) per plant.
Zucchini 6–9 gal. (30–40 liters) per plant.
Sweet peppers 1 gal. (5 liters) per plant.
Tomato 3¼ gal. (15 liters) per plant.

GROWING TIPS

• For a quick start, raise plants in cell packs rather than sowing directly into the pot.

• Never let pots dry out. Many vegetables are likely to bolt or split if the water supply is erratic.

• Line clay pots with plastic to cut down on water loss.

• Choose dwarf or miniature cultivars.

• Feed with a general or potash-rich liquid fertilizer (see p. 206) as appropriate. Seaweed extract will give a plants a boost.

• The *A–Z of Vegetable and Salad Crops*, pp. 337–366, gives the feeding requirements of individual crops. You can adapt this to container growing.

EDIBLE MIXTURES FOR POTS

The groupings listed here are each designed to be crowded into a deep, 16-in. (40-cm) pot. Even the flowers are edible!

Fitting everything in relies on regular attention, thinning out (and eating) excess plants as they grow, tying up and staking as required, and eating everything as young as possible.

Use a good-quality, rich potting soil, keep the pot well watered, and fertilize pots that include tomatoes once the first fruits have set.

Simply salads

1 x tomato 'Sweet 100' or other reliable tall (not bush) cultivar
12 x 'Sugar Lace' semileafless peas
4 x lettuce 'Red Sails' or similar looseleaf lettuce
4 x lettuce 'Oakleaf' or other compact looseleaf lettuce
4 x arugula
6 x compact, variegated nasturtium 'Alaska'

Pretty in purples

5 x purple-podded string bean 'Royalty'
5 x Chinese leaf celery
8 x baby beet 'Little Ball'
4 x chervil
1 x creeping golden thyme
3 x viola 'Johnny Jump Up'

Aztec delight

5 x mini sweet corn 'Dwarf Blue Jade'
6 x purple kohlrabi 'Purple Vienna'
3 x coriander (for leaf)
3 x parsley
3 x trailing tomato 'Basket King'
4 x summer savory

Edible delights

Tall, sun-seeking sweet corn allows plenty of room for smaller plants tucked in beneath it to grow and tumble over the rim of the pot.

Dessert apples
Choose a compact apple cultivar for successful container growing. With most apples and pears, you will need to grow two or more varieties to ensure successful pollination.

Fruit in pots

While most fruits can be grown in containers, they need regular attention if they are to flourish and will not appreciate being neglected during your summer vacation. The harvest from these plants will be less heavy than from plants in the ground, and their productive life span is considerably shorter.

Which fruits to grow

Figs, which produce successfully only when their roots are restricted, do well in containers. Apples, plums, pears, and cherries can make attractive, productive pot plants. The more tender fruits, such as apricots, nectarines, and citrus, benefit from the mobility of a pot, which can be moved into the protection of a greenhouse in winter and put outside in suitable summer conditions. Check on the pollination requirements of each fruit; if it is not self-pollinating, you may need to grow more than one plant to ensure production. There is no need to grow trees on dwarfing rootstocks; the restriction of the pot will limit size. In fact, a more vigorous stock can be the better choice because it will grow a more resilient tree. Dwarf peaches and nectarines, which make ideal patio fruits, are also available.

> ### GROWING TIPS
> • Never let the growing medium dry out.
> • Give fruit in pots a sunny, sheltered spot.
> • Rotate the pot every week or two if positioned next to a wall.
> • Thin the fruit if necessary as the plant will be able to support only a relatively small crop.

Of the soft fruit, strawberries are most suited to containers. Blueberries also do well and can be given the acid soil they need wherever you are. Gooseberries and currants trained as standards look attractive in pots and are convenient to pick. A grapevine will also make a standard (see p. 263) for a small crop of fruit. Choose autumn-fruiting raspberries if you want to grow them, as they grow on fresh new growth, but they may have to be replaced every year. Blackberries and other hybrid berries are just too vigorous for containers.

Pots and composts

Plant fruit as you would any other potted plant, into a container only 2–3 in. (5–8 cm) larger than

FRUIT TREES AND BUSHES FOR POTS

Fruit	Container growing requirements
Apple	Choose compact cultivars on rootstocks M26 or MM106; prune as a pyramid or bush.
Pear	Compact cultivars on Quince A or C rootstock; prune as a pyramid or bush.
Cherry	Self-pollinating sweet cherry cultivars on Colt rootstock; train as a pyramid.
Plum	Self-pollinating dessert cultivars on Pixy or St. Julien A rootstocks; train as a pyramid.
Peach and nectarine	Naturally dwarf "patio" cultivars or traditional cultivars on St. Julien A rootstock; train as a pyramid or bush.
Fig	Needs a 15-in. (38-cm) pot; prune to a multistemmed, shrubby habit, removing older wood to encourage young growth.
Blueberry	Needs a well-drained compost with a low pH of 4–5.5.
Currants and gooseberry	Look good trained as standards.
Grapevine	Train as a standard; replace every 3 years.
Strawberries	Use a 6-in. (15-cm) pot for each plant, or several plants in a larger pot; plant in late summer; keep outside over winter; produce for 1 year only. Plants can then be planted out into open ground if available.

the existing rootball. Increase the size of the container, if necessary, at the next repotting. A container measuring 18 in. (45 cm) in diameter and 15–18 in. (38–45 cm) deep is a reasonable maximum pot size for most fruits. Strawberries can thrive in much smaller pots. Grow several plants in a larger pot, a "strawberry tower" with planting pockets on the sides, or even in a window box.

Use a nutrient-rich, soil-based medium. Feed with high-potash liquid fertilizer when the fruits start to swell. Give the plants a nitrogen-rich fertilizer in late summer. Topdress every spring, removing the top 1–2 in. (2.5–5 cm) of medium and replacing it with

garden compost. Repot every alternate winter: Remove the plant from its pot and gently tease away as much old potting mix as you can. Cut away thick woody roots, taking care not to damage the fibrous roots, and repot into fresh compost.

This general schedule, combined with regular watering (which may mean twice a day at times) and prompt attention to problems, should ensure that fruits grow well. However, because organic methods concentrate on growing in open ground, there is relatively little experience to draw on of managing container fruit organically; you may find that with experimentation you can get better results.

CITRUS FRUITS IN CONTAINERS

With their glossy foliage and bright fruits, citrus can make attractive patio plants. Growing them in containers means that they can be given the right conditions in both summer and winter.

• Use a nutrient-rich, soil-based medium, and add 20% horticultural sand to improve drainage.

• In summer, place the pots outside in a warm, sheltered area. Water them freely, but make sure the pots drain well. Liquid-feed the plants regularly, using a high-nitrogen organic fertilizer from spring to midsummer, and then a general fertilizer until autumn (see also p. 206).

• In winter, bring the pots into a greenhouse or sunroom—the minimum temperature needed varies with the type of citrus you have, but is likely to be at least 45°F (7°C) at night, and slightly higher during the day. Water less frequently, allowing the medium to partially dry out between waterings.

• Topdress established plants with fresh medium in spring.

PLANTS FOR HANGING BASKETS

Trailing foliage plants

Helichrysum petiolare
Plectranthus australis
Plectranthus amboinicus
Various ivies (*Hedera*)
All the above are easy to grow
from cuttings (see p. 106).

Flowering plants

Convolvulus major T
Convolvulus minor U
Black-eyed Susan vine
  (*Thunbergia alata*) T
Fuchsias T/U
Dianthus chinensis U
Begonias T/U
Geraniums T/U
Petunias T/U
Impatiens walleriana U
Erigeron 'Profusion' T
Trailing lobelias T
Sanvitalia procumbens T
Scaevola aemula T

T Trailing
U Upright

Plants for winter baskets

A winter-flowering hanging
basket can be planted in
early autumn once the summer-
flowering plants have passed
their prime. A dwarf conifer
surrounded by dwarf spring
bulbs and tulips looks good.
Plant the conifer in spring to
make way for summer plants.
Other good winter choices are:

Variegated periwinkle (*Vinca
  major* 'Variegata')
Ivies (*Hedera*)
Small shrubby plants such
as *Euonymus fortunei* and
x *Chamaeycyparis pisifera*
Winter-flowering heathers

Variegated varieties, where
available, will give a brighter
show in low winter light.

Hanging baskets

Hanging baskets are an excellent way of decorating a wall or post, adding color and interest. They can also increase the growing space in a greenhouse. Ornamentals, herbs, and even tomatoes can all be grown successfully in baskets.

Go for the largest basket you can manage; buy a hanger that will hold its weight and attach it securely. A 16-in. (40-cm) basket can be awkward to handle, but is easy to care for. A 14-in. (35-cm) basket will do for general use, but a 12-in. (30-cm) basket is really too small. An open wire framework increases the planting area, which ultimately is more attractive. It needs to be lined, however, and will dry out more quickly than a solid basket.

Liners and growing media

Avoid sphagnum moss, the traditional liner, as its harvesting can cause environmental damage. Liners made from alternative, often recycled, materials are available, or you can make your own. An old sweater can be cut to fit a basket, or you can use hay twisted into ropes. Hay does tend to grow some interesting surprises during the summer; unwanted additions can be snipped off with scissors.

"Mock moss," made from wool or coir and often dyed green, is the closest alternative to real moss. It is available loose or in preformed sheets. Winter baskets can also be lined with conifer cuttings 6–8 in. (15–20 cm) long, along with a little yarn inside to fill any gaps.

A soilless medium is best because it is lighter. Improve water retention by adding an organic moisture retainer based on coarse seaweed meal. Use worm compost in the mix (up to 25% volume) to increase the level of fertility and improve the water-holding capacity.

Basket plants

Baskets look their best with a combination of trailing and upright plants, as well as plants with a long flowering season. Choose a selection of plants to suit the season and location of the hanging basket. Half-hardy plants, both foliage and flowering, are usually used in summer baskets. Trailing plants should be planted around the rim and through the mesh of wire baskets. Do not skimp on numbers if you want a really good display. With ornamentals, aim for a plant every 2–4 in. (5–10 cm) in all directions.

Caring for baskets

Water baskets daily, even in wet weather. Twice a day may be necessary in hot or dry, windy weather. Once a basket has dried out, it is very difficult to rewet. Take the opportunity when watering to look for pests and diseases, and snip off any infested foliage. If a whole plant is unhealthy, remove it and replace it with another plant. Regular deadheading helps to prolong the life of a basket display.

A weekly feeding with a high-potash organic liquid fertilizer (see p. 206) is necessary for tomatoes and flowering plants. For baskets of herbs use an all-purpose liquid fertilizer at 2-week intervals. Seaweed extract added to the feed can be beneficial.

BASKET TIPS

• Raise basket plants in root trainers (see p. 112), as the resulting root ball is an ideal size to pass through the liner into the medium.
• In cool climates, hang a newly planted basket in a greenhouse or a sheltered spot for a few weeks first to give it a good start.
• Wrap yarn or moss around the rim of a wire basket to prevent it cutting through stems.
• Avoid windy sites, such as the corner of a building; the basket will dry out more quickly.
• To prevent a basket from swinging in the wind, tie the back of it to the bracket behind.

Improvised linings
Conifer clippings make one of the cheapest linings for hanging baskets, as do discarded wool sweaters.

Gardening under cover

GREENHOUSES, SPACIOUS HOOP HOUSES, FRAMES, AND
CLOCHES—ALL SHELTERS EXPAND YOUR GROWING HORIZONS

Full house (facing page)
A modest greenhouse can provide the inspiration you need to raise your own plants—organically, of course.

Collectable cloches (below)
These beautiful, hand-blown glass cloches now have antique value, but in the organic garden are put to good use rather than gathering dust on a shelf. Our gardening forefathers expected tools and equipment to last a lifetime, and took care of them accordingly.

WALK INTO A GREENHOUSE or hoop house (polyethylene tunnel) and feel the atmosphere change—savor the different smells and marvel at the luxuriant growth. In here you can enjoy your organic garden whatever the weather. There may be new and interesting crops to care for, tender plants safe from frost, and seedlings destined for both the flower and food garden germinating weeks early.

Greenhouses and hoop houses trap the sun's energy, raising the temperature and creating an atmosphere where plants thrive. This chapter covers the selection and use of unheated structures that, with the addition of a heated bench and some winter insulation where necessary, can be used year-round with minimal energy consumption.

Protection from the elements can also be provided on a smaller scale with coldframes, cloches, and crop covers. A coldframe is a useful adjunct to a greenhouse as a halfway house for hardening off tender plants and seedlings. It can also stand alone as a place to grow tender crops such as melons in summer and lettuces in winter. A frame can also be used to provide unheated winter protection against the rain for rock-garden plants, cuttings, and autumn-sown seeds.

Cloches are movable structures, also valuable for use in hardening off and for growing tender crops that benefit from extra warmth early and late in the season. Cloches can also be used to warm up the soil to give direct-sown crops a good start, or to bring on an early strawberry crop. Although cloches are primarily employed in fruit and vegetable growing, they can also be a useful form of protection for ornamentals.

Crop covers are the simplest form of protection of all—sheets of lightweight material that are laid directly over plants to protect against adverse weather conditions and pests.

This chapter describes the range of structures and materials—from greenhouses to row covers, that are available, and how to get the best from them.

ADVANTAGES OF A COVERED SPACE
- Raise plants to flower or grow elsewhere.
- Save money on plants, especially bedding.
- Keep lettuces growing all year and produce other out-of-season crops.
- Grow fruit and vegetables that need a good, long season to succeed outdoors.
- Grow exotic and tender fruit, vegetables, and flowers that would not survive outside.
- Protect plants through adverse weather.
- Provide high-quality, organically grown plants for the house.

Lean-to greenhouse
Plants in a lean-to structure can benefit from the heat absorbed by a wall during the day, then released at night when temperatures fall.

Greenhouses and hoop houses

The biggest difference between a greenhouse and a hoop house is cost. Where limited space means only a small structure is possible, a greenhouse is the best choice. It will be more pleasing to look at, needs less maintenance, gives the best light transmission, and at this size the cost differential is less. With larger structures over 200 sq. ft. (20 sq. m), a hoop house is the best choice for cost-effective food production.

Glass is transparent, admits more light than plastic, warms the house more quickly, and retains heat longer. Plants, particularly those with a high light requirement such as tomatoes, grow better under glass than under plastic. Glass lasts indefinitely, while plastic becomes brittle and breaks down with age.

What size greenhouse?

Whatever the size of your greenhouse, there will be times when it is not large enough. A popular size is 6 ft. (1.8 m) wide and 8 ft. (2.4 m) long. A path 2 ft. (60 cm) wide down the middle allows 2 ft. (60 cm) on each side for the plants. A better arrangement is a greenhouse that is 8 ft. (2.4 m) wide and 6 ft. (1.8 m) long. This arrangement allows 3 ft. (90 cm) on either side of a shorter path, giving some additional plant space.

Where space is limited, a lean-to greenhouse may be an option. The problem of lack of light from one side can be partially alleviated by painting the wall inside the greenhouse white. A sunny wall is best for a general-purpose greenhouse. A lean-to greenhouse on a wall that does not get any direct sun is good for cuttings and for growing ferns and plants whose natural habitat is the forest floor.

Materials for greenhouse frames

The most commonly used materials are aluminum and wood. Aluminum is light and strong and needs little maintenance. Aluminum greenhouses vary a good deal in quality. Glazing bars consist of T-sections in the poorer quality ones; H-sections make for a sturdier, better-quality structure. On a windy site, the latter is advisable.

Wooden greenhouses may be manufactured from various types of wood. Cedar is very durable and does not require toxic wood preservatives. It is a good choice if you can be sure that it comes from a sustainable, managed source. Wood is a better insulator than aluminum, but the thicker glazing bars required block more light.

Greenhouse glazing

Glass is the most common glazing material, toughened for safety if necessary. An alternative is polycarbonate plastic—a twin-walled, lightweight, tough material that provides good insulation. On the down side, however, it is not "see-through" and allows only 85% light transmission, as opposed to 97% for glass. Adequate vents for good air circulation and temperature control are vital (see facing page). If you spend the day away from home, an automatic vent opening system could be a good investment. Even in spring, unexpected sun can cause a rapid temperature rise if vents are closed, and plants can suffer.

Choosing a hoop house

A hoop house consists of a framework of galvanized steel hoops. One that is short and wide is preferable to a long, narrow tunnel covering the same area, as ventilation is better with this configuration. Hoop houses have a much moister atmosphere than greenhouses, so good ventilation is vital. Install large

Side issue
Hoop houses may have vertical or sloping sides. If a house is less than 22 ft. (7 m) wide, choose a model with vertical sides so that every bit of space can be used.

doors (or double doors) at each end for maximum air flow. Sides that roll up to reveal several feet of mesh netting are another possibility.

What type of cover?

A hoop house is covered with a single plastic sheet, which is stretched over the hoops. Covers can vary in thickness, life span, light transmission, and cost. Some sheets are treated on one side to prevent drips and aid insulation. The life span of a cover varies from 3 to 7 years depending on the quality. It can be increased by a year or so by sticking anti-hotspot tape to the hoops before assembly.

Other plastic-covered structures

A solar tunnel has a P.V.C. cover, reinforced with fabric and assembled in sections. It is easier to cover, and the green color gives a more pleasant appearance. If you prefer a more traditional-looking greenhouse structure without the permanence or expense of a glass-glazed structure, you can also find many small hobby greenhouses with single-, double-, or triple-wall, polycarbonate glazing available from garden supply catalogs. Some suppliers also offer combination garden sheds/greenhouses, which act like large coldframes.

GREENHOUSE VENTILATION

Ventilation is essential for both temperature and disease control. Unlike ventilation, which can be controlled, drafts are bad for plants and should be eliminated, especially at the base and eaves. Ideally, the area of the roof vents should equal one-fifth of the floor area, but few greenhouses have this amount. Additional vents are sometimes available as an optional extra and are well worth the extra investment. A louver vent (left), placed opposite the door and near the floor, is more effective than additional roof vents because it acts as an air intake, replacing the warmed air that leaves through the roof vents.

Lime wash can be painted on glass to provide shading in the heat of summer.

A sliding door is preferable to a hinged one as it does not catch the wind and can be used as a variable vent.

Equipping greenhouses and hoop houses

The range of uses—and seasons of use—of a greenhouse or hoop house can be greatly extended by adding a few extras. Good staging (benching), a waterproof power supply (installed by a qualified electrician), a heated bench or propagator, and gutters that will direct water from the roof into a water barrel will all prove invaluable.

This chapter assumes that no heating is provided under cover other than that supplied by a heated bench or propagator, with added insulation for winter. This is the most energy-efficient way of running most greenhouses. Additional heating can be added if required.

Staging

If most efficient use is to be made of a greenhouse or hoop house, some form of staging will be needed. Slatted staging allows good air flow, which helps to control fungal disease, but it is cold in winter. A good compromise is to have slatted staging for summer use, covering it in winter with styrofoam slabs, protected by a plastic sheet. Cavity wall insulating slabs from a home improvement center are ideal for this purpose.

Plants can be protected from several degrees of frost by standing them on styrofoam and covering them with one or two layers of row cover.

Narrow shelves above staging provide additional storage for pots and trays. They are particularly useful for young plants such as tomatoes, which require a lot of light. Wide shelves should not be installed as they block light from the plants below. Stand plants on higher shelves on trays so water does not drip on plants below.

Heated bench

A heated bench is an economical and energy-efficient way of providing heat. The gentle bottom heat it provides will speed the germination of seeds early in the season, give a boost in cold weather to plants in containers, and provide protection against light frost. To make a heated bench, bury soil-warming cables in a 4-in. (10-cm) bed of moist sand. A strong bench is needed to support the weight. A lighter alternative is an aluminum tray or bench, or roll-up mat, with a flat heating element incorporated into it. A thermostat can be installed to regulate the temperature.

A box made from transparent plastic with a hinged lid that fits over a heated bench provides extra protection for raising tender plants or keeping plants frost-free over winter. Use row cover instead of plastic if desired, but plastic is best.

On a smaller scale, you can simply purchase a heated propagator, which only needs to be plugged in to provide the same bottom heat.

Insulation

Insulation in winter and early spring helps to reduce the risk of frost damage and to maintain the highest possible temperature. In a greenhouse, the best insulation for the lower half is styrofoam slabs. The upper part of the greenhouse can be lined with bubble plastic. Twin-wall plastic with large bubbles (2-in./5-cm diameter) is best. The glazing bars of

Plants on show
Although rarely possible on this sort of scale, staging makes good use of space and displays plants to best advantage.

SOIL BEDS UNDER COVER

Plants grown in a soil bed (far left) within a greenhouse or hoop house are much easier to manage and require much less attention than those grown in the restricted environment of pots and growing bags. Appropriate soil improvement, following organic principles, avoids the need for liquid feeding. Raised edges (left) allow bulky soil improvers to be added as a mulch.

A soil floor rather than a concrete one also helps to keep the atmosphere cooler in hot weather.

most aluminum greenhouses have a channel on the inside. Clips are available that lock into this channel and hold the bubble plastic in place. If the glazing bars have no channel, curtain wires can be stretched along the ridge and eaves to support sheets of bubble plastic. In wooden greenhouses, insulating curtains can easily be put up with thumbtacks. When insulation is removed, label each piece for easy refitting in the autumn. In a hoop house, hang wires to support sheets of bubble plastic.

Shading

In summer, a greenhouse may become too hot. Plants will wilt; sunlight may scorch leaves and cause tomato fruits to develop a condition known as green shoulders. Shading cuts out some sunlight and prevents overheating—but, unless it can be easily removed, it will also cut out light on cloudy days. A well-ventilated greenhouse will require minimum shading, and possibly none at all.

The simplest method of shading is to paint the outside of the glass with lime wash. Shading on the roof is more effective than on the sides. Shade the side facing the midday sun first, then check its effectiveness before applying any more. Blinds that can be raised or lowered depending on the weather are more efficient. They are installed inside the house and may get in the way of tall plants that reach the roof, however. Green plastic

sheeting, row cover, or netting installed inside on supports can be used to protect individual, vulnerable plants and seedlings. Shading is not needed in a hoop house.

Soil beds

Growing in the greenhouse soil, rather than in pots, is recommended for plants that will spend their whole lives in the greenhouse. Plants are much less trouble to care for when grown in the soil than in a pot or growing bag, particularly those that have high food and water requirements, such as tomatoes. The soil should be managed in the same way as the soil outside—using organic manures, compost, green manure, and fertilizers to build fertility as required. Liquid feeding should not be required.

Soil beds, as opposed to concrete flooring, help to keep the air in a greenhouse moist. Organize the area into beds, preferably of a size that means that you do not have to step on the soil.

A crop rotation (see also pp. 301–303) must be used to prevent pest and disease buildup in the soil. As space is limited and many greenhouse crops are related, a good rotation can be difficult to achieve. It may be necessary simply to avoid a crop for a year or two, or grow it in containers placed on a plastic sheet over the soil. If problems do build up, then it may eventually be necessary to change the soil to a depth of at least 12 in. (30 cm).

What to grow under cover

A greenhouse or hoop house can be the engine-room of the kitchen garden, providing a host of young transplants for plots outside (see pp. 111–113). Some crops are, however, traditionally grown to harvest under glass—most especially the more tender, fruiting vegetables, such as tomatoes, cucumbers, peppers, and eggplants (see pp. 224–225). However, hardy crops can also be grown out of season—either earlier or much later than they would outside. The "hungry gap," between late winter and summer, when outdoor crops are scarce, can be filled with midwinter sowings of spinach, spring cabbage, broccoli, peas, cauliflower, potatoes, and other traditional outdoor crops. Choose cultivars suited to indoor growing (see left). Crops may be either sown direct in soil beds or raised in a heated propagator or on a heated bench, then transplanted into the soil or potted up. Protect against frost where needed.

At the other end of the season, valuable greens for autumn and winter salads and stir fries can be sown, from late summer onward, up to 4 weeks later than the recommended outdoor sowing times. Suitable crops include chervil, arugula, French sorrel, giant red mustard, corn salad, endive, upland cress, and baby beets. You don't need a lot of room to produce a few meals' worth of fresh vegetables out of season. All of the projects on pp. 226–227 work on a small scale.

Flowers

A greenhouse or hoop house can supply almost continuous color for the home and garden. Bedding plants, basket plants, container plants, half-hardy border perennials, hardy perennials, biennials, pot plants, and cut flowers are all easy and rewarding to grow. As well as raising plants to flower elsewhere, grow some to add color to the greenhouse or hoop house itself. Sweet peas sown in mid-autumn will flower abundantly in spring. Half-hardy climbers such as morning glory and black-eyed Susan vine thrive in the protected conditions. Hardy annuals such as pot marigolds can be sown in autumn in pots or soil beds; they will then provide early spring color and food for beneficial insects for pest control. French marigolds are worth growing among tomatoes and other crops as they may be effective in repelling whitefly.

Fruit in the greenhouse
Sweet melons (right) and grapes are traditionally grown to fruition under glass in cool climates, but you can also give winter shelter to tender fruits in pots, such as peaches and nectarines, not to mention herbs like bay. A greenhouse or hoop house can also be used to force delicious crops of early strawberries (see p. 226).

GROWING CALENDAR*

Season	Production/Action	Crop
Spring	Crops to harvest 4–8 weeks earlier than those outdoors	Cabbage, cauliflower, broccoli, lettuce (1) Peas (2) Potatoes, spinach, cress (3) Radish, watercress (4) Carrots (3 or 4) Strawberries (in pots or growing bags)
	Flowers for cutting	Sweet Williams, stocks, spring bulbs (6); sweet peas (2)
	Plant raising for growing inside	Tomatoes, peppers, eggplants (1) Sweet corn (2) Cucumbers, zucchini, melons (5)
	Plant raising for growing outside	Bedding plants, patio and conservatory plants, basket plants[†] (1) Brassicas (1) Peas and beans (2) Zucchini, pumpkins, squashes (6)
	Plants being grown from cuttings	Hanging basket plants[†] Plants for pots and tubs
Summer	Fruit for harvesting	As sown in spring: eggplants, zucchini, cucumbers, melons, peppers, sweet corn, tomatoes
	Plants being propagated	Hardy biennials from seed Half-hardy perennials from seeds and cuttings Hardy perennials from seeds and cuttings
Autumn	Fruit for harvesting	As in summer: eggplants, zucchini, cucumbers, melons, peppers, sweet corn, tomatoes
	Flowers for cutting	Chrysanthemums, snapdragons, stocks
	Seed-sowing and planting for winter crops under cover	Carrots (4, sow early autumn) Lettuce, endive, chicory, kohlrabi, Oriental greens, other winter salads, stir-fry leaves; raise in cell packs or sow direct depending on available cropping space Plant parsley in the corner of a soil bed
Winter	Food ready for harvest	Parsley planted in autumn Crops sown in autumn: carrots, kohlrabi, winter salads, stir-fry leaves
	Flowers for cutting	Chrysanthemums, daffodils, anemones Sweet peas[‡]
	Plant raising	Broad beans and peas[‡] Onions, early cauliflowers, cabbages: sow in pots or cell packs on a heated bench; move to staging, prick off if appropriate; keep frost-free
	Plants being protected from winter cold	Half-hardy container plants such as cannas, standard fuchsias, bougainvillea Tender perennials, such as Marguerite daisy, geraniums

* These plans can be carried out in a 84 sq. yd. (72 sq. m) greenhouse or hoop house. They can be adapted for smaller structures.

Key
1 Sown in cell packs and finally transplanted into soil beds; could be sown in pots early in the season, then pricked off into the packs
2 Sown in root trainers, then transplanted into soil beds
3 Sown directly into soil beds
4 Grown from seed to maturity in containers
5 Sown individually in pots
6 Transplanted into beds the previous autumn, after summer crops have finished

[†] In late spring, hang planted-up hanging baskets inside to give them a good start. Move outside when conditions are favorable.
[‡] Sow in root trainers, germinate on heated bench, and move to regular bench as soon as germination is observed.

Fruiting crops under cover

Fine fruits (facing page)
*An unheated greenhouse or hoop house is a perfect environment for growing warmth-loving fruiting crops such as tomatoes (**1**), eggplants (**2**), cucumbers (**3**), and peppers (**4**).*

Tomatoes are a popular crop for a cool greenhouse or hoop house. Eggplants and peppers can also give excellent results, though they need slightly higher temperatures and do not give such high yields. All three belong to the same botanical family (see pp. 304–313), making crop rotation difficult. Alternate these plants with crops from another family—cucumbers or melons, for example (see facing page)—or use pots and growing bags.

Starting off
Young plants may be bought from late spring on—but for the best choice of cultivars and organic plants, raise your own on a heated bench or in a propagator. You can start tomatoes as early as midwinter if you can keep them frost-free. If not, sow in spring, 8–10 weeks before the last frost.

Tomato cultivars are available specifically for growing under cover, but most outdoor cultivars grow well in an unheated greenhouse. "Indeterminate" types make best use of limited space, making tall plants with a single vertical stem, known as cordons. Bush and trailing types do well in pots and baskets. Eggplants and peppers make more compact, bushy plants, to 30 in. (75 cm) tall at most.

Germinate seeds in a warm spot, transplanting the seedlings into 3–4-in. (7.5–10-cm) pots. Keep these growing in a warm place (54–61°F/12–16°C, depending on the plant). Once the first flowers show, they can be planted in a soil bed or into pots or growing bags.

Soil beds, pots, or growing bags?
To grow in soil beds in a greenhouse or hoop house, apply a medium-fertility soil improver such as garden or worm compost to the soil, and check that the soil temperature 4 in. (10 cm) below the surface is at least 56°F (14°C). If not, move the plants into a pot one size larger and wait. If plants are leggy, they can be planted in the soil up to 1 in. (2.5 cm) deeper than they were in the pot. Spacing will depend on the cultivar. Follow the advice on the seed packet. Never crowd plants; it encourages disease.

To grow in pots, use 8–10-in. (21–25-cm) pots filled with a rich organic potting mix. Arrange them at a spacing appropriate to the crop and cultivar.

Growing bags are another option. Two plants per bag are easier to manage and give larger yields than the three usually recommended.

Watering and feeding
Watering and feeding should be adjusted to the growth rate of the plants. Early in the season, take care not to overwater or overfeed: Both can be disastrous. Once plants are growing well, however, do not let them dry out. Production will be reduced, and tomatoes and sweet peppers may develop a condition known as blossom end rot (see p. 88). Plants in pots and bags may need watering twice a day in hot weather. Start feeding with an organic liquid feed (see pp. 206–207) once the first fruit has set. Plants grown in soil beds will not need as much watering or feeding if the soil is in good health.

Support and training
To support cordon tomatoes, attach a length of twine to the greenhouse frame above each plant, and tie the other end loosely around the stem at the base of the plant. As the plant grows, twist the tip around the string. Alternatively, tie the stem to a tall stake. Taller eggplants and peppers may also need support.

Sideshoots growing from the main stem of cordon tomatoes must be pinched off when small, leaving the single main stem to grow tall. Do not remove sideshoots from bush tomatoes, peppers, or eggplants.

Stopping
An indeterminate tomato will keep growing while conditions are suitable, but in cooler climates in an unheated greenhouse, plants are usually "stopped" after 4 or 5 flower trusses form. Simply cut off the growing tip of the plant. This encourages the development and ripening of the existing fruit, rather than new growth that will flower too late to crop. Eggplants and peppers need not be stopped, but limiting the number of fruits produces larger ones.

Harvesting
Harvest tomatoes when they are ripe. Peppers may be picked green, before they mature, or left to ripen, which will give a smaller crop. Pick eggplants when the skin is still shiny and taut.

Supporting stems
In addition to the support given by twine, canes, or frames, bottomless pots filled with medium around the base of tomato plants will encourage rooting from the stem and hence a more stable plant. It also makes directing water to the roots more efficient.

GREENHOUSE CUCUMBERS

Modern greenhouse cucumber cultivars prefer warmer, more humid conditions than tomatoes, so grow them away from the door or side vents. They are vulnerable to soilborne stem and root rots, so rotate them with other crops or grow in growing bags or 12-in. (30-cm) pots. Where greenhouse temperatures are regularly below 68°F (20°C) at night during the growing season, grow an outdoor variety instead.

• Sow seed of greenhouse cultivars sideways, one seed per 3-in. (7.5-cm) pot.

• Germinate with bottom heat of at least 68°F (20°C).

• Keep the seedlings at around 68°F (20°C); move them to 5-in. (12-cm) pots as necessary.

• Keep the growing medium moist but not waterlogged.

• Plant out when minimum night temperatures reach 68°F (20°C).

• All-female F1 cucumbers produce fruit on the main stem, so they can be grown up a single cane or string with plants 18 in. (45 cm) apart, just like cordon tomatoes. They are very productive grown in this way and take up little space. Remove all flower buds and sideshoots from the first 12 in. (30 cm) of the main stem; after this, remove sideshoots but leave the flower buds—you should get one cucumber at each leaf joint.

If you have space, train sideshoots out horizontally on netting or wires, pinching them off after two leaves and removing secondary shoots.

• Water regularly. Once fruits start to swell, liquid-feed pots and growing bags weekly.

• In hot weather, spray the greenhouse floor with water once or twice a day to maintain a humid atmosphere.

• Harvest fruit regularly to maintain production.

Other under-cover crops

Even if space is limited, there are still ways to enjoy a taste of homegrown fresh fruits, vegetables, lettuce, and even cut flowers often well before or after local garden produce is available.

Watercress

Watercress is quick and easy to grow. Germinate the seeds on a hot bench or in a propagator in a pot of multipurpose medium that is standing half-submerged in a tray of water. Transplant seedlings into cell packs or root trainers, and stand them, half submerged, in a tray of water.

Seal the small holes in a growing bag with electrical tape. Remove most of the plastic from the top of the growing bag by cutting three large square holes. Soak the medium. Plant five plants in each hole, equally spaced. Begin harvesting as soon as the shoots are large enough, and harvest regularly.

Strawberries

Strawberry plants forced under cover will produce only once, but you'll have a mouthwatering treat a month earlier than outdoor plants. In late summer, peg runners (see p. 248) from garden plants into individual 6-in. (15-cm) pots of multipurpose medium, or peg them down onto the surface of the medium using twine threaded through two drainage holes. When rooted, cut them from the parent plant and "plunge" the pots outdoors, sinking them into a bed of gravel or leaf mold to keep the roots frost-free. Strawberries need a period of cold to initiate flower bud formation. In midwinter, move the plants into the greenhouse or hoop house. When growth begins, feed once with an organic liquid fertilizer (see pp. 206–207). Cover flowering plants at night if frost is likely. Remove covers during the day to allow pollinating insects to reach the flowers. Flowers can be dusted with a cotton swab to assist pollination. After harvest, discard the plants.

Stir-fry leaves and salad mix

Make use of any spare bench space with a crop that matures quickly. Vegetables for stir-fry and salad (see pp. 332–333) can be grown on a bench in a container 6 in. (15 cm) deep, filled with an organic multipurpose medium. Sow seeds very thinly in rows every 8 weeks from early spring until mid-autumn. Water the medium without wetting the leaves. Pick individual leaves as required.

Sweet corn

Sweet corn is very successful when grown under cover. Pollination of almost 100% is achieved if at least nine plants are grown. The crop matures quickly and can use the same space occupied by early potatoes or another early crop. Some cultivars grow to 6 ft. (2 m) tall, so choose a short cultivar unless you have a lot of headroom. Sow seeds individually in deep pots or root trainers in late spring. Plant out into a soil bed in a block pattern, with plants 12 in. (30 cm) apart. If red spider mite is a problem, use a biological control (see p. 100).

Crops under cover (1)
This page, from left to right: sweet corn needs the whole height of the house to grow; watercress grown in a wet growing bag can be harvested on a cut-and-come-again basis; you may find it hard to resist picking off the short but sweet crop of forced strawberries one by one.

New potatoes for Christmas

Save a few tubers from a crop of early potatoes, such as 'Early Red Norland' or 'All Red'. Leave them in the sun to turn green, then store until late summer. Then, plant in a 3-gal. (15-liter) tub with drainage holes. Put a 6-in. (15-cm) layer of multipurpose or potting medium into the bottom of the container and place three tubers, buds up, on top. Cover with 3 in. (7.5 cm) of the medium, then water well. As the shoots grow, continue to fill the container with medium, always leaving the top of the shoots in the light. You can use the contents of used growing bags or other once-used growing media to save costs.

Water regularly, taking care not to allow the medium to dry out—feeling the weight is a good test for moisture content. The foliage can be supported with four stakes (fitted with caps to protect your eyes) pushed inside the rim of the pot, supporting two horizontal circles of string; or the stems can be allowed to trail from the pot. Protect from frost. Stop watering when the leaves and stems die off. Empty the contents on Christmas morning and harvest the new potatoes.

Chrysanthemums

Pot-grown chrysanthemums fit in well with summer greenhouse crops and will produce colorful, long-lasting blooms for cutting in mid- to late autumn, when garden flowers are scarce. Started off under cover in spring, they can go outside in summer, just when the covered space is needed for tomatoes and other fruiting crops; when these come to an end, the chrysanthemums can come in to flower. Initially you will have to buy small plants or rooted cuttings. Specialty nurseries offer the widest choice. From then on you can propagate your own plants each year from the overwintering "crown" of the previous year's plants, if healthy. Take cuttings in spring (see p. 106) and root on a heated bench or in a propagator at 55–65°F (13–18°C). When they are well-rooted, transplant each one into a 3½-in. (9-cm) pot, and grow them on the greenhouse staging.

When the plants have produced 6–8 in. (15–20 cm) of growth, pinch out the growing tips, leaving four or five leaves below. This will make the plants grow bushy. When they have filled the small pots, pot them into 9-in. (23-cm) pots using a nutrient-rich growing medium, based on garden compost (see pp. 42–49 and 52–55). Harden them off gradually before putting them outside.

As the plants grow, tie the stems to canes for support. Tie the tops of the canes to a horizontal wire to prevent the plants from blowing over. Water as needed and feed weekly with an organic liquid fertilizer. As autumn nears, watch out for early frosts; cover flower buds if necessary. In mid-autumn, bring the plants under cover for flowering.

Cut flowers when the outside petals are expanded and the center petals still tightly packed. Crush the end of the stem before placing in water. After flowering, cut off any growth above 6 in. (15 cm) and put the pots under the benches. During winter, give only enough water to prevent dehydration. In spring, bring the pots into better light and increase watering. Then, to start again, take cuttings from the new shoots and discard the parent plant.

Crops under cover (2)
This page, from left to right: compact and fast-growing lettuce crops and young stir-fry leaves are perfect gap-fillers, and many can be grown into winter (see also p. 332); new potatoes can be grown in a tub or used growing bag in a corner until ready to harvest for a midwinter treat; other late offerings from the greenhouse or hoop house can include your own chrysanthemums—either large showy blooms like these or those with cheerful sprays of open flowers.

NATURAL PEST CONTROL

The enclosed, sheltered environment of a greenhouse or hoop house provides ideal conditions for the microscopic pest predators known as biological controls. These are available to combat greenhouse whitefly (top), red spider mite, aphids, thrips, vine weevil, scale and slugs. For more details see *Plant Health*, p.100.

Film of moisture
Closing hoop house doors early will result in a layer of condensation building up on the inner side of the plastic as the outdoor air cools down in the evening, buffering sharp falls in temperature inside.

Management tips under cover

Plants under cover may be sheltered from some of the harsher aspects of life outdoors, but they are also completely reliant on you, the gardener, for water, food, and protection against harmful organisms that will also thrive indoors, with a ready supply of tender plant material and cozy hiding places. They may also suffer from the down side of being under glass or plastic—a buildup of excess heat and humidity—without your intervention. With good housekeeping you can provide the conditions that plants, rather than pests and diseases, need to thrive.

Climate control
• Control temperature by insulation and ventilation—shade only as a last resort.
• Keep row cover cut to size. During heavy frosts, cover tender plants with one or more layers.
• Invest in a maximum/minimum thermostat to monitor temperature and help you to manage appropriate ventilation and insulation.
• On mild winter days, fully open doors and vents, but remember to close them in mid-afternoon. If you are not at home, leave the doors closed.
• When warm days are followed by cold nights, close a hoop house well before sundown to obtain a layer

of condensation on the sheet. This provides some insulation against the cold.

A healthy environment
• Keep the house very tidy—store pots and other equipment elsewhere.
• Keep the glass or plastic clean—it may need to be washed down several times a year.
• Clear out and scrub down the structure at least once a year. Use hot, soapy water and finish off with a powerful rinse with a hose.
• Do not smoke in the greenhouse or hoop house.
• Prune out dead and diseased parts of plants—clean the pruning shears before moving to another plant.
• Dispose of dead plants, or those badly infected with pest or disease, immediately.

Pests and diseases
• Raise your own plants where possible to avoid the risk of bringing in pests and diseases.
• Check purchased plants and their soil. Quarantine them in another area for a week or two before introducing them to the greenhouse or hoop house.
• Use crop rotation to prevent the buildup of soilborne pests and diseases.

USING STRAW BALES

Straw bales can provide an extra root run and moisture reservoir for tomato plants. Use organic straw—tomato plants are very susceptible to chemical residues. Soak the bales in water and apply a high-nitrogen organic fertilizer over 2 to 3 weeks so that they start to decompose. Wrapping the bales in plastic can help to retain moisture and warmth, but take care in hot summers that conditions do not become too warm for plant roots. Then plant each tomato in a mound of potting soil on the surface of the bales. Feed them throughout the season exactly as you would plants in pots and growing bags.

• Inspect plants daily for signs of pest or disease. Problems build up rapidly in a closed environment.

• In summer, mist plants that are susceptible to red spider mite with a fine spray of water.

• Use yellow sticky traps to monitor pests.

• Use biological control agents (see p. 100) to deal with regular pest problems. Remove sticky traps before introducing flying biological control agents.

Soil, compost, and feeding

• Wherever possible, grow plants in soil beds rather than pots or growing bags.

• Use organic techniques to keep the soil fertile and healthy.

• Pot up plants promptly as necessary, to prevent them exhausting their medium and getting potbound. This also helps to keep pests at bay.

Watering

• The appearance of the surface of a soil bed is not always a good indication of the moisture level; check below as well. Check pots by feeling the weight.

• Make an inspection hole toward one end of a growing bag that allows medium to be tested with the fingertips.

• Whenever possible water in the morning; avoid watering in the evening.

• Wet the soil rather than the plants.

• Use a good-quality watering can with a long spout and a removable, fine rose. A can with an on/off trigger can make watering more precise.

• Use rainwater whenever possible, but water seeds and young seedlings with tap water; they are more vulnerable to disease and hence need cleaner water.

• Before use, let tap water stand in the greenhouse for a few hours to warm up and to allow excess chlorine to escape.

• Water seeds and seedlings from below, standing pots and trays in a container of water. Remove when the surface of the medium is wet.

• Periodically check the effectiveness of watering—feel the weight of pots at the front, middle, and back of benches. Check the edges of beds—they may be getting less water than the middle.

• In warm weather, "damp down" in the morning—wet paths and other surfaces to increase humidity.

• In autumn, keep foliage as dry as possible.

• In winter, use a smaller watering can to make it easier to apply a smaller quantity of water to plants in the greenhouse or hoop house.

Coldframes, cloches, and crop covers

Coldframes, cloches, and crop covers can provide valuable temporary or longer-term protection for food crops and ornamentals. They are cheaper, require less space, and are more flexible in their use than a greenhouse or hoop house.

Coldframes

A traditional coldframe is a low, wood- or brick-framed structure with a sloping roof made from glazed wooden frames, known as lights. These lights may be hinged to form a lid that can be propped up, or they may slide across or be removed entirely, allowing the degree of ventilation to be varied according to what is in the frame. This type of frame is not widely sold these days, but it is relatively cheap to make one at home, especially if recycled wood or bricks are used. Rigid plastic may be used for glazing where weight or safety must be considered. Making your own also means that the frame can be custom-built to fit the available space. Place wooden frames on bricks to prevent the wood from rotting.

The modern coldframe is a lightweight, aluminum structure with glass on all sides—very like a large cloche. These are more flexible in many ways as they are more easily moved, but they do not provide the same degree of insulation and are not as sturdy as their old-fashioned counterparts.

Position a coldframe where it will get good light in winter and spring. Shading can be added in summer and insulation in winter, if needed. If you are going to grow crops in the frame, then prepare the soil covered by the frame to suit the crop in mind. If using the frame to protect pots and trays, a layer of gravel makes a good base. This can be laid over a weedproof membrane attached around the base of the frame to help keep out slugs.

Cloches

Cloches are designed to be moved around the garden as required. They come in many different shapes and sizes and vary widely in price. Tunnel cloches, supported by wire or plastic hoops, are designed to protect a row of plants; wider versions can be used to cover the whole width of a 4-ft. (1.2-m) vegetable bed. Where pest protection is the main requirement, tunnel cloches may be covered with netting, mesh, or row cover instead of plastic. Other types of cloche may be used individually or put together to cover a row. Designs such as the traditional bell cloche (now available in clear plastic) are intended to cover individual plants.

Shape, height, width, ventilation, degree of frost protection, and ease of watering and repositioning are all points to consider when choosing a cloche. Those shaped like the letter A give plants near the edges little headroom; wider cloches with vertical or near-vertical sides are more versatile.

Filling the frame
The great advantage of a frame is that it provides both protection and excellent ventilation. This is particularly useful when hardening off plants. Coldframes can also be used to protect hardwood cuttings and trays of slow-germinating seeds of trees and other hardy plants during winter, and to give shelter from winter rains to rock-garden plants and dwarf bulbs.

GETTING THE BEST FROM A FRAME
Use your coldframe to:
• Harden off seedlings and transplants.
• Protect trays and pots of slow-germinating seeds, such as trees and wildflowers.
• Grow tender crops such as melons.
• Grow early and late lettuce crops.
• Create nursery beds for brassica transplants.
• Protect hardwood cuttings over winter.
• Protect rock-garden plants in pots from winter rains.

CLOCHES

Cloches come in all shapes and sizes (**1**); even open-weave baskets can protect against birds, rabbits, and frost at night. Simple "mini-cloches" made from sawn-off plastic bottles (**2**) will protect individual young plants. Be sure not to trap a slug inside. A Victorian glass cloche (**3**) makes an attractive addition to any garden. Polycarbonate sheeting has now largely replaced the glass panes traditionally used to make functional A-shaped cloches (**4**), good for low, bushy plants.

HARDENING OFF

Plants protected by frames and cloches must be gradually introduced to the cooler, drier outside environment, although this may not take as long as for plants grown within a greenhouse or hoop house, especially as the season progresses. First, prop up or slide off frame covers (right) for part of the day, then for the whole day, then at night as well for a couple of days before removing the plants.

Plant growth under a cloche can be especially soft and tender, as the space is so enclosed. A spell of cloudy weather is ideal for hardening them off, as they will be less likely to be scorched by strong sunlight. Remove the cloche (far right) for a short time in the evening, replacing it before nightfall for several days.

THE MANY USES OF CLOCHES

• Warm up soil in spring prior to planting or sowing.
• Help to establish newly set out transplants.
• Protect plants from birds, rabbits, and other mammals.
• Protect plants from insect pests.
• Protect half-hardy crops from light frost and cold winds.
• Harden off plants grown in a greenhouse or hoop house.
• Cover parts of rows of lettuce to stagger maturity times.
• Protect food crops such as parsley and cabbage over winter.
• Protect autumn-sown flowers (for example, larkspur and cornflower) over winter.
• Force bulbs such as daffodils in early spring.
• Extend the season into early winter for herbs and lettuces.
• Protect cuttings of hardy perennials in winter.
• Protect strawberry flowers from frost— remove in daytime for insect pollination.
• Cover herbs in late winter for an early crop.
• Keep hardy lettuces producing over winter.

Choosing cloches

Traditional glass cloches are attractive and give better light transmission and frost protection than plastic ones. It is also easier to see what is going on inside without removing the cloche. Plastic-covered cloches, however, are relatively cheap, lightweight, and less likely to break. The disadvantages of plastic cloches are that they give less frost protection (unless double-walled) and are more likely to blow away in the wind. Plastic also has a shorter life span. Exposure to sunlight decays it, causing it to become opaque and brittle. Better-quality cloches use plastic that is more resistant to damage by sunlight.

Cloche practicalities

Most cloches have to be removed to water the plants beneath. A few models incorporate features that allow watering without removal, but it is always important to check plants regularly. Adequate ventilation is also essential in cloches—simply to prevent plants from overheating, to facilitate hardening off, or perhaps to give pollinators access to flowers like strawberries. Some cloches have holes in the ends, covered by "hit-or-miss" discs. For these to be effective, the holes have to be large in relation to the area of the ends. It is, however, equally important that a cloche can be closed at both ends, or it can become a wind tunnel.

Floating row cover

Row cover is a lightweight, synthetic fabric, bonded rather than woven, that can be laid directly over plants. It lets in air, light, and water. It is easily damaged and may only last a couple of seasons. Thicker grades can last longer. Outdoors, row cover can be used as a temporary cover to protect vulnerable plants against the elements and pests until the plants are sturdy enough to survive alone. To keep pests out, it is advisable to cover the seeds or plants right from the start. When the plants are to be uncovered, remember to remove the row cover gradually, replacing it at night at first, to harden plants off.

For short-term protection, for example when frost is forecast and could harm new bedding plants, strawberries in flower, or tender crops in a greenhouse or hoop house, the row cover can be put on overnight and then removed during the day. Row cover can also be used to form windbreaks for young or vulnerable plants.

Limitations of row cover

Row cover can be used long-term to protect a crop throughout its life—for example, it makes an excellent barrier to carrot fly—but this does have disadvantages. Weeds will thrive under row cover, as will diseases that are encouraged by the more humid atmosphere. And, since the material is opaque, it has to be removed in order to check what is going on underneath. Frequent removal and replacement will be necessary to weed and inspect for pests and disease problems. Some of these disadvantages can be avoided by using fine plastic mesh instead of row cover to cover crops.

Mesh fabrics

Lightweight, fine mesh plastic net fabrics are also available for garden use to protect plants. Much tougher than row cover, this type of material can last for 10 years or so. It can be laid directly over plants or stretched over tunnel cloche hoops. These fabrics do not give as much protection against frost as row cover does, but they do give plants some protection against the elements and from the same range of pests. Most pests will be excluded by the standard mesh size, but to form a barrier against tiny creatures such as flea beetle, ultrafine mesh (0.8 mm) should be used.

A covering of fine mesh has the advantage of being see-through, so you can check the progress of plants (and weeds) without continually removing the covering. Conditions are less humid too, so diseases are less likely to develop. Mesh can be left in place throughout the life of a crop, or until it outgrows the height of supported covers and tunnels—but do this only if absolutely necessary. In general, it is best to remove coverings as soon as plants can survive without them.

Pests excluded by crop covers

Row cover and mesh, securely anchored, will protect crops from flying pests such as carrot fly, flea beetle, cabbage root fly, cabbage white butterflies, aphids, and onion fly. Rabbits will also be deterred, but not slugs and other soil-dwelling pests, which attack crops from below.

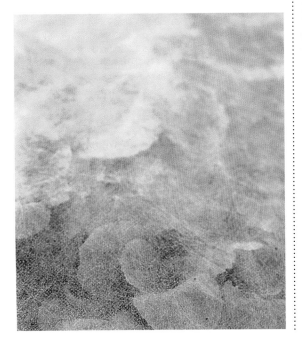

ATTACHING ROW COVER

Weigh row cover down with small bags of soil or boards, or use commercial plastic pegs sold for this purpose. Alternatively, staple the edges to two wooden battens. Unwind the fabric to release extra material. With wood-edged raised beds, you can pin or staple the row cover directly to the edging (top) on one side.

To make a windbreak, tuck the row cover under a horizontal length of twine looped between canes (bottom). Catch the row cover under the twine when you wind it around the canes to help prevent slipping.

Covered crop
Row cover provides good protection against many pests, including cabbage root fly, carrot fly, whitefly, and flea beetle. Lay it loosely over the plants and hold it down all around. Tuck some slack in at the edges and release this as the plants grow.

Grow your own

ENJOY THE FRESHEST, MOST DELICIOUS ORGANIC PRODUCE

Growing fruit

BLOSSOM IN SPRING, SHADE IN SUMMER, AND ABUNDANCE AT
HARVEST—FRUIT IS THE TREASURE TROVE OF THE GARDEN

FRUIT HAS BEEN part of our diet since we gathered our harvest from the wild forests. Now tamed, improved, and cultivated, fruits offer instant gratification as the original nutritious fast food, straight from the plant. Associations with time and place, accumulated history, myth, and folklore all add to the spice—for example, apples, once associated with the fall of Adam and Eve, were held in low esteem from the 13th century until their rehabilitation as the just fruits of honest toil in the 16th century. In our times, too, fruit surely earns its place in a garden.

All fruits are attractive in blossom; some are also deliciously scented to give promise of the juicy bounty to come. Fruit is versatile enough to be restricted and managed to fit even a small garden—trained against a wall or fence, for example. Where there is space, however, the crown of an apple or pear tree provides dappled shade and much sought-after medium height to the plant architecture of the garden. Finally, the harvest is both luscious and beautiful. There may be no fruit in some years, but generally there is enough to share with friends—and with wildlife.

All-around attraction (facing page)
Every garden should have an apple tree—not only productive but beautiful in flower, leaf, and fruit, with silvery bark on branches that become ever more gnarled and full of character with age. Even at the end of its life it yields fragrant logs for burning.

Currants and berries (below)
Soft fruits from the supermarket cannot compare with those warmed and ripened by the sun and grown in your own garden.

WHY GROW FRUIT ORGANICALLY?

- **Fast food** Fruit is the ultimate fast food: It can be eaten straight from the plant.
- **Produced without pesticides** Organically grown, there is no need to peel or scrub the fruit before eating.
- **Connect with the seasons** Summer strawberries, autumn apples—harvesting your own fruit connects with the living seasons.
- **Endless choices** With hundreds of apples to choose from, the range of fruits and cultivars is amazing.
- **Fresh and tasty** Home-grown fruit can be harvested and eaten at the appropriate time—not when it suits the stores.
- **Less work for more** Growing most fruit takes little time in comparison with the returns.
- **Local production** Saves on food miles; allows you to taste fruits and cultivars that would never make it to the stores.
- **Enhance the garden** Fruit trees and bushes can be attractive garden plants in their own right.
- **Anyone can do it** Fruit can be planted in even the smallest of yards.
- **It can be fascinating** Growing fruit can be a rewarding hobby.

Deciding what to grow

This chapter deals with a range of fruits suitable for temperate climates. This includes low-growing fruiting plants such as strawberries, cane fruits, and small-berried bush fruits as well as tree fruits such as apples, pears, plums, figs, cherries, peaches, and even hazelnuts.

You will have personal preferences for the fruits you like. It is important also to know what will succeed in your conditions and what you have space for. The information that follows explains the needs of different fruits and will help you make successful choices. Once you have considered all the potentials and pitfalls of your site, as well as the local weather, you will be in a good position to decide what to grow and where. You may have walls or fences in your garden. These may be open to the sun most of the day, sunny for part of the day, or cold, facing away from the midday sun. You may have a garden with limited space. There are possibilities for all these situations.

Some fruits may benefit from growing against a wall, especially in less favorable conditions, but most fruit also grows well in the open garden. The free flow of air in this situation helps to reduce disease infections.

Many fruits are very attractive to birds, squirrels, and foxes and will need to be grown inside a netted cage or netted individually. These include cherries and all the soft fruits—currants and berries.

Coping with the elements

Although most of the fruits described in this book are hardy, few, if any, will cope with frost when in blossom or in early fruit. It is vital to avoid planting into frost pockets and to avoid creating new frost pockets by erecting fences or establishing plantings that trap and hold frost rather than letting it drain away. Frost, being cold, drains downward to the lowest point. Fruit trees and bushes can, therefore, be planted above the danger level and thus escape damage. It is worth remembering also that some fruit, such as some cultivars of strawberry, need a period of frost in winter to initiate flowering for the next year's crop.

Wind has the obvious effect of damaging branches. Less obvious is the fact that pollinating insects cannot settle in blustery weather and this will affect the size of the harvest. Some gardens are naturally sheltered. If not, thought needs to be given to creating shelters against the wind.

Without doubt, the greatest contribution to a successful harvest comes from the sun. Sunshine provides energy for plants to grow, ripens wood, and improves the flavor and color of fruits. If your garden receives little sun, you will be greatly limited in what you can successfully grow.

Geography also affects choice of fruits. The farther away from the equator you are, the shorter your summer will be, and it simply may not be long enough to ripen some fruits. If you live in a cool region with a short season, you are unlikely to ripen good dessert grapes without a greenhouse, for example. Other fruits often grown under cover in cooler areas (see also pp. 216–229) include figs, peaches, and apricots. In warm regions these fruits bear bountiful crops without protection; on the other hand, in these areas apple varieties from cooler climates will struggle with the heat.

Altitude above sea level is another important consideration. At higher altitudes the season is shorter and there is simply insufficient warm daylight time to ripen some crops. Above 400 ft. (120 m) the possibilities are more limited: damsons, early ripening and cooking varieties of apples, currants, strawberries, and most cane fruits will be the main choices.

Arctic raspberry
This unusual fruit is very unlikely to be in the stores, but like alpine strawberries it is easy to grow, and ornamental, too. The flavor of the berries produced by these mat-forming herbaceous perennials is subtly different from that of the conventional raspberry. Plants reach a mere 6–8 in. (15–20 cm) tall, and die back in winter. To ensure good pollination grow more than one cultivar.

How much space?

If your garden is small, you may have to adapt your plans for fruit to fit the available space. Many types of soft fruits are popular with birds and will need netting. This is easier to do when they are grown in a plot together. You may decide that even just two raspberry plants, grown up each side of a freestanding post, are better than none. Even in the smallest garden, however, you can grow plentiful supplies of strawberries along the edge of a border or path, or in containers. Many tree fruits will also, with careful maintenance, be productive in a pot (see also *Container Gardening*, pp. 212–213).

A single fruit tree can, when mature, produce a generous crop, but some cultivars of tree fruit need other trees nearby that are compatible pollinators in order to set fruit. A single pear tree of the variety 'Comice' or 'Cascade' in your garden, for example, is unlikely to produce—unless your neighbor has a compatible cultivar.

But remember that, thanks to the development of dwarfing rootstocks for many fruit trees and their amenability to training (see pp. 244–245), two or more trees need not dominate a garden. If you are very partial to apples, want to plant several cultivars, but have limited space, you could use a wall or fence to grow cordons which need only 30 in. (75 cm) between trees.

Will it grow in my soil?

Fortunately, most soils are perfectly suitable for growing fruit. Shallow or high pH soils, however, do pose problems that are hard to fix because the topsoil is too shallow for good rooting, or because it is too alkaline. Some fruit can still be grown in these conditions but raspberries, in particular, will struggle.

Blueberries and cranberries need very acid conditions (pH 5.5 or less), and most fruit thrives in slightly acid soil. However, the majority of fruits will tolerate alkaline conditions. Raspberries are an exception and become iron-deficient in soils with a pH higher than 6.5. Young leaves on new growth turn yellow and ultimately the potential life of the plant is decreased from 12–14 years to as few as 8. You will still be able to harvest an adequate crop in this time, however, so all is not lost. It is very difficult to make alkaline soils more acid, but very acid soils can be made less acid

by applying ground limestone or dolomitic lime.

The acidity of the soil is not the only factor. The structure of soil is also important. In good, friable soil, plant roots are able to spread freely and deeply and make good use of the nutrients already present.

It comes as no surprise, perhaps, that fruit prefers a deep rich loam that is well-drained but moisture-retentive. You may not have these conditions to offer, but much can be done to improve soil structure, open up heavy soils, and increase the water-holding capacity of light soils (see *Soil and Soil Care*,

Space-saving forms
Cordons and espaliers can be grown against walls and fences and also freestanding, with the support of a strong post-and-wire system. They can also form attractive screens.

pp. 33–61). If you have a very poor soil, start to improve it a year in advance of planting.

Drainage

Fruits are composed largely of water, so adequate supplies are essential. In very wet locations, on the other hand, the main concern will be drainage (see also p. 64). Roots will rot and fungal pathogens attack where drainage is poor. Perhaps the most dramatic effect can be seen in raspberry plantings, where phytophthora root rot can rapidly run along waterlogged rows, killing canes as it spreads.

Preparing the site

Fruit is a long-term investment. In the case of fruit trees you may expect 50 years or more of production, depending on the rootstock used (see p. 242). You might imagine that maintaining such a crop will need regular application of organic fertilizers, manure, and compost. This is not necessarily the case. Giving fruit a good start is, on the other hand, of utmost importance. It is difficult to improve conditions after planting, whereas prior to planting there is ample opportunity to create the soil structure and fertility to give trees,

bushes, and canes a running start. A well-established plant has an extensive root system that can forage for nutrients more efficiently than a weak plant. Details of soil improvement using well-rotted manure and garden compost are given under individual fruits. For alternatives and further information, see *Bulky organic soil improvers*, p. 40.

Supplementary fertilizers

Spraying with dilute seaweed extract (see p. 207) is extremely beneficial for fruit, especially in spring and early summer. Both trees and bushes will take up nutrients more effectively, receive a full range of trace elements, and have enhanced hardiness to frost damage if given regular seaweed sprays.

Watering needs

If you have only a small number of fruit trees and bushes you may be able to water adequately with a watering can or hand-held hose. Where this is impractical, the best solution is to install permanent irrigation lines of soaker hose (see p. 68). A mulch (see below) of straw or other organic matter applied in late spring will help conserve water. Large, established trees should not need watering.

Mulches

Specific recommendations for planting and feeding are given for each fruit type on the following pages. As a general rule, however, with the exception of strawberries and some others, you will not need to add compost or fertilizers more than once every 2 or 3 years. An important addition to this is the use of organic mulches.

The most common materials used for mulching fruit are straw and hay, although weathered and part-composted shredded prunings and wood chips are excellent if enough is available. You can use your own shreddings or buy in bagged product.

Mulches need to be applied thickly to damp soil in late spring when it has had a chance to warm up. Apply hay and straw up to 4 in. (10 cm) deep and shreddings 2 in. (5 cm) deep, keeping a clear area of about 6 in. (15 cm) in diameter around tree trunks and the base of plants to deter voles and mice from chewing at the bark. Mulches not only suppress weeds and retain moisture but can also contain significant levels of nutrients. Hay and straw, for

FRUITS FOR SUN AND SHADE

Must have sun
Apples
Apricots
Figs
Grapes
Hybrid berries
Peaches
Pears
Plums
Nectarines
Strawberries
Sweet cherries

Will tolerate light or part shade
Blackberries
Black currants
Damsons and gages
Gooseberries
Jostaberries
Raspberries
Red and white currants
Sour cherries

Mulching
Fruit trees benefit from a thick strawy mulch in late spring, but keep it away slightly from the actual trunk. Rake off and compost the straw in winter to remove any pests and disease spores lurking within.

example, will release considerable amounts of potassium during the course of a season. Shreddings contain fewer nutrients but add to organic matter levels and improve soil structure. Light-colored mulches should be removed in winter to allow dark soil to absorb heat on early spring days and radiate it up into branches at night, protecting fragile emerging blossoms. Removing the mulch will also clear away some disease spores and overwintering pests.

Plant health

The best approach to maintaining healthy fruit crops is to be watchful, keeping a regular check on how plants are growing. This way, signs of any problems are seen early on and can be dealt with before they become serious. Incipient disease infections can often be pinched or pruned out and pest colonies removed with a wipe of the thumb. See right for general guidelines to keep your fruit healthy. Potential pests and diseases of fruits, with more detailed advice, are in the *A–Z of Plant Problems* (see pp. 367–395).

Weeds—tolerance or zero tolerance

Control of weeds for fruit is just as important as for vegetables, except where fruit trees are growing on vigorous rootstocks. If we recognize that many weeds are, in fact, wild flowers, we instantly change their status. Many of them are valuable in attracting beneficial insects and have an important place in orchards. In close proximity to bush and cane fruits and low-growing fruits such as strawberry and alpine raspberry, however, they are less beneficial, competing with the crop plants for light, water, and nutrients; if very abundant, they can reduce air flow and increase the likelihood of fungal attack.

Hoeing and hand-weeding are still the most effective ways of removing weeds growing in open soil. There is often a flush of weed growth before mulches are applied in spring. Once mulches are in place, they should severely curtail weed growth. Some perennial weeds may penetrate the mulch; these will have to be removed by hand.

Since perennial weeds are so awkward to remove from growing fruit, it pays to do your utmost to clear ground well before planting (see pp. 78–79).

Imported currantworm larva
This pest can rapidly strip the foliage from both gooseberry and red currant bushes. When young, the larvae are very small and prefer to feed in the center of the plant. You need to look carefully and regularly right into the heart of bushes in order to find and pick off the pests before they can do too much damage.

FRONT LINE DEFENSE
Prevention is the key to healthy fruit.
• Plant pest- and disease-resistant cultivars.
• Choose the right site.
• Never plant fruit where similar fruit has been growing.
• Prune plants to create an open growth habit to allow good airflow between branches.
• Do not overfeed with nitrogen.
• Remove damaged and diseased fruit, shoots, and foliage.
• Remove mulches over winter.
• Use a liquid seaweed foliar spray.
• Protect from birds with netting or a fruit cage.
• Provide shelter and the right kind of plants and flowers for creatures that eat pests.
Encourage these pest predators:
  Anthrocorid bugs (see p. 98)
  Earwigs (see pp. 93 and 192)
  Lacewings (see pp. 98 and 192)
  Lady beetles and their larvae (see pp. 99 and 192)
  Hoverfly larvae (see pp. 98 and 197)
Most need no more welcome than an unsprayed garden, but in many cases providing appropriate habitats and food plants will make all the difference (see *Gardening for Wildlife*, pp. 186–202).

Choosing cultivars

There is more to choosing a cultivar than liking the name. There are fruit cultivars for different seasons, different climates, different flavors; there are also cultivars with known resistance to some pests and diseases. When making your selections you should bear the following points in mind:

• **Season of harvest and use** If you have room, you may wish to extend your season of harvest with cultivars that succeed each other in maturing or fruits that are suitable for storing. There are late-fruiting cultivars of apples and pears that do not actually ripen until stored for a while.

• **Disease and/or pest resistance** If you have a particular local problem, such as apple canker, you should look for resistant or less-susceptible varieties.

• **Suitability for your local climate** Cultivars that do well in a warm climate may perform poorly when planted in a garden with a shorter, cooler season and vice versa. Some older cultivars have strong local associations; these are worth seeking out for general robustness and reliability.

• **Flavor** Not all cultivars have good flavor, and personal tastes vary. If you can, try before you buy.

• **Pollination requirements** See below and under individual fruits for further information.

Pollination

Fruit will not form unless flowers are pollinated. Many fruits, including the majority of soft fruits, are self-fertile: They do not need pollen from another plant or tree to set flowers. Many cultivars of plum and a few cherries are self-fertile; many apples are to some extent self-fertile but benefit greatly from cross-pollination with another apple cultivar. Some cultivars are not able to set fruit on their own and need to be planted within bee-flying distance of another cultivar that is both compatible and in flower at the same time. If you are short of space, a neighbor's yard is usually close enough.

Some apples are referred to as "triploids." This refers to their genetic structure and means that the flowers are "male sterile," producing little or no pollen. These generally need two pollinators, of different cultivars, to set a good crop.

Cherries are particularly complex as, apart from the few self-fertile cultivars such as 'Stella', they all need pollinators and are extremely fussy, in general, as to who supplies the pollen. There are several instances of total incompatibility, and no fruit can result from these matches.

Because trees differ in their blossoming time and the amount of viable pollen they produce, it's critical to choose cultivars carefully. Mail-order catalogs that sell fruit trees will suggest good pollinators for all of the trees they sell that require a pollinator.

Rootstocks

Most fruit trees are not grown on their own roots. Instead, they are grafted in the nursery onto the roots of compatible trees, usually of the same type. Apricots, however, are grafted onto plums, and pears

Cordon companions
A row of apple or pear cordons, here trained against post-and-wire supports, can be made up of different cultivars to fulfill pollination needs.

onto quinces. Rootstocks enable propagation of cultivars that do not root from cuttings and help to control the size of the tree. Depending, for example, on the rootstock selected, the same cultivar of apple might grow 8 ft. (2.4 m) tall, or 30 ft. (9 m). Further information on rootstocks is given under each fruit.

Own-root trees

Figs are always grown on their own roots, and all other tree fruits can be. They need careful managing as they can be enormously vigorous, resulting in trees up to 35 ft. (10.5 m) tall that take 5 to 8 years to fruit. In collaboration with fruit breeder Hugh Ermen, H.D.R.A. has been working for some years on establishing systems for growing trees on their own roots. Providing that vigor can be controlled, there are benefits for the organic gardener in better health and longevity (for the tree!) and less need for scrupulous weed control, as the trees will grow strongly despite competition, once established. In due course, apple trees on their own roots will become available to gardeners.

There is room for experimentation and innovation with these own-root trees. Orchards of such trees allow for imaginative floral underplantings, as the resulting competition for water and nutrients helps to control the natural vigor of the fruits.

Family trees

Two or more cultivars can be grafted onto the same rootstock to produce a single tree that bears different fruits on different branches; not only a novel conversation topic, but also a practical way of growing cultivars needed to pollinate each other in a small space.

Newly grafted fruit trees

Specialty fruit nurseries graft many hundreds of young trees each year, binding shoots from chosen cultivars onto the roots of other trees that will control height and vigor. The plant tissue fuses naturally at the graft point or "union."

Pruning and training

All fruit needs to be pruned for best results. Pruning aims to achieve a number of objectives:
• **Removal** of dead, diseased, and damaged material.
• **Creating a balance** between light penetration and light interception. With too many leaves, sunlight cannot enter the crown to ripen fruit; too little foliage and not enough photosynthesis takes place.
• **Opening up** the branch framework to allow better air circulation and lessen risk of fungal infection.
• **Pruning** out colonies of pests.
• **Shaping** the trees.
• **Controlling** vigor.

Before starting to prune, it is important to understand how trees and bushes grow. There are essentially two phases of growth. In spring there is a surge of new growth as each tree tries to ensure that it can compete for light with its neighbors. In midsummer this growth slows down and energy is then devoted to ripening the fruit already on the trees and producing new fruit buds for next season. Late in the summer there may be a short, second phase of leafy growth. You can take advantage of this pattern by pruning in winter if you want a plant to make more growth, and in summer if you need to

FREESTANDING TREE FORMS

Open center
A rounded or goblet shape with an open center: no central trunk beyond the point where the canopy branches. The restricted height makes for easy picking. Good for apples, Asian pears, and peaches, as well as sour cherries in warm areas or sites.

Central leader
A tree with a central trunk and branches arranged in tiers from top to bottom to give a somewhat pyramidal shape. Suited to apples, pears, plums, and sweet cherries.

Container fruit
Small bushes and standards can be created to grow in pots, useful where tender fruit needs to be under cover in winter. Most types of fruit can be used including red currants and gooseberries.

Standard tree
The traditional form for orchards of full-size apples and pears. The crown can be above head height on a full standard, making ladders a necessity for picking and pruning. Not suitable for small gardens.

control vigor. Formally trained fruit trees—fans, espaliers, pyramids, cordons, and palmettes—are thus pruned mainly in summer to keep tight control of the shape. Formative pruning of young trees is, on the other hand, usually done in the winter, with the exception of peaches, which are highly susceptible to cytospora disease infection in winter.

It is important with tree fruit to recognize a flower/fruit bud from a leaf or shoot bud. The latter are generally fairly flat and pointed and lie close to the stem. Fruit buds are usually rounder and fatter and point slightly away from the branch. Some fruit types produce flowers on 1-year-old wood, others on older wood—see the individual pages for details.

Trained forms

The craft of training fruit into architectural forms has its origins in France and Belgium. In Britain, the Victorians embraced the idea of formal shapes with enthusiasm, creating boats, goblets, winged pyramids, and candelabra in ever more elaboration. The most common and useful forms for modern gardens are oblique or upright cordons (single stem), fans, and espaliers. These shapes suit many soft fruit types, too. Apart from the attractiveness of the shapes achieved, training trees in this way allows fruit to be grown on a wall or on wires, thereby taking up less space. It suits small gardens admirably and makes productive and attractive use of walls and fences.

FLAT-TRAINED TREES

A system of parallel horizontal wires is used to support all these forms.

Cordon
A single trunk with clusters of short fruiting shoots, or spur systems, along its length. They can be vertical but are usually set at an angle. Cordons trained with two or more parallel main stems are known as double or multiple cordons. Good for apples, pears, and plums.

Espalier
A central trunk with opposing pairs of horizontal arms. Most usually 3-, 4- or 5-tiered. A low, single-tiered espalier is also called a "stepover." Suited to apples and pears.

Palmette
Similar to an espalier, but the arms radiate upward at a 45° angle. A very formal shape, popular in Victorian Britain. Suited to apples and pears.

Fan
Branches divide and radiate outward from a point 2–2½ ft. (60–75 cm) above the ground. The branches are not parallel but spread like fingers to cover the wall space allocated. Best suited to plums, cherries, figs, peaches, and apricots, but can also be used for apples and pears.

Restoring overgrown fruit trees

An old, tangled fruit tree is not an uncommon sight in gardens. Planted by an enthusiastic gardener or a relic of an older orchard, the tree has been neglected and left unpruned for many years. Some such neglected trees are tall and wide on their vigorous rootstocks; others are weak, stunted, and sickly. The latter type rarely become productive and are usually riddled with disease.

Decisions to make

Since renovating a tree is laborious, it is worth deciding in advance whether the effort is justified. Consider the following questions:

• **How diseased is the tree?** High levels of canker, mildew, and scab are not good signs.

• **Are there signs of vitality and vigor?** If extension growth annually is negligible, pruning hard may stimulate new growth (but this is not always the case).

• **Does it fruit, and are the fruits of good flavor?** Not all old trees are of rare or sought-after cultivars. Flavor is a matter of personal preference, and each gardener will need to decide for him- or herself.

• **Does the tree contribute to the overall design of the garden?** Gardens have become smaller, and occasionally large trees are left that are not in scale with the plot and create excessive shade. It may be better to start again with a new tree on a dwarfing rootstock or several trees trained as cordons.

Apples and pears

With few exceptions, large old trees were originally formed as open-centered, goblet-shaped bushes. The aim is to restore them to this with a basic framework of six to eight main permanent branches spaced evenly around the tree. This work should be done in winter.

• Start by removing all growth below the point at which the main branches start. Cut or pull out all suckers growing at the base.

• Examine the tree from below and choose the main branches that you will retain.

• Saw off all strong upright branches, any growing across the center, and any damaged or diseased ones.

• The center of the tree should be open to air and light. Remove any growth in the center to leave the main branches free of laterals for the first 2 ft. (60 cm) of the trunk.

• Now remove all other large branches that are not wanted for the framework that arise from the trunk or near the center of the tree.

• Work along each retained branch with pruning saw and shears, shortening sideshoots and thinning spur systems (the knobbly clusters of short stems) to leave up to three or four well-spaced, fat fruit buds on each spur system and no rubbing, crossing, or congested branches.

• With time, branches can get very long. If a long branch droops, growth at the tip will slow down or stop. Restoring vigor to old trees is part of the health package. If this has happened, prune back the leader to a single, strong, outward-pointing shoot. As you prune, cut out any diseased tissue.

The following summer there may be considerable growth around the pruning cuts. This must be managed, or the tree will, in a few years, revert to its former state.

• In midsummer, rip off any new young shoots in the center of the tree or below the point where the main branches start.

• In winter, thin out new sideshoots at major pruning cuts to leave single young laterals that will form new fruiting spurs in 2 years.

Thereafter prune the tree as an open center bush (see p. 268).

Plums

Restoring overgrown plums requires less dramatic pruning. Trees do not need to be as open and airy as apples and pears. The work must be carried out before buds open in spring to minimize the spread of diseases. The ideal time is just after fruit production.

• Reduce the height and width of the tree to a manageable size by sawing off large branches to a point where an outward-facing shoot or branch arises.

• Remove all damaged, diseased, crossing, and rubbing branches.

• Thin out the remainder of the canopy if necessary so that light can penetrate and no shoots are touching.

USEFUL EQUIPMENT

Once you have decided to restore a tree, you will need to be properly equipped. Minimum requirements are:

• Bow saw—for large branches over 1½ in. (4 cm) diameter.
• Pruning saw—for branches up to 1½ in. (4 cm) diameter.
• Pruning shears—for thinning out laterals. Since you may be climbing in the tree or up a ladder, a holster for the shears is very useful.
• Ladder—steps are dangerous in this work; an extension ladder is required, with rope to lash it to branches and prevent slipping. If you have several fruit trees, a specialized fruit tree ladder, tapering at the top and with a supporting leg (see left), is a very useful investment.

It is always advisable to work with someone else in case of accident and to help pull out tangled branches.

As with fruits pruned routinely, wounds on properly pruned fruit trees will heal perfectly adequately without the use of wound paints.

CULTIVAR CHOICE

Early
'Earliglow', 'Early Red',
'Honeoye', 'Northeaster',
'Sunrise', 'Surecrop'

Mid-season
'Allstar', 'Guardian', 'Jewel',
'Midway', 'Red Chief',
'Redcoat'

Late
'Bounty', 'Robinson', 'Sparkle'

Ever-bearing (perpetual)
'Ft. Laramie', 'Ogallala',
'Ozark Beauty'
(Note: ever-bearing or
"perpetual" types are generally
grown for a late harvest. To
achieve this, you must remove
all flowers that form until late
spring. Otherwise they will
produce nearly all of their fruit
in summer.)

**Resistant to powdery
mildew**
'Chambly', 'Jewel', 'Red Chief',
'St. Clair', 'Tristar'

**Resistant to verticillium
wilt**
'Allstar', 'Lateglow', 'Red
Chief', 'Tribute', 'Tristar'

Resistant to red stele
'Allstar', 'Cavendish',
'Earliglow', 'Lateglow',
'Quinault', 'Red Chief',
'Tribute', 'Tristar'

Tucking straw under fruits
*Keeping the fruit clean and dry (right)
will reduce the risk of spoilage by rots
and mildew.*

Pegging down runners
*You can peg a few runners into pots
(far right) to root to increase your
stocks of plants, provided that the
parent plant shows no sign of disease.*

Strawberries

The taste of the first strawberry of the year is undoubtedly more exciting than the sight of the first robin. You could be harvesting your first crop within 12 months of planting.

The earliest cultivars start bearing in late spring—even earlier if grown under cover. The main season then extends through the summer with late season "perpetual" types continuing the harvest into autumn. By choosing appropriate cultivars (see left) it is possible to harvest outdoor strawberries from early summer until the first frosts of autumn. In a small garden, however, limit yourself to one or two varieties, as fewer than 12 plants of each provides a frustratingly small harvest. The healthy, productive life of a strawberry plant is about 3 years. Strawberries are generally hardy in Zones 3 to 10.

Strawberries do not freeze well except as a purée and cannot be stored as whole fruit. Eat them immediately or refrigerate for a day or two.

Site and soil
Strawberries need winter cold to initiate flowering and summer sun to grow and ripen fruit. An open site in full sun is best. Relatively unfussy about soil, strawberries will grow in an acid soil with a pH as low as 5.5. Well-drained, slightly acidic, sandy loams with good levels of organic matter suit them best. High fertility is not a good idea as it will tend to encourage big leafy plants at the expense of fruit. Good drainage, however, is extremely important, as is adequate water at most stages of growth. If your soil is not a sandy loam, you can still grow good strawberries by attending to soil structure and drainage (see pp. 38–41). Strawberries can also be grown in containers (see pp. 212–213).

Buying plants
Strawberries are bought in various forms: bareroot runners, pot-grown plants, and cold-stored runners. This allows for flexibility in planting times.

Strawberries reproduce by sending out long stems (runners), at the end of which young plantlets form. These root while still attached to the parent. The traditional bareroot runners are best planted as soon as they become available in summer. They can be planted as late as autumn, but should then be deflowered in their first year as they will be weakened by growing a crop while still so young.

Pot-grown plants can be planted in autumn or early winter and can even be held back for planting until late spring if weather conditions are not suitable. If bought in winter, keep them out in the cold to ensure flowering. They can be allowed to fruit in their first year.

Cold-stored runners are held back in growth by keeping them artificially cool. They are sold in early summer for immediate planting, when they rush into growth and produce a crop late in the season. They will then fruit normally in the following years.

Preparation and planting

Before planting, dress the bed with 1 in. (2–3 cm) of leaf mold and lightly work it in. If your soil is particularly poor, add either well-rotted manure— one wheelbarrowful to 8–10 sq. yd. (8–10 sq. m)— or garden compost at twice that rate.

• **Space plants** 12–18 in. (30–45 cm) apart in the row with 30 in. (75 cm) between rows.

• **Scoop out** holes large enough to spread out bare roots or to fit a potted rootball.

• **Set the plants** with the crown above the soil level (do not bury the center of the plants) and firm soil with the fingers or knuckles.

• **Water** the plants well.

Caring for the crop

Be alert for problems, and take precautions to prevent damage to the fruits (see right). In dry weather keep plants well watered, especially while fruit is swelling. If soil has been well prepared, strawberries will not need additional feeding during the season. Remove all runners that form; up to three runners on a healthy plant can be retained, however, to make new plants.

Harvest fruits when they are fully colored all over and eat them right away—not that you will need prompting! After all the crop has been picked, trim off all foliage to leave 1 in. (2.5 cm) or so of stalk to protect the newly emerging leaves. Put all this, with the straw, on the compost pile. This will take away any lingering pests or diseases and reduce the risk of reinfection.

A light dressing of garden compost soon after tidying up foliage, at the rate of one 2-gallon bucket per sq. yd. (10 liters per sq. m), will stimulate healthy new growth.

Looking ahead

You will need to plan to move your strawberry bed somewhere new every 3 years. Ideally you should allow 6 years before returning strawberries to a strawberry bed or planting raspberries there, as they share many soilborne diseases. In small gardens you may have to settle for 3 years. In the interim the bed could be used to grow annual flowers, lettuce, or other short-lived plants. This means you will need to identify at least two plots for strawberries over the long term.

PROTECT THE CROP

Plant certified disease-free plants, or runners from a crop known to be healthy. Make pest- and disease-resistant cultivars your first choice where possible.

Plant in an appropriate site, where strawberries or raspberries have not been grown for 6 years or more. This is to avoid persistent soilborne problems such as red stele and verticillium wilt.

Don't overcrowd plants; a damp atmosphere can encourage gray mold (botrytis), which spoils the fruit. To keep fruits clean and dry, lay a 2-in. (5-cm) mulch of straw around plants, tucking it under the foliage. Pick off diseased fruit and foliage as seen. Powdery mildew symptoms on leaves are more likely in dry weather. Use a drip or soaker hose watering system to avoid wetting the foliage.

Net the crop before the fruits ripen. This will exclude birds, but squirrels and foxes may also take the fruit. Slugs love ripening strawberries. Encourage natural predators, put down slug traps, or use biological control (see p. 100) if necessary.

Check plants regularly for aphids and red spider mite. The latter is more likely in hot, dry locations, and under cover. Biological controls can be used against red spider mite and vine weevil, which can cause sudden death of individual plants as they eat the roots.

Viruses and strawberry red stele disease can cause stunted growth. Remove the plants; do not replant with strawberries or raspberries.

See the *A–Z of Plant Problems*, (pp. 367–395) and *Plant Health* (pp. 84–103) for more information.

CULTIVAR CHOICE

Summer-bearing red
'Algonquin', 'Boyne', 'Canby',
'Festival', 'Gatineau', 'Hilton',
'Latham', 'Liberty', 'Newburgh',
'Willamette'

Autumn-bearing red
'Amity', 'Autumn Bliss',
'Heritage', 'Redwing',
'Summit'

Black raspberries
'Allen', 'Black Hawk', 'Bristol',
'Cumberland', 'Haut',
'Lowden', 'Munger'

Purple raspberries
'Brandywine', 'Clyde', 'Royalty',
'Success'

Yellow raspberries
'Fall Gold', 'Golden Summit'

Raspberries

Raspberries follow the strawberry season with
perfect timing. They are normally grown in rows, but
even a small garden can find room for two or three
plants grouped around a single 5-ft. (1.5-m) stake.
As well as cultivars spanning the summer season you
will also find autumn-fruiting types. These produce
fruiting canes in a single year, providing a harvest
from late summer until the first frosts of autumn.
Summer raspberries grow on canes grown the
previous year, so their first crop will be harvested in
the second season after planting. Autumn-fruiting
types will produce a small crop in the first year.
Raspberries are generally hardy in Zones 3 to 9.

Raspberries freeze well, but otherwise will keep
for only 1 or 2 days in a refrigerator.

Site and soil

Raspberries grow in relatively cool areas with
shorter summers, as well as in warmer climates. They
prefer fertile, well-drained soil with a pH of 6.5 or
below. Raspberries are not happy in alkaline soil
so don't amend your soil with lime. They will suffer
permanently from iron deficiency (see p. 89), which
cannot be corrected easily. They need sunshine for at

least half the day but can tolerate breezy locations
provided they are well staked and tied.

Good drainage is vital as raspberries are prone to
an aggressive root rot that thrives in waterlogged
soils. Equally important is adequate water in summer
as raspberries root close to the surface and can
quickly suffer from water shortage.

Buying plants

Raspberries are usually sold as bareroot plants
for winter planting. It is essential to buy certified
virus-free stock from a reputable supplier, as
raspberries are very prone to viruses. Good-quality
stock will produce for up to 14 years if well
managed, perhaps 8 if your soil is alkaline.

Soil preparation and planting

Raspberries, blackberries, and strawberries share
some unpleasant soilborne diseases. For this reason
these fruit types should not replace each other when
a planting becomes exhausted. If planting into
previously cultivated soil, you will need to do little
more than add garden compost or well-rotted
manure at the recommended rate (see p. 40).

Remove all perennial weeds before planting, then erect a post-and-wire support. A double support system (see below) allows more canes but takes more space. Set the plants 15–18 in. (35–45 cm) apart (or for more vigorous cultivars, such as 'Autumn Bliss', around 20 in./50 cm apart) in a line under the wires up to the soil mark on the cane stub.

In spring, buds will break first on the cane stub before new growth emerges from below ground. As soon as this happens, cut off the stub to soil level.

Caring for the crop

Address weeding, watering, and any pests and disease problems (see right) as soon as possible. Feeding during the season should not be necessary. An annual dressing of compost after harvest and fertilizer in spring (see below) should be sufficient. If growth is weak, plants may be showing infection by virus rather than lack of nutrition, and they need to be removed and burned.

By early summer the new canes will be growing well and a small forest of new growth, known as suckers, will be emerging. Keep hoeing or cutting off any suckers forming outside of the row until the soil is warm enough to mulch heavily. Use straw or hay. Newspaper six or seven pages thick under the mulch will smother out unwanted suckers and weeds, but it does hinder rain penetration.

Thin out the new canes to 10 or 12 per 3 ft. (1 m) of row when they are about 30 in. (75 cm) tall, removing weak or diseased canes first. Canes of autumn-fruiting types do not need thinning. Restrict them to a band about 12 in. (30 cm) wide. Tie the canes loosely to the wire supports as they grow.

After the harvest

As soon as possible after fruiting, cut down all fruited canes of summer crops to ground level. Try not to leave an untidy stub, which can be an entry site for pests and diseases. Spread garden compost along the row to help decompose the dead stubs.

Thin the new canes if necessary to leave about eight to ten for every 3 ft. (1 m) of row, and tie them firmly to the wires. Leave autumn-fruiting types loosely tied, even after harvest. In autumn, loop over the top of each cane and tie it to the top wire. This makes canes more stable in windy weather. In late winter, untie the cane tips and prune back to a bud just above the top wire. At the same time, cut back all canes of autumn-fruiting crops to ground level and mulch with garden compost to cover the stubs and help them rot. Remove the old straw mulch and compost it before adding compost. In alternate springs, spread seaweed meal at 4 oz. per sq. yd. (125 g per sq. m) and a general organic fertilizer, according to label instructions, to give plants a boost.

PROTECT THE CROP

Start with healthy, virus-free stock, planted where no cane fruit or strawberries have been grown for 6 years or more. Culitvars resistant to aphids are available. A soil pH of 6.5 or less and good drainage are vital. Check for aphids during the season; squash by hand or spot-treat with a soap spray. Net ripening fruit against birds.

Small raspberry fruitworms may be found in ripe fruit—spray with pyrethrins when flower buds appear. Removing mulches and lightly cultivating soil around canes in winter will help to control this beetle and also cane borers. Borer damage can be an entry point for diseases.

Throughout the season, check canes for signs of raspberry spur blight, cane blight, and cane spot. Cut out and burn diseased canes. Use Bordeaux mixture as a preventative spray at bud break where these diseases have occurred.

See the *A–Z of Plant Problems*, p. 367, and *Plant Health*, p. 84, for more information.

Summer raspberries
The fruiting canes are tied to support wires, while new canes grow up in the spaces between, to be tied when the fruited canes are pruned out.

CULTIVAR CHOICE

Blackberries
'Helen' (T)
'Loch Ness' (T) (shown below)
'Marion'
'Waldo' (R)(T)

Hybrid berries
'Boysenberry' (T)
'Tayberry'

R good disease resistance
T thornless

Blackberries and hybrid berries

Blackberries grow wild, but if you want to have your own personal supply of this usually heavy-cropping, juicy, late summer fruit, then grow your own. Blackberries can be hardy from Zones 5 to 10, depending on the cultivar.

In the 20th century many crosses, principally between raspberries and blackberries, were carried out to produce a range of interesting hybrid berries. These include loganberries, tayberries, boysenberries, and many others. These fruits are mostly earlier-producing than blackberries and sweet, but with a similar growing habit.

You will harvest your first crop in the second summer after planting and can anticipate full production the year after that.

Site and soil

Most blackberries and hybrid berries are vigorous, if not rampant, growers and need plenty of space. The ideal situation is against a wall, fence, or post-and-wire arrangement similar to that used for raspberries (see p. 251). It is important to give plants sufficient space for the long canes to be tied. Beds prepared at the base of walls or fences should be at least 3 ft. (1 m) wide.

Blackberries are easy to grow and are not fussy about soil. Hybrid berries generally need more

Blackberries are vigorous and easy to grow, and are not fussy about soil

warmth and similar conditions to raspberries—a well-drained, slightly acid soil.

It is possible to grow blackberries in partial shade or a site facing away from the sun, but hybrid berries grow best in full sun.

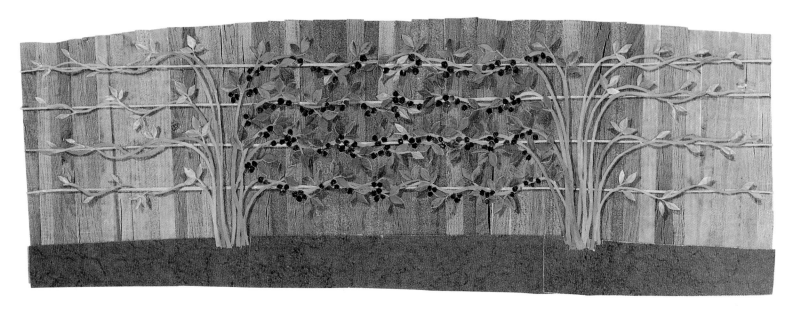

Buying plants

Plants are sold as bareroot canes in the same way as raspberries. If you have a small garden, look for some of the less vigorous cultivars, such as 'Marion'. Most cultivars are thorny but a few are thornless. These are, in some cases, also less vigorous but seem to have less flavor than the thorned cultivars. The season for these berries extends from midsummer through to late autumn.

Preparation and planting

Prepare the soil as for raspberries (see p. 251). Each plant may need as much as 24 ft. (7.2 m) of space to tie the canes, depending on the cultivar. Erect posts as for raspberries and set wires 9 in. (23 cm) apart, from 2 ft. (60 cm) above soil level up to about 5 ft. (1.5 m). If you are planting against a fence or wall, a similar wiring arrangement will be needed.

Plant a single plant at the center of the support, or space plants according to vigor (see *Cultivar Choice*, facing page) if you are growing several. Bury each plant up to the soil mark on the stub and firm the soil.

In spring, buds will form on the stub; later, new growth will emerge from below soil level. As soon as this happens, cut off the old stub at soil level.

Pruning and training

In the first year, only a few canes will grow. Tie all these to one side as they develop. By midsummer you will need to attend to this weekly because growth is rapid.

There are three methods of tying: roping, where the canes are divided into equal numbers and tied as they develop in loose "ropes" along each wire; weaving, where canes are trained individually in informal loops up and down the wires; and fans, which are used for stiff-stemmed types like 'Oregon Thornless', where the canes are tied in a rough fan shape across the framework. If cane tips touch the soil, they may root and produce a new plant.

In the second year, this growth will flower and fruit, and new canes will grow. Tie the new canes to the opposite side, following one of the methods above. This is known as the "alternate bay" system (see above). Allow up to 30 new canes per plant, although some cultivars produce many fewer.

After fruiting, cut all fruited canes to the ground and spread garden compost over the cut stubs to help them decompose quickly.

Caring for the crop

After a few years the plants will throw up suckers away from the main clump. These can be hand-pulled as they appear.

Blackberries need little feeding. If vigor declines, apply garden compost, well-rotted manure, or alfalfa meal. Hybrid berries will benefit from a dressing of garden compost every 2 to 3 years.

Keep the crop well watered. In early summer, mulch the soil with straw or hay as for raspberries (see p. 251). Root spread is extensive, so all exposed soil around the plant should be covered to at least 3 ft. (1 m) from the plant.

"Alternate bay" training
The simplest way to train blackberries is with the fruiting canes tied on one side, and the new growth on the other. With several plants, alternate the sides so that fruiting canes meet fruiting canes, and new growth grows toward new growth.

PROTECT THE CROP

Plant healthy, virus-free stock in an appropriate spot. Netting against birds may be needed. Train new canes away from old ones (see above) so that diseases such as rust and purple blotch are not transferred from old to new foliage. Cover stubs of cut-down canes with compost to help them decompose.

Remove mulch in autumn to allow birds access to the soil to help clear up capsid bugs and raspberry beetles.

Pests and diseases are less likely to be a problem where plants are growing in appropriately managed soil and where the garden environment encourages natural predation. See the *A–Z of Plant Problems*, p. 367, for more details.

**"Destructive" method of
pruning black currant
bushes (right)**
*This method works well only if you
have three plants or multiples of three.
Divide the bushes into three groups
of equal number. Starting in the
autumn after the first crop has been
harvested, prune off all growth on all
plants in one of these groups. Leave
the others unpruned. Rotate your way
through all three groups in successive
years so that eventually, in any year,
you will have one set of plants
growing new branches and two sets
cropping. This system is reasonably
effective at reducing disease infections.*

Black currants

Black currants, nutritious and rich in flavor, are hardy and reliable, although late frost can damage blossoms and reduce the crop. The berries can be eaten raw, cooked, or pressed for their juice. Black currants have a particularly high vitamin C content and, as with all soft fruits, are best consumed soon after picking to gain maximum nutritional benefit. However, they are suitable for freezing and make excellent preserves.

Black currants are always grown as bushes. You will harvest a moderate crop after 2 years, reaching full production after 3 or 4 years.

Site and soil
As black currants are pruned hard, they generally need quite fertile conditions but are otherwise unfussy about soil types. They do grow into quite broad bushes even with pruning and are not suited to trained shapes such as fans in the way that red currants are. A single bush can be quite productive, so you can still grow black currants if you have a small garden. Choose a spot in full sun most of the day for best results. Bushes become stunted and spindly in a too-shady spot. Plants are generally best grown in Zones 3 to 6.

Buying plants
Black currants are generally sold as 1-year-old plants. A good plant will have a few branches and a strong, fibrous root system. Some nurseries may sell container-grown young plants, which can be planted at any time of year when the ground isn't frozen, provided enough water is given to help establish

them. It is always preferable, however, to plant in early winter or, if that is not possible, very early in spring when the soil is workable and not too wet.

There are cultivars that are resistant to some of the pests and diseases of black currants, particularly to American gooseberry mildew and white pine blister rust (see *Protect the Crop*, facing page). Others are particularly valued for their flavor and extra-high vitamin C content.

Preparation and planting
It is important to prepare the ground well.
• Mark out an area large enough to accommodate the number of bushes you plan. Allow a spacing of 5–6 ft. (1.5–1.8 m) apart—unless you are using the "hedge" system (see facing page)—or 5 ft. (1.5 m) in all directions for a single bush.
• Clear the site of all perennial weeds and, if drainage is poor, double-dig the plot (see p. 322). If digging a bed in lawn, dig the sod under, carefully removing dandelion or other perennial weed roots.
• Just before planting, work in well-rotted manure at the rate of one 2-gallon (10-liter) bucket to every 20 sq. ft. (2 sq. m), or garden compost at twice that rate. If organic matter levels are low and you are not digging in sod, apply about 1 in. (2–3 cm) of leaf mold as well and lightly dig it in.
• Set the plants 5–6 ft. (1.5–1.8 m) apart (or use the alternative closely spaced "hedge" method, see facing page) and plant them about 2 in. (5 cm) deeper than the soil mark to encourage further roots to form on the buried stems. Cut back the branches, leaving one or two buds on each above soil level.

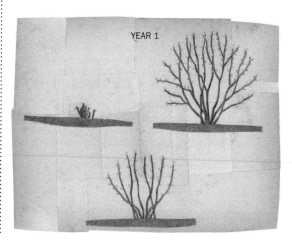

YEAR 1

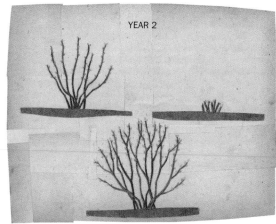

YEAR 2

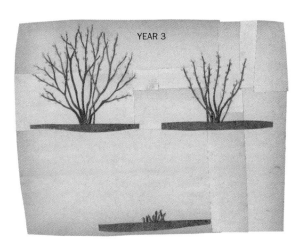

Currant events
Apart from the harvest of luscious, juicy fruits (left), the key time in the black currant year is winter, when they should be pruned—traditionally, as above, by sawing out thick, old branches at the base to leave younger wood that will produce well in coming years.

Feeding

Feed bushes with garden compost, well-rotted manure, or organic fertilizers at least every 3 years at the rate recommended, or every other year on poorer soils. A well-managed planting should last over 20 years. Mulch bushes in late spring with straw or hay.

Pruning

Black currants fruit mainly on the previous season's wood. The aim of any management is, therefore, to encourage as much healthy new growth as possible to fruit the following year. It is not necessary to create an open center to the bush. In the first year, the new plants will produce branches from above and below ground and there will be no crop. No pruning is necessary. In the second year, the existing branches will fruit and grow. New branches also grow from below ground. They are pruned in autumn, traditionally by removing up to one-third of the oldest branches as close as possible to soil level (see above). This process does not start until the autumn of the third year. Start with those lying closest to the ground. In some cases, a good new shoot can be found near the base of an old branch. Prune back to this if it is well placed.

Alternatives to traditional pruning

These include the "destructive" method (see left), which prunes bushes in groups of three on a 3-year cycle, and the "hedge" method. With this method it is possible to gain a bigger harvest early in the life of a new planting by close planting at 36 in. (90 cm) apart. Once the bushes start to become crowded, you can either remove every other bush in winter and thereafter use the "traditional" method, or sustain the system by removing all fruited wood every autumn.

Red and white currants

A red currant bearing a full crop of ripe berries is truly stunning. These berries may not be as sweet as strawberries, but they are an essential summer dessert, make excellent jelly and wine, and, with their high pectin content, are very useful for mixing with fruits that set poorly when making jam. They also freeze well.

There are cultivars available to span a season of harvest during the main summer months. The red currant is, perhaps, more dramatic in fruit, but some connoisseurs prefer the white for its slightly sweeter flavor. All the advice given here for red currants also applies equally to white currants. Both perform best in Zones 3 to 6.

Unlike black currants, which fruit almost exclusively on wood grown the previous year, red currants crop on short shoots that grow from a permanent framework of branches. They can thus not only be grown as bushes but also as cordons and fans, and even as standards (see p. 263).

Red currants will start producing as soon as there are branches that are 2 years old. The crop will increase annually, and peak after 5 years or so. A well-managed bush might last up to 30 years, although 15 to 20 is more usual.

Site and soil
Although closely related to black currants, red currants have a different habit of growth and rather different requirements, needing less fertile conditions. They are fully hardy, tough, reliable, and rather unfussy about soil. They are well suited to growing as cordons or fans and will even produce fruit in cool locations where they receive only short amounts of direct sunlight.

If you plan to grow these currants as cordons or fans, you will need a fence or wall equipped with horizontal wires, or a post-and-wire structure to support them (see also *Blackberries*, p. 252). Birds enjoy these fruits, so you will need to net them.

Buying plants
Plants are usually sold bareroot or container-grown as 1-, 2-, or 3-year-old plants. To grow as bushes, look for plants with a good fibrous root system, a short single stem, and three or more young branches of about pencil-thickness at the base. For trained shapes, start with 1-year-old plants.

Preparation and planting
For bushes, mark out a site large enough to accommodate the number of bushes you plan. Allow for a spacing of 4–5 ft. (1.2–1.5 m) apart. Space cordons 15–18 in. (40–45 cm) apart. A fan will grow to about 6 ft. (2 m) wide.

To prepare the soil, follow the advice given for black currants. Just before planting, work in garden compost or any other medium-fertility soil improver

except farmyard manure, at the rate of one 2-gallon (10-liter) bucket to every 10 sq. ft. (1 sq. m). Heavy dressings of manure are not recommended for red currants, as plants grow too vigorously and branches can tear away in high winds.

Plant bareroot bushes in winter; pot-grown plants can be planted at any time but will establish better if planted in winter. Dig a hole large enough to accommodate the roots comfortably and spread the roots out evenly in the hole. Replace the soil, ensuring that the plant is planted at the level of the original soil mark. If a 1-year-old plant has more than one stem arising from the base, remove all but the best; a branched 2- or 3-year-old bush should have a single "leg," or length of clear trunk, below the point where the branches form.

Pruning and training

Unlike black currants, red currants fruit on wood that is at least 2 years old. Whether grown as trained forms or bushes, red currants are pruned to encourage short, stubby fruiting shoots known as spurs. Winter pruning (see below) forms and maintains the basic shape and size of the plants, while additional summer pruning restricts the amount of growth on them by shortening all shoots on the main framework branches. Summer pruning also helps to remove disease and any aphids present.

Summer pruning

To summer prune, first identify the leading shoot of each branch (the one at the tip that extends the length of the branch) and do not prune it. (If the leading shoot is exceptionally long, choose a shorter shoot below it and leave this unpruned.) Prune all other sideshoots to five leaves. This pruning is important because:

• It removes pest colonies at shoot tips.
• It removes soft sappy growth, which is most susceptible to American gooseberry mildew and other fungal infections.
• It improves air circulation, reducing the risk of infection by mildew and other diseases, which thrive in still air between congested growth.
• It controls vigor, restricting stem and leaf production in favor of promoting fruit and fruit bud development.

Caring for the crop

Mulch all plants in late spring with hay or straw. This will conserve moisture and suppress weeds. Do not overfeed red currants. A dressing of garden compost every 3 years should be adequate for their needs. Clear away suckers (shoots growing around the base of the plant) to leave a single clear stem by pulling, cutting, or chopping them away, ideally when they are still small.

PROTECT THE CROP

The currant aphid can colonize undersides of leaves from bud burst. Encourage natural aphid predators. Pick off badly infested leaves, or spray with canola oil-soap spray if widespread. Check from mid-spring for imported currantworm larvae, which can defoliate a plant. Pick off, or spray with canola oil-soap spray. Clear up fallen leaves in autumn.

PRUNING AND TRAINING RED CURRANTS IN WINTER

Bush	Cordon	Fan
At planting Cut back all branches by one-half to an outward-facing bud. Shorten any sideshoots to two or three buds.	**1** Only one upright stem should be retained. In the winter after planting, cut this back by up to one-half of the new growth and reduce sideshoots to two or three buds.	**1** After planting, reduce to a single stem and prune this back to leave a short "leg" of about 10 in. (25 cm).
Years 1 and 2 Repeat this process in subsequent years until a bush is formed with eight to ten main branches, each with a strong leading shoot and spur system forming lower down. Keep the center of the bush open by pruning out shoots growing toward the center. Start summer pruning (see above).	**2** Repeat this process each winter until the plant has reached the desired height. Start summer pruning from the third year (see above).	**2** After the first growing season, a number of branches will have grown out. Remove any growing toward or away from the wall or supports. Tie the four best-placed branches, using canes to keep them straight, in a fan shape. Leave the center open. Cut all four branches back by one-half. Remove all others.
Subsequent years Once the bush is formed, each winter prune back the leading shoot by up to one-half and continue to reduce all side growth to two or three buds. Remove any old, congested, and weak spur systems.	**3** Thereafter in winter cut back the leader to one or two buds of new growth or prune back to a new leader slightly lower down the stem. Remove old, congested, and weak spur systems. To create a double or triple cordon, allow two or three stems to grow upright, training them parallel to each other.	**3** In the next year, allow two good branches to grow from the buds near the tip of each of the existing branches and tie them. Spur back all growth lower down to two or three buds in winter.
		4 Continue this process until the space is filled, leaving at least 6 in. (15 cm) between the tips of branches at the outside of the fan. Do not allow any strong upright branches to grow, as these will tend to dominate and reduce vigor on lower-angled branches. Start summer pruning (see above) once the fan is formed.
		5 Thereafter each winter, prune the new spurs as above, occasionally reducing or removing spur systems. After several years, the lowest two branches may become weak. These can be removed and the next tier brought down to replace them.

CULTIVAR CHOICE

American gooseberries (R)
'Downing' (green)
'Houghton' (red)
'Oregon Champion' (green)
'Pixwell' (pink)
'Poorman' (red)
'Welcome' (red)

European gooseberries
'Chautauqua' (green)
'Fredonia' (dark red)
'Hinnomaki Yellow' (yellow)
  (R)
'Whitesmith' (pale green to
  white)

R resistant to American
gooseberry mildew

Gooseberries

If you claim to have no interest in gooseberries, there is a fair chance it is because you have never tasted a fine dessert fruit, packed with flavor.

Gooseberries can be grown as bushes, cordons, fans, and standards. Hardy in Zones 3 to 7, a well-managed bush will last 15 to 20 years and will produce the second summer after planting. Gooseberries freeze well but otherwise do not store for long.

Site and soil

Gooseberries and red currants are closely related, and advice on site and soil for red currants (see p. 256) is equally applicable for gooseberries. Gooseberries can also be grown with little direct sunlight, except that choice dessert cultivars are better grown where they will receive sunlight for at least half the day.

Buying and planting

Buy, plant, and prepare the soil following the general advice given for red currants (see p. 256). Gooseberries can be rather droopy in habit and it is important to keep fruit away from contamination by

Winter pruning
Gooseberries are "spur-pruned" as red currants are: Sideshoots are shortened to short fruiting spurs.

CLOSE RELATIONS

The jostaberry (*Ribes nigridolaria*) is a cross between the gooseberry and black currant. Hardy in Zones 3 to 7, it is a vigorous, thornless bush, with round, tangy-sweet fruit. Jostaberries are best eaten when perfectly ripe, soon after picking.

Plant in full sun or part shade, spacing bushes 8 ft. (2.4 m) apart. Each winter, cut off any shoots that are more than 3 years old and thin to leave 6 shoots per plant. Jostaberries are resistant to gooseberry mildew and white pine blister rust.

soil, which can in turn lead to fungal infections or attack by slugs and snails. Plant gooseberries where there is a good airflow, keep the bushes pruned to an open center, and push in four stakes around each bush, about 12 in. (30 cm) away from the stem and angled slightly outward. Join them with string or light wire at a height of about 16–18 in. (40–45 cm) so that new branches are forced to be more upright. In subsequent years these canes can be moved outward and the wire raised or removed. The other option is to train plants as cordons.

Caring for the crop

Feeding and watering Follow the mulching and feeding information for red currants (see p. 257).
Pests and diseases Gooseberries share the same pests and diseases as red currants (see p. 257). American gooseberry mildew and the imported currantworm are the two main problems. Mildew-resistant cultivars are an effective method of avoiding this disease. In spring, look for and cut out mildewed shoots and leaves, then developing fruit. Check from mid-spring for imported currantworm larvae, which can defoliate a plant. Pick off where practical, or spray with canola oil-soap spray. Finally, watch for aphids on young shoots in spring; squash these by hand, wash off with water, or spray with soap.

Pruning

Gooseberries are pruned and trained as for red currants (see p. 257), except that spurs are left longer in winter and pruned to three or four buds rather than two to allow more fruits to grow.

Blueberries

Unlike many of the fruits we grow, blueberries are a native American crop. Gardeners can choose highbush blueberries (Zones 4–7), lowbush blueberries (Zones 2–6), midhigh cultivars (Zones 3–7), or rabbiteye blueberries (Zones 7–9). Unfortunately blueberries thrive only in very acid soils, meaning major soil modifications or growing in pots for some of us.

Fruiting will start in the second summer after planting, reaching full production after 5 or 6 years. The season lasts from mid- to late summer.

Site and soil

Blueberries need damp but not waterlogged soil with high organic matter levels and a soil pH between 4 and 5.5. Choose a sunny site, although some shade will not be a problem. Protection from late frost is important.

Buying plants

A single plant will produce fruit, but better results will be achieved with two or more bushes to cross-pollinate. Buy 2- or 3-year-old plants, usually pot-grown, checking that they are not rootbound.

Preparation and planting

Never forget that blueberries need very acid conditions. You will need to test the pH of any compost or manure that you use. Garden compost is frequently alkaline and manure cannot be guaranteed to be acid. Use only rainwater when watering plants. If you do not have suitable soil conditions, grow blueberries in a large pot or tub.

Plant bushes in late autumn or early winter, spacing them 5 ft. (1.5 m) apart. Mulch with composted bark or pine needles.

Caring for the crop

Feeding and watering Keep the mulch topped up annually. Remember not to use tap water on plants.

Pests and diseases Problems are rare.

Harvesting Fruits ripen over a period of weeks and should be picked when they are soft, fully blue, and come off the branches easily. Fruits can be frozen successfully or are suited to preserving.

Pruning

Blueberries fruit on 2- and 3-year-old branches. The aim of pruning is to keep a good supply of new branches, removing a number of branches that are 4 years old or more each year. In the first 2 or 3 years, prune out any very weak growth or branches growing in a more horizontal plane close to the soil.

In subsequent years, continue to remove weak growth; cut out crossing branches and wood that has stopped fruiting. Prune out branches growing close to soil level or pointing downward.

CULTIVAR CHOICE

American grapes
'Canadice' (red), 'Concord' (blue), 'Delaware' (red), 'Mars' (blue), 'Niagara' (white), 'Reliance Seedless' (red)

European and hybrid grapes
'Aurore' (pink), 'Himrod' (white), 'Interlaken Seedless' (golden), 'Madeleine Angevine' (golden), 'Pinot Noir' (dark blue), 'Thompson Seedless' (white)

Grapes

Grapes make a wonderful treat straight from the vine, or preserved as jelly, juice, or wine. They thrive in full sun, with good drainage and protection from late frosts.

Selection

There are four main types of grapes grown in North America: European, or wine grapes (*Vitis vinifera*); American, such as 'Concord' (*V. labruscana*); hybrids between European and American; and muscadine (*V. rotundifolia*).

Early settlers to North America found native grapes growing rampantly. Many good fresh-eating and juice grapes have been selected from the native species, including 'Concord' and 'Niagara'. Hardy in Zones 4 to 7, American grapes have a strong grape or "foxy" flavor and slipskins, which means that the berries can easily be squeezed out of the skins.

European (vinifera) grapes produce most of the world's table grapes, wine, and raisins. They are not as hardy as their American cousins (Zones 6 or 7 to 10), are much more susceptible to diseases, and require more work to harvest a satisfactory crop.

Plant breeders have crossed and recrossed European and American species and created grapes to satisfy almost every taste and use. Many of them are as hardy as their American parent and have good disease resistance.

Most of us would love to be able to grow sweet, seedless grapes such as the 'Thompson Seedless' or 'Flame Seedless' grapes found in grocery stores. Unfortunately, growing seedless grapes isn't simple. These vinifera cultivars grow well only in hot, dry regions. Also, commercial growers spray the vines with synthetic growth regulators and girdle the vines at fruit set to make the berries large. Without such treatment, these cultivars produce disappointingly small grapes. If you still yearn for seedless grapes from your backyard, try planting seedless American cultivars such as 'Mars' (blue), 'Himrod' (white), or 'Canadice' (red). If you live in the Deep South, you may be able to grow only muscadine grapes. Hardy in Zones 7 to 10, they make good jelly and juice and a distinctive, sweet wine.

American and hybrid grape cultivars can be grown on their own roots. European grape roots are very susceptible to phylloxera, a sucking insect native to the eastern and southern United States and now spread throughout the world. Choose vines grafted on American rootstocks. Certain American rootstock cultivars are also resistant to nematodes and the virus diseases they transmit.

Buying plants

Grapevines are available either as bareroot or container-grown plants, usually about a year old. American, hybrid, and muscadine grapes can be grafted or grown on their own roots. In most areas, European grapes must be grafted onto phylloxera-

Double Guyot

This technique works well with European grapes. Train the vine so that the vertical fruiting shoots are well spaced to allow plenty of sun to fall on the fruits. Ensure that you have a group of three strong shoots in the center. When the fruiting arms are pruned out, two of these can be tied down along the bottom wire to form next year's structure. The third is a reserve in case one shoot fails. If by any chance two or all of the central shoots are lost, you can retain last year's rods, cutting back the vertical fruited shoots to two or three buds.

resistant rootstock. In the Deep South, choose rootstocks or cultivars resistant to Pierce's disease. All grapes are self-pollinating—their flowers will pollinate each other—making it possible to grow just one vine and still get a good crop.

Planting and care

Prepare the site a year before planting the vines. Remove perennial weeds, and have the soil tested. Dig the site deeply, adding lots of garden compost and any amendments needed to correct deficiencies. Grapes do best at a pH of 5-6. Nitrogen, potassium, and magnesium are most likely to cause deficiencies. In the absence of a soil test, add seaweed meal at the rate of 4 oz. per sq. ft. (125 mg per sq. m).

Plant dormant, 1-year-old vines in the spring before their buds begin to swell and open. Soak roots in a bucket of water for 1 to 2 hours before planting. Prune each vine back to leave two live buds before planting; also cut back long roots so they'll fit easily into the hole without bending. Leave 1-2 in. (2.5-5 cm) of trunk above ground and make a shallow basin around the vine to hold water. If you are planting grafted vines, be sure to keep the graft union above ground level.

Fertilization and watering

On most sites, careful soil preparation before planting eliminates the need for heavy fertilization. Mulch lightly with compost in late winter each year. Compost tea and dilute seaweed extract sprays are good general foliar fertilizers. Keep in mind that overfertilizing can cause grapevines to grow rampantly and produce little fruit.

Keep vines well irrigated in summer, but stop watering once the grapes begin to ripen in late summer. A mulch of straw applied in late spring and removed in autumn will keep down weeds and help conserve moisture, as well as providing some potash.

Training and pruning

There are many ways to prune grapes. Two of the most common methods for home gardeners are cane pruning and spur pruning. You can train cane- or spur-pruned vines on an existing fence or wall. If you're planning to plant several vines, you'll probably need to build a trellis. Each vine will need about 8 ft. (2.4 m) of trellis. To construct a trellis, set 8-ft. (2.4-m) cedar or locust posts 24 ft. (7.2 m) apart and 2 ft. (60 cm) into the ground. Install guy wires from the end posts to keep them from being pulled over.

TRAINING GRAPES

	Cane-Pruned Vines	Spur-Pruned Vines
First winter	Prune the vine in late winter after the coldest weather is past. If the vine didn't grow as high as the top wire on the trellis, cut it back to two buds, just as you did when you planted it. If the vine did reach the top wire of the trellis, it is time to select a trunk. Choose the straightest, sturdiest cane that is at least as tall as the top trellis wire. Cut off all other canes flush to the chosen cane. Tie that cane loosely to the trellis, then cut it off just above the top trellis wire.	Training is the same as for cane-pruned vines at this stage.
Second summer training	Let the topmost five buds develop into sideshoots and grow sideways along the trellis. Carefully break off any lower sideshoots, but not the leaves, that form on the trunk. Remove any flower clusters that form.	Training is the same as for cane-pruned vines at this stage.
Second winter pruning	In late winter, select two sturdy, pencil-size canes, one headed each way along the trellis. Tie them loosely to the trellis wire every 1 ft. (30 cm) or so. Rub off extra buds along these canes, leaving one bud every 4–5 in. (10–12 cm). Then cut the canes so that each cane has just ten buds. Cut all other canes off flush with the trunk.	Training is the same as for cane-pruned vines at this stage.
Third summer pruning	Each of the buds of the canes you left at winter pruning time will produce a fruiting shoot this summer. Remove most of the flower clusters, leaving just five on each cane. Also, rub off any shoots that sprout below the top 2 in. (5 cm) of the trunk. On grafted vines, rub off all shoots that sprout below the graft union.	Training is the same as for cane-pruned vines at this stage.
Third winter pruning	In late winter, cut the ties that held last year's main branches to the trellis. Examine the canes that have grown along these main branches. On each main branch, select one pencil-size cane near the trunk to become the new main branch. Cut off all the other canes, including last year's main branches. Make cuts flush with the trunk or the new main branches. Tie the new main branches loosely to the trellis wire every 1 ft. (30 cm) or so. Rub off buds on the branches, leaving one every 4–5 in. (10–12 cm). Cut back the branches so each has just ten buds.	In late winter, renew the ties that held the main branches to the trellis. Cut each of the canes that have sprouted from these branches back to two buds. When you're done, there will be a two-bud spur every 4–5 in. (10–12 cm) along the main branches. Cut any extra spurs flush with the main trunk.
Fourth summer pruning	Each of the buds left after the winter pruning will produce a new shoot. Rub off any shoots that sprout below the graft union on grafted vines.	Training is the same as for cane-pruned vines at this stage.
Fourth winter pruning	In this and subsequent years, prune your bearing vine in late winter as described for pruning in the third winter. If the previous season's canes are about as big around as a pencil and 5–6 ft. (1.5–1.8 m) long, keep the same number of buds as you did last year. If the canes are shorter, leave four fewer buds than you did last year; if the canes are longer, leave four more buds.	In late winter, renew the ties that hold the main branches to the trellis. Select one pencil-size shoot near the base of each two-bud spur and cut it back to two buds. Cut the other shoot that emerges from the spur off flush with the spur. Cut any extra shoots flush at their source.

Stretch 9- or 10-gauge galvanized wire between the end posts, 30 in. (80 cm) above ground level, another wire at the top of the posts, and one or two additional wires between them.

Thinning the fruit

Thinning is not essential for grapes grown for wine. For best results, table grapes should be thinned when the grapes are no bigger than a small pea. Use a small pointed stick and pointed scissors. Avoid touching the fruits with your fingers as it removes the waxy "bloom," spoiling the finish and increasing the possibility of infection by gray mold (botrytis). Cut off about half of the berries to leave plenty of space between each grape in a broad-shouldered bunch. Further thinning may be necessary in midsummer if the berries are still too tightly packed.

Summer care

Use small paper bags to protect fruit clusters from insects, diseases, and birds. In early summer, cut a tiny hole in the bottom corner of a paper bag to allow water to escape. Slip the open end of the bag over the cluster. Fold the top of the bag tightly around the stem. Be sure that there's enough space in the bag for the fruit to enlarge, then staple the bag closed without crushing the stem. Another option is to drape netting over the vines in late summer to keep birds from pecking at the ripening fruits.

If you had past problems with grape mealybugs, this is a good time to scrape all loose bark off your vines to expose the mealybugs to bright summer sun and heat, which will kill them.

In late summer, pull or cut off a handful of leaves around every cluster so air can circulate around developing fruits, minimizing diseases such as bunch rot. Be sure to leave one leaf over each cluster to prevent sunscald. Or attach pieces of row cover onto the vines so that they cover the clusters and protect the berries from intense sunlight.

Harvesting

Grapevines bear by their third or fourth growing season. Harvest when the fruit tastes ripe. Support the cluster with one hand and cut its stem with pruning shears. Handle clusters gently, and lay them in a basket or shallow tray as you harvest. If picking large quantities, morning is the best time; gather small quantities any time during the day. Move picked fruit to a cool, protected place as soon as possible. Grapes keep well in your refrigerator. Some European cultivars such as 'Emperor' and 'Ribier' will keep as long as 6 months. Other grapes will last 2 months at most.

Spot-pick muscadine grapes every 2 days because they ripen unevenly and tend to drop when very ripe. They are the most perishable grapes and will keep no more than 3 weeks, even under refrigeration.

Winter protection

There are grape cultivars that will tolerate severe winter cold. You can grow cultivars beyond their normal northern limit by training trunks only 1 ft. (30 cm) high and covering the vines with mulch during the winter, or by bending whole vines over and burying or mulching them for the winter.

Once grape buds begin to swell in the spring, they become more frost tender. All species are susceptible to frost damage at temperatures below 32°F (0°C). Cover with floating row cover if late frost threatens. Autumn frosts seldom cause damage to grapes because the high sugar content of the berries keeps them from freezing and the outer canopy protects both the foliage and the fruit beneath it. If you live in an area with short seasons, plant an early-ripening cultivar.

A STANDARD GRAPEVINE

Grapevines grow extremely well in containers, trained in many shapes—but a simple standard works well. The main stem will need the support of a sturdy stake about 4 ft. (1.2 m) tall that extends down to the base of the pot. Attach a wire-framed hanging basket upside-down on top of the stake (a small, spoked wooden wheel could also be used); this will give extra support to the fruiting shoots and allow them to cascade down in an attractive fountain shape.

A generous-size pot is essential, filled with a soil-based medium with added sand (see p. 205, and pp. 114–117) to give weight and stability. Feeding will be required (see also *Container Gardening*, p. 206) and regular, plentiful watering during summer.

To form the standard, in the first year train a single stem vertically as for the double Guyot. In winter, if the stem is strong and extends well above the stake, prune it to a healthy bud at the height of the top of the stake. (If growth is weak, cut back the leading shoot by one-half and complete the above process the following winter.) Rub off all but the top three or four buds on the stem, completely removing any sideshoots at the same time. Each subsequent year, as shoots grow, train them over the support (up to 12 as the vine becomes established), and let each bear one or two bunches of fruit, then in winter, cut them back to two or three buds.

PROTECT THE CROP

Prevention and good sanitation are the best ways to avoid grape problems. Choose grape types that are naturally suited to your climate. Keep the area under vines well mulched to prevent spores from splashing up onto plants from the soil, and control weeds to maintain good air circulation around the vines.

Fungal disease—downy and powdery mildew and botrytis (gray mold)—are the major problems on vines. Look for resistant cultivars. If necessary, spray or dust with sulfur to prevent the spread of these diseases.

Grape berry moths lay eggs on flower clusters. Their greenish or purplish larvae spin silver webs and feed on buds and flowers. Many other caterpillars feed on grape leaves, too. Control by spraying with BT (*Bacillus thuringiensis*). Pick off Japanese beetles and drop into soapy water; spray serious infestations with pyrethrins.

Harvesting table grapes
Create a handle for each bunch by cutting the stem on either side of it so that you do not need to touch and spoil the fruit.

Apples

Providing a harvest from a succession of cultivars, from midsummer to the fruit that stores until spring, apples must offer one of the longest periods of fresh supply of any fruit. There is so much interest in apples that the range of cultivars runs into the thousands, with many historic cultivars still stocked by specialty nurseries.

Over many centuries, apples have evolved and been selected and bred to suit a very wide range of situations. There are now cultivars to suit warm and cool climates (Zones 3 to 9) with rootstocks to match. The rootstocks (see below) determine the ultimate size of the tree, the age it starts fruiting, and its useful life expectancy.

Site and soil

In general, this fruit grows best on rich, well-drained soil with a pH of 6.5. If your soil is less fertile you can compensate by treating your soil and by using a more vigorous rootstock or even growing the tree on its own roots. Plant on an open site in full sun that is protected from the wind. Avoid frost pockets. Apples do not perform well at altitudes above about 400 ft. (120 m) in cool regions.

Apples are suited to growing as formal, trained shapes against walls and fences or, for improved air flow, on freestanding post-and-wire supports. Walls that face the setting sun are ideal; cooking apples can be grown on a cool wall. Avoid very hot conditions.

Buying plants

The ideal time to buy trees is in late autumn or early spring for immediate planting. They are usually sold bareroot, but container-grown trees can be found at most times of year (though cultivar choice is likely to be limited).

To ensure healthy, good-quality trees, buy plants that are guaranteed to be free of virus. Buy 1-year-old trees, known as "maidens" (single, unbranched vertical stems) or "feathered maidens" (with a few small sideshoots). Plants of this age are relatively cheap and can be pruned to your preferred shape from the outset. It is also possible to buy more expensive, preformed young bush or espalier trees that are 2 or 3 years old.

The shape of the trees

Freestanding trees may be grown as central leader trees (the most popular shape, easy to form and maintain). Standard or full-size trees, with a tall clear trunk, are seen today only on large estates and in traditional orchards, as their height makes them difficult to prune and pick.

Central-leader trees are shaped much like Christmas trees (one main trunk with many side branches). During its first few years of growth, the goal is to help the tree develop a framework of strong, well-positioned branches. Part of creating this framework involves spreading each branch so the

Feast of fruits (facing page)
Top row, from left to right: 'William's Pride', 'Liberty', 'Enterprise'. Middle row: 'Pristine', 'Redfree', 'Gold Rush'. Bottom row: 'Dayton', 'Rajka', 'Jonafree'.

CULTIVAR CHOICE

Summer
'Lodi', 'Earligold', 'Jerseymac', 'Paulared', 'Pristine', 'Redfree'

Autumn ripening
'Cortland', 'Empire', 'Golden Delicious', 'Granny Smith', 'Mutsu', 'Northern Spy', 'Winesap'

For fresh eating
'Honeycrisp', 'Honeygold', 'Jonagold', 'Liberty', 'McIntosh', 'Regent'

For cooking
'Cortland', 'Freedom', 'Idared', 'Rhode Island Greening', 'Rome Beauty'

Good for storage
'Enterprise', 'Idared', 'Jonathan', 'Liberty', 'Newtown Pippin'

When selecting apple cultivars, keep in mind that most need cross-pollination, so you need to choose at least two different cultivars. Mail-order suppliers can tell you which cultivars will pollinate each other.

APPLE ROOTSTOCKS

Rootstocks	Effect	Height	Planting	Notes
M27	Very dwarfing	5–6 ft. (1.5–1.8 m)	4–6 ft. (1.2–1.8 m)	Needs permanent staking; fruits very early in life.
M9	Dwarfing	6–10 ft. (1.8–3 m)	8–10 ft. (2.5–3 m)	Needs a fertile, rich soil and permanent staking; produces fruit very early in life.
M26	Dwarfing	8–12 ft. (2.4–4 m)	10–15 ft. (3–5 m)	Good on lighter soils; strong root system; produces fruit after 2 or 3 years.
MM106	Semi-dwarfing	12–18 ft. (4–5.5 m)	12–18 ft. (4–5.5 m)	Suitable for poor soils or traditional orchards; strong root system; produces fruit after 2 or 3 years.
MM111	Vigorous; semi-vigorous in poor soil	20–28 ft. (6–9 m)	18–24 ft. (5.5–7.5 m)	Strong root system; produces fruit after 2 or 3 years; suitable for traditional orchard.
Own-root trees	Vigorous	Over 28 ft. (9 m) unless grown at close spacing	Best grown as cordon 30 in. (75 cm) apart or leader at 8 ft. (2.5 m) apart	Very strong root system; needs summer pruning to control vigor; produces fruit after 3 or 4 years.

CRAB APPLES

These small-fruited apple trees can be grown as cordons but are usually grown as informal trees, valued for the ornamental features of their blossoms, attractive foliage, and fruits. Crab apples make good pollinators; *Malus* x *zumi* 'Golden Hornet' is popular for orchards. *Malus* 'John Downie' makes particularly good crab apple jelly.

habit and pruning needs best, although fans and palmettes are also possible. Trees that will be trained flat need a strong framework to support them and hold the branches in place. Buy ready-made metal supports, or erect a post-and-wire system. Wires can also be strung across walls or fences. Set the top wire or rail at a height of about 6 ft. (2 m), although on a wall this could be higher. Set wires 12 in. (30 cm) apart, starting at 30 in. (75 cm) from the ground.

Cordons are usually planted obliquely at an angle of 45–60°, pointing up the slope on sloping ground, as this helps control vigor. Space trees 30 in. (75 cm) apart and use M26 or MM106 rootstocks. Use M27 for vigorous cultivars such as 'Golden Delicious'.

With espaliers, it is possible to have tiers of branches ascending as high as space and inclination permits, but it is most usual to have three tiers at 18-in. (45-cm) intervals. It is also possible to have a single tier ("step-over") at 30–36 in. (75–90 cm) above the ground. For a three-tier espalier, erect a post-and-wire support structure with wires at 2 ft., 3½ ft., and 5 ft. (60 cm, 1.1 m, and 1.5 m).

Planting distances for espaliers will depend on the rootstock (see p. 265). All rootstocks except M9 are suitable; use only M27 where you plan a single tier espalier or "step-over."

To form and maintain central-leader trees and espaliers, see p. 268.

angle between the trunk and branch is between 45° and 60°. To widen narrower angles, you can insert items such as toothpicks (for young shoots), clothespins, or wood strips with notched ends to spread the branches. Another option is to hang weights from the branches to pull them into the proper position.

Apples trees can also be trained flat. The cordon and espalier shapes (see p. 245) suit their growth

Good neighbors (facing page)
Cordons (main picture) not only look beautiful but also are a useful way of growing several apple cultivars in close proximity, where space for several freestanding trees cannot be found. Coordinating the flowering time of cultivars is crucial in achieving good cross-pollination and thus heavy crops. (Pictured, from left to right: 'King of the Pippins', 'Kidd's Orange Red', and 'Red Devil' in flower.)

PLANTING AN APPLE TREE

• Prepare a hole at least 3 ft. (1 m) in diameter in light soil, twice that size in poor-draining, heavy clay, or silt soil. You will need a stake 3 ft. (1 m) long, a hammer or mallet, a tree tie, some well-rotted manure, leaf mold if the soil is particularly heavy or light, bone meal, seaweed meal, and any organic fertilizers required to amend inherent deficiencies (see p. 61).
• Mark a circle to the desired size.
• If planting in grass, slice off the sod and stack it to one side.
• Dig out topsoil to a spade's depth and stack it separately.
• Loosen the soil in the bottom of the hole with a garden fork. Also, in heavy soil, lightly loosen soil in the sides of the hole.
• Hammer in the stake off center on the side from which the prevailing wind blows.

• Either drop sod upside down in the hole and chop it with a spade, or, if you do not have sod, add a bucket of leaf mold.
• Half-fill a 2-gallon (10-liter) bucket with well-rotted manure, mix in 5 oz. (135 g) each of seaweed meal and bone meal and any other fertilizers required, and then mix this into the set-aside topsoil.
• Place the tree in the hole and attach it loosely to the stake so that it will be planted no deeper than the original soil mark. A stake placed across the hole will help you gauge the depth.
• Return half the soil to the hole, untie the tree, and shake it gently to settle soil around the roots. Add a little more and tamp the soil gently to firm the tree in.
• Return the remainder of the soil, firm it in, and attach the tree to its stake.

PRUNING AND TRAINING APPLES AND PEARS

When	Central-leader tree	Cordon	Espalier
On planting (maiden or feathered maiden) and in the first year	**On planting** Cut the main trunk back to 24–30 in. (60–75 cm). Cut off about one-third of each side branch. **Summer** When the new side branches are 12–18 in. (30–45 cm) long, it's time to select three or four main branches and prune off the others. Choose branches that point in four different directions. Each branch should be 4–8 in. (10–20 cm) above or below the nearest branch. Cut off all other branches at the main trunk (the central leader). Spread branches if needed (see p. 266).	**On planting** Attach a stake to the wires for each tree at an angle of 45–60° (see also p. 245). Prune the stem by about one-half to a strong bud facing along the line of the stake. **Late summer** Tie the tree to the stake.	**On planting** Prune back to a point just above the lowest wire with three well-placed buds below it and tie it to the wire. Tie in a stake on each side at 45° to the wires, facing opposite directions to support the growing branches. Allow the three buds to grow. **Late summer** Tie in one shoot to each stake, leaving the central one to grow vertically. Tie this to the second wire.
After 1 year (year 1)	**Late winter** Shorten each branch, cutting off one-third to one-half of the length. This will encourage side branches to grow. Remove any new shoots that are growing at a narrow angle and competing with the central leader. If the central leader has grown very tall, cut it back to about 2 ft. (60 cm) above the crotch of the uppermost side branch. **Summer** When new side branches are 12–18 in. (30–45 cm), select another "layer" of three or four main branches about 18 in. (45 cm) above the previous season's main branches. Cut off other new branches, including any water sprouts (vertical shoots) or suckers (sprouts near the soil line). Spread the chosen branches as needed.	**Late winter** Prune back the previous year's growth on the main stem by between one-third and one-half. Reduce all laterals arising directly from the trunk to three buds. **Late summer** Tie the extension growth of the leader to the stake.	**Late winter** Pull down the new branches to horizontal, but leave the tips pointing slightly upward. Move the stakes out to these tips, retaining the 45° angle. Prune to a bud just above the second wire as at planting, and attach angled stakes to make the second tier.
After 2 years (year 2)	**Late winter** Shorten side branches to encourage branching. Remove one-third to one-half of the previous season's new growth. Remove any new shoots that are growing at a narrow angle and competing with the central leader. If necessary, cut back the central leader to about 2 ft. (60 cm) above the crotch of the uppermost side branch. **Summer** Depending on the vigor and size of your tree, it may not start bearing for 3 or more years. Continue to prune and spread branches as you did during the previous summer.	**Midsummer** When growth of new wood slows and begins to turn brown at the base, cut back all shoots arising directly from the main stem to three leaves above the cluster of leaves right at the base. Prune growth arising from last year's laterals that is longer than 10 in. (25 cm) to one or two leaves. **Mid-autumn** Cut back shoots over 10 in. (25 cm) to one or two leaves. Any new growth since the summer pruning should be removed at the base. **Late winter** Cut back the leader by about one-third.	**Summer** Tie in the new growth on both tiers as in year 1. Repeat the winter training and pruning for the third tier. Start pruning laterals as for cordons (see left).
In subsequent years	**Late winter** Continue pruning as you did the previous winter, until your tree begins bearing large crops. After that, winter pruning is minimal. Over time, your tree may develop a "hole" or empty spot in the outside shell of the branch tips. If this happens, trim back branch tips on the inside of the hole, making cuts just above buds that face toward the hole, to help it fill in. **Summer** When growth slows and stops in mid- to late summer, cut off any vigorous vertical shoots, leaving a ⅛–¼ in. (3–7 mm) stub. Each of these stubs will tend to form a fruiting spur next season. Use thinning cuts as needed to remove branches to open up the tree to light and air. Cut back branches that are pointing straight downward to a more horizontal branch. Cut or rub off suckers from near the soil line any time.	**Late winter** Continue winter-pruning the leader until it has reached the desired height. Thereafter it can be pruned in summer at a leaf to 1¼–2 in. (3–5 cm) of growth. When spur systems become very complex or excessively long, reduce them or remove them. **Summer** Prune all laterals and sub-laterals every summer as for year 2 (see above).	**Summer** Once branches have reached the end of their wires, the stakes can be removed and summer pruning can be carried out from then on as for cordons. After 10 years or more, the lowest tier may be considerably less vigorous than the top tier. This can be remedied by completely removing the top tier and training in two new branches in the following years. Old and congested systems can be renovated as for cordons.

Looking after the fruit

It is important to keep weeds under control around trees, especially during their early years of establishment. They compete for food and, more importantly, nutrients. For weaker rootstocks, M27 and M9, good weed control under the canopy is essential throughout the life of the tree. Thick straw mulches 3–4 in. (8–10 cm) deep help to smother weeds and conserve moisture. Lay this in late spring, removing it in winter to the compost pile (see also p. 240). Grass can be allowed to grow up to the trunk of well-established standard trees on MM111.

Feed trees that show signs of decline with well-rotted manure or garden compost applied in early spring. This is likely to be about every 3 years for M26, more frequently for M9 and M27 trees. Trees on MM106 and MM111 will not need feeding after the first 10 years unless they are growing in particularly poor soil.

Pruning

Once established, all tree forms benefit from winter pruning, which aims to keep a balance between older fruiting wood and new, vigorous growth. Trained forms—cordons, espaliers, and fans—need extra pruning in summer to keep their shape. See facing page for details. To renovate neglected trees, see pp. 245–246.

Thinning the fruits

It is normal in summer for many fruitlets to drop naturally, but these may not be the ones you would have selected. For the best quality and size of fruit it is important to thin fruitlets early. Start thinning about 6 weeks after most petals have dropped.
• Remove the "king fruit" at the center of the cluster. This is usually slightly larger and distorted.
• Thin the remaining fruitlets to leave one per cluster and 4–6 in. (10–15 cm) between each fruitlet. Select the best fruitlet, discarding any that are affected by pests, damaged, or distorted.
• If fruit set is poor and the crop is light, leave two fruitlets in some or all of the clusters.

Harvesting

The first indication of ripeness will be when the skin colors and a few windfalls are on the ground. Test by gently lifting and twisting individual fruits

in the palm of your hand. If they come away easily they are ready for picking. Fruit of early cultivars can be eaten from the tree; later cultivars need time to develop their flavor after picking.

Storing fruit

Late cultivars will not ripen until they have been in store for a while. A refrigerator is ideal for storing apples but a frost-free shed, cellar, or attic will be adequate. Aim for cool, dark, slightly damp conditions. Store only perfect fruits.
• **Slatted boxes or shelves** Traditionally apples were stored in custom-made slatted boxes or drawers. A good substitute is a vegetable crate. Lay apples in a single layer, not touching each other.
• **Individual wrapping** Wrap each apple in a square of tissue paper or newspaper, ensuring each fruit is completely covered. Fruit can be placed in boxes or vegetable crates in layers.
• **Plastic bags** Use large polyethylene bags, making four small holes in the lower part of the bag with a pen or pencil. Fill each bag with about 4 lb. (2 kg) of fruit, and fold the neck of the bag loosely; do not tie it. Do not store different cultivars in the same bag or box; ethylene given off by the earlier cultivars as they ripen will affect the later ones. Check fruit in store regularly and discard or use any that show signs of deterioration.

CULTIVAR CHOICE

European pears
'Anjou'
'Bartlett'
'Bella de Guigno'
'Bosc' (RF)
'Butirra Precoce Morettini'
'Comice' (RF)
'Gorham'
'Harrow Delight' (RF)
'Highland'
'Kieffer' (RF)
'Moonglow' (RF)
'Seckel' (RF)
'Spalding' (RF)
'Warren' (RF)

Asian pears
'Chojuro' ('Old World')
'Ichiban'
'Korean Giant'
'Mishirasu'
'Nijisseiki' ('Twentieth
  Century')
'Shinseiki'
'Yakumo'
'Yongi'

RF resistant to fireblight

Pears

Melting and buttery or crisp and flavorful, a ripe pear is a special treat. These versatile fruits keep well in storage, and they dry, freeze, and can successfully, too. Hardy in Zones 4 through 9, the trees are handsome in the landscape, with white spring flowers, shiny leaves, and vivid fall color. They are long-lived and less troubled by pests and diseases than many tree fruits.

Pears are quite long-lived trees, but the quality and size of the fruit starts to decline after 30 or 40 years. The earliest cultivars are ready in midsummer and can be eaten straight from the tree. The majority are picked from early to mid-autumn and need at least 2 or 3 weeks after picking to ripen. Late-storing cultivars will keep well into winter. Unlike Asian pears, most European pears should not be left to ripen on the tree, as they will be less flavorful.

Site and soil

Plant pears in early spring or fall, on a sunny site with plenty of air flow. Pear trees prefer a moderately fertile soil with a pH between 6 and 6.5. They thrive in the same conditions that apples do, but tolerate poorly drained soil slightly better.

Buying plants

The pears that are most familiar to us are European pears (*Pyrus communis*). Their cousins, the Asian pears (hybrids of *P. pyrifolia*, *P. ussuriensis*, and *P. bretschneideris*), are gaining popularity and are equally easy to grow. Their fruits are often round and have a crisp, sweet, juicy flesh.

Pears need to be pollinated by another compatible cultivar, so grow at least two cultivars. A few cultivars don't produce viable pollen; if you select one, you'll need to plant three different cultivars to ensure good fruit set. Your mail-order supplier can advise you as to the pollination requirements of the cultivars you are considering.

Pruning and training

Start training your pear trees as soon as you plant them. Be sure to spread the branches (see pp. 265–266) because pears tend to grow up, not out, if left on their own. If you develop a strong, spreading framework, it will be easier to prune and the trees will bear earlier. Train European pears to a central leader system, as cordons, or espaliers as you would for apples (see *Pruning and Training Apples and Pears*, p. 268).

Asian pears are best trained to an open-center system. At planting time, cut the main trunk back to 24–30 in. (60–75 cm) and trim back any side branches by one-third to one-half their length. During the growing season, when the new growth reaches 12–18 in. (30–45 cm) long, choose four main branches that emerge in different directions and are separated along the trunk by 4–8 in. (10–20 cm). Cut off all other branches and cut off the main trunk just above the top branch. You may choose to leave the main trunk for an extra season to let it shade the center of the tree. Shorten branches by about one-third of their length to encourage branching. Spread branches as needed.

PEAR ROOTSTOCKS

Rootstock	Effect/Notes	Eventual max. height	Planting distance
Quince C	Dwarfing; suitable for all forms of tree	8–10 ft. (2.4–3 m)	10–13 ft. (3–4.5 m)
Quince A	Semi-dwarfing; suitable for bush, trained forms on poor soils, traditional orchards	12–13 ft. (3.6–4.5 m)	12–13 ft. (3.6–4.5 m)
'Bartlett' pear	Vigorous; suitable for traditional orchards	28–40 ft. (9–12 m)	30–40 ft. (10–12 m)
'OH' x 'F' ('Old Home' x 'Farmingdale' pear)	Offers fireblight resistance	12–13 ft. (3.6–4.5 m)	12–13 ft. (3.6–4.5 m)

In the third and fourth years, snip back branch tips in late winter or early spring to encourage plenty of smaller side branches. From then on, cut out a few of the side branches each summer to help shape the framework of the tree and to remove overly crowded or short and weak branches. And always prune out any diseased stems, cutting back well into healthy wood.

Both European and Asian pears can be subject to fireblight, a bacterial disease that spreads through the vascular system. If the bacteria reach the main trunk and roots, the entire tree may die. Where fireblight is a major problem, try training your pears to have multiple trunks. If one or more of the trunks become diseased, you can prune off the infected wood, and save the rest of the tree.

To create a multiple-trunk tree, allow four or five well-spaced branches to grow vertically during the first summer after planting. (Don't use branch spreaders.) These branches will all serve as trunks. In the second year, choose and spread side branches that point outward from each of the trunks. Remove all side branches that point into the tree's interior. Thereafter, just imagine that the trunks are one large trunk and prune according to the directions on p. 268 for a central-leader tree.

Caring for the crop

Pears need the same feeding, watering, and mulching as apples (see p. 269). The trees are likely to set more fruit than they can handle. Unthinned fruits will be small, and the heavy fruit load may break branches or prevent flowering the following year. A month or two after bloom, thin the fruits to leave one or two per cluster.

Harvesting and storing

Not all pears have strong skin coloring, so judging ripeness can be difficult. When the approximate picking time arrives, start testing individual fruits. Hold the bulbous end of the fruit in the heel of your hand with your index finger on or near the stalk. Tilt the fruit gently upward. It will come away easily when ready for picking. With the exception of very early cultivars, pears need to ripen off the tree.

Pears are more difficult than apples to store well. It is important to know when a cultivar is likely to ripen, but outward signs are not dramatic; there will be a slight yellowing of the skin color. Bring batches in to room temperature to complete ripening—it may take a further 2 to 3 weeks. When ripe, pears are soft at the stalk end and will give when pressed gently.

PROTECT THE CROP

Pears have one unique problem insect: the pear psylla. Also, they are generally more susceptible to fireblight than apples and other fruits are.

Pear psyllas are tiny, red or green insects that suck plant juices. As they feed, they release a sticky honeydew that supports the growth of black sooty mold. The black mold is usually the first symptom.

Sooty mold looks a bit like the blackening caused by fireblight. To diagnose the cause of a black coating on pear leaves, rub an affected leaf with a wet fingertip: Sooty mold washes off, but fireblight doesn't.

Soft, succulent growth promotes both problems, so limit fertilizer applications to your pear trees. Pruning can also stimulate succulent growth. Whenever possible, use branch spreaders rather than pruning cuts to keep your tree open to light and air. Plant resistant cultivars to reduce the risk of fireblight. If damage does appear, cut off blighted twigs at least 1 ft. (30 cm) below the decay, on a dry day. Sanitize pruning tools between cuts.

If you find pear psyllas on your trees during the growing season, spray insecticidal soap to control them. Next season, spray with horticultural oil in early spring and again when the buds start to show green.

Plums

Unless you live in a truly frigid climate or in the tropics, you can find a plum suited to your garden. Although there are many species, the most important from the gardener's standpoint are the European plum (*Prunus domestica*), the damson plum (*P. institia*), the Japanese plum (*P. salicina*), and various species of wild American plums (*Prunus* spp.). American plums are the most cold-hardy (Zones 4 to 8), followed by European and damson plums (Zones 5 to 9), then Japanese plums (Zones 6 to 10).

Hybrids between American and Japanese plums combine the cold hardiness of the former with the fruit quality of the latter. With such a broad genetic base, cultivated plums offer diverse characteristics: sweet, melting dessert fruits or tangy, firm cooking fruits, in shades from yellow to blue to almost black.

Site and soil

Plums need full sunlight to remain healthy and produce top-quality fruit. The blossoms open early, so slopes are ideal sites. North-facing slopes are best because they warm up later in spring and delay flowering for a few days. Avoid sites where frosty air collects. Soil needs to be fairly well drained, but plums will tolerate less perfect drainage than peaches or sweet cherries will. Japanese and American cultivars prefer sandy or loamy soil, while European cultivars do well in clayey soil.

Buying plants

For Japanese plums, choose a 1-year-old tree that is ½ in. (1 cm) in diameter. For European plums, choose 2-year-old trees. Select a cultivar that is

CULTIVAR CHOICE

European plums
'Cambridge Gage'
'Coes Golden Drop'
'Early Laxton'
'French Petite' (sf)
'Golden Transparent Gage' (sf)
'Green Gage' (sf)
'Kirke's Blue'
'Long John'
'Seneca'
'Stanley' (sf)
'Valor' (sf)
'Victoria' (sf)

Japanese plums
'Beauty' (sf)
'Burbank'
'Hollywood' (sf)
'Santa Rosa' (sf)
'Shiro'

Japanese–American hybrid plums
'Methley' (sf)
'Pipestone'
'Superior'
'Toka'
'Underwood'

sf self-fertile (sets fruit when grown alone, although most of these will produce even better yields when planted with a compatible pollinator)

PRUNING AND TRAINING

	Central-leader tree	Plum cordon (from a maiden)	Plum fan (from a maiden)
After planting	**On planting** Cut the main trunk back to 24–30 in. (60–75 cm). Cut off about one-third of each side branch. **Summer** When new side branches are 12–18 in. (30–45 cm) long, select four main branches that point in four different directions and prune off the others.	Cut back the main stem by about one-third, cutting to a bud, and reduce all sideshoots to three buds.	In spring, reduce the young stem to either two sideshoots or two buds about 30 in. (75 cm) from the ground. Tie them in to stakes on supporting wires at an angle of 45° on each side. Tie two further in at an angle of 60° on each side.
In the first year	**Right after bloom** Shorten each branch by up to one-half. Remove shoots competing with the central leader. **Summer** When new side branches are 12–18 in. (30–45 cm), select three or four main branches about 18 in. (45 cm) above the previous season's. Cut off other new branches.		**Late summer** Cut back branches by half the new growth to a leaf, and tie to stakes. Set a stake below each branch and two above to begin forming a fan. Remove shoots crossing the center.
After a year's growth	**Right after bloom** Shorten side branches. Remove one-third to one-half of previous season's growth. Remove new shoots growing at a narrow angle and competing with the central leader. **Summer** Your tree may not start bearing for 3 or more years. Continue to prune and spread branches.	**Early summer** Pinch out all new growth on sideshoots to leave six leaves. **Late summer** Reduce sideshoots further so that only three leaves are left. **Late autumn** Tie in the new leader to a cane at an angle of 45° or train it upright.	**Summer** Allow three laterals to grow out from these branches on each side and tie them, one to each stake. Remove all others. At the end of the summer, reduce these new branches by half the growth they have made.
In subsequent years	When growth slows and stops in mid- to late summer, cut off any vigorous vertical shoots, leaving a ⅛–¼ in. (3–7 mm) stub. Each of these stubs will tend to form a fruiting spur next season. Thin as needed to open the tree to light and air.	**Every summer** Prune as above. Once the leader reaches the desired height, cut it back annually to a single leaf of new growth. Tie this shoot to the cane. If spur systems become long, crowded or complex, thin, reduce, or remove them.	Allow laterals to form; prune annually as for cordons (see left). Prune back leaders once they reach the required length. Allow new branches to fill any vacant space, and tie to stakes, but leave the center open. Any upright growth in the center will tend to dominate, weakening growth on the other fingers of the fan.

suited to your winter temperatures and that has resistance to common diseases in your region.

Most European plums will set some fruit without cross-pollination, but nearly all will yield better when cross-pollinated by another European cultivar. Japanese plums must be cross-pollinated by either a Japanese or American type. American plums also need cross-pollination for best yields.

TWO PLUM ROOTSTOCKS

Pixy
Dwarfing; suitable for all gardens. Allow to fruit after 3 years.
Eventual height: 6½–8 ft. (2.1–2.5 m).
Spacing: 8–10 ft. (2.5–3 m) for a central-leader tree or bush; 15 ft. (5 m) for a fan.

St. Julien A
Semi-dwarfing; suitable for larger trees and orchards. Allow to fruit after 3 or 4 years.
Eventual height: 10–12 ft. (3–4 m).
Spacing: 12–15 ft. (4–5 m) for a bush or central-leader tree; 17½ ft. (5.5 m) for a fan.

Rootstock choice can also influence your tree's success. Select 'Damas', 'Myrobalan', or 'Mariana'—the most winter-hardy—plum rootstocks for heavy or poorly drained soils. Peach rootstocks may be better on sandy soil. If you want a very small tree, buy one grafted on 'Pixy' rootstock.

Caring for the crop
- **Preparation, planting, and general care** Follow general advice given for apples (see p. 269). For fans and cordons, prepare supporting wires as for apples.
- **Pruning** To form central leaders, cordons, or fans, see above. Japanese plums grow well with open-center training (see pp. 270–271).
- **Thinning** In a good year, some cultivars will set a great deal of fruit. After the natural fruit drop in early summer, thin the remaining fruitlets with scissors to 2–5 in. (5–10 cm) apart to keep branches from breaking under the weight of the crop.
- **Harvesting** Ripe plums are fully colored (but note that they come in many colors, including green) and soft. Fruits will pull away easily.
- **Storing** Fruits do not store for long, but they can be frozen or used in preserves. Once picked, keep them cool until you are ready to use them.

PROTECT THE CROP

One common plum problem is black knot. This fungal disease produces swollen, knobby, black galls (shown below) on branches. Prune out affected branches in winter, then spray lime-sulfur as buds swell in spring, and again a week later.

Bacterial leaf spot causes small, angular black spots on leaves. Leaves may turn yellow and drop early. Spray lime-sulfur every 10-21 days until leaf drop if weather is wet or humid or if spots are spreading.

CULTIVAR CHOICE

Sweet cherries—early
'Black Tartarian'
'Sam'

Sweet cherries—mid-season
'Bing'
'Emperor Francis'
'Lapins'
'Napoleon' ('Royal Ann')
'Ranier'
'Schmidt'
'Stella' (self-pollinating)
'Van'

Sweet cherries—late
'Black Republican' ('Black
  Oregon')
'Hedelfingen'
'Lambert'
'Windsor'

Sour cherries
'Early Richmond'
'Meteor'
'Montmorency'
'Northstar'

Sour cherries of the amarelle
or Kentish types, including
'Early Richmond', 'Meteor',
and 'Montmorency', have light-
colored flesh and colorless
juice. Morello or griotte types,
such as 'Northstar', have dark
flesh and red juice.

Cherries

Cherries are normally referred to as either sweet or sour. Sweet cherries are eaten straight from the tree and have either white ("white heart") or dark ("black heart") flesh. Skin color also varies from "white," which is actually usually flushed with scarlet, to very dark. Sweet cherries ripen in midsummer; sour (tart) cherries ripen slightly later. Sour cherries are grown for culinary use and are very sour eaten raw.

Initial pruning to shape trees is similar for each type. Thereafter it is very different, as sour cherries fruit on branches produced the previous year, whereas sweet cherries fruit on older branches and are pruned as for plums.

Most sour cherries are self-pollinating, as are a few sweet cherries. In general, however, sweet cherries are not and have very complicated compatibilities for pollination. (Check with your supplier for recommendations.) Cherries will start to produce in their third year.

Sweet cherries

• **Site and soil** Hardy in Zones 5 to 9, sweet cherries flower even earlier than plums. The blossom is not frost-tolerant, so it is advisable to give cherries the warmest spot in the garden. Sweet cherries are sometimes grown as a fan against a wall that receives sunshine for most of the day. Wires will be needed, spaced 12 in. (30 cm) apart. In regions where late spring frosts are not a problem, it is possible to grow cherries as informal, "open-center" trees. Cherries have similar soil requirements to plums (see p. 272).
• **Rootstocks** Good dwarfing rootstocks for cherries are gradually becoming more widely available (see below). This is important because tall trees are difficult or impossible to net—and birds love cherries. Wall-trained cherries are easily netted and ideal for the garden.
• **Buying plants** For general advice, see plums and apples (pp. 265 and 272). Be sure to choose cultivars that will pollinate each other or are self-pollinating. Sour cherries will pollinate sweet cherries in appropriate flowering groups.
• **Preparation and planting** As for apples (see p. 266).
• **Pruning and training** Central-leader trees are formed as for apples (p. 268), fans as for plums (p. 273).
• **General care** Follow advice for apples (see p. 269). Keep at least 3 ft. (1 m) around each tree free of weeds.
• **Thinning** Cherries do not need thinning.
• **Harvesting** Cherries should be picked as soon as they are ripe. Pull by the stem, not the fruit. Either eat immediately or refrigerate. Cherries do not store but can be frozen.

Sour cherries

• **Site and soil** The requirements of sour cherries are not very different from sweet types. They do, however, flower later and can therefore be grown on cool walls, although a warmer location is preferable. In warmer regions they grow successfully as bushes out in the open, but netting is necessary as for sweet cherries. Late frosts will damage blossom. Fan-trained trees will need wires 6 in. (15 cm) apart.
• **Buying plants** As for sweet cherries. The most common cultivar is 'Montmorency'. This, like most other sour cultivars, is self-pollinating.

ROOTSTOCKS

Rootstock	Effect	Eventual height	Planting distance
Gisela 5	Dwarfing; modern successful rootstock, allowing for the first time really dwarf cherry trees	6–8 ft. (2–2.5 m)	8–10 ft. (2.5–3 m)
Mahaleb	Slightly dwarfing; winter hardy; resists crown gall	25–35 ft. (8–11 m)	30 ft. (10 m)
Mazzard	Vigorous, well-anchored; resistant to root-knot nematodes	30–40 ft. (10–12 m)	35 ft. (11 m)

Cherry fan
Fan-trained cherries are a great deal easier to net against birds than freestanding trees.

PROTECT THE CROP

Pests and diseases are less likely to be a problem where plants are growing in appropriately managed soil, and where the garden environment encourages natural predation.

Cherry fruit fly larvae burrow into cherry fruits and feed near the pit. Infested fruits are shrunken and drop early. Collect and destroy fallen fruit daily. Hang red sticky ball traps for adult flies (see below; 1–6 per tree) in May; remove traps when fruit colors. Plant white clover as a groundcover to attract predators.

Cherry fruits may split open if they take up too much water too fast. Some cultivars are more susceptible than others. Harvest and refrigerate ripe fruit immediately after rain.

Protect the crop from birds by covering with netting before it ripens. Allow birds access at other times to help control pests.

- **Rootstocks** Sour cherries are grown on the same rootstocks as sweet cherries.
- **Preparation and planting** As for apples (see p. 266).
- **Pruning and training** Although extremely similar to the sweet cherry, the sour cherry has a very different growth habit. Unlike sweet cherries, sour cherries fruit on wood produced the previous year. Initial training is similar to plums but thereafter differs markedly.

Form an open-center tree as for an Asian pear (see pp. 270–271). Once established, prune cherry bushes by removing a proportion of older 3- and 4-year-old wood to a younger side branch.

For a fan, initial pruning and training are similar to plums. The aim is to have, after 2 or 3 years, a basic framework of short permanent branches, filling half the space available with the center half empty. In the following year, allow new shoots to grow from this framework and fill the available space, tying them into a fan shape with branch tips about 5–6 in. (12–15 cm) apart.

In subsequent years, fruit will form on these 1-year-old shoots. At the same time new shoots will grow as laterals. Choose two of these for each branch close to the base and about 6 in. (15 cm) apart. Remove all others. After harvest in mid- to late summer, cut the fruited wood back to the best of the two shoots retained, with a preference for the lower one. If there is space, keep both new branches. Tie in the new growth.

After some years, the framework branches will become extended as replacement wood never forms exactly at the base. Some branches may need pruning back harder to a dormant bud. Do this on a few branches successively over a period of years.

- **General care** As for sweet cherries.
- **Harvesting** Sour cherries do not pull away easily from the tree. Use scissors or pruners to cut the stems close to the branch. Fruit is ready when it is very dark in color and soft to the touch. Fruits can be used to make jam or wine, preserved in a jar of brandy, or cooked for immediate use. Cooked cherries can be frozen.

Peaches and nectarines

PROTECT THE CROP

Peach leaf curl infects new leaves in spring, causing red blistering and distortion. Pick and destroy affected leaves when symptoms appear. Spraying trees with kelp once a month during the growing season may reduce future damage. Look for resistant cultivars.

Gummy residue on immature fruit and pinkish caterpillars inside fruit are signs of oriental fruit moths. Pick and destroy fruit with signs of damage. See also *Apricots* (facing page).

Peaches and their "fuzzless" relative, nectarines, are popular home fruit trees in Zones 5 though 9. Most gardeners are familiar with yellow-fleshed, freestone peaches, but there are other types that grow well in backyards. White-fleshed peaches are deliciously sweet, while firm-fleshed golden clingstones have aromatic flesh and good canning quality.

The best choice for most gardens is a full-size peach tree pruned to 10–12 ft. (3–4.2 m) high.

Site and soil

Choose a site with full sun, fertile soil, and a pH between 6 and 7. Alkaline soils tend to induce yellowing of the leaves (chlorosis). Avoid low spots.

Buying plants

Most peaches and nectarines are self-pollinating. Every peach cultivar needs a specific period of cold weather before it will resume growth and flower in spring. Once that requirement is met, the tree will open its flowers on the first warm day. Therefore, it's important to match cultivars carefully to the length and severity of winter in your area. In Zone 5 and the colder regions of Zone 6, choose a "high-chill" cultivar, such as 'Reliance', that will

not open its buds until spring arrives in earnest. In Zones 8 and 9, choose a "low-chill" cultivar, such as 'Desert Gold'. Call your local Cooperative Extension Service office to find the best cultivars for your conditions.

Any peach tree you buy will be grafted onto a rootstock. Most are grafted onto peach seedlings. If nematodes are a problem in your area, select trees grafted onto 'Nemaguard' or 'Okinawa' rootstocks. If your winters get cold and stay cold, 'Siberian C' rootstock will make your trees more cold-hardy. However, if your winter weather fluctuates between warm and cold, stick with seedling rootstocks.

Preparation and planting

Start preparing the soil a full year before you plan to plant peach trees. Have the soil tested and adjust the pH if necessary. Dig out every perennial weed. Plant a cover crop, such as buckwheat, over the entire planting area. If you're planting only one tree, prepare and plant a cover crop on a 10-ft. (3-m) diameter circle of ground. During the preparation year, mow the cover crop whenever it reaches 8–10 in. (20–23 cm) in height.

Plant peach and nectarine trees in early spring or fall. Avoid fall planting in Zones 5 and 6. Follow the general advice given for apples (see p. 266). If you have any doubts about how well the soil drains, build up the site into a raised bed. Set full-size trees 15–20 ft. (4.5–6 m) apart. Plant trees with dwarfing rootstocks 10 ft. (3 m) apart and genetic dwarfs as close as 3 ft. (90 cm) apart.

General care

Peaches are trained to an open-center form. Follow directions for Asian pears (see pp. 270-271) for the basic framework and general management.

Caring for fruit

• **General care** As for apples (see p. 269).
• **Thinning** Thinning is essential. Do this in two phases: When fruitlets are the size of grapes, thin to one fruit per cluster; when they are walnut-size, leave one fruit every 6 in. (15 cm).
• **Harvesting** Ripe fruits are soft to the touch and fully colored. They bruise easily.

Apricots

Apricots, delicious as they are, are not as commonly grown as peaches. This is probably because they need both adequate water and a long, warm, dry growing season, making them labor-intensive. If you can meet the conditions, they are well worth trying. Hardy in Zones 5 to 9, apricots are all self-pollinating, so you can easily grow just one tree. The season lasts from mid- to late summer.

Unlike most fruits covered so far, apricots prefer a slightly alkaline soil. Good drainage is essential, especially for heavier soils. Dieback, a common disease in apricots, is more aggresive in cold, wet winters and waterlogged soils.

Apricots flower in late winter. Except in warm areas, it is therefore usual to grow them as a fan against a sunny wall, where the blossom can be protected from frost damage. Where frosts at flowering time are rare, they can be grown as freestanding, open-center trees.

Buying plants

Follow the general advice given for apples and plums (see pp. 265 and 272). Apricot cultivars are all self-pollinating. A number of rootstocks are available (see below).

Preparation and planting

As for peaches (see facing page).

Forming trees

For establishing open-center trees, follow the advice given for Asian pears (see pp. 270–271) to create the basic framework and for general management. For fans, follow the directions for plums (p. 273). Fruit forms at the base of 1-year-old shoots as well as older wood.

Fans Once a fan is established, follow the advice for plums to prune and train new shoots and sideshoots that grow from the basic framework. Remove entirely any shoots growing toward the fence or wall. In cool regions there is very likely to be varying amounts of dieback. Prune to healthy wood as soon as you see it, and train a new shoot in summer.

After some years, long and congested spur systems should be shortened, thinned, or removed with a sloping cut that faces upward.

Pollination

In cooler areas, hand-pollination will improve fruit set.

Looking after the fruit

General care Follow the advice on watering, feeding, and weeding for other tree fruits.

Thinning In warmer regions, there may be excessive blossom. This will lead to a tendency to biennial cropping, bearing only every other year, if not thinned. After the main natural spring drop of fruitlets, take out any remaining damaged fruitlets. Thin the trusses to leave one fruit per cluster about 3–4 in. (7–10 cm) apart only if the set is heavy.

Harvesting Fruits part easily from the stem and are soft to the touch when ripe. They will not store.

CULTIVAR CHOICE

'Alfred'
'Farmingdale'
'Harglow'
'Moorpark'

PROTECT THE CROP

Apricots have a similar range of pests and diseases to peaches but are generally healthier and do not suffer from leaf curl.

The most common problem is dieback, a fungal problem that is prevalent in cool climates and soil is often very wet. Whole branches die back and sap oozes out of wounds near the branch base; avoid winter pruning and keep trees growing strongly to reduce infection. Prune out all affected branches to healthy wood.

Brown rot and gray mold (botrytis) can cause fruits to rot. Remove infected fruit, and prune to allow good ventilation. Brown rot fungus can also cause blossom wilt and dieback.

Pests and diseases are less likely to be a problem where plants are growing in well-managed soil and the garden environment encourages natural predation.

ROOTSTOCKS			
Rootstocks	**Effect**	**Eventual height**	**Planting distance**
St. Julien A	Semi-vigorous; suitable for bushes and fans	12–13 ft. (4.2–4.5 m)	13–17½ ft. (4.5–5.5 m) for fans or bushes
Seedling peach	Vigorous; tolerates wetter conditions than seedling apricot; freestanding trees	20–25 ft. (6–8 m)	15–20 ft. (5–6 m)
Seedling apricot	Vigorous; freestanding trees	23–28 ft. (7.5–9 m)	17½–22 ft. (5.5–7 m)

Figs

It is not difficult to grow figs, exotic though they may seem. The main problems in cooler temperature climates are to restrain their vigor and to bring them into fruitful production. In a Mediterranean climate figs may fruit twice in a year but in cooler situations once a year is more usual. Figs will not produce successfully in cool, short summers. No pollination is necessary as the flowers form inside the embryo fruits and are self-pollinating. Figs are grown on their own roots and not grafted onto rootstocks.

Site and soil

Figs do best in warm, dry, sunny locations with a long growing season (Zones 8 to 10). In cooler climates (Zones 6 and 7), figs are best grown against a wall receiving maximum sunshine. The wall needs to be at least 10 ft. (3 m) high as figs are vigorous and each fan tree will take up to 10–12 ft. (3–4 m) in width. Horizontal wire supports will be needed at 12-in. (30-cm) intervals. Alkaline soils suit figs better but it is not necessary to add lime unless the pH is less than 6.

One way to restrict fig tree roots, and therefore the tree's vigor, is to grow it in an excavated pit 24–36 in. (60–90 cm) square, lined with concrete blocks or bricks. The pit should be dug 24 in. (60 cm) deep and the bottom 12 in. (30 cm) filled with stones. Trees restricted in this way fruit much

Ripening figs
New embryo pea-size fruitlets form as the current season's figs ripen. These fruitlets will overwinter and then start to swell during summer.

PRUNING AND TRAINING

	Fig bush	Fig fan
On planting	The basic framework is formed as for a central-leader plum (see p. 273).	Advice for fans outside or indoors is almost identical, but greenhouse-grown figs need a more open branch structure with more widely spaced arms. Initial pruning to create the basic framework is as for peaches and sour cherries (see p. 275), but allow about 12 in. (30 cm) between the skeleton branches.
In subsequent years	**Spring** Remove all branches growing into the center to keep it open. Cut out any frost-damaged wood and thin out branches to prevent crowding. The most productive branches are young, short, and thick. All spindly growth should be removed. The aim is to produce an open framework of flattish branches to allow maximum light penetration. In warmer climates, where hot sun is more of a problem than frost damage, aim for a more upright shape to help shade the center. After a while, some long bare branches will form in the tree. Cut these back in spring to one bud to generate a new branch.	**Spring** After all danger of severe frost is past, start by removing all frost-damaged wood, crossing or badly placed branches, and weak spindly growth. Clear away all suckers arising at or below ground level. Cut out all old branches that have produced fruit to one bud, and prune back a number of 1-year-old shoots near the center of the fan similarly to encourage new branches. Tie the remaining unpruned sideshoots to an open fan shape, filling the wall but leaving the center slightly open. Do not allow any strong upright growth in the center. **By midsummer** New shoots will have arisen along the length of the branches. Except where replacement branches will be needed, pinch these back to five leaves. Embryo figs will then form on these to grow and ripen the following year. **Autumn** Remove all part-formed or unripened figs to leave only pea-size embryo figs on the tree.

Container culture
In cold-winter climates, a large pot lets you move your fig to protect it from low temperatures. You'll need a sturdy dolly to bring the fig to a protected spot in the fall and back into the garden each spring.

more readily. In hot, dry climates this practice will not be necessary. Trees can be grown as a freestanding bush with unrestricted roots. They may eventually reach 25 ft. (8 m) in height. Figs are well suited to container growing (see pp. 212–213).

Buying plants

Look for 2-year-old container-grown specimens with two good branches for a fan, three or four for a bush, about 24 in. (60 cm) above soil level. Unless you live in a warm region or have the opportunity to grow figs in a greenhouse, choose an early or mid-season variety.

Preparation and planting

For freestanding bushes, follow advice for apples. For fruit grown in the ground, it is important to provide adequate nutrition to give the tree a good start. Once the planting hole is prepared, add to the soil to be returned:
• One 2-gallon (10-liter) bucket of garden compost
• One small spadeful of chopped, well-rotted manure (or use alfalfa meal applied in spring)
• 2 oz. (75 g) bone meal
• 2 oz. (75 g) seaweed meal
• Ground limestone, if the soil pH is below 6.

Tease the roots out from the potting medium. Set the tree in the hole and work in the above mixture around the roots, planting the tree level with the original soil mark. To train and prune as a bush or fan, see above.

Feeding and weeding

Keep wall-trained trees free of weeds at all times. Freestanding trees can be vigorous, and you can surround them with grass once established. Unrestricted trees will not need feeding. Pit-grown trees will, however, need feeding annually as their roots are restricted. Every other spring, apply one 2-gallon (10-liter) bucket of garden compost or half a bucket of well-rotted manure to the surface. In alternating years, apply a balanced organic fetilizer and 2 oz. (75 g) seaweed meal.

Regular watering will be necessary for trees grown indoors, in a container, or against a wall outside in dry weather.

Picking the fruit

In a temperate climate, fruits outdoors will ripen in late summer. Fruits hang down when ripe and are very soft to the touch. They may have split skins. Figs are best eaten fresh or can be dried.

PROTECT THE CROP

Outdoor-grown figs are relatively problem-free. Fruit may need protection from birds. In autumn, protect the embryo figs from frost damage if this is likely to occur. Pick off any diseased fruits and leaves; cut out any branches that have died back, cutting well back into healthy wood.

Figs growing indoors or in a very hot, dry situation—against a wall, for example—may suffer from red spider mite, soft scale, and other greenhouse pests. Check plants regularly, and introduce the relevant biological control agent. Prune and train to give an open shape to reduce the risk of gray mold developing.

Clear up fallen leaves and debris at the end of the season, and remove any figs that have not ripened (but not the tiny embryo fruits that will produce the next season's crop).

See the *A–Z of Plant Problems*, p. 367, for more details.

Snapped stems
Snapping or "brutting" filbert stems reduces vigor and helps nuts to ripen. It also makes the plant more likely to bear female flowers.

Filberts

In America, cultivated hazelnuts are generally referred to as filberts, although in Britain the name "cobnut" is more common.

Site and soil
Filberts grow best in full sun and a well-drained soil with a pH of 6–7. While adequate fertility is important, too much will lead to large, unproductive trees. The trees are fully hardy but flower extremely early. It is important, therefore, to choose a frost-free site. Commercial nut "plats" (plantations) are frequently sited on hillsides and slopes to ensure that frost "drains away."

Although nuts are wind-pollinated, they need protection from strong winds and will benefit from windbreak hedges.

Buying plants
Spacing for nut trees is wide; each tree will eventually take up an area of 11 ft. (3.5 m). Buy 2- or 3-year-old well-rooted trees.

For good-quality, easy-to-pick filberts, grow a single-stemmed tree

Filberts are not self-pollinating and need to be pollinated by another cultivar; not all cultivars are mutually compatible for this purpose. If you have wild hedgerow or woodland filberts nearby, you should have no problem with pollination. *Cultivar Choice* (see left) includes advice on compatibility.

Preparation and planting
Follow the general guidelines for apples (see p. 266), allowing a cultivated weed-free area at least 3 ft. (1 m) in diameter around each tree.
• Prepare the site in autumn so it will be ready for planting soon after leaf fall.
• Just before planting, add bone meal at the rate of 4 oz. per sq. yd. (125 g per sq. m).
• If rabbits are a problem, install a spiral tree guard on the trunk.
• Plant the tree to the same depth as it was in the nursery (look for the soil mark), and tamp it well.

Forming the tree
Filberts can be allowed to grow as a multiple stemmed, bushlike tree, as wild nut trees do. However, a single-stemmed tree, or standard, with an open, goblet-shaped crown produces better-quality nuts that are easier to pick. It is also easier to weed and mulch a single stem. To train a standard:
After planting
• Remove all shoots growing from below ground to leave a single main stem. Prune off any growth to a height of about 18 in. (45 cm) above soil level. The crown can then form naturally above this point.
In subsequent years
• In late summer each year, snap in half any lateral branches of 12 in. (30 cm) or more of the current season's growth (see photo, below left). The snapped portion is left hanging down to aid location in winter. This process, called "brutting," reduces vigor, helps nuts ripen, and encourages weaker growth, more likely to bear female flowers.
• Regularly prune out any shoots growing around the base of the tree.
• In winter, prune any strong upright growth, damaged branches, and "brutted" laterals to three or four buds.
• Keep the tree to a height convenient for picking by pruning back tall branches to a suitable outward-facing lateral.

Caring for the plants
Keep trees free of weeds and mulch with straw early in autumn. Remove this mulch in winter. Apply well-rotted manure every 3 years in spring at the rate of one wheelbarrowful to 9 sq. yd. (10 sq. m), increasing the frequency only if growth is poor. Nuts do not need thinning.

Harvesting the crop
The harvesting period is from late summer, when the husks are still green and the nuts are juicy, through mid-autumn, by which time the shells and husks are brown and the kernels firm and full-flavored. The last crop to be harvested can be stored until midwinter. Filberts cannot normally be stored for long as they dry out more quickly than other nuts. For short-term storage, keep nuts refrigerated.

PROTECT THE CROP

Fungal leaf spots and powdery mildew may appear on the leaves in summer. Mulch plants well, and water in very dry weather. Pick off or cut out badly infected leaves and shoots; clean up all plant debris in the autumn.

Both Eastern and Western filbert blight kill branches. American filberts have some tolerance for the Eastern blight fungus, so look for resistant cultivars that have been bred from these plants. Western filbert blight is a bacterial disease most common in the Pacific Northwest. It causes small, angular leaf spots that start out with a water-soaked appearance and turn reddish brown. Cankers also form on the branches. Prune out infected twigs in winter. Older plants are less affected than younger ones.

The major problem of filberts in many areas is the squirrel, which harvests ripe nuts. Little can be done against this creature. Filbertworms may attack young nuts, creating a round exit hole in the ripe nut. The percentage of the crop attacked is usually too small to warrant attention.

Pests and diseases are less likely to be a problem where plants are growing in appropriately managed soil, and where the garden environment encourages natural predation.

Growing herbs

KNOWN FOR THEIR FRAGRANCE, FLAVOR, AND HEALING
PROPERTIES, HERBS ARE EASY TO CULTIVATE ORGANICALLY

**Choosing herbs
(facing page)**
*Plant a selection of herbs that reflects
your own taste. Choose plants for
their fragrance, foliage, culinary use,
or simply for their beauty alongside
garden ornamentals.*

WALK INTO ANY HERB GARDEN for a sensory
experience—the plants it contains will have been
selected for their scent as well as their appearance.
Many also have rich associations with human
history. Here are plants that have, over many
centuries, helped people to sleep, soothed pain,
repelled insects, calmed fractious babies, and flavored
intoxicating drinks. Herbs are still grown today
for their useful qualities as well as their beauty.
This chapter will tell you about growing herbs
organically, along with information about how to
harvest, store, and use various herbs. It also includes
details about which herbs are suitable for different
soil types and situations, as well as how to stop
invasive herbs from taking over the garden.

What is an herb?

The broadest definition of an herb is a plant that
people use or have used for a specific purpose.
Nowadays herbs are most commonly known for
their culinary, medicinal, aromatic, and decorative
qualities. In earlier times, people relied on herbs for
an even greater number of uses: Some were utilized
in dyeing and cleaning fabrics; others had a role in
ritual and ceremony; and many were used in
everyday life as flavorings for food and drink, to
promote good health, and to cure illness.

Annuals, biennials, perennials, bulbs, shrubs,
climbers, and trees can all have herbal value. In many
cases, it is the leafy part of the plant that is used as
an herb, but other parts, such as roots, fruits, seeds,
flowers, and even the bark of some trees, are used
and classified as herbs.

Herbs are plants that people have found useful throughout history

Most (but not all) herbs are safe to handle and
consume. Some herbs can be toxic to humans
and animals even in small doses, so they need to be
treated with respect. Never use anything that you are
not sure is completely safe, and consult a doctor or
other medical expert first if you want to use herbs
for their medicinal properties.

Growing herbs organically

Herbs are easy to grow, beautiful to look
at, and, in many cases, free from pest and disease
problems. Growing them yourself means that you
can have fresh supplies on hand when you need
them, and using organic methods means you can
be sure they have not been treated with pesticides.

Growing herbs of any kind will increase the
diversity of a garden, one of the key principles
behind a successful organic system. With such a
huge range of herbs to choose from, there is almost
certainly one for every situation. Herbs can be
selected to climb, creep, tumble, form dense carpets,
or be trained up walls. Some will be happy in boggy
soil, others on top of walls, between paving stones,

Herbs at hand (below)
*Both decorative and practical, a terra-
cotta strawberry jar on the doorstep
keeps favorite culinary herbs nearby
for a quick snip to flavor your meals.*

HERBS TO ATTRACT WILDLIFE

For bees
Borage, chives, lungwort, sage, thyme, teasel, mint

For beneficial insects
Pot marigold, fennel, yarrow, dandelion, angelica, coriander, feverfew, tansy

For butterflies and moths
Evening primrose, catmint, hemp, agrimony, valerian, lavender, coltsfoot, purple loosestrife

For birds
Poppy, rose, teasel, elder, hawthorn

See p. 289 for an index of common and botanical names

Out of the blue
Borage flowers are characteristically blue, but more unusual white flowers can sometimes be found.

under trees, or in meadows—success depends on matching the right plant to the available conditions. They also vary in size: from the tiny, ground-hugging Corsican mint *(Mentha requienii)* to stately giants such as angelica or lovage, which reach 6 ft. (2 m) high. Herbs can be grown for their appearance alone. Some plants have spectacular flowers, some are valued for their foliage, and they all have something to contribute to a garden.

Many herbs attract wildlife: Birds eat the seeds and berries, butterflies and bees enjoy the nectar and pollen, while beneficial insects will lay their eggs near sources of aphids and other pests. Some examples are given above. Dense plantings of ground-covering herbs such as thymes provide habitats for many beneficial creatures, including beetles, spiders, and even frogs and toads.

Growing herbs for flavor

Herbs impart an enormous range of flavors to both sweet and savory dishes. They can be added to soups, sauces, stews, salads, casseroles, pies, breads, and anything else you can eat! Although it is easy to buy dried herbs, their flavor is far better when fresh. Recipes that list dried herbs can be adapted for fresh

herbs just by doubling the quantities given. With practice, you should be able to judge quantities according to taste. A good suggestion is to start with just one or two fresh herbs in a recipe until you become familiar with the flavors and learn how to combine them for the best effects.

Preparations and decorations

Another tradition is the use of aromatic herbs to repel moths or insects and to keep stored clothes or linen smelling sweet. These mixtures are effective and still popular today, either sewn into bags or stored loose in containers as potpourri.

Herbs are also an important part of the cosmetics industry, finding their way into bath oils, shampoos, creams, and lotions. Many old-fashioned preparations are simple to make yourself and much cheaper than buying products off the shelf.

The role of herbs in rituals and ceremonies was more evident in ancient times, but vestiges still remain, such as the way we decorate our homes with mistletoe, ivy, and holly in midwinter. Other herbs are appreciated today simply for their decorative role, either in the garden or in fresh or dried flower arrangements.

Where to grow herbs

Herbs grow well in all sorts of situations, from a few culinary herbs planted in a window box to a rambling wild garden full of teasels, nettles, and brambles. Plant according to your personal taste and how you intend to use the herbs: A few herbs can be scattered throughout a garden, but if you plan to go into large-scale production of herbs for cooking or drying, it will be easier to dedicate a separate area to them. For best results, group herbs by their growing requirements rather than by their use.

Creating an herb garden
Formal herb gardens are based on a system of paths and beds, often edged with low-growing hedges. To remain neat, this type of garden requires quite a bit of maintenance, with hedges trimmed two to three times a year and careful attention to weed control. Thorough preparation of beds and paths at the outset is essential to prevent weed problems later on.

Group herbs by their growing requirements rather than by their use

An informal herb patch is equally attractive, or herbs can be mixed in among other flowers, shrubs, and even vegetables. Put them in beds and borders, against walls and fences—in fact, anywhere that you have space!

Shade-tolerant herbs
Herbs that enjoy dappled shade thrive on the edges of shrub masses or by patches of small trees. Add a low-fertility soil improver on an annual basis in order to mimic the decayed leaf layer that occurs naturally in woodland areas. Vigorous groundcover herbs can become rampant in favorable conditions, so cut them back regularly, remove runners to control their spread, or plant them in containers.

Drought-tolerant herbs
Drought-tolerant herbs look stunning growing together in a location where they will have full sun in well-drained soil. A naturally dry part of the garden will be ideal. Use a gravel mulch around the plants to help control weeds and keep the area immediately around the base of the plants dry. These herbs will also grow well in containers, where you can provide ideal soil conditions for them, and which you can move around the garden to make best use of the sunniest spots.

Herbs for damp soil
Herbs that like damp soil will grow well in a naturally boggy area, or you can create one by the edge of a pond (see *Ponds for Wildlife*, pp. 198–201). In dry summers you will need to keep up the water levels in the pond or bog garden. Again, some of these species can become invasive once they are established in the garden.

Herbs for walkways
Choose low-growing herbs that thrive in dry conditions for planting between stepping-stones. Fill the cracks with compost and sow the seed directly into the soil in spring. Keep watered and avoid walking on the herbs until they become established.

Herbs for a vegetable patch
Leafy herbs such as chervil, coriander, summer savory, and dill all enjoy the slightly richer soil normally found in a vegetable garden. These types of herb are best sown direct in the spring once the soil is warm enough.

Herbs in containers
Many herbs grow well in containers, which is a good way of providing suitable conditions if your soil is not ideal (see also *Container Gardening*, p. 210). Use any container with drainage holes and a minimum depth of about 12 in. (30 cm).

Put a few stones at the bottom of the container, then fill it with all-purpose organic potting medium (see pp. 114–115). For herbs such as rosemary, which prefer a light soil, mix in some fine gravel to ensure adequate drainage. Use no more than 1 part gravel to 5 parts growing medium, depending on the herb's requirements. Check moisture levels at least once a day in sunny weather, and water if necessary.

PLANTS FOR PLACES

Herbs for formal hedging
Boxwood
Hedge germander
Wall germander
Winter savory
Rosemary (choose *Rosmarinus officinalis* 'Miss Jessop's Upright')
Lavender (especially *Lavandula angustifolia* 'Munstead' and 'Hidcote')
Hyssop

Herbs for informal edging
Alpine strawberry
Chives
Parsley
Common thyme
Lavender cotton (santolina)

Shade-tolerant herbs
Bugle
Creeping Jenny
Dwarf comfrey
Periwinkle
Sweet violet
Lungwort
Woodruff
Lily-of-the-valley
Foxglove

Drought-tolerant herbs
Artemisia
Lavender
Rosemary
Sage
Thyme
Lavender cotton (santolina)
Curry plant

Herbs for damp soil
Hemp agrimony
Meadowsweet
Water mint
Valerian

Herbs for walkways
Lady's mantle
Corsican mint
Creeping savory
Creeping thymes

See p. 289 for an index of common and botanical names

Caring for herb plants

Most herbs are relatively easy to grow organically. Follow these guidelines to ensure successful cultivation of your chosen herbs.

Soil preparation and planting

Check the preferred soil conditions of your chosen herbs (see p. 288) before planting. Many herbs thrive in a well-drained, low-nutrient soil. If your soil is heavy, incorporate a low-fertility soil improver to improve drainage. Constructing raised beds will also help. For a short-term solution, add a couple of handfuls of sand or gravel to the bottom of the planting hole. Other herbs that prefer a more fertile soil may benefit from the addition of a medium-fertility soil improver. Remove any weeds, especially perennial weeds such as quack grass.

Maintenance

Remove flowering stems from shrubby herbs such as lavender and sage after flowering. Prune these herbs in the spring to control the size of the plant and to prevent them becoming bare and woody at the base.

Always remove flowers if you want to harvest the maximum quantity and quality of leaves. Pinch off growing tips to encourage bushy growth, and cut out any plain shoots on variegated herbs. Established clumps of perennials are best divided every 2 to 3 years, in spring or autumn (see *Dividing Perennials*, p. 173). It can be worth taking cuttings each year from tender shrubby herbs such as some lavenders, which may not survive the winter.

Propagation

Many herbs are easy to raise in the garden. Annuals and biennials such as parsley and basil are grown from seed. Some perennials, such as fennel and chives, are also easy to raise from seed and may self-sow. Remember that cultivated varieties do not always grow from seed or produce seed. In this case, vegetative propagation is the only option—by cuttings, layering, or division, depending on species.

Invasive herbs

Vigorous herbs will take over if left to their own devices. These species are excellent for growing in wild areas, where they will be controlled by equally vigorous neighbors. In other situations, they need to be restricted: Bury a large plant pot or a bucket with the bottom removed or with extra drainage holes, and plant invasive herbs inside. Cut back any vigorous growth and rooted creeping stems, and divide every 2 to 3 years. Some invasive herbs are prolific self-seeders: Remove flowerheads before seeds form, or hoe off the seedlings in spring.

Tough and tender
Known for their versatility, hardy pot marigolds (Calendula, below right) grow vigorously in most soils, although they prefer fine loam. They self-seed readily, so remove any dead flowerheads if you want to prevent too much seed dispersal. By contrast, the tender herb basil needs warmth, sun, and protection from wind, frost, and scorching. Grow seedlings (below) under cover and plant out only when the weather is warm enough. In cooler climates, basil may be best grown in a greenhouse or hoop house.

VIGOROUS HERBS

Invasive herbs
Chinese lantern
Comfrey
Creeping Jenny
Mint
Soapwort
Bee balm
Horseradish
Tansy

Vigorous self-seeders
Chives
Evening primrose
Lady's mantle
Lemon balm
Sweet cicely
Teasel
Coltsfoot
Jacob's ladder
Feverfew
Pot marigold
Borage

See p. 289 for an index of common and botanical names

Border invader
With its large, robust rosette of leaves, borage is an opportunistic self-seeder. Although it is a beautiful plant, it will crowd smaller neighbors.

POPULAR HERBS

◁ BASIL

Tender perennial grown as an annual. 12–18 in. (30–45 cm). Cultivars vary in leaf size, color, and flavor.

Ideal location Greenhouse, hoop house, or sunny, sheltered spot outdoors. Light, well-drained, fertile soil. Grows well in containers.

Cultivation Sow under cover in late spring and early summer at 55°F (13°C). Apply a medium-fertility soil improver before planting out. Pinch off tips for bushy growth; remove flowers to promote leaf production.

◁ BAY

Evergreen shrub or small tree. Frost-tender, especially when young. Golden-leaved 'Aurea' is particularly tender. 10–20 ft. (3–6 m). Can be pruned to limit size. Good for topiary.

Ideal location Sheltered, sunny spot in light, well-drained soil. Good in pots.

Cultivation Add a medium-fertility soil improver when planting and mulch every spring. Prune in summer if necessary. In exposed areas protect from wind and frost. Prone to attack by scale insects.

CHIVES ▷

Hardy perennial. 12 in. (30 cm). Both leaves and flowers can be used. The pinkish flowers are attractive to bees.

Ideal location Sunny, moist, fertile soil, but tolerates shade and most soils.

Cultivation Add a medium-fertility soil improver before planting. Cut back to 2 in. (5 cm) after flowering to promote fresh growth. Sow seed in late spring. Divide established clumps in spring or autumn.

FENNEL ▷

Hardy perennial. 6 ft. (2 m). Leaves, stems, and seeds are all used. The flowers attract many beneficial insects. The cultivar 'Purpureum' has bronze foliage.

Ideal location Sunny position, in well-drained, fertile soil.

Cultivation Add a medium-fertility soil improver when planting. Cut back dead flowering stems in spring. Sow seed in spring; may self-seed. Established plants may be divided in spring or autumn.

◁ LAVENDER

Hardy, evergreen shrub. 24–39 in. (60–100 cm). Flowers are very popular with bees and butterflies. Many forms, including tender prostrate, dwarf, pink- and white-flowered varieties.

Ideal location Sunny, sheltered spot with light, well-drained soil. Will not tolerate waterlogged ground.

Cultivation Trim in spring. Remove flower spikes after flowering. Plants may need replacing every 3–5 years. Take cuttings in spring or summer, or layer in spring.

◁ MINT

Hardy perennial. 1–39 in. (3–100 cm). Many types available, including ginger mint, spearmint, peppermint, and pennyroyal. Invasive habit, spreading by runners and seed. Plant in containers to limit spread.

Ideal location Light shade; moist but not waterlogged soil.

Cultivation Add a medium-fertility soil improver when planting or dividing. Cut to ground level in autumn. Divide every 2–3 years. To propagate, take root cuttings or divide established plants.

PARSLEY ▷

Biennial. Quite hardy, but needs winter protection in cold regions. 12 in. (30 cm). Curly and flat-leaved varieties.

Ideal location Partial shade and moist, fertile soil. Good in containers.

Cultivation Sow in cell packs in gentle heat (65°F/18°C is ideal) or directly into the ground when soil is warm. Sow in spring and summer for summer harvest, and in late summer for a winter crop grown under cover. Vulnerable to carrot fly and virus.

ROSEMARY ▷

Evergreen shrub. 4–5 ft. (1–1.5 m). Many types, of varying hardiness, including dwarf, prostrate, and variegated cultivars. Dwarf types can be clipped for hedging.

Ideal location Sheltered, sunny spot. Well-drained, low-fertility soil. Cannot tolerate waterlogged soils.

Cultivation Prune in spring. Tender cultivars need winter protection. Take softwood cuttings in spring, semi-hardwood in summer. Layer established branches in spring.

◁ CORIANDER

Annual. To 28 in. (70 cm). Grown for leaves and seed. Special selections for leaf production available.

Ideal location Sunny, in light but fertile soil. Benefits from cloche or hoop house protection in cool climates.

Cultivation Sow direct from spring to autumn for continuous supply of leaves. Goes to seed quickly in hot weather. Add a medium-fertility soil improver before sowing. Pick leaves regularly for use or leave to flower for seed production.

THYME ▷

Evergreen shrub. 12 in. (30 cm). Many types, including lemon-scented, golden, and variegated. Creeping thymes make good groundcover.

Ideal location A dry, sunny spot with poor, well-drained soil. Dislikes wet winter conditions. Grows well in gravel, paths, and rock gardens.

Cultivation Trim after flowering. Layer in spring, or take cuttings in early summer. Creeping thymes may be divided.

◁ SAGE

Evergreen shrub. 24–36 in. (60–90 cm). Many types, including purple and variegated cultivars. The flowers attract bees.

Ideal location: Sunny. Poor, light, well-drained soil.

Cultivation Prune in spring. May not always survive the winter, so take cuttings. Prone to powdery mildew. Take cuttings from new growth in spring and early summer.

FRENCH TARRAGON ▷

Perennial. 24 in. (60 cm). Popular for flavoring vinegar. Has a much finer flavor than Russian tarragon, which can be invasive.

Ideal location: Sunny, in light, well-drained, poor soil. Cannot tolerate waterlogged soil.

Cultivation Remove flower spikes to encourage leaf growth. Protect roots from damp over winter. Cannot be grown from seed. Divide or take root cuttings in spring.

COMMON AND BOTANICAL NAMES

Specialty herb nurseries usually sell herbs under their botanical names. In most garden centers you may also find that, apart from a small selection of culinary herbs, the plants are scattered about under their botanical names. Many plants that are used as herbs are beautiful garden plants in their own right. Look at the list below and you may well find that you are already growing a number of these herbs (or their close relatives). Always check whether an herb is edible before use.

Alpine strawberry *Fragaria vesca*
Angelica *Angelica archangelica*
Artemisia *Artemisia*
Basil *Ocimum basilicum*
Bay *Laurus nobilis*
Bee balm *Monarda*
Borage *Borago officinalis*
Boxwood *Buxus*
Bugle *Ajuga reptans*
Catnip *Nepeta cataria*
Chamomile *Chamaemelum nobile*
Chervil *Anthriscus cerefolium*
Chinese chives *Allium tuberosum*
Chinese lantern *Physalis alkekengi*
Chives *Allium schoenoprasum*
Coltsfoot *Tussilago farfara*
Comfrey *Symphytum officinale*
Comfrey, dwarf *Symphytum grandiflorum*
Coriander *Coriandrum sativum*
Corsican mint *Mentha requienii*
Creeping Jenny *Lysimachia nummularia*
Curry plant *Helichrysum italicum*
Dandelion *Taraxacum officinale*
Dill *Anethum graveolens*
Elderberry *Sambucus nigra*
Evening primrose *Oenothera biennis*
Fennel *Foeniculum vulgare*
Feverfew *Tanacetum parthenium*
Foxglove *Digitalis*
Garlic *Allium sativum*
Garlic chives *Allium tuberosum*
Ginger mint *Mentha x gracilis*
Hawthorn *Crataegus monogyna*
Hemp agrimony *Eupatorium cannabinum*
Honesty *Lunaria annua*
Horehound *Marrubium vulgare*
Horseradish *Armoracia rusticana*
Hyssop *Hyssopus officinalis*
Jacob's ladder *Polemonium caeruleum*
Lady's mantle *Alchemilla mollis*
Lavender *Lavandula*
Lemon balm *Melissa officinalis*
Lily-of-the-valley *Convallaria majalis*
Lovage *Levisticum officinale*
Lungwort *Pulmonaria officinalis*
Madder *Rubia tinctorum*
Marjoram *Origanum majorana*
Marshmallow *Althaea officinalis*
Meadowsweet *Filipendula ulmaria*
Mint *Mentha*
Oregano *Origanum*

Orris *Iris germanica* subsp. *florentina*
Parsley *Petroselinum crispum*
Pennyroyal *Mentha pulegium*
Peppermint *Mentha x piperita*
Periwinkle *Vinca major, V. minor*
Pineapple mint *Mentha suaveolens*
Poppy *Papaver*
Pot marigold *Calendula officinalis*
Purple coneflower *Echinacea purpurea*
Rose *Rosa*
Rosemary *Rosmarinus officinalis*
Rue *Ruta graveolens*
Sage *Salvia officinalis*
Santolina *Santolina chamaecyparissus*
Sea holly *Eryngium*
Soapwort *Saponaria officinalis*
Southernwood *Artemisia abrotanum*
Spearmint *Mentha spicata*
Summer savory *Satureja hortensis*
Sweet Cicely *Myrrhis odorata*
Sweet violet *Viola odorata*
Tansy *Tanacetum vulgare*
Tarragon, French *Artemisia dracunculus*
Tarragon, Russian *Artemisia dracunculus* subsp. *dracunculoides*
Teasel *Dipsacus fullonum*
Thyme, common *Thymus vulgaris*
Thyme, creeping *Thymus serpyllum, T. praecox*
Valerian *Valeriana officinalis*
Wall germander *Teucrium chamaedrys*
Water mint *Mentha aquatica*
Winter savory *Satureja montana*
Woodruff *Galium odoratum*
Yarrow *Achillea millefolium*

Harvesting and preserving herbs

Small amounts of herbs can be picked throughout the growing season and used immediately. Harvesting large amounts of herbs for drying or using in some other way requires a different approach. Whichever you do, always harvest thoughtfully, without stripping a plant bare. As a general rule, never harvest more than about one-third of a plant at any one time. Vigorous plants, such as mint and comfrey, can be cut back to ground level two or three times a season without doing them any harm.

Saving seeds (below)
Tie a bunch of harvested herbs, wrap them gently in newspaper or a paper bag, and then dry them upside down to collect the seeds.

HERBS TO PRESERVE

Culinary herbs that dry well
Bay
Mint
Rosemary
Sage
Tarragon
Thyme

Herbs to dry for decoration
Chinese lantern
Honesty
Poppy
Sea holly
Teasel
Yarrow

Herbs for freezing
Basil
Borage flowers
Chervil
Chives
Fennel leaf
Parsley
Summer savory

Herbs to flavor vinegar
Elderflowers
Chive flowers
French tarragon
Garlic
Lavender flowers

See p. 289 for an index of common and botanical names

Knowing when to harvest

Allow perennial herbs to become established before harvesting them. This will usually be in or after the second year of growth. Never harvest from plants that look weak or are struggling to grow.

The majority of leafy herbs reach their maximum flavor just before the flowers open. After that point, the texture and flavor of leaves change as the plants put energy into flower and seed production. Remove all flowers to extend the production of tender leaves unless you are growing the herbs for flowers or seed.

Herbs harvested for drying need to be collected with as little moisture on them as possible. The ideal day for this is dry, warm, but not too sunny. The ideal time is after overnight moisture has dissipated but before strong sunlight has caused the volatile oils to evaporate. In most cases this is around mid-morning, depending on the climate and weather conditions.

Always use sharp pruners or scissors to harvest the herb in order to avoid damaging the plant unduly. Collect your plant material quickly, and then bring it indoors immediately to minimize any deterioration in flavor and quality.

Preparing herbs for storage

Drying is an excellent way of preserving herbs for use out of season. Many leaves and seeds keep their flavor well and, stored correctly, should last up to a year. Providing the ideal range of temperatures and ventilation for drying individual herbs is not easy in a domestic situation, and if you dry herbs at home you may find that the drying process results in some loss of flavor and color. Some herbs do not retain their flavor well when dried, and are best used fresh or preserved in some other way (see facing page). Check all the plant material carefully before you dry it and discard any parts that are diseased or damaged.

There are two main methods of drying herbs: suspended in bunches, and lying flat on racks or trays. Electric dryers are available to buy. Whichever method you use, it is best to dry each type separately because they dry at different rates. Choose a dark, clean, dry, well-ventilated location, free from dust and insects. Always dry herbs out of direct sunlight, which causes loss of color and flavor.

Poppy seedheads
Dried poppy seedheads can look very decorative. When the "pepperpot" tops of the seedheads open, the seeds can be shaken out.

Drying in bunches

Keep the bunches of herbs small; a good guideline is to gather up no more than enough stalks to fit comfortably in your hand. Hang the herbs upside down; this helps to preserve their appearance if you are planning to use them for decorative purposes. Use rubber bands to tie up the bunches as these will shrink with the herbs. Be aware that these rubber bands will eventually break and need to be replaced. Finally, tie a large paper bag or sheet of newspaper loosely over the flowerheads (see facing page) if you want to collect the seeds.

Drying on racks or trays

To dry herbs flat, strip the leaves from each stem and arrange them in a single layer on a rack or tray. Try to inspect the herbs regularly to ensure they are drying properly, and turn any of the larger leaves frequently to ensure that they dry evenly. Look also for anything that shows signs of mold or decay and remove it. The herbs are ready when they are crisp to the touch but not brittle. They should crumble but not shatter when you crush them.

Once dried, store the herbs in airtight containers to prevent them from reabsorbing moisture from the air. Glass jars, cans, or screw-top containers are all suitable. Keep them in the dark in a cool, dry place. Most dried herbs will retain their flavor for up to a year, but are best renewed after that time.

Freezing

Freezing retains the flavor but not the appearance of herbs. It is an excellent way of preserving leafy herbs that do not dry well, such as basil, parsley, fennel leaf, and chives. To freeze these herbs, wash, chop, and place them in ice-cube trays. Cover with water and freeze. Remove the cubes from the trays and store in plastic bags or boxes in the freezer until needed. To use, add to dishes at the end of the cooking time. They are particularly good for soups, stews, and sauces.

Herb-flavored vinegar

Some herbs have traditionally been used to flavor vinegars. These vinegars make excellent ingredients in mayonnaise, salad dressings, and any other recipe that requires vinegar. Use a mild-flavored vinegar such as cider or white wine vinegar; balsamic vinegar is not suitable as its flavor is already too strong.

Place the chopped or crushed herbs in a bowl and pour the vinegar over them. Cover and leave for about 2 weeks for the flavor to develop, making sure the herbs stay immersed. Strain the mixture through muslin or a coffee filter, and check for flavor. If it is not strong enough, repeat the process with a new bunch of herbs. If it is too strong, dilute with plain vinegar. Store in clean bottles or jars, but make sure the vinegar does not come into contact with metal lids as this will cause corrosion.

DRIED HERB RECIPES

A simple potpourri
Rose petals
Lavender flowers and leaves
Lemon balm leaves
Pot marigold petals
Use equal amounts of these dried herbs. Mix together and put in a bowl or closed container. As the aromas fade, you can add a few drops of an essential oil of your choice to restore the fragrance.

Soothing bath bag
1 tablespoon chamomile flowers
1 tablespoon lavender flowers
2 tablespoons oatmeal or cornmeal
Mix the ingredients well, then place in the center of a square of muslin, or a fine, large handkerchief. Gather the edges together, and tie securely with ribbon or string.

Hang the bag in the flow of the hot water as the bath is running. You can also use the bag as a gentle body scrubber, which releases a soothing, milky juice from the oatmeal or cornmeal.

Sweet bag for linen or clothes
Make a small sachet of fine muslin. Fill with equal amounts of dried herbs selected from the following, according to preference (both flowers and leaves can be used):
Lavender
Artemisia
Rosemary
Lavender cotton (santolina)
Sage
Pennyroyal
Lemon balm

Growing vegetables

VEGETABLES ARE THE LOGICAL STARTING POINT FOR PEOPLE
WHO WISH TO TAKE CONTROL OVER THE FOOD THEY EAT

THERE EXISTS NO STRONGER connection with the living soil, the earth, and the changing seasons than eating food you yourself have sown, nurtured, and harvested. Vegetables can be grown virtually anywhere—a garden in the traditional sense is not essential to produce safe, healthy food. The results with some types of vegetable growing are quick—sprouted seeds, for example—and will be ready to eat in a matter of days. Most can be harvested within a few weeks or months, although some can take longer to begin bearing. The desire to grow fruit follows on logically as knowledge and experience with vegetables grow. If you are new to both, it pays to start small and gradually expand your edible horizons.

Growing vegetables organically is a positive, empowering, rewarding, and (for some) spiritual experience. Above all it is deeply satisfying, enjoyable, and fundamental to our very existence, with many health benefits. The shared enthusiasm for growing food cuts through barriers of class, race, and culture like no other. Plants of all types can bring people and communities together, but none succeed quite like those that we eat. However much food you decide to grow, or whatever constraints you have to work with, growing at least some of your own vegetables organically satisfies more than the fundamental human desire to eat healthy, fresh, uncontaminated produce—it is also a way of minimizing our impact on the wider environment.

The bigger picture

Many common fruits and vegetables travel for thousands of miles around the planet before they reach their final destination. Transport is often by air, followed by road, both of which consume vast amounts of fossil fuels that contribute to atmospheric pollution leading to global warming.

The number of so-called "food miles" traveled by supposedly "fresh" produce can be enormous, resulting in much food being eaten a long way from where it was grown. Cultivars created for the rigors of travel and longevity—rather than nutritional value and flavor—are the direct fallout of worldwide monocultures and the move toward increased globalization. These growing systems depend almost exclusively on high, unsustainable inputs of energy, artificial fertilizers, and synthetic chemical pesticides. Concerns over food safety are increasingly frequent, ranging from worries over pesticide residues to the many uncertainties surrounding the widespread use of genetically modified food crops.

Environmental benefits

Growing your own vegetables, and growing them organically, provides not only safe, uncontaminated food but also has significant environmental benefits. Food miles are virtually eliminated, organic waste can be recycled through techniques like composting, and threats to our health are reduced. Increasing attention is being focused on the "localization" of food, where produce grown locally, using environmentally friendly and sustainable, organic techniques, is sold directly to the people of that region. Such initiatives reconnect people with where their food actually comes from, but growing your own is still the ultimate in "locally grown" food.

**Food for the soul
(facing page)**
Whether you grow vegetables in a community garden with the companionship of other gardeners or in the seclusion of your own yard, nurturing your own crops to harvest can provide a peaceful, satisfying, and healthy respite from the stresses and strains of everyday life.

WHY GROW YOUR OWN ORGANIC CROPS?

- Produce is fresher
- Grow crops you cannot buy
- Better flavor and higher nutritional value
- A positive, empowering, healthy activity
- Helps to educate future generations about where food comes from
- Helps build communities
- Many environmental benefits
- Control over what you eat
- You can do it anywhere
- Kinder to nature

GENETICALLY MODIFIED ORGANISMS (G.M.O.s)

All organisms contain genes, which pass the blueprint for that particular organism on from one generation to the next. In nature, unrelated species cannot interbreed, so the genes of a fish could never end up in a plant—but this bizarre notion is now a reality. Genetic engineering (G.E.) has made cross-species transfer of genes possible: The characteristics carried by the introduced gene become part of the new organism. Vitamin A-enhanced rice, for example, contains genes from a daffodil.

There are both ethical and safety concerns about G.M.O.s. Although the developers and others are happy that the technology is safe for human health and the environment, others disagree. This is why G.M. plants and animals are not organically acceptable.

G.M. crops have been introduced rapidly, without extensive testing, on the grounds that they are similar to unengineered crops. But the process involves creating gene combinations that could not have occurred naturally. Once released into the environment, genes that "escape" from the G.M. parent plant, via soil bacteria or cross-pollination, will be impossible to retrieve. Once incorporated into wild plants, we can only surmise what the outcome might be.

At the time of this writing, no G.M. crops are available to gardeners, but developments on the horizon include peculiar colors, such as blue carnations and roses, grass that does not need mowing, and novel perfumes. This novelty may prove to be more costly than we can possibly imagine.

International flavor
Here, Chinese cabbages grow next to English lavender; experimenting with crops from different cultures is part of the fun.

Past, present, and future

Organic gardening is not about simply looking back or nostalgia for what came before, especially where vegetables are concerned. Successful organic growing techniques have been developed over many generations through observation, trial, and error. Working in harmony with nature allows us to observe natural systems closely and learn from them all the time, as we discover new approaches to growing food and develop fresh, often innovative techniques. Growing organically is about putting into practice the findings of the latest scientific research, choosing cultivars that are naturally resistant to pests or diseases, using proven cultural practices alongside new, experimental ones, and encouraging and fostering nature's own checks and balances.

A rich heritage

Preserving and maintaining the best of the past for future generations is inextricably linked to organic gardening. Many "heirloom" or "heritage" vegetable cultivars are the result of selective breeding over many generations and are specifically suited to the unique growing conditions found in a particular locality. Preserving this genetic diversity ensures that a rich and varied gene pool remains available for future breeding, as well as giving us a fascinating insight into our global vegetable heritage.

Making space for food

It is possible to grow organic vegetables successfully in virtually any space that receives sunlight. In the developed world, most of us live and work in towns and cities where space is usually at a premium, but this need not be a barrier to growing your own food. Growing vegetables in a limited space does at times require a degree of ingenuity and innovation,

> Becoming partially self-sufficient in certain kinds of food, especially vegetables, is a realistic option available to us all

but coupled with patience, experience, and a willingness to learn, you will succeed.

The image of self-sufficiency still held by many remains a distant dream. Total self-sufficiency, tarnished as its image often is by crankiness and eccentricity, is impractical for most of us. Whether you simply grow a supply of fresh lettuce in a pot on a windowsill or plant an entire garden with a cornucopia of edible plants, you will have taken an important step that is good for both you and the world around you.

Getting started with vegetables

You can read books, talk to other gardeners, and think about it forever, but the best way to start growing vegetables is simply to do it. Your first few successes will give you confidence, and you will soon start to get a feel for what works well in your conditions.

Deciding what to grow

There are so many possibilities when first starting to grow vegetables that it is helpful to ask yourself a few questions, set priorities, and then plan accordingly. Would you like to produce staple vegetables, or unusual types not easily available in stores? Do you have facilities to store vegetables over winter? If so, consider growing suitable ones for storage or freezing. How much time do you have to spare? Some vegetables need more attention than others. Take a look at the section on vegetable families (pp. 304–313) to find out more about the range that can be grown. The *A-Z of Vegetable and Salad Crops* contains more detail for individual crops.

Where to grow vegetables

The ideal place to grow vegetables is often described as a fertile, well-drained, moisture-retentive soil, in a flat, sunny, but sheltered position. Most gardeners do not have these "perfect" conditions, but still grow excellent vegetables by making the best of what they have. When selecting a site for your vegetables, consider the following points:

• **Sun and shade** Deep shade will severely limit the growth of vegetables, but some can tolerate light shade, including lettuce, chard, beets, and kohlrabi. In cool climates, position tall vegetables so that they will not cast a shadow on lower-growing ones, but in hotter climates use them to provide welcome shade.

• **Drainage** Vegetables will not thrive in a waterlogged site, which is better used for something else, such as a pond or bog garden. Improve heavy soil gradually by adding low-fertility organic material and consider growing in raised beds (see p. 322).

• **Shelter** Protect exposed sites with permanent or

Choice crops
Below, clockwise from top left: radishes, easy to grow; sweet corn, a family favorite; 'Lollo Rosso' lettuce; the showy black kale 'Tuscana'.

CROPS AND CLIMATE

On the following pages, references to warm and cool climates are intended as a general guide to help you to decide which vegetables to grow, in what part of the garden, and whether they need some form of protection. The information is tailored to suit temperate climates, which have a relatively narrow range of temperatures. "Cool climate" refers to mild-to-cool summers and cool-to-cold winters, where rainfall occurs all year round and summer and winter are linked by intermediate spring and autumn conditions. "Warm climate" refers to warm-to-hot, often longer summers and cool winters. The terms "under cover" or "unheated protection" indicate where vegetables can be grown successfully under some form of unheated cover—cloches, frames, or a greenhouse or hoop house (see *Growing under Cover*, pp. 216–233).

TOOLS AND EQUIPMENT

Handle tools before buying to assess which model feels most comfortable. The following basic items will make lighter work of jobs around the vegetable garden:

• Compost bin and leaf mold container—for recycling green waste to make soil improvers.
• Fork—for general cultivation, lifting root crops, aerating soil, and moving and incorporating bulky organic material.
• Hoe—for surface weed control, creating seed drills, mounding soil, and surface cultivation, depending on type.
• Labels—for naming plants and cultivars, recording dates.
• Rake—for breaking up and leveling soil, seedbed preparation, covering seed holes.
• Spade—for digging, general cultivation, deep weed control. Use a "border" spade, with a smaller head, if you have back problems.
• Sticks, string—for marking rows.
• Trowel or hand fork—for hand-weeding and making planting holes.
• Watering can—for irrigation.
• Wheelbarrow—for collection and transportation of bulky materials.

Starting small
A small plot is easy to manage and can still produce a good range of vegetables. Being overambitious may result in more crops than you are able to care for successfully, which can lead to disappointment.

temporary windbreaks such as hedges, fences, or netting. Protect individual crops with barriers, cloches, or other covers, especially when young.
• **Slopes** Use terracing to prevent soil erosion. Position rows or beds across the contours of a site, rather than up and down. Be aware that the bottom of a slope can be a frost pocket.
• **Space** Select vegetables to suit the space available. Even quite small areas can be very productive, using vertical as well as horizontal growing space. Remember to allow space for making leaf mold and compost when planning the layout.
• **Dogs and footballs** Depending on what else you use your garden for, you may conclude that growing vegetables is just not compatible with the other demands on it. In this case, consider having a vegetable plot in a community garden.

Growing methods
There are many ways of growing vegetables: in rows, beds, or containers; on their own; or mixed with flowers and shrubs. Both this chapter and others will help you choose the method that suits you.

Preparing the ground
You may already have a clear piece of land suitable for growing vegetables, but if not, there are various organic methods of preparing it. You could dig up part of the lawn, remove existing plants from flowerbeds, or use a light-excluding mulch to clear a weedy patch. (See *Weeds and Weed Control*, p. 79, and *The No-Dig Approach*, p. 328, for more details.)

Before you start growing, find out more about your soil and start to treat it organically. Use organic soil improvers and fertilizers as necessary to build the fertility. (See *Soil and Soil Care*, pp. 32–61, for all the information you need.)

Plans and records
Even if you are growing only a few vegetables to start, it makes sense to draw up a simple plan for a crop rotation (see pp. 301–303). Keep a close eye on what happens through the season so you can deal with any problems and adjust growing conditions accordingly.

Keep records. This is helpful for all gardeners, not just beginners. At its most basic level, this could simply mean writing the cultivar name and sowing date on a plastic label used to mark a row. Soon you will be able to record information on yields, pests and diseases, weather conditions, and what grew well where. Don't worry if not everything goes according to plan! Even experienced gardeners will tell you that they still get surprises.

Planning the produce year

Planning ahead can help you to get the best results from growing vegetables, put your fantasies into practice, and harvest fresh produce all year round. Thinking about the whole year ahead also helps to spread the workload. It enables you to put time aside for important jobs such as making compost, collecting autumn leaves, incorporating green manures, and applying soil improvers, as well as the more obvious tasks of sowing, planting, and harvesting.

Spread the harvest

The majority of vegetables from a spring planting are ready to harvest between early summer and late autumn. Crop and cultivar choice, combined with a

> Some vegetables have a range of cultivars that produce at different times of the year

range of sowing and planting times, make it possible to avoid summer gluts and to spread the harvest over a longer period. In cool climates, grow crops under cover and use protective barriers to further extend the cropping season at both ends. (See *Gardening under Cover*, pp. 216–233.)

The hungry gap

In cool climates, the period between late winter and late spring is known traditionally as the "hungry gap" because there is not much to harvest from the garden at this time. To fill this gap, grow vegetables that are hardy enough to withstand winter with some protection, such as leeks or kale, or that mature very quickly from an early spring sowing, such as radish or seedling lettuces.

One of the difficulties in filling the hungry gap with hardy vegetables is that they need to be in their final growing position by midsummer, when the ground may still be occupied by summer crops. In this case, allocate less space to summer vegetables, or try interplanting smaller summer crops with winter ones (see p. 318 for more about interplanting).

Cultivar choice

Some vegetables, such as cabbage (see below, right), carrot, cauliflower, leeks, lettuce, onions, and peas, have a range of cultivars for different seasons; some can even be available to harvest all year. Cultivars described as "quick" or "early" are especially useful at both the beginning and the end of the growing season, as they produce a crop more quickly than main crops. Others have been bred to tolerate cold conditions in winter.

Successional sowing is another way of spreading the harvest, particularly suitable for fast-maturing crops. This means that you sow a small amount of the same crop at intervals of 2 to 3 weeks. A good rule of thumb is to sow the next batch of seeds when the previous ones are just starting to show as seedlings. Suitable vegetables include arugula, corn salad, kohlrabi, lettuce, radish, spinach, spring onions, and turnips.

Storage

Crops such as potatoes, pumpkins, and onions can be stored in good condition for many months over winter (see pp. 334–335). Freezing can also help to extend the "eating" season of some vegetables.

CABBAGE THROUGH THE YEAR

- **Spring cabbage** Sow in late autumn; plant out under protection in early winter; harvest in late spring and early summer. Suitable cultivars: 'Early Jersey Wakefield', 'Grenadine'.
- **Summer cabbage** Sow in mid- to late spring; plant out in early summer; harvest in late summer and early autumn. Suitable cultivars: 'Danish Ballhead', 'Golden Acre'.
- **Winter cabbage** Sow in mid- to late spring; plant out in midsummer; harvest in mild climates from late autumn until late winter. Suitable cultivars: 'Rapid Ball', 'Sanibel', 'Savoy Ace'.

Vegetable & salad crop planning chart

Organic vegetables and salad greens can be picked fresh—from the garden, from under a cloche, or from an unheated greenhouse or hoop house—at most times of year except in very harsh climates. Add to this your stored veggies (but not the freezer) and the out-of-season selection expands further.

The key to all-year-round fresh vegetables is good planning, and this chart will help you to do just that. It shows when crops can be sown, when they will be growing, and when they vacate the space for another crop to move in. It is also a useful overview of the sheer range of crops that you can grow in the garden.

Inevitably the chart gives an overview, rather than specific dates and times for specific areas. Exact timing will depend on growing conditions in your location (and in that year), the cultivars you grow, and the stage at which you harvest your crops.

CROP		Jan	Feb	Mar	Apr	May	Jun	Jul	Aug	Sep	Oct	Nov	Dec	See page
Artichoke, globe	+ * PE				P—P									338
Artichoke, Jerusalem	PE		P————P											338
Arugula			SU Ss				Ss		Ss		Ss SU			SC 338
Asparagus—from seed	+ M PE		SH S———S			T								338
Asparagus—1-year-old crowns	+ PE			P——P										339
Asparagus pea	* M					S———S								339
Bean, broad—spring-sown				Ss———Ss										339
Bean, broad—autumn-sown											SP———SP			340
Bean, hyacinth	M					SH P-P								309
Bean, runner	*						S———S							340
Bean, string	*				SP	Ss———Ss								340
Beet	* M			Ss			Ss							341
Beet, leaf/perpetual spinach	* M			S———S			S———S SU							SC 341
Broccoli—calabrese	* M				Ss				Ss	S–S TuP				342
Broccoli, 9-star (perennial)	M PE				S———S T———T									342
Broccoli—sprouting	* M				S——S	T———T								342
Brussels sprouts	M		SH—SH	S——S			T—T	S——S						343
Cabbage—spring	M									SU	TuP—TuP			343
Cabbage—early summer	* M		SH———SH	T————T										343
Cabbage—summer (including red)	* M			S——S T———T										343
Cabbage—autumn (including red)	* M					S——S	T———T							343
Cabbage—winter	M					S——S	T———T							343
Cabbage, Chinese	* M						Ss————Ss		TuP					344
Cardoon					S——S									344
Carrot—early cultivars	* M		Ss———Ss											344
Carrot—main crop					Ss———Ss									344
Cauliflower—spring	M					SP		T						345
Cauliflower—early summer	M		SH	T—T							SP			345
Cauliflower—late summer	M			S——S		T								345
Cauliflower—early autumn	M				S		T							345
Cauliflower—autumn	M					S		T						345
Cauliflower—winter	M						S		TuP					345
Cauliflower—mini	* M				Ss————Ss									345

Key to symbols and colors used

S	Sow outdoors into the soil
Ss	Successional sowing/cropping outdoors into the soil
SsU	Successional sowing/cropping in unheated greenhouse/hoop house
SH	Sow in heated protection
SU	Sow in unheated protection, e.g., unheated greenhouse/hoop house
SP	Sow under outdoor protection, e.g., cloche, frame, low hoop house
P	Plant outdoors
PI	Plant indoors, e.g., greenhouse or hoop house

PP	Plant outdoors under protection, e.g., cloche, frame, low hoop house
TuP	Transplant to unheated greenhouse/hoop house
T	Transplant directly to garden
+	Full production begins second season after sowing/planting
*	Optional earlier sowing in heated protection
M	Can be raised in cell packs and transplanted
PE	Perennial
SC	Suitable as a seedling cutting crop

———	Duration of sowing/planting period
(shaded)	Actual period of growth
(white)	Area *not* occupied
(light)	Fresh harvest period
(hatched)	Forcing period
(dark)	Available from store

CROP			Jan	Feb	Mar	Apr	May	Jun	Jul	Aug	Sep	Oct	Nov	Dec	See page
Celeriac				SH———	SH SU	———	SU P–P								346
Celery—self-blanching					SH——SH		P–P								346
Chard	*	M			S————	S			S———S SU					SC	347
Chervil, turnip-rooted										S———S					347
Chicory—red						Ss———			——Ss						347
Chicory—sugarloaf, for mature heads		M					S———		——S						347
Chicory—sugarloaf, seedling crop				SsU———SsU Ss———					——Ss SsU				SC	347
Chicory—Witloof/forcing							S——S			TuP					347
Corn salad					S———S			S———S SU———SU						348
Cress, upland					Ss———			——Ss							348
Cucumber—indoor						SH	SU PI								348
Cucumber—outdoor	*	M					SH P–P								348
Dandelion		PE				S———S									332
Eggplant				SH———SH		PI–PI P–P									349
Endive	*	M			SH———SH PP Ss——Ss SP								SC	349
Florence fennel	*					S———S								SC	350
Garlic				P——P						P———P				350
Good King Henry	+	PE			S———S									351
Hamburg parsley					S———S			S—S						351
Kale	*	M			S———S T——T								SC	351
Kohlrabi	*			Ss———Ss Ss———Ss SU										352
Komatsuna							Ss———Ss SU					SC	352
Leeks	*	M		SH S———S									SC	352
Lettuce—summer and autumn	*	M			Ss———Ss								SC	353
Lettuce—indoor winter crop		M							SsU———SsU				353
Lettuce—protected winter crop		M							S———S				353
Melon, sweet		M				SH——SH PP								353
Mibuna greens		M			SsU Ss———			——Ss SsU				SC	354
Mitsuba		PE		P——P					P——P				354
Mizuna greens		M			SsU Ss———			——Ss SsU				SC	354
Mustard, cress (incl. Greek)					Ss———			——Ss SP——SP				SC	332
Mustards, oriental		M					Ss———Ss TuP				SC	354
New Zealand spinach	*	M				S									355

CROP		Jan–Dec activity	See page
Okra		SH—SH PP—PP	355
Onion—bulb, sown early in heat	M	SH—SH P	355
Onion—bulb, sown outdoors		S—S	355
Onion—bulb, from spring sets		P—P	355
Onion—bulb, sown in autumn		S—S	355
Onion—bulb, from autumn sets		P—P	355
Onion, spring and pickling		S—S	356
Onion, Welsh/bunching		Ss—Ss S—S	356
Oriental saladini		SU Ss—Ss S—S SU	SC 333
Pak choi	M	Ss—Ss SP	SC 357
Parsley—leaf	M	SH—SH S—S P S—S	288
Parsnip		S—S	357
Peas—early, spring-sown	* M	S—S	357
Peas—early, autumn-sown		SU—SU	357
Peas—main crop		Ss—Ss Ss—Ss	357
Pepper, sweet/chili		SH—SH P-P	358
Potato—early, in unheated protection		P	358
Potato—early		P—P	358
Potato—main crop		P—P	358
Potato—autumn crop		P—P	358
Pumpkins and winter squashes	*	SH T S	359
Purslane, summer		SU—SU S—S	SC 360
Purslane, winter (claytonia)		S—S S—S SU	SC 360
Radish—daikon		S—S	360
Radish—summer		SP Ss—Ss Ss SP—SP	360
Radish—winter		S—S	360
Red orach		Ss—Ss S—S	SC 361
Rhubarb—from crowns	+ PE	P—P P—P	361
Rutabaga		SP—SP S—S	362
Salsify		S—S S—S	362
Scorzonera		S—S	362
Seakale—forced in the ground	+ PE	S P	363
Shallots		P—P P—P	363
Sorrel	PE	S—S S—S	364
Spinach—summer crop		SU Ss—Ss	SC 364
Spinach—winter crop		Ss—Ss SU	364
Sweet corn		SH—SH P-P	364
Tomato—outdoor/unheated protection		SH—SH PP P-P	365
Tomato—indoor with heat		SH—SH PI-PI	365
Turnip		SP Ss—Ss	366
Watercress	M	Ss—Ss	226
Zucchini and summer squash	M	SH T S	366

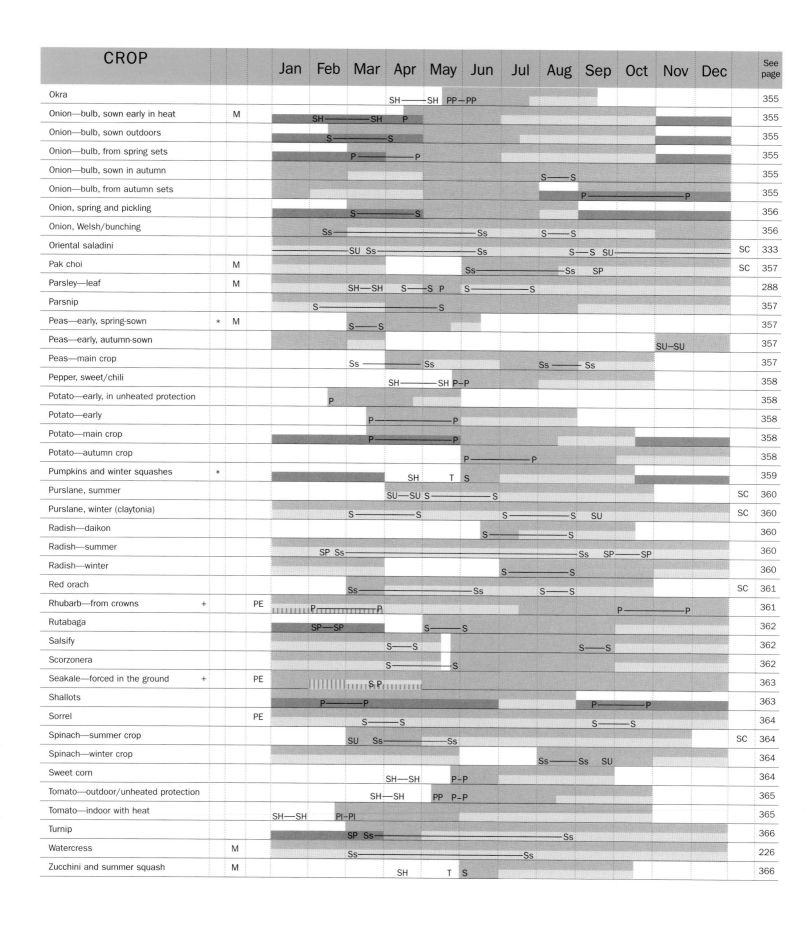

Crop rotation

Crop rotation is the practice of growing related vegetables in different areas in consecutive years. Vegetables from the same botanical family (described in detail in the pages that follow) are susceptible to the same pests and diseases. Parsnips, for example, belong to the same family—the Apiaceae—as carrots, and are also a favorite of the carrot fly.

Some vegetable relationships are easy to grasp: The peas and beans all belong to one family, as do the onion, shallot, and garlic tribe. But the parts of the plant eaten—their shape and flavor—are not always a good basis for guesswork. Brussels sprouts, for example, would obviously seem to belong with cabbages in the Brassicaceae family, which they do—but so do rutabagas, radishes, and turnips. Beets, on the other hand, are related to spinach and chard. Sometimes it is only when vegetables flower that clear family resemblances can be seen; the flowers of the Solanaceae—tomatoes, potatoes, peppers, and eggplants—are remarkably similar (see p. 312).

If members of the same family are grown in the same place year after year, there is a tendency for soilborne pests and diseases to become established. In small plots, moving vegetables just a few yards may not have much effect on pest and disease control, but it is still worth doing for other benefits.

• **Nutrient availability** Vegetables differ in their nutrient requirements, so moving them around the growing area helps prevent the soil from becoming depleted locally and makes best use of the soil.

• **Soil treatments** Some crops need soil amendments to do well; others make good use of residual fertility left by a previous crop. Grow crops with similar requirements together so you can apply the appropriate soil treatments for them. This means that all parts of the vegetable area will receive the same treatment over the period of the rotation.

• **Weed control** Some vegetables, such as pumpkins and potatoes, produce weed-suppressing foliage and are easy to weed. Others, like onions and carrots, are more difficult to weed and do not have a growth habit that competes well. Alternating vegetables with these characteristics helps keep weeds under control.

• **Soil structure** Plant roots occupy different levels of the soil. Alternating deep- with shallow-rooting vegetables has a positive effect on soil structure.

How long is a crop rotation?

Three or 4 years is the usual recommended minimum for a crop rotation, but it can certainly be longer. If you know that your soil has a serious, persistent problem, such as nematodes, onion pink root, or clubroot, you may need a much longer rotation to grow susceptible crops with any success.

Planning a crop rotation

Plan your own rotation according to the crops you want to grow, or use the examples on pp. 302–303 to get started. Remember that you do not have to grow the same vegetables every year, although there will be some favorites you want to repeat.

• **Make a list** of the vegetables you want to grow over a whole season, and in roughly what quantities.

• **Group vegetables together** according to botanical family (see pp. 304–313 for details).

• **Draw a plan** of the growing area. Divide it into equal sections according to how many years the rotation is to last. If using several different areas of the garden for growing vegetables, treat each one separately, changing the crop each year for the period of the rotation. Distribute the vegetables around the sections, keeping families together. If one family does not fill a whole section, try to combine it with another that requires similar soil conditions. Fast-maturing crops and those from miscellaneous families (see above right) can fill in the gaps.

NO ROTATION

The following crops do not belong to any of the main vegetable families and can fill gaps in a rotation plan.
• Chinese artichoke (Lamiaceae)
• Corn salad (Valerianaceae)
• New Zealand spinach (Aizoaceae)
• Summer and winter purslane (claytonia) (Portulacaceae)
• Sweet corn (Poaceae)
Many green manures are brassicas or legumes, but the following are "miscellaneous":
• Buckwheat (Polygonaceae)
• Winter rye (Poaceae)
Perennial vegetables are not included in rotations simply because they remain in place for several years. Some fall within the main crop families.
• Asparagus (Liliaceae)
• Cardoons (Asteraceae)
• Globe artichokes (Asteraceae)
• Good King Henry (Chenopodiaceae)
• 9-star broccoli (Brassicaceae)
• Rhubarb (Polygonaceae)
• Seakale (Brassicaceae)
• Sorrel (Polygonaceae)

Vegetable families
Keep crops in the same family together (here, potatoes and tomatoes, both Solanaceae), moving them from plot to plot each year.

BASIC COOL-CLIMATE ROTATION
Move the crop groups around the plots counterclockwise each year.

Plot 1: Solanaceae, Cucurbitaceae

Compost in spring, then grow potatoes, tomatoes, and zucchini. After harvest, sow/plant garlic, leeks, and/or a green manure for soil improvement.

Plot 4: Apiaceae, Chenopodiaceae

Carrots, parsnips, celery, beets, spinach, chard (below), with lettuce between. Use winter rye or buckwheat as a green manure over winter.

Plot 2: Alliaceae, Papilionaceae

After harvesting the garlic and leeks planted the previous year (see Plot 1), grow peas and beans. Plant the green manure common vetch to overwinter, liming beforehand if necessary as brassicas will follow.

Plot 3: Brassicaceae

Grow summer brassicas, then plant autumn brassicas with lettuce and other interplantings between. Add compost in spring and summer. Mulch autumn brassicas with leaf mold over winter.

ROTATION FOR A WARMER CLIMATE

Plot 1 Add compost in spring. Grow tomatoes, eggplants, and peppers, then garlic or onions to overwinter.

Plot 2 Onions or garlic planted the year before (see Plot 1). Grow lettuce over winter. Add leaf mold in spring.

Plot 3 Add manure in spring, then grow pumpkins, squashes, and zucchini.

Plot 4 Sweet corn, interplanted with lettuce in the early season. Follow with a green manure.

• **Be flexible** and prepared to adapt your plans, while sticking to the rotation principles. Unexpected weather and other crop disasters can affect everyone.
• **Keep records** of what you planned and what actually happened. This will be useful information if you want to adjust the rotation in following years.

Soil treatments in a rotation

• **Compost and other medium- to high-fertility soil improvers** Use for heavy feeders such as potatoes, leeks, cabbage family, and squash. Apply in spring before planting.
• **Lime** Add to cabbage family section to control clubroot in the autumn before planting, but only if necessary to raise pH. Do not lime when growing potatoes, as it can encourage scab.
• **Leaf mold and other low-fertility soil improvers** Beneficial preceding root crops; apply anywhere as a mulch to improve structure, especially over winter.
• **Green manures** Consider the family that green manures belong to and use them to follow a crop from the same one. In this way, any problem affecting that family is more likely to appear in the green manure rather than the crop. Use them over winter, sowing in late summer or autumn, or as catch crops (see p. 318) in spring and summer. Do not use winter rye before sowing seeds direct as it inhibits germination when it decomposes.

Growing perennial vegetables

Perennial vegetables, which can stay in the same spot for many years, obviously do not fit into the usual crop rotation. Asparagus and rhubarb are best given their own separate beds. Others, such as globe artichokes and seakale, make beautiful border plants, given sufficient space. Good King Henry and sorrel, much smaller plants, can be tucked into a border, too.

As with all perennial plants, appropriate soil preparation, including removal of all perennial weeds, is essential before planting (see p. 170, and also the *A–Z of Vegetable and Salad Crops*, p. 337). When replacing them, do not replant on the same site. Check for pests and diseases on perennial crops, especially those such as nine-star broccoli that are related to other vegetables. Pests and diseases that become established on perennial crops can be a source of infection for other plants.

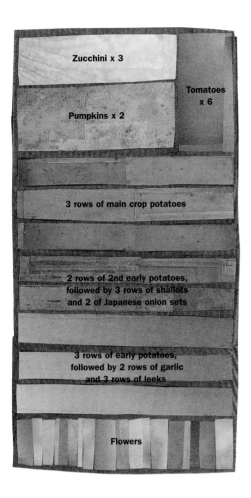

Zucchini x 3

Tomatoes x 6

Pumpkins x 2

3 rows of main crop potatoes

2 rows of 2nd early potatoes, followed by 3 rows of shallots and 2 of Japanese onion sets

3 rows of early potatoes, followed by 2 rows of garlic and 3 rows of leeks

Flowers

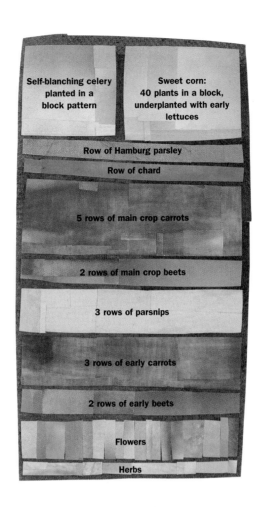

Self-blanching celery planted in a block pattern

Sweet corn: 40 plants in a block, underplanted with early lettuces

Row of Hamburg parsley

Row of chard

5 rows of main crop carrots

2 rows of main crop beets

3 rows of parsnips

3 rows of early carrots

2 rows of early beets

Flowers

Herbs

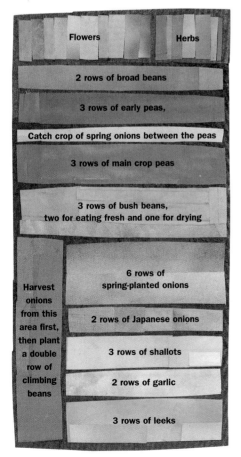

Flowers

Herbs

2 rows of broad beans

3 rows of early peas,

Catch crop of spring onions between the peas

3 rows of main crop peas

3 rows of bush beans, two for eating fresh and one for drying

Harvest onions from this area first, then plant a double row of climbing beans

6 rows of spring-planted onions

2 rows of Japanese onions

3 rows of shallots

2 rows of garlic

3 rows of leeks

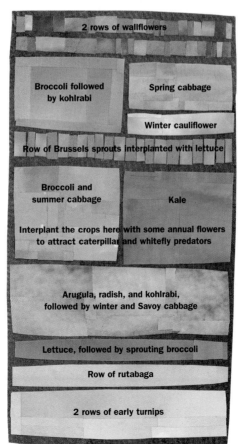

2 rows of wallflowers

Broccoli followed by kohlrabi

Spring cabbage

Winter cauliflower

Row of Brussels sprouts interplanted with lettuce

Broccoli and summer cabbage

Kale

Interplant the crops here with some annual flowers to attract caterpillar and whitefly predators

Arugula, radish, and kohlrabi, followed by winter and Savoy cabbage

Lettuce, followed by sprouting broccoli

Row of rutabaga

2 rows of early turnips

4-YEAR COOL-CLIMATE ROTATION FOR A LARGE PLOT (Scale: 1:50)

This plan will supply a good range of seasonal vegetables, fresh and stored. Flowers are for cutting and herbs for the kitchen; both will attract beneficial insects. Crops stay in their groups and move plot clockwise each year:

Year One
1 4
2 3

Year Two
2 1
3 4

Year Three
3 2
4 1

Year Four
4 3
1 2

The Group 1 crops (top left)
Big feeders from the Solanaceae and Cucurbitaceae. In spring, dig in the winter rye (see Group 4), then apply compost for them. After harvesting the early potatoes, plant Alliaceae to grow over winter; they need no feeding.

The Group 2 crops (below left)
Peas and beans, as legumes, fix their own food, but benefit from a leaf mold mulch. Harvest some overwintered onions early to make way for climbing beans. Spring-planted onions join their overwintered relatives. Follow on with common vetch to fix nitrogen for next year's brassicas; lime in autumn if the soil needs it.

The Group 3 crops (below right)
Brassicas and salads. Dig in the vetch, or add garden compost or equivalent in spring. Mulch with leaf mold in the autumn to make a good seedbed for next year's root crops.

The Group 4 crops (top right)
Mostly root crops, which need no extra feeding, using up last year's leftovers. Apply compost in spring where celery, chard, and sweet corn are to grow. Follow with winter rye for winter cover.

Brassicaceae—the cabbage family

Family members

Agricultural mustard★ (*Sinapis alba*)

Arugula• (*Eruca vesicaria*)

Broccoli (*Brassica oleracea* Italica Group)

Brussels sprout (*Brassica oleracea* Gemmifera Group)

Cabbage (*Brassica oleracea* Capitata Group)

Cauliflower (*Brassica oleracea* Botrytis Group)

Chinese cabbage (*Brassica rapa* Pekinensis Group)

Cress• (*Lepidium sativum*)

Hanover salad• (*Brassica napus*)

Kale (*Brassica oleracea* Acephala Group)

Kohlrabi (*Brassica oleracea* Gongylodes Group)

Mizuna greens• (*Brassica rapa* var. *nipposinica*)

Mustard• (*Brassica hirta*)

Oriental mustards• (*Brassica juncea*)

Pak choi• (*Brassica rapa* Chinensis Group)

Radish• (*Raphanus sativus*)

Rutabaga (*Brassica napus* Napobrassica Group)

Seakale (*Crambe maritima*)

Sprouting broccoli (*Brassica oleracea* Italica Group)

Turnip (*Brassica rapa* Rapifera Group)

Upland cress (*Barbarea verna*)

★ *Green manures* • *Suitable as a seedling cutting crop*

Members of the large and diverse brassica family are grown for their leaves, buds, roots, stems, or shoots. They thrive in cool, moist climates and are very nutritious, rich in minerals and vitamins. Many familiar "western" vegetables, such as cauliflower and cabbage, belong to the brassica tribe; it also includes oriental vegetables like Chinese cabbage and mizuna greens. Some, such as kales, sprouting broccoli, and Savoy cabbage, need a long growing season, but they are very hardy and provide useful winter food. Empty soil between larger winter brassicas is useful for catch cropping and interplanting. However, careful choice of cultivar and close spacing can produce smaller, meal-size heads of vegetables such as cabbage and cauliflower. Some brassicas make good seedling cutting crops for livening up green salads (see p. 332).

Soil treatment and crop rotation

Brassicas need a firm, moisture-retentive soil; they won't thrive where moisture is limited. In a crop rotation, this family follows the nitrogen-fixing pea and bean tribe (see p. 308). A green manure crop of common vetch or clover gives leafy brassicas all the nitrogen they need. In the absence of a green manure, a medium-fertility soil improver, such as compost, can be applied to the brassica bed. Acid soils should be limed in autumn prior to growing brassicas.

Brassicas are easily raised from seed or by planting ready-grown "starter" plants. Western brassicas tend to be sown in spring and summer; many oriental types, which tend to bolt in hot, dry conditions and when the day length is increasing, are best sown in the shortening days after midsummer—providing useful autumn crops. Fast-growing crops like arugula and radish, directly sown, will be ready quickly; kohlrabi and broccoli can produce in as little as 8 weeks. A succession of sowings will maintain a supply. Many brassicas, however, take months to reach maturity. Avoid tying up the growing space for this long by sowing in a nursery bed or cell packs, and transplant when the ground becomes available.

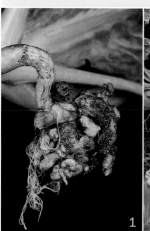

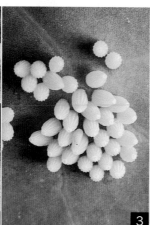

MEET THE FAMILY

The members of this diverse group, which includes annuals, biennials, and perennials, will all ultimately produce the same characteristic flower, with four petals arranged in a cross.

Some forms of brassica can be picked at almost any time of year. Leafy crops include kales (**1**) and cabbages for winter (**2**), spring (**3**), and summer use (see p. 297). The immature flowerheads of calabrese, cauliflowers (**4**), and sprouting broccoli are eaten; Brussels sprouts develop small, cabbagelike heads along a tall stem.

Cress, mustard, radish, and Hanover salad are used as sprouted seeds, and many can be eaten as seedling crops. The perennial vegetable seakale is grown for its forced shoots, harvested in mid- to late winter. Kohlrabi produces crisp and juicy swollen stems. Radishes can even be grown for their peppery seed pods.

Root crops include rutagabas, turnips, and radishes. Spring and summer radishes tend to have small roots, apart from the long white Daikon types. Winter radishes are much larger.

Oriental brassicas, such as pak choi and oriental mustards, are fast-growing, producing tasty, nutritious leaves and shoots that are good in salads and stir-fries.

Some brassicas have a typical strong, mustardy flavor, but others, such as kohlrabi and broccoli, are more delicate. Many can be eaten raw, as well as cooked or pickled.

Brassicas may not be an obvious choice for an ornamental garden, but some are very attractive. Red, curly, and "ragged-leaved" kales can look stunning over winter. Kohlrabi, in purple or green, makes an interesting addition, and the glaucous green of many cabbages and cauliflowers makes a perfect foil for brightly colored annuals. Oriental mustard greens and some "mini" cabbages could be grown as bed edging.

Alliaceae—the onion family

Family members

Garlic (*Allium sativum*)

Leek (*Allium porrum*)

Onion (*Allium cepa*)

Shallot (*Allium cepa* Aggregatum Group)

Welsh onion (*Allium fistulosum*)

Tree onion (*Allium cepa* Proliferum Group)

Plants in the onion family have a pungent flavor and many produce typical "drumstick" flowerheads if left to flower. Crops include tiny pickling onions, multi-colored shallots, slim young spring onions, pungent garlic, and red, white, and yellow globe onions. All are hardy, cool-climate crops.

Spring onions, a quick filler crop, are eaten as slim young plants, leaves and all. Onion, shallots, and garlic are usually harvested once they are mature; when dry, they can store well for many months (see p. 335). Leeks, which do not produce a bulb, are grown for their long white, cylindrical "shank." They can be left in the ground to harvest in the winter months.

The herbs chives and garlic chives (see p. 289) also belong to this family; eat their leaves and flowers. The perennial Egyptian or tree onion bears aerial bulbs in place of flowers, and these may sprout and grow in the soil. Flowers of leeks and garlic may also produce tiny bulbs in place of seed.

Growing the crop

Members of this family are simple to grow. By choosing a range of types and cultivars, they can be available all year round, either fresh or stored. Spring onions and leeks are grown from seed, the latter raised in a seedbed for transplanting in early summer (see p. 315). Onions and shallots are grown from seed or sets (immature bulbs), and garlic is planted as cloves only. Garlic must undergo a period of cold to produce well, which is why it is traditionally planted in autumn. Shallots may also be planted in autumn, and late summer is the time to sow or plant the Japanese onion cultivars for an early crop.

Soil and spacing

Members of this family prefer a well-drained, relatively fertile soil. Avoid rich feeding, which encourages disease and cuts down on storage life. Soil that has been fed for a previous crop, such as potatoes or brassicas, should suffice. Leeks can benefit from a medium- to high-fertility soil improver in poorer soils.

Bulb onions and leeks respond well to variations in plant spacing (see p. 316), which can be used to supply the size of plant you prefer. A crop of slender gourmet leeks, for example, can be grown as close as 2 in. (5 cm) apart.

PROTECT THE CROP

Onion white rot (center) attacks bulbs and can survive in the soil for 20 years or more. Try to avoid introducing it on plants and soil, and use a crop rotation.

Where onion fly is a problem, the maggots tunnel into bulbs. Protect the crop with a lightweight row cover.

Various fungi may attack onion foliage. Downy mildew (top) is common in wet seasons; its dark spores turn leaves black. Clear up infected debris and use a crop rotation. The orange pustules of leek rust (bottom) appear in summer. It may look alarming, but plants will often grow out of the disease in autumn.

Cucurbitaceae—the cucumber family

Family members

Zucchini, marrow, summer squash (*Cucurbita pepo*)

Cucumber, gherkin (*Cucumis sativus*)

Luffa (*Luffa cylindrica*)

Melon (*Cucumis melo*)

Pumpkin, gourd, winter squash (*Cucurbita maxima*, *C. moschata* or *C. pepo*)

Watermelon (*Citrullus lanatus*)

Members of the cucumber family, also known as cucurbits, are typically vigorous plants with big, bold leaves and yellow, trumpet-shaped flowers. They require a lot of space. Trailing cultivars can be trained to scramble over arches or up netting. Bush cultivars are more compact.

This family is grown mainly for its fruits, which may be eaten young or mature. They come in a wonderful array of shapes, colors, and sizes. Flowers and seeds can also be eaten. All are tender annuals that need warm conditions to do well. In cool climates, zucchini (also known as courgettes), pumpkins, squashes, and cucumbers can produce outdoors if raised in warmth and transplanted into warm soil, after the last frost. In warmer regions they can be sown direct outside. Melons need warm conditions and may need to be grown in a cool greenhouse or coldframe. Greenhouse cucumbers also need the warm, humid conditions provided in a greenhouse or hoop house.

Cucumbers, zucchini, and summer squashes are eaten young and picked regularly to maintain the supply. They tend to have a mild flavor. Melons are picked when ripe, and pumpkins and winter squashes are left to mature on the plant, to develop a tough skin for storage. Some are bland and watery while others develop a sweet, rich, densely textured flesh—excellent for soups and stews.

Growing the crop

All members of this family benefit from a dressing of medium-fertility soil improver, such as compost, on planting. Unless you are growing in a container, no further feeding is required. In an outdoor crop rotation, they can be included in the potato or brassica beds, or given their own section.

Once planted, most outdoor cucurbits need little attention and make good weed-suppressing plants. Melons and greenhouse cucumbers will require more training, watering, and feeding.

In most cases, the flowers—which are either male or female—must be pollinated to set fruit. Greenhouse cucumbers will, however, be bitter if pollinated. "All-female" hybrid cultivars avoid the task of removing male flowers to prevent pollination.

PROTECT THE CROP

Some cultivars show some resistance to cucumber mosaic virus (above). Protect young plants from slugs. Powdery mildew may be a sign of a dry soil; late in the year it will not affect the crop. Under cover, biological controls can be used to control pests like red spider mite. Crop rotation, good ventilation, and hygiene are the best defense against diseases such as mildew and sclerotinia.

Fascinating fruits

All of the cucurbits, even the common or garden zucchini (far left), are striking in appearance. Squashes show some of the widest variety of form, from the glowing lanternlike spheres of 'Atlantic Giant' (center) to the curious, infolded 'Turk's Cap' (below).

Papilionaceae—the pea and bean family

PROTECT THE CROP

Use crop rotation to avoid a buildup of root rot.

Early spring-sown seed of peas and beans may be eaten by mice. Traps can be set under wire netting; later sowings may be safer.

The pea and bean weevil eats notches out of leaves from early spring. Plants growing well can usually withstand the damage; if necessary, young plants can be protected with a row cover put on at sowing time.

The black bean aphid first appears on the tips of broad beans. Nip out infested shoots. Early sowings are less prone. Early and late sowings of peas can be made to miss the pea moth, whose larvae eat peas.

Broad bean chocolate spot is an early-season disease, common in wet soil. Powdery mildew on peas tends to occur in dry soils, later in the season.

Young string and runner beans are attractive to slugs and snails. In cooler areas, the first crop is best transplanted, rather than directly sown, with individual bottle cloches added for extra protection.

For more advice see the *A–Z of Plant Problems*, p. 367.

Pea and bean flowers
The Papilionaceae take their name from the Latin for butterfly, based on the appearance of their flowers (right, pea; far right, broad bean). Sweet peas, lupines, and clovers are also members of this family.

Family members

Alfalfa ★ (*Medicago sativa*)
Asparagus pea (*Lotus tetragonolobus*)
Broad or fava bean (*Vicia faba*)
Clover ★ (*Trifolium* spp.)
Common vetch ★ (*Vicia sativa*)
Fenugreek ★ (*Trigonella foenum-graecum*)
Field bean ★ (*Vicia faba*)
Hyacinth bean (*Dolichos lablab*)
Lupine ★ (*Lupinus angustifolius*)
Pea (*Pisum sativum*)
Runner bean (*Phaseolus coccineus*)
String bean (*Phaseolus vulgaris*)
Trefoil ★ (*Medicago lupulina*)

★ *Green manures*

The vegetables in this family, once known as Leguminosae, are still widely referred to as legumes. They are grown primarily for their fleshy pods and/or seeds. Legumes characteristically develop root nodules containing bacteria that fix nitrogen gas from the air. When the nodules decay, nitrogen is released into the soil, which is why the green manures in this family are so valuable.

Peas and broad beans are hardy, cool-season crops, growing best below 59°F (15°C). String and runner beans are frost-tender and need warmer conditions to thrive.

Young broad bean pods and shoot tips can be eaten, but the green, white, or red seeds are the main crop. Traditionally, peas are shelled from their pods, but snow and sugarsnap pea pods are eaten whole.

Peas can vary in height from 2 ft. to 10 ft. (60 cm–3 m), and most are supported with twiggy branches or wide-mesh pea netting. "Leafless" cultivars, with more tendril than leaf, are self-supporting when grown in a block.

Dwarf bush beans are ideal for small spaces and containers. Climbing cultivars (known as pole beans) will twine up canes or sticks in a tepee or double row. They do best in warm-to-hot weather and are much more tolerant of dry conditions than runner beans.

Runner beans are generally climbers, although dwarf cultivars are available. The edible flowers can be red, white, salmon-pink, or bicolored red and white, making an attractive feature trained up a trellis or tepee. The pods are long and green.

Soil and crop rotation

Legumes thrive in a well-drained but moisture-retentive soil that has been fed for a previous crop such as potatoes. In a rotation they can be followed with brassica family crops, which will make use of the nitrogen provided by the pea and bean nodules, provided that roots have been left in the ground.

LEGUME MEDLEY

There is more to string beans than green pods. Pods also come in purple, yellow, green with red flecks, and other combinations. If left to fatten up, plump fresh beans may be podded like peas, or they can produce dry beans—a high-protein crop for winter use. The range of colors and patterns of dried seed reveal their true diversity. Saving seed is easy—which is probably why so many heirloom cultivars still exist.

Climbing beans were originally grown as ornamentals and still can be today. 'Trionfo Violetto', for example, has purple stems and edible deep purple pods (left), stunning grown with annual climbers such as morning glory or the firebrand flower clusters of *Ipomoea lobata* (*Mina lobata*). Tall peas also make an attractive feature. The showy, scarlet runner bean can provide a blast of color all summer.

The hyacinth bean is one of the most attractive, with its purple-pink flowers set against green-bronze leaves. Maroon pods follow (below), edible when cooked. It is a tender plant, however, and needs a minimum temperature of 64°F (18°C).

Chenopodiaceae—the beet family

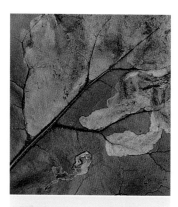

PROTECT THE CROP

The crops in this family are relatively trouble-free, although some tend to bolt in adverse conditions. Beet leaf miner (above) has little effect on beet roots, but can spoil leaf beet crops. Remove affected leaves, and squash the maggots within the "mines." Downy mildew can be a problem on young spinach when the air is moist.

Concentrated color
Rich, dark colors of both roots and leaves (below, of ruby chard and spinach) are a hallmark of this family.

Family members

Beet (*Beta vulgaris* subsp. *vulgaris*)
Chard, Swiss chard, or seakale beet (*Beta vulgaris* Cicla Group)
Good King Henry (*Chenopodium bonus-henricus*)
Leaf beet, perpetual spinach, or spinach beet (*Beta vulgaris* Cicla Group)
Red orach or mountain spinach (*Atriplex hortensis* 'Rubra')
Spinach (*Spinacea oleracea*)

This family includes both leaf and root crops suitable for warm and cool climates. Spinach and red orach are fast-growing, leafy "catch" crops. Spinach is best sown in the cool temperatures of spring and autumn as it rapidly goes to seed in hot, dry weather. Sow little and often for a good supply.

Beets

Beets are grown for their substantial, juicy roots, commonly dark red, but gold, white, and bicolored types are available. The deep green and magenta leaves are decorative and can be eaten when young, either raw or lightly cooked. Fast-growing baby beets are eaten when 1–2 in. (2.5–5 cm) across. Larger roots of main crop cultivars can be stored for winter use. "Bolt-resistant" cultivars are used for early sowings.

The leafy beets

Leaf beet and chard are known by a confusing range of names. The former has large, medium green leaves; the latter tends to have a dark green glossy leaf with a wide, prominent midrib, which can be eaten as a separate vegetable. The midrib color ranges from white through yellow, orange, and luminous pink to glowing red. Leaf beet and chard are easy to grow, much less prone to bolting than spinach, can be picked over a period of many months, and withstand low winter temperatures. Two sowings, one in spring and one in autumn, should give a year-round supply.

The little-known perennial Good King Henry is an old-fashioned salad plant. Its leaves can be picked early in the year; the flowering shoots are also eaten. It prefers a good rich soil and tolerates some shade.

Growing the crops

Crops in this family all prefer a fertile soil that does not dry out easily. They are often included in the "roots" section of a rotation, in soil that has been improved for a previous crop. They may appreciate a mulch of a medium-fertility soil improver in poorer soils. Spinach beet and chard can be raised in cell packs for transplanting, and beets are suitable for multi-sowing (see p. 317). All can be grown in a cool greenhouse for out-of-season production.

Asteraceae—the lettuce family

Family members

Cardoon (*Cynara cardunculus*)

Chicory (*Cichorium intybus*)

Endive (*Cichorium endivia*)

Globe artichoke (*Cynara scolymus*)

Jerusalem artichoke (*Helianthus tuberosus*)

Lettuce (*Lactuca sativa*)

Salsify (*Tragopogon porrifolius*)

Scorzonera (*Scorzonera hispanica*)

Vegetables in the Asteraceae family range from the compact annual lettuce to the magnificent perennial globe artichoke, which can grow to 8 ft. (2.5 m) tall. Depending on the crop, the leaves, shoots, flower buds, roots, or stem tubers may be eaten.

Lettuce is perhaps the most widely grown member of this family, eaten, along with chicory and endive, as a salad. All three can be very decorative, with leaves in diverse shapes and colors. Some lettuce cultivars produce a hearted lettuce; individual leaves can be picked from the "looseleaf" types over several weeks. Chicory and endive are often blanched to reduce their bitterness, and chicory roots can be forced to produce pale young shoots known as chicons. Using a selection of cultivars and cloche protection, these crops can provide leafy salad all year round. They also do well in an unheated greenhouse and are useful as seedling crops, for interplanting, and for growing in containers.

Jerusalem artichokes are simple to grow, producing starchy, edible stem tubers and stems up to 8 ft. (2.5 m) tall. Some cultivars produce a rather unexpected "sunflower," with the characteristic flower form of this family—masses of small ray petals surrounding a central boss of florets.

Perennial globe artichokes and cardoons, very similar in appearance, produce large, thistle-like blooms if allowed to flower. The stems of cardoons are blanched in autumn; the large, immature flower buds of the globe artichoke are eaten in early summer.

Salsify and scorzonera are little-grown root crops, the former white-skinned, the latter black. They are harvested in autumn, or lifted as required in winter. The following spring, the shoots can be blanched for eating, or left to produce edible flower buds.

Soils and situations

The plants in this family prefer well-drained soils. The leafy crops can be fitted into a vegetable plot rotation or put among ornamentals. Cardoons and globe artichokes need a lot of space and would not look out of place in an ornamental border. The roots can join other root crops in a crop rotation, while Jerusalem artichokes make a good windbreak.

PROTECT THE CROP

Lettuce is the most pest- and disease-prone member of the Asteraceae. Common pests include slugs, cutworm, leaf aphids, and root aphids. Young plants can be protected against slugs by barriers and traps. Crushed eggshells may have a short-term effect as a barrier (see above).

Under cover, downy mildew (top) and gray mold (botrytis) can be a real problem, especially in cool, damp conditions. Crop rotation, good hygiene, and ventilation can reduce the problem.

Cultivars with resistance to aphids, downy mildew, and various physiological disorders are available.

Lettuce alone

The Asteraceae family includes not only crops but also many ornamentals, including asters (as the name would suggest) and chrysanthemums, and weeds such as dandelions, too. Far left: lettuces growing with related ornamental daisies; left: salsify flowerhead going to seed.

Solanaceae—the potato family

Family flowers
Below, from left to right: flowers of eggplant, potato, and tomato.

Family members

Potato (*Solanum tuberosum*)

Tomato (*Lycopersicon esculentum*)

Pepper, sweet (*Capsicum annuum* Grossum Group)

Pepper, chili (*Capsicum annuum* Longum Group)

Pepper, hot (*Capsicum frutescens*)

Eggplant (*Solanum melongena*)

Potatoes, despite being frost-tender, produce well in cool climates. Other members of this family—tomatoes, eggplants, and peppers—need warmth and good light levels for reliable production. They are popular crops for a cool greenhouse or hoop house (see pp. 224–225), but may also be sown indoors, then transplanted outside when conditions are right.

Potatoes aplenty

Potatoes need quite a lot of space but are easy to grow, and the amateur grower has a far wider choice of cultivars than is ever seen in grocery stores. They store well for winter eating.

Potatoes are planted as tubers. Always use certified "seed" tubers. Spring planting is the norm; a late summer planting can, with protection, give a winter crop (see p. 227). Some potatoes will produce true seed, in small, green, tomato-like fruits, but these are rarely used for growing (and are poisonous if eaten).

Tender fruit crops

Homegrown tomatoes, left to ripen on the plant, surpass anything store-bought in flavor. Again, the diversity available to the gardener is staggering—from compact, manageable, bushy plants to "indeterminate" cultivars that can grow many feet tall; from tiny, cherry-size fruit to those that make a meal in themselves, in red, yellow, orange, and green. Tomatoes can be grown in pots, baskets, and growing bags. More vigorous cultivars are easier to manage when grown directly in the soil.

The taste of peppers can be sweet or hot-to-blistering, the latter known as hot or chili peppers. Sweet peppers can be picked when green or left to ripen to red, yellow, orange, or purple. Hot peppers usually produce smaller, longer, more pointed fruit.

Eggplant fruits are now typically a dark, shiny purple, but the originals were a very egglike white. Modern cultivars bearing no more than four or five fruits per plant make cropping more reliable. Both eggplants and peppers grow well in containers or in the soil, doing best under cover in cool climates.

Soil and rotation

All do best in a fertile soil, rich in organic matter, where rich compost has been applied. They follow a winter rye green manure well.

Apiaceae—the carrot family

Family members

Carrot (*Daucus carota*)

Celeriac (*Apium graveolens* var. *rapaceum*)

Celery (*Apium graveolens*)

Florence fennel (*Foeniculum vulgare* var. *dulce*)

Hamburg parsley (*Petroselinum crispum* var. *tuberosum*)

Parsley (*Petroselinum crispum*)

Parsnip (*Pastinaca sativa*)

Skirret (*Sium sisarum*)

Turnip-rooted chervil (*Chaerophyllum bulbosum*)

This is a diverse group of crops with a range of flavors. The family likeness appears when they flower—tiny individual flowers are produced in creamy white, umbrella-shaped flowerheads, known as umbels (see the carrot flowers below). They are very attractive to beneficial insects.

Carrots and parsnips are traditional root crops; Hamburg (turnip-rooted) parsley, turnip-rooted chervil, and skirret are less well known. Celery and celeriac leaves and stems have the same distinctive flavor, as does the knobbly swollen stem base of celeriac, which is eaten more like a root crop. Florence fennel "bulbs" (in fact, stem bases) have a crisp texture when raw and a mild licorice flavor.

Its attractive feathery foliage can be used in place of the herb fennel. Best sown after midsummer, Florence fennel is the fastest of these crops to grow. Most others need a long growing season. Parsley, an herb, is often grown along with these vegetables.

Growing the crop

Carrots and parsnips are direct-sown hardy crops that may be left in the ground for use over winter, or harvested for storage. Early carrots, quicker to produce, are eaten fresh. Both crops prefer a light soil that has been fed for a previous crop, such as brassicas. In stony or heavy soil, consider growing early carrots in a container (see p. 210).

Celery and celeriac will bolt if growth is checked. They are best sown in cell packs and transplanted when the soil has warmed up. The soil should be rich in organic matter so it never dries out, and dressed with a medium- to high-fertility soil improver.

Although the members of this family have differing soil requirements, they are kept together in a traditional rotation as they are prone to the same problems. On a bed system, where the ground may be divided up into more than four distinct areas, they can be given separate beds.

PROTECT THE CROP

Root crops may fork (top) in stony soils. The major pest of this family is carrot rust fly; the larvae feed on the roots of all members. Discolored foliage (center, on parsley), may be noticed before root damage (below, on a carrot). Barriers and row covers are the most effective way to prevent damage.

Parsnip canker, a disease of parsnips only, is exacerbated by carrot fly damage. Good drainage and close spacing can prevent it.

Root rot affects this and several other crop families, especially in wetter soils. Avoid growing susceptible plants on an infected site for at least 4 years.

Sowing and planting vegetables

F1 HYBRIDS

You will see some cultivars in seed catalogs marked "F1." This means that they are F1 hybrids—obtained by crossing two specifically selected parents. F1 hybrid plants are usually very vigorous and uniform in appearance and can perform very well. They often show good resistance to certain pests and diseases, and some are available as organically produced seed. One of the main drawbacks with "F1s" is that plants from a single sowing tend to all produce at once. Sowing smaller amounts of seed but at more frequent intervals avoids this.

Alternatives to seed
Just as potato tubers left in the light will sprout both roots and shoots (right), so other crops multiply by vegetative means. Jerusalem artichokes are grown from tubers, like potatoes; seakale from sections of fleshy root. Onions and shallots can be grown not only from seed but also from small bulbs known as "sets." Garlic is always grown this way. Asparagus, globe artichokes, and rhubarb produce much more quickly if grown from divisions or "offsets" taken from a mature plant (see also p. 106) rather than seed.

This section looks at growing vegetables outdoors. Plants can also be raised in a greenhouse or other protected situation to avoid adverse outdoor conditions, or simply for convenience. For more details, see *Raising Plants*, p. 104; *Gardening under Cover*, p. 216; and the *A–Z of Vegetable and Salad Crops*, p. 337.

Choosing seeds

Organic seed is produced to recognized organic standards, without the use of artificial fertilizers or pesticides. "Conventional" seed is produced using artificial fertilizers and pesticides, and its use is acceptable when organic alternatives are unavailable.

Where possible, use good-quality organically grown seeds from a reliable source, or save your own. If organic seed is not available, check the seed packet to make sure that the seed you use has not been treated with pesticide dressings after harvest.

Heritage or heirloom varieties (see p. 16) are available from seed exchanges. Cultivars developed using genetic modification (G.M.) techniques (see p. 294) are not appropriate in an organic garden.

Seed formats

Most vegetable seeds are sold dry and loose inside a foil or paper packet. Various treatments and formats can make sowing easier and enhance performance.

• **Coated/pelleted seed** Each seed is coated in clay or diatomaceous earth to make handling and sowing easier. Check that no pesticide is present in the coating.

• **Primed seed** Seeds are germinated under ideal conditions, then "dried back" before being prepared for immediate sowing or storing at 41°F (5°C). Emergence is rapid, even, and unaffected by fluctuating soil temperatures. Primed seeds include carrot, celery, leek, parsley, and parsnip.

• **Seed tapes** Seeds are embedded in a biodegradable paper tape, which is laid in a row. These tapes make sowing quick and easy and always produce perfect rows. Thinning is unnecessary.

Always keep seed in a cool, dry place. For details on seed storing and life span of seeds, see p. 121.

Alternatives to seed

Some vegetables are raised vegetatively—from tubers or offsets, for example. This may be because they rarely set seed, because seed-raised plants are very variable, or because vegetative propagation is faster. Even where seed raising is possible, you may prefer to buy plants. This may be to save waiting time—asparagus, for example, doesn't produce until its third year, so 1-year-old plants, known as crowns, are usually planted.

Crops such as tomatoes and cucumbers need to be raised in warm conditions, which you may not be able to provide. Buying plants avoids the problem and may not be any more expensive if you need only a few plants. Even the very basic crops such as cabbage and Brussels sprouts can be purchased as pack-grown "starter" or "plug" plants. These are useful where space, time, and conditions for plant raising are limited. They may be available locally or by mail order. When buying mail order, open plants on receipt, water, and place them in a well-lit spot. Always buy organically grown plants, sets, and tubers wherever possible.

Sowing vegetables

When sowing outdoors, seed may be sown directly, where the crop will grow and mature, or in a nursery bed or seedbed for transplanting later. A seedbed is used primarily for brassicas that take up a lot of space for a relatively long time. Plants can also be raised in a greenhouse, on a sunny windowsill, or in another protected situation to avoid adverse outdoor conditions or simply for convenience.

Warming the soil

Cool-climate vegetables like beets will germinate in spring as soon as soil temperatures reach 41°F (5°C) or above. Warm-climate crops like French beans need at least 55°F (13°C) and must not be sown or planted out until all risk of night frost has safely passed. Soil can be warmed prior to sowing using cloches, row cover, or black plastic. A dark mulch also warms up quickly in spring. Nonpermeable materials like plastic also help to keep the soil dry—seeds will rot in cold, wet conditions.

On a bed system (see p. 322), an entire bed can be warmed for early spring sowings using row cover (see also p. 233). It can be pulled back, seeds sown into the warmed soil (or young plants planted), and then replaced.

Thinning

Unless seeds are sown very thinly or multi-sown (see p. 318), some seedlings need to be removed to allow others space to develop. Thin in stages, leaving each seedling just clear of the next until the recommended spacing is reached. Water before and after thinning, disturbing the soil as little as possible. Plants in nursery beds may also need thinning prior to transplanting.

Transplanting from nursery beds

Water young plants thoroughly before transplanting to minimize root damage. Always handle plants by their leaves. Loosen the soil with a fork and keep as much soil on the roots as possible. Lift plants in cool conditions and transplant immediately into holes just large enough to take the roots, with the lower leaves just above the soil. Firm the soil, then water and keep moist. Wilting is common, but plants soon recover. In very hot weather, cover new transplants with a lightweight material, such as row cover, that will provide some shade. Remove it after a few days when the plants have perked up.

Thinning carrots
Most vegetables need thinning if seed germination has been successful. Carrots are sown as thinly as possible to avoid the need for thinning and thus reduce the risk of attack by carrot rust fly. Thinnings of some crops (though not carrots) can be replanted to fill any gaps, or used in salads.

Transplanting leeks
Slow-growing vegetables can be sown in pots or cell packs until the harvest of early crops makes space available in beds. Leeks can be raised in pots or seed trays, or closely spaced in a seedbed in a spare patch of soil. Water them well before transplanting to individual blocks of planting holes, 6 in. (15 cm) deep and 6–9 in. (15–23 cm) apart. Drop a single plant into each hole, but do not fill the hole with soil. Instead, water thoroughly to settle soil gently around the roots.

Using space effectively

Using spacing techniques combined with suitable cultivars and, where possible, a bed system of growing (see p. 322) will help make the best use of any growing space. Where there is no need to walk between rows, vegetables can be grown using closer than traditional spacings. The practice of growing vegetables in long rows, with the soil between them hoed regularly, grew out of changes to agricultural practice during the 18th century. This system still has its merits used on a small plot, but in most gardens better results can often be achieved by block planting, spread out evenly across the bed or growing area, using equal or square spacing.

Good use of space

On narrow beds, no space is wasted on paths between rows of crops. Vegetables can be grown in rows spaced more closely, or spaced equally in either a square or staggered formation.

• **Equal spacing** Plants are grown in staggered rows and each plant is an equal distance apart from all the others. The between-plant spacing is an average of the recommended in-row and between-row spacings. For example, plants normally grown 6 in. (15 cm) apart in rows 12 in. (30 cm) apart can be grown equidistantly at 9 in. (23 cm) apart each way. Plants receive equal amounts of light, moisture, and nutrients and soon form a canopy over the soil, which helps to reduce weeds.

• **Square** Plants are grown at the same spacing in the row as between the rows, resulting in a square pattern. This is useful where only two or three plants can fit across a bed. A planting "grid" can easily be made by pressing a straightedge into the soil to mark out evenly spaced lines at right angles to each other. Sow or plant where the lines cross.

Achieving the pattern

To achieve the desired plant layout using transplants, simply plant out at the required spacings. For vegetables sown direct, either station-sow, planting 2–3 seeds at each position where a plant is required, and thin later to leave just a single plant; or sow in rows and carefully thin seedlings in each row. Crops such as beets can also be multi-sown direct to a desired pattern.

The effect of plant density

The spacing of vegetables such as onions and cabbages affects their final size; up to a certain limit, allowing them more space means they grow larger. By reversing this and growing them more densely, with less growing space, the result is vegetables of a smaller, often more convenient size. In most cases overall yield is also increased. There is a lower limit below which closer spacing becomes counter-productive because plants are simply too close together to be able to develop to a harvestable size. Using equal spacing is generally the most effective way to influence plant size and can be varied to suit different vegetables.

Bulb onions illustrate the influence of spacing on size. For large bulbs, an equal spacing of 8 x 8 in. (20 x 20 cm) is ideal. By reducing this to 6 in. (15 cm) between plants each way, smaller, medium-size onions are produced. At an equal spacing of 2 ft. (60 cm), summer cabbage will produce the largest heads possible, but if the spacing is reduced to 1 ft. (30 cm) there will be a higher total yield of smaller heads, which are generally more convenient for use in the kitchen. Recommended in-row and block spacings for individual vegetables can be found in the *A–Z of Vegetable and Salad Crops*, p. 337.

"Mini-vegetables"

An extreme example of how very close spacing can succeed is the use of "mini," "baby," or "high density" vegetables. These are cultivars selected because they respond well to very close spacing. They are useful for very small beds, such as the square-foot garden (see below) and containers (see p. 210). The between-plant spacing for a crop such as leeks can be as little as ½ in. (13 mm). Mini vegetables produce small, meal-size harvests over a long period if sown little and often.

"Square-foot" gardening

Using this technique, modest harvests of a wide range of vegetables are possible over a long period. The idea of square-foot gardening was developed in the U.S. It requires little space or time and can also be a good "start-up" technique for a child or adult who has not grown vegetables before. A useful harvest can be achieved from an area no more than 4 x 4 ft. (1.2 x 1.2 m). The area is divided up into 16 squares of 12 x 12 in. (30 x 30.cm) using string. Different vegetables are grown in each square, at close, equal spacings. Various cultivars, including the "mini" types, are suitable. Taller and climbing crops are grown on the side of the bed farthest from the sun to avoid shading others. Crop rotation principles are followed (see also p. 301).

Multi-sowing

Multi-sowing simply means sowing several seeds in the same place, either direct or in 2-in. (5-cm) cell packs, and allowing all to grow to fruition. The seedlings are left unthinned and, if pack-grown, are planted out as a complete cell "unit," spacing them at around twice the normal spacing. The result is several smaller roots or bulbs instead of one large one. Crops suitable for multi-sowing include beets, leeks, and bulb onions (4–5 seeds sown per station

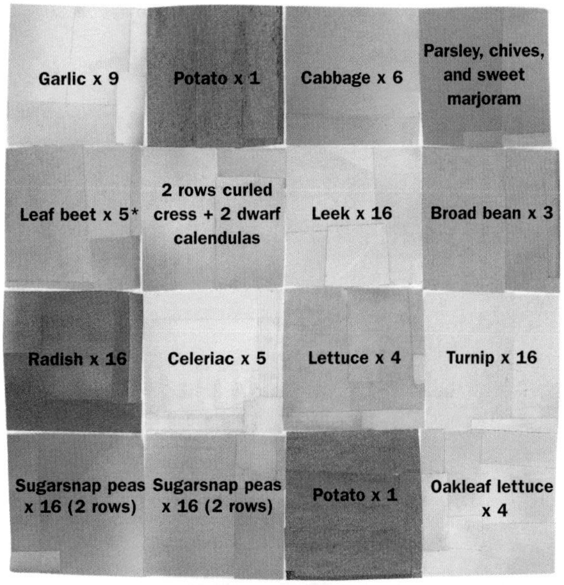

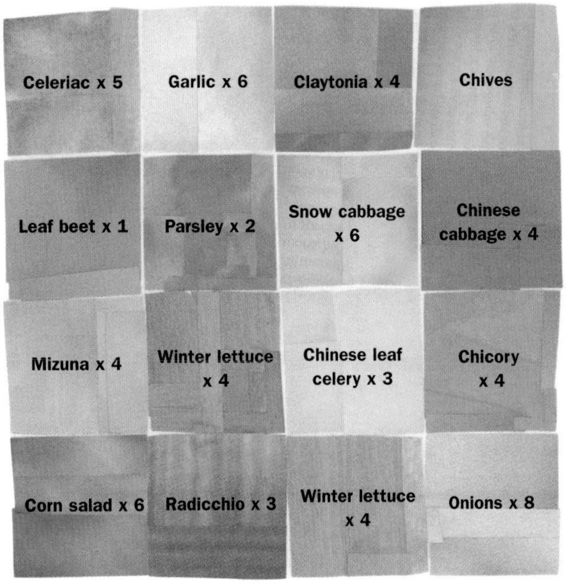

Top plot

Garlic x 9	Potato x 1	Cabbage x 6	Parsley, chives, and sweet marjoram
Leaf beet x 5*	2 rows curled cress + 2 dwarf calendulas	Leek x 16	Broad bean x 3
Radish x 16	Celeriac x 5	Lettuce x 4	Turnip x 16
Sugarsnap peas x 16 (2 rows)	Sugarsnap peas x 16 (2 rows)	Potato x 1	Oakleaf lettuce x 4

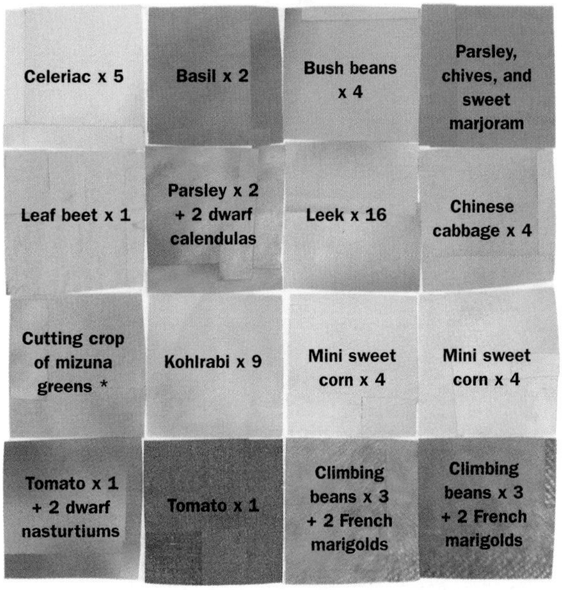

Center plot

Celeriac x 5	Basil x 2	Bush beans x 4	Parsley, chives, and sweet marjoram
Leaf beet x 1	Parsley x 2 + 2 dwarf calendulas	Leek x 16	Chinese cabbage x 4
Cutting crop of mizuna greens *	Kohlrabi x 9	Mini sweet corn x 4	Mini sweet corn x 4
Tomato x 1 + 2 dwarf nasturtiums	Tomato x 1	Climbing beans x 3 + 2 French marigolds	Climbing beans x 3 + 2 French marigolds

Bottom plot

Celeriac x 5	Garlic x 6	Claytonia x 4	Chives
Leaf beet x 1	Parsley x 2	Snow cabbage x 6	Chinese cabbage x 4
Mizuna x 4	Winter lettuce x 4	Chinese leaf celery x 3	Chicory x 4
Corn salad x 6	Radicchio x 3	Winter lettuce x 4	Onions x 8

A YEAR IN A SQUARE-FOOT PLOT

These plans show one way to take a 4-ft. (1.2-m) square plot through the year. At the height of the season it should provide at least three or four servings a week of various crops, and at the least productive times will supply salad greens, herbs, and garnishes. The plot even includes edible flowers.
• Grow taller and climbing plants on the side farthest from the sun to avoid shading others.
• Thin out plants as they fill the square, and eat the thinnings.
• Harvest plants at the earliest possible moment.
• Whenever a new crop is planted, add compost or leaf mold, according to its needs. Mulch potatoes with compost.
• Have pack-grown plants ready to fill empty squares for continuity of cropping.

Top
Planting of the crops shown here begins in late winter and continues through the spring, to produce in spring and summer.
★ Thin leaf beet to one plant only to produce later.

Center
The plot in summer and early autumn, with new crops growing in almost every square.
★ Leave four plants of mizuna to grow larger for late crops.

Bottom
Mid- to late autumn, with hardy leaf and salad crops, and the garlic cloves and onion sets planted to overwinter.

Recommended cultivars:
Broad bean 'Aquadulce' and 'Sweete Lorane'
Cabbage 'Charmant'
Celeriac 'Brilliant'
Leek 'King Richard'
Sugar pea 'Sugar Ann'
Potato 'Yukon Gold'
Radish 'Easter Egg II' and 'French Breakfast'
Sweet corn 'Dwarf Blue Jade'
Turnip 'Tokyo Cross'

Multi-sowing
These red-skinned bulb onions have been multi-sown, five seeds to each 2-in. (5-cm) module cell, then transplanted to a bed. As the cluster of plants develops, each bulb finds its own growing space and reaches only a modest size.

or module cell), round cultivars of carrot (4 seeds per cluster), and salad or spring onions and chives (10 seeds per cluster).

Interplanting and underplanting

Interplanting is the sowing (or planting) of fast-growing or small vegetables, in rows or patches, on unused ground between slower-growing main crops. Many combinations of plant and interplant can be used, but the guiding rule must always be that the "interplant" should not be allowed to thrive at the expense of the main crop and must be harvested before the slower crop needs the space. Spring onions, small lettuces, and many other summer and autumn salad crops are particularly good interplants. The space between late-crop brassicas can be usefully filled with a wide range of interplants. Tall plants like sweet corn, which cast little shade, can be underplanted with lower-growing plants like bush beans, lettuce, or mizuna, or spreading vegetables such as zucchini and pumpkins, to make maximum use of space. Shade-tolerant vegetables like lettuce and spinach can be sown between rows of climbing beans.

Catch and double cropping

Catch crops are fast-maturing vegetables sown on spare ground between the clearance of one main crop and the planting of another. Leaf lettuce, radish, arugula, seedling cutting crops, and fast-growing green manures are good examples. With double cropping, seeds of fast-maturing crops are sown between slower-growing crops such as parsnips, and harvested before the latter need the space.

Successional sowing

Sowing fast-maturing vegetables like lettuce and radishes little and often, at 2–3 week intervals, avoids gluts and gives a continuous supply over many months. Suitable crops also include arugula, calabrese, corn salad, kohlrabi, seedling salads (see p. 332), spinach, spring onions, and turnips.

GOOD CROPS FOR INTER- AND UNDERPLANTING

Arugula
Chicory
Corn salad
Endive
Lettuce (right, among leeks)
Mizuna
Pak choi
Radish
Seedling cutting crops
Spinach
Spring onion

Zucchini, squashes, and pumpkins also make good weed-suppressing underplantings for tall plants such as sweet corn (far right) and runner beans.

Vegetable care

Once established, many crops need little maintenance. Check them regularly, and provide any extra care they need to ensure high yields.

Watering

Stress caused by lack of water can cause bolting, make plants more susceptible to pest and disease attack, and reduce yields. Seedlings and transplants should never dry out. Once established, watering thoroughly but infrequently is more effective than little and often. Water that soaks down into the soil encourages deep rooting and helps plants draw on reserves during dry spells. Some crops benefit from water at particular stages of growth (see below). Do not overwater; excessive, unnecessary watering can reduce the flavor of crops such as tomatoes.

Apply water at the base of plants in the evening, when evaporation is less (or if slugs are a problem, early in the morning). Use a can with a fine rose for small seedlings, or a watering wand attached to a hose. Crops needing lots of water, such as runner beans, can have bucketfuls poured around their roots, or use a soaker hose (see *Water and Watering*, pp. 67–68).

Feeding

If the soil has been prepared appropriately in advance, most crops should need no extra feeding. Long-term crops may benefit from mulching with a medium- or high-fertility soil improver.

Hoeing (above)
A hoe with a sharp blade is used to skim over the surface of the soil, cutting through seedling weeds, which then shrivel and die in the sun. As crops mature and cover the soil with a leafy canopy, the need for hoeing is reduced.

KEY STAGES FOR WATERING

If the weather is dry during the critical periods below, plants must have water to produce well.
• String beans, broad beans: at start of flowering; when pods are forming.
• Lettuce: 7–10 days before harvest.
• Summer cabbage, summer and autumn cauliflower: 2–3 weeks before harvest.
• Zucchini: once fruits begin to form.
• Peas: when flowering and as pods form.
• Potatoes: when tubers are marble-size.
• Sweet corn: when flowering starts and when cobs are swelling.
• Runner beans, tomatoes: flowering onward.
• Broccoli, celery, spinach: whenever dry.

Close planting (left)
In this dense planting of lettuces in a block, the close canopy of leafy rosettes shades the ground well, reducing the loss of soil moisture and hence the need to water. Weeds are also suppressed.

Attracting predators
Grow flowers in the vegetable patch to attract beneficial insects that will aid pollination and keep down pests.

Plant supports (1)
This page, left to right: Broad beans are easily kept from flopping by enclosing them in twine tied to stakes. Climbing pole beans will quickly cover an open tower of woven willow and twine. Short twigs pushed in the soil are the ideal support for peas.

Mulching and weed control

Mulching bare soil reduces water loss through evaporation and prevents germination of weed seeds. If a high- to medium-fertility soil improver is used, this also adds plant nutrients. Apply mulches to warm, moist soil in spring and summer.

Weeds compete for food, light, and moisture—so keep vegetables as weed-free as possible. Sow your seeds in rows or stations so you can distinguish them from annual weeds; only broadcast-sow vegetables that you can readily identify at the seedling stage, such as carrots. Vigorous crops may need only a single weeding before they outgrow competition. See *Weeds and Weed Control* (pp. 73–83) for mulches and techniques suitable for a vegetable plot.

Plant problems

Healthy, well-grown plants are more resistant to pest and disease attack. Use pest- and disease-resistant cultivars where problems are known to exist. Pests attack vegetables above and below soil. They range from large animal pests such as rabbits, which cause general damage, to microscopic nematodes that attack specific crops such as potatoes. Knowledge of pest life cycles aids control, as can timing of sowing to avoid pest-prone periods of the season. Pest control can range from hand-picking slugs and snails to using natural biological controls. Physical barriers can prevent some pests laying their eggs near crops. Do everything you can to prevent disease, as it can spread rapidly. Viral diseases are difficult to control and plants should be destroyed. The risk of infection with some fungal diseases can be reduced by raising soil pH (see pp. 61, 302). Crop rotation (see p. 301) plays an important role in reducing the severity of other soilborne diseases and some pests.

Certain problems with vegetables are caused by bad cultural practice or mineral deficiencies in the soil. Bolting happens when plants "run to seed" prematurely and is caused by drying out, sudden fluctuations in temperature, sowing at the wrong time, or pack-grown plants becoming rootbound. Poor fruit or pod set can be caused by lack of pollination, drought, or erratic watering.

Plant protection

Half-hardy vegetables planted in spring are vulnerable to cold and frost. They can be protected with cloches or row cover. Protection can also be given to vegetables such as outdoor tomatoes in early autumn to help ripen late fruits.

Training and support

Vegetables such as pole beans will spiral up canes, although they may need to be guided to their supports and tied in until they start to climb. Peas

have tendrils that will cling to twigs or wide-mesh pea netting. Trailing pumpkins, cucumbers, and squashes use tendrils to climb up trellises, over fences, and into trees.

Tall nonclimbing vegetables, such as taller varieties of Brussels sprouts, broad beans, and cordon tomatoes, will need the support of sturdy stakes.

Blanching and forcing

Some vegetables such as endive and celery can be made more palatable by blanching—excluding light from all or part of a growing plant for a certain period, which turns the leaves pale and yellow. Curly endive is sweeter-tasting if blanched for around 10 days. Rhubarb, seakale, and Witloof chicory are forced in complete darkness from a "dormant" state to produce tender leaves and shoots. Where perennial crops such as rhubarb are forced regularly, grow several plants so that the forced plant can be rested for a season or two before being forced again. Seakale can be harvested annually. Chicory is discarded once the "chicons" are harvested.

Harvesting

Harvesting requirements vary widely. Leeks, potatoes, and some cultivars of other vegetables will stay in good condition for weeks. Others, such as early cabbage and broccoli, need to be picked almost as soon as they are ready. Peas and runner and string beans will stop producing more pods if not picked regularly. Get to know your crops so you can get the very best from them. Whatever you are harvesting, try to eat it as soon as possible. Fresh produce has the best flavor and the highest nutritional value. Sweet corn must be the most extreme example of this, tasting best if cooked within 15 minutes of picking. On the other hand, vegetables such as winter squashes and onions can be kept in good condition for months. See *Storing Vegetables*, p. 334.

Traditional rhubarb forcers
These pots have been left on long after the forcing period is over simply because of their ornamental value.

Plant supports (2)
This page, left to right: Squashes scramble over a support of canes tied together with twine. Indeterminate tomatoes need a sturdy support such as a bamboo cane. Runner beans will spiral up a frame of bamboo canes.

Growing in beds

Growing vegetables in narrow beds divided by access paths has many advantages over traditional row planting. In a traditional vegetable plot, soil improvers and fertilizers are applied across the whole area, and then dug in. The soil between the rows is compacted as crops are watered, fed, weeded, and harvested. A "bed system" breaks with this constant cycle of compaction followed by cultivation.

The most important factor when setting up beds for vegetable growing is that you should be able to reach the center of the bed easily without over-stretching or having to walk on the soil. Although rectangular beds are easy to set out and manage, beds can be of any shape as long the center is reachable from the path.

Beds can be flat or raised, edged or with no edging, dug, double-dug, or not dug at all. Choose the combination that suits you.

Flat or soil-level beds

A flat bed without any edging is the simplest and least labor-intensive to set up. Each corner of the bed is marked with a post, and string is tied between them to define the edge. The height of the bed relative to the paths will increase, however, if the soil is medium to heavy, and it is well dug (see below). Soil improvers will also tend to raise it, while the paths become lower due to compaction. Flat beds are best suited to light soils, which would tend to dry out rapidly if raised up.

Raised and edged beds

Edging provides a neat, sharply defined boundary between bed and path. It contains the soil on the bed and any mulching material on the path. Edging is recommended on medium to heavy soils where the level of the bed tends to rise above the path. Where topsoil is thin, edging allows the bed to be built up with soil that can be dug out from the paths or imported from elsewhere. Raised beds are especially useful in heavier soils where drainage is poor.

An edge 4–12 in. (10–30 cm) high is adequate in most situations. Beds raised to 2 ft. (60 cm) are useful where there is difficulty in bending, if cultivation is done from a wheelchair, or where

EDGING MATERIALS SUITABLE FOR RAISED BEDS

Upside-down bottles
Bricks
Concrete blocks/slabs
Logs★
Roofing tiles
Slates
Lumber★
Synthetic "wood" (see p. 131)
Woven willow or hazel (see
    p. 141) ★★

★ Should be untreated, or treated with environmentally friendly preservative (see p. 130).
★★ Soil along bed edges may dry out rather quickly.

Beds on show (facing page)
Entire beds can easily be covered with sheets of row cover or fine mesh, low plastic tunnels, or cloches in order to warm soil, raise earlier and more tender crops, extend the growing season, provide winter protection, and protect crops from certain pests.

ADVANTAGES OF A BED SYSTEM

• Beds help maximize even the smallest growing space.
• Beds can look very attractive, giving a tidy, organized appearance to a vegetable-growing area.
• All work is done from the paths, avoiding compaction and damage to soil structure.
• Soil improvers, fertilizers, and water are concentrated on the growing areas, not wasted on paths.
• Drainage is improved and the soil warms up faster in spring.
• Rounded beds with a convex profile have an increased surface area.
• Lack of compaction reduces the need for digging—and only the growing area, not the paths, need be dug.
• Vegetables can be grown at close, equal spacings, increasing yields from the area.
• Spacing can be manipulated to vary the size of individual vegetables such as onions.
• Close, even spacing creates a dense canopy of leaves, smothering out weeds.
• Crop rotation (see p. 301) is much easier to plan and manage.
• Crops can be harvested in any weather without damaging the soil.

there are serious drainage problems. The main drawbacks with raised beds are the initial cost of materials, the labor required, and drying out at the bed edges. Choose the edging material to create the look you want (see far left).

"No-dig" or double-dug?

The soil in a bed is treated the same as the soil in an open plot. If the soil is dug regularly, this is done working from wide wooden boards to avoid compaction. Beds are particularly appropriate where a no-dig system is used (see p. 326). At the opposite extreme is the intensive deep bed—prepared by double digging and incorporating soil improvers to a depth of around 2 ft. (60 cm). A low-fertility soil improver such as leaf mold can be incorporated as the bed is dug initially. This deep cultivation is useful where the soil is compacted. It results in a deep,

fertile zone with an open, well-drained structure into which roots can easily penetrate. Medium- to high-fertility materials, if required, should be mixed only into the top 6–8 in. (15–20 cm). Increases in yield are noticeable and plants are more tolerant of drought. Loosening of the soil and the addition of soil improvers can produce a noticeable increase in bed height, so edging may be required.

Planning a bed system

For most purposes, square or rectangular narrow beds, 3–4 ft. (90–120 cm) wide, allow easy access to the center of the bed, although the exact width will depend on your height and reach. An average bed length of 10 ft. (3 m) avoids having to walk too far to reach the other side. Beds can be grouped formally where food production is the main objective, or in patterns for a decorative "potager" effect.

Paths

Paths should be a minimum of 1 ft. (30 cm) wide, with some up to 2 ft. (60 cm) for wheelbarrow access. Bare paths will require hoeing to control weeds. Light-excluding natural-fiber carpet covered with wood chips or sawdust is effective and clean to walk on. A porous membrane covered with gravel, pine needles, bark, or similar material can also be used. More formal paths of slabs or bricks can look

more elegant but are more expensive. Grass paths can be effective between vegetable beds, provide an all-weather surface, and look attractive. If grass is used, the paths should be set up to the width of your lawn mower, and brick or other permanent edging should be used to act both as a mowing edge and to prevent grass from invading the beds. The clippings can be used as a mulch.

The addition of soil amendments tends to raise the beds, while paths sink as they become compacted

Siting and orientation

Beds should be in an open, sunny position. Wherever possible, rectangular beds should run north–south to minimize shade from taller crops. In other situations, grow tall-growing crops on the side of the bed farthest from the sun.

Sowing and planting

Always work from the paths or from a wide wooden plank across the bed. A length of wood that fits inside the edge of raised beds is ideal for marking out seed holes and planting positions. For more information on spacing techniques suitable for beds see *Using Space Effectively*, p. 316.

If several different crops are to be grown in the same bed, keep each together in a block, at equal spacings, or with the rows running across the bed. Tall crops that need support, such as climbing beans, can be grown in rows down the middle of beds running north–south, with smaller crops on either side. In beds running east–west, tall crops are better grown in separate beds or in blocks with rows running across the bed, to minimize shading. Plant wide-spaced vegetables such as Brussels sprouts in staggered rows along rather than across beds, with other vegetables interplanted between.

Watering

Water by hand or use a semi-automatic system of soaker hose (p. 68) if all the vegetables in the bed have the same watering requirements. Soil near the sides of raised beds may need extra water.

Small beds with brick paths
Brick paths roughly 18 in. (45 cm) wide allow access to crops in all weather and are convenient for wheelbarrows. They look good, too.

Growing mushrooms

Mushrooms of various types, from the familiar white button mushroom to the more exotic oyster mushroom and the shiitake, can be grown relatively easily by the gardener. Several are available year-round. They are eaten raw or cooked and some can be dried. Different types can be grown successfully in shaded and cool parts of a garden as well as in sheds or cellars. There is no need for soil or light, but production can be sporadic and unreliable if the required conditions are not met.

What is a mushroom?

Mushrooms are fungi—plants which, lacking chlorophyll, are unable to manufacture their own food. They rely on other organisms—living or dead plants or even animals—for their needs. Suitable materials, or "substrates," on which to grow mushrooms include logs, untreated sawdust, wood chips, coffee grounds, strawy manures, or even newspaper and cardboard. The fungi break the substrate down to compost in the process of digesting it for food.

For most of its life a fungus exists as a network of fine filaments—the mycelium—growing through a substrate. The edible part, the mushroom, is a "fruiting body," which produces spores. This appears only when conditions of nutrition, humidity, temperature, and light are correct.

Growing mushrooms

To grow your own mushrooms, you will be supplied with live "spawn"—the mycelium—growing in a suitable substrate. In some cases this simply has to be put in the correct location to grow; alternatively, you may use the spawn to inoculate a substrate, such as hardwood logs, a pile or bed of compost, or even a roll of paper towels.

Organic kits for growing the familiar cultivated mushroom, consisting of a container filled with an inoculated compost, are quite widely available. Starter kits for other, less usual species are available from specialty suppliers.

Growing on logs and sawdust

Hardwood logs, 2–6 in. (5–15 cm) in diameter and cut in the dormant season, are inoculated in spring. Birch, beech, and oak give the most reliable results.

Small wooden dowels, which are supplied already colonized with mushroom mycelium, are inserted into predrilled holes. The logs are kept in warm, moist conditions while the mycelium colonize the wood. It can take 6-12 months from inoculation to fruiting, which can then continue for several years.

Bags of moist sawdust from untreated lumber can be mixed with spawn, then kept in a warm spot while the mycelium grow. These are then moved to a bright, cool location for fruiting.

Growing on bulky organic material

Growing methods vary with each type of mushroom, but in general spawn is mixed with moist, well-rotted manure, compost, straw, or other organic material (which should be free of other fungi) and placed in bags. Mycelium growth is then encouraged in moist conditions at a temperature of around 68°F (20°C). Fruiting begins several weeks later.

GROWN ON ORGANIC MATERIAL

Field mushroom (*Agaricus campestris*) White cap, pink to brown gills on underside.
Morel (*Morchella esculenta*) Gray-brown, spherical cap; strong, aromatic flavor.
Parasol (*Lepiota procera*) Large cap has brown scales on a pale background.
Shaggy mane (*Coprinus comatus*) Elongated egg-shaped shaggy cap; disintegrates to black and inklike. Delicious eaten young.
Shiitake (*Lentinus edodes*) Widely cultivated; strong, smoky flavor. Dries well.
White button (*Agaricus bisporus*) The common cultivated mushroom.
Wood blewit (*Clytocybe nuda*) Dense flesh; young caps blue-violet, violet underneath.

GROWN ON LOGS OR SAWDUST

Chicken of the woods (*Laetiporus sulphureus*) Yellow brackets; texture and taste of chicken.
Pearl oyster (*Pleurotus ostreatus*) Large, oyster-shaped fruiting bodies. Widely cultivated.
Lion's mane (*Hericium erinaceum*) Waterfalls of iciclelike spines; mild, sweet flavor.
Nameko (*Pholiota nameko*) Orange-brown cap; delicious Japanese mushroom.

MUSHROOMS IN THE GARDEN

Integrated into the garden, mushrooms look good as well as producing a tasty crop. The common white cultivated mushroom (*Agaricus bisporus*), for example, may appear on its own in your garden, especially if you have amended your soil with spent mushroom compost. It fruits in the autumn and may crop for several years if the conditions are right. The sides or corners of wood-edged raised beds can be replaced with hardwood logs, which are then inoculated with mushroom spawn. A slow compost pile can be used to produce shaggy manes. This species will also grow, along with the king stropharia (*Stropharia rugoso-annulata*), in a border mulched with wood chips or straw.

A note of caution
Mushrooms often appear at a considerable distance from where they were first introduced. The identity of any unfamiliar-looking mushroom must always be checked before eating. Many species are poisonous.

The "no-dig" approach

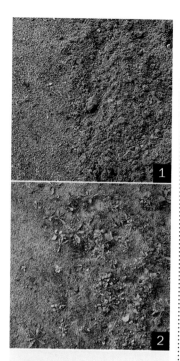

THE EFFECT OF DIGGING

This demonstration shows how digging the soil can increase weed numbers by bringing dormant seeds from lower levels to the surface, where they will germinate. On a bare piece of ground (**1**), the soil on the right is cultivated, while that on the left is left untouched. Three weeks later (**2**), many more weed seedlings have germinated on the dug soil than on the undisturbed side. Fewer weeds, and therefore less time spent weeding, is one of the great benefits of the no-dig approach.

"No-dig" is an organic technique that can be used for growing all types of vegetables. In no-dig, after any initial cultivation required, the soil is never turned over. Soil improvers, which in a no-dig system often have a dual role as a mulch, and fertilizers are spread over the soil surface but are not incorporated—this job is left to earthworms and other organisms. Earthworms improve drainage through their burrowing activities, while their crumbly, aerated casts enhance soil structure. Soil organisms further decompose what the worms drag down, releasing food for the growing plants and forming humus. Some soil disturbance is inevitable when sowing, planting, and harvesting, but this is minimal compared with that caused by digging. In the long term, digging is detrimental to soil structure, resulting in increased losses of soil moisture and organic matter.

The main drawbacks of no-dig are that it can take longer to improve a poor soil and that soil-inhabiting pests are not exposed to predators. Combining the best elements of digging with no-dig techniques is generally the most pragmatic approach. The soil may need initial cultivation before going no-dig—for example, if it is badly compacted—and it can still be turned over occasionally, such as when incorporating green manures. No-dig is particularly successful when combined with a bed system, where the soil is not walked on (see p. 322).

Contrary to popular opinion, a no-dig plot does not require huge quantities of mulch materials. Compost and manure are added in the same quantities as on a dug plot. Potatoes (see facing page) are the only crop that must have an extra-thick mulch; it is essential to prevent green tubers.

Getting started

To get the best results from no-dig, the soil should be in a reasonable condition, structurally, at the outset. This may involve digging to improve drainage and relieve any compaction. If you are unsure about the condition of your soil, the information in *Soil and Soil Care* (pp. 32-61) will help you determine whether digging is necessary and what soil treatments may be required.

> ### THE BENEFITS OF A NO-DIG SYSTEM
> • The repeated effort of labor-intensive digging is no longer required.
> • Soil structure is preserved and, in time, enhanced.
> • Soil organisms flourish in the stable conditions of undisturbed soil.
> • Losses of organic matter and moisture are greatly reduced.
> • Fewer weed seeds are brought to the surface.

In soil that does not have any major problems, the no-dig approach can be adopted right away. If the plot is weedy or you are converting a patch of lawn, it can be cleared without digging using a sheet mulch (see p. 328). Before sowing or planting, appropriate soil improvers are spread evenly over the soil or are concentrated on planting positions for widely spaced crops such as zucchini. Organic fertilizers and lime, if required, can be lightly raked in before spreading any bulky soil improver.

Sowing and planting

Most crops are grown in the same way as they would be on a dug bed. In an established no-dig system, the surface soil will be fine, crumbly, and ideal for seed sowing. Seed is sown in holes or stations. Transplants are set into holes made with a trowel. Any layer of soil improver or mulch should be scraped back prior to sowing or planting, then spread as the plants begin to grow.

Weeds and weeding

On a no-dig plot, weeds are drastically reduced as dormant seeds are not brought to the surface. An organic mulch further reduces weed numbers and retains soil moisture, but is not essential.

Light hoeing is effective on bare soil and gradually depletes the reserve of weed seeds. Any perennial weeds should be loosened with a fork and lifted out, disturbing the soil as little as possible.

Harvesting

You may be able to simply pull root crops out of the ground. If not, use a fork to loosen them gently, causing minimal disruption to the soil.

GROWING NO-DIG POTATOES

In climates where potato foliage is at risk from frost damage, it is usually advisable to plant a no-dig crop slightly later than normal. The mulch tends to reduce soil temperature, and the plants may be more susceptible to frost damage.

Planting

1 Hoe off, cut, or mow down any vegetation on the growing area.

2 Soak the ground well if dry. Spread manure, compost, or a nitrogen-rich organic fertilizer over the ground at the appropriate rate (see p. 40).

3 Lay out seed tubers on the ground at the required spacing. Where there is a risk of frost, plant them into a trowel hole.

4 Cover each row with a 3-in. (7.5-cm) layer of hay or old straw. Mark the position of each row to avoid standing on the tubers.

As they grow

1 Check regularly for shoots emerging through the mulch, and ease any through that are pushing up the mulch rather than growing through it.

2 Replenish the mulch as the plants grow, covering the area between the rows, too.

3 When the plants are close to meeting across the row, cover the mulch with a thick layer of grass clippings to exclude light and keep the tubers from turning green.

4 Add more grass as necessary. Birds love to pull the mulch apart but will play a useful role in controlling pests at the same time.

Harvesting

To harvest a few potatoes, simply pull back the mulch and pick as many tubers as you require. They will be sitting on the soil surface. Replace the mulch and leave the rest to keep growing. To harvest the whole crop, lift or rake off the mulch. Lift all tubers, checking for any that may have developed below ground level.

Green manures and no-dig

Green manure crops (see p. 56), which are usually dug into the soil, can still be grown in a no-dig plot. Annual green manures, such as mustard, are cut down or hoed off and left as a mulch. Perennial green manures such as clover and winter rye (which will tend to regrow if cut down even though they are annuals) are cut down and killed off with a light-excluding mulch or by growing a no-dig crop of potatoes.

Sheet mulching

Sheet mulching with various materials (see below) is an easy, highly effective way of clearing ground such as a weedy plot or a lawn. It is particularly useful when establishing a no-dig system. You can harvest a crop in the first year, without any digging. Where resources are limited, concentrate on clearing a small, manageable area first.

MATERIALS FOR SHEET MULCHING

A sheet mulch is made up of two or three layers.

Base layer
(Biodegradable; excludes light)
Large sheets of cardboard
Cardboard boxes, flattened
Newspapers, full thickness

Middle layer
(Soil improver; anchors base layer)
Garden compost
Grass clippings
Leaf mold or fallen leaves
Well-rotted manure
Mushroom compost (Note: high lime content)
Shredded soft prunings
Spent straw or hay

Top layer—optional
(Retains moisture; looks good)
Straw
Hay

Mulch when soil is warm and after heavy rain. Mulching cold soil delays warming up, slowing plant growth and increasing the risk of slug damage. These chard plants (right) have been raised in cell packs and planted through a sheet mulch.

Laying a sheet mulch

Cut down any vegetation first, and dig out any woody weeds. Lay the base layer, overlapping the "joints" between sheets of cardboard or paper by 12 in. (30 cm) to exclude light. This is best done on a still day; the soil must be warm and moist.

To hold this layer down so it smothers weeds, add a covering layer no more than 4 in. (10 cm) deep, especially along overlapping edges. The choice of material for this depends on what is available and the fertility of the soil. Ground that has been uncultivated for some time, or which was a lawn, is often very fertile and crops will grow surprisingly well with no additional feeding. If the ground is poor, use a medium- or high-fertility soil improver, such as well-rotted manure or garden compost, for the covering layer. Fresh or spoiled straw can be spread as a 2-in. (5-cm) layer over the top to keep it looking neat and tidy and to help conserve moisture. Watering the entire area will settle the layers and keep materials from blowing away.

As the base layer decomposes, the covering layer sinks onto the soil surface, where it is incorporated into the soil by worms, increasing soil fertility.

Growing through a sheet mulch

In the first year potato tubers and transplants such as brassicas, zucchini, and pumpkins can be planted through the mulch into the soil in pockets loosened with a trowel; mix in some compost if available. Initially, plants may need more frost protection than usual as the mulch cuts off the warming solar radiation that usually comes from the soil at night. Use row cover or, alternatively, plant a little later.

Small seeds and root crops are unsuitable for sheet mulches in the first year, but in the following season the surface of the ground should be crumbly and very suitable for sowing all types of seed. It is useful to continue to keep the soil mulched to prevent the germination of weed seeds, protect the soil from crusting after heavy rain, and conserve moisture.

Perennial weeds such as docks and thistles may push up through a sheet mulch. To remove them, simply loosen the soil around their roots and ease them out. A second year of sheet mulching may be needed to control them completely.

Once a sheet mulch has cleared the ground, the area can be maintained using no-dig techniques.

Edible landscaping

Many vegetables are not just delicious to eat but also gorgeous to look at. Edible landscaping takes account of the ornamental aspects of edible plants alongside their practical value. It also means you can grow edible plants in a garden without the need for a separate vegetable area.

An edible landscape can be large or small, formal or relaxed, and include fruit, vegetables, herbs, and flowers. A famous example is at Villandry in France, designed to complement the Château on a grand scale, where vegetables provide blocks of color within a formal layout of paths and beds edged with clipped hedges. At the other extreme is a mixed border, where both edible and ornamental plants all tumble about in merry confusion.

Potager gardens

A potager is an edible garden planted specifically for its ornamental as much as its edible qualities. Maintaining a balance between appearance and yield can be difficult, and careful planning is needed to keep it looking good all year. Planning for either summer or winter is easier, with the garden "at rest" during one of these seasons.

Creative planting

Edible landscaping offers the creative gardener the opportunity to try out all sorts of unusual planting combinations. Vegetables are appreciated for their color, leaf shape, texture, overall form, and as visual statements. They can be trained up screens, trellises, or other plants to provide height, or used to create colorful shapes and patterns at ground level. Allowing some vegetables to go to seed often results in unexpected delights; lettuces, for example, turn into elegant tapering towers up to 4 ft. (1.2 m) high. They are no good for eating at that stage but look delightful! Onions and leeks left to run to flower produce ball-shaped flowerheads at the top of tall stems: striking, colorful, and attractive to bees.

Tower power
Red and green lettuce make attractive spires when left to go to seed. The display may be short-lived, but this is a cheap and cheerful way to improvise a formal effect.

Beautiful plants are healthy plants

Plants in an edible landscape need to be healthy and flourishing to look their best. Pay careful attention to maintaining the soil in good condition and, just as you would in a traditional vegetable plot, remember the principles of rotation (see p. 301) when planning from one year to the next to produce best results. Replacement or substitute plants kept in reserve at varying stages of growth will be useful to take the place of any damaged or unhealthy plants, keeping the display looking good.

Eating the landscape

Harvesting inevitably leaves gaps in an edible landscape. Solve this problem by using varieties that can be picked over a long period, such as kale or looseleaf lettuces. In addition, select crops that still look good after the edible part has been harvested, such as French and runner beans or zucchini. It helps to grow "temporary" plants beside others that will expand to fill the gaps. Raise extra plants in pots or cell packs as replacements for those you eat.

Potager style
Colorful crops planted in patterns can rival the brightest bedding displays and are edible, too.

VEGETABLES AND HERBS FOR EDGING

For summer into autumn
Compact lettuce, especially 'Lollo Rosso' and 'Lollo Verde'
Curly endive
Curly parsley
Red-leaved plantain
Strips of seedling crops
Dwarf Savoy cabbage

For autumn into winter
Lamb's lettuce
Mizuna
Ornamental cabbage and kale
Rosette pak choi

Perennials
Chives
Garlic chives
Marjoram
Salad burnet
Sage, purple and green varieties
Thyme
Winter savory

BEAUTIFUL VEGETABLES

Vibrant colors

Asparagus pea (red flowers)

Beet 'Bull's Blood'(dark red
foliage)

Broccoli 'Romanesco' (lime
green curds)

Crimson-flowered broad bean

Eggplant (purple flowers and
rich purple fruits; or try 'Easter
Egg', with white fruits)

Giant red mustard (red/green
leaves)

Kale 'Red Russian' (pinkish
gray leaves)

Kale 'Tuscano' (greenish
black leaves)

Leek 'St. Victor' (purple/blue)

Pumpkin (orange fruits)

Purple- and yellow-podded
pole beans

Radicchio (red/white leaves)

Rainbow chard (yellow, white,
red, pink, and orange stems)

Red cabbage (purple/blue leaves)

Ruby chard (above left)

Height and drama

Cardoons

Cucumber, trellised

Globe artichokes (above right)

Green and bronze fennel

Pole beans

Pumpkins and squashes, trained

Radishes grown for seed pods

Runner beans

Seakale

Good leaf shape or texture

Endive, curled

Kale, frilly

Lettuce, oakleaved or frilly

Mizuna

Parsley, curled

Pumpkin (below left)

Zucchini

Edible flowers

Borage (blue or, rarely, white)

Calendula (orange)

Chives (pink or purple)

Cowslip (yellow)

Lavender (mauve, white, or pink)

Nasturtium (below right;
yellow/orange/red)

Rose (pink/red flowers taste best)

Sage (purple/pink)

Viola (purple, rarely white)

LEAFY SALAD CROPS

All these plants can be grown as seedling crops. Those marked ★★ are best grown only as seedlings when used for salads; all others can be grown as seedlings, semi-mature, or mature plants.

Mild
Chard ★★
Chervil
Chinese cabbage
Coriander
Corn salad ★
Dill
Leaf beet ★★
Lettuce
Pak choi
Spinach ★★
Summer purslane
Winter purslane (claytonia) ★

Bitter
Chicory ★
Dandelion
Endive

Hot
Garden cress ★★
Garden mustard ★★
Greek cress ★★
Mibuna
Mizuna ★
Oriental mustard ★
Radish leaf ★★
Rocket ★
Snow cabbage ★
Upland cress ★
Watercress

★ Good for an autumn crop in a cool climate
★★ Best grown as seedling crops for salads

More detail on growing these crops can be found in the *A–Z of Vegetable and Salad Crops*, p. 337.

Cutting lettuce
Harvest seedling lettuce when about 4–6 in. (10–15 cm) high, leaving a short stem to regrow.

Growing greens

A great number of vegetables can be used to make delicious salads, but for gardeners the term "salad plants" normally refers to leafy greens that are suitable for eating raw. These vary widely in their origins, flavors, colors, and textures. Some flowers are also edible (see p. 331) and make colorful additions to salad mixtures.

Salads all year

It is possible to harvest something fresh and leafy almost year-round, with a bit of planning. Salads are perhaps especially welcome in winter when fewer fresh vegetables are available.

Spring and autumn Choose quick-maturing varieties that will produce a crop within weeks of sowing. Protect with cloches or row cover, or grow in a greenhouse or hoop house to extend production.

Summer The widest range of salad greens can be grown in summer, both seedlings and mature plants. Make sure they never lack water at this time of year to discourage premature bolting. Some greens are mild, many more are stronger, so grow a mixture for a blend of flavors. Chicory, endive, and dandelion are all quite bitter, but blanching mature plants will produce milder, more tender leaves. Cover flat varieties with a plate and upright ones with a pot or bucket—or tie the leaves together. It takes 1 to 3 weeks, depending on the season.

Winter Salads sown in late summer will be ready to harvest in early winter, and with protection or in mild winters, some can be harvested right through the winter. In harsh climates, grow seedling crops indoors on windowsills in shallow trays or pots.

Techniques

Salad plants can be grown to maturity, harvested at the seedling stage, or when semi-mature. Seedling or semi-mature crops can be harvested much earlier, within a few weeks, and the harvest can go on over a longer period.

Seedling greens

Seedling greens are harvested when immature. Seeds can be mixed before sowing, providing an instant mixed salad. Seedling crops are shallow-rooting, so will grow well in containers with a minimum depth of about 4 in. (10 cm) as well as in the soil. They do not need particularly fertile conditions, but do benefit from a soil or growing medium that retains water well. These crops have a high water requirement, so make sure you can water them easily in dry conditions. Weed-free conditions are important. If weeds are a problem, use the stale seedbed technique (see p. 75).

Sowing seedlings

Sow seedlings direct into a fine seedbed or container, either broadcast over the whole area or in shallow holes approximately 4 in. (10 cm) wide. Aim for a spacing of about ¾ in. (2 cm) between seeds. Water well to encourage germination. In hot, dry, or windy conditions, it is helpful to cover the seeds with row cover or windbreak netting until they germinate.

• **Interplanting and catch cropping** Quick-growing seedling crops make good use of space among slower growing, widely spaced vegetables such as cabbages, potatoes, or zucchini. They will be ready to harvest long before the larger crop needs

MESCLUN AND ORIENTAL SALADINI

Mixed salad seeds are sometimes sold as mesclun, misticanza, or saladini. These mixtures contain different types of chicory, endive, lettuce, with perhaps arugula, leaf radish, dandelion, and cress. Most mixtures are suited to spring and summer sowing.

Oriental saladini contains oriental vegetables, such as mizuna, mibuna, oriental mustards, Chinese cabbage, and pak choi. These do well at the beginning and end of the season in cool climates, and can last through the winter with some protection.

You can also make your own mixtures according to taste and to suit your conditions.

the space. Another option is to sow seedlings when the ground is empty for short periods.

• **Successional sowing** Sow a new batch of seeds every 2–3 weeks to ensure continuity of harvesting.

Harvesting

Seedling greens are ready to harvest as soon as they are about 4–6 in. (10–15 cm) high, usually within a few weeks. Use a sharp knife or scissors to cut the leaves, or pick by hand, leaving a stem of about ¾ in. (2 cm). The plants can regrow, and you will be able to cut them two or three times over the following

weeks. The life of a seedling patch varies depending on weather conditions and season. Seedling crops do not stay fresh for long once harvested, so pick them just before you want to eat them.

Semi-mature salads

Sow seeds at a wider spacing than for seedling crops, leaving about 6–8 in. (15–20 cm) between plants. Alternatively, sow in cell packs and plant out, or simply transplant some seedlings to a similar spacing. To harvest, pick individual leaves from the outside as the plants develop, leaving the growing tip intact.

Storing vegetables

Certain vegetables can be stored through the winter to eat fresh when produce from the garden is scarce. Some very hardy crops, such as parsnips and Jerusalem artichokes, can be left in the ground over winter, but there are disadvantages to this. It increases the likelihood of pest damage, and any disease present will have the opportunity to spread. In addition, the soil may freeze solid in cold weather, making harvesting difficult.

Many vegetables can be stored successfully without any special equipment as long as you are able to provide the right conditions. Once your vegetables are in storage, they need to be inspected regularly. Adjust conditions if necessary, and remove anything that shows signs of decay to keep it from spreading to the other vegetables.

Harvesting for storage

Best results will be obtained from main crop cultivars that mature toward the end of the season and are harvested in cool conditions.

• **Harvest vegetables just as they reach maturity** Picking too early means they will not have developed their full flavor; leave it too late and they become fibrous and woody.

• **Only store best-quality produce** Anything that is blemished or has pest and disease damage will only deteriorate, and may also spread rots to other fruits and vegetables.

• **Handle with care** Even quite sturdy crops, such as potatoes, are easily bruised. The damage may not be apparent at first, but it may allow rots to set in once stored.

Where to store vegetables

The ideal storage conditions for individual vegetables vary according to type. In general, the best place is somewhere cool and dry, with an even temperature, and free from mice and other pests. A basement or cellar is ideal, but an unheated shed, garage, or room in the house is also suitable. Lift storage containers off the floor on boxes or pallets, and keep a supply of old blankets, sacks, or rugs for extra insulation if required.

Storage requirements

Details of storage conditions for crops that last well through the winter are given opposite. Some other crops can also be stored for shorter periods:

• **Tomatoes** Harvest green tomatoes at the end of the growing season, before the first frost. Whole vines can be uprooted, then hung in a cool, dry place to continue to ripen slowly. Alternatively, harvest fruit individually, wrap in paper, and store on trays or in boxes. To encourage ripening, place tomatoes in a closed paper bag or box with a ripe apple or banana.

• **Cabbages** Firm red and white winter cabbage will store for several months if harvested before the first frost. It is crucial to leave the roots intact, or cut leaving a 6-in. (15-cm) stem. Place on pallets or slatted shelves and keep at 32–39°F (0–4°C). Cover with straw, sacks, or thick layers of newspaper if temperatures drop.

• **Leeks and Brussels sprouts** Both can normally be left in the ground all winter, but if very harsh weather is forecast you can bring a temporary supply into the house for convenience. Dig up entire plants with roots intact, and place in a bucket with just enough water to cover the roots. In a cool place, they should stay fresh for up to a week.

Drying and storing beans
Choose varieties recommended for storage, such as these cranberry beans. Leave the pods on the vine until dry and crisp. Shell the beans and store in an airtight container.

CROPS TO STORE

1 Potatoes

Lift and leave exposed to dry for a few hours. Store in heavy paper bags, tied or folded loosely at the neck. Potatoes must be stored in the dark to prevent them turning green and developing high levels of solanine, a toxic alkaloid. Frost protection is essential. Ideal temperature 41–50°F (5–10°C).

2 Onions, shallots, and garlic

Harvest garlic when the first 4–6 leaves turn yellow. Leave onions and shallots until all the leaves have fallen over naturally. Lift carefully, and leave in a warm, dry place for a couple of weeks. In fine weather, do this outdoors, lifted off the ground on racks or pallets. Otherwise, bring them under cover to finish drying. Bulbs are ready to store when the skins are papery and rustle when handled. Braid into ropes or hang in net sacks in a place where air circulates freely. Ideal temperature 36–39°F (2–4°C).

3 Carrots, parsnips, beets, celeriac, and rutabaga

Remove excess soil gently; do not wash or scrub as this may damage the skin. Remove leafy tops by twisting close to the crown. Place in shallow trays or boxes, separating layers with moist sand, untreated sawdust, fine leaf mold, or sieved soil. Ideal temperature 32–39°F (0–4°C).

4 Pumpkins and winter squash

These need a few weeks of sunny weather at the end of the season to develop a tough skin for optimum storage. Harvest before the first frost. Cut with a long stalk, leaving part of the vine attached. As this dries, it hardens and protects the stem, which is otherwise vulnerable to rotting. Store in a dry, airy place, if possible on slatted shelves or in nets for good air circulation. Can last 6–9 months if well-ripened at harvest. Ideal temperature 50–59°F (10–15°C); storage at higher temperatures causes the flesh to become fibrous.

A–Z of Vegetable & Salad Crops

Notes on the entries

- **Botanical name and family** These tell you more about plant relationships—how the crop fits in, if at all, to a rotation plan and whether it may share preferences and weaknesses with other crops (see also pp. 301–313). This is followed by a general description of the crop.
- **Seed to harvest** The usual time taken to achieve a crop. Sometimes Planting to Harvest, for crops that are vegetatively propagated.
- **Crop diversity** In some cases none at all, especially for crops that do not lend themselves to commercial cultivation and those, like some of the salad leaves, that are only one step away from the wild. Other crops are bewilderingly—or perhaps excitingly—diverse, with a huge array of cultivars to choose from; in some cases recommendations are given.
- **Site** All crops will perform better for you if given the site and soil conditions they prefer.
- **Soil treatment** The recommendations given are suggestions for an "average" soil, if such a thing exists. What is actually needed will depend on many factors. If your soil contains good organic matter levels and you grow green manures, you can cut down on the use of soil improvers and fertilizers—unless you are looking to grow bumper-size crops. A dry, poor soil might require more improvement than is suggested, especially if you need to increase its water-holding capacity. See also *Soil and Soil Care*, pp. 33–61, and *Growing Vegetables*, pp. 293–296; also individual vegetable families (pp. 303–313).
- **Ideal pH range** See pp. 37 and 61 for more information.
- **Sowing** Covers timing and options for both outdoors and under cover. Methods are described in more detail in *Growing Vegetables*, pp. 314–318 (including techniques such as multi-sowing and interplanting), and in *Raising Plants*, pp. 104–123. Minimum germination temperature figures give an idea of when and where a particular crop can be sown—direct in the soil, or raised in the warmth of a propagator or under plant lights, for example. Knowing when the soil outside is warm enough for sowing does come with experience, but if you are new to vegetable growing or have moved to a new area, a soil thermometer can be useful.
- **Spacing** For rows, the recommended distance between plants in the row is given first, and then the distance between rows. Block planting refers to equidistant planting, and indicates the space each way that each plant will need. For a further explanation of growing in beds and rows, see p. 322.
- **Plant care** See also pp. 319–323. Problems referred to here are covered in detail in the *A–Z of Plant Problems*, beginning on p. 367.
- **Harvesting** Personal preference sometimes plays a part in deciding when to harvest, but general recommendations are given here, together with an indication of whether the crop is best eaten fresh or can be stored short- or long-term.

Keeping records

These entries are a great starting point for growing vegetables, but keep in mind that growing conditions vary widely, so not all of the advice will work for your climate. The best thing you can do to improve your success rate is to keep careful notes about what you do in your vegetable garden and when you do it. Good records are invaluable to gardeners who are serious about their soil, their crops, and their time. Knowing what went wrong one year will help you avoid making the same mistake the next. Records will also help you build on the previous year's successes. You may think you'll remember all of this without bothering to write it down, but you'd be surprised how many useful lessons you will end up learning a second time simply because you forgot.

Some gardeners keep a loose-leaf notebook or notepad with their gardening supplies, where it is handy for jotting down observations and thoughts. Others use a calendar. Your records can be as formal or informal as you choose, but try to keep them up to date. A good method is to take a once-a-week walk through the garden, not for the purpose of doing any weeding or harvesting but just to observe, smell, and touch. You will notice more details when you're not there to do any work, and it can be one of the most pleasurable times you spend in the garden.

Artichoke, globe

Cynara scolymus ASTERACEAE

This perennial plant—4–5 ft. (1.2–1.5 m) tall with a 36-in. (90-cm) spread—is easy to grow but produces a relatively small crop for the space, making it more suitable for a larger plot. It makes a fine addition to an ornamental planting. The large spiky heads (flower buds) are eaten. Allowed to open, they become inedible, but bees love the magnificent, peacock-blue thistle flowerheads. Globe artichokes are hardy in Zones 8 to 10; grow as an annual in cooler climates.

PLANTING TO HARVEST Around 28 weeks in the first season. Thereafter, produce in summer.
CROP DIVERSITY Heads usually green, but there is a purple form.
SITE Sunny, sheltered. Avoid heavy or wet soils, where it is less likely to survive the winter.
SOIL TREATMENT Apply a high-fertility soil improver, plus a low-fertility soil improver on dry soils.
IDEAL pH RANGE 6.5–7

Sowing
Can be raised from seed or grown from offsets (or divisions) taken from plants in April. Select only the best for division and discard the rest.

Spacing
At least 3 x 5 ft. (1 x 1.5 m).

Plant care
Water until established. Mulch with hay or compost. Protect from frost by covering the crown with straw. Remove in the spring

before growth starts. The productive life of artichokes is 3–4 years, so take offsets from a third of your plants every year to keep supplies going.
PROBLEMS Usually trouble-free. Aphids may be a nuisance but can be washed off using a hose.

Harvesting
Globe artichokes produce several large heads from July to September. Harvest them when plump but still tender, with scales still tight, and eat fresh. Removing side buds will increase the size of the main head. Cook heads whole and eat the fleshy pads at the base of the scales. Before eating the heart at the top of the stem, remove all of the fibrous "choke."

Artichoke, Jerusalem

Helianthus tuberosus ASTERACEAE

Not for small gardens, this perennial (Zones 2 to 9) crop provides good cover for birds and amphibians, crowds out many weeds, and makes a useful summer windbreak. It usually produces pretty sunflowerlike blooms. The edible parts are the knobby tubers that grow in the soil.

PLANTING TO HARVEST 16–20 weeks.
CROP DIVERSITY Tubers are smooth or knobby, creamy yellow or red.
SITE Sun or partial shade. Avoid poorly drained soils.
SOIL TREATMENT Apply a

medium-fertility soil improver before planting. High-fertility materials produce larger tubers.
IDEAL pH RANGE 6–7.5

Sowing
Plant tubers 6 in. (15 cm) deep in February or March.

Spacing
ROWS 12 in. x 3 ft. (30 cm x 1 m)
BLOCK PLANTING 18 in. (45 cm)

Plant care
Support with stout stakes and wires or individual canes in windy areas. Mound up 1½–4 in. (4–10 cm) of soil around the roots in early summer for additional support. Watering in dry weather and removing flower buds will increase the yield. When leaves turn yellow in late summer, cut stems to 6 in. (15 cm).
PROBLEMS Usually trouble-free. Occasionally attacked by slugs and wireworms.

Harvesting
Tubers do not store well once harvested so they are best dug when needed, after the leaves have turned yellow. Replant some for the next season if required. Remove all tubers if you want to clear the area.

Arugula

Eruca vesicaria BRASSICACEAE

Also called salad rocket, a fast-growing crop of spicy salad leaves that can be cut as little as 3 weeks after sowing. The flowers are also edible. It makes a good quick catch crop and

grows well in containers. Arugula can be grown for most of the year. Early and late sowings can be made under cloches or in a hoop house or greenhouse. It likes moisture-retentive soil and partial shade. Apply a low-fertility soil improver on light soils. Make regular sowings direct into soil February–June and late August–October. Plants sown in high summer tend to bolt. Broadcast thinly in wide rows or blocks for a seedling crop for cutting. Space at 6 x 6 in. (15 x 15 cm) for larger leaves. Pick or cut leaves as required. Water in dry weather. Flea beetle is often a problem, but plants can be grown under mesh or row cover. As a brassica, arugula is also vulnerable to clubroot and must be included in a crop rotation.

Asparagus

Asparagus officinalis LILIACEAE

A perennial crop in Zones 2 to 9, easy to grow once established. It provides a gourmet harvest of delicious spears from April–June. Yields are relatively small for the growing area needed, but a bed can produce for 20 years. It is vital that all perennial weeds are cleared before planting.

SEED TO HARVEST 2–3 years.
CROP DIVERSITY Plants are either male or female. Traditional cultivars produce a mixture of both. All-male F1 cultivars give slimmer spears in larger numbers over a longer season. Female spears are said to be more succulent. Most spears are green,

---

Cultivar choice
Globe artichoke 'Green Globe'; 'Imperial Star'; 'Violetto'—purple-tinged buds.
Jerusalem artichoke 'Dwarf Sunray'—shorter cultivar, has a sunflowerlike flower; 'Fuseau'—smooth tubers.
Asparagus 'Mary Washington'; 'Purple Passion'—purple spears. All-male cultivars: 'Jersey General' F1; 'Jersey Knight' F1.

Globe artichoke

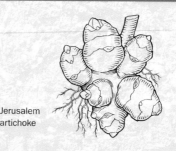

Jerusalem artichoke

Arugula

but a purple cultivar is available.

SITE Will grow in a wide range of not too fertile soils. Good drainage is essential, as is a deep root run. Lime if pH is below 6. Foliage can grow to over 36 in. (90 cm) tall, so avoid windy sites.

SOIL TREATMENT Dig site well, removing all weeds. Add a medium-fertility soil improver in the winter before planting.

IDEAL pH RANGE 6.5–7.5

Sowing

Can be raised from seed. To shorten time to production, buy 1-year-old plants, known as crowns.

UNDER COVER F1 hybrid seed is costly, so it is advisable to sow it under cover. Sow in large cell packs or 3½-in. (9-cm) pots in February. Maintain a temperature of 55–61°F (13–16°C) until plants are 4–6 in. (10–15 cm) tall. Harden off and plant out in June.

OUTSIDE Sow open-pollinated asparagus seed March–April on a prepared seedbed 1 in. (2.5 cm) deep in rows 18 in. (45 cm) apart. Thin to 6 in. (15 cm). Select the best seedlings to plant out in spring as 1-year-old crowns.

MINIMUM GERMINATION TEMPERATURE 50°F (10°C)

Planting

PACK-GROWN TRANSPLANTS Plant up to early summer, at a depth of 4 in. (10 cm).

1-YEAR-OLD CROWNS Plant without delay in March and early April. Dig a trench 10 in. (25 cm) deep, 12 in. (30 cm) wide, forming a mounded ridge of soil along the bottom. When sitting on this mound the crowns should be 4 in. (10 cm) deep. Spread out the fragile

roots carefully, then gently fill in the trench to the level of the crowns. Keep filling as they grow, always leaving 3–4 in. (8–10 cm) of stem showing.

Spacing

ROWS Asparagus grown in single rows will produce for longer as it takes more time for the bed to become congested. Space plants 12–16 in. x 6 ft. (30–40 cm x 2 m).

BEDS Asparagus is traditionally grown in 3-row beds, with 12 in. (30 cm) between plants and rows, and 4½ ft. (1.3 m) between beds.

Plant care

Keep watered in the first year to establish. Protect young shoots with row cover in cold springs. Well-grown plants may need support in summer. Weeding is a crucial job—once perennial weeds are established they are almost impossible to eradicate. Mulch once the spears have emerged with a medium- or low-fertility soil improver (the

latter on fertile soil) to control weeds and feed the foliage, or fern. Hand-weed as necessary; do not hoe as asparagus is shallow-rooted. Cut the fern close to the ground once it turns yellow in the autumn. Asparagus beetle can overwinter in old stems, so prompt removal is important.

PROBLEMS Asparagus beetle, slugs, Fusarium wilt.

Harvesting

Cut spears sparingly at first until crowns are established. Hybrid cultivars can be cut lightly in the second year after planting as crowns or pack-grown plants. In the third year harvest for 6 weeks, and from then on for 8 weeks if plants are growing well. Asparagus is ready to cut when spears are 6 in. (15 cm) tall. Cut the spears 1–2 in. (2.5–5 cm) below soil level. Cut all spears during the harvest period to maintain a supply. Asparagus is best eaten fresh. Refrigerate for no more than 3–4 days.

Asparagus: The 4-year Sacrificial Crop

Useful if you have sufficient land, especially in a spot with a known weed problem or where you do not want to tie up an area for 10 years or so. Once this system is established, the asparagus can be fitted into a normal vegetable crop rotation pattern, with a much shorter wait for the crop to come into harvest.

YEAR 1 Prepare a bed and on it station-sow open-pollinated seed, 4 in. x 10 in. (10 cm x 25 cm) apart. Keep the plants weed-free as they grow and develop, and cut the fern back in autumn.

YEAR 2 Prepare and sow another bed. Cut a few of the fattest spears (not more than one per 18 in. (45 cm) of row) from the first bed.

YEAR 3 Sow another bed. Cut about one-third of the fattest spears from the first plot, and a few from the second.

YEAR 4 Sow another seedbed. Cut all spears from the first plot, which can then be dug over and used for a different crop; harvest the 1- and 2-year-old beds as above.

Asparagus pea

Lotus tetragonolobus
PAPILIONACEAE

An attractive half-hardy annual with small, winged, edible pods. Its bright green leaves and crimson flowers make it worth growing for its appearance alone. It enjoys light but fertile, open soils and a sunny site, and will succeed in hot, dry soils where true peas fail. It can also be grown in containers. No soil treatment is needed before sowing if soil was improved for a previous crop. Otherwise, apply a low- or medium-fertility soil improver depending on soil conditions. Sow under cover in May and June in trays or cell packs, barely covering the seed. Harden off and plant outside 6 weeks after sowing. Sow outside from mid-April to the end of May, ¾ in. (2 cm) deep. Space in rows 4–6 in. x 12 in. (10–15 cm x 30 cm) or in blocks 8 in. (20 cm) each way. Watering once flowers have set makes pods more tender. Cropping starts 8–10 weeks after sowing. Pick pods regularly when 1 in. (2–3 cm) long; they quickly become stringy and tough. Picking is easiest in the evening, as the leaves fold down.

Bean, broad

Vicia faba PAPILIONACEAE

The broad or fava bean is a hardy, reliable crop that thrives in cool conditions. It can be sown in autumn (under shelter) or spring for midsummer

Asparagus

Asparagus pea

harvest. Dwarf and shorter varieties can be grown in large containers. Broad beans will fix nitrogen in the soil and are often grown as cover crops.

SEED TO HARVEST Spring-sown crops: 12–16 weeks. Autumn-sown crops: 28–35 weeks.
CROP DIVERSITY Dwarf and tall cultivars with green, white (pale green), or red seeds. Green-seeded plants are said to be tastier than white. Longpod varieties tend to be hardier than shorter-podded "Windsors." Most broad beans produce white flowers.
SITE Open, sunny site; winter crops need shelter. Will not do well on dry or waterlogged soils. Lime-tolerant.
SOIL TREATMENT Apply a low-fertility soil improver to light soils before sowing.
IDEAL pH RANGE 6–7

Sowing
MINIMUM GERMINATION TEMPERATURE 41°F (5°C)
UNDER COVER In late autumn, sow extra-hardy cultivars in a frame or hoop house. For early crops, sow in boxes or biodegradable tubes; transplant with 3–4 true leaves. Rapid growth of young plants limits root diseases; also useful if mice tend to eat seeds.
OUTSIDE In spring, sow from March–April. Plants stop growing well at temperatures above 59°F (15°C).

Spacing
ROWS Usually grown in double rows, 6–9 in. (15–20 cm) between plants, 24 in. (60 cm) between rows.
BLOCK 8–12 in. (20–30 cm).

Plant care
Pinch out the growing tips once the bottom flower clusters have opened to deter black bean aphid. Earlier sowings are usually less prone to attack. Tall varieties may need a support of stakes and string when pods swell, especially on windy sites.
PROBLEMS Mice; pea and bean weevil; black bean aphid; broad bean chocolate spot; broad bean rust; root rot.

Harvesting
Harvest pods when beans can just be felt through them, before they get large and tough. Young pods may be eaten whole. Broad beans freeze well.

Bean, runner

Phaseolus coccineus PAPILIONACEAE

A frost-tender perennial, usually grown as an annual. A prolific cropper, with attractive flowers and long, rough pods that are eaten young before the seeds develop. Easy to grow. Most climb to 10 ft. (3 m) or so, making a useful and attractive screen, if grown in a row, or tepee. Runner beans produce a tuber, which can be stored over winter (or may survive in light soil) to produce plants the next season. These may be less vigorous than those grown from seed.

SEED TO HARVEST 12–16 weeks.
CROP DIVERSITY Flowers can be scarlet, white, bicolored, or salmon. Pods are always green, but seeds may be white, black, or purple-speckled. Dwarf cultivars, growing to around 15 in.

(38 cm) tall, are available.
SITE Sheltered, sunny, with moisture-retentive soil to allow deep rooting. Dwarf cultivars can be grown in containers.
SOIL TREATMENT Grow on soil improved for a previous crop. Where necessary, apply a low-fertility soil improver to ensure a good water supply, or grow on a "compost trench" (see p. 48).
IDEAL pH RANGE 6.5

Sowing
MINIMUM GERMINATION TEMPERATURE 54°F (12°C)
UNDER COVER Sow in May in deep trays, biodegradable tube pots, or root trainers. Transplant after the last frost in warm soil.
OUTSIDE Station-sow, 2 seeds per station, from late May to early July once the soil has warmed up; a second sowing for a later crop is worthwhile.

Spacing
ROWS In double rows—6 in. x 2 ft. (15 x 60 cm), or up a cane tepee. Bush varieties—6 in. x 2 ft. (15 x 60 cm).
BLOCK PLANTING Dwarf cultivars only, 12 in. (30 cm).

Plant care
The plants need a strong framework of 8-ft. (2.5-m) bamboo canes to support the fully grown plants and their crop. Mulch well once plants are established. Water regularly in dry weather once the first flower buds appear to encourage more flowers. The flowers must be pollinated to produce pods.
PROBLEMS Birds; slugs; root aphids; bean seed fly; root rots; halo blight. Poor pod set (see also *Poor/No Fruit Set*, p. 387)

can be due to frosts at flowering time, water shortage, poor weather reducing the activity of pollinating insects, a site too exposed for the insects, or birds pecking at flowers.

Harvesting
Pick young pods 7 in. (17 cm) or so in length. Regular picking encourages more pods to form.

Bean, string

Phaseolus vulgaris PAPILIONACEAE

These produce good crops (often more reliably than runner beans) in a relatively small space but need warm conditions for a successful start. Usually eaten as young fresh pods, in drier regions these can be used to produce a crop of dry beans. Also called snap, pole, or bush beans.

SEED TO HARVEST 7–13 weeks. Dwarf cultivars start earliest. 16–18 weeks for dry beans.
CROP DIVERSITY Available in climbing or dwarf cultivars, with round (pencil) or flat pods. The lilac, purple, and white flowers are decorative; the pods can be striped, violet, or yellow as well as green. Yellow pods have a more waxy texture and a good flavor. For growing under cover, pick a compact bush variety, or if space allows grow a climbing variety, which may be less prone to disease as there is a better flow of air around the plants.
SITE Warm site and soil, sunny and sheltered. Can be grown in an unheated greenhouse or hoop house, or in containers.
SOIL TREATMENT None needed

Cultivar choice
Runner bean 'Scarlet Emperor'—traditional cultivar from 1906; 'Apricot Runner'—peach-colored flowers; 'Painted Lady'—scarlet-and-white blooms.
String bean Bush: 'Blue Lake'—a classic, uniform ripening; 'Gold Mine'—yellow pods; 'Purple Queen'—purple pods turn green when cooked; 'Dragon Tongue'—good for fresh eating or as a dry bean. Pole beans: 'Kentucky Blue'—stringless pods; 'Asparagus'—exceptionally long, slender pods; 'Trionfo Violetto'—deep purple pods.

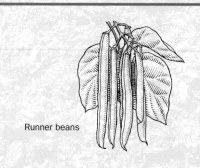

Runner beans

on a reasonable soil or one improved for a previous crop. If not, add a medium-fertility soil improver before sowing.
IDEAL PH RANGE 6.5–7.5

Sowing

MINIMUM GERMINATION TEMPERATURE 55°F (13°C)
UNDER COVER To get an early start for plants for dry bean production and for early crops, sow in May under cover in deep wooden boxes lined with newspaper, or in biodegradable tubes, root trainers, or 3½-in. (9-cm) pots. Harden off before planting outside only after the last frost.
OUTSIDE Sow from early summer, when the soil is warm enough, until late June. Warm the soil with cloches or black plastic to benefit early sowings. The last sowings, which should be dwarf varieties, may need cloche protection. Sow 2 in. (5 cm) deep. Expect about 75% germination—always put a few extra beans in at the end of a row for transplanting into gaps.

Spacing

ROWS Dwarf beans: 2–3 in. x 18–24 in. (5–7 cm x 45–60 cm), depending on cultivar. Climbing beans: Grow up tepees or in double rows 24 in. (60 cm) apart, with 5 ft. (1.5 m) between double rows. Sow 2 seeds per support, with 4–5 in. (10–12 cm) between supports. Closer spacing is possible in containers but does increase risk of disease.
BLOCK PLANTING Dwarf beans: 6–8 in. (15–20 cm). Close planting delays harvesting by a week or so.
UNDER COVER Use wider spacing to lessen the risk of disease.

Plant care
Use bottle cloches to prevent pests taking the seeds and eating seedlings. Use tall stakes or pole supports for climbing beans. Taller dwarf cultivars may benefit from the support of twigs. Watering as the pods develop increases yield.
PROBLEMS Mice; Mexican bean beetle; slugs; red spider mite; black bean aphid; halo blight; viruses.

Harvesting
Pick fresh beans as soon as they are large enough. Check plants at least every other day, as beans develop very quickly and plants can stop producing as soon as a single pod is allowed to mature. Purple and yellow pods are easier to spot than the green ones. The beans freeze well and can also be turned into chutney. Do not pick fresh beans from a drying crop as this will delay maturity. Leave the pods to dry on the plants until they rattle. Drying can be completed indoors in bad weather. Hang whole plants upside down in a warm, airy place until dry.

Beet

Beta vulgaris subsp. *vulgaris*
CHENOPODIACEAE

Easy and quick to grow, beets can be sown outdoors over a long period, from March to June.

SEED TO HARVEST 7–13 weeks.
CROP DIVERSITY Roots can be red, yellow, or white, and round, cylindrical, or long. Bolt-hardy cultivars (resistant to bolting

caused by cold weather when young) are good for early sowings. The green and red foliage is attractive and edible, but the old cultivar 'Bulls Blood', with its deep red foliage, is most colorful. Suitable for mini-veg.
SITE Open, sunny. Beets are salt-tolerant—useful in coastal gardens—but do not tolerate an acid soil. The round "ball" cultivars grow well in containers.
SOIL TREATMENT Nothing required on a fertile soil or one improved for a previous crop. Apply a low-fertility soil improver to light or heavy soils.
IDEAL PH RANGE 6.5–7.5

Sowing
Seeds are usually multigerm: each produces several seedlings. Monogerm types are specially bred to produce a single seedling from each seed.
MINIMUM GERMINATION TEMPERATURE 45°F (7°C)
UNDER COVER Start sowing in late February or early March. Sow in cell packs, 2 seeds (or 2–3 monogerm seeds) per cell. Thin to strongest seedling. For multisowing, allow 4–5 seedlings per module. Use a small-rooted cultivar. Harden off when plants have 3–4 true leaves before transplanting outside.
OUTSIDE Sow from March or April until late June, or 2 weeks later in mild areas. To grow beets for storage, sow globe or long cultivars in May and June.

Spacing
Spacing can be adjusted to some extent depending on the cultivar and size of root required.

ROWS Early and quick crops: 4 x 9 in. (10 x 23 cm). Main crops: 3 x 12 in. (7.5 x 30 cm). Mini-beet: 1 x 6 in. (2.5 x 15 cm). Multisown: 9 x 9 in. (22 x 22 cm).
BLOCK PLANTING 5–6 in. (12.5–15 cm) apart.

Plant care
Water often in hot, dry weather or the roots will become woody.
PROBLEMS Usually trouble-free.

Harvesting
Harvest roots as soon as they are the right size. For storage, harvest in autumn. Roots can be left in the soil over winter but may become tough and slug-eaten. Twist, rather than cut, the tops off. Store beets in a cool, dark, humid place, such as a box of moist sand.

Beet, leaf

Beta vulgaris Cicla Group
CHENOPODIACEAE

Also called perpetual spinach or spinach beet, with edible stems and leaves. It can crop year-round. Similar in flavor to spinach, but more reliable.

SEED TO HARVEST 8–12 weeks.
CROP DIVERSITY None.
SITE Tolerates salt-laden winds and some shade. A good winter crop under cover.
SOIL TREATMENT Apply a low-fertility soil improver if soil was amended with compost for a previous crop. Otherwise use a medium-fertility improver, or a low-fertility material with a nitrogen-rich organic fertilizer.
IDEAL PH RANGE 6.5–7.5

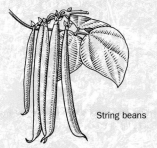
String beans

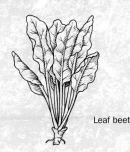
Leaf beet

Cultivar choice
Beet 'Lutz Green Leaf'—exceptionally large roots; 'Red Ace F1'—good disease resistance; 'Golden'—bright gold roots; 'Chiogga'—red-and-white striped flesh.

Sowing

MINIMUM GERMINATION TEMPERATURE 46°F (8°C)

UNDER COVER Sow the "multigermed" seeds in cell packs in March and April. Thin to the strongest seedling, or plant in clumps for a seedling crop. Harden off before planting outside. For a winter crop under cover, sow in August.

OUTSIDE Station-sow, half a thumb deep, in March and April to crop over the summer and autumn. Sow in July and August to crop over winter and spring.

SEEDLING CUTTING CROP Broadcast thinly in early autumn for cutting in winter under cover.

Spacing

ROWS 9 x 15 in. (23 x 38 cm)

BLOCK PLANTING 9 in. (23 cm)

Plant care

Water in dry weather. Mulch to retain moisture; use a medium-fertility soil improver.

PROBLEMS Beet leaf miner; beet leaf spot.

Harvesting

Pick leaves from the outside first as soon as they are big enough to eat. Cutting crops are ready very quickly; take the first cut at about 2 in. (5 cm) tall. Allow to regrow slightly taller before the next cut. To rejuvenate older plants, cut all the leaves off just above the soil.

Broccoli

Brassica oleracea Italica Group BRASSICACEAE

Broccoli is a tasty, fast-maturing, green-headed vegetable, producing from early summer to autumn. It is less hardy than sprouting broccoli, but produces larger, denser heads. Sprouting broccoli is hardy and easy to grow. It is in the ground from midsummer until the next spring. Each plant can take up to 10 sq. ft. (1 sq. m) of ground, but repays this by producing when other vegetables are scarce.

SEED TO HARVEST Regular broccoli: 11–14 weeks; sprouting broccoli: 8–12 months.

CROP DIVERSITY Regular broccoli cultivars are early, mid-season, and late-maturing. There used to be little choice with sprouting broccoli, but modern cultivars can be earlier to crop, with larger spears.

SITE Open, but protected from strong winds. Broccoli will crop on less fertile soils than other brassicas; is suitable for early and late cropping under cover.

SOIL TREATMENT Apply a medium-fertility soil improver, or a low-fertility soil improver with a general organic fertilizer in the spring before planting—or plant after a nitrogen-fixing, green manure crop.

IDEAL pH RANGE Regular broccoli 6.5–7.5; sprouting broccoli 6–7.5.

Sowing

MINIMUM GERMINATION TEMPERATURE Regular broccoli 41°F (5°C); sprouting broccoli 45°F (7°C)

UNDER COVER Regular broccoli resents root disturbance and must be sown in cell packs or biodegradable pots. For an early crop, sow in March. Harden off and plant outside 4–5 weeks after sowing. Overwinter a late summer sowing of an early-maturing cultivar in an unheated hoop house or greenhouse to crop the following spring. Sow sprouting broccoli in cell packs or in a seedbed from April to mid-May. Harden off before planting out.

OUTSIDE Station-sow regular broccoli, 2–3 seeds per station, thinning to a single seedling. Sow April to July to crop from early summer through to autumn. Sow sprouting broccoli in a seedbed from mid-April to mid-May. Scatter seed thinly in rows ¾–1 in. (2–2.5 cm) deep, aiming for 3 in. (7.5 cm) between plants. Transplant in June and early July.

Spacing

Transplant deeply (with lowest leaf on the surface of the soil) to reduce the danger from cabbage root fly and encourage a good root system; firm around plants after planting.

ROWS With regular broccoli, close spacing produces small heads maturing at once. Wider spacing gives more sideshoots and larger central heads over a longer period. Close spacing: 3–24 in. (8–60 cm). For maximum yield: staggered rows, 6–12 in. (15–30 cm). For largest central heads: 8–18 in. (20–45 cm). Sprouting broccoli: 24 in. (60 cm) apart, allowing 30 in. (75 cm) between rows for easy picking.

BLOCK PLANTING Regular broccoli: 8 in. (20 cm); sprouting broccoli: 24 in. (60 cm).

Plant care

Protect young plants from cabbage root fly (see p. 372); use row cover or mesh to keep out other pests. Water regular broccoli routinely in dry weather. If water is restricted, one good soak 2–3 weeks before harvest is best. Mulch with compost after cutting the central heads to encourage sideshoot production. Sprouting broccoli may need staking over winter; mounding soil on stems during the growing season encourages extra rooting.

PROBLEMS Cabbage root fly, mealy cabbage aphids, cabbageworms, clubroot; flea beetle; birds. Regular broccoli may also get downy mildew.

Harvesting

Cut the central head of regular broccoli before flowers open. Expect 2–3 further pickings of small sideshoots. Snap off sprouting broccoli shoots when buds show but before they open. Regular picking encourages more shoots. Harvesting period can last up to 2 months.

Broccoli, 9-star

Brassica oleracea BRASSICACEAE

A short-term perennial producing small, cauliflowerlike heads. Sow seed in mid-spring. Thin to 6 in. (15 cm), then transplant into a rich, firm soil in early autumn. Leave 36 in. (90 cm) between plants. Each plant produces 6–9 heads to harvest in the spring. Pick all heads, even if inedible, to stop them from going to seed. Apply a medium-fertility soil improver each year after harvesting. Replace plants after 3 years. Control diseases and

---

Cultivar choice

Broccoli 'Packman' F1—uniform heads, early to mature; 'Rosalind'—purple-tinged heads; 'Small Miracle'—compact plants, can even grow in pots. Sprouting: 'De Cicco'.

Brussels sprouts 'Diabolo' F1; 'Trafalgar' F1—excellent for fall-winter harvest; 'Oliver' F1—early to mature; 'Rubine'—purple-red sprouts.

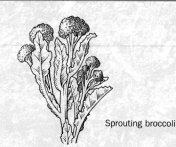
Sprouting broccoli

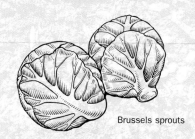
Brussels sprouts

pests, especially mealy cabbage aphid and cabbage whitefly, as they can spread to other brassica crops.

Brussels sprouts

Brassica oleracea BRASSICACEAE

A hardy, cold-weather crop for autumn and winter harvest from a spring sowing. Needs a long growing season, but crops over a long period. Mature plants are very hardy. Their wide spacing leaves room for interplanting (see p. 318) when young.

SEED TO HARVEST 20 weeks.
CROP DIVERSITY Early, mid, and late season; dwarf (14 in./35 cm) and tall (30 in./75 cm) cultivars. Modern cultivars produce tighter, more compact sprouts. Green and red cultivars available.
SITE Open, full sun, in firm soil.
SOIL TREATMENT Add a medium-fertility soil improver, or a low-fertility improver plus a general organic fertilizer, in the spring before planting—or plant after a nitrogen-fixing green manure crop. Mulch with grass mowings or apply a complete organic fertilizer mid–late July if plants are not growing vigorously.
IDEAL PH RANGE 6.5–8

Sowing
MINIMUM GERMINATION TEMPERATURE 45°F (7°C)
UNDER COVER For the earliest crop, sow in March in a seedbed or large cell trays. Harden off and plant 6 weeks after sowing.
OUTSIDE Sow from mid–March to mid–April, starting with the early cultivars. Sow thinly in rows, 1½ in. x 8 in. (4 cm x 20 cm), in a seedbed. Plant out from late spring to early summer.

Spacing
Transplant deeply (with the lowest leaf on the surface of the soil) to reduce the danger from cabbage root fly; firm around plants well after planting.
ROWS Space short cultivars 18 in. (45 cm) apart, tall cultivars 24–36 in. (60 cm–1 m) apart; allow 30 in. (75 cm) between rows for ease of picking. Closer plantings give more uniform maturity of smaller sprouts.
BLOCK PLANTING 18–30 in. (45–75 cm) depending on cultivar.

Plant care
Stake well on windy sites. Mound soil up stems as they grow. Remove diseased leaves.
PROBLEMS Flea beetle; mealy cabbage aphid; cabbage root fly (may also affect the sprouts); cabbage whitefly; birds; cabbage caterpillars; clubroot; downy mildew; brassica white rust.

Harvesting
Sprouts taste best after a frost. Harvest from the bottom of the stem, leaving those higher up to develop. To harvest a week's supply, pull a plant up and put it outside with its roots in a bucket of water to keep fresh. Can be frozen, but best eaten fresh.

Cabbage

Brassica oleracea BRASSICACEAE

A hardy crop that thrives in cool conditions and can be available year-round. Can grow large; choose varieties or change plant spacing for smaller heads.

SEED TO HARVEST 20 weeks.
CROP DIVERSITY Spring cabbage: sow under cover in autumn, eat in spring as loose leaves—"spring greens"—or once hearts have developed. **Summer and autumn cabbages:** sow in spring to mature in 4–6 months. May be ball- or pointed-headed.
Winter cabbages May be white or Dutch—large, very tight, white heads, harvested during autumn and winter from a spring sowing, storing for months once cut—or Savoy: bubble-textured, with dark green leaves, very hardy, and can stand into winter from a spring sowing. Crosses between these two types are also very hardy. Red cabbage, distinctive in looks and flavor, is usually grown to mature in late summer and autumn. It is often not as hardy as overwintering types but stores well if kept frost-free. **Mini-veg:** Some cultivars can also be grown as mini-veg.
SITE Open, sunny site. Tolerant of exposure. Some cabbages, such as smaller Savoys, look attractive in a flower garden.
SOIL TREATMENT Apply a medium-fertility soil improver, or a low-fertility soil improver plus a general organic fertilizer, before planting—or plant after a nitrogen-fixing green manure. Do not overfeed cabbages that will overwinter. If growth is too lush it may not survive frost.
IDEAL PH RANGE 6–8

Sowing See table below.
MINIMUM GERMINATION TEMPERATURE 45°F (7°C)
UNDER COVER For extra-early crops sow an early summer cultivar in cell packs or trays in February or March. Harden off and plant out as soon as the soil is workable. An early crop can also be grown under cover. Later sowings can be made in trays or cell packs under cover.
OUTSIDE Sow thinly in a seed-bed. Transplant 5–6 weeks later.

Plant care
Protect seedlings and young plants from cabbage root fly (see p. 372). Water transplants until established.

SOWING AND SPACING FOR CABBAGE

Type	Sow in	Spacing in rows & blocks*
Spring	September	12 in. (30 cm), or 4 x 12 in. (10 cm x 30 cm) thinning to 12 in. (30 cm); eat the thinnings as spring greens.
Early summer	February, March	14–18 in. (35–45 cm)
Summer	March	14–18 in. (35–45 cm)
Autumn	May	20 in. (50 cm)
Winter	May	20 in. (50 cm)

* Spacing can vary depending on variety choice and size of final head required (see also p. 316).

Spring cabbage

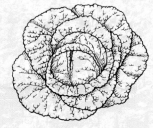
Savoy cabbage

Cultivar choice
Cabbage Spring: 'Golden Acre'—fast-maturing. Early summer: 'Charmant' F1. Summer: 'Tendersweet' F1—superior flavor; 'Dynamo' F1—compact heads for mini-cabbage. Autumn: 'Stein's Late Flat Dutch'; 'Danish Ballhead'. Red cabbage: 'Ruby Ball' F1—resistant to splitting.

PROBLEMS Cabbage root fly; mealy cabbage aphid; cabbageworms; flea beetle; clubroot; brassica white blister.

Harvesting

Cut as needed. Spring cabbages in fertile soil can give two crops: after cutting the head, make a crosscut on the remaining stalk, and several small cabbages will develop. Autumn and winter cabbages can be stored (see p. 334).

Cabbage, Chinese

Brassica rapa var. *pekinensis*
BRASSICACEAE

Chinese cabbage has an upright head and is dark to pale yellow green in color. A quick-growing and mild-flavored late summer and autumn crop, good stir-fried and raw in salads. Prone to bolting if growth is checked by transplanting or drought.

SEED TO HARVEST 8–10 weeks.
CROP DIVERSITY Heads may be dense or loose, short and barrel-shaped, or taller and cylindrical.
SITE Humus-rich, moisture-retentive soil. Tolerates some shade in summer. Good as a late-season crop under cover.
SOIL TREATMENT Apply a low-to medium-fertility soil improver before planting.
IDEAL pH RANGE 6.5–7

Sowing

MINIMUM GERMINATION TEMPERATURE 50°F (10°C)
UNDER COVER Sow in cell packs from May to August;

choose bolt-resistant cultivars to sow before midsummer. Harden off before transplanting. Late crops can be planted out under cover in September.
OUTSIDE Station-sow, or sow thinly from mid-June to August.

Spacing

ROWS 12 x 18 in. (30 x 45 cm)
BLOCK PLANTING 14 in. (35 cm)

Plant care

Water regularly in dry weather. Mulch with a low-fertility soil improver to retain moisture. Grow under row cover or fine netting if flea beetle is a problem.
PROBLEMS Flea beetle; caterpillars; slugs; clubroot.

Harvesting

Cut semimature or mature heads. Stumps may sprout new leaves.

Cardoon

Cynara cardunculus ASTERACEAE

A large perennial, closely related to globe artichokes, 4–5 ft. (1.2–1.5 m) tall with a 3-ft. (90-cm) spread. It is easy to grow, but produces a small crop for the space. Although a perennial, cardoon is grown as an annual in Zones 6 to 9, for eating. The stems, when blanched, are the edible parts. It is beautiful in flower in its second year if not harvested.

SEED TO HARVEST 34 weeks.
SITE Sunny, sheltered. Avoid heavy or wet soils. Can be grown in large pots and mixed borders.
SOIL TREATMENT Apply a high-fertility soil improver, plus a

low-fertility soil improver on dry soils. Can be grown on a compost trench (see p. 48).
IDEAL pH RANGE 6.5–7

Sowing

MINIMUM GERMINATION TEMPERATURE 55°F (13°C)
UNDER COVER In spring, sow 2–3 seeds in a 3½-in (9-cm) pot in a sandy compost in gentle heat. Thin to one seedling and harden off. Transplant after the last frost when plants have 3–4 leaves.
OUTSIDE Cardoons can be sown direct. Station-sow 3–4 seeds, 1 in. (2.5 cm) deep, in April.

Spacing

20 in. x 5 ft. (50 cm x 1.5 m)

Plant care

Cardoons need regular watering and a compost or hay mulch to produce large succulent stems. On a dry day in early autumn, blanch stems by pulling them into a bundle. Wear gloves. Tie with soft string. Wrap a collar of cardboard or thick newspaper around leaves to exclude light. Tie tightly. Stake the collar on exposed sites.
PROBLEMS Usually trouble-free. Aphids are an occasional nuisance but can be washed off using a jet of water from a hose.

Harvesting

Cardoons are ready after about a month of blanching, and will stand blanched until hard frosts. Lift plants with a fork, cut off the roots and outer leaves. If the weather turns cold, cut and store in a dark, frost-free place. Eat tender inner stalks and leaf midribs raw, braised, or dipped in batter and sautéed.

Carrot

Daucus carota APIACEAE

Carrots are not suited to all soils and can be a challenge to grow. Using a selection of cultivars, you can harvest carrots almost all year round. They can be closely spaced, giving a good yield from a relatively small area.

SEED TO HARVEST Early cultivars: 9 weeks. Main crop cultivars: 20 weeks.
CROP DIVERSITY Early cultivars are used for the quickest crops, sown throughout the season, and for crops under cover and in containers. Main crop cultivars have larger roots, for summer and autumn harvest; also suitable for winter storage. Root shape can be small and round, slender or broad, short or long, cylindrical or tapering. Most are orange, red, or yellow; purple and white cultivars are available, mainly through seed exchanges. Can be grown as mini-veg.
SITE Medium to light, stone-free soil in a sunny, open site. Shorter varieties grow well in containers. Early and late crops can be grown under cover.
SOIL TREATMENT No additional feeding is needed on reasonable soil, or on soil amended with compost for a previous crop. Mulching with a low-fertility soil improver in the previous winter can be beneficial. Do not sow immediately following a winter rye green manure crop.
IDEAL pH RANGE 6.5–7.5

Sowing

Germination is often slow and uneven. Improve by using

Cultivar choice
Chinese cabbage 'China Express'—good bolt resistance.

Cantaloupe see Melon, sweet

Cardoon 'Gigante'; 'Tenderheart'.
Carrot 'Danvers Half Long'; 'Nantes Half Long'—slim, cylindrical roots; 'Royal Chantenay'—sweet flavor, tapering roots; 'Little Finger'—perfect for containers; 'Thumbelina'—short, round roots, great for containers.

Chinese cabbage

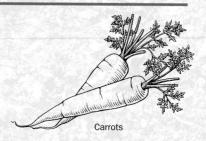

Carrots

pelleted seed (p. 314), or gel-sowing pre-germinated seed (see p. 110).

MINIMUM GERMINATION TEMPERATURE 45°F (7°C)

UNDER COVER Best sown direct as roots do not develop well if disturbed. Round-rooted cultivars may be started off in cell packs; short-rooted cultivars may be raised in biodegradable tubes, which are transplanted whole. For growing under cover, sow from February to August; February to June for transplanting outdoors.

OUTSIDE Start sowing early cultivars as soon as soil is warm enough, in February or March. Main crops can be sown from April to June. For winter storage, sow in late May or June so the roots are not too large when they are lifted in the autumn. Scatter seed thinly in shallow rows, ¾ in. (2 cm) deep, or station-sow 3–4 seeds per station.

Spacing

Early (quick) cultivars are often grown at wider spacing than main crops to aid rapid growth.

ROWS Sow thinly in rows 6 in. (15 cm) apart. Thin early carrots to 3 in. (7 cm). Thin medium-size main crop roots to 1½ in. (4 cm), up to 3 in. (7 cm) for larger roots.

BLOCK PLANTING Sow broadcast; thin to 3–6 in. (7–15 cm).

MINI-VEG ½ in. (1 cm) x 6 in. (15 cm).

Plant care

Keep weed-free when young. Water well in dry weather.

PROBLEMS Diseases and disorders are rare. The main pest is carrot rust fly: to avoid it, grow the crop under row cover or fine netting. Carrots sown in early June miss the first generation of fly attack and are large enough to survive a second-generation attack. Carrot rust fly may be attracted by the scent of crushed carrot foliage, so sow thinly to minimize the need for thinning. Thin in the evening, not in bright sun when carrot rust flies will be active. Onions may offer protection. Grow 4 rows of onions for every row of carrots.

Harvesting

Pull roots while young. Main crop roots may be left in the ground over winter and dug as required. In cold areas protect with a straw mulch. Storage in the ground is not advisable in heavy soils or where carrot fly is a problem. Lift October–November for storage.

Cauliflower

Brassica oleracea BRASSICACEAE

Cauliflowers can be difficult to grow successfully. They need moisture throughout the growing season, so autumn- and spring-heading types are easier to cultivate. Most are large plants that can be in the ground for up to a year. For small gardens, early summer and mini-cauliflowers are best.

SEED TO HARVEST Summer and autumn cauliflowers—16 weeks. Winter cauliflower—40 weeks. Mini-veg—15 weeks.

CROP DIVERSITY A wide range of cultivars is available, suited to different growing and producing seasons from early summer to winter. Most are white, but can also be orange, green, and purple-headed. Suitable for mini-veg.

SITE Open, sunny site; avoid frost. Fertile, moisture-retentive soil.

SOIL TREATMENT Apply a medium-fertility soil improver, or a low-fertility soil improver plus a general organic fertilizer, before planting—or plant after a nitrogen-fixing green manure.

IDEAL pH RANGE 6.5–8

Sowing

Best sown in cell packs or pots to reduce transplanting check. For sowing times and spacings, see the table below. Harden off and transplant as soon as possible—around 6 weeks after sowing. Can also be sown outdoors in a seedbed, leaving at least 2 in. (5 cm) between seedlings.

MINIMUM GERMINATION TEMPERATURE 45°F (7°C)

Spacing

See table below.

Plant care

Cauliflowers resent any check to growth. Mulch, and water in dry weather to keep growth active. Firm around plants in frosty or windy conditions. Protect heads against frosts, rain, and heavy dew in autumn by tying up leaves. This will also keep curds white. Modern varieties often have leaves that naturally protect the heads.

PROBLEMS Clubroot (see p. 374). Protect against cabbage root fly, whitefly, and caterpillars with a fine mesh cover. Small, premature, and deformed heads are usually the result of a check to growth, often by transplanting or drought. "Whiptail" (narrow leaves, curds fail to develop) is

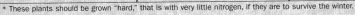

SOWING TIMES AND SPACINGS FOR CAULIFLOWER

Harvest	Sow indoors	Sow outdoors	Spacing in rows	Spacing in blocks
Early summer	Early October; early February		18 in. (45 cm) x 24 in. (60 cm)	21 in. (53 cm)
Late summer	March	March (sheltered sites only)	18 in. (45 cm) x 24 in. (60 cm)	21 in. (53 cm)
Early autumn	Late April	Late April	22 in. (50 cm) x 24 in. (60 cm)	22 in. (55 cm)
Autumn	Mid-May	Late June	24 in. (60 cm) x 26 in. (65 cm)	25 in. (63 cm)
Winter, frost-free areas only		Late May	28 in. (70 cm) each way	28 in. (70 cm)
Spring *		Late May	24 in. (60 cm) x 26 in. (65 cm)	25 in. (63 cm)
Mini-cauliflowers	April to early July	April to early July	4 in. (10 cm) x 9 in. (23 cm)	5 in. (12.5 cm)

* These plants should be grown "hard," that is with very little nitrogen, if they are to survive the winter.

Cauliflower

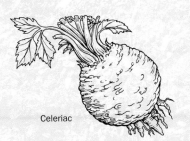

Celeriac

Cultivar choice
Cauliflower 'All the Year Round'—a classic, dependable; 'Fremont' F1; 'Snow Crown' F1—matures quickly for early harvest; 'Violet Queen' F1—rich purple heads; 'Romanesco'—pointed yellow-green heads.

caused by boron deficiency, usually when soil is too acid.

Harvesting

Select tight, small-curded heads. Curds starting to separate or turn yellow or brown are a sign of overmaturity. Mini-cauliflowers will not stay in good condition for long. Cauliflowers keep for a week in the fridge, or hang upside down for up to 3 weeks in a cool, dark shed—occasionally mist with a fine water spray.

Celeriac

Apium graveolens var. *rapaceum*
APIACEAE

Celeriac produces a large, celery-flavored "bulb"—a swollen stem. Leaves can also be used to season dishes. A close relative of celery. Easier to grow, though it still needs a long season of unchecked growth to grow well.

SEED TO HARVEST 26 weeks.
CROP DIVERSITY There is little variation. Some cultivars are less prone to discolor when cooked.
SITE Needs a fertile, moisture-retentive soil to do well. Will grow in sun or semi-shade.
SOIL TREATMENT Apply a medium- to high-fertility soil improver, or a low-fertility soil improver with a nitrogen-rich organic fertilizer.
IDEAL pH RANGE 6.5–7.5

Sowing

MINIMUM GERMINATION TEMPERATURE Germinates best at 50–66°F (10–19°C)
UNDER COVER Sow in gentle heat (65°F/18°C) in February

and March, or April and May if no heat available. Sow in trays or cell packs, thinning or transplanting into individual pots when large enough to handle. Harden off before planting out after the last frost. Take care not to bury the crown of the plant.

Spacing

12–15 in. (30–38 cm) each way.

Plant care

Water in dry spells. Mulch to retain soil moisture. From midsummer onward, remove lower leaves to expose the crown.
PROBLEMS May suffer from the same pests and diseases as celery, but is generally trouble-free.

Harvesting

Harvest from late summer to the following spring, starting when bulbs are large enough. Store in the ground if possible, covering with dry straw for protection. Can be lifted and stored indoors, but quality will deteriorate.

Celery

Apium graveolens APIACEAE

Celery produces crisp, crunchy, succulent stems. Traditional trench celery is quite demanding of soil conditions and requires attention over a long growing season. Self-blanching celery is less labor-intensive and easier to grow but is not as hardy, nor so delicate in texture or flavor.

SEED TO HARVEST Self-blanching and green celery—11–16 weeks. Trench celery—9 months.
CROP DIVERSITY Trench celery

is a traditional crop for late autumn with white, pink, or red stems that are blanched before use. Self-blanching cultivars have creamy yellow stems, paler when grown in a block. American green cultivars have green stems that are not blanched.
SITE Must have fertile, moisture-retentive, well-drained soil. Prefers an open site, but tolerates some shade. Grows well in deep containers.
SOIL TREATMENT Apply a high-fertility soil improver, or one of low- to medium fertility with a nitrogen-rich organic fertilizer. For trench celery, in early spring dig a trench 15–18 in. (38–45 cm) wide, 12 in. (30 cm) deep. Mix soil improvers, as above, into the soil removed, then fill in the trench to a depth of 3–4 in. (7.5–10 cm). Use the remaining soil to blanch the celery as it grows. Trenches should be 4 ft. (1.2 m) apart. Apply a general organic fertilizer to the trench before planting if needed.
IDEAL pH RANGE 6.5–7.5

Sowing

MINIMUM GERMINATION TEMPERATURE Germinates best at 50–66°F (10–19°C).
UNDER COVER Sow in trays or cell packs in gentle heat in March and early April, no more than 10 weeks before the last frost. Sow on the surface of the compost, or cover only lightly. Germination can be slow and erratic. Gel sowing (see p. 110) can improve it. Transplant into biodegradable pots. Thin cells to one seedling as early as possible. Plant out when conditions are warm enough. Plants may bolt if subjected to temperatures below

50°F (10°C) for more than 12 hours when young. Protect with cloches if necessary. If seedlings are growing fast and the weather is unfavorable for planting out, snip them down to 3 in. (8 cm) tall with scissors to slow growth. Keep the plants under cover until outdoor conditions are suitable.
MULTI-SOWING Self-blanching celery only. Sow 6–8 seeds per cell, thinning to 2–3.

Spacing

ROWS Trench celery—12–18 in. (30–45 cm) between plants, 4 ft. (1.2 m) between trenches.
BLOCK PLANTING For self-blanching celery: 6–12 in. (15–30 cm). Closer spacing gives a high yield of more slender stems.
MULTI-SOWING Self-blanching celery only: 8 in. (20 cm).

Plant care

Water frequently and regularly in the growing season. Remove discolored outer leaves. Blanch trench celery stems (see Cardoon) once plants are 12 in. (30 cm) tall. Surround a block of mature, self-blanching plants with straw to blanch outer rows.
PROBLEMS Celery crown rot; celery leaf miner; slugs; celery leaf spot; calcium deficiency caused by irregular water supply.

Harvesting

Harvest trench celery in the autumn, about 9–10 weeks after blanching begins. Blanched celery will stand in the ground for about a month in good condition, but is a magnet for slugs. Harvest self-blanching celery July–September. Celery is not totally hardy and will not survive prolonged frosts.

Cultivar choice
Celeriac 'Brilliant'—flavorful, early-maturing, 'Diamant'—stores well.
Celery Trench: 'Giant Red'—heirloom cultivar; 'Tall Utah 52-70R Improved'—dependable producer; 'Ventura'—extra-vigorous.
Self-blanching: 'Golden Self-Blanching'.

Celery

When severe cold is forecast, lift plants and store in a cellar or in cool, moist sand. Can be lifted and heeled in in a dark coldframe. Keeps for a week in the fridge.

Chard

Beta vulgaris Cicla Group
CHENOPODIACEAE

Easy-to-grow beet relative also called Swiss chard, grown for its stems and leaves. It produces for many months. Leaves have thick, often beautifully colored midribs. The plant is attractive enough for an ornamental plot.

SEED TO HARVEST 8–12 weeks.
CROP DIVERSITY Chard typically has white midribs but some have midribs in ruby-red or a rainbow of colors.
SITE Will tolerate salt-laden winds (useful for seaside gardens) and some shade. A good winter crop in an unheated hoop house or greenhouse.
SOIL TREATMENT Apply a low-fertility soil improver if soil was amended with compost for a previous crop. Otherwise use a medium-fertility improver, or a low-fertility material with a nitrogen-rich organic fertilizer.
IDEAL pH RANGE 6.5–7.5

Sowing
MINIMUM GERMINATION TEMPERATURE 47°F (8°C)
UNDER COVER Sow individual seeds in cell packs during March and April. The seeds are "multi-germed," with several seedlings emerging from one seed. Thin to the strongest seedling, or

plant as a clump for cutting as a seedling crop. Harden off before planting outside. For a winter crop under cover, sow in August; for a seedling cutting crop, broadcast thinly in early autumn.
OUTSIDE Station-sow about half a thumb deep in March and April to produce in summer and autumn. Sow in July and August to produce over winter and the following spring.

Spacing
ROWS 9 x 18 in. (23 x 45 cm).
BLOCK PLANTING 12 in. (30 cm).

Plant care
Water if necessary in dry weather. Mulch to retain moisture. Use a medium-fertility soil improver if growth needs a boost. Over-wintered crops can stand some winters unprotected but give a finer crop with the protection of cloches or row cover.
PROBLEMS Beet leaf miner.

Harvesting
Pick leaves from the outside as soon as they are big enough. Rejuvenate older plants if leaves have become coarse by cutting all the leaves off just above the soil. Cutting crops are soon ready; take the first cut when about 2 in. (5 cm) tall. Allow to grow slightly taller before the next cut.

Chervil, turnip-rooted

Chaerophyllum bulbosum
APIACEAE

An unusual root vegetable; although very slow to germinate,

it is easy to grow.
SITE Sunny, open, fertile soil.
SOIL TREATMENT Apply a medium-fertility soil improver, or grow on land amended with compost for a previous crop.
IDEAL pH RANGE 6.5–7.5

Sowing
Sow outside as it needs a period of cold for germination. Sow in late summer–early autumn, covering seed lightly. Seeds will not germinate until spring.
GROWING IN ROWS 6–8 in. x 12 in. (15–20 cm x 30 cm).
BLOCK PLANTING 8 in. (20 cm).

Plant care
Once germinated, plants have a relatively short growing season; do not let them suffer growth checks. Water regularly in dry conditions, and keep weed-free.
PROBLEMS Usually trouble-free.

Harvesting
When leaves die back after mid-summer, roots are nearly mature. Start to use when leaves are quite withered, twisting off remaining leaves. Roots are said to improve in quality if left in the ground for a few weeks. Dig as required on light, well-drained soils. Otherwise, lift and store in damp leaf mold or sand. Eat roots boiled.

Chicory

Cichorium intybus ASTERACEAE

A hardy perennial, usually grown as an annual. Chicories have a distinctive, slightly bitter taste and are a useful, colorful salad crop for the winter. Their leaves come in a wide range of shapes

and colors; some produce hearts, and some can be forced or blanched to reduce bitterness. Good ornamentals in containers.

SEED TO HARVEST Variable.
CROP DIVERSITY Witloof chicory is grown primarily for forcing. Roots are lifted and forced in the dark in winter to produce blanched plump shoots, knows as chicons (called Belgian endive). Red chicory (also known as radicchio) has red or variegated leaves. Some cultivars have a compact heart, others remain loose-leaved; some can be forced. Individual leaves can also be picked. The best color develops with shortening days and cool nights, though new cultivars are naturally red. Not always hardy in cold winters. Cutting chicory produces small rosettes of leaves for cutting. Sugarloaf chicories look rather like large, green cos lettuce when mature, and are harvested in autumn. Plants are drought-resistant once established, and withstand light frosts. Can be grown as a seedling cutting crop.
SITE Avoid very light or heavy soils. Tolerate some shade. Witloof chicories need deep soil to produce good roots for forcing. Grow nonforcing types in a cool hoop house or green-house for early and late crops, and over winter. Chicories are decorative enough for containers or at the front of a border.
SOIL TREATMENT None needed on most soils, especially on soil improved for a previous crop.
IDEAL pH RANGE 5.5–7.5

Sowing
See table on p. 348.

Chicory "chicons"

MINIMUM GERMINATION TEMPERATURE 50°F (10°C). Germination rates are usually high; use thinnings for salads.

Plant care

Water until established in dry weather, then should survive dry conditions without watering. May need row cover or cloches if hard frosts are forecast. Dig roots to start blanching suitable varieties in late autumn and winter. PROBLEMS Usually trouble-free. Slugs can be a problem on forced and blanched chicories.

Harvesting

FORCED CHICORY Cut chicons when tips show through soil (if blanched with soil) or 4–5 in. (10–13 cm) tall under cover. Cut 1 in. (2.5 cm) above the neck. Roots may grow another shoot. SUGARLOAF Cut when large enough. The stump may resprout. RED CHICORY Cut once hearts form, leaving stumps to resprout,

or pick individual leaves. Quite frost hardy; cover with a cloche to harvest over winter. Harvest seedling cutting chicory when about 1 in. (2.5 cm) tall.

Corn salad

Valerianella locusta
VALERIANACEAE

Small, hardy annual salad plant also known as lamb's lettuce or mache, with a mild flavor. Usually grown for autumn and winter use, it can be grown in a cool greenhouse or hoop house over winter. The large-leaved English or Dutch type has more elongated leaves. The French type is a more compact rosette of a plant with smaller leaves. Extremely hardy, corn salad grows almost anywhere; no special soil treatment is required and it is generally trouble-free. Sow it in rows, or broadcast in

wide rows; thin to 4–6 in. (10–15 cm) each way. Sow in March and April for summer cropping; July and August for winter use; or August and September for winter production under cover.

Pick individual leaves when large enough, or cut whole plants. Good for interplanting. Corn salad will self-sow freely in the garden if you let it flower. Seedlings can be transplanted.

Cress, upland

Barbarea verna BRASSICACEAE

A hardy biennial with a strong watercress flavor. Fast-growing, it can be harvested almost all year. Does best on more fertile soils. Summer crops need light shade. A useful winter salad grown under cover; suits an ornamental bed. Will self-seed if left to flower. Apply a medium-fertility soil

improver if soil has not been improved for a previous crop. Sow in cell packs, or direct. Sow in July and August for cropping winter to spring; in August for winter cropping under cover; March–June for summer cropping. Row spacing: 6 x 8 in. (15 x 20 cm); block planting 6 in. (15 cm). Water in dry spells. Flea beetle may be a problem. Start picking individual leaves when they are large enough. Will produce over a long period.

Cucumbers and gherkins

Cucumis sativus CUCURBITACEAE

Cucumbers are tender annual, trailing plants, grown outdoors or under cover for summer cropping. Gherkins are short-fruited types, harvested young and usually pickled.

SOWING TIMES AND SPACING FOR CHICORY

Chicory type	Crop type	Sowing time	Location	Final spacing in rows
Witloof and other forcing types	Roots for forcing	Mid-June to early July	Outside	8 x 12 in. (20 x 30 cm)
Sugarloaf	For mature heads in autumn	June and July	Outside	10 x 12 in. (25 x 30 cm)
Sugarloaf	For smaller heads, or semimature cutting crop over winter	July and August	In cell packs, to transplant into soil beds or containers under cover	10 x 12 in. (25 x 30 cm)
Sugarloaf	Seedling cutting crop	January and February, September	Under cover	Sow broadcast, or in bands 6–8 in. (15–20 cm) wide, 8 in. (20 cm) apart
Sugarloaf	Seedling cutting crop	March–August (midsummer crops may be rather tough)	Outside	Sow broadcast in patches
Red chicory, early cultivars	Leaves and hearts in summer	Late April and May	Outside, or in cell packs under cover	8–14 in. (20–35 cm)
Red chicory	Leaves and hearts in autumn	June and early July	Outside	8–14 in. (20–35 cm)
Red chicory	Protected winter crop	August	In cell packs; transplant under cover	8–14 in. (20–35 cm)

Cultivar choice
Chili peppers *see* Peppers
Corn *see* Sweet corn

Corn salad 'D'Etampes'; 'Valgros'—large leaves; 'Verte de Cambrai'; 'Vit'–good for spring, fall, or overwintering.

Corn salad

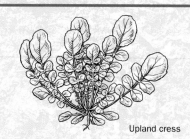
Upland cress

SEED TO HARVEST 12 weeks.
CROP DIVERSITY Outdoor cucumbers: Traditional cultivars are rough, spiny fruits, 4–6 in. (10–15 cm) long; newer cultivars (usually F1 hybrids) have smoother skins and are longer. There are trailing and bushy types of outdoor cucumber, often needing to be pollinated to set fruit. Apple cucumbers are ridge types with round, yellow fruits. Grow them outdoors, in a hoop house or under cloches. European or greenhouse cucumbers have long, smooth fruits, setting without pollination. They become bitter if pollinated, in fact, so all-female cultivars have been bred to avoid pollination. They are for growing under cover.
SITE Grow outdoor crops in a warm, sheltered site, with fertile, moisture-retentive soil. Outdoor types need average temperatures around 64–86°F (18–30°C) and are damaged below 50°F (10°C), tolerating some shade in summer. Greenhouse cultivars need high humidity and night temperatures of at least 68°F (20°C). They can be grown in border soil, large containers, growing bags, or on straw bales. Cucumbers can be an unusual ornamental feature if grown up a fence or archway.
SOIL TREATMENT Apply a low- to medium-fertility soil improver before planting, or grow on a compost trench (see p. 48). On heavy soils, mound up the earth before planting on the mound.
IDEAL PH RANGE 5.5–7

Sowing

Sow under cover in a heated propagator or similar to maintain a temperature of at least 68°F (20°C) until the seeds germinate.

Seedlings must be kept where the night temperature is at least 60°F (16°C) for outdoor cultivars, and 68°F (20°C) for greenhouse cultivars. Use cell packs or bio-degradable pots to avoid disturbing the roots. Sow seeds on their side at a depth of ½ in. (1.5 cm). Start outdoor crops May–June, no more than a month before the last frost is expected. Sow in April for a greenhouse/hoop house crop, or in May if no additional heat can be supplied. Harden off before transplanting outside; outdoor plants may need cloches after planting to establish well. When planting, leave the rootball slightly above the soil surface to reduce risk of stem rot.
MINIMUM GERMINATION TEMPERATURE 68°F (20°C)

Spacing

ROWS Trellised: 18 x 39 in. (45 x 100 cm). Grown on the ground: 24–30 in. (60–75 cm) x 4–5 ft. (1.3–1.6 m), depending on the cultivar.
BLOCK PLANTING About 30 in. (75 cm) depending on cultivar.

Plant care

Train trailing types up netting, wires, canes, or strings; nip out the growing point when plants reach the top of the support. Ridge types will also grow on the ground; pinch out the growing point when 5–6 leaves have formed to encourage bushy growth. Water regularly throughout the growing season, and mulch plants grown on the flat with straw to keep fruit clean. Remove any male flowers appearing on greenhouse cucumbers. All-female types may produce male flowers,

particularly if stressed—take these off at once. Do not remove male flowers from ridge cucumbers or gherkins. Check the seed packet for which cucumber type you have.
PROBLEMS Slugs and aphids (mainly outdoors); red spider mite; cucumber beetles; powdery mildew; cucumber mosaic virus; stem rots.

Harvesting

Cut fruits once large enough— check regularly for any hidden fruits. Best kept in a cool room, wrapped in plastic film, rather than a fridge. They pickle well.

Eggplant

Solanum melongena SOLANACEAE

This heat-loving annual crop thrives in warm-summer areas. Can also be grown inside in cooler climates, though it must be sown indoors. Plants are relatively compact and bushy.

SEED TO HARVEST 16–24 weeks.
CROP DIVERSITY Most cultivars have purple fruits, and may be round, long, or oval. Some have egglike, white fruits.
SITE Well-drained, fertile soil. Grow in a very warm, sheltered site, or in a cool hoop house or greenhouse. Eggplants need temperatures of 75–86°F (25–30°C) for good production. Growth is stalled below 68°F (20°C). Eggplants also do well in containers, which can stand outside in good weather.
SOIL TREATMENT Apply a medium-fertility soil improver before planting into soil. In pots,

use a rich multipurpose medium.
IDEAL PH RANGE 6.5

Sowing

MINIMUM GERMINATION TEMPERATURE 70°F (21°C). Sow under cover in gentle heat from mid–February to March. When the leaves are large enough to handle, prick out into 4-in. (10-cm) pots, and keep at 60–64°F (16–18°C). When first flowers appear, plant in a soil bed under cover or into 8-in. (20-cm) pots. Put plants outside only when there is little risk of frosts.

Spacing

16–18 in. (40–45 cm) each way.

Plant care

Tall plants may need a stake for support. For good-size fruits, allow only 4 to 6 to grow on a plant. Keep well watered. Feed container plants with a high-potash organic liquid feed once fruits have started to set.
PROBLEMS Red spider mite and whitefly; aphids.

Harvesting

Harvest once required size is reached, when skin is still shiny.

Endive

Cichorium endivia ASTERACEAE

A slightly bitter-tasting salad vegetable related to dandelions and chicory. It is easy to grow and can be harvested most of the year. It withstands a light frost, but a winter crop needs protection. Eat as a seedling crop, picked as loose leaves, or as blanched, mature heads.

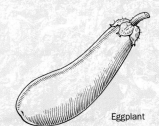

Eggplant

Fares better than lettuce in the low light levels of winter. Suitable for containers.

SEED TO HARVEST 7–13 weeks for mature heads. Quicker for seedling and looseleaf harvest.
CROP DIVERSITY There are two types. Escarole, also called Batavian endive, is a broad-leaved, hardy, upright plant, good for winter cropping. Frisee or curled endives are short, squat plants with frizzy leaves, more heat-tolerant and mostly used for summer and autumn crops.
SITE Not fussy, but winter crops need a well-drained, sheltered site on relatively infertile soil. Light shade tolerated in summer. The Frisee types are very attractive. A useful winter crop in a cool greenhouse or hoop house.
SOIL TREATMENT None needed where soil has been improved for a previous crop. Otherwise, apply a low-fertility soil improver.
IDEAL pH RANGE 5.5–7.5

Sowing

If temperatures fall below 40°F (5°C) for 20 days or more, then endive seedlings will bolt.
MINIMUM GERMINATION TEMPERATURE 68°F (20°C)
UNDER COVER Sow in April for growing under cover, May for transplanting outdoors. Best raised in cell packs for transplanting. Sow again in autumn for a protected winter crop.
OUTSIDE Sow June–early July in shallow rows for autumn harvest. Sow in August for a winter crop (protected under cloches or in frames). Sow April–September for harvest as a seedling crop, or as young leaves. Grow early and late sowings under cloches

or in an unheated hoop house or greenhouse.

Spacing
ROWS 12 x 14 in. (30 x 35 cm)
BLOCK PLANTING 12 in. (30 cm)

Plant care
Water in dry weather. Use cloches in cold weather. Mature plants can be blanched (p. 332).
PROBLEMS Slugs; aphids. Basal rots can be a problem in winter—grow in well-drained soil, and keep leaves dry.

Harvesting
Cut seedling crop when 4–6 in. (10–15 cm) tall. Pick leaves as needed or when of convenient size. Cut mature heads, blanched if preferred. Cut stems may regrow to provide another crop of leaves.

Florence fennel

Foeniculum vulgare var. *dulce*
APIACEAE

An unusual vegetable that can be difficult to grow well. The edible part is the licorice-flavored, swollen, white base of the leaf stalk. The fine, feathery leaves are also delicious. Its short growing season makes fennel, or finocchio, a useful catch crop, though it tends to bolt if growth is checked by drought or cold. It can withstand light frost.

SEED TO HARVEST 10–15 weeks.
CROP DIVERSITY Modern cultivars, resistant to bolting, are available for earlier sowing.
SITE Warm and sunny, with a well-drained, moisture-retentive

soil. Avoid heavy soils. Pretty enough to grow in a flower garden. Suitable for growing in a cool hoop house or greenhouse for an early or late crop.
SOIL TREATMENT Enjoys soil amended with compost for a previous crop. Add a low-fertility soil improver before planting.
IDEAL pH RANGE 5.5–7.5

Sowing
MINIMUM GERMINATION TEMPERATURE 59°F (15°C)
UNDER COVER Resents root disturbance so cell packs or bio-degradable pots are preferable to trays. Sow April–July, using bolt-resistant cultivars before mid-June. Sow mid-July–early August for a late crop to grow under cover. Thin to one seedling per cell; harden off before transplanting when they have 3–4 true leaves.
OUTSIDE Sow from May to July using bolt-resistant varieties before mid-June. Station-sow in pinches ½ in. (1 cm) deep at 2-week intervals for a succession of crops until the first frosts.

Spacing
ROWS 12 x 12 in. (30 x 30 cm)
BLOCK PLANTING 12 x 12 in. (30 x 30 cm)
MULTISOWING Fennel is sometimes eaten as a seedling crop, stir-fried with other edible greens. When growing seedling fennel, station-sow at 2 in. (5 cm) by 12 in. (30 cm) and do not thin.

Plant care
Early and late sowings may require frost protection. Mulch with a low-fertility soil improver. Water regularly for maximum tenderness and size, and to avoid the plants bolting. When bulbs

are egg-size, mound up soil to one-half their height to keep them white and succulent.
PROBLEMS Slugs; bolting. Grow bolt-resistant varieties; do not transplant; water regularly.

Harvesting
Cut bulbs just above ground level when the size of a flattened tennis ball. Cut stems often grow a second crop of tasty leaves for use in salads. Fennel keeps for 2 weeks or more in the fridge, but tends to shrivel if stored too long.

Garlic

Allium sativum ALLIACEAE

An easy, surprisingly hardy crop that needs a long growing period to produce well but takes up little space in the yard. Garlic is grown from cloves rather than seed. Buy garlic specifically for planting, rather than that sold for eating. The latter may carry diseases and is unlikely to be a cultivar adapted to your particular region. However, garlic will adapt to the local day length and temperature over the years, so you can develop your own strain by saving cloves to plant (from healthy plants only).

PLANTING TO HARVEST 16–36 weeks. Not raised from seed.
CROP DIVERSITY The diversity can be bewildering, including pink-purple and white-skinned cultivars. Some are short-dormancy, storing only until Christmas. These tend to produce larger cloves and bulbs than the long-dormancy cultivars, which should keep until the following spring or later. Some produce

---

Cultivar choice
Fava beans see *Beans, broad*

Florence fennel 'Fino', 'Perfection'—resists bolting.
Garlic Softneck: 'Inchelium Red'—mild flavor; 'Polish Softneck'—very hardy, large cloves, strong flavor; 'Western Rose'—stores well. Hardneck: 'German Extra-Hardy'—very hardy, stores well; 'Siberian'—very cold-hardy; 'Spanish Roja'—popular heirloom cultivar.

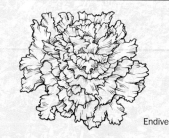
Endive

Florence fennel

well from a spring planting, but most must be planted in autumn. Most garlic sold in grocery stores is soft-necked and does not flower. This makes it ideal for braiding. Hard-necked garlic—also known as rocambole—bears a flowerhead, but this does not detract from production.
SITE Open situation. Garlic is usually grown over winter, so it needs a soil that does not become waterlogged. It can easily be tucked into an ornamental garden and can also be grown in containers.
SOIL TREATMENT Soil improved for a previous crop is ideal. Do not plant in freshly manured soil.
IDEAL pH RANGE 6–7.5

Planting
Divide bulbs into cloves immediately before planting. To produce good-size bulbs, most cultivars need 1–2 months when the soil is below 50°F (10°C), so it is best planted in late autumn. Some cultivars can be planted in February. Plant cloves, pointed end up, into position with the tip 1–4 in. (2.5–10 cm) below the soil surface—more shallowly in heavier soil. Where soil is likely to be very wet over winter, plant in pots filled with a free-draining, loam-based medium and stand outside.

Spacing
ROWS 3–4 in. x 10–12 in. (7.5–10 cm x 25–30 cm)
BLOCK PLANTING 7 in. (18 cm)

Plant care
Water in spring if dry. To improve yields of stiff-stemmed garlic, cut back the flowering stem by one-half 2–3 weeks before harvest.

PROBLEMS Onion white rot; onion rust.

Harvesting
Harvest in July or August once leaves begin to turn yellow. Dig up carefully before leaves have died back to keep the skin around the bulb intact. Leave to dry in the open, or in a cool, dry shed. Lay out on a slatted shelf or hang up. Once dry, braid into ropes or tie in bunches.

Good King Henry

Chenopodium bonus-henricus
CHENOPODIACEAE

An old-fashioned perennial salad plant, growing 36 in. (90 cm) tall. It prefers a moist soil and tolerates some shade. Sow in spring with 16 in. (40 cm) between plants. Harvest young leaves and flowering shoots in the second year. Ready early in the year. Divide plants every 2 to 3 years.

Hamburg parsley

Petroselinum crispum var. *tuberosum*
APIACEAE

Grown for its white, parsniplike roots, harvested in late autumn and winter. The leaves can be used for parsley flavoring.

SEED TO HARVEST 30 weeks.
SITE Moisture-retentive soil where it can root deeply. Can be grown in light shade.
SOIL TREATMENT None needed where soil was improved for a previous crop. Benefits from a

low-fertility soil improver applied as a mulch over the previous winter.
IDEAL pH RANGE 6.5–7

Sowing
MINIMUM GERMINATION TEMPERATURE 45°F (7°C)
UNDER COVER Not appropriate.
OUTSIDE Sow March–April in rows ½ in. (1 cm) deep. Germination can be slow. Cover with cloches or clear plastic to speed it up. Can also be sown in July for an early crop the next year.

Spacing
ROWS 8 x 12 in. (20 x 30 cm)
BLOCK PLANTING 8 in. (20 cm)

Plant care
Keep weed-free when young—sowing a few quick-germinating radishes will mark the row until the parsley shows. Mulch established plants for moisture retention and weed control. Cover crops left in ground over winter with straw.
PROBLEMS Parsnip canker.

Harvesting
Dig from early autumn through to the following early spring. Flavor is better if stored in the ground, rather than lifted for indoor storage.

Kale

Brassica oleracea Acephala Group
BRASSICACEAE

Kale is one of the hardiest winter vegetables, easy to grow, and tolerant of a range of adverse conditions. Best eaten

after frost early in the year when fresh crops are scarce, but can be available from late summer on. Useful for growing after an early crop such as broad beans or early peas.

SEED TO HARVEST 7 weeks for the quickest types. Will stand in good condition for a long time, giving a long harvest period.
CROP DIVERSITY Kales range in height from 12 in. (30 cm) to 3 ft. (90 cm) or more. Leaves may be curly, plain, ragged, fringed, or blistered, in plain green, purple, or both.
SITE Does better in poorer soils than other brassicas. Does not need to grow into a large plant to produce a useful crop. Will tolerate exposed sites and some shade, but not poorly drained soil.
SOIL TREATMENT Apply a medium-fertility soil improver, or a low-fertility soil improver plus a general organic fertilizer—or plant after a nitrogen-fixing green manure. Do not make soil too rich; the resulting lush late growth may not be frost hardy.
IDEAL pH RANGE 6.5–7.5

Sowing
MINIMUM GERMINATION TEMPERATURE 45°F (7°C)
UNDER COVER Sow in trays or cell packs in February for a summer crop, May for a winter crop.
OUTSIDE Sow thinly in a seedbed in April–May, in shallow rows. Transplant 6–8 weeks later. Siberian kale, also known as Hanover salad, may be sown direct as late as July or early August. Station-sow 3–4 seeds and thin to 1 seedling when large enough.

Garlic

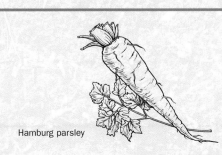
Hamburg parsley

Spacing

Dwarf cultivars: 12–18 in. (30–45 cm). Tall cultivars: 24–30 in. (60–75 cm). Some taller cultivars can be spaced only 18 in. (45 cm) apart if harvested when young.

Plant care

Water seedlings until established. **PROBLEMS** Cabbageworms; cabbage whitefly; cabbage root fly; mealy cabbage aphid; clubroot.

Harvesting

Pick leaves as needed from mature plants, or from young plants for a quicker harvest. Often tastier after a hard frost.

Kohlrabi

Brassica oleracea Gongylodes Group BRASSICACEAE

A small, fast-growing member of the brassica family, with an unusual appearance. The spherical swollen stems, sitting just above ground level, are picked at tennis-ball size. Can be sown and harvested almost all year round. Makes a good catch crop or an interesting addition to an ornamental garden. Can be grown in containers.

SEED TO HARVEST 5–9 weeks.
CROP DIVERSITY Green cultivars are usually grown for spring and summer crops, the hardier purple cultivars for autumn and winter use. New hybrid cultivars grow larger without becoming woody.
SITE Open. Suitable for early and late production under cover.

SOIL TREATMENT Apply a low-fertility soil improver or one of medium fertility on poor soils.
IDEAL pH RANGE 6–7

Sowing

Sow every few weeks for a regular supply as kohlrabi will not stand in an edible condition for long once ready.
MINIMUM GERMINATION TEMPERATURE 50°F (10°)
UNDER COVER Sow in cell packs from late February through to August. Plant out when no more than 2 in. (5 cm) high. Sow in September to grow under cover.
OUTSIDE Sow direct March–August. Use the hardier purple varieties for later sowings.

Spacing

ROWS 7 x 12 in. (18 x 30 cm)
BLOCK PLANTING 10 in. (25 cm)

Plant care

Water in dry weather. Kohlrabi is fast-growing and tends to be problem-free—though it is susceptible to the same pests and diseases as other brassica plants.
PROBLEMS Flea beetle, cabbage root fly; mealy cabbage aphids; clubroot.

Harvesting

Quick to mature, so check and harvest regularly. Cut older varieties when no larger than a tennis ball. Modern kohlrabi varieties can grow to 4 in. (10 cm) in diameter without getting woody. Late crops can be left in the ground unless heavy frost is forecast, or store for up to 2 months in boxes of moist sand. Has a fresh, crisp, juicy taste eaten raw or lightly cooked.

Komatsuna

Brassica rapa var. *perviridis* or var. *komatsuna* BRASSICACEAE

This versatile, leafy Japanese crop, also known as mustard spinach, has a milder "bite" than the Chinese mustards, but more flavor than the cabbages. It can be sown almost all year round and eaten at any stage from seedling to large plant. Mature plants can be 7 in. (18 cm) tall by 20 in. (50 cm) wide. It can be sown from early spring to autumn outdoors, from mid-winter to late autumn under cover. Soil conditions and pest and disease problems are the same as for Chinese cabbages.

Leeks

Allium porrum ALLIACEAE

A hardy crop for an autumn and winter harvest. Leeks do not take up much space, and are generally easy to grow. They can be harvested over a long period as they will stay in the ground in good condition for many months. Their strong root system does wonders for soil structure.

SEED TO HARVEST 16–20 weeks.
CROP DIVERSITY Early cultivars: for late summer and autumn use. Usually taller and slimmer and less hardy than later cultivars. Late cultivars: for winter use. Usually shorter and fatter. A few cultivars have decorative purple foliage. Can be grown as mini-leeks, a milder alternative to the spring onion.
SITE Open site in fertile soil that

retains moisture but does not become waterlogged in winter.
IDEAL pH RANGE 6.5–7.5
SOIL TREATMENT High-fertility soil improver; medium-fertility if following a pea crop; or low-fertility improver with nitrogen-rich organic fertilizer.

Sowing

MINIMUM GERMINATION TEMPERATURE 45°F (7°C)
UNDER COVER Multisown leeks only. From February sow 4 seeds per cell. Plant out, unthinned, when 8 in. (20 cm) tall.
OUTSIDE Sow from March to early May in a seedbed. Sow seeds 1 in. (2.5 cm) deep, 1 x 6 in. (2.5 x 15 cm). Transplant to final site. Sow mini-leeks direct in position; do not transplant.

Planting

Transplant at 10–15 weeks old, 8 in. (20 cm) tall—though they can be transplanted when larger. The main planting time is in June, but it can go on into early August if waiting for other crops to finish and clear the site. Water seedbed well before digging up transplants; do not trim roots or leaves. Make holes 6 in. (15 cm) deep. Drop a single leek into each hole and water in (see p. 315). Do not fill in the hole.

Spacing

ROWS 3–6 in. x 12 in. (7.5–15 cm x 30 cm).
BLOCK PLANTING 6–9 in. (15–23 cm) each way.
MULTISOWN 9 in. (23 cm)
MINI-LEEKS ¾ x 6 in. (2 x 15 cm)

Plant care

Water until established if dry.
PROBLEMS Leek moth; leek

Cultivar choice
Kohlrabi 'Early White Vienna'—pale green; 'Express Forcer' F1—extra-early, green; 'Kolibri' F1—purple; 'Kossak'—extra-large, green.

Lamb's lettuce *see Corn salad*

Leek Early to mid-season: 'Albinstar'—for mini-veg; 'King Richard'. Late-season: 'Laura'—very hardy; 'Leekool'; 'Titan'.

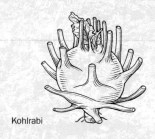

Kohlrabi

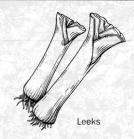

Leeks

rust, which shows as bright orange pustules on the leaves. It often disappears in the autumn, once the weather has turned cool and damp.

Harvesting

Lift leeks as required. Generally they will stand in the ground for many weeks in good condition, though early cultivars may not survive really hard weather.

Lettuce

Lactuca sativa ASTERACEAE

This universal salad ingredient has undergone a revolution in the last decade or so. Crisp or butterhead, hearted or looseleaf, frilly or plain, there is a lettuce to fit every taste, season, and garden.

SEED TO HARVEST 4–14 weeks, depending on cultivar and season.
CROP DIVERSITY Butterheads: hearted lettuces with soft, almost greasy leaf. More tolerant of drought and heat than other types so usually grown in summer.
Crispheads: crunchy crisp leaves forming solid hearts. Heat-tolerant for summer production. Some are suitable for winter growing in an unheated greenhouse. **Romaine or cos:** upright habit with more substantial, crisp, tasty leaves and a loose heart. Slower to mature than butterhead and crisphead types. Better grown in cooler weather in a humus-rich, moist soil. Hardier than most lettuces; some can be grown outside over winter. Many are suitable for seedling cutting crops.
Looseleaf, leaf lettuce, salad

bowl: Nonhearting, with a diverse range of leaf color and shape. Individual leaves can be picked over many weeks. Slow to bolt. Suitable for seedling crops.
   Some lettuce cultivars can overwinter in a cool greenhouse or hoop house. Cultivars resistant to root aphid and tolerant of downy mildew are available.
SITE Most soils, except dry or poorly drained. Appreciates light shade in the summer. Suitable for interplanting between rows of peas or brassicas or underneath tripods of runner beans. Also good for growing in containers and in an ornamental garden.
SOIL TREATMENT None needed where soil is regularly improved for vegetable growing. On poor soil apply a medium-fertility soil improver.
IDEAL pH RANGE 6–7

Sowing

Choose an appropriate cultivar to suit the sowing time.
MINIMUM GERMINATION TEMPERATURE 41°F (5°C). Germination is inhibited in hot weather, above 77°F (25°C).
UNDER COVER For summer and autumn crops, sow in cell packs or trays from February to early July. Once temperatures rise, outdoor sowings are likely to be more successful. For continuous supply, sow at 2-week intervals or select a range of types and cultivars. After hardening off and planting out, protect early and late sowings with cloches—or grow in an unheated greenhouse as necessary. For overwintering crops, either outdoors or in an unheated greenhouse, sow in late August or early October,

depending on the cultivar.
OUTSIDE Sow a 3-ft. (1-m) row of each cultivar at 2-week intervals from April, when the ground is warm enough, until early September. Thin out when large enough to handle, using the thinnings as transplants if required. Bareroot transplants will not do well in summer. When temperatures are high and likely to inhibit germination, sow between 2 PM and 4 PM and water well. The critical period is a few hours after sowing.
   Seedling cutting crops are most useful at the start and end of the season: Make early sowings under cover in late February and March; sow outside when conditions are suitable. Avoid summer months, then sow again in late August outside, and under cover in September. Broadcast seed thinly in patches at 3-week intervals.

Spacing

ROWS 6–15 in. x 8–14 in. (15–38 cm x 20–35 cm), depending on cultivar.
BLOCK PLANTING 8–14 in. (20–35 cm), depending on cultivar.

Plant care

Water until established and in dry periods, to prevent leaves becoming tough and bitter. Keep greenhouses and hoop houses well ventilated to reduce the risk of mildew and botrytis in overwintering crops.
PROBLEMS Slugs—if these are a real problem, raise the lettuce in cell packs and plant out as sturdy young plants, protected with bottle cloches; aphids; lettuce root aphids; cutworm;

downy mildew; gray mold; bolting, which can be a problem in hot weather, so choose bolt-resistant cultivars for growing in high summer.

Harvesting

HEARTED LETTUCE Cut as soon as they have hearted as they will quickly bolt. Cos types will stand a little longer.
LOOSELEAF Pick leaves from the outside of the plant as they are required.
SEEDLING CUTTING CROPS Harvest when 2 in. (5 cm) tall, about 4 weeks after sowing; 2–3 subsequent cuts can be made.

Melon, sweet

Cucumis melo and *Citrullus lanatus* CUCURBITACEAE

Sweet melons grow on a trailing vine in the same fashion as their close relative, cucumber. Melons are tropical plants that need temperatures of 77–86°F (25–30°C) to grow well.

SEED TO HARVEST 12–20 weeks.
CROP DIVERSITY What we call cantaloupes are actually muskmelons. Their skin is covered with shallow veins, and the fragrant flesh ranges from salmon to green. Honeydew melons have larger, more oval fruits and waxy skins. Watermelons fall under a different botanical classification, but they thrive in the same conditions that other melons require.
SITE Grow under cloches, in a coldframe, or in a greenhouse/ hoop house, in a warm, well-drained soil rich in organic

Head lettuce

matter, but not too fertile.
SOIL TREATMENT Apply a medium-fertility soil improver, or low-fertility soil improver plus a general organic fertilizer.
IDEAL pH RANGE 6.5–7

Sowing
MINIMUM GERMINATION TEMPERATURE 64°F (18°C)
UNDER COVER Sow in spring, usually late April or May, about 6 weeks before the last frost. Sow in 2½–3½-in. (6–9-cm) pots, with the seed sown on its side. With expensive F1 seed, sow 1 per pot only. Thin, if necessary, to 1 seedling per pot. Once germinated, keep light and warm—55–61°F (13–16°C). Do not sow too early, as you do not want plants to become potbound. Transplant into 5-in. (13-cm) pots if necessary.

Planting
Put cloches in place a few weeks in advance to warm the soil. Plant out in June into a slight mound, about 1½ in. (4 cm) high, to help keep the stem just above ground and therefore dry and free from rot. Water in rather than firming the soil.

Spacing
GROWN ON THE GROUND 3 ft. x 3–5 ft. (1 m x 1–1.5 m)
TRAINED UP STAKES OR NETTING 15 in. (38 cm) for a single cordon, 24 in. (60 cm) for a double cordon.

Plant care
Protect from cold weather. Once fruiting, shade from hot sun. As flowering starts, allow pollinating insects access to plants under cover, or hand-pollinate. Water

plants regularly. Feed those in containers with a high-potash feed once flowers have set.
PROBLEMS Aphids; cucumber beetle; powdery mildew; bacterial wilt; squash vine borer.

Training
PLANTS GROWN ON THE GROUND Plants can be left to scramble over the ground, on a bench, or up netting. After 5 leaves have developed, pinch out the growing tip. Allow 4 lateral shoots to develop, spacing them out so they grow in different directions. If space is short, under cloches for example, allow only 2 laterals to grow.
TRAINED PLANTS Allow 1–2 shoots to grow per plant, training them up stakes or netting. Pinch out the growing tip when 6 ft. (2 m) long to encourage sideshoots to grow. Tie in these sideshoots, and pinch out their growing tip after 5 leaves to encourage further sideshoots to grow; these will flower. Support fruits, when tennis ball-size, with a netting sling.
ALL PLANTS Pinch out the growing tip of each flowering shoot at 2 leaves beyond the flower. Leave 4–5 fruits of uniform size to grow on each plant, picking off the rest when grape-size.

Harvesting
Melons are ready to pick in late summer and early autumn. Ripe fruits are sweet-smelling.

Mibuna greens

Closely related to Mizuna greens (see below). They grow more or

less in the same way, but are less vigorous and less tolerant of heat and cold.

Mitsuba

Cryptotaenia japonica APIACEAE

A hardy evergreen plant, also known as Japanese parsley. The delicately flavored stems and leaves are used raw in salads. Mitsuba, a woodland plant, enjoys moist soil and light shade. Sow direct in spring or autumn, leaving 6 in. (15 cm) between plants, or grow under cover for winter cropping.

Mizuna greens

Brassica rapa var. *nipposinica* BRASSICACEAE

Attractive leafy crop, with a mild mustardy flavor, eaten raw or lightly cooked. Its green feathery leaves can be cut as a seedling crop, picked individually from larger plants, or cut as a whole head. Makes pretty edging. Will grow over winter with protection.

SEED TO HARVEST Seedling crop 3 weeks; semimature plants 6–8 weeks; mature plants 8–10 weeks.
CROP DIVERSITY Green- and purple-leaved cultivars.
SITE Soil must not dry out. Summer crops can take light shade. Good for interplanting when kept small. Suitable for winter cropping under cover.
SOIL TREATMENT None needed if soil improved for a previous crop. On light soils, use a low- to medium-fertility soil improver.

Sowing
MINIMUM GERMINATION TEMPERATURE 45°F (7°C)
UNDER COVER Sow in cell packs from March/April for transplanting outside. Sow direct or in cell packs September to March for growing under cover.
OUTSIDE Sow April to August.

Spacing
Seedling cutting crop: Sow thinly in bands or patches. Semi-mature plants: 4–8 in. (10–20 cm). Mature plants: 12 in. (30 cm).

Plant care
Water in dry weather.
PROBLEMS Clubroot; slugs; flea beetle. Where flea beetle is a problem, grow under row cover or fine mesh netting.

Harvesting
Cut seedlings when a few inches high. Pick individual leaves when plants are large enough, or cut the whole head.

Mustards, oriental

Brassica juncea BRASSICACEAE

Mostly hardy, leafy greens, with a hot mustardy flavor. Pick individual leaves for salads and stir-fry in autumn and winter. Can be grown as a seedling crop for cutting. Useful for interplanting.

SEED TO HARVEST 6–13 weeks.
CROP DIVERSITY Variety of leaf shapes and colors are available.
SITE Open site. Suitable for late cropping in an unheated greenhouse/hoop house, or containers.

Cultivar choice
Oriental mustards 'Green Wave'; 'Osaka Purple'—purple-tinged leaves.

Mizuna greens

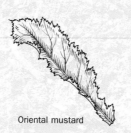
Oriental mustard

New Zealand spinach

SOIL TREATMENT None needed if soil improved for a previous crop. If not, apply a low- or medium-fertility soil improver. **IDEAL pH RANGE** 6.5–7

Sowing

MINIMUM GERMINATION TEMPERATURE 45°F (7°C). Best sown direct but can be transplanted from cell packs. Some cultivars can be sown in spring and late summer; others are for late summer sowing only.

Spacing

For harvesting young leaves: 6 x 6 in. (15 x 15 cm). Larger plants: 14 x 14 in. (35 x 35 cm). As a seedling cutting crop: Broadcast seed thinly.

Plant care

Water as necessary in dry weather. **PROBLEMS** Clubroot; flea beetle—to protect against flea beetle, grow under row cover or mesh.

New Zealand spinach

Tetragonia tetragonioides AIZOACEAE

Unusual-looking half-hardy perennial usually grown as an annual. Unlike true spinach it thrives in hot, dry conditions. Seed is slow to germinate and is best soaked in water for 24 hours before sowing. Raise in cell packs and plant out after the last frost, or sow direct once the risk of frost has passed. Plants are low and sprawling; space at least 18 in. (45 cm)

apart. The thick, fleshy leaves and shoot tips are picked as required, starting around 6–7 weeks after sowing. Usually pest- and disease-free.

Okra

Abelmoschus esculentus MALVACEAE

Okra is a traditional southern favorite, but you don't have to live in the South to grow it. If your summers are long and warm enough for raising sweet corn, you can grow okra, too.

SEED TO HARVEST 50–65 days. **CROP DIVERSITY** Look for early-maturing cultivars if your summers are short. If your skin is sensitive to okra's spiny pods, look for spineless cultivars. Okra normally bears green pods; red-podded types are also available. **SITE** Full sun and fertile, well-drained soil. **SOIL TREATMENT** Will grow in ordinary garden soil but does particularly well after a nitrogen-fixing green manure crop. **IDEAL pH RANGE** 6.5–6.8

Sowing

MINIMUM GERMINATION TEMPERATURE 68°F (20°C). **UNDER COVER** In short-season areas, start seeds indoors 3 to 4 weeks after the last frost date. Sow in 2-in. (5-cm) pots, 3 seeds per pot. Keep the pots at 80–90°F (27–32°C) until the seedlings emerge. Grow the seedlings at 75–80°F (24–27°C). Thin to leave 1 seedling per pot. **OUTSIDE** In mild areas, sow seeds 2–3 in. (5–8 cm) apart when the soil has warmed to 68°F (20°C).

Spacing

2–3 ft. x 2–3 ft. (60–90 cm x 60–90 cm)

Plant care

When plants are 4 in. (10 cm) tall, mulch to keep out weeds and conserve moisture. Water during dry spells. Every 3–4 weeks, sidedress with compost. **PROBLEMS** Cutworms; corn earworms; nematodes.

Harvesting

Use a sharp knife to harvest pods when they are 1–6 in. (3–15 cm) long and still tender. Harvest at least every other day to keep plants producing until frost. Okra does not store well, so eat fresh, freeze, or pickle the same day as harvesting.

Onions, bulb and globe

Allium cepa ALLIACEAE

A popular long-season, frost-tolerant crop. Simple to grow from sets, and undemanding if you want to grow kitchen-size bulbs. In mild areas with low summer rainfall, autumn-planted onions may be more reliable.

SEED TO HARVEST Spring-sown seed: 20–24 weeks; autumn-sown seed: 42 weeks; spring-planted sets: 18–20 weeks; autumn-planted sets: 36–38 weeks.

CROP DIVERSITY Can be oval or cylindrical in shape, with red, white, or golden brown skin. Long-day types need the 13–16 hours of summer daylight found

in more northern latitudes; short-day onions thrive in southern climates with only 12 hours of daylight. Day-neutral cultivars will form bulbs in both areas. Seed offers the greatest choice of cultivars. **SITE** Onions prefer an open, sunny situation but tolerate a little shade. Autumn sown/planted onions need full sun and must have good drainage. Onions can look good among other plants, but dislike being crowded. **SOIL TREATMENT** None needed if soil was improved for a previous crop. If not, add a low- to medium-fertility soil improver, depending on the soil condition. **IDEAL pH RANGE** 6–7

Sowing

MINIMUM GERMINATION TEMPERATURE 45°F (7°C) *If sowing in spring, for a late summer harvest:* **SEED, UNDER COVER** Sow in trays or cell packs in February/March. Harden off and plant out when about 4 in. (10 cm) tall. Multisowing: sow 6 seeds per cell and do not thin. **SEED, OUTSIDE** Station-sow several seeds per station, as soon as soil is warm enough, usually by April. Thin to 1 seedling; leave several to grow if multisowing. **SETS** Plant sets March/April. They need a period of cold to initiate root formation, so plant as early as possible once soil is workable. Push sets into the soil, so just the tips are visible, with the pointed end upward. *If sowing in late summer/autumn for early summer harvest:* **SEED** Timing of sowing to suit geographical location is critical to ensure that seedlings will

Globe onion

survive the winter but not bolt early in spring. Sow in August—in the 2nd week in the north, the 4th in the south. Sow thinly in rows. Thin to 1 in. (2.5 cm) in autumn, and in stages to the final spacing in spring.

SETS Plant from September to November, when the ground is fit to walk on. Push sets in as for the spring-planted crop.

Spacing

ROWS Bulb size is influenced by spacing. For medium-size bulbs: 1½ x 12 in. (4 x 30 cm); for larger bulbs, 4 x 12 in. (10 x 30 cm) **BLOCK PLANTING** 4–6 in. (10–15 cm)
MULTISOWN 10 in. (25 cm).

Plant care

Hand-weed carefully as roots are very shallow. In spring, apply a nitrogen-rich fertilizer to over-wintered onions if required.
PROBLEMS Onion fly; onion thrips; onion downy mildew; onion neck rots; onion white rot; bolting (fluctuating weather conditions often the cause; red cultivars are especially prone).

Harvesting

Harvest to eat fresh when large enough. When onions stop growing, the leaves fall over and turn brown. Allow them to fall naturally; do not bend them over. Gently pull the onions up. In dry weather, spread them out on slatted trays or a bench in the sun for the skins to ripen. In wet conditions dry off under cover. Avoid bruising bulbs. Once skin is rustling dry, hang onions in nets or string into ropes. Store in a cool, airy location. Use thick-necked bulbs first, as they rarely store well. Autumn-sown onions should not be stored long-term.

Onions, spring and pickling

Allium cepa ALLIACEAE

Onions that are harvested after only 8 weeks or so. European spring or bunching onions form a slim plant with a white or red shank, mild-flavored for salads. Pickling or mini-onions have small bulbs used fresh or for pickling.

SEED TO HARVEST 8 weeks.
CROP DIVERSITY Red and white cultivars. Hardy cultivars of spring onions are grown over winter.
SITE Open site preferred but will tolerate a little shade. Can be grown under cover for an early crop. Spring onions can be grown over winter. Suitable for growing in containers.
SOIL TREATMENT No treatment needed if soil was amended with compost for a previous crop. If not, apply a low- to medium-fertility soil improver, depending on the soil. Pickling onions tolerate poorer soils than other types.
IDEAL pH RANGE 6–7

Sowing

MINIMUM GERMINATION TEMPERATURE 41°F (5°C)
UNDER COVER Sow in early spring and late summer direct into soil beds.
OUTSIDE Spring onions: sow in spring and summer every 3 weeks for a continuous supply. For an early spring crop, sow suitable cultivars in August. Pickling onions: sow in March and April.

Spacing

Sow thinly in rows 4 in. (10 cm) apart, or in bands 3–4 in. (7–10 cm) wide, 6 in. (15 cm) apart. Aim for ½–1 in. (1–2.5 cm) between seeds.

Plant care

Water in dry conditions. Protect winter crops in severe weather.
PROBLEMS Onion fly; onion white rot; onion downy mildew.

Harvesting

Pull spring onions to eat when 6 in. (15 cm) tall. Pickling onions are harvested when the foliage has died back, or used fresh.

Onions, Welsh/ bunching

Allium fistulosum ALLIACEAE

Perennial Welsh onions grow in clumps like chives, with hollow leaves up to 18 in. (45 cm) tall. The base of the leaf is thickened at and below ground level. A useful winter vegetable, eaten raw or cooked, surviving temperatures as low as 14°F (−10°C). Developed from the Welsh onion, the Japanese or Oriental bunching onion is a ubiquitous Chinese vegetable. A perennial usually grown as an annual or biennial, the plants are harvested at any stage from seedling to fully grown. They tend to be more vigorous and productive than Welsh onions.

CROP DIVERSITY Japanese bunching onions: multi- and single-stemmed, white or red.

SITE See Onions, bulb, and globe. Will grow in containers. Flowering forms of Welsh onion look good in large pot, and make attractive green edging to a vegetable patch. Japanese bunching onions can be interplanted with other plants.
IDEAL pH RANGE 6–7.5

Sowing

MINIMUM GERMINATION TEMPERATURE 45°F (7°C). Oriental bunching onions can be sown in cell packs for transplanting, or sown direct.
UNDER COVER Sow Welsh onions in cell packs in April; harden off and transplant about 6 weeks later.
OUTSIDE Sow in spring or summer. Sow in shallow rows, a pinch of 3–4 seeds every 2 in. (5 cm), allowing 8 in. (20 cm) between rows. Transplant to rows 9 x 12 in. (23 x 30 cm), in blocks 8 in. (20 cm). Divide established clumps and replant younger outer sections.

Harvesting

To harvest as small leafy shoots, sow year-round under cover; from spring to autumn outside. Sow thickly in wide rows. Harvest when around 6 in. (15 cm) tall, 30–40 days after sowing.

To harvest as larger scallions/small bunching onions, sow year-round under cover; from spring to early autumn outside. Sow thinly in wide rows, thinning to 1½ in. (4 cm), or multisow, 6 seeds per cell, to transplant. Harvest when 12 in. (30 cm) tall, after 60–80 days.

To harvest as larger bunching onions, sow in cell packs in

Cultivar choice
Onions, spring and pickling Spring onions: 'Evergreen White Bunching'; 'White Lisbon Bunching'; 'Red Baron'—red stalks. Pickling onions: 'Crystal White'. *Pak choi* 'Joi Choi' F1—vigorous, pure white stems; 'Mei Qing Choi' F1—very compact.

Parsley *see p. 288*

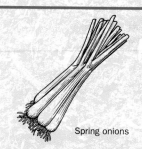
Spring onions

Pak choi

spring and early summer. Transplant after 4–8 weeks for a late summer/autumn harvest. Sow late summer to transplant in early autumn for harvesting the following spring. Row spacing 3 x 12 in. (7.5 x 30 cm), in blocks 8 in. (20 cm). Ready to harvest in 3–4 months. Use the thickened white stem and the green leaves.

Plant care

For winter harvests in cold areas, protect Welsh onions with cloches or frames. Divide established clumps every 4–5 years. Remove spent flowerheads from cultivars that flower.
PROBLEMS Thrips; stem and bulb nematodes; downy mildew; onion white rot.

Pak choi

Brassica rapa var. *chinensis*
BRASSICACEAE

Pak choi leaves have a wide mid-rib and form a loose head. A close relative of Chinese cabbage, eat raw or lightly cooked at any stage from seedling to mature plant. Leaves, stems, and flowering shoots are all edible. Grow spring sowings as seedling crops as early sowings run to seed quickly. Will stand light frost.

SEED TO HARVEST Mature plants: 5–8 weeks; seedling crops: 2–3 weeks.
CROP DIVERSITY White-, green-, and purple-stemmed cultivars in varying sizes. Some are more resistant to bolting.
SITE Humus-rich, moisture-retentive soil to ensure the fast

growth needed for a good crop. This quick growth makes it good for interplanting between slower plants. Suitable for growing as a late-season crop in an unheated greenhouse or hoop house.
SOIL TREATMENT Apply a medium-fertility soil improver or a low-fertility one with organic fertilizer before planting.
IDEAL pH RANGE 6.5–7

Sowing

MINIMUM GERMINATION TEMPERATURE 50°F (10°C)
UNDER COVER Sow in cell packs for transplanting June–August. Some cultivars can be sown earlier. The latest sowings can be planted under cover.
OUTSIDE Sow June–August.

Spacing

For harvesting young leaves: 5–6 in. (13–15 cm). For medium-size plants: 7–9 in. (18–23 cm). Large plants: 18 in. (45 cm). As a seedling cutting crop—broadcast thinly. Spacing will also depend to some extent on cultivar.

Plant care

Water if needed in dry weather. If flea beetle is a problem, grow under row cover or mesh netting.
PROBLEMS Flea beetle; slugs; clubroot.

Parsnip

Pastinaca sativa APIACEAE

Long, white parsnip roots make a deliciously sweet winter staple. They are utterly hardy and easy to grow, but do need a long growing season. Germination is

slow—it may take 3 weeks or so—and fresh seed must be used every year. Harvest in the late autumn and winter. Leave a parsnip in the ground over winter and it will produce a majestic flower spike the following year, a magnet for beneficial insects. Sow parsnips mixed with radish seed to mark the area. The radishes will be ready to harvest when the parsnips are just starting to emerge.

SEED TO HARVEST 16 weeks.
CROP DIVERSITY Long- and short-rooted cultivars, but otherwise little variety. Modern cultivars tend to be smaller and faster-growing. May also be grown as a mini-vegetable.
SITE For good roots, parsnips need a well-worked, stone-free soil, in an open, sunny position.
SOIL TREATMENT Parsnips do best in soil amended with compost for a previous crop. They will benefit from a low-fertility organic mulch, applied in the winter before sowing.
IDEAL pH RANGE 6.5–8

Sowing

MINIMUM GERMINATION TEMPERATURE 35°F (1.5°C); maximum 63°F (17.5°C). Sow outdoors whenever possible.
UNDER COVER Sow in biodegradable tubes, to avoid disturbing the roots.
OUTSIDE First sowings can be made in February, but as they germinate slowly later sowings in warmer soil (until May) may be more successful. Fluid-sowing can improve the germination rate. Sow thinly in shallow rows, or station-sow, 3 seeds per station, thinned to 1 per station.

Spacing

Root size depends on spacing.
ROWS For small roots: 4 x 8 in. (10 x 20 cm). For larger roots: 6 x 12 in. (15 x 30 cm).
BLOCK PLANTING 6–8 in. (15–20 cm).

Plant care

Keep seedlings weed-free until established.
PROBLEMS Carrot fly; root rot; parsnip canker. Canker is more of a problem in nitrogen-rich and acid soils. Early sowings are most prone to attack.

Harvesting

Flavor improves after a frost. Lift as required when leaves start to die. Can be left in the ground over winter, but harvest by late winter as older roots will develop a hard, woody core.

Peas

Pisum sativum PAPILIONACEAE

Peas are well suited to cooler climates. By growing a range of types and varieties, peas can be harvested from May to September. The climbing, edible-podded types fit into almost any garden, producing attractive flowers and tasty pods. Pea roots fix nitrogen, boosting soil fertility. In cool climates, peas are more reliable than beans for drying.

SEED TO HARVEST Early cultivars: 11–12 weeks. Main crops: 13–14 weeks.
CROP DIVERSITY Shelling peas: Early main crops and main crops: mostly 18–48 in. (45–120 cm) tall, but old cultivars, to 8 ft.

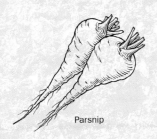
Parsnip

Peas

(2.5 m) tall or more, are still available. Pods usually green, some purple. Round-seeded peas are hardier but less productive and not so sweet-tasting as wrinkle-seeded types. Petit-pois are selected smaller pea cultivars. **Edible-podded peas**: Snow peas are eaten when immature pods are flat. Sugar, or snap pod, peas are picked when pods are thick-walled and plump. Both grow 2–5 ft. (0.6–1.5 m) tall. **SITE** Soil that does not dry out in summer, but is not waterlogged in winter. Summer crops tolerate some shade. Tall peas make an attractive screen. The leafless types look decorative in small clumps or containers. **SOIL TREATMENT** Apply a low-fertility soil improver before sowing. **IDEAL pH RANGE** 6–6.8

Sowing

Grow a range of varieties for a regular crop through summer. Early and late sowings are less likely to be attacked by pea moth. **MINIMUM GERMINATION TEMPERATURE** 50°F (10°C) **UNDER COVER** Start the earliest crops in deep cell packs or pots under protection from March. Harden off and transplant when about 4 in. (10 cm) tall. **OUTSIDE** Peas do not germinate well in cold, wet soil, so delay spring sowings until the soil is warm, or sow under cloches. Sow until early June; summer sowings thrive only if the soil does not dry out. Sow round-seeded cultivars in November in mild areas.

Spacing

ROWS Sow in broad rows, 9 in. (23 cm) wide, or in double rows of two rows 2 in. (5 cm) wide and 9 in. (23 cm) apart, spacing seed 2 in. (5 cm) apart each way in the row. Leave 24–36 in. (60–90 cm) between rows, depending on height of cultivar. **BLOCK PLANTING** Suitable for semi-leafless and shorter cultivars: 2–3 in. (5–7 cm) apart.

Plant care

Provide supports for plants early on. Peas have tendrils that cling to twiggy sticks, wire mesh, or pea netting. Leafless and semi-leafless types need little support if grown in a block. Mulch to keep soil moist. Water regularly in dry conditions from when flowers first open. Watering before will not improve the crop, but just encourage lots of leafy growth. **PROBLEMS** Birds (pigeons, pheasants, jays); mice; pea and bean weevil; pea moth; pea thrips; root rots.

Harvesting

Pick snow peas as soon as of convenient size. Keep picking to encourage production. Harvest sugar peas when pods are plump. Pick shelling peas when the peas can be felt through the pod, before they get too large. Fresh peas freeze well. Peas for drying should be left to hang on plants until rattling dry. Shell peas to finish drying. Keep in airtight jars.

Pepper

Capsicum annuum Grossum Group (sweet) and Longum Group (chili) SOLANACEAE

Pepper choices—ranging from crispy sweet to fiery hot, from big and blocky to long and skinny—increase each year. This native American vegetable is second only to tomatoes as a garden favorite, and its cultivation is much the same. Just keep sweet peppers, often called bell or green peppers, at some distance from hot ones, since the two can sometimes cross-pollinate.

SEED TO HARVEST 20–28 weeks. **CROP DIVERSITY** Sweet peppers: Mature fruits may be green, red, yellow, or purple; oblong or tapered in shape. Some have thicker walls and are slower to mature. Compact cultivars grow well in containers. Chili peppers vary in heat, shape, and color. Orange-, red-, and purple-fruited cultivars are available. **SITE** Peppers need a minimum temperature of 70°F (21°C) to produce well. In cool climates, this means peppers are normally grown in a cool greenhouse or hoop house or in a very warm, sheltered site in milder regions. A fertile soil that warms up early is essential. **SOIL TREATMENT** Apply a medium-fertility soil improver. **IDEAL pH RANGE** 6–6.5

Sowing

MINIMUM GERMINATION TEMPERATURE 70°F (20°C). Sow seed in gentle heat in pots or cell packs, in April or May. Transplant into 3–3½-in. (8–9-cm) pots; as soon as the roots have filled the pots, move into 4–5-in (10–13-cm) pots. Keep temperatures at 54–61°F (12–16°C) during this period.

Planting out

Plant out into greenhouse soil or large pots or growing bags when first flowers appear. Plant outside only after the last frost. Protect plants as necessary to maintain them at a temperature of at least 59°F (15°C), and no higher than 86°F (30°C).

Spacing

12–18 in. (30–45 cm), depending on the cultivar.

Plant care

Support tall plants with a stake. Water regularly in dry weather, and feed plants in pots with a high-potash liquid fertilizer. Maintain high humidity in the greenhouse by damping down when necessary—possibly twice a day in hot weather. **PROBLEMS** Aphids; red spider mite; whitefly; blossom end rot.

Harvesting

Pick sweet peppers when still green to encourage more fruits to form, or leave for 2–3 weeks to develop a mature color and a sweeter flavor. At the end of the season, when frost is forecast, pull up all the plants whole and hang them upside down in a frost-free shed. The fruits will continue to ripen. Chilis should be left to ripen on the plant. They can be stored dry, preferably in an airtight jar, in the dark.

Potato

Solanum tuberosum SOLANACEAE

Potatoes are easy to grow. They require a fair amount of space

---

Cultivar choice
Pepper Sweet pepper: 'Blushing Beauty' F1—shades of cream, orange, and red when fully ripe; 'Chocolate Bell' F1—deep purple skin; 'Gypsy'—very early, compact plants; 'Sweet Banana'—heirloom cultivar, long, yellow-green fruits. Hot pepper: 'Ancho' ('Poblano') and 'Big Thai'—relatively mild; 'Jalapeno'—moderate heat; 'Habanero' and 'Thai Dragon' F1—ultrahot.
Potato 'Kennebec'—late-season, white flesh; 'Red Norland'—early, red skin; 'Rose Gold'—midseason, pink skin, yellowish flesh; 'Swedish Peanut'—late-season, golden skin and flesh; 'Yukon Gold'—early–midseason, yellowish flesh.

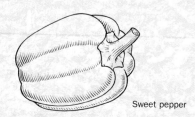

Sweet pepper

but can give a good return. The work involved is a rewarding way of clearing ground. Frost-tender, potatoes are usually planted in spring for an early and late summer crop, or in summer for an autumn crop. Potatoes are usually grown from small tubers called "seed" potatoes. Always buy certified seed potatoes, grown to a strict standard to ensure they are healthy. Reject shriveled, soft, or damaged tubers. They can also be grown from micropropagated plants—usually old or scarce cultivars. Potato flavor can vary widely depending on where grown, so try a selection to discover what suits you and your soil.

SEED TO HARVEST 13–20 weeks from planting.

CROP DIVERSITY There are dozens of cultivars of seed potato available in the U.S. Early, second early, and main crop cultivars are classified by the time taken to mature. Earlies are the quickest, but lowest-yielding. Main crops store well. Skin colors include pink, yellow, purple, and red, and flesh colors are usually yellow or white, but there are purple-fleshed cultivars. Textures vary from floury, high dry-matter cultivars (good for roasting and chips) to waxy salad potatoes. Cultivars with resistance to blight and nematodes are available, and well worth choosing to help combat these problems.

SITE Open, sunny, site, though will tolerate a little shade. The ideal soil is deep, fertile, humus-rich, and preferably acid. Avoid poorly drained sites. Can be grown in large containers. An extra-early crop to harvest in late April or May can be grown in an unheated greenhouse/hoop house or under cloches if given adequate frost protection.

SOIL TREATMENT Apply a high-fertility soil improver to the soil or planting trenches, or use a low- or medium-fertility soil improver, depending on the soil, with a nitrogen-rich organic fertilizer. **IDEAL pH RANGE** 5–6

Planting

Seed potatoes are sprouted or "chitted" before planting to help them grow quickly. To produce sturdy short shoots, put potatoes in trays or egg cartons, rose end (the end with most eyes) upward, in late winter or very early spring. Put in a light, warm place, 64°F (18°C), out of direct sunlight until shoots have just started to grow. Move to a cooler position for about 6 weeks before planting outside.

GROWING UNDER COVER Plant mid-February. Protect from frost.

GROWING OUTSIDE Plant into trenches or individual holes, 3–6 in. (7–15 cm) deep, and cover with at least 1 in. (3 cm) of soil. Potatoes can also be grown on the soil surface under a mulch using the no-dig technique (see p. 327). Plant mid-March–May. Tubers suffer if planted into cold, wet soil; if weather conditions are uncertain, delay planting. Protect early plantings from frost if necessary.

Some growers prefer to grow their potatoes in hills. To plant a hill, pile up a 3–4-ft. (90–120-cm) wide mound of soil 4–6 in. (10–15 cm) high. Space seed potatoes 6 in. (15 cm) apart near the center of the hill and bury with 4–5 in. (10–13 cm) of soil. Continue covering the tubers as they develop. Another option is to form the hills in autumn with a 3–4-ft. (90–120-cm) thick mound of leaves. The next spring, plant the seed potatoes on top of the partially decomposed mound and cover with 1 ft. (30 cm) of straw or hay, adding more as the vines mature.

Spacing

ROWS Early cultivars: 11–14 in. (28–35 cm) apart, with 15–20 in. (38–50 cm) between rows. Second earlies and main crop cultivars: 14–18 in. (35–45 cm) apart, with 26–30 in. (65–75 cm) between rows.

BLOCK PLANTING Early cultivars: 12 in. (30 cm). Second earlies and main crop cultivars: 14 in. (35 cm).

Plant care

FROST PROTECTION Early potatoes are most at risk. Cover foliage with soil, straw, newspaper, or row cover overnight if frost is likely.

EARTHING UP Mound soil on potatoes as they grow, bringing the soil up around the shoots. This helps control weeds, prevents the tubers from turning green, and gives some protection against tuber blight. Start when plants are 6 in. (15 cm) tall, leaving a small amount of foliage showing. Mound up again just before the foliage meets across the rows. Mounding soil is not possible with closer spacing, but the plants shade themselves. Alternatively, plants can be mulched with a thick layer of hay, straw, leaf mold, or grass clippings, which also helps to conserve moisture.

SOIL MOISTURE AND WATERING For the highest yield of good-size tubers, keep the soil moist throughout the season. Watering is most effective when tubers are the marble size (which usually coincides with flowering). Water the soil, not the foliage.

PROBLEMS Slugs (mainly tubers); potato cyst nematode (tubers); wireworm (tubers); potato blight (foliage and tubers); scab (tubers); potato blackleg (stems); black-heart and hollow heart (tubers); internal browning (tubers); rust spot (tubers); magnesium and potassium deficiencies (foliage).

Harvesting

Start harvesting early varieties in late June and July. Flowering is an indication that tubers will be large enough, but not all cultivars flower. Main crops should be dug as the foliage dies down, usually in September. Second earlies somewhere between the two. All tubers must be removed to reduce the risk of disease. Harvest on a dry day, if possible, and rub off excess soil before storing in paper or burlap sacks. Keep the tubers cool, between 45–50°F (7–10°C), frost-free, and dark. Allow slight humidity and air to circulate.

Pumpkins and winter squashes

Cucurbita maxima and *C. moschata* CUCURBITACEAE

Large, very vigorous, half-hardy plants, with a diversity of

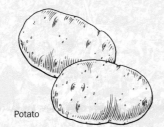

Potato

shapes, colors, and sizes of fruit. Undemanding and rewarding to grow. Heat-tolerant.

SEED TO HARVEST Ready to pick 12–20 weeks after planting, depending on the cultivar.
CROP DIVERSITY Pumpkins and winter squashes are delightful in their diversity. Fruits may be several to the pound, or weigh in at several dozen pounds each. Color ranges from orange, to green to gray—sometimes with multiple colors in one fruit—and the skin may be smooth or warty. The flesh may be watery but is usually dense and sweet. All store well. Both trailing and bush types are available.
SITE Sheltered, in full sun. Small-fruited varieties look good trained up a pergola or archway.
SOIL TREATMENT Apply a low- or medium-fertility soil improver, depending on soil conditions. Rich soil or over-generous feeding encourages foliage at the expense of the fruit. Can be grown in a compost trench (see p. 48).
IDEAL pH RANGE 5.5–6.8

Sowing

MINIMUM GERMINATION TEMPERATURE 55°F (13°C)
UNDER COVER Sow in late spring, 3–4 weeks before your last frost date. Push 2 seeds into each 3½-in. (9-cm) pot; remove the weaker seedling. Harden off well before planting outside after all danger of frost has passed. Transplant carefully to avoid root disturbance.
OUTSIDE Sow direct in early summer in mild areas. Protect with bottle cloches for extra warmth at the start.

Spacing

These vigorous plants typically grow to fill all available space. When transplanting, mark the center of each plant so you will know where to water if needed. They will grow happily beneath runner beans or sweet corn.
ROWS Bush cultivars: 24–36 in. x 36–48 in. (60–90 cm x 90–120 cm). Trailing cultivars: 4–6 ft. x 6 ft. (1.2–1.8 m x 1.8 m).
BLOCK PLANTING Bush cultivars: 36 in. (90 cm). Trailing cultivars: 4–6 ft. (1.2–1.8 m).

Plant care

Trailing cultivars can be trained up a support, or pegged out into a circle to keep them under control. Keep weed-free until established. Water only until established; plants root deeply and need little further watering. When the plants are growing well, mulch with straw, hay, or a low-fertility soil improver. Allow only 3–4 fruits per plant to mature on large pumpkin cultivars. In wet seasons, fruits may rot where in contact with the soil; to avoid this, slip a board underneath them.
PROBLEMS Aphids; cucumber beetle; squash vine borer; bacterial wilt; mosaic virus; powdery mildew.

Harvesting

Shoots, young leaves, flowers, fruits, and seeds can all be eaten. Pumpkins and winter squashes intended for storage should be left on the plant as long as possible to develop a hard skin before the first frosts. When fruits feel hard and sound hollow if tapped, cut them from the vines and expose the underside to the sun for 10 days or so to complete the ripening process. Well-ripened fruit will store for 6–12 months in an airy place at 45–50°F (7–10°C).

Purslane, summer

Portulaca oleracea
PORTULACACEAE

An attractive, half-hardy plant with succulent, bright green or golden leaves and stems, which are excellent in summer salads. Needs warm conditions, so grow in a warm, sheltered spot with light, well-drained soil. Sow direct in May and June. Can also be sown in cell packs in April to plant out. Space 6 in. (15 cm) between plants. Earlier and later seedling crops can be grown under cover. Pick young leafy shoots after 4–8 weeks, leaving at least 2 leaves on the plant, which should resprout.

Purslane, winter

Montia perfoliata PORTULACACEAE

Mild-flavored hardy annual salad plant, also known as miner's lettuce and claytonia. Leaves, stems, and flowers are all edible; valuable for spring and autumn use, and as a winter salad grown under cover. Plants have attractive bright green, fleshy, triangular leaves and a white flower; they are small, and ideal for interplanting and edging. They grow wild in some areas. Best on a light sandy soil, but not really fussy and will also grow in light shade. No special soil treatment is needed. Sow March and April for summer use; July and August for autumn cropping; and September for cropping over winter under cover, in seed trays, or cell packs. Transplant when large enough. Broadcast thinly for a seedling cutting crop, or sow in rows. Winter purslane will self-sow freely if you let it flower, so you may need to sow it only once. Thin plants to 4–6 in. (10–15 cm) apart. Cover with a cloche to produce through winter—though winter purslane may survive without. Pick individual leaves as soon as large enough. Plants continue to grow for many weeks. They are usually trouble-free.

Radish

Raphanus sativus, Raphanus sativus Longipinnatus Group
BRASSICACEAE

A diverse crop, suited to cool climates. Typical salad radishes grow in as little as 4 weeks in summer. Hardy autumn and winter radishes have substantial roots that can be harvested over a long period and eaten raw or cooked. If the roots are left to produce a flowering stem, the immature seedpods can be eaten, too. They are crisp and hot. Radish can also be grown as a seedling cutting crop (see p. 332). Leave a radish to go to seed. A single plant will provide a good supply of seed.

SEED TO HARVEST Summer types: 4 weeks. Daikon types: 7–8 weeks. Autumn and winter

---

Cultivar choice
Radicchio *see Chicory*

Radish 'Easter Egg Blend II'—red, pink, purple, or white roots; 'French Breakfast'—heirloom cultivar, cylindrical roots; 'Sparkler'—scarlet-and-white, fast-growing; 'Summer Cross' F1—daikon type, heat-tolerant, disease resistant.

Summer purslane

Winter purslane

types: from 20 weeks.

CROP DIVERSITY Summer cultivars: small pink, red, white, or bicolored roots; round, elongated. or long. Daikon: large, long, hot white roots, grown to maturity in late summer/autumn. Autumn and winter cultivars: large, round, or elongated roots, with black, pink, or red skins. Autumn and winter radishes are frost-tolerant.

SITE Open site generally, but prefers light shade in summer. Avoid soil prone to drought. Summer types are good for interplanting, growing in containers, and as early and late crops under cover.

SOIL TREATMENT Prefer a soil that has already been improved for a previous crop. Apply a low-fertility soil improver to light soil.

IDEAL PH RANGE 6.5–7.5

Sowing

Not suitable for transplanting.

MINIMUM GERMINATION TEMPERATURE 41°F (5°C)

UNDER COVER For early and late crops, sow summer cultivars under cloches or row cover, or in the soil in a cool greenhouse or hoop house. Sow February–March and September–October. Sow Daikon types in August for a winter crop.

OUTSIDE Summer cultivars: Sow thinly in rows, or broadcast. For succession, sow in late February–September at 10-day intervals. Avoid hot, dry months. Daikon cultivars: midsummer onward. Winter cultivars: July–August.

Spacing

ROWS Summer cultivars: ¾–1 in. x 4–6 in. (2–2.5 cm x 10–15 cm). Daikon: 4 x 10 in (10 x 25 cm).

Winter cultivars 8 x 12 in (20 x 30 cm).

BLOCK PLANTING Summer cultivars: broadcast thinly; thin to 4 in. (10 cm). Daikon cultivars: 9–10 in. (23–25 cm). Winter cultivars: 8–12 in. (20–30 cm).

Plant care

Do not allow to dry out, but avoid overwatering, which encourages leafy growth.

Harvesting

SUMMER CULTIVARS Harvest as soon as roots are large enough. They turn woody and go to seed quickly.

DAIKON CULTIVARS Harvest in mid–late summer. Will stand for several weeks.

WINTER CULTIVARS Harvest in autumn–early spring. Protect from frost with straw or store in sand in a frost-free shed. Leave a large root in the soil to flower and produce pods the next year. Pick pods when young and juicy.

Red orach

Atriplex hortensis
CHENOPODIACEAE

Also known as mountain spinach, this is a tall, decorative annual. It self-seeds at will. Sow in spring and summer, leaving 8 in. (20 cm) between plants. Eat the mild-flavored leaves lightly cooked.

Rhubarb

Rheum x *cultorum* POLYGONACEAE

One rhubarb plant can take up a lot of space, but it is usually all a family needs. It is simple and trouble-free to grow, well-suited to cool temperate climates. As it is the young, pinky red stalks that are eaten, botanically this fruit is classed as a vegetable. It makes an attractive ornamental. Rhubarb leaves are poisonous to eat, but quite safe to compost. The toxic oxalic acid they contain breaks down harmlessly during the composting process.

CROP DIVERSITY Some cultivars are more suited to forcing and early cropping than others.

SITE Fertile, fairly heavy soil in sun or light shade. Tolerant of all soils except waterlogged soils.

SOIL TREATMENT Dig deeply. Apply a medium- to high-fertility soil improver before planting. Mulch with a low-fertility soil improver after planting.

IDEAL PH RANGE 5–6

Sowing and planting

Most easily grown from "sets" or crowns, but can be raised from seed—although the results will be variable and take some time.

MINIMUM GERMINATION TEMPERATURE 55°F (13°C). Sow under cover in February, 2–3 seeds to a 3½-in. (9-cm) pot. Harden off and plant out once frosts have passed. Sow outside in spring, 1 in. (2.5 cm) deep in rows 12 in. (30 cm) apart. Thin to 6 in. (15 cm). Plant in permanent position in autumn.

PLANTING Buy virus-free plants or divide existing plants that are at least 3 years old in winter. Plant sets in October–November and February–March. The bud should be just below the soil surface. Firm soil well after planting. Sets may be grown on in pots for a few months before planting to give them a better start. Pot-grown plants can be planted at any time if the soil conditions are suitable.

Spacing

At least 36 in. (90 cm) each way.

Plant care

Water until established. Remove flower stems as they appear. Clear up leaves after foliage has died down. Mulch in late winter or early spring with a medium- to high-fertility soil improver.

PROBLEMS Usually trouble-free. May suffer from crown rot or viruses, for which there is no cure. Remove infected plants and do not replant on the same site.

Forcing

Established plants can be forced in early spring for pale pink, delicately flavored stems. Plants can be dug up and brought under cover, or blanched.

UNDER COVER Lift crowns over 2 years old in November or December and leave on the soil surface to expose them to the cold. In January, place crowns close together in deep boxes or pots packed with soil. Keep in a warm, dark shed or garage, or under greenhouse benches. Keep moist and warm, covering with an upturned bucket to exclude light. Discard after cropping.

OUTSIDE From February, cover crowns with a bucket or blanching pot. To speed up the process, pile fresh manure mixed with leaves or half-made compost around the blanching cover. Harvest after 6 weeks or so. Do not take another crop from forced plants for at least 2 years.

Cultivar choice
Rhubarb 'Crimson Red'; 'Glaskin's Perpetual'; 'Victoria'.

Rhubarb

Harvesting

Harvest 12–18 months after planting. Take only a few stems in the second year. From then on, harvest until June or July. If you sow seed early enough there is often enough to harvest from surplus seedlings from a late winter sowing. Twist off, rather than cut, stalks. Harvest lightly in autumn if you have not taken a crop in spring.

Rutabaga

Brassica napus Napobrassica Group
BRASSICACEAE

A very hardy root crop with a long growing season. It needs cool, damp conditions to do well. Roots can be left in the ground until the end of the year for autumn and early winter harvest. Delicious, sweet-flavored orange flesh.

SEED TO HARVEST 26 weeks.
CROP DIVERSITY Flesh color is usually yellow, though may be white. Skin color is purple or creamy brown, or a combination of both. Some cultivars are resistant to mildew and clubroot.
SITE Open site. Fertile, well-drained soil that does not dry out.
SOIL TREATMENT Apply a low-fertility soil improver if soil has been amended with compost for a previous crop. If not, treat also with a general organic fertilizer or use a medium-fertility soil improver. Do this in good time to let soil settle before sowing.
IDEAL pH RANGE 5.5–7

Sowing
MINIMUM GERMINATION TEMPERATURE 40°F (5°C)

UNDER COVER Sow suitable cultivars under row cover in February for an early crop of small-to-medium roots.
OUTSIDE Sow outside in early May in cooler areas, late May and early June in warmer regions. Firm the soil first if loose. Sow thinly in rows ¾ in. (2 cm) deep. Thin seedlings when no more than 1 in. (2.5 cm) high. Sow under row cover or fine mesh to protect against flea beetle and cabbage root fly where necessary.

Spacing
ROWS 9 x 15 in. (23 x 38 cm)
BLOCK PLANTING Early crops 6 in. (15 cm); main crops 12 in. (30 cm).

Plant care
Water regularly in dry weather, or may turn woody. Roots are also likely to split if watered suddenly after a dry period.
PROBLEMS Cabbage root fly; flea beetle; boron deficiency; root rot; clubroot; downy mildew; powdery mildew.

Harvesting
Harvesting can start as soon as roots are large enough, usually in early to mid-autumn. They can be left in the ground and dug as needed, but tend to be woody after December. Rutabagas can be stored in boxes (see p. 335) in a cool location.

Salsify

Tragopogon porrifolius
ASTERACEAE

An easy-to-grow root vegetable that is also known as vegetable oyster. It needs a long growing season but can be harvested all winter and takes up relatively little space. Can be blanched to give a spring crop.

SEED TO HARVEST 20 weeks
CROP DIVERSITY Little.
SITE Well-cultivated soil free of stones in open, sunny position. Makes compact clumps to fit among other crops or in a border. Unharvested plants will bear glorious mauve dandelion flowers in their second year—a favorite of hoverflies.
SOIL TREATMENT No additional feeding needed on reasonable soil that has been improved for a previous crop.
IDEAL pH RANGE 6–7.5

Sowing
MINIMUM GERMINATION TEMPERATURE 45°F (7°C).
Sow outside in April. Use fresh seed every year. The large seeds are easy to station-sow, 2–3 seeds per station at ½ in. (1 cm) deep. A second sowing can be made in September. Germination may be erratic, but it usually takes about 20 days.

Spacing
ROWS 8 x 12 in. (20 x 30 cm)
BLOCK PLANTING 9 in. (23 cm)

Plant care
Little needed. Hand-weed or mulch for weed control. Hoeing can damage the roots.

Harvesting
ROOTS Lift in autumn when the leaves have died. The long roots are brittle, so dig carefully. Keeps for a week in the fridge. Survives most winters left in the soil.

SHOOTS Roots left in the soil sprout in late spring. Remove dead leaves and mound up the soil around shoots to a depth of 6-8 in. (15-20 cm) or cover with straw or leaves. Cover with an upturned bucket if you only have one or two plants. Blanched shoots taste similar to chicory and resprout for 2–3 cuttings.

Scorzonera

Scorzonera hispanica ASTERACEAE

An uncommon, hardy perennial root crop, usually grown as an annual. The edible roots are black-skinned with white flesh.

SEED TO HARVEST 18 weeks.
CROP DIVERSITY Little.
SITE Deep, light soil is essential for long roots to develop.
SOIL TREATMENT No additional feeding is needed on reasonable soil improved for a previous crop.
IDEAL pH RANGE 6–7.5

Sowing
MINIMUM GERMINATION TEMPERATURE 45°F (7°C).
Sow direct in April and May as soon as the soil warms up.

Spacing
4 x 8 in. (10 x 20 cm)

Plant care
Hand-weed or mulch for weed control. Hoeing can damage the roots. Generally trouble-free.

Harvesting
Allow roots to grow for at least 4 months. Harvest from autumn to spring. Roots that have not reached a reasonable size can be

---

Cultivar choice
Rutabaga 'American Purple Top'; 'Gilfeather'—heirloom cultivar, white skin and flesh; 'Joan'—yellow flesh.
Salsify 'Sandwich Island Mammoth'—heirloom cultivar.
Scorzonera 'Large Jan'—long, uniform roots.

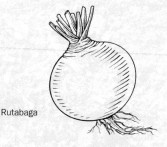

Rutabaga

left for another year. Cover with straw or leaves in early spring to produce fresh greens. This blanches emerging leaves, which can be cut when 4 in. (10 cm) tall. Scorzonera produces flowers in its second season, and the flower buds can be eaten.

Seakale

Crambe maritima BRASSICACEAE

This Victorian favorite is a perennial vegetable that can be grown in a demanding or relaxed fashion. The blanched shoots are harvested in mid- to late winter. With its large gray leaves and sweet-scented fountains of white flowers, seakale is an attractive ornamental and should produce well for 7 years.

SEED TO HARVEST 2 years.
CROP DIVERSITY Little.
SITE Open, permanent site in reasonably fertile soil. A deep, well-drained, slightly alkaline soil rich in organic matter is best.
SOIL TREATMENT Clear all weeds, especially perennials, and apply a medium-fertility soil improver. Lime the previous autumn if soil is acid.
IDEAL pH RANGE 6.5–8

Sowing

Plants from seed tend to be more vigorous than those propagated from root cuttings (*see below*).
MINIMUM GERMINATION TEMPERATURE 45°F (7°C)
UNDER COVER Seed can be slow to germinate; sandpaper it lightly to get it started. Sow in early spring in 3½-in. (9-cm) pots or in soil in a coldframe. Select the strongest-looking plants, harden off, and transplant to final position when they have 3–4 leaves.
OUTSIDE Sow in a seedbed in mid-March, 1 in. (2.5 cm) deep, in rows 12 in. (30 cm) apart. Thin to 6–8 in. (15–20 cm).

Planting root cuttings

Seakale is often raised from offsets or root cuttings. Root cuttings can be taken in late fall from plants that are at least 3 years old. Cut lateral root branches off in 3–6-in. (7.5–15-cm) lengths in winter. Buds grow from the end nearest the main root. Cut that end square and the other slanted, so you know which is which. Stand bunches of prepared root cuttings, square cut upward, in moist sand in a cool shed. Plant outdoors in late March, by which time buds should have appeared. Rub out all but the strongest bud, and plant in a dibble hole with the buds 1 in. (2.5 cm) below the soil surface.

Spacing

12–15 in. x 18–24 in. (30–38 cm x 46–60 cm)

Plant care

Apply an annual topdressing of medium-fertility soil improver or seaweed meal to permanent plants in late spring once stems are cut. Remove yellowing foliage and flowering shoots so the plant's energy goes into the roots.
PROBLEMS Slugs on young shoots; clubroot; root rot in soggy soil.

Forcing to harvest

Allow plants to grow for at least 1 full year before harvesting.
OUTDOOR METHOD In February or March, clear away leaf debris from plants and cover them with an upturned bucket (at least 15 in./38 cm deep) or a forcing pot. Cover with leaves or straw to protect young shoots from cold. Cut blanched pale stems low down, with a little piece of root attached, when 4–8 in. (10–20 cm) long. Stop cutting in May. Take 3–4 shoot cuttings from each established plant—this can be done annually.
FORCING INSIDE Forcing indoors allows a prolonged cutting season. Lift plants over 18 months old in late fall after the first frosts. Remove any side roots of pencil thickness from crowns to make cuttings for replanting in spring. Store the crowns (plants) in sand until required for forcing over the winter. Force a few at 2–3 week intervals. Plant 3 crowns in a 9-in. (27-cm) flowerpot, with the tops just showing, in a mixture of leaf mold and loam. Cover with an upturned bucket or flowerpot with the hole covered. Keep in a cool shed or cellar no less than 50°F (10°C); in 5 or 6 weeks the shoots will be ready to cut. After forcing, plants are exhausted, so discard. Seakale does not store.

Shallots

Allium cepa Aggregatum Group ALLIACEAE

A hardy, easy crop, less demanding than onions. Shallots raised from sets form a clump of small bulbs. Plants raised from seed produce a single bulb. Ready from July, they may keep in store for up to a year.

SEED TO HARVEST From seed: 20 weeks; from sets: 20–24 weeks.
CROP DIVERSITY A range of shapes, sizes, and skin colors.
SITE Open, sunny situation preferred, but tolerates a little shade.
SOIL TREATMENT No treatment needed if soil was improved for a previous crop. If not, apply a low- to medium-fertility soil improver, depending on soil condition.
IDEAL pH RANGE 6–7

Sowing

Shallots are usually planted as sets (*see below*) but a few cultivars can be raised from seed. Sow in March and April. Broadcast seed thinly in wide rows, aiming for 1–2 in. (2.5–5 cm) around each plant. Thin if necessary.
MINIMUM GERMINATION TEMPERATURE 45°F (7°C)

Growing from sets

Plant in February and March when soil conditions are suitable. Can be planted in September and October for an earlier crop in mild areas with well-drained soil. Push sets gently into a light soil. Otherwise make a small hole or take out a row. The tip of the set should be at soil level. Cultivars such as 'Wintergreen' dislike cold soil and are best planted later, in April.

Spacing

ROWS 6 x 8 in. (15 x 20 cm)
BLOCK PLANTING 8 in. (20 cm). Plant small sets 1 in. (2.5 cm) apart in autumn for an early crop used as spring onions.

Plant care

Little attention needed. Water in dry weather when bulbs swell.

Seakale

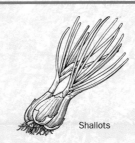

Shallots

PROBLEMS Onion problems may also affect shallots, but they are usually trouble-free. They often bolt if weather conditions fluctuate. Some cultivars are less prone to bolting; choose these for early planting.

Harvesting

Harvest when leaves are dying back, usually from July onward. Lift bulbs and leave them to dry. Once totally dry, separate individual bulbs and store in nets or on slatted trays in a cool, dry place.

Sorrel

Rumex acetosa POLYGONACEAE

Hardy perennial with sharp, lemony leaves to harvest early in the season. Sow in spring or autumn, either direct or in trays for transplanting, leaving 12 in. (30 cm) between plants. Remove flower spikes to encourage leaf production. Renew plants every 3–4 years. Sorrel has such a sharp flavor that the leaves are best mixed with something milder.

Spinach

Spinacia oleracea CHENOPODIACEAE

A quick-growing, leafy crop, best grown in cool temperatures. Goes to seed rapidly in hot weather.

SEED TO HARVEST 5–10 weeks.
CROP DIVERSITY Some cultivars are suited to spring and autumn sowing, while others, more resistant to bolting, can also be

grown in summer.
SITE Prefers light shade in summer, making it a useful interplant. Or, grow in an open site on a fertile soil that does not easily dry out. Can be grown in containers in light shade, and in an unheated greenhouse or hoop house for early or late crops.
SOIL TREATMENT Apply a low-fertility soil improver or a medium-fertility soil improver on poor soil.
IDEAL pH 6.5–7.5

Sowing

Successional sowing of suitable cultivars can give a crop over a long period. Sow as the previous batch is just coming through.
MINIMUM GERMINATION TEMPERATURE 45°F (7°C). Will not germinate above 86°F (30°C).
UNDER COVER Sow direct in early spring and early autumn under cloches or in an unheated greenhouse or hoop house.
OUTSIDE Sow thinly in rows in early and late spring, then in late summer and early autumn.

Spacing

ROWS 3–6 in. x 12 in. (7–15 cm x 30 cm)
BLOCK PLANTING 6 in. (15 cm)

Plant care

Water in dry weather. Can be prone to downy mildew.

Harvesting

As soon as plants are over 2 in. (5 cm) tall, start picking single leaves. Pull whole plants when 6–8 in. (15–20 cm) tall, or cut 1 in. (2.5 cm) above ground; they may resprout. Rapidly goes to seed. Use fresh or freeze. Mainly problem-free as it grows so fast.

Sweet corn

Zea mays POACEAE

A grain crop, unrelated to any other usually grown in the garden. Half-hardy, it is easy to grow in a good summer, less successful in a cold or wet year. Grows up to 5½ ft. (1.7 m), each plant producing one or two cobs. Eaten within a few minutes of picking, their flavor is unrivaled by anything you can buy.

SEED TO HARVEST 10–15 weeks.
CROP DIVERSITY The fresh kernels of traditional sweet corn cultivars store carbohydrate as sugar, not starch. Once cut, the sugar changes to starch, which is why sweet corn should be eaten as fresh as possible. Supersweet varieties are less hardy than the usual sweet corn. The two types should not be planted together, as the super-sweetness is lost if the plants cross-pollinate. Mini-corn is grown by close planting of selected, early cultivars.
SITE Warm, sheltered, sunny, with well-drained soil. Can also be grown under cover. Mini-corn can be grown in pots.
SOIL TREATMENT Grow on soil that has been improved for a previous crop or apply a medium-fertility soil improver.
IDEAL pH RANGE 5.5–7

Sowing

MINIMUM GERMINATION TEMPERATURE 50°F (10°C). Sweet corn needs to germinate in warm temperatures to do well.
UNDER COVER Sow in April. Sweet corn resents root disturbance, so raise transplants in root trainers or biodegradable

tubes. Harden plants before planting out. Planting through black plastic will speed growth.
OUTSIDE In warm areas, sow direct into soil warmed under cloches or black plastic if needed before sowing. Station-sow 2–3 seeds, 1–1½ in. (2.5–4 cm) deep. Thin to 1 seedling.

Spacing

Sweet corn is wind-pollinated, so plant in blocks, with 14 in. (35 cm) between plants. For mini-corn, leave 6 in. (15 cm) between plants, or grow 4 plants in a 12-in. (30-cm) pot. Grow supersweet cultivars at least 25 ft. (8 m) from other types to avoid cross-pollination.

Plant care

May need support on exposed sites. Stems can be mounded with soil to encourage more rooting for extra support. If necessary, water when corn starts to swell. Hand-weed or mulch for weed control.
PROBLEMS Mice; birds; slugs; corn earworms; European corn borer.

Harvesting

Corn is ripe when "silks" turn brown. Press a thumbnail into a corn grain—a milky juice means it is ripe. Can be frozen or pickled. Pick mini-corn when cobs are 3 in. (7 cm) long.

Tomato

Lycopersicon esculentum SOLANACEAE

A popular, short-season, half-hardy summer vegetable,

Cultivar choice
Spinach 'Bloomsdale Long-Standing'—heirloom cultivar, slow to bolt; 'Melody' F1; 'Space' F1—smooth leaves; 'Tyee'—crinkled leaves, slow to bolt.

Squash see *Pumpkins and winter squashes* and *Zucchini and summer squash*

Sweet corn 'Dwarf Blue Jade' F1—blue kernels turn green when cooked, very compact plants; 'Early Sunglow' F1—quick to mature; 'Fantasy' F1—great flavor; 'Golden Bantam'—heirloom cultivar, yellow kernels; 'Indian Summer' F1—multicolored kernels; 'Silver Queen' F1—white kernels.

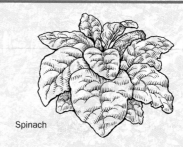

Spinach

relatively easy to grow without a greenhouse anywhere that has a reasonable summer. For earlier cropping and/or higher yields per plant, use a greenhouse or hoop house (for more information on growing tomatoes under cover, see p. 224).

There are literally hundreds of cultivars. Disease-resistant cultivars are good for greenhouse growing where a long crop rotation is not practical. Yellow cultivars may be more resistant to potato blight than others. Those listed below are suited to growing both outside, in warmer regions, and under cover (unless otherwise stated).

SEED TO HARVEST 7–12 weeks.
CROP DIVERSITY From the gardener's viewpoint there are 2 main types of tomato:
Indeterminate (sometimes called cordon or tall) varieties produce a single main shoot that grows indefinitely in warm conditions and is normally trained up a central support. Sideshoots are pinched off. Some cultivars of this type are for the greenhouse, but most grow outdoors.
Determinate or bush varieties have no leading shoot but develop many side branches, forming a sprawling bush—the most common form of outdoor tomato. Trailing or extra-dwarf cultivars are selections of this type chosen for containers. There are also cultivars that are semi-determinate.

Tomato fruits can be round, plum-shaped, or ribbed, from cherry size to fruits that weigh 16 oz. (450 g) or more. Color is even more variable, including red, white, yellow, orange, green, purple, and striped. The larger-fruited beefsteak and plum cultivars tend to ripen later. Plum cultivars are thick-walled and good for making sauces. Cultivars resistant to various pests, diseases, and ripening disorders are available.
SITE Warm, sheltered, in full sun with fertile, well-drained soil. Under cover, tomatoes are easiest to manage in soil beds but can also be grown in large containers, indoors or out. Bush varieties can even be grown in a hanging basket.
SOIL TREATMENT Apply a medium-fertility soil improver, or a low-fertility soil improver combined with a general organic fertilizer.
IDEAL pH RANGE 5.5–7

Sowing

MINIMUM GERMINATION TEMPERATURE 60°F (16°C). Seedlings can withstand cooler temperatures. Sowing under cover, in gentle heat, is the best method of getting consistently successful crops in cool climates. For growing in a heated greenhouse, start sowing in January. For an unheated greenhouse/hoop house, or growing outside, sow 6–8 weeks before the last frost. Sow in trays (pricking out into pots), cell packs, or 3½-in. (9-cm) pots. Plants may need potting up again before transplanting outside. Harden off once danger of frost has passed.

Tomato cuttings

Sideshoots are easily rooted as cuttings to provide several plants from a single seed. Cut off sideshoots when 6 in. (15 cm) long. Insert into 3-in. (8-cm) pots filled with equal parts of leaf mold and sharp sand. Cover with a plastic bag or bottle. Provide bottom heat at 60–62°F (15–16°C) early in the season. Cuttings root in 10–14 days. Pot up or plant out as appropriate. Remove the first truss of flowers if a plant is not growing strongly.

Planting out

Plant out when first flowers show. To fruit well, tomatoes need temperatures of around 70–75°F (21–24°C). If these temperatures are unlikely in summer, plant in a greenhouse/hoop house. Leggy plants can be planted slightly deeper than in their pot. Under cover, interplant with French marigolds to reduce the risk of whitefly attack.
PLANTING OUTSIDE Harden off and transplant once all danger of frost has passed. Soil temperature should be at least 50°F (10°C) and air temperature a minimum of 45°F (7°C). Protect with row cover or cloches if necessary. To warm the soil and encourage fruit to ripen earlier in cooler regions, plant through a black plastic mulch.

Spacing

ROWS Tall, indeterminate, and semi-determinate types: 15–18 in. x 18 in. (38–45 cm x 45 cm); allow 3 ft. (90 cm) between pairs of rows. Train as cordons with a single stem. Bush types: 18–20 in. x 18–24 in. (45–48 cm x 45–60 cm). Extra-dwarf bush types: 10–12 in. x 12–14 in. (25–30 cm x 30–35 cm). Bush types are usually left to sprawl.
BLOCK PLANTING 18 in. (45 cm)

Plant care

Protect from low temperatures and frost, but remember to allow access for pollinating insects once flowers open. Mulch for moisture retention. Once fruit has formed, water plants in very dry weather. Plants in containers need regular watering, even twice a day in hot weather, and supplementary feeding with a high-potash organic liquid fertilizer. Plants grown in a well-managed soil should not need additional feeding. Mulch with a medium-fertility soil improver or comfrey leaves. Overwatering or overfeeding reduces the flavor of a crop. Train indeterminate types up a string or sturdy support. Pinch out sideshoots. In late summer, or earlier in cooler regions, pinch off the growing tip to encourage development and ripening of the fruit. Do not pinch off sideshoots of bush cultivars. To keep the crop clean, support plants with canes or similar, or mulch with straw. Shade greenhouses in summer.
PROBLEMS Potato and tomato blight; Colorado potato beetle; aphids; whitefly; red spider mite; hornworms; fusarium wilt; gray mold (botrytis); tobacco mosaic virus; tomato leaf mold; verticillium wilt; blossom end rot; magnesium deficiency.

Harvesting

Pick fruits as they ripen fully, reaching the color appropriate to the cultivar. Cut the fruit stalk, leaving the calyx attached to the fruit. Toward the end of the season, pull up outdoor plants still fruiting and hang by their roots in a frost-free shed or garage. The fruit will continue to

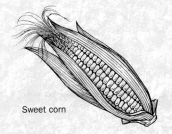

Sweet corn

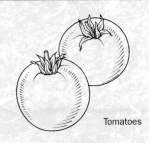

Tomatoes

ripen. Alternatively, when frost threatens, pick all fruit and place green ones in a single layer in a drawer or box in a cool place to ripen. Healthy fruits continue to ripen until the New Year. They can also be bottled, frozen, or made into sauce.

Turnip

Brassica rapa Rapifera Group
BRASSICACEAE

A root vegetable in the cabbage family, turnips are suited to moist, cool conditions and tolerate mild frosts. Young turnip leaves make excellent spicy spring greens. Their flesh can be white or yellow, and the skins white, yellow, pink, or red. Early cultivars are small and white, fast-growing for spring and summer crops. Main crop cultivars are hardier, used fresh in summer and winter; also for winter storage. Quick-maturing cultivars are good for catch-cropping. Turnips can take some shade. Apply a low-fertility soil improver if soil has been improved for a previous crop. Otherwise use a medium-fertility soil improver, or low-fertility soil improver with a general organic fertilizer.

The earliest sowings of quick cultivars can be made under row cover or cloches in early March, as soon as the soil is workable. Sow thinly in rows or station-sow. Sowing under row cover or fine mesh will protect against flea beetle and cabbage root fly. Sow early/quick cultivars outside in March and April every 3 weeks for successional cropping.

May/June sowings are possible if weather is cool and wet. Sow main crop cultivars in July and August. To ensure good root formation, thin to required spacing as soon as possible: 4 x 9 in. (10 x 23 cm) for quick cultivars; 6 x 12 in. (15 x 30 cm) for main crop cultivars; 6 in. (15 cm) when block planting. Water regularly in hot, dry weather or plants may bolt. Turnips are also vulnerable to turnip gall weevil, cabbage root fly, flea beetle (seedlings), clubroot, downy mildew, powdery mildew, root rot, and boron deficiency.

Pull early turnips when 1½–2 in. (4–5 cm) across. Harvest main crop turnips when tennis-ball size or keep in the ground until New Year. Any still growing can be used for greens by cutting tops at 4–6 in. (10–15 cm) high. Tops will usually crop several times.

Zucchini and summer squash

Cucurbita pepo CUCURBITACEAE

Large, often very vigorous, half-hardy plants, with a diversity of shapes, colors, and sizes of fruit. Undemanding and rewarding to grow. Heat-tolerant.

SEED TO HARVEST Ready to pick anywhere from 6 to 8 weeks after planting.
CROP DIVERSITY Soft-skinned and smooth fruits, available in all shapes, from round "patty pan" squashes to the crookneck types. Zucchini are typically dark green but can also be yellow; they usually produce long, straight fruits but may also be globe-shaped. Usually eaten fresh; summer squash and zucchini do not store well. The flowers are edible, too. Both trailing and bush types are available.
SITE Sheltered, in full sun. The foliage and fruits of bush varieties can look stunning in an ornamental garden. Zucchini and summer squash can be grown under cover for an early crop.
SOIL TREATMENT Apply a low- or medium-fertility soil improver, depending on soil conditions. Rich soil or over-generous feeding encourages plants to produce a lot of foliage at the expense of the fruit. Can also be grown in a compost trench (see p. 48).
IDEAL pH RANGE 5.5–6.8

Sowing

MINIMUM GERMINATION TEMPERATURE 59°F (15°C)
UNDER COVER Sow in late spring, 3–4 weeks before your last frost date. Push two seeds into each 3½-in. (9-cm) pot; remove the weaker seedling. Harden off well before planting outside when all danger of frost has passed. Transplant carefully as plants dislike root disturbance.
OUTSIDE Sow direct in early summer in mild areas. Protect with bottle cloches for extra warmth at the start.

Spacing

Trailing cucurbits are vigorous plants; where space is limited, choose compact bush cultivars. Trailing cultivars will grow well beneath tall crops, such as runner beans or sweet corn.
ROWS Bush cultivars: 24–36 in. x 36–48 in (60–90 cm x 90–120 cm). Trailing cultivars: 4–6 ft. x 6 ft. (1.2–1.8 m x 1.8 m).
BLOCK PLANTING Bush cultivars: 36 in. (90 cm). Trailing cultivars: 4–6 ft. (1.2–1.8 m).

Plant care

Keep weed-free until established. Water only until established. When the plants are growing well, mulch with straw, hay, or a low-fertility soil improver. Trailing cultivars can be trained up a strong support, or pegged out into a circle. Early in the season, or in response to stress, plants may temporarily produce only male flowers. Zucchini and other summer squash growing under cover may need hand-pollination (see p. 120).
PROBLEMS Aphids; cucumber beetle; squash vine borer; bacterial wilt; mosaic virus; powdery mildew.

Harvesting

You can pick zucchini and other summer squash as soon as you see them (even with the flower still attached) for use as baby vegetables. For cooking, 6–8 in. (15–20 cm) is a good length for zucchini and crookneck cultivars; pick rounder types at 4–8 in. (10–20 cm) in diameter. The fruits ripen quickly, and plants will stop producing once they mature, so pick every day or two to keep the harvest coming. Zucchini are notorious for hiding their fruits, so check carefully when you harvest. Zucchini and summer squash fruits will keep in the fridge for 2–3 weeks.

Cultivar choice
Turnip 'Hakurei' F1—white root, early; 'Purple Top White Globe'—a reliable favorite; 'Tokyo Cross' F1—fast-growing, disease resistant.

Watercress see p. 226
Watermelon see Melon, sweet

Zucchini and summer squash 'Black Beauty'—a classic zucchini with near-black fruits; 'Condor'—dark green zucchini, nearly spineless stems for easy picking; 'Gold Rush' F1—bright yellow zucchini; 'Peter Pan'—summer squash with flattened, light green fruits; 'Ronde de Nice'—rounded green zucchini; 'Seneca Prolific' F1—yellow straightneck summer squash'; 'Yellow Crookneck'—bright yellow summer squash.

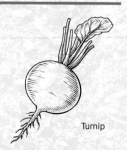

Turnip

A–Z of Plant Problems

THE FOLLOWING REFERENCE SECTION, while it cannot be completely comprehensive, covers the majority of plant problems that you may encounter in the garden and under cover, in greenhouses and hoop houses. It may also help in diagnosing and dealing with similar problems on houseplants, too.

Entries are arranged by common name; additional common names may be listed at the bottom of each page. For pests and diseases, to avoid any confusion, scientific name(s) are also given. Each entry briefly describes the problem, whether a cultural disorder, a disease, or a pest. Plants susceptible to the problem are then listed; in some cases these are quite specific, but, in others, groups of related plants or any plant growing under similar conditions may be affected. The most commonly seen symptoms are described.

For each problem, measures for prevention and control are then given—if any are necessary. This latter point cannot be overstresssed. Above all, never use sprays, even "organic" ones, unless essential.

Best practice for healthy plants
Use the following general measures to encourage healthy, problem-free plant growth and reduce the need to use controls.
• Provide appropriate food and shelter to encourage natural predators (see *Gardening for Wildlife*, pp. 186–201).
• Create a good soil structure (see *Soil and Soil Care*, pp. 33–39).
• Feed the soil with composted organic soil improvers (see also *Soil and Soil Care*, pp. 40–61).
• Grow plants that suit the site.
• Do not sow or plant when temperatures are too low.
• Practice good hygiene—clear away pest-ridden and diseased foliage and plants, both in the garden and under cover (see also *Management Tips under Cover*, pp. 228–229).
• Encourage good airflow around plants by thinning out and pruning.
• Do not overfeed, particularly with nitrogen, which causes lush growth that is attractive to pests.
• Use a crop rotation when growing vegetables (see pp. 301–303).
• Pick off pests and diseases as they appear.
• Grow resistant cultivars where there is a known problem.

Spraying—best practice
Never:
• Spray if another method is available.
• Mix different sprays together.
• Spray on a windy day.
Always:
• Identify the problem correctly so the right spray is used.
• Check that the product is legally and organically approved for the job. Regulations are frequently updated.
• Spray at dusk to avoid harming bees.
• Follow the instructions on the bottle or packet.
• Wear protective clothing and use a good-quality sprayer.
• Avoid spraying predators.

Other useful references
Most of the techniques and materials listed here for prevention and control are given fuller descriptions and often pictured in the chapter on *Plant Health*, pp. 84–103—including biological controls, traps and barriers, and "organic" sprays. Other useful references are:
• Crop covers—row cover and mesh, pp. 230–233.
• Mineral (nutrient) deficiencies and soil pH: pp. 36–37 and p. 61.
• Soil testing and analysis, pp. 33–37.

Getting more help
If you cannot determine the cause of a particular problem, free advice is available from the Cooperative Extension Service. This service was established in 1914 to provide an educational link between the public, the United States Department of Agriculture, and land-grant colleges (state colleges built on land donated by the government). Extension offices provide gardening advice tailored to your particular climate, soil, and growing conditions through publications, classes, workshops, and one-on-one consultations. Most offices are listed in the government section of the phone book. Look for the headings Cooperative Extension, Agricultural Extension, or University Extension under the county government listing, or check for the same headings under the listing for your state land-grant college.

Anthracnose

Various anthracnose diseases are caused by fungi. They affect many different plants and cause a variety of symptoms.

SUSCEPTIBLE PLANTS Many kinds of woody and herbaceous plants. Vegetables such as beans, cucumbers, melons, peppers, and tomatoes are particularly susceptible. Anthracnose-prone trees include dogwoods, maples, and sycamores.

SYMPTOMS On leaves, these fungal diseases generally appear first as small, irregular, yellow or brown spots that darken as they age. These spots may also expand and join to cover the leaves. On vegetables, anthracnose diseases produce small, dark, sunken spots in the skin. As the disease progresses, the spots may spread. Pinkish spore masses appear in the center of the spots in moist weather. Fruit eventually rots. On trees, infection can begin before the leaves appear, killing the tips of young twigs, or it can produce brown spots on young leaves. In the latter case, defoliation may occur, forcing the tree to produce a new set of leaves in the summer and severely weakening it.

PREVENTION AND CONTROL Avoid anthracnose on vegetables by selecting resistant cultivars when available, buying healthy transplants, planting in well-drained soil, and not touching plants when they are wet. Remove and destroy infected plants. On trees, prune out the dead wood and the water sprouts. Avoid drought stress by watering trees during dry spells and keeping the root zone mulched. Gather up and destroy infected leaves.

Fungicide spray: A dormant spray of Bordeaux mix may provide some control.

Aphids

Small, soft-bodied, sap-feeding insects ½₂–⅛ in. (1–3 mm) long. Sometimes called greenfly or blackfly, depending on their color; they may be winged or wingless, with long legs and antennae, and prominent tubelike structures at the end of the abdomen. Body color is red, orange, yellow, green, brown, or black, depending on species. In favorable conditions, females when only a week old give birth to live young so colonies can build up rapidly.

SUSCEPTIBLE PLANTS Most plants may be attacked by aphids. Many aphid species are plant-specific, such as the lupin aphid, while others, such as the peach potato aphid, will attack hundreds of different types of plants. Aphids may spend the summer on certain plants, moving to a different host species for the winter.

SYMPTOMS Tender young growth is most prone to attack, but aphids will also colonize leaves, stems, and, in some cases, roots. Leaves and shoots become distorted. Heavy infestation can kill a plant. Leaves are often coated with honeydew, a sticky substance produced by aphids. Black sooty molds grow on the honeydew, inhibiting photosynthesis and spoiling appearance. Root aphids can cause plants to wilt. Aphids also transmit viruses.

PREVENTION AND CONTROL Tolerate aphid colonies where they are not causing damage. They will act as a "nursery" for aphid predators and parasites to feed and breed on. To control aphids, rub them off or pick off infested shoots. Grow attractant flowers and create suitable habitats for birds, earwigs, lady beetles, hoverflies, spiders, ground beetles, parasitic wasps, lacewings, and other natural enemies of the aphid. Allow natural predators time to work. Do not overfeed plants with nitrogen; soft, sappy growth is a magnet to aphids. Keep containers adequately fed and watered, and pot up plants as necessary. Use crop rotation to avoid buildup of root aphids. Grow resistant cultivars.

Biological controls: Under cover, *Aphidius* and *Aphidoletes*—both need a minimum temperature of 50°F (10°C) and at least 2 hours at 64°F (18°C) every day to stimulate activity. Lacewing larvae are ideal trouble-shooters when an aphid infestation has gotten out of control. Use them to reduce the pest population to manageable levels, then introduce the other controls. They need a minimum temperature of 50°F (10°C). They may be used outside from early May; or use lady beetle larvae from April.

Pesticide sprays: Insecticidal soap; pyrethrin; canola oil. All of these must hit the aphids to work. Once leaf curling has occurred and pests are concealed, a spray is unlikely to be effective.

See also Cabbage aphid; Lettuce root aphid; Woolly aphid.

Apple maggot

Rhagoletis pomonella

The adult apple maggots are ¼-in. (6-mm) flies with yellow legs and transparent wings patterned with dark, crosswise bands. They lay eggs just beneath the skin of the fruit, and the larvae tunnel within. The larvae are white, ¼-in. (6-mm) maggots in fruit. Apple maggots are found throughout the eastern United States and Canada, as well as northern California.

SUSCEPTIBLE PLANTS Apples, blueberries, and plums. A similar pest affects cherries.

SYMPTOMS Maggots tunnel through the fruit flesh. Fruit drops prematurely. Early-ripening cultivars are most affected.

PREVENTION AND CONTROL Grow late-maturing cultivars of susceptible crops. Collect and destroy dropped fruit daily until September, then twice a month in autumn. Hang apple maggot traps in trees from mid-June until harvest (one per dwarf tree, six per full-size tree). Plant white clover as a groundcover around susceptible plants to attract beetles that prey on the pupae.

Apple powdery mildew

Podosphaera leucotricha

Fungal disease that overwinters in buds. Infected buds open

Apple bitter pit *see Calcium deficiency*

Apple capsid *see Capsid bugs*

Never mix different pesticide sprays together.

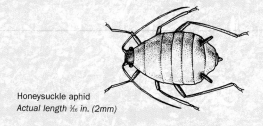
Honeysuckle aphid
Actual length ¹⁄₁₆ in. (2mm)

later than healthy ones.
See also Powdery mildew.

SUSCEPTIBLE PLANTS Apple; also pear, quince, peach, *Photinia*, and medlar.
SYMPTOMS A powdery white coating on buds, leaves, and stems. Flowers drop; leaves distort, wither, and fall. Early infections cause weblike russetting on fruit.
PREVENTION AND CONTROL Grow resistant cultivars. Mulch under trees to stop soil drying out. Water trees in dry weather. In winter, cut out infected shoots. In spring, remove infected leaves and shoots. Spray with seaweed extract to promote strong growth.
Fungicide spray: Sulfur, although it can harm some apple cultivars. Check the label before use.

Apple scab

Venturia inaequalis

This fungal disease overwinters in leaf debris and is spread to new leaves in spring by wind and rain. In severe cases the disease can overwinter in twig lesions. Apple scab is worse when the weather is cool, wet, or overcast in spring and early summer, especially at flowering time.

SUSCEPTIBLE PLANTS Apple.
SYMPTOMS Dark brown/green blotches appear on the leaves; these may expand along the veins and run into each other. Leaves may drop prematurely. Dark spots, which develop into corky patches, appear on the fruit skin. Fruit may crack but

does not rot. In severe cases, twigs blister, swell, and burst to produce brown-green pustules in spring.
PREVENTION AND CONTROL Grow resistant cultivars. In autumn, water fallen leaves on the ground with high-nitrogen liquid (nettle brew, manure tea), as this will help to kill spores and decompose leaves. Mow the ground below trees to shred leaves and speed decomposition, or collect leaves and compost them. Cut out and burn diseased twigs. Prune apple trees to maintain good air circulation.

Asparagus beetle

Crioceris asparagi

The adult beetles are up to ¼ in. (6 mm) long, with distinctive yellow and black wing cases. Larvae are gray-black with a humped back. Adults hibernate under stones, in soil, and in plant debris, emerging in spring to feed on asparagus foliage. Eggs are laid in June. There may be two or three generations in a year.

SUSCEPTIBLE PLANTS Asparagus.
SYMPTOMS Foliage eaten. Growth may be checked.
PREVENTION AND CONTROL Pick off larvae and adults. Clear plant debris where beetles may overwinter.

Bacterial canker

Pseudomonas mors-prunorum

In autumn and winter canker bacteria, spread by rain-splash

from the leaves, enter twigs through leaf scars to cause canker lesions. In spring and summer the foliage is attacked, but no new cankers are formed.

SUSCEPTIBLE PLANTS Plum and cherry.
SYMPTOMS Dark brown spots appear on leaves in the late spring. These drop out leaving a "shot hole" appearance. Cankers usually occur on plum tree trunks and cherry branches. Initially, amber-colored gum exudes from a slight depression. Leaves become yellow and stems die back.
PREVENTION AND CONTROL Not an easy disease to control. Try to avoid damaging the bark of trees. Make sure trunks will not rub on any supporting stake, take care when cutting surrounding grass, and do not leave rough pruning cuts.

Bacterial soft rot

Erwinia carotovora

A common disease caused by a soil-dwelling bacteria. It does not appear to survive in the soil but can survive on plant debris. Infection enters through wounds such as those caused by slugs or carrot root fly.

SUSCEPTIBLE PLANTS Brassicas, especially turnip and rutabaga; also celery, cucurbits, leeks, lettuce, onion, parsnip, potato, tomato, and cyclamen.
SYMPTOMS Water-soaked lesions around a wound that rapidly enlarges. The infected stem, leaf base, or storage organ disintegrates into a foul-smelling, slimy, brownish rotting

mass. The skin of most storage organs is not affected, although cracks may appear through which the slimy interior may seep.
PREVENTION AND CONTROL Ensure that land is well-drained. When growing vegetables use a strict crop rotation—minimum 3 years, but preferably 4 or 5. Control wound-forming pests like wireworms, slugs, and root-damaging larvae. Once rot has started there is no cure. Dispose of or bury infected plant material.

Beet leaf spot

Cercospora beticola, Ramularia beticola

This fungal disease overwinters in residue from diseased plants or on seed. It is spread by rain-splash, wind, insects, tools, and by hand. High humidity and warm temperatures encourage disease development.

SUSCEPTIBLE PLANTS Red beet, spinach beet; also sugar beet.
SYMPTOMS Small, more or less circular spots with a pale ashen center and brown-purple margins appear on leaves.
PREVENTION AND CONTROL Clear up crop debris; use fresh seed. Damage is rarely significant.

Black knot

Dibotryon morbosum

This fungal disease appears as a cancerous black or greenish growth on stems. Wild plum and cherry trees can be a source of infection.

Asparagus beetle
Actual length ¼ in. (6 mm)

Bacterial canker

Apple replant disease *see Replant disease*

Grow resistant cultivars if possible where there is a known problem.

SUSCEPTIBLE PLANTS Cherries and plums.

SYMPTOMS Black knot appears as unsightly swellings on twigs and branches. These swellings are usually black, but they may appear velvety green in early spring. Tips of infected branches often die back. Severe infections can kill whole limbs, and the tree may be stunted.

PREVENTION AND CONTROL Look for resistant cultivars. In fall or late winter, prune off infected limbs, 6–12 in. (15–30 cm) below the knots; disinfect pruners in between cuts with a 10% bleach solution (1 part bleach to 9 parts water). Destroy the prunings.

Fungicide spray: Remove any wild plum or cherry trees nearby. For persistent infections, apply 2 sprays of lime-sulfur, 7 days apart, before the buds begin to grow in spring.

Black vine weevil

Otiorhynchus sulcatus

Adults are wingless, dull, dark brown-black, about ⅜ in. (9 mm) long, covered in small buff-yellow specks. They emerge in May and June, feeding by night. Virtually all are female and each lays several hundred eggs in soil around host plants from late July. The larvae are creamy white "C"-shaped grubs with brown heads and can be up to ½ in. (1 cm) long. They feed on plant roots until the following spring, when they pupate in the soil. Most adults die at the end of the season, but some

overwinter. In a greenhouse, adult weevils may emerge in the autumn and lay eggs over a longer period.
See also Weevils.

SUSCEPTIBLE PLANTS A wide range of plants in the garden, greenhouse, and house. Plants in pots are particularly at risk.

SYMPTOMS Adult weevils eat irregular holes around the edges of leaves. This damage is more cosmetic than life-threatening. Larvae are the main problem as they feed on plant roots. If a plant is growing poorly or wilts suddenly and dies, check in and around the rootball for this pest. It may show no leaf symptoms.

PREVENTION AND CONTROL Inspect plants regularly for adult weevils, particularly at night. Inspect newly purchased plants for adults and larvae before planting out. Protect individual pots and greenhouse bench legs with sticky tape smeared with nondrying glue, and renew these barriers regularly.

Biological control: Outdoors and under cover, use *Heterorhabditis megidis*, a parasitic nematode; minimum soil/compost temperature 54°F (12°C). Under cover it may be used year-round as long as soil temperatures are adequate. Outside it is best applied in April/May, and August/early September.

Boron deficiency

Root crops are most susceptible to this disorder; also cabbages, cauliflowers, celery, pears, strawberries, and carnations.

SYMPTOMS Growing tips die, plants are bushy and stunted. Beets—rough, cankered patches appear on roots; may cause a brown rot internally. Cabbage—leaves distorted; hollow areas in stems. Cauliflower—curds develop poorly and may develop brown patches. Stem, leaf stalks, and midribs roughened. Celery—leaf stalks develop cracks on the outer surface; inner tissue is reddish brown. Pears—fruits develop hard, brown flecks in the flesh; may be distorted. New shoots may die back in spring. Rutabaga and turnip—brown or gray areas, often in concentric rings, develop internally in the lower parts of the root. Strawberries—plants stunted. Leaves small, yellow, and puckered at tips. Fruits small and pale, developing a "waist" close to the stem end.

CAUSES A true soil deficiency is fairly rare; it may occur when the bedrock contains granite, which is low in boron. Leaching from light soils in heavy rainfall, excess liming/high pH, and very dry soils may also be the cause.

PREVENTION AND TREATMENT Improve moisture retention of light soils. Measure pH before liming; keep pH below 7. Rake borax into the soil at 1 oz./sq. yd. (35 g/sq. m). Use a foliar spray on pears: 2 oz. in 5 gallons of water (70 g in 22 liters).

Boxwood psylla

Psylla buxi

These insects lay their eggs in late summer in slits in leaf axils

and twigs. They hatch in mid-spring. Their young feed on growing points and young shoots from late spring onward. There is one generation each year.

SUSCEPTIBLE PLANTS Boxwood.
SYMPTOMS The leaves at the tip of infected shoots arch inward to form tight, cabbagelike clusters. Growth can be checked if infestation is severe. Sticky honeydew and black sooty molds may be present.

PREVENTION AND CONTROL Control is only necessary on young plants if they become stunted. Clip regularly, particularly in early spring, to remove infested shoot tips.

Brassica white rust

Albugo candida

Fungal disease spread by wind, insects, and rain-splash. It can remain dormant in the soil for several months, where it overwinters.

SUSCEPTIBLE PLANTS Vegetables and ornamental brassicas; the annual weed shepherd's purse.
SYMPTOMS Small, smooth, white blotches resembling white paint spots appear on leaves and stems. These spots later become powdery. Distortion of affected areas or the entire plant follows. Commonly associated with brassica downy mildew.

PREVENTION AND CONTROL Destroy diseased plants. Use a strict crop rotation—minimum 3 years but preferably 4 or 5 years.

Beet leaf miner *see Leaf miners; also p. 310*

Pick off or prune out pests and diseases as they appear.

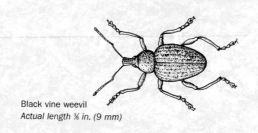

Black vine weevil
Actual length ⅜ in. (9 mm)

Broad bean chocolate spot

Botrytis fabae

This fungal disease thrives in damp and overcrowded conditions. Spores can overwinter on infected plants and plant debris. The disease is more likely to be a problem where soil is short in potassium.

SUSCEPTIBLE PLANTS Broad bean, field bean.
SYMPTOMS Round, chocolate-brown spots develop on leaves, stems, pods, and seed coats. These may merge until totally blackened parts of the plant die.
PREVENTION AND CONTROL Provide ample spacing between plants. Grow in well-drained soil. Avoid autumn sowing if this disease is a regular problem. Spring-sown beans are more likely to recover than plants infected later in the season. Improve potassium levels if low.

Brown rot

Sclerotinia fructigena, S. laxa

Airborne fungal disease that infects plants through wounded bark. Caterpillars, birds, support stakes, or hailstones can cause the initial damage. It spreads quickly throughout the plant and cankers may develop. The fungus overwinters on infected fruit and cankers. A form of this fungus also causes blossom wilt.

SUSCEPTIBLE PLANTS Apple, peach, almond, nectarine, cherry, quince, plum, and pear.
SYMPTOMS A very common

fungal problem that produces soft, brown patches on fruit (see p. 91). Concentric circles of white fluffy growth also develop on these areas while fruit is on the tree or in storage. Fruit may turn black. Some fruit on the tree will shrivel, become "mummified," and remain attached throughout the winter.
PREVENTION AND CONTROL Prune out affected branches and remove fruit from the tree. Pick up windfalls. Do not compost any of this material. Take care not to damage fruit that is to be stored. Do not store any diseased fruit. Cut out cankers and diseased spurs during normal winter pruning.

Cabbage aphid

Brevicoryne brassicae

Adults of this pest are gray-green in color and are covered in a powdery white mealy wax. Overwintering eggs, laid on stems and leaves of brassicas, hatch in spring. Infestations occur from midsummer onward, reaching a peak in early to mid-autumn.
See also Aphids.

SUSCEPTIBLE PLANTS Brassicas.
SYMPTOMS Dense colonies of aphids cause distortion and discoloration of leaves. A severe infestation can check growth and can kill shoot tips and young plants.
PREVENTION AND CONTROL Remove overwintering brassica plants as soon as they have finished cropping. This should be done by mid-spring. Bury plant debris deep in a compost

pile or in a compost trench. Examine young plants regularly from early summer to early autumn and squash any colonies of eggs or young.
Pesticide sprays: Insecticidal soap; pyrethrin; canola oil.

Cabbage caterpillars

The cabbage white or large white butterfly (*Pieris brassicae*) is a creamy white butterfly, with a broad black tip to the forewing, appearing in April and May. Clusters of bright orange eggs are laid on and under leaves of susceptible plants. The distinctive yellow and black caterpillars, often found in large clusters, grow up to 2 in. (5 cm) long, feeding for a month or so (see p. 304). There are two or three generations a year. The spring brood of the small cabbage white butterfly (*Pieris rapae*) is white, with slightly clouded black tips on forewings. The summer brood have darker tips and black markings on the wings. Eggs are laid singly, under leaves. The caterpillars, which grow up to 1½ in. (3.5 cm) long, are velvety green, making them difficult to spot, especially when lying along the vein of a leaf. They are often found feeding in the heart of a plant. There can be three generations in a year, with the severest attacks in late summer.

SUSCEPTIBLE PLANTS Brassicas; large whites may also attack nasturtiums (*Tropaeolum* spp.).
SYMPTOMS Foliage eaten. A

plant may be quickly stripped to a skeleton.
PREVENTION AND CONTROL Examine plants regularly when the butterflies have been seen. Squash eggs, pick off caterpillars. Wasps are particularly effective at controlling this pest. Grow crops under fine mesh netting to exclude the butterflies.
Biological control: Apply *Bacillus thuringiensis* (BT) as a spray to infested plants.

Cabbage looper

Trichoplusia ni

Adults are gray moths with a silver spot in the middle of each forewing. They emerge from overwintering pupae in May and lay light green, dome-shaped eggs on the undersides of leaves. The larvae are green, 1½-in. (4-cm) caterpillars with two white lines down their backs, one along each side. They feed for 2 to 4 weeks, then pupate 10 days in cocoons attached to stems or leaves. There are three to four generations per year.

SUSCEPTIBLE PLANTS Brassicas (cabbage, cauliflower, and broccoli, for example), as well as many other vegetable crops.
SYMPTOMS Larvae chew large holes in leaves and may destroy whole plants.
PREVENTION AND CONTROL Hand pick larvae several times weekly and drop them into soapy water. Till crop residues into the soil before adults emerge in spring. Attract native parasitic wasps by planting pollen- and nectar-rich flowers.

Small cabbage white butterfly

Black spot *see Rose black spot*
Blossom end rot *see Calcium deficiency*

Biological control: Spray larvae with *Bacillus thuringiensis* var. *kurstaki* (B.T.K.).

Cabbage root fly

Delia radicum

Adults of this flying insect are ¼ in. (6 mm) long and resemble small horseflies. They lay eggs in soil near, or occasionally on, host plants. Legless white larvae, up to ⅜ in. (8 mm) long, feed on roots. Pupae overwinter in the soil. Damage is usually worse in late spring and early summer, but a second and even third generation may continue to damage plants into autumn. Transplants raised in seedbeds, pots, and cell packs are also prone to attack.

SUSCEPTIBLE PLANTS Brassicas; also related ornamentals such as wallflowers and stocks.
SYMPTOMS Young plants wilt or grow poorly, and are easily pulled out of the ground. Established plants may show no obvious symptoms. Damage to root crops (radish, rutabaga, turnip) may make them inedible. Larvae occasionally found inside Brussels sprouts.
PREVENTION AND CONTROL Cover with nonwoven row cover or fine mesh netting directly after sowing or planting. Or, protect individual plants with a cabbage root fly mat (see p. 304)—a 5-in. (12-cm) square of soft woven material or rubber carpet underlay, or purchased equivalent. Plant into a slight hollow; in the event of an attack, mound soil to boost new root growth. Interplant with bush or dwarf broad beans.

Calcium deficiency

A disorder common on acidic soils, and on plants growing in containers where the water supply is erratic.

SYMPTOMS Curling of young leaves or shoot tips, poor growth. Apple—"bitter pit." Fruit skins pitted; brown spots in flesh, which tastes bitter. Large fruits are particularly susceptible. Symptoms may develop in storage. Brussels sprouts and cabbage—internal browning. Carrot—"cavity spot." Oval spots on roots develop into cracks and craters. Organisms may invade, causing rapid root rotting. Celery—central leaves blackened, plants stunted. Tomatoes, sweet peppers—"blossom end rot" (see picture, p. 88). A dark brown/black patch appears on blossom end of developing fruit. Not all fruit on a truss or all trusses on a plant need be affected.
PREVENTION AND TREATMENT A true calcium deficiency is rare, though it can occur in some acid soils. Symptoms are more commonly the result of disruption in the supply of calcium. This may be caused by a shortage of water, which slows the transport of calcium to the plant, and also by excessive use of potassium or magnesium-rich fertilizers. Add lime to acid soils, where appropriate, up to a pH of 6.5. Apply organic matter to soil to maintain conditions that allow a steady water supply throughout the season. Never let container-grown plants dry out.

Capsid bugs

Small, active, sap-feeding winged creatures, up to ¼ in. (6 mm) long. Nymphs (the young) are similar to adults but without wings. Color varies with species. These creatures are rarely seen as they quickly drop to the ground or fly away when disturbed.

SUSCEPTIBLE PLANTS A wide range of wild and cultivated plants, including runner bean, black and red currants, apple, chrysanthemum, dahlia, fuchsia, and rose.
SYMPTOMS Most species feed on plants, causing small ragged holes in leaves, particularly at shoot tips. The damage is distinctive. Leaves develop a characteristic tattered appearance as they grow. Buds and shoots may be killed; flowers and fruit deformed. Apple fruits develop raised bumps and scabby patches. Some capsids are useful predators of small pests, particularly on fruit.
PREVENTION AND CONTROL Encourage birds to feed near apple, pear, plum, and hawthorn trees in winter by hanging suet and bags of nuts from branches. If damage is extensive, tidy up under hedges over winter, raking out leaf litter and clearing away any plant debris. Control is not always easy as adults are elusive, but damage is not usually severe.

Carrot rust fly

Psila rosae

Small, shiny black flies lay eggs in small clusters near host plants, starting in late spring. The larvae are creamy white, up to ½ in. (1 cm) long. Pupae, and sometimes larvae, overwinter in soil and roots of carrot and parsnip. There are two or three generations per year, the first causing most damage.

SUSCEPTIBLE PLANTS Carrot, celery, chervil, parsley, and parsnip.
SYMPTOMS Young seedlings can be killed. The first sign of attack on mature plants is often a reddening of the foliage and stunted growth. The roots have rusty brown irregular tunnels eaten away just below the skin. Larvae may be visible.
PREVENTION AND CONTROL Avoid growing carrots in sheltered sites, the preferred areas of weak-flying carrot flies. Delay sowing until June to avoid first generation attack. Harvest crops by late autumn. Some cultivars are said to be less susceptible. Sow seed thinly to avoid the need for thinning; the fly can be attracted by the smell of bruised foliage. If thinning is necessary, remove all thinnings immediately and water to firm the soil. Grow one row of carrots between four rows of onions to mask the smell of carrots. This is only effective before the onions begin to form bulbs in early to midsummer and may not be effective on a small scale. Cover with row cover or a fine mesh netting immediately after sowing. Grow under the cover throughout the life of the crop. Can also be grown within a topless enclosure of fine mesh netting, maximum 3 ft. x 10 ft. x 30 in. (90 cm x 3 m x 75 cm) high. Turn over

---

Barriers and crop covers can protect many crops from pest damage. See p. 101, and also pp. 230–233.

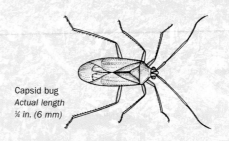

Capsid bug
Actual length
¼ in. (6 mm)

soil in winter where damage has occurred to expose overwintering larvae.

Caterpillars

Caterpillars are the larvae of butterflies and moths. Their bodies are segmented. The first three segments behind the head carry a pair of jointed legs, making up the thorax, while the remaining ten segments make up the abdomen, which may have up to five pairs of fleshy legs. Sawfly larvae, similar in appearance but not related, have at least six pairs of legs on the abdominal segments.
See Cabbage caterpillars; Codling moth; Cutworm.
See also Sawflies, for comparison.

Cedar-apple rust

Gymnosporangium juniperi-virginianae

Cedar-apple rust completes its life cycle only where the fungal spores can travel back and forth between cedar and apple trees. Spores from cedar trees send spores to infect apple trees, but infections on the apple tree do not spread within the tree; they can only send the disease back to infect cedar.

SUSCEPTIBLE PLANTS Eastern red cedars and other species of junipers; apples and crab apples.
SYMPTOMS On cedars, hard, brown swellings appear on branch tips. These galls do not seriously damage cedar trees, but they can mar the plants'

appearance. Warm, moist weather in spring causes these galls to swell dramatically, and they produce gelatinous horns that release rust-colored spores. The spores then infect apple trees. The symptoms on apples show up in spring as tiny yellow spots, which later expand and turn orange. These spots form on upper leaf surfaces and on fruit. Brown spots may appear on the undersides of leaves.
PREVENTION AND CONTROL Rust fungi need moisture, so promote drying through pruning for good air circulation around the branches and by selecting an airy planting site. Prune off and destroy galls on cedars before late winter. Plant apple trees only if cedar trees are at least 4 miles (6.4 km) away; this will reduce the chance of the disease spreading. If you want to grow both cedars and apple trees, choose rust-resistant species and cultivars of these plants. Many fungicides, including sulfur and lime-sulfur, that are effective against other fungal diseases are not very effective against rust diseases.

Celery late blight

Septoria apiicola

Seed is the main source of infection by this fungal disease. The germinating seedlings are infected; the disease spreads to other plants by rain-splash.

SUSCEPTIBLE PLANTS Celery; also celeriac.
SYMPTOMS Brown spots with a

lighter or darker border develop on older leaves. These soon spread to other foliage and occasionally to leaf stalks. Spots can be numerous and may merge, causing leaf death.
PREVENTION AND CONTROL Clear away diseased leaves and other debris. Never save seed from infected plants.

Chrysanthemum leaf miner

Chromatomyia syngenesiae (*Phytomyza syngenesiae*)

Small, inconspicuous dark flies lay up to 100 eggs in small incisions in leaves during summer months from which larvae hatch and feed within the leaves; most damage occurs in late spring to midsummer. In heated greenhouses, breeding continues for most of the year.

SUSCEPTIBLE PLANTS Chrysanthemum, cineraria, calendula, lettuce, groundsel, sow-thistle, and other related members of the Asteraceae family—indoors and outside.
SYMPTOMS First symptoms are a white spotting of leaves caused by the feeding of adult females. Narrow white tunnels appear between the upper and lower leaf surface. These later widen and meander toward the leaf midrib. After approximately 2 to 3 weeks, small dark bumps can be seen on the lower leaf surface.
PREVENTION AND CONTROL Examine plants regularly. Pick off and destroy infected leaves. Control weeds, especially

groundsel and thistle, as these can support populations of chrysanthemum leaf miner.

Chrysanthemum white rust

Puccinia horiana

This fungus is encouraged by a moist, humid atmosphere. It may persist from year to year on overwintering plants.

SUSCEPTIBLE PLANTS Chrysanthemums, in greenhouses and outdoors.
SYMPTOMS Yellow to pale green spots on upper leaf surfaces, corresponding to pustules on lower leaf surface, initially dirty buff in color, later white. Leaf spots gradually turn brown and dead in the center.
PREVENTION AND CONTROL Choose less susceptible cultivars, and destroy affected plants immediately. Do not propagate from diseased plants.

Clematis wilt

Ascochyta clematidina

This fungal disease originates from the soil or other plants. It is thought infection occurs in conditions of high humidity. Infection enters through small wounds caused, for example, by birds, insects, and bruising by plant ties.

SUSCEPTIBLE PLANTS Clematis.
SYMPTOMS Sudden drooping of young growth. Affected leaves next to the stalks blacken, then wither and die. Dark lesions may

Canker, cherry and plum *see Bacterial canker*

Canker, parsnip *see Parsnip canker*

Carrot cavity spot *see Calcium deficiency*

Avoid spraying unless essential.

Yellow-tailed moth caterpillar

be seen on the stem at or near ground level. Patchy blackening can occur on otherwise healthy leaves. Large-flowered hybrids are most susceptible to this disease, especially those with *Clematis lanuginosa* in their parentage.
PREVENTION AND CONTROL Plant newly purchased clematis 6 in. (15 cm) deeper than originally grown. *Clematis viticella* cultivars are said to be much less susceptible. Avoid mechanical damage to stems, particularly when securing ties. Cut back infected growth to soil level or below. New healthy growth should emerge from ground level. If symptoms recur, remove the soil to a depth of 12 in. (30 cm) and destroy the infected plant. Replace with fresh soil and replant.

Clubroot

Plasmodiophora brassicae

This soilborne fungal disease can survive in the soil for up to 20 years in the absence of a suitable host. Clubroot thrives in damp, acid conditions. It is less of a problem in alkaline soils; in hot, dry seasons; and in spring-maturing crops. The disease is spread on infected plant material and contaminated soil. It is easily carried in soil on tools, machinery, footwear, and infected transplants, which may not show symptoms.

SUSCEPTIBLE PLANTS Brassicas; wallflower, stocks, and candytuft.
SYMPTOMS Plants wilt on hot, sunny days but may recover at night; they may become stunted and develop red tints on foliage.

Roots develop swollen galls—either a single large gall or several smaller swellings. Plant growth and crop yields are severely reduced.
PREVENTION AND CONTROL This disease is very difficult to control, so avoidance is very important. Buy transplants from a reliable source, or raise your own. Build up good soil fertility and improve drainage. Lime acid soils. Where clubroot is present, liming to a pH of at least 7.0 may help. Remove all infected roots as soon as possible, preferably before the galls disintegrate; do not compost. Mound fresh compost around crops that have been attacked to encourage them to develop new healthy roots. If clubroot is present on your land, raise plants in pots using disease-free potting mix.

Codling moth

Cydia pomonella

The adult moth, ⅜ in (8 mm) long, mottled gray-brown in color, lays its eggs on fruits and leaves in early and midsummer. Single caterpillars tunnel into a fruit, often through the eye, leaving no obvious signs. The caterpillar, pinkish white with a black or brown head, grows to ¾ in. (2 cm) in length, as it eats its way to the core of the fruit. After a month or so, it leaves the fruit to pupate under loose bark, tree ties, and similar locations. In a hot summer, there may be two generations.

SUSCEPTIBLE PLANTS Apple; less frequently pear and quince.

SYMPTOMS Caterpillars cause extensive tunnels through fruit, spoiling it. Damaged fruit may ripen and drop prematurely.
PREVENTION AND CONTROL Hang sticky pheromone traps in trees from mid-May to late July, or early September in a hot year. Traps may reduce damage on isolated trees—or can be used to monitor the presence of the moth, so a spray can be timed accurately, before the caterpillars move into the fruit. Earwigs are predators.
Biological control: *Bacillus thuringiensis* (B.T.) is partially effective.

Colorado potato beetle

Leptinotarsa decemlineata

Adults are yellowish orange, ⅜-in. (8-mm) beetles with 10 lengthwise black stripes on the wing covers and black spots on the thorax. Overwintering adults emerge from the soil in spring to feed on young plants. After feeding, females lay up to 1,000 eggs during their several-month lifespan. The eggs are bright yellow ovals, standing on end in clusters on the undersides of leaves. They hatch in 4 to 9 days. The dark orange, humpbacked grubs feed for 2 to 3 weeks, then pupate in the soil. Adults emerge in 5 to 10 days. There are two generations a year in most areas, three generations in southern areas.

SUSCEPTIBLE PLANTS Potatoes, tomatoes, eggplants, and related plants, including petunias.

SYMPTOMS Both adults and larvae chew holes in foliage. Their feeding can kill small plants and reduces the yields of mature plants.
PREVENTION AND CONTROL When overwintering adults begin to emerge, shake adults from plants onto a dropcloth in the early morning. Dump the beetles into soapy water. Attract native predators and parasites by planting pollen- and nectar-rich flowers. Mulch plants with deep straw layer. Cover plants with row cover or mesh until midsummer.
Biological controls: Release two to five spined soldier bugs per square yard (sq. m) of plants. Release *Edovum puttleri* in southern areas to attack second-generation larvae. Apply parasitic nematodes to the soil to attack the larvae as they prepare to pupate. Apply double-strength sprays of *Bacillus thuringiensis* var. *san diego* (B.T.S.D.) on larvae.
Pesticide sprays: As a last resort, spray weekly with pyrethrin or neem.

Corn earworm

Heliocoverpa (Heliothis) zea

Adults are tan moths that emerge in early spring, migrating long distances to find food, if necessary. Females lay white, ribbed, and round eggs on leaves or in the tips of corn ears. Eggs hatch in 3 days. The larvae are 1–2 in. (2.5–5 cm) long, light yellow, green, pink, or brown caterpillars, with yellow heads and black legs, and white and dark stripes along their

Cherry bacterial canker *see Bacterial canker*

For more information on biological controls, see p. 100.

sides. The larvae feed for 2 to 4 weeks, then pupate in the soil. Adults emerge in 10 to 25 days. There are one to four generations per year.

SUSCEPTIBLE PLANTS Corn and tomatoes are the main targets, but the larvae will also feed on a broad range of vegetable crops, fruits, and flowers.

SYMPTOMS On corn, the larvae feed on fresh silks, then move down the ears, eating kernels and leaving trails of excrement as they go. Early and late cultivars are most affected. On tomatoes (where the larvae are called tomato fruitworms), the larvae burrow into ripe fruits, eat buds, and chew large holes in leaves.

PREVENTION AND CONTROL Plant corn cultivars with tight husks to prevent larvae from entering, or open the husk ends and dig out any larvae in the tip before they damage the main ear. Squirt mineral oil on the tips of the ears. Attract native parasitic wasps and predatory bugs.

Biological controls: After corn silks start to dry, spray *Bacillus thuringiensis* var. *kurstaki* (B.T.K.) into the tips of the ears, or apply granular B.T.K. Spray B.T.K. on leaves and fruit of plants where fruitworms are feeding. Squirt parasitic nematodes into tips of corn ears. Release lacewings or minute pirate bugs.

Pesticide control: Paint pyrethrin-and-molasses bait (3 parts spray solution to 1 part molasses) around the base of plants to kill adults as they start to emerge.

Crown gall

Agrobacterium tumefaciens

This common bacterium enters plants through wounds, such as those that occur during transplanting. The bacteria may be transmitted from one plant to another on a trowel or shovel, which can wound a plant during digging. The bacteria may also survive on dead plants for years in infested soil, waiting for a suitable host plant.

SUSCEPTIBLE PLANTS A wide range of woody and herbaceous plants. Those commonly attacked include peaches, pear, cherries, grapes, brambles, euonymus, chrysanthemums, and roses.

SYMPTOMS Above ground, the plant is stunted with yellowing leaves. Just beneath the soil line of an infected plant (or sometimes just above the soil line), you will see the tuberous swellings that upset the mineral- and water-conducting vessels, causing the aboveground symptoms.

PREVENTION AND CONTROL Inspect nursery plants carefully before you buy to avoid infected plants. Protect healthy plants by dipping their roots in a solution of *Agrobacterium radiobacter* (sold as Galltrol-A and Norbac 84C) before planting. To control mild infections, prune off diseased growth; disinfect your pruners in between cuts with a 10% bleach solution (1 part bleach to 9 parts water). Remove and destroy severely infected plants. Avoid replanting the area with susceptible plants.

Cucumber beetles

Diabrotica undecimpunctata howardii and *Acalymma vittatum*

Spotted cucumber beetles are greenish yellow, ¼-in. (6-mm) beetles with 11 black spots on their wing covers. Overwintering adults emerge from under crop residues in spring and lay eggs in the soil close to plants. Their larvae, also known as southern corn rootworms, are white grubs with brown heads and brown patches on the first and last segments. They feed for 2 to 4 weeks, then pupate. There are one or two generations per year in northern areas, three in southern areas. Striped cucumber beetles are a similar size but have black heads and three wide black stripes on their wing covers. They emerge in April to early June, eat weed pollen for 2 weeks, then lay eggs in the soil at the base of plants. The eggs hatch in 10 days. The larvae—slender white maggots—feed on roots for several weeks, then pupate in early August. Adults emerge in 2 weeks to feed on blossoms and fruit. One or two generations per year. The larvae and adults of both species can transmit cucumber mosaic virus and bacterial wilt as they feed.

SUSCEPTIBLE PLANTS Squash-family plants, sweet corn, other vegetable crops, and flowers.

SYMPTOMS Southern corn rootworms feed on corn roots, often killing young plants and weakening older ones. Striped cucumber beetle larvae feed on the roots of squash-family plants only, killing or stunting the plants. Adults of both species feed on leaves, stems, flowers, and fruit of squashes and other crops.

PREVENTION AND CONTROL Remove and destroy crop residues where adults overwinter. Rotate garden crops with green manures such as alfalfa. Cover seedlings and plants with row cover or mesh, hand-pollinating squash-family plants.

Biological control: Apply parasitic nematodes to the soil weekly to control larvae.

Pesticide spray: As a last resort, spray adults with pyrethrin.

Cucumber mosaic virus

Viral disease spread primarily by aphids; it may also be spread by handling diseased plants and on contaminated tools. Infection usually occurs when plants are about 6 weeks old. *See also* Viruses.

SUSCEPTIBLE PLANTS Cucumber, squash, melon; also celery, beans, and peppers. Ornamentals include anemone, aquilegia, begonias, campanula, dahlia, lily, and primula.

SYMPTOMS Vary according to plant affected. In cucurbits, the virus causes mottling or mosaic patterns (shown on p. 91) and distortion on the leaves. Flowering is reduced; plants are stunted and may die. The fruits will be small, dark, and pitted,

---

Chocolate spot *see Broad bean chocolate spot*

Practice good garden hygiene— clear away pest-ridden and diseased foliage and plants.

and may develop bright yellow blotches.
PREVENTION AND CONTROL Grow resistant cultivars. Remove infected plants as soon as symptoms are identified. There is no cure.

Cutworm

Noctuidae

Various nocturnal moth caterpillars are grouped under the general name of cutworm. These soil-living larvae tend to be fat, and will curl up as a "C" when disturbed. They may be brown, yellow, or green with dark markings. Cutworms feed at night, and can be found at almost any time of year, both outdoors and within the greenhouse.

SUSCEPTIBLE PLANTS Young vegetable plants, especially lettuce and brassicas; also carrot, celery, beets, potato, strawberries, and many ornamentals.
SYMPTOMS Stems of seedlings and young plants eaten through at ground level. Roots, corms, tubers, and leaves may also be damaged.
PREVENTION AND CONTROL Cultivate infested soil in winter to expose caterpillars to predators, or allow chickens to scratch it over. Keep ground weed-free, as weeds provide sites for egg laying. In the greenhouse, soak the soil thoroughly, then cover and leave overnight. This will bring cutworms to the surface, where they can be picked up. On a small scale, locate caterpillars in soil or feeding on plants at night, and destroy. Protect susceptible transplants with a collar—such as a cardboard or plastic tube, or tin can with the base removed—pushed down into the soil around the plant.

Cytospora canker

Cytospora leucostoma

Also known as valsa or leucostoma canker, this fungal disease can be a serious problem on trees.

SUSCEPTIBLE PLANTS A wide range of woody plants. Some of the most susceptible trees include stone fruits (such as peaches and plums), apples, pears, spruces, maples, poplars, and willows.
SYMPTOMS New shoots turn yellow, wilt, and die back. The inner bark on infected twigs may show black or reddish brown discoloration. Gummy cankers form on trunks and branches and increase in size until they girdle and kill the affected part.
PREVENTION AND CONTROL Plant resistant cultivars when available. Vigorously growing trees are less susceptible to this disease. Prune out infected branches during dry weather; disinfect your pruners between cuts. Avoid making unnecessary wounds in the bark, which can provide an entry for the fungus. On stone fruits, it is particularly important to avoid winter damage, which can be caused by fertilizing the trees late in the season.

Damping off

Rhizoctonia solani and *Pythium* spp.

There is a wide range of these troublesome soil-dwelling fungal diseases. Some survive on decaying plant debris, others exist as spores in the soil. They will multiply rapidly in cool, wet, poorly ventilated situations.

SUSCEPTIBLE PLANTS Seeds, seedlings, cuttings, roots, and vegetable parts at or below soil level, such as carrot and celery. Will spread rapidly through trays of seedlings.
SYMPTOMS Seeds fail to germinate. Seedlings are attacked at soil level or below; stems become water-soaked, blackened, and thin. Seedlings collapse and die. Reddish brown root lesions form on seedlings and mature plants, initially just below the soil surface. Rootlets of older plants die. Vegetables such as potatoes, cucurbits, and beans may become infected during extended wet periods. This results in a cottony fungal growth followed by the disintegration of the vegetable interior into a soft watery mass. *Rhizoctonia* also causes brown patches on lawns and fine turf.
PREVENTION AND CONTROL Always ensure pots and trays are scrubbed clean before sowing seed or taking cuttings. Use a sterile medium for seed sowing. Ensure drainage is good—waterlogged plants are more prone to pest and disease attack. Do not overcrowd seedlings, cuttings, or older plants—good ventilation is essential to reduce humidity, which will encourage disease. Sow when soil has warmed up well in the spring. This will encourage plants to grow quickly and without check.
See also Phytophthora root & stem rots.

Downy mildew

Disease caused by a range of related fungi that attack specific plants or groups of plants. These include *Peronospora destructor* on onion; *Bremia lactucae* on lettuce; *Peronospora sparsa* on rose; *Plasmopara viticola* on grapevines, and *Peronospora violae* on pansies. These fungi survive in the soil, in crop debris, and on infected plants, not all of which will show symptoms.

SUSCEPTIBLE PLANTS Many plants, particularly when they are young.
SYMPTOMS Yellow patches on upper leaf surface, with corresponding patches of mold beneath in damp weather. Large areas of a leaf may be infected and the leaf may die. Onions rot in store. The disease is most common in damp and humid growing situations.
PREVENTION AND CONTROL Grow resistant lettuces such as 'Sangria' or 'Little Gem'. Use a 5-year rotation for onions where downy mildew has occurred. Improve ventilation and air flow. Remove infected leaves or individually affected plants. If it continues, remove and destroy all infected plants.
See also Onion downy mildew.

Common green capsid *see Capsid bugs*
Common scab *see Potato common scab*
Cuckoo spit *see Froghopper, common*

Identify problems correctly so that the right spray, if necessary, is used.

Earwigs

Forficula auricularia

The earwig can be a pest in some situations, but it is also a useful predator, particularly of apple pests such as codling moth and aphids, feeding at night. It has an elongated, reddish brown body, 1 in. (2.5 cm) long, with pincers at tip of the abdomen. Earwigs lay eggs in the soil in late winter, which hatch in early spring. There may be a second generation.

SUSCEPTIBLE PLANTS Dahlia, clematis, chrysanthemum, delphinium, and other flowers.
SYMPTOMS Young shoots and flowers are eaten, leaving large ragged holes. Earwigs are often found in cavities in damaged tree fruits, but do not usually initiate the damage.
PREVENTION AND CONTROL Earwigs do not usually travel far, so clearing up debris where they might hide and trapping can make a local difference. Trap in upturned flower pots stuffed with straw and placed on top of a cane, in lengths of dry broad bean stalk, or in a "lacewing hotel" (*see* p. 192) Shake traps into a bucket of soapy water to kill the earwigs, or liberate them on fruit trees.

Edema

Disorder affecting a wide range of plants, particularly greenhouse plants such as begonias, brassicas, cacti and succulents, solanum, tomato, pelargonium, camellia, capsicum (peppers and ornamental winter cherries), peperomia, and grapevines.

SYMPTOMS Small, wartlike growths on the undersides of leaves and sometimes on stems. Upper leaf surface has pale blotches. At first greenish white, the swellings become rusty and have a corky texture.
CAUSES Caused by overwatering during cloudy, humid weather, when the plant takes up more water than it can lose through the leaves.
PREVENTION AND CONTROL Reduce watering. Improve drainage and air circulation. Do not remove affected plant parts; this will just make the symptoms worse. The condition is not infectious.

European corn borer

Ostrinia nubilais

Adult females are pale yellowish brown moths with darker zigzag patterns across their wings; males are darker-colored. The adults emerge in early June and lay white eggs in late June to mid-July, in masses of 15 to 20 on the undersides of leaves. The eggs hatch after 1 week into beige, brown-spotted caterpillars up to 1 in. (2.5 cm) long. They feed for 3 to 4 weeks. At the end of the season, the larvae overwinter in plant residue and pupate in early spring. There are one to three generations per year.

SUSCEPTIBLE PLANTS Many vegetable crops.

SYMPTOMS Young larvae feed on corn leaves and tassels and beneath husks, damaging the ears. Older larvae burrow in corn stalks and ears; damaged stalks may break. Larvae also tunnel in the stems or pods or beans, onions, peppers, potatoes, tomatoes, and other crops.
PREVENTION AND CONTROL Plant resistant corn cultivars, and rotate crops. Remove tassels from two-thirds of corn plants before they begin to shed pollen. Pull out and destroy all infested crop residue immediately after harvest. Attract native parasites by planting flowers between corn rows.
Biological controls: Spray *Bacillus thuringiensis* var. *kurstaki* (B.T.K.) on the undersides of leaves and into the tips of the ears, or sprinkle the granular form into ear tips.
Pesticide spray: For severe infestations, spray pyrethrin when larvae begin feeding.

European red mite

Panonychus ulmi

Tiny, sap-sucking creatures, oval in shape. Their tiny, round, red-brown eggs (⅟₂₀₀ in./0.15 mm across) overwinter on host plants in clusters and hatch from April to June. There may be five more generations in a season.

SUSCEPTIBLE PLANTS Apple and plum; also cotoneaster, hawthorn, pear, and rowan.
SYMPTOMS Leaves become speckled and dull green, then bronze, and may fall prematurely.

Severe attacks in June or July can reduce fruit bud formation.
PREVENTION AND CONTROL Encourage natural predators. Do not overfeed plants.
Pesticide spray: Insecticidal soap.

Fireblight

Erwinia amylovora

Don't confuse this bacterial disease with sooty mold, a relatively harmless, black leaf fungus that rubs off easily. Fireblight bacteria enter the tree at the growing tips. They may travel down toward the roots and kill the whole tree.

SUSCEPTIBLE PLANTS Many plants in the rose family, especially pears, apples, and quinces.
SYMPTOMS Flowers usually show symptoms first, turning brown and then shriveling. Leaves turn brown or black, and the dead leaves cling to the twigs. Symptoms progress from the tips of the shoots toward the roots. Shoot tips turn black, wilt, and curl downward. Fruit on affected shoots turns black and may cling to the tree. As the growing season progresses, fireblight bacteria grow within the blighted shoots, down branches, and toward the roots. During autumn, the bacteria form a sunken, dark canker in which to overwinter.
PREVENTION AND CONTROL Plant resistant cultivars, or choose fruit trees grafted onto blight-resistant rootstocks. Do not prune susceptible woody plants too severely or overfeed

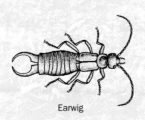

Earwig

Encourage good air flow in and around plants by thinning out and pruning. It can reduce the risk of some diseases.

them because both of these practices encourage succulent, disease-susceptible growth. To further discourage succulent growth on mature trees, grow grass right up to the trunk; if needed, also allow the grass to grow longer than normal. Prune out infected branches, along with 6–12 in. (15–30 cm) of healthy tissue. Disinfect pruners between cuts by dipping them in a 10% bleach solution (1 part bleach to 9 parts water).
Pesticide spray: Spray with Bordeaux mix during dormancy.

Flea beetle

Family *Chrysomelidae*
Small shiny black beetles, ⅛ in. (3 mm) long, that jump when disturbed. They hibernate in mulches and plant debris. Feeding starts in spring. Eggs are laid in soil near susceptible plants in late spring and early summer. There is one generation a year.

SUSCEPTIBLE PLANTS Brassicas, such as radish, rutabaga, turnip, arugula, and Oriental brassicas, particularly when seedlings. Also ornamentals such as nasturtium, alyssum, anemone, and godetia.
SYMPTOMS During spring and summer, adult beetles eat small holes in leaves and stems. A severe attack will check growth and kill young plants. Damage is always more severe in dry weather. Larvae feed on plant roots or in leaf mines.
PREVENTION AND CONTROL Encourage quick, vigorous seedling growth. Sow at the right time, prepare the site well, and never let plants lack

water. Sow under row cover or ultrafine mesh netting (0.8 mm mesh). Some crops can be uncovered once established; others such as Chinese cabbage, radish, and arugula, may need to be covered until harvest. Japanese radish may tolerate some flea beetle attack and divert the pest away from other more sensitive crops.

Froghopper, common

Philaenus spumarius
Also called the "spittlebug," this sap-feeding pest ranges in color from yellow to greeny brown. It grows up to ¼ in. (6 mm) long, with a blunt, wedgelike appearance with large eyes. Adults jump when disturbed. Young nymphs on plant stems cover themselves with a distinctive froth—"cuckoo spit"—for protection.

SUSCEPTIBLE PLANTS Roses and rosemary; also numerous outdoor and undercover plants.
SYMPTOMS Young shoots may become distorted and wilt. Flowers may be damaged. The white "cuckoo spit" if extensive may be disfiguring.
PREVENTION AND CONTROL Damage is rarely a problem. Spittle and nymphs can be removed by spraying with a high-pressure jet of water.

Frost damage

Tender plants are the most susceptible to this disorder.

Normally hardy plants can also be damaged if a hard frost follows a period of warm weather that has encouraged new growth, or if a frost occurs in the summer, for example. Plants that receive early morning sun, which melts the frost rapidly, are also vulnerable.

SYMPTOMS Frost symptoms appear overnight, and may affect many unrelated plants. Flowers and buds are discolored, usually brown. Frosted blooms may not produce fruit. Leaves and stems turn brown or black; young growth toward the outside of the plant will be most affected. Apple skins may be russetted, usually at the flowering end of the fruit opposite the stalk. Damage may not be noticed until the fruit has developed.
PREVENTION AND CONTROL Protect susceptible plants with row cover, sheets of newspaper, or other cover during risk periods. Harden off plants before planting out. Keep tender plants indoors until risk of frost is past. Select later-flowering cultivars. Avoid planting susceptible plants in frost pockets or where they will receive the early morning sun.

Fungus gnat

Sciara and *Orfelia* spp.
Also known as mushroom fly and sciarid fly. Adult flies, dark brown, midgelike, up to ⅛ in. (3 mm) long, are found on the surface of moist potting media, running quickly and vibrating their wings rapidly. They fly up when disturbed. Eggs are laid in

the medium. Transparent white larvae, up to ½ in. (1 cm) long with shiny black or brown heads, hatch a week later. They feed on plant roots. The whole life cycle can be completed within 4 weeks at a temperature of 68°F (20°C). Breeding can continue year-round in suitable temperatures.

SUSCEPTIBLE PLANTS Potted plants under cover; also mushrooms. Seedlings, cuttings, and young plants are most at risk.
SYMPTOMS Seedlings and young plants may collapse and die. Mature plants will grow poorly where infestation is high. Plants in growing media based on high levels of coir, peat, or other types of organic matter are more prone to attack.
PREVENTION AND CONTROL Always water from below, and keep watering to a minimum without allowing plants to dry out. Pot up plants as necessary, using a loam-based growing medium. Cover the potting medium with a ½-in. (1-cm) layer of sand or grit to discourage infestation. Yellow sticky traps and insectivorous plants, such as Mexican butterwort (*Pinguicula caudata*), will trap flying adults. Check new plants for presence of fungus gnats before introducing into house or greenhouse. Remove severely infested plants.
Biological controls: Use the predatory mite *Hypoaspis miles* at temperatures above 52°F (11°C). *Steinernema feltiae*, a parasitic nematode, requires moist soil and a lower minimum temperature, 57°F (14°C).

Fusarium wilt *see Wilt diseases*

Never spray on a windy day.

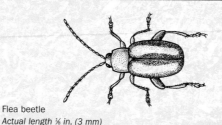
Flea beetle
Actual length ⅛ in. (3 mm)

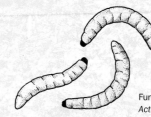
Fungus gnat larvae
Actual length ¼ in. (5 mm)

Grasshoppers

Family *Acrididae*

Adult grasshoppers are brown, yellow, or green, 1–2-in. (2.5–5-cm) insects with leathery forewings and enlarged hind legs. Many have brightly colored underwings. In late summer, females deposit elongated masses of eggs in the soil. The eggs hatch in spring, and the nymphs (which look like tiny adults) develop for 40 to 60 days until molting to adults. They feed until killed by cold weather.

SUSCEPTIBLE PLANTS Adults eat any kind of vegetation.
SYMPTOMS Large holes in leaves, flowers, or shoots; whole plants devoured.
PREVENTION AND CONTROL Grasshoppers are usually killed by natural enemies (blister beetle larvae, ground beetles, birds, parasitic nematodes, and fungal diseases), so control measures generally aren't necessary in organically managed gardens. Cultivating in autumn will kill overwintering eggs.

Gray mold

Botrytis cinerea

This fungus survives on plant debris and in the soil. Spores are spread by air currents, rain, or water splash. Infection is usually through a wound of some sort.

SUSCEPTIBLE PLANTS Most living or dead plant material including fruits, flowers, and leaves.
SYMPTOMS Fluffy, grayish white mold grows on infected areas (see p. 90). Where stems are infected, growth above the infection will yellow and wilt. Flowers, for example strawberries, may be infected, but no symptoms may show until the fruit starts to ripen.
PREVENTION AND CONTROL Good general hygiene. Remove all dead and dying plants or plant parts as soon as infection is noticed. Ensure good ventilation around plants.
See also Peony blight; Onion neck rot.

Greenhouse thrips

Heliothrips haemorrhoidalis
See Thrips

SUSCEPTIBLE PLANTS Azalea, citrus, ferns, fuchsia, orchids, and zantedeschia; also other greenhouse and house plants.
SYMPTOMS Infested plants may be marked with globules of red/brown liquid caused by feeding thrips.
PREVENTION AND CONTROL Maintain a humid atmosphere. Check plants before bringing into the house or greenhouse. Tap plant over white paper; thrips will fall onto the paper.
Biological control: The predatory mite *Amblyseius cucumeris*; optimum temperature 77°F (25°C).

Greenhouse whitefly

Trialeurodes vaporariorum
These insects will breed year-round in a greenhouse if plants are present. They may move out into the garden in the summer, but will not survive winter outdoors. Can transmit viruses. *See also* Whiteflies.

SUSCEPTIBLE PLANTS Tomato, cucumber, and many other greenhouse and houseplants.
SYMPTOMS Leaves may develop yellow spots and other discolorations. The plant may become sticky and stunted. In bright sunlight the leaves can wither and die.
PREVENTION AND CONTROL Hang yellow sticky traps near plants to control small infestations, and for monitoring the appearance of whitefly where biological control agents are to be used. Remove sticky traps before introducing biological control agents. Dispose of badly infested plants. Clean greenhouses thoroughly in early spring. Wash down all surfaces, including benches.
Biological control: Under cover, use *Encarsia formosa*, a parasitic wasp (works best at 64-77°F/18-25°C; not recommended below 50°F/10°C); or *Delphastus*, a predatory beetle; optimum temperature 70–82°F (21-28°C).
Pesticide spray: Insecticidal soap. Spray directly onto whiteflies in early morning when temperatures are low and adults less mobile. Apply once a week for 3–4 weeks for best results.

Holly leaf miner

Phytomyza ilicis
Adults of this pest are small, inconspicuous flies. Eggs are laid from late spring onward on the underside of holly leaves near the midrib. Larvae hatch and tunnel into leaves, remaining there until the following spring. There is one generation each year.

SUSCEPTIBLE PLANTS Holly.
SYMPTOMS Not a serious pest, but the damage it causes can be unsightly. First symptoms show as straight, narrow, light green tunnels burrowed between the upper and lower leaf surface. These develop into blotches or "mines" as the larvae continue feeding between leaf layers.
PREVENTION AND CONTROL Where infestation is light, pick off and destroy affected leaves.

Imported currantworm

Nematus ribesii

Larvae of this pest are green with black spots and a shiny black head, reaching 1¼ in. (3 cm) long when fully grown. Eggs are pale green/white, about ¹⁄₃₂ in. (1 mm) long, laid on the underside of leaves along the main veins, usually low down in the middle of a bush. There are two or three generations a year, with damage starting in April or May. Larvae of the third generation overwinter as cocoons in the soil.

SUSCEPTIBLE PLANTS Gooseberries and red and white currants.
SYMPTOMS The first symptoms are tiny holes in the leaves made by the young larvae. Newly

Holly leaf miner damage

Gooseberry sawfly *see Imported currantworm*
Greenfly *see Aphids*

For tips on reducing pest and disease problems in the greenhouse, see pp. 228–229.

hatched larvae feed at the center of a bush for 1 to 2 weeks, then progress outward. They can quickly strip a whole bush of foliage leaving only a skeleton of leaf veins. Repeated defoliation may reduce fruiting.

PREVENTION AND CONTROL Grow plants as a cordon or fan to make location and removal of larvae easier. Inspect bushes carefully for pinhole-size holes in mid-spring, early to midsummer, and early autumn. Destroy any eggs or larvae found. If infestation is heavy, remove the whole leaf. Daily inspection is advisable. Remove mulches in late autumn/winter and cultivate lightly around bushes.
See also Sawflies.

Iris borer

Macronoctua onusta

Adults are moths with dark brown forewings and yellowish hind wings; wingspan is 2 in. (5 cm). They emerge in summer and lay eggs. The eggs overwinter on old leaves and hatch in late April or early May. The larvae are fat, pinkish borers up to 2 in. (5 cm) long, with brown heads and a light stripe down the back, and rows of black dots up the sides. They enter the leaves, feed for several weeks, then pupate in the soil near rhizomes. Iris borers are found in the eastern United States west to Iowa, and in Quebec and eastern Ontario.

SUSCEPTIBLE PLANTS Iris, especially bearded types.
SYMPTOMS Leaves may show irregular tunnels under the leaf surfaces. The larvae enter a fan of leaves at the top and tunnel down toward the rhizome, where they may eat the whole interior without being noticed. Borers often introduce soft rot bacteria into rhizomes as they feed, causing a wet, slimy, smelly rot.

PREVENTION AND CONTROL In fall, remove dead, dry leaves, which often carry borer eggs, and destroy badly infested fans in spring. You can also crush borers in the leaves by pinching toward the base of the telltale ragged-edged leaves or by running your thumb between the leaves and squashing any borers that you find. Check rhizomes when you divide the clumps for this pest. If you find a few borers, try cutting them out; destroy badly infested rhizomes.
Pesticide control: In spring, dust the base of the plants with pyrethrin to kill emerging larvae.

Iron deficiency

Also known as lime-induced chlorosis. Has very similar symptoms to and often occurs with manganese deficiency.

SUSCEPTIBLE PLANTS Pears, raspberries; acid soil-lovers such as camellias and azaleas growing on alkaline soils, but any type of plant can be affected.
SYMPTOMS Leaves turn yellow or brown around the margins. This extends between the veins (see p. 89). Young leaves may be totally yellow or bleached white, with no green showing. Fruit quantity and quality are poor.
CAUSES Soil pH too high for acid-loving plants. Waterlogging. Excessive use of phosphates.
PREVENTION AND CURE Choose plants to suit the soil type. Apply well-rotted manure or compost.

Japanese beetle

Popillia japonica

Adult Japanese beetles are chunky, metallic blue-green, ½-in. (1-cm) beetles with bronze wing covers, long legs, and fine hairs covering their body. They emerge in midsummer and lay eggs in late summer. These eggs hatch into plump, dirty white, brown-headed grubs that overwinter deep in the soil. They move toward the surface in spring to feed on roots, then pupate in early summer to start the cycle over again.

SUSCEPTIBLE PLANTS Adults eat the flowers and skeletonize the leaves of a broad range of plants; the plants may be completely defoliated. Larvae feed on roots of lawn grasses and garden plants.
SYMPTOMS Holes in flowers and leaves, or leaves skeletonized completely (with only the leaf veins remaining).
PREVENTION AND CONTROL In early morning, shake beetles from plants onto dropcloths, then drop them into soapy water to kill them. Cover crop plants with row cover or mesh. Plant pollen- and nectar-rich flowers to attract native species of parasitic wasps and flies.
Biological control: Apply milky disease spores or parasitic nematodes to sod to kill larvae.

Lace bugs

Family *Tingidae*

Adults are tiny, oval or rectangular buds with lacy wings and wide, flattened extensions on the thorax. They insert their conelike eggs along the midribs on the undersides of leaves. They hatch into nymphs, which are smaller and darker than the adults, and covered with spines. They feed for several weeks before molting to adults. There are three or more generations per year. Most species overwinter in the egg stage, the rest as adults under the bark of trees.

SUSCEPTIBLE PLANTS Flowers, trees, and vegetable plants.
SYMPTOMS Adults and nymphs suck juices from the undersides of leaves, spotting the foliage with excrement and leaving speckled white or gray, blotchy appearance on leaf surfaces.
PREVENTION AND CONTROL
Pesticide control: Spray superior oil (not on chrysanthemum flowers), or spray pyrethrin as a last resort.

Leaf miners

Larval pests that tunnel around feeding within leaves, creating characteristic maze patterns. They can be squashed in their "mines" between finger and thumb, or leaves can be picked off. Damage tends to be more unsightly than harmful, except on

Feed the soil with composted organic soil improvers (see pp. 40–41).

leafy crops. See Chrysanthemum leaf miner, Holly leaf miner.

Leafhoppers

Family *Cicadellidae*

Adults are small, wedge-shaped, slender, green or brown insects; a forward point above the head is very pronounced in some species. Some have brightly colored bands on the wings; all jump rapidly into flight when disturbed. Overwintering adults start laying eggs in spring when leaves begin to appear on trees. (Some species do not survive winter in the northern United States and in Canada; they migrate from the south every summer.) Females lay eggs in leaves and stems. The eggs hatch in 10–14 days. The pale, wingless nymphs are similar to adults and hop rapidly when disturbed. Most species have 2–5 generations per year, overwintering as adults or eggs.

SUSCEPTIBLE PLANTS Most fruit and vegetable crops, also some flowers and weeds.
SYMPTOMS Adults and nymphs suck juices from stems and the undersides of leaves. Their toxic saliva distorts and stunts plants and causes tipburn and yellowed, curled leaves with white spots on the undersides. Fruit may be spotted with drops of excrement and honeydew. Pests may spread viral diseases as they feed.
PREVENTION AND CONTROL Wash nymphs from plants with stiff sprays of water. Attract natural enemies (predatory flies and bugs and parasitic wasps).
Pesticide sprays: As a last

resort, spray with insecticidal soap or pyrethrin.

Leatherjackets

Tipula and *Nephrotoma* spp.

The larvae of the crane fly: legless, brown to grayish black, fat, soft-bodied, up to 2 in. (5 cm) long, with no distinct head. In late summer, adult flies lay up to 300 eggs in grassland or in soil near plants. Eggs hatch approximately 2 weeks later. Larvae feed on roots during the autumn and the following spring and summer. Adults emerge in late summer to early autumn.

SUSCEPTIBLE PLANTS Lawns; also brassicas, strawberries, lettuce, and various ornamentals.
SYMPTOMS Yellowing patches on lawns in dry weather. Starlings may be seen probing lawns in search of leatherjackets. Larvae also feed on roots of young plants in spring. Plants turn yellow, wilt, and may die. Symptoms can be confused with cutworm damage and also root-infecting fungi; it is important to confirm the presence of leather-jackets before taking action.
PREVENTION AND CONTROL Raise plants in pots to produce a vigorous root system. Do not plant susceptible plants on newly cleared land. Trap leatherjackets on lawns by thoroughly watering yellow areas and covering overnight with burlap, tarpaulin, or a similar material. Larvae will come to the surface under the covering. Pick off and destroy the following morning. This method can be used on cultivated land, by

placing a layer of grass mowings under the cover. Leave for 1 or 2 days, then pick off and destroy any leatherjackets that surface. Repeat, then fork the soil lightly to expose larvae that remain.
Biological control: Outdoors, use *Steinernema feltiae*, a parasitic nematode. Apply mid-September, to moist soil.

Lettuce root aphid

Pemphigus bursarius

Small, yellow-white, wingless, waxy aphid pests with small dark spots on abdomen, found among lettuce roots during summer. Overwinters mainly on Lombardy poplar, moving in June to lettuce and sow-thistle. Root colonies can persist into the winter, and may survive in the soil until the next season. *See also* Aphids.

SUSCEPTIBLE PLANTS Lettuce, sow-thistle. Lombardy poplar is a winter host.
SYMPTOMS A severe infestation will cause lettuce plants to wilt suddenly, then die.
PREVENTION AND CONTROL Grow root aphid-resistant cultivars, such as 'Dynamite'. Rotate crops.

Magnesium deficiency

Disorder particularly affecting potato, tomato, black currant, apple, gooseberry, raspberry, rose, and chrysanthemum.

SYMPTOMS Symptoms develop first on older leaves, spreading to young leaves later. Leaves turn yellow (or sometimes red, purple, or brown) between the veins and around the margins, while veins remain green.
CAUSES Acid soil. Magnesium is easily washed out of light soils by heavy rain. Overuse of high-potash fertilizers can make magnesium unavailable to plants.
PREVENTION AND CONTROL For immediate effect, foliar-feed every 2 weeks with Epsom salts diluted at the rate of 8 oz. per 2½ gallons of water (200 g per 10 liters) after flowering. Reduce the use of potash fertilizer if appropriate. Treat with dolomitic limestone (if pH is too acidic).

Manganese deficiency

Disorder particularly affecting French bean, pea, onion, apple, cherry, and raspberry. *See also* Iron deficiency.

SYMPTOMS Leaves become yellow, with the smallest leaf veins remaining green to produce a checkered effect. Youngest leaves affected first, though the plant may grow away from the problem so that new leaves may seem least affected. Brown spots appear scattered over the leaf surface. Severely affected leaves turn brown and wither.
CAUSES Most common on soils with a pH of over 7.5, and also those with poor drainage and high organic matter levels.

Lime-induced chlorosis *see Iron deficiency*

Leatherjacket (cranefly larva) *Actual length 2 in. (5 cm)*

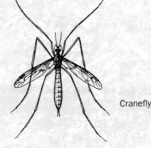
Cranefly

Grow plants that suit the site.

PREVENTION AND CONTROL
Grow plants suited to the soil
type. Improve soil structure.

Mealybugs

Pseudococcus and *Planococcus* spp.
The adult female of this pest
is small, up to ⅛ in. (3 mm)
long, and powdery gray. Eggs are
laid in batches of 100–150, with
a protective covering of woolly
wax. Newly hatched mealybugs
crawl over plants for a few days
then settle down to feed. Adult
males have wings and can
appear in large numbers during
the breeding season. Populations
are usually highest in the
autumn and early winter. In very
cold areas they are restricted
to greenhouses, but in warmer
areas they spread outdoors.
Breeding can be continuous
in greenhouses and in the home.

SUSCEPTIBLE PLANTS Sprouting
potatoes; cacti, succulents, plus
many tender indoor plants;
glasshouse plants such as jasmine,
asparagus fern, and oleander.
SYMPTOMS Severe infestations
on young growing shoots can
weaken plants. Wax-covered
colonies are often found in leaf
axils and on cacti spines. Leaves
may be covered in sticky
honeydew. This may in turn be
covered in black sooty mold.
PREVENTION AND CONTROL
Cut out and burn severely
infested shoots and branches.
Wash out inaccessible colonies
with a powerful jet of water
or remove with a paintbrush as
appropriate. Repeat inspection
and removal of mealybugs two
or three times at twice-weekly

intervals. Examine all new plant
introductions; ideally, quarantine
new plants for a month.
Biological control: The
predatory lady beetle
Cryptolaemus montrouzieri;
optimum temperature 68–77°F
(20–25°C).
Pesticide spray: Insecticidal
soap. Disturb the waxy coating
covering colonies before spraying.

Mexican bean beetle

Epilachna varivestis
Adults are oval, yellowish brown,
¼-in. (6-mm) beetles with 16
black spots on the wing covers.
They overwinter in leaf litter in
nearby fields. In spring, females
lay clusters of oval, yellow eggs
on the undersides of bean
leaves. Eggs hatch in 5 to 14
days, into plump, yellowish
orange grubs with long,
branching spines. They feed for
2 to 4 weeks, then pupate on
leaves. There are one to three
generations per year.

SUSCEPTIBLE PLANTS String
beans and soybeans.
SYMPTOMS Adults and larvae
feed on the undersides of leaves,
leaving lacy-looking patches on
the leaf surface. Severely
defoliated plants may be killed.
PREVENTION AND CONTROL
Plant early-season bush beans to
avoid main beetle generations.
Plant soybeans as trap crops, then
destroy them when infested with
larvae. Handpick larvae and
adults daily in small bean patches.
Cover plants with row cover or
mesh until plants are large

enough to withstand damage.
Dig in crop residues as soon as
plants are harvested. Attract native
predators and parasites by leaving
flowering weeds between rows or
by interplanting flowers and herbs.
Biological controls: Release
spined soldier bugs (*Podisus
maculiventris*) to control the early
generation; release parasitic
wasps *Pediobius foveolatus* when
the weather warms.
Pesticide spray: As a last
resort, spray weekly with
pyrethrin or neem.

Mineral deficiencies

It is unwise to treat soil for a
deficiency unless you are sure
that it really is deficient in that
particular element, as this may
simply exacerbate the condition.
Deficiency symptoms often
occur as a result of over-liming,
excessive fertilizer use, or poor
soil structure—rather than a
true shortage in the soil. Cold
weather, drought, and waterlogging can also cause a
temporary deficiency in a plant.
True shortages of elements are
much less common. A soil or
plant analysis may be necessary
to identify a deficiency accurately.
See also Boron, Calcium, Iron,
Potassium, Phosphorus,
Nitrogen, Magnesium, and
Manganese deficiencies.

Moles

Scalopus aquaticus
Adult moles are about 6 in.
(15 cm) long, with dense, dark

brown fur. Females raise a litter
of four or so per year. They do
not feed on plants, but their
activities can undermine them,
disrupting growth and making
lawn mowing difficult.

SYMPTOMS Moles create
mounds of loose soil ("mole
hills") on cultivated land,
lawns, and rough ground.
Light, well-drained soils are
most affected. Damage is
generally greatest in late
winter and early spring.
PREVENTION AND CONTROL
Trapping is the only certain way
to control this pest. The best time
to trap moles is in late winter
and early spring when runs
can be more easily located. First
locate permanent mole runs by
careful observation, probing, and
excavation. Place a mole trap in
the run, choosing a straight length
of run within 6–8 in. (15–20 cm)
of the soil surface. Examine the
trap at least once a day; if it fails
to catch a mole within 4 days,
move it to another run. It may be
possible to deter moles for a brief
length of time by using repellents
that create strong smells or by
using a device to produce a
vibration in the run.

Nectria canker

Nectria galligena
This fungal disease is spread by
wind and rain-splash, and enters
the plant through cracks in the
bark, leaf scars, or pruning cuts.
Diseased fruit left on trees can
also be a source of infection.

SUSCEPTIBLE PLANTS Apple,
pear, hawthorn, and poplar.

Mildew, downy *see Downy mildew*

Mildew, powdery *see Powdery mildew*

Nutrient deficiencies *see Mineral deficiencies*

Canker is a particular problem on poorly drained or wet sites. **SYMPTOMS** Tree bark shrinks and cracks, often in concentric rings with the central piece of bark falling away. Deep lesions develop on the branches. Swelling can occur around the canker, and young twigs may die back. Cream-colored pustules may be seen in summer; red spots are more common in autumn. Papery bark can result. Uncontrolled canker can ring an entire stem. Fruit skins crack; some fruits dry and can remain, "mummified," on the tree. **PREVENTION AND CONTROL** Do not grow trees on wet sites or badly drained clay soil. Improve drainage. If a young tree becomes affected, it may be advisable to remove it. Once a tree is established, sow a grass seed mixture up to the main stem to reduce the risk of infection by rain-splash. Cut out cankers and diseased branches. Do not use poplar or hawthorn as a windbreak near apples.

Nematodes

Microscopic worms, invisible to the naked eye. Some attack plants, while others are beneficial, attacking slugs and larvae of weevils and other pests. *See also* Potato cyst nematodes.

Nitrogen deficiency

All vegetables except nitrogen-fixing legumes are prone to this disorder, as are apples, plums, currants, and many other plants.

SYMPTOMS Plants grow poorly; leaves are pale green or in some cases, such as brassicas, with yellow, red, or purplish tints. Lower leaves show symptoms first. Flowering and fruiting may be reduced and delayed. **CAUSES** Shortage of available nitrogen in the soil. This can occur on any soil, but is more likely on light soils, low in organic matter, where rainfall is heavy. Cold weather, especially early in the season, can cause a temporary shortage. Adding wood shavings and similar woody material to the soil can cause "nitrogen robbery"— where soil organisms are mopping up any available nitrogen to help them break down the woody material. **PREVENTION AND CONTROL** Build up organic matter levels in the soil. Grow a green manure, such as winter rye, over winter to reduce leaching of nitrogen from the soil. Grow nitrogen-fixing green manures such as common vetch. Apply composted green waste and animal manures. Mulch plants with grass clippings. Apply nitrogen-rich organic fertilizers.

Onion downy mildew

Peronospora destructor

A fungal disease that survives in the soil for up to 5 years, and in crop debris and on infected plants, not all of which will show symptoms. It can, for example, overwinter in seemingly healthy autumn-planted onions, acting as a source of infection for the spring-planted crop.

SUSCEPTIBLE PLANTS Onion, Egyptian onion, and shallot. **SYMPTOMS** Leaves turn dark gray, wither, and collapse. Bulbs may rot in store. The disease is worst in cool, wet seasons. **PREVENTION AND CONTROL** Use a 5-year rotation where onion downy mildew has occurred. Do not save seed from infected onions. Break the cycle—give up growing autumn- and spring-planted onions for a year or two. Remove infected plants as soon as they are noticed. Remove weeds to encourage good air flow around plants.

Onion fly

Delia antiqua

Adults of this pest emerge in May from pupae overwintering in the soil. Eggs are laid on young leaves, stems, or soil near plants. White larvae, up to ⅜ in. (8 mm) long, feed in stems and on roots and bulbs for 2 or 3 weeks before pupating. There may be three or four generations in a single year.

SUSCEPTIBLE PLANTS Onion; also shallot, garlic, and leeks. **SYMPTOMS** Young plants wilt and die; leaves and stems of more established plants become soft and rotten. Larvae bore into onion bulbs, which then tend to rot. Attacks are most severe in early to midsummer. May be confused with stem nematodes and onion white rot.

PREVENTION AND CONTROL Grow under row cover or fine mesh netting, put in place immediately after sowing or planting. Remove infested plants as soon as onion fly is discovered. Use a crop rotation and cultivate the soil in winter to expose pupae to predators.

Onion neck rot

Botrytis allii

Fungal disease favored by wet, cool summers. The main source is infected seed. The fungus also survives in soil and crop debris for 3 to 4 years. Infection does not spread between bulbs in store, but symptoms do not all develop at the same time.

SUSCEPTIBLE PLANTS Onion. **SYMPTOMS** Onions appear healthy when growing, but bulb scales become soft after 8–12 weeks in store. Brown, sunken lesions and a fluffy gray mold develop in the neck. The upper part of the bulb is soft when pressed, with brownish black discoloration under the dry outer leaves. The fungus spreads downward through the bulb, which in severe cases may decay completely and be covered with fluffy, gray mold. Sides and base of bulbs are rarely affected unless outer scales have been damaged before or during harvest. **PREVENTION AND CONTROL** Buy seed and sets from reputable suppliers. Use wide spacing during growth to allow air movement around the crops. Avoid damage before or during harvest, and allow tops to fall over

Onion fly larva *Actual length ⅜ in. (8 mm)*

Provide appropriate food and shelter to encourage natural predators (see pp. 186–202).

naturally. Dry well in an airy, warm dry atmosphere until the onion skins rustle. Do not store damaged bulbs. Store in cool, dry, airy conditions and remove bulbs that develop symptoms as they occur. Use a crop rotation of at least 4 years.

Onion rust

Puccinia allii

Fungal disease that survives on crop debris and wild *Allium* species. May be worse in nitrogen-rich soil or where potassium levels are low.

SUSCEPTIBLE PLANTS Leeks, onions, chives, garlic, and other *Allium* species; ornamental alliums are less susceptible.
PLANT SYMPTOMS Dusty reddish orange pustules appear on leaves and stems during summer. In a severe attack the leaves may turn yellow and die. Plant size and therefore crop yield may be reduced. Later growth may be disease-free as infection declines in the cooler weather of autumn. In mild autumns, the disease may continue to develop.
PREVENTION AND CONTROL Check nitrogen and potassium levels in soil. Improve the drainage of soil, if necessary. Use a crop rotation—minimum 3 years but preferably 4 or 5 years. Clear away any diseased plant debris.

Onion thrips

Thrips tabaci
See Thrips

SUSCEPTIBLE PLANTS Onion and leeks.
SYMPTOMS *See* Thrips.
PREVENTION AND CONTROL Outdoors, crops can withstand a light infestation. Water plants well during dry spells. Remove and destroy crop debris after harvest.
Pesticide sprays: Canola oil.

Onion white rot

Sclerotium cepivorum
Onion white rot is caused by a highly persistent soil-living fungus. The resting bodies (sclerotia) can survive for 15 years in the soil without a suitable host plant. The fungus is active when the soil temperature is around 50–68°F (10–20°C). Autumn-planted garlic and winter onions are particularly susceptible in mid- to late spring when soil temperatures are ideal. By this time they have a well-developed root system, extensive enough to stimulate the sclerotia into germination.

SUSCEPTIBLE PLANTS Bulb onions and garlic; also spring onions, leeks, chives, and shallots.
SYMPTOMS Plants suddenly start to die. Older leaves turn yellow; roots become stunted or rotten. Seedlings keel over; larger plants can easily be pulled out of the ground, and garlic stems pull away easily from the bulb. A few plants in a small patch may be affected at first, and then a whole row may show signs as the disease spreads. As the disease progresses, a white, cottony-looking fungal growth will be seen around the base and up the side of bulbs, with tiny black globules, like poppy seeds, among the fungus. These are the fungal resting bodies of white rot, known as sclerotia.
PREVENTION AND CONTROL Grow onions from seed, not sets, so the root system will be small when disease activity is at its highest. Grow garlic purchased from a reputable source, and avoid infecting clean ground. Clean tools and boots well after cultivating contaminated soil or after use in another garden. Use a strict crop rotation, ideally at least 8 years if onion white rot is present. Space plants widely; when stimulated by nearby plants, white rot can spread sideways through the soil and intertwined roots will also move infection along a row. Clumps of multisown onions should be 12 in. (30 cm) apart. If the area of infection is small, remove and dispose of affected and adjacent plants, and the surrounding soil. In areas known to be infected with white rot, try growing garlic in 4-in. (10-cm)-diameter holes filled with uncontaminated soil. Leeks are worth trying, even on badly infected ground.

Oriental fruit moth

Grapholita molesta
Adults are small, dark gray moths with dark brown, mottled forewings. They emerge in early May to mid-June. The females lay flat, white eggs on twigs or the undersides of leaves; these hatch in 10 to 14 days. The first-generation larvae—white to pinkish gray, brown-headed caterpillars—bore into tender stems and twigs, feed for 2 to 3 weeks, then pupate. Second-generation adults appear in mid-July; second-generation larvae bore into young fruit and don't feed on twigs. A third generation of larvae arrives by the end of August in the northern United States; these bore into the stem ends of mature fruits and feed on the pits.

SUSCEPTIBLE PLANTS Apple, apricot, cherry, peach, pear, and other fruit trees.
SYMPTOMS In spring, young larvae bore into green twigs, causing the twigs to wilt and die back. The tree may look unusually bushy from growth of new lateral shoots below the damaged parts. Second-generation larvae bore into developing fruit, leaving masses of gummy castings. Later generations enter the stem end of maturing fruit, leaving no external signs of damage; perfect-looking fruit injured through stem entry will usually break down in storage.
PREVENTION AND CONTROL When possible, plant early-maturing peach and apricot cultivars that are harvested before midsummer. To destroy overwintering larvae, cultivate the soil 4 in. (10 cm) deep around trees in early spring. Attract native parasitic wasps and flies with flowering cover crops planted around trees. Disrupt mating with pheromone patches applied to the lower limbs of trees (one patch for every four trees).

Never spray when bees are working—the evening is usually the safest time.

Biological control: Repeated sprays of *Bacillus thuringiensis* var. *kurstaki* (B.T.K.) may help control the larvae.
Pesticide spray: Spray superior oil to kill eggs and larvae.

Parsnip canker

Itersonilia perplexans, Mycocentrospora acerina, and *Phoma* spp.

There are three main types of parsnip canker: black, orange-brown, and purple. All cause damage to the root. Wet sites exacerbate them. Black canker is spread by rain-splash from diseased spots on the leaves. Spores then enter through damaged roots. Carrot rust fly wounds may create entry points. Orange-brown canker is possibly caused by soil-inhabiting organisms. Purple canker occurs in soils high in organic matter.

SUSCEPTIBLE PLANTS Parsnip.
PLANT SYMPTOMS Black canker produces dark lesions, often on lateral roots. Orange-brown canker produces a brown coloration on the skin, initially on the shoulder of the main root. Purple canker produces a purple lesion with brown water-soaked margins.
PREVENTION AND CONTROL Grow in a well-drained site. Grow a resistant variety such as 'Gladiator'. Mound soil in summer to stop the spores of black canker from reaching the roots. Use close spacing to produce uniformly smaller roots that may be less susceptible to some forms of canker. Control carrot fly. Use a crop rotation.

Pea and bean weevil

Sitona lineatus

Adults, brown-gray and ¼ in. (5 mm) long, overwinter in plant debris and vegetation, moving on to plants to feed in early spring. Eggs are laid in the soil, and the larvae feed on root nodules for a few weeks, pupating in the soil. Adults emerge in June or July. There is one generation a year. *See also* Weevils.

SUSCEPTIBLE PLANTS Peas, broad bean; also related plants.
SYMPTOMS Characteristic scalloped holes are eaten out of the edges of leaves in spring and summer. Young plants may be severely damaged early in the season when growth is slow. Otherwise, healthy plants can usually tolerate the damage.
PREVENTION AND CONTROL Avoid using vetch as an overwintering green manure. Prepare ground well before sowing to encourage strong, fast growth. Cover young plants with a barrier of row cover or mesh, immediately after sowing.

Peach leaf curl

Taphrina deformans

Spores of this fungal disease are spread by rain. The disease is worse following cold, wet springs and in cool, damp areas.

SUSCEPTIBLE PLANTS Peach; also almond, nectarine, and rarely apricot. Both edible and ornamental types may be affected.
SYMPTOMS In early spring, new leaves thicken and start to twist and curl, becoming yellow or orange-red in color. Red blisters appear on leaves in early summer. Infected leaves develop a pale bloom, turn brown, and fall prematurely. Regular attacks will reduce vigor and the production of fruit, and spoil the appearance of the tree.
PREVENTION AND CONTROL Cover wall-grown specimens from mid-winter to mid-spring to prevent rain-splash spreading the disease to developing buds and young foliage. Construct a lean-to frame of wood and clear plastic sheeting, rather like a rectangular coldframe window, but make the vertical pieces long enough so that they can be inserted in the soil. This cover can be attached to a wall or fence and secured in the ground. Do not plant susceptible trees in cool, damp situations. Avoid sites near ponds. Pick off diseased leaves on sight. Keep trees well fed and watered to encourage the development of new healthy growth.
Fungicide spray: Spray with Bordeaux mixture just after autumn leaf fall, and again as buds begin to swell in late winter or early spring.

Peachtree borer

Synanthedon exitiosa and *S. pictipes*

Adults are blue-black, 1¼-in. (3-cm) moths with a yellow or orange band across the body and narrow, translucent wings. They resemble wasps and, unlike most moths, they are active during the day. The first adults emerge in July, and emergence continues into early fall. In late summer, females begin laying eggs on tree trunks or in cracks in soil within a few inches of trunks. Eggs hatch in 10 days, and new larvae—white caterpillars with dark brown heads—burrow into tree trunks to feed and overwinter until next year. In spring, they spin brown, silken cocoons at the surface of their burrow or in the soil.

SUSCEPTIBLE PLANTS Peaches, primarily; also apricot, cherry, nectarine, and plum trees.
SYMPTOMS Larvae bore beneath the bark of trees at the base, as well as into main roots near the surface, often girdling the trees. Burrow entrance holes exude gum mixed with sawdustlike material. Young or weak trees may be seriously damaged or killed; older trees are less affected.
PREVENTION AND CONTROL Adult peachtree borers are attracted to weak trees, so keep plants vigorous and avoid damaging them. Attract native parasitic wasps and predators. Beginning in late summer and into fall, inspect tree trunks from 1 ft. (30 cm) or so above ground level to 2 in. (5 cm) below ground level, digging away soil to expose the trunk area below the ground surface. Kill borers in exposed burrows by inserting a fine, flexible wire. In fall and spring, cultivate soil around the base of the trunk to expose and destroy larvae and pupae.

Pear psylla

Cacopsylla pyricola

Adults of this pest overwinter on twigs and branches. Their eggs

For more information on organically approved fertilizers, see p. 61.

Pea and bean weevil
Actual length ¼ in. (6 mm)

Pear psylla *Actual length 1/16 in. (2 mm)*

are laid in April on spurs and shoots and hatch a few weeks later. Nymphs (the young) are pink to orange, with pink/red eyes. They feed on young buds and leaves. There are three generations a year.

SUSCEPTIBLE PLANTS Pear, plus a wide range of trees and shrubs. **SYMPTOMS** Leaf and blossom buds are damaged in spring. Summer feeding results in large deposits of honeydew and the growth of sooty mold. Damage to fruit buds forming in late summer reduces the next year's fruit crop. Severe infestation causes premature leaf fall. **PREVENTION AND CONTROL** Prune off and burn the most severely infested shoots. Grow flowers such as corn marigold and cornflower to attract predators.

Pear sawfly

Caliroa cerasi
Adults are tiny, shiny, black-and-yellow insects that resemble houseflies. They emerge in late May, and their eggs hatch in a week. The young larvae resemble green-black, ½-in. (1-cm) slugs; older larvae are yellow and segmented. They feed for 3 to 4 weeks, then pupate in the soil. Second-generation adults appear in late July, with larvae hatching in mid-August.

SUSCEPTIBLE PLANTS Cherries, cotoneasters, pears, and plums. A related species attacks roses. **SYMPTOMS** Larvae skeletonize upper leaf surfaces, leaving scorched-looking areas. Young

trees may be defoliated and eventually killed. Second-generation larvae cause the most damage. **PREVENTION AND CONTROL** Spray trees with a strong stream of water to remove larvae. **Pesticide spray**: As a last resort, spray with pyrethrin.

Pear scab

Venturia pirina
Fungal disease similar to apple scab but infection also occurs frequently on bud scales. Scab is worse in cool, wet periods in spring and early summer.

SUSCEPTIBLE PLANTS Pear. **PLANT SYMPTOMS** Dark scabby spots, similar to apple scab symptoms, appear on shoots, leaves, fruit, and buds. Fruit spotting can be more severe than on apples, causing fruit to become deformed with deep clefts. Twigs develop conspicuous swellings which later burst. **PREVENTION AND CONTROL** *See* Apple scab.

Peony blight

Botrytis paeoniae
Also known as peony wilt, this fungal disease persists in the soil and can survive on infected plant debris. It thrives in humid conditions.

SUSCEPTIBLE PLANTS Peony and lily-of-the-valley. **SYMPTOMS** Stems develop dark brown coloration at soil level. Gray mold develops on young buds and flowers, which darken.

Stems wilt and collapse. Flowers may fail to open. **PREVENTION AND CONTROL** Space plants widely to promote good air flow. Plants that are infected should be cut down to ground level in the autumn. Clear away all diseased plant debris. Carefully remove a layer of topsoil around infected plants and replace with fresh soil.

Phosphorus deficiency

All plants may be prone to this disorder, but it is not common.

SYMPTOMS Poor growth. Leaves turn bluish green with purple tints, but not yellow. Fruits small and green, with acid taste. Not easy to diagnose, and can be confused with drought, root damage, or nitrogen deficiency. **CAUSES** Soil may be naturally deficient in phosphorus—particularly acid soils, poor chalk soils, and in areas of high rainfall. Cold weather can cause a temporary deficiency. **PREVENTION AND CONTROL** Apply organic sources of phosphorus like rock phosphate or bone meal.

Phytophthora root & stem rots

Phytophthora spp.
Various species of these soilborne fungi cause root and stem rots in plants. Plants in wet soils are more likely to be infected. Some strains of the

fungus are host-specific, others attack a range of plants.

SUSCEPTIBLE PLANTS Azalea, rhododendron, Lawson cypress, beech, heather, apple, raspberry, yew, linden, ornamental *Prunus* spp., sycamores, and other woody plants. **SYMPTOMS** Sparse yellowing foliage, partial dieback of twigs, whole branches, or one side of a shrub or tree. On fruit-bearing trees, fruit becomes smaller and sparser. Infected trees increase little in height or diameter and die within 3 to 10 years of initial infection. Tongues of dead bark can extend up the stem from soil level. On examination, roots at that point will be dead. On smaller specimens lower leaves may drop and the entire plant wilts. Difficult to diagnose. Can be confused with other, less severe problems. **PREVENTION AND CONTROL** Never plant in land known to have *Phytophthora*; replace the soil. Avoid transferring contaminated soil on boots and equipment. Make sure land is well-drained. Some plants are less susceptible: crab apples and *Quercus robur* (English oak) seem to be resistant. There is no cure.

Plum curculio

Conotrachelus nenuphar
Adults are dark, brownish gray, ¼-in. (6-mm) beetles with warty, hard wing covers, a prominent snout, and white hairs on the body. They overwinter under fallen leaves, stones, logs, or other garden debris, flying to trees just as the blossoms

Peony wilt *see Peony blight*

Use a crop rotation when growing vegetables.

open. Adults feed and lay round, white eggs just under the skin of fruit. The eggs hatch in 5 to 10 days into plump, white grubs with brown heads. These larvae feed within fruits for 2 to 3 weeks; when the fruit drops, they exit and pupate in the soil. Second-generation adults emerge in late July to late October, feed on ripe or fallen fruit until fall, then move to shelter to hibernate.

SUSCEPTIBLE PLANTS Plums and apples primarily, but also apricots, cherries, and peaches.
SYMPTOMS Adult females deposit a single egg just under fruit skin, leaving a crescent-shaped scar at each egg-laying site. Newly hatched larvae feed inside the fruit, causing it to drop, rot, or develop deformed growth.
PREVENTION AND CONTROL Knock beetles out of trees onto a dropcloth by sharply tapping branches with a padded stick; gather fallen beetles and drop into soapy water. For this control to be effective, you must do it twice a day throughout the growing season. Every other day, pick up and destroy all fallen fruit. Keep chickens around fruit trees to feed on dropped fruit.

Poor/no fruit set

Disorder especially affecting fruit, squash, and runner beans.

SYMPTOMS Plants fail to fruit, or fruit poorly. Raspberry and strawberry fruits may be distorted or have dry areas. Plants otherwise growing well.

CAUSES Frost at flowering time. Lack of suitable pollinator in the vicinity (apples and pears). Lack of flowers as a result of inappropriate pruning. Male flowers not open at same time as female flowers (cucurbits). Poor weather at flowering time, hindering pollinating insects. Dry soil.
PREVENTION AND CONTROL Identify the cause and then remedy, if possible.

Potassium deficiency

Disorder also known as potash deficiency, caused by a shortage of potassium in the soil. Most common on light, sandy soils, and those with a low clay or high peat content.

SUSCEPTIBLE PLANTS Potato, tomato, apple, currants, pear, and other edible and ornamental fruiting plants.
SYMPTOMS Brown scorching on leaf tips and margins, which may curl up. Purple-brown spots may appear on the underside. Poor flowering and fruit set. Plants may be more prone to frost damage and disease.
PREVENTION AND CONTROL Improve soil structure. Plant-based potash fertilizers, seaweed meal, comfrey leaves, and comfrey liquid can be used to supply potassium. Apply well-rotted manure that has been stacked under cover, or compost. Add wood ash, which has a good potash content, to the compost pile. Do not add it directly to the soil as it is very soluble.

Potato blackleg

Erwinia carotovora

The bacteria that cause this disease overwinter in potato tubers, plant debris, and soil. Tubers are invaded through damaged skin. Poor drainage, potassium deficiency, or excess nitrogen exacerbate the condition.

SUSCEPTIBLE PLANTS Potato.
SYMPTOMS First seen as small water-soaked lesions on stems. Stems turn brown or black 4 in. (10 cm) above and below soil level, becoming mushy. Leaves roll, wrinkle, and blister. Lower stem disintegrates and can be foul-smelling. Tubers can also be attacked, resulting in a gray, slimy rot. This disease can affect isolated individual plants and even isolated stems on one plant. It is more likely during prolonged wet conditions.
PREVENTION AND CONTROL Plant in well-drained soil. Lift crops during dry weather if possible to prevent cross-infection of healthy tubers at harvest. Avoid wounding tubers. Never save tubers from infected plants for seed. Maintain storage temperatures at 39°F (4°C) to inhibit new infections.

Potato common scab

Streptomyces spp.

A widespread bacterial disease, common on light, sandy, alkaline soils and encouraged by hot, dry weather. Serious attacks can occur on newly cleared grassland. Following initial infection, the scab lesions produce further spores, which persist in the soil. The disease is usually present in most soils but is only active given the correct conditions.

SUSCEPTIBLE PLANTS Potato.
SYMPTOMS Scabby, angular spots of corky tissue appear on the skin of the tuber (shown on p. 91). Spots can almost cover the skin surface and may be either superficial or form deep pits. Yield is seldom affected but wastage is increased with the extra peeling needed.
PREVENTION AND CONTROL Do not apply lime; this will increase scab incidence. Water potato crops in dry weather, especially when in flower. Add organic soil improvers to increase the water-holding capacity of the soil. Grow resistant cultivars.

Potato cyst nematode

Heterodera spp.

The golden cyst nematode (*H. rostochiensis*) and the white cyst nematode (*H. pallida*) are microscopic worms, which feed in the roots of tomatoes and potatoes. They survive in the soil in the form of pinhead-size cysts, each containing hundreds of eggs. Cysts can remain dormant for 10 years or more, hatching in the presence of exudates from the roots of potatoes and related plants. New cysts—which can be white, yellow, or brown—may be seen on roots from late June to August. A hand lens is usually

Potash deficiency *see Potassium deficiency*

If you have to spray, always read the label first and follow the instructions carefully.

needed to see the cysts. Common on plots where vegetables have been grown for many years.

SUSCEPTIBLE PLANTS Potato and tomato.

SYMPTOMS Plants yellow and die back prematurely, sometimes in patches. Crop yields reduced. In severe cases, growth may be poor and the crop minimal.

PREVENTION AND CONTROL Plant certified seed potatoes. Avoid bringing in soil on plants or tools from sites that may harbor the pest. Grow resistant potato cultivars. Use as long a crop rotation as possible. Feed the soil with bulky organic soil improvers to encourage natural predators. On infested land, the no-dig technique (see p. 326) may give a better yield. Early cultivars may produce a reasonable crop before the pest attack takes effect.

Potato late blight

Phytophthora infestans

This fungal disease overwinters on infected potato tubers and surviving plants. Plants growing from volunteer tubers (potatoes left in the ground at harvest time) are a common source of infection. It spreads rapidly to new crops in warm, damp weather. Spores are washed from leaves down into the soil by rain to infect potato tubers. Resistant spores which can survive in the soil may also be produced—but it is not known yet how commonly they occur.

SUSCEPTIBLE PLANTS Potato and tomato.

SYMPTOMS A common and serious fungal problem in warm, wet seasons when it spreads rapidly. Less frequent in dry conditions. Potato—dark blotches on leaves, mainly tips and edges, and on stems. White mold develops under leaves in humid conditions. The whole plant may collapse quickly. Infected tubers develop dark sunken lesions, which become firm and dry. Tubers may decay to a foul-smelling mush as a result of invasion by bacterial soft rots. Tomato—foliage symptoms similar to potato but less severe. Green fruit and stems show dark markings, mature fruit quickly develop a dry, leathery rot. This may only become evident days after harvest. A whitish gray mold may also develop over the rot.

PREVENTION AND CONTROL Plant good-quality seed potatoes from a reputable source. Grow tolerant potato cultivars such as 'Katahdin' and 'Kennebec'. Destroy volunteer plants including self-set tomatoes and potatoes growing on compost piles and similar sites. Mound soil around potatoes or mulch them to reduce the likelihood of spores being washing down onto tubers. Smooth the sides of the ridges to prevent spores being washed into the soil through cracks. If blight appears on the foliage, remove all affected leaves immediately. Cut off all foliage and stems in a bad case. Compost only in a hot pile. Do not harvest the potato crop for at least 3 weeks to avoid infecting tubers with spores

during lifting. Harvest all tubers and do not save tubers for seed from blighted potatoes or seed from infected tomatoes.

Powdery mildew

Erysiphe, *Sphaerotheca*, and *Podosphaera* spp.

The distinctive symptoms of powdery mildew can be caused by a range of related fungi. Each mildew species affects only a specific group of plants. Most common when conditions are warm and dry during the day and cold at night, and on dry soils.

SUSCEPTIBLE PLANTS Almost any: specific mildews attack apple, apricot, cherry, and plum; brassicas, cucurbits, gooseberry, blackcurrant, grapevines, roses, strawberry, and raspberry.

SYMPTOMS A white to gray powderylike coating may develop on almost any part of a plant.

PREVENTION AND CONTROL Prune out any infected shoots of perennials in spring and late summer. Make sure plants are supplied with correct amounts of water and nutrients at all times. Prepare the ground well before planting. Mulch plants to retain moisture. Do not overdo nitrogen-rich fertilizers, as this can encourage soft growth more easily infected by the fungus. New cultivars that show some degree of resistance to mildew are constantly being developed. *See also* Apple powdery mildew.

Fungicide spray: Sulfur. This may harm young leaves, and some gooseberry and apple cultivars. Check the label before use.

Psylla

Small, sap-feeding pests that feed on flowers, leaves, young buds, and shoots of plants, causing distorted growth. Plants may be covered in sticky honeydew leading to black sooty mold growth. It is the young nymphs that cause most damage. They have wide, flattened bodies, with prominent wing buds and eyes. Adults, $\frac{1}{16}$–$\frac{1}{8}$ in. (2–3 mm) long, resemble winged aphids; they can jump and fly.

See also Boxwood psylla; Pear psylla.

Rabbits

Oryctolagus cuniculus

Burrowing animals that live in tunnels excavated in hedge banks and similar situations. They feed at night, early morning, and late afternoon on a wide range of plants. A rabbit can eat 1 lb. (0.5 kg) of vegetation per day, so a large colony can cause extensive damage.

SUSCEPTIBLE PLANTS A wide variety of fruits, vegetables, grasses, and flowers.

SYMPTOMS Rabbits graze on young shoots. Plants can be eaten to ground level and bark stripped from trees. Most damage is done in spring and early summer.

PREVENTION AND CONTROL If rabbit numbers are high, erect a rabbitproof fence around important plants. Use a mesh size of 1–1¼ in. (2.5–3 cm). The fence should be 3–4 ft. (1–1.2 m) high with a further 1 ft. (30 cm) buried below ground level and

Do not overfeed plants, especially with nitrogen, which causes lush growth attractive to pests.

angled outward. It should be well supported by posts and straining wires and should be inspected regularly for holes. If the local rabbit population is small, protect individual plants with netting or tree protectors. Surrounding plants with spiky plant clippings will also deter grazing rabbits. Electric fencing may also be used. Some plants are said to be less attractive to rabbits (see pp. 157 and 172).

Raspberry cane blight

Leptosphaeria coniothyrium

Soilborne fungal disease, which enters through cracks in bark or pruning wounds. It is spread by rain-splash and on tools.

SUSCEPTIBLE PLANTS Raspberry; also blackberry, hybrid berries, and strawberry. **SYMPTOMS** Leaves shrivel and die. Dark patches and cracked bark develop on canes just above the soil. Within the patches, masses of pinhead-size pustules develop. Canes become brittle. **PREVENTION AND CONTROL** Handle canes with care to avoid damage. If the canes are infected, cut back to below soil level. Burn all infected material. Disinfect tools after use.

Raspberry cane and leaf spot

Elsinoe veneta

From late spring to early summer, this fungal disease infects young canes. Spores overwinter on host plants. Fruiting canes develop lesions from infection the previous year.

SUSCEPTIBLE PLANTS Raspberry; blackberry, loganberry, and other hybrid berries. **SYMPTOMS** Attacks young growth. Purple spots are found on canes, leaves, blossom, and stalks. Leaves may drop, bark can split, and small cankers form. Fruit yield is reduced. Severe infection will cause distortion and death. **PREVENTION AND CONTROL** Cut out and burn infected canes. **Fungicide spray:** Bordeaux mixture when buds on fruiting canes open, then 10 days later.

Raspberry spur blight

Didymella applanata

This fungal disease is spread in wet conditions by rain and wind, especially in a damp spring.

SUSCEPTIBLE PLANTS Raspberry and loganberry. **SYMPTOMS** Leaves may develop dark brown lesions in early summer. In late summer, purplish blotches appear on stems around buds, turning brown-black to silver in winter. Diseased canes become dotted with tiny black fruiting bodies. Plants rarely die as a result of this disease but fruit yield is reduced. A dry summer can cause the canes to become dry and shriveled. **PREVENTION AND CONTROL** Cut out and burn diseased

canes. In spring, thin canes to reduce overcrowding. Cultivars 'Boyne' and 'Festival' have some resistance to this disease. **Fungicide spray:** Where this disease has been a problem, spray with Bordeaux mixture at 14-day intervals in spring when the buds are ½ in. (1 cm) long.

Red spider mite

Tetranychus urticae

"Red" can be misleading as these tiny pests, up to ¹⁄₆₄ in. (0.5 mm) long, become red only during autumn and winter. They are also known as the two-spotted mite; for most of the year, they are pale green/yellow with two dark spots. They thrive in hot, dry conditions, reproducing in as little as 8 days at 80°F (26°C). The mites hibernate in cracks and crevices, leaf litter, and garden canes. In the greenhouse they may breed year-round if the temperature remains above 54°F (12°C).

SUSCEPTIBLE PLANTS A wide range of plants in greenhouses and indoors. May also attack outdoor plants in a hot, dry season: strawberries, peach, grapevine, cucumber, string and runner beans, eggplant, carnation, fuchsia, and impatiens. **SYMPTOMS** Leaves initially show a fine speckling. As the attack continues, they take on a bronzed appearance and may wither and die. A fine webbing is produced, strung between parts of the plant or under the leaves. Using a magnifying glass, mites and their tiny eggs can be seen on the undersides of leaves.

In an unheated greenhouse the most severe attacks occur from June to September, but mites can be active all year round. **PREVENTION AND CONTROL** Spray plants, if appropriate, with a fine mist of water, twice daily. Ensure all plants have the best growing conditions possible. Red spider mite can be severe on plants that are potbound or overcrowded, or growing poorly in hot and dry conditions. Discard badly infested plants. In spring clean out the greenhouse and scrub down benches. Use a high-pressure hose on cracks and crevices. **Biological control:** Under cover and in warm areas outside use *Phytoseiulus persimilis*, a predatory mite; optimum temperature 64–75°F (18–24°C). **Pesticide sprays:** Insecticidal soap; canola oil.

Replant disease

Exact causes are still not known. Soil-dwelling nematodes and fungal diseases are probably responsible. It is thought that the level of these organisms increases in proportion to the size or age of the plant, and that they can coexist with the strong woody roots of mature plants, but new plants with soft root tissue are overwhelmed by the level of these organisms in the soil.

SUSCEPTIBLE PLANTS Cherry, rose, viola, China aster, apple, peach, pear, plum, and strawberry. **SYMPTOMS** Effects occur when a new plant is placed in a site once inhabited by a related

Avoid spraying predators.

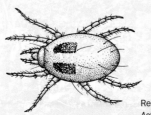

Red spider mite
Actual length ¹⁄₆₄ in. (0.5 mm)

plant. In the first year, the new plant grows poorly. Root systems are weak and may become blackened. Plants may fail to establish.

PREVENTION AND CONTROL
Avoid planting susceptible plants where the same or a related plant has recently been removed. If you must replant in the same spot, dig out a large hole, remove the soil and replace it with fresh soil from a site where susceptible plants have not been grown. Plants grown in large containers, with a large rootball at planting-out time, may have more chance of survival.

Rose black spot

Diplocarpon rosae
Fungal disease spread by rain-splash, on hands, and on tools. Attacks are worst in warm, moist conditions. Overwinters on stems, fallen leaves, and soil.

SUSCEPTIBLE PLANTS Rose.
SYMPTOMS Small to large black spots develop on the leaves. Eventually they merge to produce large irregular patches. Affects both leaf surfaces. Edges of leaf spots may turn yellow. Leaves fall prematurely. Bushes become weak if disease is severe.
PREVENTION AND CONTROL
Clear up fallen leaves. Prune infected stems hard in spring. Grow resistant cultivars such as 'Veilchenblau', 'New Dawn', and 'Knock Out'. Mulch plants with compost or leaf mold before buds burst in spring to reduce the risk of overwintering spores splashing up from the ground.

Fungicide spray: Sulfur. This may harm some young leaves. Check the label before use.

Rose rust

Phragmidium spp.
Spores of this fungal disease overwinter on fallen leaves. They germinate in spring, reinfecting bushes through wind and rain-splash. Spores also survive on the soil surface, plant stems, fences, stakes, and plant debris.

SUSCEPTIBLE PLANTS Rose.
SYMPTOMS Initially, bright orange pustules appear on leaf stalks, branches, lower leaf surfaces, especially along veins, and on any hips persisting from the previous year. During summer, yellow–orange pustules develop on lower leaf surfaces away from leaf veins. Later pustules become speckled with black spores, the overwintering stage of the disease. *Rosa pimpinellifolia* is particularly susceptible.
PREVENTION AND CONTROL
Grow healthy plants in well-drained soil. Keep well pruned to encourage good air circulation. Grow resistant cultivars. Clear away any diseased plant leaves and other debris. Prune out stems showing symptoms as soon as they are seen in spring. Cut well back beyond the point of infection.

Sawflies

Adults sawflies are small, inconspicuous, dark-bodied flies up to ½ in. (1 cm) long. The

larvae, which damage plants, vary in color from cream to green and brown and resemble moth or butterfly caterpillars. They range in size from ½–1¼ in. (1.5–3 cm) long. (*See also* Caterpillars, for comparison.) The larvae feed on leaves, stems, and fruit of a wide range of wild and cultivated plants. If infestation is severe the plant is often reduced to a skeleton. *See also* Imported currantworm.

Scale insects

Sap-feeding pests that move only when newly hatched, when they crawl about looking for a suitable feeding site. These young "crawlers" settle to feed near the leaf veins or stem of the affected plant, developing a waxy shell (scale). Adults resemble tiny limpet shells and when young can be mistaken for small brown flecks. Two species are most likely to be found on plants in the greenhouse, conservatory, or house. Hemispherical scale (*Saissetia coffeae*) is dark brown in color, dome-shaped, ⅛ in. (3 mm) long. Soft scale (*Coccus hesperidum*) is light green/brown in color with a darker center spot; oval and flat in shape, about ¼ in. (5 mm) long. Breeding can take place year-round if temperatures are suitable.

SUSCEPTIBLE PLANTS A wide range of plants, particularly under glass and indoors.
SYMPTOMS Plants are weakened by the feeding scales, and leaves may fall. Scale insects excrete a sticky substance, known as honeydew, which drops from

the feeding area onto leaves below. Black sooty molds may grow on it. Appearance is marred, and growth inhibited.
PREVENTION AND CONTROL
Check plants regularly, especially the undersides of the leaves, for the presence of scale. Where an infestation is light, individual scales can be removed easily with a fingernail or a cotton bud. Check new plants carefully for signs of scale before introducing them into the house or greenhouse.
Biological control: In warm, sunny conservatories and greenhouses use *Metaphycus helvolus*, a parasitic wasp. Optimum temperature 68–86°F (20–30°C). Needs high levels of sunshine to be really effective.
Pesticide spray: Insecticidal soap.

Scorch

Disorder affecting soft and hairy-leaved plants.

SYMPTOMS Bleached-looking or pale brown patches on leaves. Damaged areas may crisp.
CAUSES Strong sunlight. Made worse by water droplets on foliage, concentrating the rays.
PREVENTION AND CONTROL
Avoid wetting foliage in strong sunlight. Always water susceptible plants from below. Provide shade.

Slugs

Soft-bodied, slimy pests, which move on a slimy, muscular foot and leave a characteristic slime

---

Root aphids *see Aphids*
Root rots *see Damping off, Phytophthora root & stem rots*
Rose powdery mildew *see Powdery mildew*
Rose sickness *see Replant disease*
Scab *see Apple scab, Pear scab, Potato common scab*

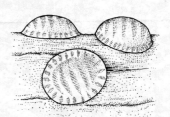

Scale Actual length
1/16–1/4 in. (2–5 mm)

trail. They can vary in color from pink to black, and in size up to several inches. Some, like the gray-brown field slug, live and feed mainly above ground; others inhabit the soil. In the daytime slugs may be found in cracks and crevices and under any shelter where it is cool and damp. At night, especially when damp, slugs will be found feeding and crawling over plants. Slug eggs are laid in clusters in soil cavities. They are spherical, opaque or translucent, and colorless.

SUSCEPTIBLE PLANTS A huge range of plants are liable to be attacked, particularly seedlings, young plants, annuals, and herbaceous perennials. Slugs will also attack tubers and fruit.
SYMPTOMS Irregular holes eaten in roots, stems, bulbs, tubers, buds, flowers, fruit, and leaves of a wide range of plants. Seedlings fail to come up or are eaten off. Most damage occurs at night. Telltale slime trails may be seen.
PREVENTION AND CONTROL There is no one single, simple method of controlling slugs. Use a range of techniques to protect susceptible plants, especially when young. When sowing seeds, water the bottom of the hole, then cover with dry soil. Encourage quick germination and growth of seedlings and young plants. Plant out sturdy, indoor-grown transplants rather than sowing directly. Water in the morning; damp soil and plants in the evening encourage slugs and snails. Do not mulch young plants. Protect individual young plants with plastic bottle cloches. Hoe regularly to disturb slime trails that may be used by other slugs and snails to locate edible plants. Dig in winter to expose slugs and eggs to weather and predators. Grow varieties of potato less susceptible to slugs; harvest all potato tubers by early autumn. Hand-pick slugs at night and destroy. Use traps baited with beer, milk, or grape juice; ensure the lip is raised ¾–1¼ in. (2–3 cm) above the soil surface to avoid trapping beetles. Surround susceptible plants with bran; remove slugs found in it. Lay a ring of comfrey leaves around any susceptible plants. This will act a decoy but is ineffective after midsummer. Provide alternative food—such as lettuce leaves (preferably under bricks or slates to keep them moist)—when transplanting into an empty bed. Plant sacrificial plants, such as French marigolds. Protect pots and larger plants with copper-coated tape. Encourage natural enemies such as frogs, toads, beetles, and centipedes. Hens can help to clear slugs from empty ground or in a greenhouse.
Biological control: Outdoors and under cover, use *Heterorhabditis megidis*, a parasitic nematode; minimum soil/compost temperature 54°F (12°C).

Snails

These creatures have a conspicuous hard shell which they withdraw into when threatened. They move on a large, slimy, muscular foot and leave a characteristic slime trail. Active from spring to autumn, snails usually hide under hedges and in cool, damp places during the day. They feed at night, especially during damp weather. The garden snail (*Helix aspersa*) is the most common pest, with a gray-brown shell up to 1¼ in. (3 cm) across. Banded snails (*Cepaea nemoralis*) are not normally a serious pest. Their shells have white, yellow, gray, or pink bands with darker stripes, or are sometimes entirely pale yellow.

SUSCEPTIBLE PLANTS A wide range of plants.
SYMPTOMS Irregular holes eaten in roots, stems, bulbs, tubers, buds, flowers, fruit, and leaves. Seeds fail to come up and seedlings are eaten. Most damage occurs at night.
PREVENTION AND CONTROL Some of the methods suggested for slugs may also work for snails. Do not grow very susceptible plants near locations like walls, rocks, and wood piles, where snails hide.

Sooty molds

Cladosporium spp. and others

Sooty mold fungi grow on sugary honeydew excreted by sap-feeding insects. They do not directly damage plants but are unsightly and block out light needed for photosynthesis. Leaves may fall; in severe cases the plant may be weakened.

SUSCEPTIBLE PLANTS Camellia, bay laurel, birch, ornamental citrus, linden, oak, plum, rose, tomato, vines, willows, and many others, outdoors and under glass.
SYMPTOMS Black or brown sootlike deposits appear on upper leaf surfaces and other plant parts. Plants will also be infested with sap-feeding pests such as aphids, whiteflies, scale insects, or mealybugs.
PREVENTION AND CONTROL Control the pests that are producing the honeydew. Spray or sponge leaves with water. When cleaned of mold, fruit will still be edible.

Sowbugs

Armadillidium vulgare, Oniscus asellus, Porcellio scaber, and other spp.

Mid- to dark gray, hard-bodied, jointed, terrestrial crustaceans up to ¾ in. (2 cm) long. Young sowbugs are lighter in color, depending on age, and much smaller. They hide during daylight under seed boxes, pots, stones, and other debris, emerging at night to feed. Batches of 20 or more eggs are laid and held in brood pouches by the adult female. The young disperse and feed for a year or so before they mature.

SUSCEPTIBLE PLANTS Seedlings and young plants.
SYMPTOMS The main source of food for the sowbug is dead or decaying plant matter, not living plants. They can, however, eat off seedlings at soil level.
PREVENTION AND CONTROL Sowbugs are such ubiquitous creatures that trying to eliminate them would be impossible and is rarely necessary, except perhaps in greenhouses and garden frames in spring where seed-raising is going on. Destroy large colonies by pouring boiling water over them. Control survivors by

For more information on watering problems, see pp. 63–64.

Slug

Snail

setting baits of bran, dried blood, boiled potato, grated cheese, or sugar under a plank of wood, a box, or other dark location. Collect and destroy. Keep greenhouses clear of decaying plant debris. Do not mulch susceptible young plants.

Splitting

Disorder affecting cabbage, carrot, cherries, onion, parsnip, plum, potato, rutabaga, and tomatoes.

SYMPTOMS Fruits, heads, roots, and stems split lengthwise. This can allow organisms that cause dieback or rotting to enter. Apple fruits may become hollow. **CAUSES** Rapid growth, especially when rain or watering follows a very dry period; also wide fluctuations in temperature. **PREVENTION AND CONTROL** Improve waterholding capacity of soil. Mulch soil.

Strawberry crown rot

Phytophthora cactorum

Fungal disease, soilborne and spread by rain-splash onto the fruit. Spores also enter through damaged plant parts.

SUSCEPTIBLE PLANTS Strawberry. **SYMPTOMS** Droughtlike effects. Young leaves wilt, older leaves develop a red coloration. Plants die. When cut through, the crown is brown and dead. **PREVENTION AND CONTROL**

Remove infected plants. Apply a good layer of straw or other protective material to keep fruit off the soil surface. Plant new crops far from the previous growing site.

Squash bug

Anasa tristis

Adults are brownish black, flat-backed, ½-in. (1-cm) bugs covered with fine, dark hairs. They give off an unpleasant smell in defense. Unmated adult insects overwinter in garden litter, vines, or boards to emerge, mate, and lay shiny, yellow to brown eggs in groups on the undersides of leaves in spring. The nymphs are whitish green or gray, similar in shape to adults, with a darker thorax and abdomen as they mature; they are usually covered with a grainy white powder. Nymphs take all summer to develop, molting five times before maturity.

SUSCEPTIBLE PLANTS All cucurbit crops; winter squash are the most severely affected. **SYMPTOMS** Both adults and nymphs suck plant juices, causing leaves and shoots to blacken and die back; attacked plants fail to produce fruit. **PREVENTION AND CONTROL** Maintain vigorous plant growth. Handpick all stages of this pest from the undersides of leaves. Support vines off of the ground on trellises. Attract native parasitic flies with pollen and nectar plants. Cover plants with row cover or mesh (hand-pollinate flowers).

Squash vine borer

Melittia cucurbitae

Adults are narrow-winged, olive-brown, 1–1½-in. (2.5–4-cm) moths, with fringed hind legs, clear hind wings, and a red abdomen with black rings. They emerge in spring and lay eggs on stems and leaf stalks near the base of the plant. The brown-headed, white larvae feed in vine stems for up to 6 weeks, then pupate in the soil.

SUSCEPTIBLE PLANTS Squash, pumpkins, cucumbers, melons, and gourds. **SYMPTOMS** Larvae bore into the vines, chewing the inner tissue near the base and causing vines to wilt suddenly. Girdled vines rot and die. **PREVENTION AND CONTROL** Early in the growing season, cover vines with row cover or mesh; uncover later for pollinators, or hand-pollinate flowers. To save attacked vines, slit infested stems and remove the borers, then heap soil over the vines to induce rooting. **Pesticide spray:** If squash vine borers have been a serious problem in previous years, spray the base of susceptible plants with pyrethrin to kill young larvae before they enter vines.

Stink bugs

Family Pentatomidae

Adults are shield-shaped, green, tan, brown, or gray, ½-in. (1-cm) bugs. Most species are smooth, but a few are spiny or rough-

textured. They overwinter in weeds in waste areas. Females lay 300–500 barrel-shaped eggs each when the weather warms. They hatch in a week into oval-shaped, wingless nymphs that look similar to the adults. Nymphs develop to adults in about 5 weeks.

SUSCEPTIBLE PLANTS Brassicas, beans, peas, sweet corn, tomatoes, and peaches. **SYMPTOMS** Adults and nymphs suck plant sap from leaves, flowers, buds, fruit, and seeds. Feeding punctures in fruit cause scarring and dimpling known as cat-facing. **PREVENTION AND CONTROL** Control weeds in susceptible crops; remove or mow weedy areas adjacent to garden beds. Attract native parasitic wasps and flies by planting small-flowered plants.

Strawberry red stele

Phytophthora fragariae var. *fragariae*

Spores of this fungal disease are released into the soil from the decaying roots of infected plants. The spores can lie dormant for at least 12 years. Infection of healthy roots occurs in wet conditions. It is spread on contaminated plants and on soil on tools and boots.

SUSCEPTIBLE PLANTS Strawberry. **SYMPTOMS** Leaves develop a brownish purple tinge. A reddish band appears around the

Spittlebug *see Froghopper, common*

Stem rots *see Damping off*

For more information on improving soil structure and drainage, see pp. 38–41.

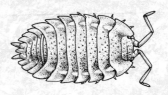

Sowbug

leaf edges; this may color the entire central leaf area. Growth can be patchy, with individual plants becoming weak and stunted. Roots are stunted and dark brown or black in color, and the outer layers are easily peeled off. When the root is split open, the classic symptom is a red core running down the center. It is most noticeable in spring and autumn but less defined during summer.

PREVENTION AND CONTROL Always plant certified, healthy planting stock. Make sure the growing site is well-drained. Grow cultivars with resistance to particular strains of red stele. Check with a reputable fruit nursery for suitable cultivars. Do not grow strawberries on the same land again; spores can lie dormant for many years.

Tarnished plant bug

Lygus lineolaris

Adults are small, oval, light green to brown, mottled bugs. Each forewing has a black-tipped yellow triangle. Adults overwinter under bark or leaf litter, emerging in early spring to lay eggs in leaf tissue. They hatch in 10 days. The nymphs are yellow-green and wingless; they look similar to adults. Nymphs feed for 3 to 4 weeks, then molt into adults. Besides tarnished plant bugs, several other plant bug species (Family *Miridae*) also damage garden plants.

SUSCEPTIBLE PLANTS Most flowers, fruits, and vegetables.

SYMPTOMS Adults and nymphs suck plant juices, causing shoot and fruit distortion, bud drop, wilting, stunting, and dieback.
PREVENTION AND CONTROL Cover plants with row cover or mesh. Attract native predators (bigeyed bugs, damsel bugs, and pirate bugs) with groundcovers and pollen-rich flowers.
Biological control: Try releases of minute pirate bugs.

Thrips

Insect pests that attack a wide range of plants, indoors and out. They are small, elongated, cylindrical insects, up to ⅛ in. (4 mm) long. Color ranges from white/yellow to brown/black. Larvae resemble adults but without wings. Various species of thrips are found throughout North America. They feed in large numbers on the upper side of leaves, and on flowers and buds of a wide range of plants, indoors and out, causing a characteristic silvery mottling and some distortion. They can reproduce in as little as a month, laying eggs on plants. Adults and young stages overwinter in soil, leaf litter, and plant debris.
See also Greenhouse thrips; Onion thrips.

Tomato hornworm

Manduca quinquemaculata
Adults are large, gray moths with a 4–5-in. (10–13-cm) wingspan. They emerge in June and July

from soilborne pupae, then lay eggs on the undersides of leaves. The eggs hatch in one week into green caterpillars up to 4½ in. (11 cm) long, with a black horn on the tail and eight diagonal white marks along the sides. They feed for a month, then pupate in the soil until the following summer. The tobacco hornworm (*Manduca sexta*), a related species, has a red horn and seven white marks on the sides.

SUSCEPTIBLE PLANTS Nightshade-family plants, including tomatoes and potatoes.
SYMPTOMS Larvae of both species consume leaves, stems, and fruit. Feeding can kill young plants.
PREVENTION AND CONTROL Handpick caterpillars from plants, unless they are covered with small, white, ricelike projections, which are actually the cocoons of parasitic wasps.
Biological control: Spray with *Bacillus thuringiensis* var. *kurstaki* while caterpillars are still small.

Viruses

Viruses, invisible to the naked eye, exist in living plant material, where they do not necessarily cause symptoms. They are spread by sap-sucking insects, such as aphids, by contact (on hands and on tools, especially cutting tools such as pruners), by birds, and by propagation from contaminated plants. Some viruses are plant-specific while others will infect a number of unrelated plants.

SUSCEPTIBLE PLANTS A huge range of plants are vulnerable to some form of virus.
SYMPTOMS Many and varied, including stunting, mottled and mosaic-patterned leaves, distorted fruits, and even death. Yield of perennial crops will fall.
PREVENTION AND CONTROL Control the agent that transmits the virus. Grow resistant cultivars. Plant certified virus-free planting material. Use a crop rotation for viruses transmitted by soil-living organisms. There is no cure for infected plants. Dig up infected plants. Burn woody plants.
See also Cucumber mosaic virus; Zucchini yellow mosaic virus.

Waterlogging

This is a common disorder of houseplants and other pot-grown plants; also plants in poorly drained soils.

SYMPTOMS Yellowing of leaves, dry angular blotches on leaves, general stunting of growth. Root-rotting diseases may also be encouraged.
CAUSES Overwatering, especially when growth is slow. Poor drainage.
PREVENTION AND CONTROL Adjust watering according to plant species and time of year. Improve drainage of soil; ensure that pots can drain well. Grow plants that thrive in waterlogged soils.

Weevils

Beetles with a characteristic snout and clubbed antennae.

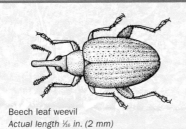

Beech leaf weevil
Actual length ¹⁄₁₆ in. (2 mm)

Tomato blight *see Potato late blight*
Two-spotted mite *see Red spider mite*
Verticillium wilt *see Wilt diseases*

They range in size from 1/16 in. (2 mm) to 1 in. (2.5 cm), depending on species. The larvae have a soft white body and obvious head; they are otherwise featureless.
See also Black vine weevil; Pea and bean weevil.

Whiteflies

Adults of this pest, 1/16 in. (2 mm) long with white wings, fly up from plants when disturbed. Eggs, laid on host plants, hatch into "scales"—oval, immobile larvae found on the undersides of leaves. Both scales and adults are sap-feeders and excrete sticky honeydew, which drops on to the upper surface of leaves below. Sooty molds develop on this. A severe infestation may stunt growth.
See also Greenhouse whitefly.

Wilt diseases

Fusarium and *Verticillium* spp.

A common and widespread group of fungal diseases with similar symptoms. Damage is usually caused by a blockage of the water-conducting tissues of the stem, starving the leaves of water. The disease may persist in the soil for several years, depending on the particular causal organism, and can enter plants through wounds. Commonly associated with nematode attack. Some wilts, such as those affecting China asters and peas, are host-specific, while others will attack a wide range of edible and ornamental plants.

SUSCEPTIBLE PLANTS Fruit, vegetables (especially legumes, tomato, cucurbits), ornamentals.
SYMPTOMS Wilting, which often starts on lower leaves, with some recovery at night initially. A dark discoloration can be seen in the middle of the stem when cut well above soil level.
PREVENTION AND CONTROL Mound soil around infected plants. If infection is severe, remove all infected plants and associated soil. Do not compost any of the plant material. Do not grow susceptible plants on the same site for at least 6 years.
See also Clematis wilt; Peony blight.

Wind rock

Disorder that often affects young trees and shrubs and also herbaceous plants that have far more foliage than roots.

SYMPTOMS Plants are rocked to and fro but not completely uprooted. This produces a hollow around the base of the stem, which can fill with rainwater that may freeze. This will damage the base of the stem and allow access to disease.
CAUSES Strong winds.
PREVENTION AND CONTROL Firm in any wind-rocked plants as soon as possible. Stake plants if appropriate.

Wind scorch

Disorder affecting many plants.

PLANT SYMPTOMS Browning of foliage on the side of a plant facing the prevailing wind. Individual leaf margins or tips may be markedly browner than the leaf centers. Apples and other fruit may show a red/brown russetting on the skin surface.
CAUSES Severe winds, especially salt-laden. Buildings can create a wind tunnel or a particularly drafty spot in a garden.
PREVENTION AND CONTROL Grow plants suitable for windy positions—usually, plants for coastal areas are suitable, but check the hardiness of these for inland and northern areas. Grow or erect a windbreak.

Wireworms

Agriotes and *Limonius* spp. and others

Wireworms are the larvae of click beetles. They are tough-skinned, slender, cylindrical, 1 in. (2.5 cm) in length and golden/yellow to orange/brown in color. They have three pairs of legs at the head end of the body. Eggs are laid in grassland and weedy soil from early to midsummer and larvae may feed for up to 5 years. Because they dislike disturbance, they are usually found on grassland and newly cleared ground.

SUSCEPTIBLE PLANTS Potato, strawberry, brassicas, beans, beets, carrot, lettuce, onion, and tomato; also ornamentals including anemone, carnation, dahlia, gladioli, and primula.
SYMPTOMS The roots, corms, tubers, and stems of many plants are attacked, most severely in the spring and autumn, but damage can occur throughout the year. Potatoes show small entry holes 1/16–1/8 in. (2–3 mm) across and when cut open a network of tunnels run through the tuber. Later these holes may be enlarged by slugs or millipedes.
PREVENTION AND CONTROL Damage is most severe on newly cultivated land. Cultivate the soil during winter to expose larvae to birds and other predators. Lift potatoes in early autumn to limit damage. In greenhouses trap wireworms on spiked pieces of potato or carrot buried in the soil. Remove regularly and destroy. Expose homemade compost to birds and other predators before use if it is infested with wireworm. Grow the green manure mustard on the area. It is said to speed up the life cycle.

Woolly aphid

Eriosoma lanigerum

This small brown aphid lives in colonies on stems and branches, protected by a white waxy substance that looks like cotton wool. They are most conspicious in late spring and early summer, but present all year. Young aphids overwinter in cracks in bark and in galls.

SUSCEPTIBLE PLANTS Apple, cotoneaster, hawthorn, ornamental *Malus*, pyracantha, and other related plants.
SYMPTOMS Leaves and fruit become disfigured; galls may develop on twigs and branches. Canker may enter through cracks in the bark and dieback may result.

For information on hedges, windbreaks, and fences, see pp. 136–140 and 148–149.

PREVENTION AND CONTROL
Use a stiff brush to remove woolly colonies. Cut out and burn badly infested branches. *See also* Aphids.

Yellow jackets

Vespula spp.

Adults of this pest are winged, with conspicuous yellow and black markings, up to ¾ in. (2 cm) long. They construct large, papery nests in cavities in soil, walls, buildings, and compost piles. Early in the year, wasps are valuable predators, feeding their young on small caterpillars and other pests. Most wasps are killed by frosts in autumn. Queen wasps overwinter in dry protected areas such as outbuildings, sheds, and under loose bark of trees.

PLANTS ATTACKED Ripening fruits of apples, pears, grapes, peaches, and plums.
SYMPTOMS Holes eaten in ripening fruit in summer and early autumn, usually extending damage caused by other factors. The stems of dahlias may be damaged and in dry weather the pods of runner beans may be damaged by the wasps scraping at them with their mouthparts.
PREVENTION AND CONTROL
Tolerate wasps where possible. Protect fruits with bags made of muslin, nylon tights, or similar. If abolutely necessary, accessible nests can be destroyed. This is best done after dark and should not be considered if you are allergic to wasps. Pay very strict attention to safety; keep not only children but also pets well away. Full protective clothing must be worn to cover every part of the body. Knock an aerial nest into a plastic bag. Tie tightly, then place in freezer to kill the wasps. Nests in the ground or in compost piles can be sealed by placing a glass bowl over the entrance, then pushing it down into the earth to seal it. Wasps will starve in a few weeks. The safest option is to call in a pest-control expert. Ask them to use a soap or synthetic pyrethroid spray, rather than carbamate or organophosphate compounds.

Yellows

Commonly transmitted by leafhoppers as they feed, these diseases are caused by mycoplasmalike organisms. There is no cure for infected plants.

SUSCEPTIBLE PLANTS A wide range of woody and herbaceous plants. Aster yellows affects many plants, including carrots, lettuce, tomatoes, China asters, and gladiolus. Elm yellows (also known as elm phloem necrosis) attacks several species of elms.
SYMPTOMS This disease produces a gradual yellowing of the leaves. Plants often appear dwarfed. Plant parts, including roots and flowers, may be deformed. On trees, leaves turn yellow, then brown, and may drop early. Symptoms appear over the whole crown of the tree. Plants may die in a single growing season.

PREVENTION AND CONTROL
Controlling leafhoppers (see p. 381) will reduce the chances of this disease. Remove weeds that provide overwintering sites for the pathogen, including thistles, Queen Anne's lace, dandelions, and wild chicory. Remove and destroy infected plants.

Zucchini yellow mosaic virus

Viral disease transmitted by aphids.

SUSCEPTIBLE PLANTS Zucchini, marrow, and squash.
SYMPTOMS Bright yellow mosaic pattern on leaves. Plants stunted and distorted. Fruits knobby and distorted.
PREVENTION AND CONTROL
Remove infected plants as soon as symptoms are noticed. There is no cure.

If spraying, check that the product is legally and organically approved for the job. Regulations may have changed since this information was compiled.

U.S.D.A. Plant Hardiness Zone Map

Revised in 1990, this map is recognized as the best indicator of minimum temperatures available. Look at the map to find your area, then match its pattern to the key at the right. When you've found your pattern, the key will tell you what hardiness zone you live in. Remember that the map is a general guide; your particular conditions may vary.

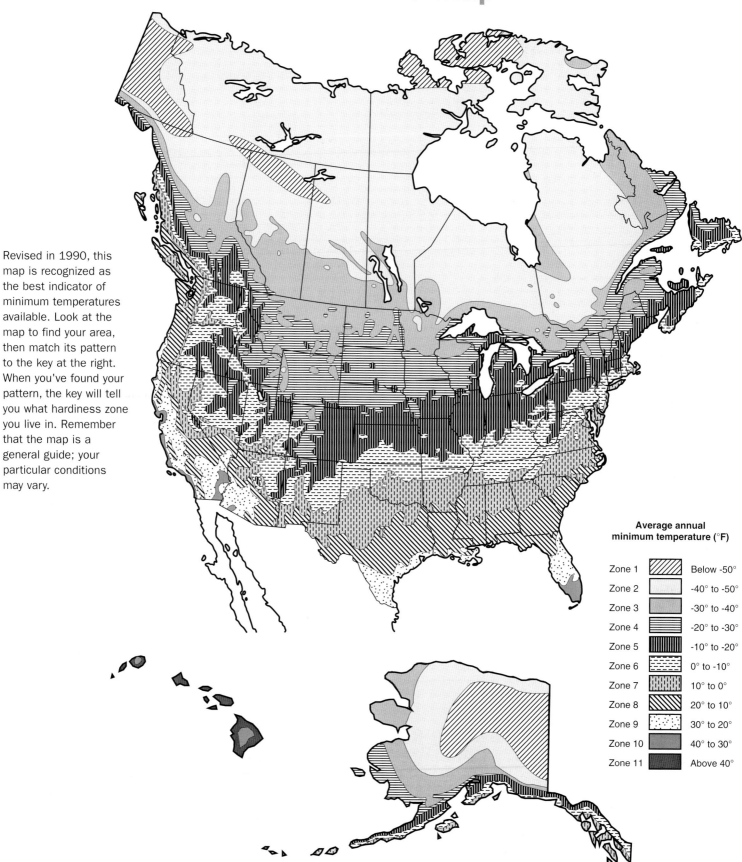

Average annual minimum temperature (°F)

Zone 1		Below -50°
Zone 2		-40° to -50°
Zone 3		-30° to -40°
Zone 4		-20° to -30°
Zone 5		-10° to -20°
Zone 6		0° to -10°
Zone 7		10° to 0°
Zone 8		20° to 10°
Zone 9		30° to 20°
Zone 10		40° to 30°
Zone 11		Above 40°

H.D.R.A. Organic Guidelines for Gardeners

Henry Doubleday Research Association supports whole-heartedly the concept of a common organic standard. The H.D.R.A. Organic Guidelines for Gardeners follow closely the organic standards set for commercial organic growers by the British organic movement, the U.K. government, and the European Union (E.U.). The H.D.R.A. Guidelines have been produced because existing commercial standards do not always apply and do not cover all aspects of gardening. In almost all cases, H.D.R.A. Guidelines match E.U. organic standards.

As knowledge changes and grows, the Guidelines will be adjusted accordingly. The H.D.R.A. Organic Guidelines have no legal standing. They are purely advisory, to be used by anyone interested in organic gardening methods. They are designed for all types and sizes of garden.

The Guidelines divide gardening practices and materials into four categories:

Best practice
Recommended for organic gardening—the ideal to aim toward.

Acceptable
Acceptable for use in an organic garden but not as ideal as those above.

Qualified acceptance
Less acceptable for regular use in an organic garden.

Not recommended
Not considered suitable for use in an organic garden.

For footnotes, see p. 401.

Soil management

A healthy, fertile soil is the basis of all effective organic growing. The soil should be managed in ways that develop and protect its structure, its fertility, and the millions of tiny creatures for which it is home.

Caring for the soil organically involves the use of organic residues, in the form of animal manures and plant and animal remains. This is to improve soil structure and maintain humus levels; to feed the soil life, whose activities are essential for soil health; and to provide plant nutrients. Attention is paid to drainage and maintenance of appropriate pH. Green manure cover crops are grown to protect and feed the soil. Cultivations are kept to a minimum and timed to avoid damage to soil structure.

Best practice
• Keep the soil covered with a protective covering of vegetation, such as a green manure or other plants, or a surface mulch.
• Apply manures and plant wastes only as detailed in other sets of Guidelines.
• Loosen subsoil to break up compaction if present.
• Improve drainage as necessary.
• Keep pH at appropriate level.
• Use a rotation system for annual plants.

Acceptable
• Soil cultivations, where necessary. These should be carried out only when the soil conditions are neither too wet nor too dry. Do not mix subsoil layers with topsoil. Keep soil cultivations to a minimum to avoid damaging soil structure.

Qualified acceptance
• Rotary tilling[1].

Not recommended
• All other practices.

Manures and waste plant materials

Organic materials should be recycled within the garden, producing compost and leaf mold to feed the soil where necessary. These can be augmented with materials brought in such as manures and other "waste" materials and commercial gardening products. Ideally these inputs should be from organic growing systems, but where this is not possible, materials from non-organic sources can be used.

Manures from intensive production systems should never be used. They may contain unwanted contaminants, and there are ethical considerations concerning the way in which the animals are kept.

Fresh manures and other waste products should be composted or otherwise processed before use.

Best practice
• Plant and animal wastes[2] from the house and garden, after being composted[3] or, if autumn leaves, made into leaf mold.

Acceptable
• Composted or well-rotted[4] strawy farmyard, horse, and poultry manures from organic sources.
• Plant waste materials and by-products from organic food processing industries.
• Commercial manures and composts carrying an organic symbol.
• Straw and hay from organic sources.
• Sawdust, shavings, and bark from lumber untreated after harvest.
• Microbial and plant extract compost activators.
• Autumn leaves collected from parks and other public areas not adjacent to busy roads.
• Organic mushroom compost.
• Wool products not containing organophosphate residues.
• Feathers from acceptable production systems[5].

Qualified acceptance
• Straw, hay, and farmyard and horse manures from non-organic sources after being composted for 3 months or stockpiled for 6 months[6].
• Composted green and household waste from centralized composting plants, not containing unacceptable levels of PTEs (see footnote 12).
• Poultry manure and deep litter from less intensive, non-organic systems[7] after being composted for 6 months or stockpiled under cover for 12 months.
• Seaweed from unpolluted beaches[8].
• Manures from non-organic straw-based pig production systems after being properly composted for 6 months or stacked for 12 months[9].
• Plant wastes and by-products from non-organic food processing industries, after being properly composted.
• Mushroom and worm composts made from non-organic animal manures, except those from unacceptable intensive systems (see footnote 17).
• Commercial gardening products such as bagged manures and garden composts from non-organic sources except those from unacceptable production systems (see footnote 17) and those containing peat[10].

• Processed animal products from slaughterhouses, except where cattle or sheep are likely to graze.
• Processed waste products from the fishing industry.
• Sewage sludge, effluent, and sludge-based composts, suitably treated and free of potentially toxic elements[11].

Not recommended
• Any materials containing levels of potentially toxic elements (P.T.E.s) greater than those permitted[12].
• Leaves and leaf mold collected from woodland[13].
• Leaves collected from busy roadsides[14].
• Peat and coir[15] as a soil conditioner[16].
• Commercial manure and garden compost products containing coir or peat.
• The use of animal residues and manures (other than processed animal products from slaughterhouses and fish industries) from intensive livestock systems[17].

Storage and application of manures and composts

Manures, composts, and other materials containing plant foods should be stored, and applied in ways that avoid leaching out of plant foods. Leaching both wastes nutrients and pollutes waterways and groundwater.

Best practice
• Store and compost manures and other materials that contain plant foods indoors or under a waterproof cover[18].
• Apply no more than one wheelbarrow-full of well-rotted strawy manure, or two of compost, per 6 sq. yd. (5 sq. m) of ground each year[19] (the

equivalent of, approximately, 11 gal./50 liters of manure or 22 gal./100 liters of compost per sq. ft./0. 3 m).
• Apply manures and compost only to growing plants, or to soil where plants are soon to be grown.

Acceptable
• Autumn/early winter applications of composted manures to an actively growing green manure crop.
• Applications of composts and composted manures to greenhouse soils at any time.

Qualified acceptance
• None.

Not recommended
• Storage systems and practices that result in the pollution of waterways.
• Autumn application of manure to bare soil intended to be left fallow over winter.

Fertilizers and liquid fertilizers

Organic fertilizers may be of plant, animal, or mineral origin. They should be regarded as a supplement to, and not as replacement for, recycling of nutrients within the garden— through a compost pile for example—and the use of other bought/brought-in bulky organic materials. They should be applied only if adequate supplies are not available from other sources.

Liquid fertilizers should be used only on plants growing in a restricted environment such as a pot, growing bag, or greenhouse border.

In the absence of more acceptable materials, restricted use of soluble fertilizers to treat severe trace element deficiencies may be allowed. A soil analysis is recommended to

identify or confirm a particular deficiency.
The products listed below may not all be readily available to the gardener.

Best practice
• None.

Acceptable
• Liquid fertilizers homemade from plants or animal manures.

Qualified acceptance
• **Nitrogen (N)** Blood meal, in growing media and on overwintered crops in spring only; hoof and horn meals.
• **Phosphorus (P) (as phosphate, P_2O_5)** Natural rock phosphate; basic slag; calcined aluminum phosphate rock; meat and bone meals. Cadmium levels in rock phosphates should not exceed 90mg/kg P_2O_5.
• **Potassium (K) (potash)** Wood ash, added to a compost or manure pile only[20]; plant extracts such as sugar beet waste; sulfate of potash, only where soil analysis shows exchangeable potassium (K) levels are below index 2[21] and clay content is less than 20%.
• **Compound fertilizers** Fish, blood, and bone meals (supplying N, P, Ca[22]), free from nonpermitted substances; fish meals (N)[23]; meat and bone meals (P, Ca, N); seaweed meal (K, N, trace elements).
• **Liming materials** Dolomitic limestone; ground limestone; ground chalk.
• **Minor minerals** Calcareous magnesium rock, or dolomitic limestone (supplying Mg[22] and Ca); gypsum, or calcium sulfate (Ca); ground chalk and limestone (Ca); Epsom salts (Mg), for acute deficiency only; magnesium rock; sulfur; calcium chloride, for bitter pit in apples.
• **Trace elements** Dried seaweed meal; seaweed extract; limestone and chalk; rock dusts. Trace elements boron; copper; iron; manganese; molybdenum;

cobalt; selenium and zinc, following soil analysis or other evidence of deficiency.
• Commercially available liquid fertilizers, made from plants or animal manures, preferably with an organic certification symbol.

Not recommended
• Fresh blood
• All other synthetic and natural fertilizers including Chilean nitrate, urea, muriate of potash, superphosphates, kainite.
• Slaked lime, quicklime.
• The use of slaughterhouse by-products (bone meal, hoof and horn meal, etc.) where cattle or sheep are likely to graze.

Rotation

An essential aspect of soil management and weed, pest, and disease control. When growing annual plants, such as vegetables, herbs, and flowers, or replanting fruit, shrubs, and other perennials, it is unwise to reuse the same site for the same type of plant. As far as possible the position should be varied, returning to the first site only after a period of years. This practice, known as rotation, helps in the control of pests, diseases, and weeds, and in the maintenance of soil fertility, organic matter levels, and structure.

Best practice
• Plants with similar pest and disease susceptibility are separated by an appropriate time interval[24].
• A balance between fertility building and exploitative cropping.
• A nitrogen-fixing leguminous crop or green manure included in the rotation to add nitrogen where appropriate.
• Varying weed-suppressing with weed-susceptible crops.
• Rotations that minimize

the time that the soil is left uncovered.
• Perennials, especially fruit and roses, not planted where a closely related plant has recently grown.

Acceptable
• Shorter rotations where space is limited, for example in a greenhouse, as long as attention is paid to keeping the soil healthy.

Qualified acceptance
• None.

Not recommended
• Growing the same annual crop in the same location year after year.

For information on soil management and compost making, see Soil and Soil Care, pp. 32–61.

Pest and disease management

Prevention is the mainstay of an organic strategy for pest and disease management. Work with nature, rather than trying to dominate it. Encourage healthy growth by providing plants with a well-structured soil and a balanced diet, by matching site and plants, and by growing pest- and disease-resistant varieties. Natural predators and parasites help to keep pests and diseases in check. The organic garden should be designed and managed to provide a mixed environment to favor these beneficial creatures. Organic gardeners should also be aware that the presence of a pest or a disease-causing organism does not necessarily require any action. The use of killing sprays should be kept to a minimum.

Good growing practice, hygiene, barriers, traps, and scarers complete the range of pest and disease management techniques.

The following products and practices are for use both outdoors and in a greenhouse or hoop house.

Best practice
• Build soil with good structure that supplies plants with a balanced diet.
• Maintain good hygiene to minimize carry-over of pests and diseases.
• Monitor plants regularly to catch potential problems early.
• Use healthy seed and planting material, certified virus-free where applicable.
• Plant pest- and disease-resistant varieties.
• Suit plants to site and soil.
• Provide habitats to encourage natural predators and parasites.
• Grow plants and flowers to feed predators and parasites.
• Use a crop rotation.
• Select sowing/planting dates to avoid specific pests and diseases.
• Use scaring devices.
• Provide good ventilation, around and within plants.
• Balanced watering.
• Mixed and companion planting; avoid monoculture.
• Biodegradable barriers.
• Give in gracefully when necessary!
(See also Conservation Guidelines, p. 401.)

Acceptable
• Introduced biological control agents.
• Non-biodegradable barriers, reused where possible.
• Steam sterilization of buildings and equipment.

Qualified acceptance
• Sticky barriers and traps, including those with pheromone lure.
• Steam sterilization of soils.
• Plant oils.
• Disinfectants based on citric acid (from natural sources) or

peroxyacetic acid for disinfection of pots, trays, equipment, and greenhouses.
• For controlling pests where there is a threat to the plant: potassium soap (soft soap) and soaps containing plant fatty acids, *Bacillus thuringiensis*, pyrethrum[25], insecticidal soap; also neem, quassia, and granulosis virus where permitted[26].
• For controlling diseases where there is a threat to the plant: Bordeaux mixture, copper sulfate, copper oxychloride, and copper ammonium carbonate; sulfur.

Not recommended
• All other pesticides, including nicotine, phenols, aluminum sulphate, and metaldehyde.

Wood preservatives

Wood preservatives are, by their very nature, persistent and toxic. In the organic garden they should be avoided where possible. Their use should be restricted to structural members, where decay could prove a safety hazard. Wood that is in contact with both soil and air is at most risk.

Best practice
• Untreated lumber.
• Lumber from trees such as oak, cedar, and black locust, which has more resistance to decay. Check that it is from a well-managed, sustainable source.
• Concrete posts.

Acceptable
• Synthetic wood made from recycled polystyrene.
• Treating wood not in contact with the soil (such as fence panels) with linseed oil or similar water-repellent product that allows the wood to breathe.

Qualified acceptance
• Boron compounds (water-based).

Not recommended
• Creosote.
• Lumber treated with C.C.A. (copper chrome arsenic)[27], often sold as "pressure-treated."

Weed control and ground clearance

Weeds provide food and shelter for a multitude of natural creatures and a useful source of material for the compost pile. They should be allowed to grow where possible, eliminating them only where they interfere with chosen plants. There is a range of cultural techniques that can be used to clear ground and keep the garden weed-free. There are no weed-killing sprays for use in an organic garden.

Best practice
• Crop rotation.
• Varying weed-suppressing and weed-susceptible crops.
• Hoeing, hand-pulling, using the stale seedbed technique.
• Close spacing; groundcover plants and cover crops.
• Creating a good, solid foundation for paths.
• Biodegradable mulches of organic origin.

Acceptable
• Digging in, or out.
• Biodegradable mulches not of organic origin.
• Pointing joints between pavers, slabs, bricks, etc.

Qualified acceptance
• Rotary tilling[1].
• Non-biodegradable mulches, preferably those that are water-permeable, and that can be reused several times.
• Permeable, non-biodegradable mulches under path surfaces or

around perennial plants.
• Flame-weeding.

Not recommended
• Any weedkillers, including those based on glyphosate and natural fatty acids.

For more information on organic weed control, see Weeds and Weed Control, pp. 73–83.

Weed control in lawns

A lawn of one or two species of grass only, which is tantamount to monoculture, does not fit well with organic principles. A mixture of grasses and broad-leaved species is much more likely to provide a healthy lawn that will stay green year-round. Clover will also help to feed the grass. Follow a good program of lawn maintenance. If grass is encouraged to grow strongly, weed problems are minimized.

Best practice
• Cut regularly, but only when required. Do not cut lower than 1 in. (2.5 cm) for a fine lawn, 2 in. (5 cm) for an all-purpose lawn.
• Leave clippings on the lawn whenever possible, but not when soil is cold and wet, or when clippings are long.
• Scarify and aerate as necessary.
• Adjust pH and drainage and remove shade as necessary if a lawn is not thriving.
• Feed only if growth is poor and/or yellow, and drought or waterlogging is not the cause. Use an organic manure, compost, or fertilizer.
• Topdress in autumn.

Acceptable
• None.

Qualified acceptance
• None.

Not recommended
• Worm killers.
• All chemical fertilizers and pesticides.

For more information on organic lawns, see Lawns and Lawn Care, pp. 174–185.

Planting material, growing media, and container growing

The ideal is to grow your own plants from organically grown seed, using organic growing media when growing in containers. Organically grown seeds, tubers, corms, bulbs, and other planting material should be used where available. As a minimum, use seed not treated with chemicals after harvest. When buying wildflower seeds, ensure that they are indigenous, not imported from another country. Bulbs and other planting material should never be taken from the wild. There are some suppliers of organic vegetable, fruit, and ornamental plants. Use these where available, or raise your own plants.
   Wherever possible, grow plants directly in the ground. Growing conditions in a pot or growing bag are inevitably restricted, requiring additional attention and feeding with soluble nutrients. An organic growing medium, preferably peat-free, should be used when raising plants and growing in containers. Purchased growing media should, ideally, carry an organic symbol. Homemade mixtures should contain only ingredients listed in the Guidelines that follow.

For more information on growing media and making seed and potting mixes, see Raising Plants, pp. 114–115.

Sowing and planting material

Best practice
• Plants grown to organic standards.
• Organically grown seed, tubers, and other planting material.

Acceptable
• Conventionally grown seed, tubers, and other planting material not treated with chemicals after harvest.

Qualified acceptance
• Plants and planting material grown using non-organic methods.
• Rooting powders not containing fungicide.

Not recommended
• Rooting powders with fungicides.
• Plants and material from the wild.
• Seed treated after harvest.
• Seeds or plants of genetically modified (G.M.) cultivars, produced using genetic engineering.

Growing media

Best practice
• Homemade growing media consisting only of materials listed in these Guidelines.
• Commercial growing media, peat-free and carrying a recognized organic certification symbol.

Acceptable
• Organic growing media containing recycled peat, preferably with a recognized organic certification symbol.

Qualified acceptance
• Perlite, vermiculite, bentonite, and zeolites that have not undergone chemical treatment with prohibited materials.
• Organic growing media containing peat, preferably with recognized organic symbol.

Not recommended
• Growing media containing materials not listed in these Guidelines.

Growing in containers

The same principles should be applied to plants grown in pots, baskets, planters, and other containers as are applied in the organic garden.

Best practice
• Organic growing media with recycled organic waste as the major source of fertility.
• Plants and seeds as above.
• Hanging basket liners made of wool or other recycled materials.
• Pots and containers of appropriate size.
• Additional feeding, where necessary, by topdressing with composts, manures, or commercial products made of the same.

Acceptable
• Organic growing media with organic fertilizers as the main source of plant foods.
• Additional feeding with organic fertilizers.
• Additional feeding with homemade liquid fertilizers made from plants or animal manures.

Qualified acceptance
• Commercially available organic liquid fertilizers, preferably with a recognized organic symbol.

Not recommended
• Moss lining for hanging baskets.
• Other liquid fertilizers.

Conservation and the environment

Conservation and organic gardening are inextricably linked. Human activities pollute the world; habitats and wildlife are disappearing fast. Loss of diversity has particular consequences for organic gardeners, who rely on natural pest/predator networks to keep pests in check. Conservation and creation of a diverse environment, both in the garden and further afield, are essential. Diverse planting, including the use of native species and less highly bred varieties where appropriate, is also recommended. Activities that pollute, such as bonfires, dumping of organic wastes, or excessive use of non-renewable resources, have no place in an organic garden.

Best practice
• Retention and creation of traditional boundaries such as hedges, stone walls, and ditches.
• Retention and creation of habitats such as hedges, ponds, and uncut grassy areas to feed and protect wildlife.
• Native species of plants.
• Non-native species with particular features for wildlife.
• Creating wildlife corridors—linked habitats to allow safe passage for wildlife.
• Using a hedge–cutting regime, if any, that avoids disturbing nesting birds, and, where appropriate, allows the hedge to flower and produce fruit.
• Use of lumber from renewable sources.
• Recycling and reuse.

Acceptable
• None.

Qualified acceptance
• Hot, dry bonfires for disposal of diseased plant material.

Not recommended
• Bonfires other than as above.
• Clearing away all plant debris from under hedges, shrubs, etc., unless for disease control purposes.
• Storage of manures uncovered.
• Lumber from nonrenewable sources.
• Plants taken from the wild; wildflower seed from overseas sources.
• Use of materials transported over long distances, when a suitable, more local alternative can be used.

Notes

1 Tilling can destroy soil structure; it can also create an impermeable "pan" or hard layer of soil.
2 Manures from rabbits, hens, gerbils, and most other vegetarian pets should be safe to compost. Those from cats and dogs can contain parasites harmful to humans. If the latter are to be composted, particular attention to hygiene is essential when handling; their use is not advised where children could come into contact with fresh or composted material.
3 Composting is an aerobic process, converting plant and animal wastes to dark, soil-like material known as compost. Ideally the compost pile should be turned several times to keep the process aerobic. Composting converts the material into a more stable form and may also kill weed seeds and diseases.
4 "Well-rotted" means manure that has been stockpiled under a waterproof cover and left to mature for a month or more. This process converts the free nitrogen and potassium that fresh manure contains into forms that are less likely to be washed out by the rain and that cannot damage plants.
5 See note 7.
6 The extra time is to allow some breakdown of any chemical residues that might be present.
7 Poultry systems from which manure can be used in an organic garden:
a) Egg production systems (defined by E.U. Regulation No. 1274/91): free-range (maximum 400 birds/acre); semi-intensive (maximum 1,600 birds/acre); deep litter (maximum 7 birds/sq. yd.).
b) Deep litter pullet rearing systems (maximum housing density of birds 31 lb. per sq. yd./17 kg per sq. m).
c) Meat-producing systems (defined by E.E.C. Regulation No. 1538/91); free-range, traditional free-range; extensive indoor barn reared (maximum
housing density of mature birds: 12 hens or 31–46 lb. per sq. yd./17–25 kg per sq. m).
8 Fresh seaweed should be treated as a resource for local use only. Loose seaweed may be collected from the shoreline—growing seaweed should not be removed from rocks. Stripping of resources, even those that are renewable, is not recommended.
9 Regular use of non-organic pig manure is not advised; these manures can contain copper and other contaminants that can accumulate in the soil.
10 The use of peat as a soil improver is not acceptable in the organic garden. Its extraction destroys invaluable natural habitats.
11 Sewage is not allowed under E.U. or U.K. organic standards. H.D.R.A. regards sewage as a wasted resource and so has included it in these Guidelines—as long as it meets the required standards. There may not be any suitable uncontaminated sewage products available at present.
12 Potentially Toxic Elements (P.T.E.s) include heavy metals and other elements, many of which are naturally present in the soil. Some are essential to plants and animals in trace amounts but can be toxic at higher levels. There are many different standards setting maximum permissible levels in soil and materials added to the soil. The variation in these standards shows that no one really knows the answer.
13 These are part of the natural cycle of fertility in the woodland and as such should not be removed from it.
14 These are likely to be contaminated with lead and cadmium.
15 Coconut fiber.
16 For peat, see note 10. As there are many organic materials of local origin available, often recycling waste materials, the use of coir—a material that is transported across the world—as a soil conditioner is not seen as appropriate in an organic garden.
17 Including poultry battery systems and broiler units with stocking rates over 46 lb. per sq. yd. (25 kg per sq. m); indoor tethered sow breeding units; other systems where stock are not freely allowed to turn through 360°, where they are permanently in the dark, or are permanently kept without bedding.
18 To prevent washing out of nutrients by rain.
19 Excessive application of manure or compost can contribute to pollution of watercourses. On a large scale, the maximum application recommended is 20 tons per acre (50 tonnes per hectare). This translates into approximately one builder's wheelbarrow full of manure per 12 sq. yd. (10 sq. m) of ground. Obviously this figure can be only a guideline as composts and manures vary in their composition. It is included here to make the point that it is not good practice to apply excessive quantities of nutrient-supplying material to the soil. The maximum rate recommended is lower than many gardeners use.
20 The nutrients in wood ash are very soluble and quickly wash out if applied directly to soil.
21 This figure refers to results given in a soil analysis.
22 Ca = calcium; Mg = magnesium.
23 Fishmeal that is a waste product from the fishing industry is acceptable; meal from fish caught directly for the purpose is not.
24 For vegetables, a 3- to 4-year rotation is usually recommended. Where particular problems such as persistent soilborne pests and diseases occur, a longer period may be appropriate. For more specific recommendations, look at the life cycle of the particular pest or disease.
25 Ideally pure pyrethrum of plant origin should be used. Currently the only pyrethrum available contains a synergist, piperonyl butoxide, to make it more effective. This synergist also has insecticidal properties. Synthetic permethrins are not recommended.
26 The use of quassia, neem, and granulosis virus is illegal in the U.K., as they are not registered for use as pesticides.
27 Highly toxic chemicals such as copper chrome arsenate are used in this treatment, which raises the question of danger to the processor and of safe disposal. The treatment process is said to render the wood safe to use, but there is evidence to show that this may not be the case. Use of this type of wood is restricted in other countries. If burned, fumes and ash are toxic.

For further information, contact:
H.D.R.A., the organic organization
Ryton Organic Gardens,
Coventry CV8 3LG
England
Tel: +44 24 7630 3517
Fax: +44 24 7663 9229
Email: enquiry@hdra.org.uk
Visit us at www.hdra.org.uk

OR

The Rodale Institute,
611 Siegfriedale Road,
Kutztown,
PA 19530
Tel: 610-683-1400
Email: info@rodaleinst.org
Visit us at
www.rodaleinstitute.org

Resources

SEEDS, PLANTS, AND SUPPLIES

Adams County Nursery
P.O. Box 108
Aspers, PA 17304
www.acnursery.com
Fruit trees and orchard supplies

Bountiful Gardens
18001 Shafer Ranch Rd.
Willits, CA 95490
www.bountifulgardens.org
Gardening equipment and supplies; also organically grown vegetable and herb seeds

The Cook's Garden
P.O. Box 535
Londonderry, VT 05148
www.cooksgarden.com
Specializes in gourmet and heirloom vegetables and flowers

DripWorks
190 Sanhedrin Circle
Willits, CA 95490
www.dripworksusa.com
Drip irrigation supplies

Ed Hume Seeds, Inc.
P.O. Box 1450
Kent, WA 98035
www.humeseeds.com
Specializes in seeds for short seasons and cool climates

Edible Landscaping
P.O. Box 77
Afton, VA 22920
www.eat-it.com
Specializes in a wide range of fruits

Fungi Perfecti
P.O. Box 7634
Olympia, WA 98507
www.fungi.com
Mushroom-growing supplies

Gardener's Supply Company
128 Intervale Rd.
Burlington, VT 05401
www.vg.com
Gardening supplies

Gardens Alive!
5100 Schenley Pl.
Lawrenceburg, IN 47025
www.gardensalive.com
A wide range of organic pest control supplies and fertilizers

Gempler's Inc.
100 Countryside Dr.
P.O. Box 270
Belleville, WI 53508
www.gemplers.com
Tools and pest management supplies

Harmony Farm Supply & Nursery
3244 Hwy. 116 North
Sebastopol, CA 95472
www.harmonyfarm.com
A wide range of organic gardening supplies, including fertilizers, irrigation systems, and open-pollinated seeds

Henry Leuthardt Nurseries, Inc.
P.O. Box 666
East Moriches, NY 11940
www.henryleuthardtnurseries.com
Specializes in small fruits and espalier fruit trees

Irish Eyes – Garden City Seeds
P.O. Box 307
Thorp, WA 98946
www.irish-eyes.com
Specializes in potatoes, garlic, onions, and shallots

J.L. Hudson, Seedsman
Star Route 2, Box 337
La Honda, CA 94020
www.jlhudsonseeds.net
Rare seeds from around the world

Johnny's Selected Seeds
184 Foss Hill Rd.
Albion, ME 04910
www.johnnyseeds.com
Vegetable and herb seeds, plus gardening supplies

Le Jardin du Gourmet
P.O. Box 75
St. Johnsbury Center, VT 05863
www.kingcon.com/agljdg
Vegetable seeds in small and inexpensive packets; shallots

Logee's Greenhouses
141 North St.
Danielson, CT 06239
www.logees.com
Herbs and indoor plants

Native Seeds/SEARCH
526 N. 4th Ave.
Tucson, AZ 85705
www.nativeseeds.org
Southwestern native and heirloom vegetable and herb seeds

Natural Gardening Company
P.O. Box 750776
Petaluma, CA 94975
www.naturalgardening.com
A wide range of organic gardening supplies, including seeds, plants, beneficial insects, and irrigation equipment

New Earth
9810 Taylorsville Rd.
Louisville, KY 40299
www.newearth.com
Hydroponics, grow lights, and organic supplies

Nichols Garden Nursery
1190 Old Salem Rd NE
Albany, OR 97321
www.nicholsgardennursery.com
Untreated herbs and vegetable seeds

Nourse Farms Inc.
41 River Rd.
South Deerfield, MA 01373
www.noursefarms.com
Specializes in small fruits, as well as asparagus and rhubarb

Park Seed Co.
1 Parkton Ave.
Greenwood, SC 29649
www.parkseed.com
Vegetable, herb, and flower seeds

Peaceful Valley Farm Supply Co.
P.O. Box 2209
Grass Valley, CA 95945
www.groworganic.com
A wide range of gardening supplies

Pinetree Garden Seeds
P.O. Box 300
New Gloucester, ME 04260
www.superseeds.com
Inexpensive, small seed packets and many other gardening-related items

Raintree Nursery
391 Butts Rd.
Morton, WA 98356
www.raintreenursery.com
Specializes in fruits, nuts, and edible plants

St. Lawrence Nurseries
325 State Hwy #345
Potsdam, NY 13676
www.sln.potsdam.ny.us
Specializes in hardy fruits and nuts

Sandy Mush Herb Nursery
316 Surrett Cove Rd.
Leicester, NC 28748
www.brwm.org/sandymushherbs
Specializes in rare and unusual herbs

Seeds Savers Exchange
3076 North Winn Rd.
Decorah, IA 52101
www.seedsavers.org
Annual membership fee; heirloom fruits and vegetables; also home of the Flower and Herb Exchange

Seeds Trust High Altitude Gardens
P.O. Box 1048
Hailey, ID 83333
www.seedsave.org
Specializes in seeds for high altitudes and cold climates

Renee's Garden Seeds
7389 W. Zayante Rd.
Felton, CA 95018
www.reneesgarden.com
Gourmet vegetables, herbs, and cottage garden flowers

Seeds of Change
P.O. Box 15700
Santa Fe, NM 87506
www.store.yahoo.com/seedsofchange
Organic seeds

Southern Exposure Seed Exchange
P.O. Box 460
Mineral, VA 23117
www.southernexposure.com
Open-pollinated and heirloom vegetable, flower, and herb seeds

Southmeadow Fruit Gardens
P.O. Box 211
10603 Cleveland Ave.
Baroda, MI 49101
www.southmeadowfruitgardens.com
Unusual fruit cultivars

Sunrise Enterprises
P.O. Box 1960
Chesterfield, VA 23832
http://commercial.visi.net/sunrise
Specializes in Asian vegetable seeds

Territorial Seed Co.
P.O. Box 158
Cottage Grove, OR 97424
www.territorial-seed.com
Vegetable and flower seeds for the Pacific Northwest; also gardening supplies

The Urban Farmer Store
2833 Vicente St.
San Francisco, CA 94114
www.urbanfarmerstore.com
Water-conserving irrigation systems and other supplies

W. Atlee Burpee Co.
300 Park Ave.
Warminster, PA 18974
www.burpee.com
Vegetable, herb, and flower seeds

Whitman Farms
3995 Gibson Rd. NW
Salem, OR 97304
http://whitmanfarms.com
Currants and gooseberries; also unusual trees and shrubs

FURTHER READING

Ashworth, Suzanne. *Seed to Seed*. Decorah, Iowa: Seed Saver Publications, 1995.

Bartholomew, Mel. *Square Foot Gardening*. Emmaus, Pa.: Rodale Press, 1992.

Bradley, Fern Marshall, and Barbara W. Ellis, eds. *Rodale's All-New Encyclopedia of Organic Gardening*. Emmaus, Pa.: Rodale Press, 1992.

Bradley, Fern Marshall, ed. *Rodale's Garden Answers—Vegetables, Fruit, and Herbs*. Emmaus, Pa.: Rodale Press, 1995.

Bubel, Mike and Nancy. *Root Cellaring*. 2nd ed. Pownal, Vt.: Storey Books, 1991.

Coleman, Eliot, and Barbara Damrosch. *Four-Season Harvest: Organic Vegetables from Your Home Garden All Year Long*. Post Mills, Vt.: Chelsea Green Publishing Co., 1999.

Coleman, Eliot. *The New Organic Grower: A Mater's Manual of Tools and Techniques for the Home and Market Gardener*. 2nd ed. Post Mills, Vt.: Chelsea Green Publishing Co., 1995.

Creasy, Rosalind. *The Complete Book of Edible Landscaping*. San Francisco: Sierra Club Books, 1982.

Ellis, Barbara W, ed. *Rodale's Illustrated Encyclopedia of Gardening and Landscaping Techniques*. Emmaus, Pa.: Rodale Press, 1990.

Ellis, Barbara W., ed., et al. *The Organic Gardener's Handbook of Natural Insect and Disease Control*. Rev. ed. Emmaus, Pa., Rodale Press, 1996.

Gershuny, Grace, and Deborah L. Martin, eds. *The Rodale Book of Composting*. Emmaus, Pa.: Rodale Press, 1992.

Gershuny, Grace. *Start with the Soil*. Emmaus, Pa., Rodale Press, 1993.

Gilkeson, Linda, and Anna Carr. *Insect, Disease, and Weed I.D. Guide: Find-It-Fast Solutions for Your Garden*. Emmaus, Pa.: Rodale Press, 2001.
Harrington, Geri. *Grow Your Own Chinese Vegetables*. Pownal, Vt.: Storey Communications, Garden Way Publishing, 1984.

Hartmann, Hudson T., et al. *Plant Propagation: Principles and Practices*. 6th ed. Englewood Cliffs, N.J.: Prentice Hall, 1996.

Hill, Lewis. *Secrets of Plant Propagation*. Pownal, Vt.: Storey Communications, 1985.

Horst, R. Kenneth. *Wescott's Plant Disease Handbook*. 6th ed. Boston: Kluwer Academic Publishers, 2001.

Hylton, William H., and Claire Kowalchik, eds. *Rodale's Illustrated Encyclopedia of Herbs*. Emmaus, Pa.: Rodale Press, 1987.

Jeavons, John. *How to Grow More Vegetables: And Fruits, Nuts, Berries, Grains, and Other Crops Than You Ever Thought Possible on Less Land Than You Can Imagine*. 6th ed. Berkeley, Calif.: Ten Speed Press, 2002.

Lanza, Pat. *Lasagna Gardening*. Emmaus, Pa.: Rodale Press, 1999.

Larkcom, Joy. *Oriental Vegetables: The Complete Guide for Garden and Kitchen*. New York: Kodansha America, 1994.

Lovejoy, Ann. *Ann Lovejoy's Organic Garden Design School*. Emmaus, Pa.: Rodale Press, 2001.

Ogden, Shepherd. *Straight Ahead Organic: A Step-by-Step Guide to Growing Great Vegetables in a Less-Than-Perfect World*. Post Mills, Vt.: Chelsea Green Publishing Co., 1999.

Powell, Eileen. *From Seed to Bloom: How to Grow Over 500 Annuals, Perennials, & Herbs*. Storey Communications, 1995.

Reich, Lee. *Uncommon Fruits Worthy of Attention*. Reading, Mass.: Addison-Wesley Publishing Co., 1991.

Rodale, J.I., ed. *How to Grow Fruits and Vegetables by the Organic Method*. Emmaus, Pa.: Rodale Inc., 1961, 1999 (renewed).

Rodale, Maria. *Maria Rodale's Organic Gardening*. Emmaus, Pa.: Rodale Press, 1998.

Roth, Sally. *Attracting Birds to Your Backyard*. Emmaus, Pa.: Rodale Press, 1998.

Roth, Sally. *Attracting Butterflies & Hummingbirds to Your Backyard*. Emmaus, Pa.: Rodale Press, 2001.

Schultz, Warren. *The Organic Suburbanite*. Emmaus, Pa.: Rodale Press, 2001.

Weaver, William Woys. *Heirloom Vegetable Gardening: A Master Gardener's Guide to Planting, Seed Saving, and Cultural History*. New York: Henry Holt & Co., 1999.

Index

Page numbers in *italics* indicate a reference to an illustration caption.

A

Abelmoschus esculentus see okra
Acanthus mollis 164, 167
  A. spinosus 164, 167
accent plants 164–5
Acer campestre 142, *144*
  A. capillipes 144
  A. griseum 142, 144
  A. negundo 146
  A. palmatus 142
  A. pensylvanicum 144
  A. platanoides 146
  A. pseudoplatanus (sycamore) 138, 141
  A. tataricum subsp. *ginnala* 146
Achillea (yarrow) 65, 163, 172
  A. 'Coronation Gold' *167*
  A. millefolium 197
  A. 'Moonshine' 167, *173*
  A. 'Taygetea' 167
  A. vulgaris 196
acid soils 37, 38, 61, 239, 259
acid-loving plants 69, 70, 154
Aconitum (monkshood) 172
Acorus calamus (sweet flag) 199
acoustic barriers 136
admiral butterfly 195
adobe walls 136
Aegopodium podagraria (bishop's weed) 79, *80*
aerating lawns 179
Aesculus 146
  A. glabra 146
  A. parviflora 145
Agapanthus 65, 164
  A. campanulatus 165
agaves 167
Ageratum 171
Agistache anisata (anise hyssop) 196
agriculture, intensive 13, 15
Agriotes spp. *see* wireworms
Agrobacterium tumefaciens see crown gall
Agropyron repens see Elymus repens
air in soil 35
Ajuga reptans 167
Alchemilla mollis 165
alder *see Alnus*
alfalfa *see Medicago sativa*
algae
  on paths 75
  on ponds 199, 201, *201*
Alisma (water plantain) 199
alkaline soils 37, 61, 89, 239
allelopathy 75
Alliaceae 306
Allium 65, 164
  A. cepa see onion; shallot
  A. cristophii 163, *165*
  A. fistulosum see Welsh onion
  A. giganteum 170
  A. pornum see leek
  A. sativum see garlic
  A. sphaerocephalon 163
Alnus (alder)
  coppicing 138
  A. glutinosa 145
  A. incana 145
Alstroemeria 164
altitudes, fruit-growing 238
aluminum greenhouse 218
alyssum, sweet *see Lobularia maritima*
amaranth seeds 123
Amblyseus cucumeris 100
Amelanchier 142
  A. lamarckii 144, 145
American gooseberry mildew 254, 255, 258
anacharis *see Egeria densa*

Anaphalis triplinervis 164
Anasa tristis see squash bug
anemones for greenhouses 223
Anethum graveolens (dill) 195, 285
angelica 284
animal-free gardening 15
animal manure 41, *58*, 59–60
  alternatives to 60
  animal pests 93
  buying composted type 60
  as growing media 116
  liquid 206–7
  making heap 59
  obtaining 59
  storing 59
  "tea" 60
  using 60, *60*
  see also specific animals, e.g. cow manure
animal welfare 15
anise hyssop *see Agistache anisata*
annuals 160, *160*
  containers *209*
  hardy seeding 171
  planting 165
  weeds 74
Anthemis 164
  A. tinctoria 167
anthocorids 98
anthracnose 368
Anthriscus sylvestris (cow parsley) 197
ants 113
Apantales glomeratus 99
Aphidius 368
Aphidoletes 98, 368
  A. aphidimyza 100
aphids 92, *92*, 97, 100, 103, *157*, 195, 368
  black beans *99*, 308
  brassicas 371
  currants 255, 257
  greenhouses 228
  honeysuckle *368*
  lettuces 311, 381
  potatoes 312
  raspberries 251
  roses 153
  woolly 394–5
  see also specific aphids, e.g. cabbage aphid
Apiaceae 313
Apium graveolens see celery
  A. g. var. *rapaceum see* celeriac
apples *236*, 238, 240, *243*, 264, 265–9, *267*
  bitter bit 372
  calcium deficiency 372
  canker 242
  capsid *see* capsid bug
  -cedar rust 373
  codling moth 374
  containers 212
  cordons *242*
  cultivars 265
  growing problems 89, 90, *90*
  maggot 368
  pests and diseases *92*, 269
  planting tree 266
  pollination 242
  powdery mildew 368–9
  pruning 268, 269
  replant disease *see* replant disease
  restoring overgrown trees 246–7
  rootstocks 243, 265, 266, 269
  scab 90, 103, 269, 369
  storing 269
  training *245*, 266, 268
  triploids 242
  see also Malus
apricots 238, 240, 242, 245, 277
  containers 212

Arabis 196
Aralia elata 145
arbors, willow 139
Arbutus x *andrachnoides* 145
  A. unedo 144, 145, 146
archangel, yellow *see Lamium galeobdolon*
arches 139
Aristolochia (Dutchman's pipe) 195
Armadillidium vulgare see sowbugs
Armeria maritima 167
Aronia melanocarpa 144
arrowhead *see Sagittaria sagittifolia*
Artemisia 167
  A. 'Powis Castle' *165*
artichokes *see* Chinese artichokes; globe artichokes; Jerusalem artichokes
arugula 304, 333, 338
  containers 211
  crop planning 297, 298
  spacing 318
Asarum europaeum 167
Asclepias (milkweed) 195
ash *see Fraxinus*
Asimina triloba (pawpaw) 195
Asochyta clematidina see clematis wilt
asparagus 298, 301, 302, 314, *314*, 338–9
  beetle 369
asparagus pea 308, 331, 339
Aster 163, 164, 195, 197
  A. x *frickartii* 'Mönch' *197*
  A. pringlei 'Monte Casino' 158, *165*
Asteraceae 311
Astilbe 164, 172
Atriplex hortensis see red orach
Aubretia 197
Aucuba 149
  A. japonica 145, 156
Aurinia saxatilis 166
automatic watering systems 68
autumn
  color, choosing trees/shrubs for 144
  silhouette plants for 163
azaleas 154, 157

B

B.S.E. 11
baby's breath 166
Bacillus thuringiensis 103
backyard garden design 24–5
bacteria in soil 14, 35
bacterial infections 90–1, *91*
  canker 369
  soft rot 369
bags, herb 291
balance in garden 84
Balfour, Lady Eve 9, 10
bamboo 157
  coppicing 141
  fence 137
  hard landscaping 129
Barbarea vernia see cress, upland
barbecues, charcoal *138*
bareroot plants *154*
bark 41
  as growing media 116
  choosing trees/shrubs for 144
  for paths 135, *135*
  as mulch for flowers 172
  for weed control 76, 77, 82
  for wildlife 190
barley
  seed 185
  straw for ponds 199, 201
barriers against pests 101–2
basil *286*, 286, 288
  seeds 119, 123
baskets 141

baths
  herbs for 291
  water use from 70
bats 198
  excrement manure 60
  roosts 192
bay 288
bay laurel *see Laurus nobilis*
beach plum *see Prunus maritima*
beans 308
  beetle, Mexican 382
  in greenhouses 223
  'Monsoller Wild Goose' 16
  rotation 302
  seeds 109, 121
  storing 333
  trenches *48*
  watering 66, 67
  weevil 308, 385
  see also specific beans
bed system for vegetables 316, 322–4
bedding mortars 133
bedding plants 165
bee balm *see Monarda*
beech *see Fagus sylvatica*
beehive compost box *47*
bees 192, 195, *196*, 284
beet 310, 341
  'Bull's Blood' 331
  containers 210
  crop planning 298
  'Forono' 222
  germination 315
  leaf spot 369
  'Little Ball' 211
  multi-sowing 317–18
  rotation 302
  seeds 119, 123
  storing *335*
  see also leaf beet
beetles 93, 94, *99*, 103, *190*
  see also specific beetles
Begonia 214
  germination temperature 108
Belgian endive *see* Witloof chicory
bell pepper *see* pepper, sweet
benches, heated 220
bentonite lining membrane 129
bentwood trellis 139
Berberis 145, 148, 156, 157
  B. gagnepainii 149
  B. thunbergii 144
    B. t. f. atropurpurea 149
Bergenia 167
  B. cordifolia 164
berm 132
berries *237*, 240
  see also specific berries
besom 141, *174*, 178
Beta vulgaris see chard; leaf beet
  B. v. subsp. *vulgaris see* beet
Betula (birch) 144, *146*
  coppicing 141
  soil improvers 154
  B. pendula 146
biennials 160, *160*
  for greenhouses 223
  weeds 74
big bud mite 93
bindweed
  field *see Convolvulus arvensis*
  hedge *see Convolvulus sepium*
biodegradable pots for seed sowing 112
biodynamics 11
biological control of pests 19, 97–100, *228*
birch *see Betula*
birds 93, *174*, 188, 190
  attracting 97, 193–7, 284
  excrement for manure 60
  food for 195

birds (continued)
  houses for 186, 191, *191, 192*
  ponds and 198
  scarers *84, 101*
bird's foot trefoil see *Lotus corniculatus*
bishop's weed see *Aegopodium podagraria*
bitter pit see calcium deficiency
bittercress, hairy 74
black bean aphid 99, 308
blackberries *80*, 196, 212, 240, 252–3,
  252–3
black currants 107, 240, 254–5, *254–5*
black-eyed Susan vine see *Thunbergia
  alata*
black knot 273, 369–70
black leg 122, 387
black locust see *Robinia pseudoacacia*
black mold, pears 271
black plastic sheeting for seedbeds 109
black rot control 122
black spot *90*, 103, 153, 390
black vine weevil 370
blanching 321, 332
blanket weed 200, 201
blewit 325
blight
  celery late 373
  filberts 281
  potato late 388
  raspberry cane 389
blindness in vegetables 89
blinds in greenhouses 221
blister mites *87*
blossom end rot see calcium deficiency
blossom weevils 93
blossom wilt *90*
blueberries 212, 239, 259, *259*
bluebirds 191
bog gardens 64, 129
boggy areas, herbs 285
bolting 63, 89, 310, 320
bonemeal fertilizer 61
borage see *Borago officinalis*
Borago officinalis (borage) 196, *284, 287,*
  331
borax fertilizer 61
Bordeaux mixture 103
borders 162, 164–7
  accent plants 164–5
  improving existing 167
  plans for *165,* 166–7
  shrubs for 147
  siting 164
boron 36
  deficiency *89*, 370
  fertilizer 61
  rods/paste 131
botanicals 103
Botrytis allii see onion neck rot
  B. cinerea see gray mold fungus
  B. fabae see broad bean chocolate spot
  371
  B. paeoniae see peony blight
bottom heat 111
Bougainvillea for greenhouses 223
Bouteloua gracilis (mosquito grass) 209
boxwood see *Buxus*
boxwood psylla 370
boysenberries 252
bramble see *Rubus*
brandling worms 52
Brassica juncea see mustards, oriental
  B. napus see rutabaga
  B. oleracea see broccoli; Brussels
  sprouts; cabbage; cauliflower; kale
  B. rapa see Chinese cabbage; turnip
  B. r. var. *chinensis* see pak choi
  B. r. var. *nipposinica* see mizuna
  greens
  B. r. var. *perviridis* (var. *komatsuna*)
  see komatsuna
Brassicaceae 304–5
brassicas 314–15
  aphids 371
  cabbage looper 371–2

brassicas (continued)
  cabbage root fly 372
  caterpillars 371
  clubroot 374
  flea beetle 378
  for greenhouses 223
  oriental containers 210
  ornamental 305
  rotation 302, 304–5
  seeds 121
  sheet mulches 328
  white rust 370
  see also individual brassicas, e.g. kale
Bremia lactucae see downy mildew
Brevicoryne brassicae see cabbage aphid
bricks
  crushed 132
  edging *165, 182*
  glass 129
  hard landscaping 129
  paths 324, *324*
  reclaimed 134
broad beans 196, 308, *308*, 331, 339–40
  chocolate spot 308, 371
  crop planning 298
  germination temperature 108
  seeds 119, 123
  supports *320*, 321
  watering 319
broadcast sowing 110
broccoli 304, 342
  9-star 298, 301, 342–3
  crop planning 298
  harvesting 321
  'Romanesco' 331
  sprouting 304, 305
  watering 319
brooklime see *Veronica beccabunga*
broom see *Cytisus*
brooms 141
brown rot *90*, 277, 371
brushwood panels 137, 139
Brussels sprouts 304, 305, 314, 343
  calcium deficiency 372
  containers 210
  crop planning 298
  siting 324
  storing 334
  support 321
bubble-fountain 198
buckwheat see *Fagopyrum esculentum*
bud mites 93
Buddleia 157, 197
  B. alternifolia 156
  B. davidii 156
  B. x weyeriana 197
  B. x w. 'Sungold' 197
building materials 126, 128–9
  reclaimed 134, *134*
  see also specific materials
bulbils, weed *74*
bulblets 106
bulbs 160, *160,* 164
  containers *209*
  for greenhouses 223
  meadow 185, *186*
  organic 19
  planting 171
  soil 170
  weed *74*
bumblebees 195, *196*
bush beans 210, 308
bush currants 257
Butomus umbellatus (flowering rush) 199
buttercup, creeping see *Ranunculus repens*
butterflies *84*, 87, 93
  attracting 284
  flowers for 195
  food for caterpillar stage 195
  shelter for pupae 190, *190*
  see also insects *and specific butterflies*
button mushroom 325
Buxus (boxwood) 148, 149, 157
  dwarf, cuttings 107
  B. sempervirens 156

C

cabbage 297, 304–5, *304–5*, 314, 331,
  343–4
  aphids 371
  autumn, crop planning 298
  boron deficiency 370
  calcium deficiency 372
  caterpillars 371
  companion planting 95
  crop planning 298
  density 316–17
  disease control 122
  dwarf, as edging 330
  germination temperature 108
  for greenhouses 223
  harvesting 321
  'Hispi' 222
  ornamental, as edging 330
  red 343
  root fly 93, 101, *233*, 304, 372
  seeds 119, 123
  spacing 343
  spring 297, *305,* 343
    watering 319
  summer 297, 305 210
    watering 67
  winter 297, *305,* 343
  see also specific cabbages, e.g. Chinese
  cabbage
cabbage looper 371–2
cabbage white butterflies 87, *99*, 101,
  304, 371
Cacopsylla pyricola see pear psylla
cacti 63, 65
cages as protection *102,* 238
calabrese 298, 305, 318
Calamagrostis 161
  C. x acutiflora 'Karl Foerster' 163
  C. brachytricha 163
calcium 36, 37
  deficiency 64, *88, 89*, 372
calcium carbonate see limestone,
  ground
calcium magnesium carbonate see
  limestone, dolomitic
Calendula (pot marigold) *286*, 331
  containers 210
  for greenhouses 222
  seeds 123, 171
Caliroa cerasi see pear sawfly
Callicarpa dichotama 145
Callitriche (water starwort) 199
Calluna vulgaris 146, 147
Camellia
  disease 87
  layering 107
  watering 66
  C. japonica 145
Campanula lactiflora 172
  C. l. 'Prichard's Variety' *165*
  C. latifolia 172
  C. latiloba 167
  C. persicifolia 167
campion 194
candytuft see *Iberis*
cane blight 251, 389
cane borers 251
cane spot 251, 389
canker *90*, 122, 369
Canna 199, 223
Capsicum annuum see chili pepper;
  pepper, sweet
capsid bugs 92, 98, 253, 372
cardboard for weed control 76, 77, 82
cardoon 65, 298, 301, 311, 331, 344
Carex comans 209
  C. pendula 167
carnations, cuttings 107
Carpinus betulus (hornbeam) 138, 148,
  149
carrot 96, 196, 313, *313*, 344–5
  calcium deficiency 372
  companion planting 95, *95*
  containers 210

carrots (continued)
  crop planning 298
  flies 93, 95, 101, *233*
  for greenhouses 223
  'Little Finger' 210
  manure and 60
  'Planet' 210
  rotation 302
  rust fly *313*, 372–3
  seeds 110, *122*, 123
  storing *335*
  thinning *315*
  'Thumbelina' 210
Carson, Rachel 11
Caryopteris 156
  C. x clandonensis 'Heavenly Blue'
  165
Catalpa speciosa 146
catch cropping 318, 332–3
caterpillars *84*, 93, 103, 371, 373
  food for 195
catmint see *Nepeta*
cats 92, 191
cauliflower 304, *305*, 345–6
  'All the Year Round' 222
  containers 210
  crop planning 298
  for greenhouses 223
  spacing 345
cavity spot see carrot, calcium
  deficiency
Ceanothus x delileanus 'Gloire de
  Versailles' *165*
cedar
  -apple rust 373
  coppicing 138
  Western red see *Thuja plicata*
  white see *Chamaecyparis thyoides*
celeriac 299, 313, *335,* 346
celery 313, 346
  blanching 321
  boron deficiency 370
  calcium deficiency 372
  Chinese leaf 211
  crop planning 299
  germination temperature 108
  late blight 373
  rotation 302
  seeds 119
  watering 319
  wild see *Vallisnera americana*
cell packs for seed sowing 112
cement 132, 133
Centaurea cyanus (cornflower) 165, 185,
  194, 197
  C. dealbata 164
  C. montana (perennial cornflower) 196
  C. nigra (knapweed) 196
  C. scabiosa (knapweed) 196
centipedes 94, *98*, 190
Centranthus ruber (red valerian) 196
Centre for Alternative Technology in Wales
  44
Cerastium tomentosum 167
Cercidiphyllum japonicum 144
Cercis canadensis 144
Cerospora beticola see beet leaf spot
Chaenomeles 145, 146
  C. speciosa 'Nivalis' *165*
Chaerophyllum bulbosum see chervil,
  turnip-rooted
chafer beetles 93
chafer grubs 100
chairs and seating 22, 26, *130*
Chamaecyparis 149
  x *C. pisifera* 214
  C. thyoides (white cedar) for hard
  landscaping 131
chamomile 'Treneague' 106
charcoal *138*
chard 310, 347
  containers 210
  crop planning 299
  rainbow 331
  rotation 302

chemicals
  in preservatives 130
  symbols 36
Chenopodiaceae 310
Chenopodium bonus-henricus see Good King Henry
cherries 242, 245, 274–5, *275*
  bacterial canker 369
  black knot 369–70
  containers 212
  cultivars 274
  pests and diseases 275
  rootstocks 274
  sour 240, 274–5
  'Stella' 242
  sweet 240, 274
  training 275
  western sand *see Prunus besseyi*
  see also Prunus
chervil 211, 285
  turnip-rooted 299, 313, 347
chickadees 191
chicken of the woods 325
chickens
  for clearing pests 102
  manure 40, 59
chickweed 74, 181
chicons 347
chicory 311, 331, 334, 347–8
  crop planning 299
  forcing 321
  for greenhouses 223
  red 347, 348
  sowing times and spacing 318, 348
  sugarloaf 299, 347, 348
  see also Witloof chicory
children, designing for 22
chili peppers 300, 312, 358
Chinese artichokes 301
Chinese cabbages *294*, 298, 304, 333, 344
chives 286, 288, 306, 330, 331
chlorine in water 69
chlorosis *89*, 380
chocolate spot 308, 371
Chromatomyia syngenesiae see chrysanthemum leaf miner 373
chromium arsenate 130
Chrysanthemum
  for greenhouses 223, 227, *227*
  growing media 114
  staking 172
  white rust 373
  C. segetum (corn marigold) 185, 194, 197
chrysanthemum leaf miner 373
Chrysomelidae see flea beetle
Cichorium endivia see endive
  C. intybus see chicory
cinquefoil *see Potentilla*
Cirsium arvense (Canada thistle) 79, *81*
Citrullus lanatus see melon
Citrus 203
  containers 212, *213*
city garden design *21*, *29*
Cladosporium spp. *see* sooty molds
clay
  for pond lining 198
  pots for seed sowing 111–12
  soils 34, 37
  water-holding capacity 64
claytonia *see* purslane
cleavers 74
Clematis 157
  coppicing 141
  layering 107
  wilt 373–4
  C. 'Arctic Queen' *208*
  C. armandii 'Apple Blossom' *165*
  C. Comtesse de Bouchaud' *209*
  C. florida 'Flore Pleno' *209*
    C. f. 'Sieboldii' *209*
  C. montana 151
  C. 'Perle d'Azur' *165*
  C. texensis 150
  C. viticella 150, 151

click beetle larvae 394
climate
  hardiness zones in U.S. *396*
  for vegetables 295, 302
climbers 150–1
  aftercare 155–6
  choosing 150, 151
  containers *208*, 209
  cuttings 107
  for greenhouses 222
  pests and diseases 157
  planting 154–5
  propagation 157
  pruning 151 , 156–7
  selecting 154
  stakes and shelter 155
  training 151
  wildlife 188
climbing beans *see* pole beans
cloches 216, *216*, 230, *231*, 232–3
  as insect traps 102
  vegetables 320
clover 196
  companion planting 95
  crimson 57
  as green manure 56, *56*, 308, *308*
  in lawns 180
  as mulch 76
  red 57
clubroot 37, 90, 94, 302, 304, 374
cocoa shells 77, 82, 172
codling moth 195, 374
coir as growing media 116
coldframes 24, 216, 230, *230*
  seed sowing 111
  seedlings 113
Coleus cuttings 107
collars for cabbages 101, 304
Colocasia (taro) 199
color
  flowers for 166, 168–9
  trees and shrubs for 144
  vegetables for 331
Colorado potato beetle 374
columbine 119, 123, *160*, 164, 170
comfrey
  'Bocking 14' *206*
  leaves, as growing media 116, 207
    collection in pipe *207*
    concentrate 207
    for manure 206, 207
    for potting mix *51*
    as "trap" crop 102
compaction in lawns 181
  see also under soil
companion planting 95–6, *95*
compost
  in greenhouses 229
  see also garden compost; green manures; manure; municipal compost; worm compost
compost bins 19, 23, *42*, 46–7, *46–7*, 129, *165*
  blankets for *46*, *49*
  preservatives 130
  see also garden compost
concrete 132
  hard landscaping 129
  post bases 137
conifers
  clippings for lining hanging basket *215*
  containers 208
  coppicing 139
  cuttings 107
  propagation 157
Conotrachelus nenuphar see plum curculio
conservation 15, 400
construction materials, organic 26
container gardening 203–15
  feeding 205, 206–7, 208–9, 213
  fruit 212–13
  guidelines 400–1
  organic approach 203
  ornamentals 208–9
  pests and diseases 205, *205*

container gardening (*continued*)
  vegetables and herbs 210–11
  watering 66, *66*, 205, 209
  see also containers; hanging baskets
container-grown woody plants 154
containers *202*, *203*
  choosing 204
  drainage 204
  fruit trees 244
  for greenhouses 223, 224
  growing media 205, 208, 210, 213
  herbs *282*, 285
  for mini-vegetables 317
  mock stone planter *205*
  for seed sowing 111
  sizes 204–5, 208, 210, 212–13
  winter protection 205
  see also container gardening; hanging baskets
contrast in design 26
Convolvulus arvensis (field bindweed) 74, *80*
  C. major 214
  C. minor 214
  C. sepium (hedge bindweed) *81*
  C. tricolor 197, 210
Cooperative Extension Service 87
copings 133, 136
copper 36
copper arsenate 130
copper sheeting against slugs 101
coppice wood for hard landscaping 130, 138–41
coppicing 145–6
cordons 239, *239*, *242*
  currants 256, 257
  fruit trees 245, *266*, 268, 273
Coreopsis 164
  C. verticillata 165
coriander *see Coriandrum sativum*
Coriandrum sativum (coriander) 123, *197*, 211, 285, 289
corn 'Anasazi' 16
corn borer, European 377
corn cockle 194
corn earworm 374–5
corn marigold *see Chrysanthemum segetum*
corn salad 297, 301, 348
  crop planning 299
  spacing 318
cornflower *see Centaurea cyanus*
cornflower, perennial *see Centaurea montana*
Cornus (dogwood) 146
  coppicing 138, 141, 145
  cuttings 107
  for wildlife *193*
  C. alba 138, *142*, 144, 156
    C. a. 'Sibirica' 147
  C. controversa 144
  C. 'Eddie's White Wonder' 144
  C. kousa 142
    C. k. var. chinensis 144
  C. mas 146, 148, 149
  C. sanguinea 157
  C. stolonifera 156
    C. s. 'Flaviramea' 144, 147
Cortaderia (pampas grass) 157, 164, 172
Corylus (hazel) 146
  C. avellana 146
    coppicing 141, 146
    poles *138*
    screen *139*
    seeds 119
  C. maximus 'Purpurea' 145
cosmetics, herbs and 284
Cotinus coggygria 144, 146, *156*
Cotoneaster 145, 146
  coppicing 141
  pruning 156
  C. horizontalis *147*
  C. microphylla 147
courgettes *see* zucchini
cow manure 40, 205–6

cow parsley *see Anthriscus sylvestris*
cowslips 108, 331
crab apples *see Malus*
crab spiders *186*
Crambe maritima see seakale
cranberries 239
cranefly *381*
cranesbills 158
Crataegus (hawthorn) 142
  seed treatment 108
  soil improvers 154
  C. monogyna 144, 149, 197
creosote 131
cress 305, 333
  crop planning 299
  for greenhouses 223
  upland 304, 348
Crinum 172
Crioceris asparagi see asparagus beetle
Crocosmia 164, 172
  C. x crocosmiiflora 'Solfatare' *166*
crocus *186*
crop covers 216, 233
crop rotation 75, 96, 301–3, 304, 320
  in greenhouses 221
  guidelines 398–9
crop yields 10
cross-pollination 119, 120
crown gall 375
crusting of soil 109, *109*
Cryptolaemus montrouzieri 100
Cryptotaenia japonica see mitsuba
cucumber 307, 314, 331, 348–9
  'Aria' 222
  crop planning 299
  'Diva' 222
  for greenhouses 223, 224, *224*, 225
  mildew 307
  mosaic virus *91*, 307, 375–6
  seeds 121, 123
  sclerotina 307
  'Tasty Jade' 222
  training 321
cucumber beetle 375
Cucumis melo see melon
  C. sativus see cucumber; gherkin
Cucurbita maxima see pumpkin
  C. moschata see squash
  C. pepo see squash, summer; zucchini
Cucurbitaceae 307
x *Cupressocyparis* 149
  x *C. leylandii* 139, 148
curculio, plum 386–7
currants *237*, 238
  containers 212
  see also specific currants
currantworm
  imported 379–80
  larva 241, 257, 258
cutting, flowers for 164, 165
cuttings 106–7, *106*
  herbs 286
  woody plants 157
cutworms 93, 311, 376
Cyclamen 160
  C. hederifolium 165
Cydia pomonella see codling moth
cylindrical mowers 176
Cynara cardunculus see cardoon
  C. scolymus see globe artichokes
cypress
  coppicing 138
  Siberian carpet *see Microbiota*
  see also x *Cupressocyparis leylandii*
cyst nematodes 387–8
Cytisus (broom)
  coppicing 141
  seed scarifying *108*
cytospora canker 376

D

daffodils 160
  for greenhouses 223
  propagation 106

Dahlia 164
  cuttings 173
damping off 87, 113, 376, 386
damselflies *186*, 198
damsons 238, 240, 272
dandelion *see Taraxacum officinale*
Daphne 156, 157
  D. mezereum 145
Daucus carota see carrot
daylily *see Hemerocallis*
deadheading 156
  annuals and biennials 172
  hanging basket 215
  perennials 172
  roses 153
deadnettle *see Lamium*
decking 135, *135*
deerproof plants 157
Delia antiqua see onion downy mildew
  D. radicum see cabbage root fly
delphinium
  cuttings 173
  pests 92
  staking 172
desert gardens *63*
design
  edible landscaping 329–31
  hard landscaping 126–41
  for organic gardening 20–9
  walls 136
dethatching lawns 178–9
Deutzia 156
Diabrotica undecimpunctata see cucumber
  beetle
Dianthus (pinks) 65, 164, 167
  D. barbatus (sweet William) 197, 223
  D. chinensis 214
diatomaceous earth against slugs 101
Dibotryon morbosum see black knot
Dictamnus 164
Didymella applanata see raspberry spur
  blight
dieback, apricots 277
Dierama pulcherrimum 16, 167
digging 39
  for breaking compaction 64
  cutting back on 75
  effects of *326*
  weeds 79, 83
  winter 94
  see also no-dig technique for vegetables
Digitalis (foxglove) 119, 160, 164, 172
dill *see Anethum graveolens*
Diplocarpon rosae see rose black spot
diseases 90–1
  container plants 205
  control in greenhouses 228–9
    guidelines 399
    in seeds 122
  fruit growing 241
  identification 87
  killed on compost pile 45
  resistance 87, 94–5, 166
  susceptibility to 63
  vegetables 302, 320
  see also specific diseases
diversity in garden 84
diving beetles 198
division 106, 167, division 173
dock *see Rumex* spp.
dogwood *see Cornus*
domes, willow 139
Doronicum orientale 158, 164, *165*, 166,
  167
double cropping 318
double Guyot method for training grapes
  261
downspouts *70*
downy mildew 376
  beet 310
  control 122
  grapes 263
  lettuces 311
  onions *306*, 383
  roses 153

dragonflies *186*, 198
drainage
  containers 204
  fruit growing 240
  pipes for watering 68
  problems 88
  systems 64
  vegetable garden 294
drip irrigation 68
driveways 132, 135
drought, stress from *86*
drought-resistant plants *63, 64, 65, 66*
drying herbs 290–1
ducks for clearing pests 102
duckweed 200
Dutch cabbage *see* cabbage, winter
Dutchman's pipe *see Aristolochia*
dwarfing rootstocks 239

E

earwigs 92, 93, *93*, 377
Eccremocarpus scaber 150
Echinacea 167
  E. purpurea 'White Swan' *165*
Echinops 164
Echium vulgare (viper's bugloss) 196
ecosystems 84
edema 64, 89, 377
edging 129, *141*, 165
  herbs 285
  lawns 177
  tiles *126*
  vegetable beds *322*, 330
edible paradise garden design 28
Egeria densa (anacharis) 199
eggplant 312, *312*, 331, 348–9
  containers 210
  crop planning 299
  for greenhouses 223, 224, *224*
  rotation 302
  worm compost for *55*
Egyptian onion 306
Eichornia crassipes (water hyacinth)
  200
Eisenia foetida see brandling worms
Elaeagnus x *ebbingei* 149
elderberry *see Sambucus*
elm *see Ulmus*
Elsinoe veneta see raspberry cane/leaf
  spot
Elymus repens (quackgrass) 79, *80*
Encarsia formosa 100
enchytraid worms *54*
endive 311, 331, 333
  Belgian *see* Witloof chicory
  blanching 321
  crop planning 299
  as edging 330
  for greenhouses 223
  spacing 318
engineering bricks 134
Enkianthus campanulatus 146
environmental benefits of organic
  vegetable growing 293
environmental conservation 15, 400
environmental costs of building materials
  128–9, 130
environmental pollution 13
Epilachna varivestis see Mexican bean
  beetle
Epilobium angustifolium (rosebay
  willowherb) 196
Epimedium 167, 172
Epsom salts fertilizer 61
Equisetum arvense (horsetail) 79, *81*
Eremurus robustus (foxtail lily) 163
Erica (heather) 37, 146, 147, 196
Erigeron 'Profusion' 214
Eriosoma lanigerum see woolly aphid
Ermen, Hugh 243
Eruca vesicaria see arugula
Erwinia amylovora see fireblight
  E. carotovora see bacterial soft rot;
    potato blackleg

Eryngium (sea holly) 65, 164, 167, *169*
  E. alpinum 166
  E. variifolium 166
Erysimum (wallflower) 196
Erysiphe spp. *see* powdery mildew
Eschscholzia californica (California poppy)
  165, 171, 197
espalier fruit trees 245, 266, 268
Eucalyptus 65
  coppicing 141, 146
  pruning 156
  E. gunnii 144
Euonymus 146, 208
  E. alatus 144, 146
  E. europaeus 145
  E. fortunei 145, 147, 149, 214
Eupatorium cannabinum (hemp agrimony)
  197
Euphorbia (spurge) 65, 157, 172
  E. amygdaloides var. *robbiae* 167
  E. characias 167
    E. characias subsp. *wulfenii* 166
  E. x *martinii* 167
European corn borer 377
European red mite 377
European style of planting, new 163
evening primrose *see Oenothera*
evergreens 167, *203*

F

F1 hybrids 119, *314*
facing bricks 134
factory farming 15
Fagopyrum esculentum (buckwheat) 56,
  57, 75, 77, 197, 301, 302
Fagus (beech) 165
  leaf weevil *393*
  F. sylvatica 148, 149
Fallopia baldschuanica (Russian vine) 73
family garden design 27
fans 245
  apricots 277
  blackberries 253
  cherries 275
  currants 256, 257
  figs 278, 279, *279*
  plums 273
farming methods 13
farmyard manure 60
  see also specific type, e.g. cow manure
fava bean *see* broad bean
feathered maidens 265
fedge 139, 148, 188
feeding *see* fertilizers
fence posts *see* posts
fences 26, 129, 136–7
  as background 164
  preservatives 130
fennel 197, 286, 288 331
  see also Florence fennel
fenugreek 308
  as green manure 57
ferns *162*, 208
fertility rating of soil 40
fertilizers 61
  artificial, history 10
  container plants 205, 208–9
  flowers 170, 172
  fruit growing 240
    in containers 213
    in greenhouses 224
  in greenhouses 224, 229
  in growing media *117*
  guidelines 398
  hanging basket 215
  lawns 178
  organic 14, 19
    as growing media 116
  organic liquid 19, 60
    for containers 206–7, 209
  overuse 12
  vegetables 319
  see also feeding
fescue for lawns 183

Festuca glauca 209
field bean 196, 308
  chocolate spot 371
  as green manure 57
field-grown woody plants 154
figs 212, 238, 240, 243, 245, 278–9,
  278–9
figwort *see Scrophularia*
filberts 280–1, *280–1*
  bud mite 93
filbertworm 281
fir, Douglas *see Pseudotsuga mensziesii*
fireblight 377–8
  apples 269
  pears 271
fish emulsion 207
fish in wildlife ponds *201*
flame weeders, organic 19
flea beetle *233*, 378
floating plants 199, *200*
Florence fennel 299, 313
flower feeders 92, 93
flowerbeds 164–7
flowers (*general only*)
  attractive autumn/winter silhouettes
    163
  beds and borders 164–7
  buying plants 170
  color 168–9
  for cutting 164, 165
  edible 331
  for greenhouses 222
  planting and care 170–3
  planting styles 162–3
  seeds 170–1
  for wildlife 193–7
  see also specific types, e.g. herbaceous
    perennials
flowforms 71, *71*
fly larvae 93
frogs 99, *190*, 198
Foeniculum vulgare see fennel
  F. v. var. *dulce see* Florence fennel
  F. v. 'Purpureum' (purple-leaved fennel)
    163, *166*
foil-lined boxes, seed sowing 111
forcing vegetables 321, *321*
Forest Stewardship Council (F.S.C.) 130
Forficula auricularia see earwigs
forget-me-not 165
forking weeds 79, *79*, 83
Forsythia 146, 148, 149, 156
Fothergilla monticola 146
foundations
  layers 134
  mix 133
  for wood paths 135
foxglove *see Digitalis*
foxtail lily *see Eremurus robustus*
Fraxinus (ash)
  coppicing 138, 141
  F. excelsior 141
freezing, herbs for 290, 291
French beans
  'Cherokee Trail of Tears' *17*
  companion planting 95
  as edging 330
  germination temperature 108, 315
  growing problems 89
  seeds 119, 123
French marigold *see Tagetes patula*
froghopper, common 92, 153, 378
frogs 99, *190*, 198
  food for 195
  houses 191
  ponds 200
  shelter 201
frost damage 88, 378
frost pockets, fruit growing 238
fruit growing 237–81
  in containers 212–13
  cultivars 242–3
  drainage 240
  feeding 240
  for greenhouses *222*, 224

fruit growing (continued)
  mulches 240, 240–1
  organic advantages 237
  pests and diseases 92, 93, 241
  planning 23, 25, 28
  plant health 241
  poor setting 387
  pruning and training 244–5
  restoring overgrown trees 246–7
  site preparation 240
  soil pH and 37
  soil requirements 239–40
  space needed 239
  watering 240
  weeding 241
  what to grow 238–41
fruit flies 54, 275
fruit moth, oriental 384
fruit trees 239
  brown rot 371
  see also specific trees
fruitworm, raspberries 251
Fuchsia
  cuttings 107
  growing media 114
  growing problems 90
  hanging baskets 214
  standard, for greenhouses 223
  F. magellanica 146
fungal disease 90, 90–1
  vegetables 320
fungi in soil 14, 35
fungicides 103
fungus gnat 378
furniture from grass 177
fusarium wilt see wilt diseases

G

gages 240
Gaillardia 96
Galanthus (snowdrop) 160, 186
gall formers 92, 93
galls 92
Galtonia candicans 164
garden compost 40, 41
  activators 19, 44
  flowers in 172
  green and brown 42–4
  green manure in 57
  as growing media 116
  guidelines 398
  high-fiber 44
  hygiene 94, 94
  ingredients 44
  for lawns 178
  making 42–8
  pile, for wildlife 190
  planning for 23
  process 48
  time taken to make 48
  tips 48
  trench 48
  using 48
  vegetables in 326, 328
  weeds in 45
garden design see design
gardener's garters see Phalaris arundinaria
  var. picta
gardening products 18–19
garlic 306, 314, 350–1
  crop planning 299
  rotation 302
  storing 335
garlic chives 306, 330
gates 129
Gaultheria 146, 147, 157
gel sowing 110, 110
genetic modification 11, 13, 16, 294
Genista 146
Geranium 214
  F1 hybrids 170
  for greenhouses 223
  hardy 158, 172, 208
  G. macrorrhizum 167

Geranium (continued)
  G. x cantabrigiense 167
  G. x magnificum 165
germination temperatures of vegetable
  seed 108
gherkin 307
Gingko biloba 144
glass in hard landscaping 129
glass lizards 99
glazing for greenhouse 218
Glechoma hederacea (ground ivy) 80
Gleditsia 146
globe artichokes 311, 331, 338
  crop planning 298
  crop rotation 301, 302
  drought resistance 65
  flowers for bees 196
  offsets 314
golden club see Orontium aquaticum
goldenrod see Solidago
Good King Henry 299, 301, 302, 310, 351
gooseberries 240, 241, 255, 258, 258
  containers 212
  cultivars 258
  currantworm 379–80
  cuttings 107
  sawfly see currantworm, imported
gourd 307
granite 133
  bedding mortar 133
  pieces 134
grape berry moths 263
grapes 145, 240, 260, 260
  in containers 212, 263
  coppicing 141
  cultivars 260–3, 260–3
  sulfur dust for 103
  see also Vitis
Grapholita molesta see oriental fruit moth
grass
  furniture 177
  paths 177, 324
  seed 110, 182, 183
  varieties 64
grass snakes 190
grasses (ornamental) 161, 162, 163, 164,
  167
  division 173
  planting 171
  in pots 209
  soil 170
grasshoppers 195, 379
grassing down 79
gravel 129, 134
  flowers in 172
  for weed control 83
gray mold fungus 90, 379
  apricots 277
  figs 279
  grapes 262, 263
  lettuces 311
  strawberries 249
gray squirrels 191
gray water 70, 70
great pond snail 201
green manures 49, 56–7
  digging in 57
  no-dig 57, 328
  seeds, organic 19
  sowing 110
  spacing 318
  vegetables 301, 302
  for weed control 75, 83
green pepper see pepper, sweet
green shoulders 221
greenfly see aphids
greenhouses 24, 216, 216
  climate control 228
  equipping 220–1
  glazing 218
  growing calendar 223
  heated benches 220
  insulation 220–1
  lean-to 218
  management tips 228–9

greenhouses (continued)
  materials 129, 218, 219
  pests and diseases 228–9
  plants for 222–7
  seed sowing 111
  shading 219, 221
  site and space 218
  size 218
  soil beds 221
  staging 220
  thrips 379
  ventilation 219
  whitefly 379
greens see salad crops
ground beetle 35, 97
ground ivy see Glechoma
  hederacea
groundcover plants 158, 163
  planting tips 147
  shrubs 147
  for weed prevention 75, 76, 83
groundsel 74
growing bags 19, 224
growing media 114–17
  for containers 208, 210, 213
  guidelines 400
  for hanging baskets 215
  homemade 114, 117
  ingredients 116
  organic 19
  pasteurizing 114
  for potting 117
  for rooting 117
  for seeds 117
  soil-based and soilless 114, 115
guano manure 60
guards for woody plants 155
Gunnera 160
gutters 70, 129
Gymnosporangium juniperi-virginianae see
  cedar-apple rust
Gypsophila 65
  G. paniculata 164
gypsum fertilizer 61

H

Hamamelis mollis 144
Hamburg parsley 299, 313, 351
hand-picking pests 101–2
hand pollination 120
hanging baskets 214–15
  care 215
  in greenhouses 223
  growing media 215
  liners 215
  plant choice 214, 215
  watering 66
  worm compost for 55
Hanover salad 304, 305
hard landscaping 126–41
hard surfaces 132–5
hardening off 113, 232
hardiness zones in U.S. 396
hardwood cuttings 107, 107, 157
harvesting
  fruit in greenhouses 224
  seeds 121
  vegetables 321
harvestmen 99
hawthorn see Crataegus monogyna
hay mulch 41
  for fruit growing 240–1
  for weed control 77
  for wildlife 190
hazel see Corylus
hazel bud gall 93
hazelnut bud mite 93
heather, winter-flowering 214
heathers see Erica
heating mats 111
Hedera (ivy) 145, 147, 150, 208
  hanging baskets 214
  for wildlife 188
  H. helix 146, 197

hedges 26, 136, 148–9
  as background 164
  choosing plants 148, 149
  clippings 45
  cutting 149, 188
  herbs for 285
  planting tips 148
  semiformal 148
  for wildlife 188
heeling in 167
height
  flowers for 166
  vegetables for 331
Helenium 163, 164, 167
  staking 172
  H. 'Butterpat' 165
Helianthemum (rock rose) for wildlife 190
Helianthus (sunflower) 158, 164, 167, 172
  seeds 119, 123
  H. 'Lemon Queen' 165
  H. tuberosus see Jerusalem artichokes
Helichrysum petiolare 214
Helictotrichon sempervirens 167
Heliocoverpa (Heliothis) zea see corn
  earworm
Heliothrips haemorrhoidalis see
  greenhouse thrips
Helleborus 167
Hemerocallis (daylily) 164, 165
  H. citrina 165
hemp agrimony see Eupatorium
  cannabinum
Henry Doubleday Research Association
  (H.D.R.A.) 110, 111, 126, 243
  guidelines 397–401
herbaceous perennials 158–60
herbs
  caring for 286
  common and botanical names 289
  in containers 210–11, 282, 285
  definition 282
  drought-tolerant 285
  flavor 284
  growing 282–91
  harvesting and preservation 290–1
  herb garden 285
  invasive 286, 287
  organic 282–3
  shade-tolerant 285
  siting 285
Hesperis matronalis (sweet rocket) 197
Heterodera spp. see potato cyst nematode
Heterorhabditis megidis 98, 100
Heuchera 164, 167
x Heucherella 167
Hills, Lawrence D. 9, 10
Hippophae rhamnoides 149
hoeing 78, 78, 83
  fruit growing 241
  vegetables 319, 326
hoes 73
hoggin 135
holly see Ilex
holly leaf miner 379
hollyhocks 160
honesty see Lunaria annua
honey fungus 90, 90
honeybees see bees
honeydew 87, 92
honeysuckle see Lonicera
honeysuckle aphid 368
hoof and horn fertilizer 61
hoop houses 24, 216
  choosing 218–19
  condensation 228
  equipping 220–1
  management tips 228–9
  sides 219
  site and space 218
  see also greenhouses
hop, golden see Humulus lupulus 'Aureus'
hop waste 40
horehound see Marrubium vulgare
hormone rooting powder 107
hornbeam see Carpinus betulus

hornworm, tomato 394
horsetail see *Equisetum arvense*
hoses 68, *68*
    high-pressure for weed control 75
Hosta 164, *165*, 172, 173
    containers 208
    pests 92
hot water treatment of seeds 122–3
hot-mix mortar 133
houseleek see *Sempervivum*
houseplants
    watering 66, 68
    worm compost for *55*
hoverflies 98, *190*, 195, 197
humidity, water loss and 64
Humulus lupulus 'Aureus' (golden hop) 150
humus 36
hungry gap 297
hyacinth, water see *Eichornia crassipes*
hyacinth bean 298, 308, *309*
Hydrangea 146, 156, 157, 208
    H. aspera 144
    H. petiolaris 151
    H. quercifolia 144, 145
Hydrilla verticillata 200
hygiene
    in garden 94
    in greenhouses 228
Hypericum 146, 147, 156, 157, 172
    H. calycinum 146, 147
hyssop see *Hyssopus officinalis*
    anise see *Agistache anisata*
Hyssopus officinale (hyssop) *166*, 197

I

Iberis (candytuft) 65, 196
    I. umbellata 197
Ilex (holly) 145, 149
    coppicing 141
    seed treatment 108
    I. aquifolium 145, 146
    I. crenata 148
Impatiens 170
    germination temperature 108
    I. walleriana 214
indicator plants for soil type 37
insects
    attracting 284
    barrier glue 101
    food for 195, 197
    houses 192
    in meadows *194*
    mesh 101
    pollination *119*
    ponds 200
    repellents 284
    traps see *under* pest control
    see also pests
insecticides 103
insulation for greenhouses 220–1
intensive farming 13, 15
Ipomoea (morning glory) 150
    germination temperature 108
    for greenhouses 222
    I. lobata 309
Iris 162, 172, 199
    I. foetidissima 167
    I. sibirica 163
iris borer 380
iron 36
    deficiency 89, 239, 380
    fertilizer 61
irrigation systems 64, 68, 155–6
Isatis tinctoria (woad) 196
isolation cages 120
Itersonilia perplexus see parsnip canker
ivy see *Hedera*

J

Japanese beetle *86*, *92*, 93, 153, 263,
    380
Japanese onion 306, 356
Jasminum officinale 150

Jerusalem artichokes 311, 338
    crop planning 298
    propagation 106
    storing 334
    tubers 314
jostaberries 240, 258
juniper see *juniperus*
Juniperus (juniper) 65, 146
    coppicing 139, 141
    for wildlife *193*
    J. communis 139, 147
    J. horizontalis 147
    J. x *pfitzeriana* 145

K

kale 304, *305*, 351–2
    black 'Tuscano' *295*, 331
    crop planning 299
    frilly 331
    'Red Russian' 331
kaolin clay 269
Kentucky bluegrass for lawns 183
king stropharia 325
kitchen waste for worm composts 52, 53
knapweed see *Centaurea*
Knautia arvensis (field scabious) 197
Kniphofia (red hot poker) 65, 167, 172
knotweed, Japanese see *Polygonum*
    cuspidatum
Koeleria glauca 209
kohlrabi 297, 304, *305*, 352
    containers 210
    crop planning 299
    for greenhouses 223
    spacing 318
Kolkwitzia amabilis 149
komatsuna 299, 352

L

Laburnum anagyroides 142, 144
    L. x *watereri* 'Vossii' 146
lace bugs 380
lace flower see *Trachymene coerulea*
lacewings 97, 98
    houses 192, *192*
Lactuca sativa see lettuce
ladders 247
lady beetles 97, *97*, 99
Lagerstroemia indica 144
lamb's ears see *Stachys*
lamb's lettuce as edging 330
lamb's quarter 74
Lamium (deadnettle) 147, 158
    L. galeobdolon (yellow archangel) 73,
      167
    L. maculatum 167
landscape fabric *76*, *76*, 77, 82, 129,
    132, 134
landscaping the garden 126–41
    with vegetables 329–31
larch see *Larix decidua*
Larix decidua (larch) for hard landscaping
    131
Lathyrus latifolius 164
Laurus nobilis (bay laurel) 141, 149
Lavandula (lavender) 65, 197, 286, 288,
    294
    clippings for ponds 199, 201
    cuttings 107
    soil improvers 154
    L. angustifolia 'Hidcote' *166*
    L. x *intermedia* Dutch Group *166*
    L. 'Munstead' 197
lavender see *Lavandula*
lavender cotton see *Santolina*
    chamaecyparissus
lawn mowers 176
lawn rake *178*
lawns *165*, 174–85
    aerating 179
    clippings *76*, 176
    damaged edges 177
    dethatching 178–9

lawns (*continued*)
    edging 177, *182*
    feeding 178
    grass varieties for 64, 183
    improving 178–9
    making into flowerbeds 170
    mowing 176–7, 183
    new 182–3
    organic care 174
    planting in 64, 154, *155*
    problems 180–1, *182*
    renovating 180–1
    sweeping *174*
    topdressing *51*, 178, 179
    watering 183
    wear *182*
    weeds 180, 400
    wildlife 188–9
    see also grass
layering 107, 157
leaf aphids, lettuces 311
leaf beet 298, 310, 341–2
leaf collectors, wheeled 178
leaf curl 276, 277
leaf feeder pests 92, 93
leaf miners 103, 380–1
    beet *310*
    chrysanthemum 373
    holly 379
leaf mold *40*, 41, 50–1
    comfrey for 116, *207*
    in containers 50, *50*
    for flowers 172
    as growing media 116
    piles 23, 190, *190*
    for seedbed 109
    types of leaves to use 50
    using *51*
    for vegetables 302
    for weed control 77, 82
    for woody plants 154
leaf shape, vegetables for 331
leaf spot *90*
    beet 369
    control 122
    filberts 281
    plums 273
    raspberry 389
leafhoppers 381
leatherjackets 37, 100, 381
leeks 306, 352
    'Babington' *17*
    crop planning 299
    for display 329
    germination temperature 108
    harvesting 321
    mini- 317
    multi-sowing 317–18
    rotation 302
    rust *306*
    'St. Victor' 331
    seeds 119, 123
    storing 334
    transplanting *315*
legumes see *specific legumes, e.g.* peas
Leptinotarsa decemlineata see Colorado
    potato beetle
Leptosphaeria coniothyrium see raspberry
    cane blight
lettuce 297, 311, *311*, 333, 353
    'Buttercrunch' 222
    butterheads 353
    containers 210
    cos 353
    crispheads 353
    crop planning 299
    cutting *332*
    disease 87
    'Galactic' 222
    germination temperature 108
    in greenhouses 227
    leaf 353
    'Lollo Rosso' 222, *295*, 330
    'Lollo Verde' 330
    looseleaf 353

lettuce (*continued*)
    'Oakleaf' 211
    oakleaved/frilly 331
    ornamental *329* ..as edging 330
    'Red Sails' 211
    romaine 353
    rotation 302
    salad bowl 353
    seeds 119, 121, 123
    spacing *318*, *319*
    as "trap" crop 102
    watering *67*, *68*, 319
lettuce root aphid 381
Leucanthemum x *superbum* (Shasta daisy)
    196
Leucojum 172
leucostoma canker see cytospora canker
Leucothoe walteri 147
Liatris spicata 164
light for seedlings 113
Ligustrum 139, 148, 149
lilac 65
Lilium 164, 165
lime
    addition to soil 39
    in hard landscaping 129
    for lawns 178, 180
    mortars 132, 133, 134, 136
    putty 133
    stonework 133
    for vegetables 302
    wash, for glass *219*, 221
lime see *Tilia*
lime-hating plants see acid-loving plants
lime-induced chlorosis 89, 380
limestone 133
    dolomite, fertilizer 61
    ground, fertilizer 61
    as growing media 116
    for worm bins 53
Limnanthes douglasii (poached egg flower)
    96, 171
Limonium platyphyllum 164, 167
Limonius spp. see wireworms
Linaria 164
linen bag, herbs for 291
liners
    for hanging basket 215
    for ponds 198
lion's mane 325
liquid manure 206–7
Liquidambar styraciflua 142, *142*, 144
Liriope muscari 167
living spaces 22
lizards 99, 190
loam as growing media 116
Lobelia 170
    trailing 214
    L. cardinalis 196
Lobularia maritima (sweet alyssum) 96,
    197
logs
    growing mushrooms 325
    log rounds 135, *135*
    for wildlife 190, *190*
loganberries 252
Lonicera (honeysuckle) 146, 150, 157,
    196
    coppicing 141
    weaving 139
    L. nitida 149
    L. periclymenum 196
Lotus corniculatus (bird's foot trefoil) 196
    L. tetragonolobus see asparagus pea
loupe *87*
lovage 284
love-in-a-mist see *Nigella*
love-lies-bleeding seeds 119
luffa 307
lump-wall construction 136
Lunaria annua (honesty) 164, 172, 197
lupine 57, 308, *308*
lupins 172
Lupinus angustifolius see lupine
Luzula sylvatica 167

Lychnis 65, 164
Lycopersicon esculentum see tomato
Lygus lineolaris see tarnished plant bug 393

M

Macronoctua onusta see iris borer
macronutrients 36
maggots
  angler's 195
  apple 269, 368
magnesium
  deficiency 86, 261, 381
  fertilizer 61
  "locked up" 89
magnifying glasses 87
magnolia 107, 156
Mahonia 146
  M. aquifolium 145, 147
  M. 'Charity' 208
  M. repens 147
maiden apple trees 265
Malus (apple/crab apple) 266
  coppicing 141
  M. 'Adams' 145
  M. 'Golden Hornet' 142, 144, 145
  M. 'John Downie' 266
  M. 'Sentinel' 145
  M. tschonoskii 144
  M. x zumi 'Golden Hornet' 266
  see also apples
Manduca quinquemaculata see tomato hornworm
manganese 36
  deficiency 89, 381–2
manure
  guidelines 397, 398
  vegetables 328
  worms *see* brandling worms
  see also animal manure; green manure; liquid manure *and specific types, e.g.* cow manure
maple *see Acer*
Marguerite daisy for greenhouses 223
marigolds 160
  corn *see Chrysanthemum segetum*
  French *see Tagetes patula*
  pot *see Calendula*
marjoram *see Origanum*
marrow 307
Marrubium vulgare (horehound) 196
mason bees, shelter 192
Matthiola (stock) 87, 223
  M. bicornis (night-scented stocks) 192
maypop *see Passiflora incarnata*
meadow grass for lawns 183
meadows 184–5
  alternatives 185
  cutting 184, 185, 194
  for wildlife 189, 194
mealworms 195
mealybug 100, 382
Medicago lupulina (trefoil) 57, 76, 308
  M. sativa (alfalfa) 56, 57, 61, 195, 308
Melianthus major 164
Melissa 172
Melittia cucurbitae see squash vine borer
melon 307, 353–4
  crop planning 299
  for greenhouses 223, 224
  seeds 121
  worm compost for 55
Menatus ribesii see currantworm, imported
Mentha (mint) 197, 288
  M. requienii (Corsican mint) 284
mesclun 333
mesh fabrics for crop cover 233
metal containers 204
metal fences 137
Metaphycus helvolus 100
Mexican bean beetle 382
mibuna greens 299, 333, 353

mice 308
Microbiota (Siberian carpet cypress) 65
  M. decussata 147
micronutrients 36
microorganisms in soil 14, 35
microwaving seeds 123
midges 98
mignonette *see Reseda odorata*
mildew *see specific mildews*
milfoil, water *see Myriophyllum*
milkweed *see Asclepias*
mimulus 162
Mina lobata see Ipomoea lobata
mineral deficiencies 63, 89, 382
mineral particles 35
mini pots for seed sowing 112
mini-vegetables 317
mint *see Mentha*
  Corsican *see Mentha requienii*
Miscanthus sinensis 163
  'Malepartus' 161
misticanza 333
mites 93, 99
mitsuba 299, 353
mixed planting 95, 95
mizuna greens 304, 331, 333, 353
  crop planning 299
  as edging 330
  spacing 318
moisture retainer, organic 19
moles 382
Molinia 164
  M. caerulea 163
  M. c. subsp. *arundinacea* 'Transparent' 161
  M. c. subsp. *arundinacea* 'Windspiel' 161, 166
Mollison, Bill 11
molybdenum 36
monarch butterfly caterpillar 195
Monarda (bee balm) 164, 196
monkshood *see Aconitum*
Montia perfoliata see purslane, winter
morel mushrooms 325
morning glory *see Ipomoea*
mortars, types of 133, 134
Morus nigra 146
mosaic virus 375–6, 395
mosaics 129
mosquito grass *see Bouteloua gracilis*
moss
  lawns 178, 180, 181
  mock 215
moth caterpillars *see* cutworm
moth repellents 284
moths 93, 102, 190
  attracting 284
  see also specific moths, e.g. cabbage looper
mountain spinach *see* red orach
mowing grass 176–7, 183
mulches 39
  black plastic 75, 77, 82
  to conserve water retention 64
  for containers 208
  for flowers 163, 172, 172
  for fruit growing 240, 240–1
  leaf mold 51
  loose 76
  manure for 60
  membranes for weed control 76, 77, 79
    organic 19
    planting through 77
  organic 19
  for paths 135
  for vegetables 320, 328
  for weed control 75, 76–7, 82–3
  for wildlife 97, 190
  for woody plants 155, 156
mulching mowers 176
mulleins 163
multipurpose mixes 114
multi-sowing vegetable seeds 317–18, 318

municipal compost 40
  as growing media 116
  for weed control 82
municipal water 69
Muscari azureum 165
mushroom compost 172
  as growing media 116
  spent 40, 41
mushroom fly *see* fungus gnat
mushroom growing 325
mustard 304, 305, 331
  agricultural 304
  crop planning 299
  as green manure 57
  greens 305
  no-dig method 328
  oriental 304, 305, 333, 354–5
mustard spinach *see* komatsuna
mycorrhizal fungi 35, 90
Myocentrospora acerina see parsnip canker
Myrica pensylvanica 157
Myriophyllum (water milfoil) 199
  M. spicatum (Eurasian water milfoil) 200

N

nameko 325
Nandina 148
  N. domestica 149
Narcissus 164
  dwarf 186
  N. 'Tête-à-Tête' 165
nasturtium 165, 170, 171, 331
  'Alaska' 211
  germination temperature 108
  seeds 119, 123
naturalistic planting 162–3, 170
nectarines 212, 240, 276
nectria canker 382–3
neem 103
nematodes 93, 98, 320, 383
Nepeta (catmint) 107, 172
  N. racemosa 'Walker's Low' 165
Nephrotoma spp. *see* leatherjackets
Nerium oleander 149
nesting places 97
netting for ponds 200
nettle, stinging *see Urtica dioica*
New Zealand compost box 46
New Zealand spinach 299, 301, 355
newspaper for weed control 77, 82
newts 99, 190, 198, 201
Nicotiana 192
  N. langsdorfii (tobacco plant) 170
Nigella (love-in-a-mist) 121, 171, 172
night-scented stocks *see Matthiola bicornis*
nitrate pollution 13
nitrogen 36
  content of manures 40, 59, 59
  deficiency 261, 383
  fixation 35, 39, 56, 90, 308
Noctuidae see cutworm 376
no-dig technique for vegetables 322, 324, 326–8
nuthatches 191
nutrients for plants 36, 301
  deficiencies *see* mineral deficiencies
Nymphaea 199
  N. 'Chromatella' 199
  N. 'Hermine' 199
  N. pygmaea 199
  N. tetragona 199
Nyssa sylvatica 144

O

oak *see Quercus robur*
oak galls 92
oat seed 185
Oenothera (evening primrose) 65, 163
offsets 314, 314
okra 300, 355
Oleander 148, 203
onion fly 306
onion thrips 384

onions 306, 306, 314, 355–6
  companion planting 95, 95
  crop planning 300
  density 316–17
  for display 329
  downy mildew 383
  germination temperature 108
  for greenhouses 223
  harvesting 321
  multi-sowing 316–17, 317
  neck rot 383–4
  rotation 75, 302
  rust 384
  seeds 123
  sowing 110
  storing 335
  white rot 384
  see also specific onions, e.g. Welsh onion
Oniscus asellus see sowbugs
opossums 190
Orfelia spp. *see* fungus gnat
Organic Farming and Gardening 11
Organic Gardening 18
organic gardening (*general only*)
  definition 9, 14–15
  designing for 20–9
  economics 13
  food 11, 12
  guidelines 11, 15, 18 , 397–401
  principles 14
  products 11
  reducing problems 94–6
  standards 11
  strategies 86
  timing 18
Organic Guidelines for Gardeners 11, 18, 397–401
organic matter in soil 36
organic movement history 9, 10–11
organic symbol 11
oriental bunching onion 356
oriental fruit moth 276, 384
oriental greens for greenhouses 223
Origanum (marjoram) 197, 330
Orontium aquaticum (golden club) 200
Oryctolagus cuniculus see rabbits
Osmia see bees, mason
osteospermum 65
Ostrinia nubilais see European corn borer
Otiorhynchus sulcatus see black wine weevil
overwintering plants 94
Oxalis stricta (common yellow sorrel) 81
Oxydendrum arboreum 142, 144
oxygenating plants 199

P

Pachysandra terminalis 147
pads 132
Paeonia 157, 164, 172
  blight/wilt 386
  P. delavayi 146
  P. lutea 146
pak choi 304, 305, 333, 357
  crop planning 300
  as edging 330
  spacing 318
palmette fruit tree 245
pampas grass *see Cortaderia*
Panonychus ulmi see European red mite
pansy seeds 119, 194
Papaver 164, 171, 172
  field 185
  germination temperature 108
  seed 74
  seedheads 291
  seeds 119, 121, 123
  P. 'Danish Flag' 160
  P. naudicaule 164
  P. orientale 158, 166
    P. o. 'Black and White' 165
  P. rhoeas 194
paper mulch for weed control 77, 82

Papilionaceae 308
parasol 325
parrot's feather *201*
Parrotia persica 144
parsley 211, 286, 288, 313, 331
  crop planning 300
  as edging 330
  for greenhouses 223
  seeds 123
  see also Hamburg parsley
parsnips 196, 313, 357
  canker *313*, 385
  containers 210
  crop planning 300
  rotation 302
  seeds 110, 123
  storing 334 , *335*
Parthenocissus 150
  P. quinquefolia (Virginia creeper) 151,
    196
Passiflora incarnata (maypop) 195
pasteurizing growing media 114
Pastinaca sativa see parsnips
paths/paving 20, 26, 129, 132, 133, *133*
  foundation mix 133
  herbs 285
  hoggin 135
  vegetable beds 324, *324*
  weed control 75, 78, 132
  wooden 135
patios 132, 135
  containers *203*
  weeding 78
  wood 135
patty pan *see* zucchini
paving *see* paths/paving
pawpaw *see Asimina triloba*
peaches 238, 240, 245, 276, *276*
  containers 212
  leaf curl *91*, 103, 385
  ornamental *see Prunus*
  peachtree borer 385
pearl oyster 325
pears 240, 242–3, 270–1, *270–1*
  boron deficiency 370
  'Cascade' 239
  'Comice' 239
  containers 212
  cultivars 270
  pear sawfly 386
  pests and diseases 271
  pruning and training 268, 270–1
  psylla 385–6
  restoring overgrown trees 246
  rootstocks 270
  scab *90*, 386
  training 245 , 268
peas 308, *308*, *309*, 357–8
  'Alderman' *17*
  crop planning 300
  for greenhouses 223
  harvesting 321
  pea and bean weevil 308, 385
  pea moth 96
  rotation 302
  seeds 96, *108*, 109, 119, 121, 123
  'Sugar Lace' 211
  supports *320*, 320–1
  in trenches *48*
  watering 66, 67, 319
peat 34–5, 38, *115*, 116
peat-free products *115*
Pemphigus bursarius see lettuce root
  aphid
Penstemon 65, 173
peony *see Paeonia*
peppers, sweet 312, 358
  calcium deficiency 372
  containers 210
  crop planning 300
  for greenhouses 223, 224, *224*
  growing problems *88*
  rotation 302
  seeds 119, 123
  see also chili peppers

perennials
  containers 208
  dividing 173
  drought-resistant 65
  evergreen 167
  for greenhouses 223
  mulching and feeding 172
  planting 171
  rabbitproof 172
  staking 172
  tender 160
  weeds 74
  see also herbaceous perennials
pergolas 129, 139
periwinkle *see Vinca major*
perlite as growing media 116
permaculture 11
Peronospora destructor see downy mildew
  P. violae see downy mildew
Perovskia atriplicifolia (Russian sage) 65,
  196
  P. a. 'Blue Spire' *165*
pesticides 103
  accumulation 13
  disposal 18
  history 10
  organic 19
  poisoning from 12
pests 92–3, 367–95
  container plants 205
  control 94, 101–2
    barriers/traps 19, 87, *100*, 101–2, *101*
    biological control 97–100
    green manure 56
    in greenhouses 228–9, *228*, 228–9
    guidelines 399
    natural 14
    organic 19
    row covers 233
  fruit growing 241
  identification 87
  lawns 180
  resistance 87, 94–5
  seedlings 110
  seeds 122
  susceptibility to 63
  vegetables 302, 320
Petroselenum crispum var. *tuberosum see*
  Hamburg parsley
Petunia 214
pH of soil 37, 61
Phacelia tanacetifolia 171, 196, 197
  as green manure 57
  seeds 123
Phalaris arundinaria var. *picta* (gardener's
  garters) 161
Phaseolus coccineus see runner bean
  P. vulgaris see string bean
Phasmarhabditis hermaphrodita 100
pheromone traps 102
Philadelphus 146, 156, 157
Philaenus spumarius see froghopper
Phlomis russeliana 163
Phlox 164, 172
Phoma spp. *see* parsnip canker
phosphate, rock, fertilizer 61
phosphorus 36
  deficiency *89*, 386
Photinia davidiana 145
Phragmidium spp. *see* rose rust
Phragmites australis (common reed) 71
Phyllostachys aureosulcata var. *aureocaulis*
  137
  P. nigra 137
  P. vivax 137
Physostegia 164
Phytomyza ilicis see holly leaf miner
  P. syngenesiae see chrysanthemum leaf
    miner 373
Phytophorum infestans see potato late
  blight
Phytophthora cactorum see strawberry
  crown rot
  P. fragariae var *fragariae see* strawberry
    red stele

phytophthora root/stem rot 240, 386
Phytoseiulus persimilis 99, 100
Pierce's disease 261
Pieris 146
  P. brassicae/rapae see cabbage white
    butterfly
  P. japonica 145
pine *see Pinus*
pinks *see Dianthus*
Pinus (pine) 65, 146
  for hard landscaping 130, 131
  needles, for compost 61
    for weed control 83, 172
  P. bungeana 144
pisé walls 136
Pisum sativum see peas
"pitcher irrigation" 68
planning
  for flowers *165*, *166*
  for vegetables 23, 28, 296, 297–300,
    301, *303*
Planococcus spp. *see* mealybugs
plant health 84–103
plant nutrients *see* nutrients
plant protection *51*
plant selection 24
plant suppliers 402–3
plant taxonomy 87
Plantago major (broadleaf plantain) *81*
plantain, broadleaf *see Plantago major*
  in lawns 180, *181*
  red-leaved, as edging 330
  water *see Alisma*
planting
  through mulch membrane 77
  timing 96
Plasmodiophora brassicae see clubroot
Plasmopara viticola see downy mildew
plastic
  bag, for cuttings 107
  as building materials 128, 129
  bubble 220–1
  containers *204*
  covers 219
  fences 137
  pots, for seed sowing 112
  for weed control 77
  "wood" 131
pleaching 145
Plectranthus amboinicus 214
  P. australis 214
plug plants, vegetables 314
plums 240, 242, 245, 272–3, *272–3*
  American 272
  bacterial canker 369
  black knot 369–70
  containers 212
  cultivars 272
  curculio 386–7
  European 272
  growing problems 90
  Japanese 272
  ornamental *see Prunus*
  pests and diseases 273
  pruning and training 273
  restoring overgrown trees 246
  rootstocks 273
poached egg flower *see Limnanthes*
  douglasii
Podosphaera spp. *see* powdery mildew
poison ivy *see Rhus toxicodendron*
pole beans 308, *320*, 320, 324, 331
poles uses *138*, *141*
pollarding 138, 145–6
pollination 119–20, 242
pollution, environmental 13
Polygonum cuspidatum (Japanese
  knotweed) 73, 74
polystyrene "wood" 131
pond skaters *198*
pond weed 200
ponds 97, *132*
  allies *200*
  digging 199
  lining 129, 198, 199

ponds (*continued*)
  maintenance 200
  plants for *199*, 199–200
  for wildlife 198–201
Popillia japonica see Japanese beetle
poplar *see Populus*
poppy *see Papaver*
  California *see Eschscholzia*
  oriental *see Papaver orientale*
Populus (poplar) 141
Porcellio scaber see sowbugs
Portulaca oleracea see purslane, summer
posts 130, 136–7, 139
pot marigold *see Calendula*
potager gardens 329, *330*
potash
  deficiency 387
  fertilizer 61
potassium 36
  in animal manure 59
  deficiency 89, 261, 387
  overfeeding 89
potatoes 312, *312*, 358–9
  'All Red' 227
  Colorado beetle 374
  blackleg 387
  blight 90, 103, *312*, 388
  in compost 94
  in containers 210
  crop planning 300
  cyst nematode 387–8
  'Early Red Norland' 227
  for greenhouses 223, 227, *227*
  growing problems 89, 92
  harvesting 321
  mulches 326
  no-dig *327*
  organic tubers 19
  rotation 75, *301*, 302
  scab 37, 64, *91*, 387
  seed 91, *94*, *314*
  storing *335*
  watering 67, 319
potbound plants *88*
Potentilla (cinquefoil) 65
  P. fruticosa 149, 156
potpourris 284, 291
pots 9
  organic 19
  for seed sowing 111–12
  worm compost for 55
potting mixes 114, 117
  leaf mold *51*
  worm compost 55
powdery mildew 90, *90*, 103, 388
  apples 368
  cucumbers 307
  filberts 281
  grapes 263
  peas 308
  roses 153
  strawberries 249
preservation of herbs 290–1
pricking out 113
primrose seeds 119
privet *see Ligustrum*
propagating plants 104–23, 157, 170
propagators 111
pruning
  against pests 102
  apples 268
  black currants 255, *254*, *255*
  blackberries 253
  cherries 275
  climbers 151
  currants 257
  figs 279
  fruit trees 244–7
  gooseberries 258
  grapes 261–2
  hedges 149
  herbs 286
  pears 270–1
  roses 153
  woody plants 155, *156*, 156–7

prunings 41, 45
for fencing 137, 139
for mulches, fruit growing 240–1
uses 141
for weed control 77
Prunus spp. (cherry; plum) 142, 146
coppicing 141
pruning 156
for wildlife 193
P. avium (cherry) for hard landscaping 131
P. besseyi (western sand cherry) 65
P. domestica see plums, European
P. laurocerasus 145, 149
P. l. 'Otto Luyken' 157
P. lusitanica 145, 149
P. maritima (beach plum) 65
P. salicina see plums, Japanese
P. sargentii 144
P. serrula 144
Pseudococcus spp. see mealybugs
Pseudomonas mors-prunorum see bacterial canker
Pseudosasa japonica 137, 146
Pseudotsuga mensziesii (Douglas fir) for hard landscaping 131
Psila rosae see carrot rust fly
psylla 388
boxwood 370
pear 271, 385–6
Puccinia allii see onion rust
P. horiana see chrysanthemum white rust
Pulmonaria 147, 166
P. saccharata 196
P. s. 'Mrs Moon' 165
pumpkin 307, 331, 359–60
containers 210
crop planning 300
for greenhouses 223
rotation 302
seeds 119, 121
sheet mulches 328
spacing 318
storage 335
training 321
in trenches 48
see also squash
purslane 301
crop planning 300
summer 360
winter 360
P.V.C. as building material 128
Pyracantha 145
P. coccinea 151
pyrethrins 103
pyrethrum 103
Pyrus see pears
Pythium spp. see damping off

Q
quackgrass see Elymus repens
quarrying 128
Quercus (oak)
coppicing 138, 141
disease resistance 87
for hard landscaping 130
Q. coccinea 144
Q. macrocarpa 146
Q. pallustris 144
Q. robur 131
Q. rubra 144
quicklime 133

R
rabbitproof plants 157, 172
rabbits 320, 388–9
radicchio see chicory, red
radish 295, 297, 304, 305, 331, 333, 360–1
containers 210
crop planning 300
for greenhouses 223
seeds 119, 123

radish (continued)
spacing 318
'White Icicle' 222
railings 129
railroad ties 131
"rain shadow" plants 65
rainfall patterns 63
rainwater 69
raised beds 38, 132, 296, 322, 322
raking lawns 174, 178
ramshorns snails 200
Ramularia beticola see beet leaf spot
Ranunculus repens (creeping buttercup) 74, 80
Raphanus sativus see radish
raspberries 196, 237, 239, 240, 250–1, 250–1
Arctic 238
cane blight 389
cane/leaf spot 389
containers 212
cultivars 250
iron deficiency 239
spur blight 389
supports 251, 251
viruses 91
raspberry beetle 253
recalcitrant seeds 121
records for vegetable growing 296, 302, 337
recycling 13, 14, 15
building materials 128
for compost 40, 45–6
planning for 23
plastic 131
for soil additives 38
red currants 240, 241, 256–7, 256–7
cultivars 256
currantworm 379–80
red hot poker see Kniphofia
red mite, European 377
red orach 300, 310, 361
red spider mite 92, 99, 100, 103, 389
cucumbers 307
figs 279
in greenhouses 228
potatoes 312
strawberries 249
red stele disease, strawberries 249
red wigglers see brandling worms
reed, common see Phragmites australis
reed beds 70, 71
reed fence 137
reed walls 136
refrigeration of seeds 123
replant disease 389–90
Reseda odorata (mignonette) 196
Rhagoletes pomonella see apple maggot
Rheum (ornamental rhubarb) 160
R. x cultorum see rhubarb
Rhizobium bacteria 90
Rhizoctonia solani see damping off
rhizomes, weed 74
Rhododendron 145, 157
deadheading 156
hedges 149
layering 107
soils 37, 146
rhubarb 301, 302, 314, 361–2
crop planning 300
forcing 321, 321
leaves as pesticide 103
ornamental see Rheum
Rhus (sumac) 65
coppicing 141
R. toxicodendron (poison ivy) 81
R. typhina 144
rhythm in design 26
Ribes nigridolaria see jostaberry
R. sanguineum 146
river water 69–70
robin 97
Robinia 146
R. pseudoacacia 130, 131, 136–7
R. p. 'Frisia' 145

rock features 132
rock garden plants, containers 208
rock phosphate 207
rock rose see Helianthemum
rocket seeds 123
Rodale, J. I. 10, 11
Rodale Institute 18
Rodgersia 160
"rogueing out" 119
root aphids see aphids
root disease, susceptibility to 64
root fly, cabbage 372
root rot 313, 386
see also damping off; phytophthora root/stem rot
root trainers, seed sowing 112
rootfeeder pests 92, 93
rooting media 114, 117
roots, weed 74, 79
rootstocks, fruit trees 239, 242–3
ropes in hard landscaping 129
roping, blackberries 253
Rosa 146, 152–3, 331
aftercare 153
black spot 390
bush 152
climbing 150, 151
floribunda 152
growing problems 90, 90
hybrid tea 152
pests and diseases 153
planting 152
powdery mildew see powdery mildew
pruning 153, 156
Redouté 153
rust 153, 390
shrub 152
sickness see replant disease
slug 103
species 152
topdressing 60
R. banksiae 'Utea' 152
R. 'Blanc Double de Coubert' 152, 153
R. Bonica 152, 153
R. 'Buff Beauty' 152, 153
R. canina (dog rose) 196, 197
R. 'Charles de Mills' 152, 153
R. 'Climbing Cécile Brünner' 152
R. 'Country Dancer' 152
R. 'F. ßJ. Grootendorst' 152
R. 'Félicité Perpétue' 152
R. filipes 'Kiftsgate' 152, 153
R. 'Frühlingsmorgen' 153
R. Gertrude Jekyll 152, 153
R. glauca 144, 145, 152, 153
R. 'Just Joey' 152, 153
R. 'Knock Out' 152
R. 'Maigold' 152, 165
R. 'Marie Pavie' 152
R. 'Max Graf' 147
R. moyesii 145, 152, 153
R. 'Paul's Hamalayan Musk' 152
R. 'Penelope' 152
R. pimpinellifolia 146, 152
R. 'Roseraie de l'Haÿ' 152
R. rubiginosa 153
R. rugosa 145, 149
R. sericea f. pteracantha 152
R. 'Snow Carpet' 152
R. 'Sun Sprinkler' 152
R. 'Winchester Cathedral' 152
rosebay willowherb see Epilobium angustifolium
rosemary see Rosmarinus officinalis
Rosmarinus officinalis (rosemary) 165, 196, 210, 285, 288
rotary mowers 176
rotary tilling 79, 83
rotenone 103
rots see specific types
roundworms 98
rove beetles 99
row cover 101, 233, 233, 320
row sowing, vegetable seeds 316
rubble, crushed 134

Rubus (bramble) 156, 197
Rosa (continued)
R. calycinoides 147
R. cockburnianus 144
R. fruticosus see blackberry
R. thibetanus 'Silver Fern' 144
ruby chard 310, 331
Rudbeckia 164, 167
R. fulgida var. sullivantii 'Goldsturm' 163
Rumex (dock) 74, 79, 80, 328
R. acetosa see sorrel
runner bean 308, 309, 331, 340
crop planning 298
as edging 330
growing problems 88
harvesting 321
poor setting 387
scarlet 195
seeds 119, 123
support 321
watering 319
runners 74, 248
rush, flowering see Butomus umbellatus
rust 90
blackberries 253
onion 384
rose 390
white 370
see also specific rusts
rust fly, carrot 372–3
rutabaga 300, 304, 305, 335, 362, 370
rye, winter
as green manure 56, 56, 57, 301, 302, 328
for weed control 75
rye grass for lawns 183

S
safety
food 293
pruning tools 247
shredders 45–6
sprays 103
sage 286, 289, 331
containers 210
as edging 330
Russian see Perovskia atriplicifolia
Sagittaria sagittifolia (arrowhead) 199
salad burnet as edging 330
salad crops 332–3
containers 211
for greenhouses 223, 226
see also specific plants, e.g. lettuce
salad rocket see arugula
saladini, oriental 300, 333
saline soils 34, 35
Salix (willow) 146
barriers 136
coppicing 138, 139, 141
cuttings 107
fence 137
pruning 156
screen 139, 140, 148
sculptures 140
S. alba 139
S. a. 'Britzensis' 144
S. daphnoides 139
S. purpurea 139
salsify 300, 311, 311, 362
salt deposits in soil 63
Salvia 164
S. officinalis see sage
S. o. 'Purpurascens' 165
S. patens 'Cambridge Blue' 171
S. x sylvestris 'May Night' 165
Sambucus (elderberry), for wildlife 193
S. nigra 145
sand 116, 129
sand-slaked mortar 133
sandstone 133
sandy soils 34, 37
Santolina 65, 146
S. chamaecyparissus (lavender cotton) 166

Sanvitalia procumbens 214
sapsuckers 92–3, *92*
Sarcococca (sweet box) 65, 145
  S. hookeriana var. *humilis* 147
savory
  summer 211, 285
  winter 230
Savoy cabbage 343
  dwarf 330
sawdust as growing media 116, 325
sawflies 390
  caterpillars 93
  gooseberry *see* currantworm, imported
  larva *92*
  pear 386
saws, bow 247
scab *see* apples scab; pears scab;
  potatoes scab
Scabiosa 164
  S. columbaria (small scabious) 197
scabious *see Scabiosa*
  field *see Knautia arvensis*
  small *see Scabiosa columbaria*
Scaevola aemula 214
scale in design 26
scale insects 228, 390
Scalopus aquaticus see moles
scarifying
  lawns 179
  seed 108, *108*
scarlet pimpernel 194
Schizophragma integrifolium 165
Schizostylis coccinea 164
sciarid fly *see* fungus gnat
Sciara spp. *see* fungus gnat
Scilla sibirica 165
Sclerotina fructigena/laxa see brown rot
Sclerotium cepivorum see onion white rot
scorch 88–9, 390
scorzonera 300, 311, 362–3
screens 26, 129, *139*, 140, 141
Scrophularia (figwort) 197
sculptures, willow 139
scything 79, 184
sea campion *see Silene maritima*
sea holly *see Eryngium*
seakale 65, 301, 302, 304, 305, *314*,
  331, 363
  crop planning 300
  forcing 321
seakale beet *see* chard
seating areas 22, 26
seaweed fertilizer 61, 207
  fruit growing 240
  grapes 261
  hanging basket 215
  lawns 178
  seedlings 113
Secale cereale see rye, winter
Sedum 65, 164, 173
  containers 208
  S. 'Autumn Joy' *165*
  S. 'Herbstfreude' 163
  S. spectabile (stonecrop) 163, 197
  S. telephium 'Matrona' 163 *S.*
seed meadow 184–5
Seed Savers Exchange 16, 123
seed trays 112
seedbeds 109
  stale 75, 83, 109
seedheads 163. 172
seedlings *104*
  fertilizing 113
  flowers 170–1
  growing media 113
  hardening off 113
  keeping healthy 112
  light 113
  pest problems 110, 113
  problems 113
  shading 64, *112*
  space 113
  stroking 113, *113*
  temperature 113
  thinning 110, 113, 315, *315*

seedlings (continued)
  transplanting 113, *113*, 315, *315*, 316
  watering 66, 68 , 113
seeds
  cleaning 121
  collections 16
  covering *112*
  drying 123
  germination 108, 315
  grass 182, 183
  growing mixes 114, 117
  harvesting 121
  heirloom 16
  moisture content 123
  organic 19, 108
  pest and disease control 122
  saving from garden 119–21
    selection for health 119
  seed coats 108
  sowing 104, 108–13
    outdoors 109–10
    successional 297, 333
    timing 96
    under cover 111–13
    vegetables 314–18
  special treatments 108
    hot water 122–3
  storage 121, 123
  suppliers 402–3
  weed *74*
  winnowing 122
  woody plants 157
self-pollination 119, 120
self-sufficiency 294
Semiarundinaria fastuosa 137
semi-ripe cuttings 107, 157
Sempervivum (houseleek) 65, 208, *209*
Septoria apiicola see celery late blight
sets, onion 19, *314*
shade-loving plants 166, 208
shading
  greenhouses 221
  seedlings 64, *112*
shaggy mane 325
shallot 306, *314*, 363–4
  crop planning 300
  storing *335*
Shasta daisy *see Leucanthemum* x
  superbum
shears, pruning 247
sheds, wildlife and 190
sheep's sorrel in lawns 178, 180
sheet mulches for vegetables 328
shelter
  vegetables 295–6
  wildlife 191–2
  woody plants 155
shield bugs *186*
shiitake 325
shower water 70
shredders 45–6, *45*
shreddings, municipal waste *40*
shrews *190*
shrubs 142–7
  aftercare 155–6
  for attractive bark 144
  for autumn color 144
  borders 147
  choosing 146–7, 154
  containers 208, *209*
  cuttings 107
  for different soil types 146
  drought-resistant 65
  effect of water shortage on 63
  groundcover 147
  in lawn 64, 154, *155*
  for ornamental fruit 145
  pests and diseases 157
  planting 154–5
  propagation 157
  pruning *156*, 156–7
  for shade 145
  wall 151
  watering 66
  wildlife 188

sieving seeds 122
Silene maritima (sea campion) for wildlife
  190
Silent Spring 11
silica gel drying of seeds 123
silt soils 34
Sinapis alba see mustard
Sisyrinchium striatum 166, 167
site assessment 20
Sitona lineatus see pea/bean weevil
Skimmia 145, 208
  S. japonica 145, 147
skirret 313
slaked lime 133
slugs 64, 92, 93, *98*, *99*, 100, 101, 102,
  390–1
  beans 308
  cucumber family 307
  in greenhouses 228
  lettuces 311
  repellents *10*
  strawberries 249
snails 64, 92, 93, 99, 101, 391
  beans 308
  water 198, *200*, *201*
snake's head fritillary *186*
snapdragons 171, 223
snowdrop *see Galanthus*
soaker hose irrigation 68
sod
  lawns 182–3
  for topsoil *116*
soft rot, bacterial 369
soft scale 87, *87*, 100, 103, 279
softwood stem cuttings *106*, 107
soil 33–61
  acidity 61
  air and water 35
  -based mixes 114
  beds in greenhouses 221, *221*, 224,
    229
  chemistry 37, 39
  compaction 38–9, 64
  conservation 128
  content 34, 35, 36
  crumbs *35*
  crusting 109, *109*
  excess water 64
  feeding 14
  fertility, organic methods 19
  floor in greenhouses *221*
  for flowers 170
  for fruit growing 239–40
  as growing media in pots 114
  health 10, 94
  life 35
  management guidelines 397
  organic management principles 38–9
  pH 37
  poor, meadows and 184–5
  profiles 37
  protection *51*, 56
  resting, with green manure 56
  sampling 37
  for seeds 109
  structure 33, *33*, *39*, 56, 301
  temperatures 109, 111
  thermometer *109*
  type 34–5, 166
  understanding 33
  for vegetable growing 296, 301, 302
  warming 315
  water-holding capacity 64
Soil Association 10
soil improvers
  application rates 40–1
  bulky 40–1
  conserving water retention 64
  flowerbeds 170
  lawns 178
  manure as 60
  mushrooms 325
  organic 19, 38
  sources 40
  types 41

soil improvers (continued)
  vegetables 302, 322, 324, 326
  -warming cables 111
  woody plants 154
soilless mixes 114
  for containers 205, 215
Solanaceae 312
Solanum tuberosum see potato
solar tunnels 219
Solidago (goldenrod) 163, 196
Sonchus arvensis (perennial sow-thistle) *81*
sooty mold 87, *87*, 271, 391
Sophora japonica 146
Sorbus 142
  S. alnifolia 144
  S. aria 146
  S. aucuparia 145
  S. intermedia 146
  S. 'Joseph's Rock' 144
sorrel 300, 301, 302, 364
  common yellow *see Oxalis stricta*
sowbugs 35, 87, 113, 391–2
sowing *see* seed sowing
sow-thistle, perennial *see Sonchus arvensis*
soybeans 61, 382
Sphaerotheca spp. *see* powdery mildew
spiders 99, 190
  crab *186*
spiking lawns 179
spinach 297, 310, *310*, 364
  crop planning 300
  disease control 122
  for greenhouses 223
  mountain *see* red orach
  perpetual *see* leaf beet
  rotation 302
  seeds 119, 123
  spacing 318
  watering 67, 319
  see also New Zealand spinach
spinach beet *see* leaf beet
Spinacia oleracea see spinach
Spirea 208
spittlebug *see* froghopper
splitting 392
spray safety 103
spring greens *see* cabbage, spring
spring onions 297, 306, 356
  containers 210
  spacing 318
spring water 69–70
sprouted seeds 305
sprouting broccoli, crop planning 298
spur blight, raspberries 251
spurge *see Euphorbia*
square-foot gardening 317, *317*
squash *307*, 331
  for greenhouses 223
  poor setting 387
  rotation 75, 302
  seeds 119, *120*, 121, 123
  spacing 318
  summer 307, 366
    crop planning 300
  training 321, *321*
  in trenches *48*
  winter 307, 359–60
    harvesting 321
    storage *335*
  worm compost for *55*
squash bug 392
squash vine borer 392
squirrels 191, 281
Stachys (lamb's ears) 65
  S. byzantina 167
stag beetle *188*
staging 220
stains, water-repellent 136
stakes 131, 155, *155*
stale seedbed 74, 83, 109
starter plants, vegetables 314
starwort, water *see Callitriche*
station sowing 109–10, 316
steel in hard landscaping 129
Steiner, Rudolf 11

Steinernema feltiae 100
stem cuttings 106–7, *106*, 173
stem feeders 93
stem rots *see* damping off
Stephanandra incisa 145
  S. i. 'Crispa' 147
step-over apples 266
Stewartia 37, 144
sticky traps *100*
stink bugs 392
Stipa 164
  S. arundinacea 161, 163, 167
  S. calamagrostis 163
  S. gigantea 161, 163, 167, *170*
  S. tenuissima 161, *163*
stir-fry leaves for greenhouses 223, 226, *227*
stock *see Matthiola*
stone
  chippings 129 , 132, 134
  containers *204*
    mock *205*
  dust 132
  hard landscaping 129
  natural *133*
    for rock gardens *132*
  reconstituted 129, *132*, 133
  reclaimed *134*
  synthetic 133
  walls for wildlife *190*
stonecrop *see Sedum spectabile*
stools 138
stopping fruiting plants in greenhouses 224
storage
  herbs 290
  seeds 121, 123
stratification 108, 157
straw 41
  bales 136, *229*
  filter 70
  in manure *58, 60*
  mulches 190, 240–1
  for strawberries *248*
  for weed control 76, 77, 83
strawberries 238, 239, 240, 248–9, *248–9*
  boron deficiency 370
  containers 212, 213
  crown rot 392
  cultivars 248
  for greenhouses 223, 226, *226*
  red stele 392–3
Streptomyces spp. *see* potatoes scab
string bean 308, *309*, 340–1
  crop planning 298
  harvesting 321
  Mexican bean beetle 382
  'Royalty' 211
  'Trionfo Violetto' *309*
  watering 319
string trimmers 184
stroking seedlings 113, *113*
Styrax japonica 142
submerged plants 199, *200*
subsoil 37, 116
suburban orchard design *22–3*
suckers, blackberries 253
sugarloaf chicory *see* chicory
sulfur 36, 103
  container mix 208
  dust 61, *103*
sumac *see Rhus*
sunflower *see Helianthus*
sunlight, water loss and 64
sunny site
  borders *166*
  flowers *166*
  fruit 238
supplies 402–3
supports 129, 141
  blackberries 253, *253*
  for climbers 150–1
  from coppiced prunings 139
  in greenhouses 224, *224*

supports (*continued*)
  raspberries 251, *251*
  vegetables 320, 320–1
"surge tank" 71
swallows 191, *198*
swallowtail butterflies *84*
sweet box *see Sarcococca*
sweet chestnut coppicing 138
sweet corn *295*, 301, 364
  in containers *211*
  crop planning 300
  'Dwarf Blue Jade' 211
  germination temperature 108
  for greenhouses 223, 226, *226*
  growing problems 89
  harvesting 321
  rotation 302
  seeds 119, 123
  spacing *318*
  watering 67, 319
  for weed control 76
sweet flag *see Acorus calamus*
sweet peas 150, *308*
  for greenhouses 222, 223
  seeds *108*, 119
sweet rocket *see Hesperis matronalis*
sweet William *see Dianthus barbatus*
Swiss chard *see* chard
sycamore *see Acer pseudoplatanus*
Symphoricarpos 145
Synanthedon exitiosa/pictipes see peachtree borer
Syringa 146

T

tachinid flies *98*
tadpoles l200
Tagetes
  germination temperature 108
  T. patula (French marigold) 95, *95*, 170
    for greenhouses 222
    seeds 119, 123
    as "trap" crop 102
tanks for water 69
Taphrina deformans see peach leaf curl
Taraxacum officinale (dandelion) 74, 79, 80, 299, 333
  in lawns 181
tarnished plant bug 393
taro *see Colocasia*
tarragon, French 289
taxonomy 87
Taxus (yew) 65, 157
  coppicing 139
  T. baccata 148, 149, 156
tayberries 252
Tellima grandiflora 167
temperature
  for seedlings 113
  water loss and 64
tepees 139, 141
terraces *165*
terra-cotta containers *204*
Tetragonia tetragonioides see New Zealand spinach
Tetranychus urticae see red spider mite
thermal weeding 78
thermometer for soil 109
thinning seedlings 110, 113
thistles 328
  Canada *see Cirsium arvense*
  in lawns 180
thrips 93, 98, 100, 103, 393
  greenhouses 228, 379
  onion 384
Thuja 149
  T. plicata (Western red cedar) 130, 131, 136–7
Thunbergia alata (black-eyed Susan) 214, 222
Thymus (thyme) 284, 289
  containers 210
  creeping golden 211
  as edging 330

Thymus (*continued*)
  as mulch 76
  for wildlife 190
  T. serpyllum 166
ties *150*, 151, 155
tiles, reclaimed *134*
Tilia (lime) 138, 141, 146
tilth 109
timber *see* wood
Tipula spp. *see* leatherjackets
titmice 191
toads 99, *190*
  food for 195
  houses 191, *191*
  shelter 201
tobacco plant *see Nicotiana langsdorfii*
tomatoes 312, *312*, 314, 364–6
  'Basket King' 211
  blight 388
  'Brandywine' *17*
  calcium deficiency 372
  in compost 94
  containers 203, 206, 210
  corn earworm 374–5
  crop planning 300
  disease control 122
  germination temperature 108
  for greenhouses 223, 224, *224*
  green shoulders 221
  growing problems 88–9, *88, 89*
  hornworm 394
  potato blight *312*
  protection 320
  rotation *301*, 302
  seeds 119, *121*, 123
  stopping 224
  storing 334
  straw bales 229
  supports 224, 321
  'Sweet 100' 211
  training *321*
  watering 67, 319
  worm compost for *55*
tools
  for fruit tree pruning *247*
  for lawns *178*
  for propagation *104*
topdressing
  containers 208–9
  flowers 172
  fruit in containers 213
  lawn *51*, 178, 179
  roses 60
  worm compost for *55*
topsoil 37, *116*, 133
trace elements *see* micronutrients
Trachymene coerulea (lace flower) 170
Tragopogon perrifolius see salsify
trailing plants 214
training
  apples *245*, 266, 268
  blackberries 253, *253*
  cherries 275
  currants 257
  figs 279
  fruit trees 244–5
  pears 270–1
  vegetables 320–1
  see also pruning grapes 261–2
transplanting seedlings 113, *113*, 315, 316
transplants 19, 75
traps *see under* pest control
trays, organic 19
tree mats for weed control 82
tree onion 306
trees 142–7
  aftercare 155–6
  for attractive bark 144
  for autumn color 144
  choosing 142–5, 154
  containers 208, *209*
  coppicing 138 , 145–6
  for different soil types 146
  drought-resistant 65

trees (*continued*)
  effect of water shortage on 63
  in lawn 64
  for ornamental fruit 145
  pests and diseases 157
  planting 154–5
  pleaching 145
  pollarding 138, 145–6
  propagation 157
  pruning 156–7
  for shade 145
  siting 145
  for small gardens 142
  staking 131, 155, *155*
  watering 66
  see also fruit trees
trefoil *see Medicago lupulina*
trellis 139
trench seed sowing 109
Trialeurodes vaporariorum see greenhouse whitefly
Trichoplusia ni see cabbage looper
Trifolium see clover
  T. incarnatum see clover, crimson
  T. pratense see clover, red
Trigonella foenum-graecum see fenugreek
trimmer mowers 176
trimmers 79
tripods 141
Trollius europaeus 164
troughs 9
Tsuga canadensis 'Cole's Prostrate' *147*
tubers 164, *314*, 314
Tulipa 160, *160*
tunnels, willow 139
turf stack *116*
turnip-rooted chervil *see under* chervil
turnips 297, 304, 305, 366
  boron deficiency 370
  crop planning 300
  seeds 123
  spacing 318
two-spotted mite *see* red spider mite

U

Ulmus (elm) coppicing 141
unity in design 26
urine in animal manure 59
Urtica dioica (stinging nettle) *81*
  for manure 207
  nettle tea as pesticide 103

V

Vaccinium 145, 146
vacuums, garden 178
valerian, red *see Centranthus ruber*
Valerianella locusta see corn salad
Vallisnera americana (wild celery) 199
valsa *see* cytospora canker
vegetable garden, herbs in 285
vegetable oils for pesticides 103
vegetable oyster *see* salsify
vegetables 12–13, 293–36, 293–7, 301–2
  bed system 316, 322–4
  blanching and forcing 321, 332
  care 319–22
  catch/double cropping 318
  climate for 295, 302
  in containers 210–11
  cultivars 297, *317*
    for greenhouses 222
  effect of water shortage on 63
  families *301*
  feeding 319
  genetically modified 294
  ground preparation 296
  growing problems 89
  harvesting 321, 333
  for hungry gap 297
  landscaping with 329–31
  manures for 60
  mulching 320
  no-dig method 326–8

vegetables (continued)
  organic, growing benefits 293
  perennial 302
  pests and diseases 302, 320
  plans and records 23, 28, 296,
    297–300, 301, 303, 335
  pollination 120
  preserving heirloom types 16–17, 294
  protection 320
  rotation 75, 301–3, 320
  safety 293
  seed treatment 108
  siting 295–6, 324
  soil pH and 37
  sowing and planting 314–15, 316–18,
    324
  spacing 316–18, 332–3
  storing 334–5
  tools and equipment 296
  training and support 320–1, 320, 321
  transport 293
  washing water 70
  watering 67, 67, 319, 324
  weed control 319, 320
  what to grow 295
  worm compost for 55
  see also specific vegetables
vegetative propagation 104, 106–7, 157
velvet mite 186
Venturia inaequalis 369
  V. pirina see pears scab
Veratrum 172
Verbascum 65, 196
  V. olympicum 167
  V. phoeniceum 167
Verbena officinalis (vervain) 196
vermiculite as growing media 116
Veronica 173
  V. beccabunga (brooklime) 199
  V. gentianoides 'Variegata' 167
verticillium wilt see wilt diseases
vervain see Verbena officinalis
Vespula spp. see yellow jackets
vetch, common, as green manure 57,
  302, 308
Viburnum 147, 149, 156
  for wildlife 193
  V. betulifolium 145
  V. davidii 145, 208
  V. lantana 146
  V. opulus 144, 145, 146
  V. plicatum 'Mariesii' 144, 147
  V. tinus 147, 148
Vicia faba see broad bean; field bean
  V. sativa see vetch, common
Villandry, France 329
Vinca (periwinkle) 146, 147, 157, 172
  V. major 73
  V. m. 'Variegata' 214
vine
  grape see grapes
  Russian see Fallopia baldschuanica
vine eyes 150
vine weevil 93, 98, 100
  black 370
  in greenhouses 228
  grubs 205
  strawberries 249
vinegar, herbs for flavoring 290, 291
Viola 195, 331
  V. 'Johnny Jump Up' 211
  V. labradorica see V. riviniana Purpurea
    Group
  V. odorata (violet) 165, 166
  V. riviniana Purpurea Group 167
violet see Viola odorata
violet ground beetle 186

viper's bugloss see Echium vulgare
viral disease, vegetables 320
Virginia creeper see Parthenocissus
  quinquefolia
viruses 91, 91, 94, 393
  see also specific viruses
Vitis vinifera see grapes

W

walkways see paths
wallflower see Erysimum
wallpaper paste for gel sowing 110
walls 26, 129, 136–7, 136
  as background 164
  shrubs 151
  for wildlife 190
  willow 140
warblers, prothonotary 191
wasps 92, 93, 99, 395
  parasitic 99, 195
waste plant materials guidelines 397–8
waste water 70, 70
water barrels 69, 69
water boatmen 198
water
  application see watering
  conservation 63
  diverter 71
  excess 64
  loss from plants 64
  pollution 13, 63
  for ponds 198–9
  purification 71
  shortage problems 63, 88, 88
  in soil 35
  storage 69, 69
  types 69–71
  using well 66–8
water hyacinth see Eichornia crassipes
water measurers 198
water milfoil see Myriophyllum
water plantain see Alisma
water starwort see Callitriche
watercress 223, 226, 226, 300
watering 63–71
  container plants 205, 209
  excess 64, 88
  flowers 171
  fruit 224, 240
  in greenhouses 224, 229
  hanging baskets 215
  lawns 183
  overwatering 88
  plant needs 64, 66–8
  roses 153
  seedlings 113
  systems 67–8
  timing 66–7
  vegetables 319, 324
  weeds and 75
  woody plants 155–6
watering can 68
waterlily see Nymphaea
waterlogging 393
watermelon 307
wattle and daub walls 136
weasels 190
weaving 139, 141, 253
weed killers, natural 75
weeding 14, 18, 73–83
  clearing weed-infested ground 79
  to conserve water retention 64
  cutting down 79, 83
  fruit growing 241
  by green manure 56, 75
  guidelines 399–400

weeding (continued)
  by hand 78, 83
  hoeing 78, 83
  in lawns 180, 400
  mulches and 39, 76–7, 82–3, 328
  no-dig approach 326
  organic 19
  thermal 78, 83
  vegetables 301, 320
weedproof barrier see landscape
  fabric
weeds
  advantages 73
  annuals 74
  biennials 74
  control see weeding
  definition 73
  disadvantages 73
  in paving 132
  perennials 74, 328
  prevention 75
  survival and invasion 74
weevils 385, 393–4
Weigela 146
welfare of animals 15
well water 69–70
Welsh onion 300, 306, 356–7
Western flower thrip 98
whirligig beetles 198
white currants 240, 256–7, 256–7,
  379–80
white pine blister rust 254, 255
white rot 306, 384
white rust 370, 373
whitefly 92, 100, 103, 228, 394
  control 95
  in greenhouse 379
  potatoes 312
  protection against 233
wicks for watering 68
wildflowers 184–5
  plug plants 185
  for wildlife 194
wildlife 186–201
  attracting 84, 188–90
    annuals 165
    flowers 166–7
    herbs 284, 284
    meadows 184
    vegetables 320
  corridors 188
  diversity 12, 13
  food 193–8
  habitats 19, 134, 136
  overwintering 173
  planning for 24–5
  ponds 198–201
  shelters 191–2
willow see Salix
wilts 87, 88, 373–4, 394
wind
  damage to fruit 238
  pollination by 119
  rock 394
  scorch 394
  water loss and 64
windbreaks 26, 64, 148–9
windowsill seed sowing 111
winnowing 122
winter
  digging 94
  flowers 167
  hanging basket 214
  moths 101
  protection 205, 263
  silhouette plants 163
wireworms 37, 92, 93, 394

Wisteria 150, 150
  coppicing 141
  growing problems 91
  seed scarifying 108
  weaving 139
  W. sinensis 151
Witloof chicory 347–8
  crop planning 299
  forcing 321
  sowing times and spacing 348
woad see Isatis tinctoria
wood ash fertilizer 61
wood
  containers 204
  fences 136–7
  greenhouse 218
  in hard landscaping 126, 129, 130–1,
    130, 135
  mulch 135, 135
  preservatives 129, 130–1, 399
  shavings in manure 58
  synthetic 131, 137
  woodchip mulches, for fruit growing
    240–1
    for weed control 77
wood mice 190
woodpeckers 191
woolly aphid 394–5
workbench 111
worm bins 52, 52, 53
  drainage 52
  feeding worms 53
  organic 19, 23
  problems 53–4
  temperature 52
  trash can-type 52
  worms for 52
worm compost 41, 52–5
  extracting worms from 54, 54
  as growing media 116
  in hanging basket 215
  removal from bins 54
  using 54, 55
worm liquid 54–5
worms (in soil) 35, 181
wrens, house 191
wrought iron work 129

Y

yarrow see Achillea
yellow jackets 395
yellow mosaic virus 395
yellows 395
yellow-tailed moth caterpillar 373
yew see Taxus
yogurt cups for cabbage protection 101
yucca 65
Yushania anceps 137

Z

Zantedeschia 164
Zea mays see sweet corn
zinc 36
zinnia seeds 119
zucchini 307, 307, 331, 366
  containers 210
  crop planning 300
  as edging 330
  for greenhouses 223
  no-dig method 326
  rotation 302
  sheet mulches 328
  spacing 318
  watering 67, 319
  yellow mosaic virus 395

Acknowledgments

This book is dedicated to Lawrence Hills, one of the pioneers of the organic movement, who founded H.D.R.A.

The Editor-in-chief would like to thank H.D.R.A. staff, and, in particular, colleagues in H.D.R.A.'s Information and Education department for their forbearance and hard work during the production of this book. Also Kate Brown and Ned Litton.

Pauline Pears
June 2001

Dorling Kindersley would like to thank:

Pam Brown, Simon Maughan, Sue Stickland, and Joanna Chisholm for editorial assistance; Katie Butler, Nick Robinson, Ben Rafkin, David Pierson, Julian Goodfrey, and Glen Pierce for their help and support during photography sessions at Yalding, and Mike Thurloe at Audley End.

Text credits

Introduction to Organic Gardening
Alan Gear, Jackie Gear, Pauline Pears

Organic by Design
Dr. Isabelle Van Groeningen (Garden plans: Kathleen Askew pp. 27, 28, and 29; Andrew Miller pp. 21, 22–23, and 24–25)

Soil and Soil Care
Colin Shaw

Water and Watering
Owen Smith

Weeds and Weed Control
Pauline Pears

Plant Health
Dr. Martin Warnes

Raising Plants
Owen Smith

The Garden Framework
Kathleen Askew

Woody Plants and Climbers
Dr. Isabelle Van Groeningen

Garden Flowers
Dr. Isabelle Van Groeningen

Lawns and Lawn Care
Adam Pasco

Gardening for Wildlife
Sally Cunningham

Container Gardening
Bernard Salt and Pauline Pears

Gardening under Cover
Bernard Salt

Growing Fruit
Bob Sherman

Growing Herbs
Anna Corbett

Growing Vegetables
Anna Corbett and John Walker

A–Z of Vegetable and Salad Crops
Sally Cunningham, Pauline Pears

A–Z of Plant Problems
Patsy Dyer and Janet Walker, with Pauline Pears, Rebecca Potts, and Maggi Brown

Index

Michèle Clarke

Picture credits

The publisher would like to thank the following for their kind permission to reproduce their photographs: (Abbreviations key: t=top, b=bottom, r=right, l=left, c=centre, f=far)

Peter Anderson: 63b.
Charlotte De La Bedoyere: 12bfl, 13bfl, 14br, 47tl, 47tr, 47cla, 47cra, 47bl, 47br, 48tl, 55tr, 68cl, 68c, 70b, 70t, 71t, 295bl, 303tr, 304bc, 305tr, 305bl, 305br, 307br, 310br, 311tr, 313bl, 318tl, 318bl, 319bc.
Bruce Coleman Ltd: Joe McDonald 195cr.
Corbis: Gary W. Carter 18cl, 191r; Joseph Sohm; ChromoSohm Inc 86br.
Alan & Linda Detrick: 93bcl.
James F. Dill: 273, 275br.
Flowform sequence at Ruskin Mill designed by John Wilkes, photo by Laurence Snook: 71b.
FLPA – Images of Nature: D. Maslowski 85.
Garden Picture Library: Philippe Bonduel 91tr; Brian Carter 218; Christopher Gallagher 8; Juliet Greene 66b; Sunniva Harte 186cl; A. I. Lord 204bc; Mayer/Le Scanff 216; Jerry Pavia 219tl; Howard Rice 278; Janet Sorrell 204br; Friedrich Strauss 211; Juliette Wade 9b, 209tr; Steven Wooster 232tc.
Garden and Wildlife Matters: John Feltwell 81clb.
Holt Studios International: 231l, 307tr; Nigel Cattlin 35tc, 74cl, 74bc, 80tr, 86cl, 86cr, 86bl, 88bc, 89cl, 89cr, 89br, 89bfl, 89cfl, 93bl, 98tl, 98tr, 98cla, 98cra, 98crb, 99tl, 99tr, 99cla, 99cra, 99clb, 99crb, 157, 186clb, 186bl, 225tr, 303cr, 304bl, 304bfl, 304br; Alan & Linda Detrick 81tr; Rosemary Mayer 98clb, 217; Phil McLean 198bl; Gordon Roberts 59b Sarah Rowland 88br; Peter Wilson 98br.
Jules Janick: 264tl, 264tr, 264cl, 264c, 264cr, 264bl, 264br.
Stephen Josland: 144t, 163tr, 167t, 189.
Andrew Lawson: 14bfl.
S & O Mathews Photography: 42bl.
Joy Michaud/Sea Spring Photos: Sea Spring Photos 17br, 99br, 99br, 219tr, 220, 225br, 227bc, 228b, 293bc, 295c, 302tl, 308tl, 312cl.
N.H.P.A.: T. Kitchin & V. Hurst 99bl, 198bl; Rod Planck 195b.
Oxford Scientific Films: 325tr; Daybreak Imagery 193; Terry Heathcote 192tr; Geoff Kidd 335bl; Gordon Maclean 314b; John McCammon 296b; Stan Osolinski 97b.
Jerry Pavia: 191b, 264tc.
Photos Horticultural: 17tl, 80br, 87tr, 87cr, 96cr, 101tr, 198bc, 204cl, 208, 209tl, 212bl, 219b, 225bl, 226br, 230b, 232tr; Arends Nursery, Germany 203b; Wisley RHS Garden 212tl.
Raintree Nursery/Sam Benowitz: 264bc.
Rodale Stock Images: 10b.
Harry Smith Collection: 42br.

Line illustrations, pp. 338–395: **Sandra Pond**

Jacket Picture Credits
Back jacket cl: **FLPA – Images of Nature:** D. Maslowski.

All other images © Dorling Kindersley.
For further information see: www.dkimages.com